MILLION DOLLAR MOVIE

MICHAEL POWELL

MILLION DOLLAR
MOVIE

Introduction
by Martin Scorsese

Random House
New York

Grateful acknowledgment is made to the following for
permission to print both published and unpublished
material:
Estate of Cecil B. DeMille: Excerpt from a letter from Cecil
B. DeMille to Michael Powell. Used courtesy of the Estate
of Cecil B. DeMille.
Alfred A. Knopf, Inc., and David Thomson: Entry on Michael
Powell in *A Biographical Dictionary of Film,* by David
Thomson (Alfred A. Knopf, 1994). Reprinted by
permission of Alfred A. Knopf, Inc., and David Thomson.

Library of Congress Cataloging-in-Publication Data
Powell, Michael.
Million dollar movie/Michael Powell; introduction by
Martin Scorsese.
p. cm.
Includes index.
ISBN 0-679-43443-7
1. Powell, Michael. 2. Motion picture producers and
directors—Great Britain—Biography. I. Title.
PN1998.3.P69A3   1994   791.43′0233′092—dc20
[B]   94-14495

Manufactured in the United States of America on
acid-free paper
Book design by J. K. Lambert
Photo insert by Wynn Dan
98765432
First U.S. Edition

August 26 ⊚ N.Y.C.

Dear Marty — Today I finished
the First Draft of Vol II. Will
you allow me to dedicate it to you?

A PRODUCTION OF THE ARCHERS Michael.

Michael Powell to Martin Scorsese. August 26, 1989

Introduction
by Martin Scorsese

There was always a mystery about Michael Powell. He liked mystery. It complimented his own natural reserve, which I always considered part of his very English character. It was also a mark of respect, for himself and whoever was lucky enough to engage his interest. A filmmaker can't be totally accessible, too easy to reach. A director needs a little distance, for observation, for reflection, and for shelter. So, in all these ways, *Million Dollar Movie* is Michael's book to the core.

One of the many remarkable things about this second volume of Michael's autobiography, aside from the way it was written (which Ian Christie describes in his preface), is the way Michael reaches deep inside himself, writing often of things that were painful but still leaving something magical untouched. I learned a lot about him in this book, and much, too, about his heart and hopes, but I'll never be able completely to understand, or to say, why he meant so much to me, and why he will always be with me.

I've talked and written many times about first meeting Michael—he sets down his own version in these pages—but it may be hard to understand now quite how baffling a figure Michael was to me and my friends twenty years ago. I started to see his films in the late 1940s, on those small flickering black-and-white TVs: *The Thief of Bagdad*, *The Tales of Hoffmann*—glorious even without color—and *The Red Shoes*, the first Powell-Pressburger film I saw in Technicolor, in a theater. Even then, I was struck by the theatricality of the films, their *cinematic* theatricality. It wasn't theatricality of acting, but *design* of actors in the frame, the way they looked and moved, the camera movement, the angles and the lighting. Jump cuts, quick dissolves, fantasy sequences that were almost Disney-like—you got the sense that anything could happen, *was going to happen*, right there, in a Powell-Pressburger film.

And every time I saw these and all the other Archers films over and over again . . . and then again . . . through the years, the experience of excitement and mystery not only remained, it deepened. And with it came a growing curiosity. Who were Powell and Pressburger? What about that shared credit for writing, producing, and directing—it suggested that these unique films were created, significantly and appropriately, in a unique way. And why didn't Powell and Pressburger rate proper historical and critical coverage?

I started to get some answers—or, to be a little more accurate, some suggestion of answers—when Michael and I first met. There was a large glass of red wine sitting on the restaurant table in front of me, and Michael didn't say very much. I talked a long time. I was very energetic, very excited, but Michael was reserved, very quiet in his answers. I don't think he quite believed that there was a whole generation of younger American filmmakers like Francis Coppola, who not only knew his movies but revered them. I assailed Michael with questions: Where could we see complete versions of the films? What else had he and Pressburger done? What were their lives like now? What happened after *Peeping Tom*? And as I talked, and even when I listened to the answers, I remember I was thinking at the same time, "Wait till I get back to Los Angeles and New York and tell everybody, because this is quite extraordinary."

Million Dollar Movie and its predecessor, *A Life in Movies*, read like an elaboration and extension of that first conversation I had with Michael. You can hear his voice in every line, and you can get a sense of the spirit that, despite assaults from within and without, remained strong and uncompromised even in the years when it seemed he had been forgotten, even during the time—a shamefully long time, over a quarter century—when he was unable to make films. It was a spirit so strong and generous that he could share it, when he chose. I know that at periods of my own doubt, and even at times of my own desolation, his spirit supported me.

Finishing *The King of Comedy*, I was at the second major low point of my career, living alone, treating myself carelessly and dangerously, trying every day to pull as much work together as I could so I could finish the film and go on, hopefully, possibly to the next project . . . if this one didn't ruin me for good. Michael understood all this; probably he recognized all the signs and symptoms. So Michael and his wife, Thelma, would come over and cook dinner for me, and talk, and just be with me. Michael never once came out and spoke directly about me or my feelings, or what I was going through. He never pried. He was able to talk to me personally, without ever seeming as if we were having a personal discussion. It took me about a year to get a grip, and for all this time, aside from my parents, there were only Thelma and Michael who spent time with me. We'd talk, we'd ramble, I'd play him music—he enjoyed Laurie Anderson's *O Superman* tremendously—and maybe this was all his way of keeping my interest alive. Just being around him was enough to say to me, "Come on, move it! Let's get going! Let's pull ourselves together." And this was a man who hadn't made a feature in something like thirty years. It was a lot more than encouragement. It was inspiration.

We became absorbed in each other's background. I thought of Michael as a kind of nineteenth-century idealist imbued with the spirit and soul of Britain. He was an enchanter, a great storyteller, a "high priest of the mysteries," as he called himself, someone who had really grown up in an aesthetically nurturing environment. It wasn't like that for me on Elizabeth Street in New York, and Michael wanted to see and experience where I grew up. He wanted to see where *Mean Streets* came from. So Bob De Niro and I took Michael downtown, showed him Chinatown and the old St. Patrick's Cathedral. He not only absorbed that atmosphere, he assimilated it. I have always hoped it was a way for him to get into my movies, and what I was trying to do, just as spending time with Michael gave his films even more resonance for me.

The night Bob and I took Michael downtown, we stopped in a favorite Chinese restaurant, a mad place where the waiters throw the food down at your table and everyone screams at everyone else. We were in the middle of this din, talking about the script of *Raging Bull,* and Michael said, "You can't use that Shakespeare ending. Even though Jake LaMotta did it on stage, you can't have him reciting Shakespeare." He was very quiet about it. We had to strain to hear him in the restaurant racket. But he was very firm. Shakespeare, he was saying, was not part of the iconography we were constructing in the film. It didn't fit the story we were telling. So I thought of the "I could've been a contender" speech from *On the Waterfront,* which Jake had also done on the stage, but it was a hard prospect; Budd Schulberg by way of Kazan by way of Brando by way of De Niro by way of me and Jake and De Niro again. An endless reflecting mirror. It was a dangerous step, but Michael made it clear it was a step in the right direction.

I was always nervous about showing Michael scripts and rough cuts, because we had become friends. I was afraid he'd be partial. That fear was groundless. He was too rigorous, too much the artist, for that kind of falsehood, that easy social politeness. He did not understand why I wanted to make another film about gangsters until Thelma read him the script of *GoodFellas.* His eyesight was failing then, but I think as he listened he could see the film. "It's the most visual script I've read in twenty years," he said. "You *must* make it." He encouraged me to be open with him as well, and dealt with my comments as freely and intimately as I did with his. When I expressed some serious reservations about one of his many dream projects, he said to Thelma, "Wonderful! Wonderful!" He thought that if I disliked it so much he must be on the right track, because it aroused an anger, kindled some passion.

I loved to watch movies with Michael, but he didn't always love the movies I loved. He didn't know Sam Fuller's work, so we screened *Forty Guns*—a mistake. I should have eased him into the work, showing him some of Fuller's earlier films first—like *Pickup on South Street, The Steel Helmet, House of Bamboo* . . . all the way to *Shock Corridor*. Anyway, Michael walked out after twenty minutes of *Forty Guns* and sent a note the next day: "I'm sorry, but I couldn't stand to see my religion practiced under such circumstances." Later, after he'd met Sam, I believe he began to reconsider; he saw the sophistication and invention under Sam's carefully nurtured rough edges.

Michael was careful to make very clear what he didn't like about a finished film of mine. He wasn't always gentle, but he wasn't ever disrespectful, either, or competitive. There were several things that concerned him about *The Last Temptation of Christ*, but in my view, he was totally wrong, and knew what I felt. If he had directed the film he would have done it very differently, I know. But I'd already made my choice, and once you do that, you go with your choice all the way. It's not a lesson I learned expressly from Michael; but it's one in which he encouraged me, and strengthened me.

He did this by force of example as much as anything. He had not worked at his art, remember, for decades, and had endured, besides, the cruel exile of indifference. Lindsay Anderson, Karel Reisz, Tony Richardson, and all the British New Wave were making extraordinary films and, for a time, obliterating the past. Michael was from another time, another epoch, a world that England was trying to leave behind. "A country's films, like a country's poets, are one of its greatest cultural assets," Michael writes, but just as Colonel Blimp refused to accept what he viewed as the coarsening of society, so did Michael decline to adopt the naturalism of the British New Wave. He had fitted no better into the cynical world of postwar film production, where the pressure to succeed commercially became almost unbearable. Michael lived film as art, and art was his religion. To abandon his cherished creative freedom was impossible; it was like losing sight of the Grail.

So Michael began to write, and to travel, and to dream of film. Once, he'd been able to catch those dreams on three-strip Technicolor, make them real for all of us to share, but when this became impossible he did not stop dreaming, or caring. No matter what the circumstances, he would always have a plan for a picture: *Beowulf* as a silent film; a series of interrelated short films called *Thirteen Ways to Kill a Poet; A Waiting Game,* a story with its roots in Ireland's bloodstained history. He never gave up and never gave in, and when circumstance denied him the chance to direct again, he turned to writing and produced two extraordinary books. Like Kazan, Renoir, and Bergman, his autobiography is at once an extension and a completion of his work. It was very much Michael's view, romantic and completely unapologetic, that there is no separation between life and art. Michael's way of seeing was also a way of being.

It was his way, distinctive and proud, and he was wise enough to encourage me, and others, to blaze their own trail, not follow in his path. Looking back now, I see Michael at so many turnings: walking in while we were looping actors for *GoodFellas,* sitting in the back of the room and talking loudly because he really couldn't see what we were doing; showing up for the graveyard shift on the sound mixing of *Last Temptation,* carrying Häagen-Dazs ice cream bars and staying all night with us, to the very last, seeing the film to rest . . . and then, during the tumult of the film's opening, confronting protesters outside the theater, having little conversations with them, trying to work out precisely what their problems were. Seeing the film to rest.

He never wavered. That was one of his greatest qualities and, for me, his most cherished legacy. He was steadfast. He reassured that in me most of all: You believe in an idea, a concept, a story, a statement you want to make, and that's the foundation of the film. You do not waver from it. Whether it takes you all the way down, whether it takes you to the edge, then pushes you off, even to the point of not making another film for thirty years, you do not waver. You'd better make that picture, even if you know it's suicide.

Las Vegas, January 1995

PREFACE

Conventionally, it could be said that Michael Powell's second volume of memoirs was written in the teeth of adversity. His impaired sight in the last few years of his life made reading and writing impossible, so he dictated and listened, while his wife, Thelma Schoonmaker, transcribed, read back, and helped him revise. And where Thelma's work as Martin Scorsese's editor on films like *After Hours, The Last Temptation of Christ,* and *GoodFellas* took her, Michael went too. Parts of the book were written in San Quentin, New York, Chicago, even Moscow (while Michael labored on *Pavlova*), and back in England in Avening, Gloucestershire. The concentration required must have been prodigious, and, however frustrating, it may ultimately have had its compensations. Like a musician composing a score, Michael had to hold the overall shape and relationship of themes in his mind across a mass of detail. No doubt the gifted writer that Michael Powell was would have made even bolder final revisions if he could have worked directly on the manuscript, but what we gain is the sense of dialogue. For in an era of ghosted and suave "as told to" memoirs, this is a rare book *spoken* with love, to its muse.

For this American edition, Thelma has added notes explaining what Michael took for granted. The result is an even richer portrait of cinema anxiously entering its second half century.

Few of those who came to know Michael Powell during his later years of recognition ever realized how many disappointments and rebuffs he had suffered, the price he paid for espousing art and eschewing compromise. Many thought, naively, that it was all because of the scandal of *Peeping Tom,* and railed against the conservative Blimps who failed to back Britain's boldest director. But this second volume of memoirs reveals that failure and frustration began much earlier. So early, in fact, that we should probably regard the glorious heyday of The Archers, from 1941 to 1948, as a temporary aberration in the long saga of Britain's habitual mistreatment of filmmakers rather than as a regime that could have lasted.

It was the war that had helped to remove Alexander Korda from the British production scene he had dominated in the 1930s (he spent most of World War II in Hollywood) and accelerated the Methodist flour-miller Arthur Rank's unlikely involvement in cinema. Under Rank's benign patronage, The Archers and their fellow "Independent Producers" flourished. Interference was minimal, and there existed a British cinema-going public avid for films that spoke from and to their experience of war. The normal assumption that Hollywood would provide "real" entertainment was temporarily suspended, even reversed.

When the war ended, many kinds of "reality" reappeared with a vengeance. One was the undimmed confidence of Hollywood, with its markets enlarged by the scale of American involvement in the war. Another was the endemic weakness of British cinema, now exacerbated by postwar economic problems. A misguided attempt by Clement Attlee's Labour government to help the balance of payments by imposing a heavy tax on American cinema earnings in Britain led to an export ban by the powerful Motion Picture Association of America in 1947. Both Rank and Korda rushed to fill the gap, but when a settlement was reached between the two countries after eight months, they found themselves seriously overextended. Rank's deficit of some £16 million in 1948 and Korda's even more parlous situation (without Rank's assets and other profitable activities) ushered in an era of compromise and retrenchment. A National Film Finance company was formed, largely to bail out Korda.

It was against this grim background that The Archers saw their revolutionary *The Red Shoes* derided by Rank executives and denied even a limited theatrical release. Insulted, Powell and Pressburger returned to Korda's fold, knowing that his charm concealed deviousness and downright treachery. But at least he had style. *Million Dollar Movie* begins with the bitter discovery that The Archers had become pawns in Korda's survival plan. This meant deferring to the "independent" moguls of Hollywood, and hawking their wares around like traveling salesmen. Yet who can fail to be impressed by the energy and enterprise that Powell brought to this new role, or by the diplomacy and resourcefulness that Pressburger contributed to their increasingly strained relationship? And who could not be moved by the waste of imagination, talent, and time that both experienced?

Million Dollar Movie is by no means a balanced account of Michael Powell's achievements. Indeed, it often seems to dwell more on his *non*-achievements, perversely avoiding those peaks that another autobiographer might have gratefully paused upon. It's still the inside story he promised (although composed by one who was never an insider) of what it meant to be a filmmaker in the second half of the century of cinema.

What we learn from it is that to be a director—to have that total self-confidence, natural authority, patience, and resourcefulness—is something that can survive even a dearth of backers and worthy projects. Through all the reverses and disappointments of the years chronicled in *Million Dollar Movie*, there is the same shrewd, shaping passion; a way of picturing and understanding the world that belongs to that uniquely twentieth-century artisan, the film director.

Million Dollar Movie takes its title from the American TV series that first introduced The Archers to a movie-struck young Martin Scorsese. Powell's dedication of this book to Scorsese reflects more than respect and gratitude; for Martin has staunchly supported Thelma's work to bring this book to fruition, taking a keen interest in furthering a fellow director's "final cut." David Hinton, whose collaborative *South Bank Show* profile of Powell, shown on British television in 1986, gave Michael renewed hope that he would again direct, also worked closely on the final manuscript. William K. Everson in New York and David Meeker in London contributed their formidable expertise in cinema history. Michael's sons also played a valued part: Kevin verified details of the Australian episodes, and Columba helped select the pictures from his father's rich legacy.

Neither this book, however, nor its predecessor would have reached final form without Thelma Schoonmaker's devotion. To work with two of the greatest filmmakers of all time is a rare privilege; to do so simultaneously would be impossible for anyone but Thelma. Unlike poor Vicky in *The Red Shoes*, she has happily survived to bring us the tale. We are profoundly in her debt.

IAN CHRISTIE
British Film Institute
London, 1995

ACKNOWLEDGMENTS

My deepest thanks go to Ian Christie. He, among all of Michael's friends who advised and supported me during the final editing of this book, worked the hardest on the manuscript. In long late-night telephone calls across the Atlantic, he gave me the benefit of his twenty-year study of, and love for, the work of Powell and Pressburger. Without his constant encouragement and steading hand, this book could not have been completed.

I am most grateful to Harry Evans at Random House for taking the gamble on publishing in America this second volume of autobiography, and to Helen Morris for her determination to make the American edition special by adding footnotes and new photographs. Her enthusiasm and amazing patience have sustained me during this past year.

Ian Christie and Markku Salmi of the British Film Institute have generously updated their Powell/Pressburger filmography for this edition, a gift to all of us. My thanks to Melanie Tebb and Kevin Macdonald for their research on the footnotes, and to everyone at Cappa Productions my gratitude for their help during these last few years, particularly Raffaele Donato, Kent Jones, and Deanna Avery.

To Martin Scorsese I owe everything, for he introduced me to my husband and has tirelessly campaigned to bring recognition to the work of Powell and Pressburger. A guiding spirit on this book, and an invaluable sounding board when difficult decisions had to be made, he has contributed to it most profoundly by giving us, in his introduction, an extraordinary glimpse of his remarkable friendship with Michael Powell.

THELMA SCHOONMAKER POWELL
Las Vegas, January 1995

CONTENTS

ILLUSTRATIONS

A model of the *Graf Spee* blown up for *The Battle of the River Plate*

Dirk Bogarde and David Oxley in *Ill Met by Moonlight*, 1956

Freddie Francis, Christopher Challis, and Michael Powell, on location for *Ill Met by Moonlight*

Cyril Cusack in *Ill Met by Moonlight*

Karl-Heinz Böhm (Carl Boehm) in *Peeping Tom*, 1960

Karl-Heinz Böhm and Pamela Green in *Peeping Tom*

Michael Powell and Columba on the set of *Peeping Tom*

David Niven in the south of France

Michael Powell with Alastair Dunnett and Bill Paton in Scotland

Walter Chiari in *They're a Weird Mob*, 1966

Michael Powell and James Mason filming *The Age of Consent*, 1969

Charles Little, John Meillon, Slim DeGrey, and Ed Devereaux in *They're a Weird Mob*

Michael Powell and Emeric Pressburger

Akira Kurosawa, Michael Powell, and Senkichi Taniguchi, 1952

Michael and Thelma Schoonmaker Powell

Martin Scorsese, Michael Powell, and Jerry Lewis during the filming of *King of Comedy*, 1981

Michael Powell and Johnson

Michael Powell at Lee Cottages

Michael and Thelma Schoonmaker Powell on their wedding day, 1984, page 402

Michael Powell and Emeric Pressburger on the set of *Oh . . . Rosalinda!!*, 1955, page 572

All photographs courtesy of the Michael Powell estate

"All art is one, man—one!"

Rudyard Kipling,
The Wrong Thing

MILLION DOLLAR MOVIE

ONE

THE COMPOSED FILM:
Michael Powell and
Sir Thomas Beecham
on the set of *The Tales
of Hoffmann*.

What of the bow?
The bow was made in England:
Of true wood, of yew-wood,
The wood of English bows.

Arthur Conan Doyle's heroic verse was one of the inspirations for The Archers' famous trademark—a target bristling with arrows. Sometimes the target was empty, awaiting the verdict of our public; sometimes the arrow would land arrogantly and squarely in the gold. In the early days the target was black and white. In later days it was in color, but always with the words "A Production of The Archers" superimposed. The public we had created for our films waited for it. They knew that The Archers' target promised something different.

In the films that Emeric Pressburger and I made together, The Archers' logo was the first thing to hit the screen. This was followed by the credits for the artists with whom we worked: painters and designers like Alfred Junge, Hein Heckroth, Arthur Lawson, Vincent Korda; cameramen like Georges Perinal, Jack Cardiff, Erwin Hillier, Christopher Challis, Otto Heller; editors like David Lean, John Seaborne, Reginald Mills, Noreen Ackland; production managers and associate producers like Sydney Streeter, George Busby; chief electricians like Bill Wall. Last of all the credits, and the first title before the story started, came: "Written, Produced and Directed by Michael Powell and Emeric Pressburger." This bold and arrogant title maintained our claim of complete independence from our sources of finance and distribution, and from all white-collared inhabitants of boardrooms, whom Bill Wall designated as "chair polishers."

You who have read the first volume of these memoirs will know how we used, or misused, this unique privilege throughout World War II. Here is the list of the films we planned and made together, from 1939 to 1947, and for which we were solely responsible:

Contraband
49th Parallel
One of Our Aircraft Is Missing
The Silver Fleet
The Volunteer
The Life and Death of Colonel Blimp
A Canterbury Tale
I Know Where I'm Going!
A Matter of Life and Death
Black Narcissus
The Red Shoes

From 1945 onward, the famous J. Arthur Rank gong was given a prominent place in our credits. In 1948, the gong was replaced by the Big Ben of Sir Alexander Korda and London Films.

≡

New readers start here.

By the time that World War II was won, The Archers had made ten films together: ten arrows in the target, nine of them in the gold, and crowned by the first Royal Film Performance, when our King and Queen and the young Princesses came to Leicester Square, London, accompanied by about twenty thousand of their loyal subjects, to see *A Matter of Life and Death* on the screen at the Empire Theatre. The names of Michael Powell and Emeric Pressburger were known in the land. Emeric and I had had the opportunity, while running in harness with the Ministry of Information, to raise our chosen medium to hitherto unheard-of heights of influence and authority. But war was the spur, and when that sharp incentive was removed we ceased our mad gallop and started to look around us. We felt as horses feel when turned out to grass after a long winter of servitude. First we had a good roll, free of all constraint, by which metaphor I mean our *Black Narcissus,* with its theme that there are more ways than one of serving God. It was followed by a glorious canter around the field, ending in taking a couple of stiff fences in company with a redheaded filly called Moira Shearer. Then we began to notice, as we lazily cropped the grass, that it was greener across the river at Shepperton Studios than at Pinewood. It was time for The Archers and their followers to move across the river and into the trees.

The Archers' new head offices were now to be at 148 Piccadilly, at Hyde

Park Corner itself, in the house where the Duke and Duchess of York had lived and brought up their two young daughters before being called to Buckingham Palace to be Their Majesties King George VI and Queen Elizabeth. This choice of head office for London Films and its associates and subsidiaries was typical of Alex Korda. To hang his Monets in a room where the future Queen of England had romped upon the carpet . . . you could hardly be more snob than that. The two houses, knocked into one, were tall, elegant, and inconvenient—but the tall windows looked out on Hyde Park Corner, on Constitution Hill, and the Mall, which leads to Buckingham Palace. Here was the heart of England, and Alex felt it deeply. As a ruthless adventurer who had been brought up in the last years of the Austro-Hungarian Empire, Alex understood the mystique that surrounds royalty. He had tasted luxury and power in other countries, but had decided to remain an Englishman. His knighthood, masterminded by Churchill during the war, clinched it. This sunset period of Alex's wonderful life has been magically evoked in *Charmed Lives* by Michael Korda, his nephew and Vincent Korda's son. For the boy, Michael, it had been as wonderful as entering the world of the Arabian Nights, and he shared his wonder with his readers, opening door after door, from the closely guarded Penthouse above Claridge's to the luxurious cabin of Alex's oceangoing yacht, appropriately named *Elsewhere.*

When Emeric and I looked back on those last years of London Films, we shared his nephew's affection and admiration for Alex. But the late 1940s was a time of disappointment and frustration for The Archers, although we had enormous fun in making the four films we did make for London Films.

We left Pinewood Studios with regret, although we had never had the same affection for Pinewood as we had for Denham. Rank had offered his independent producers the choice of either studio after the war, and we had chosen Pinewood, but I think we made a mistake. Pinewood had been occupied by the services during the war, and when it returned to civilian life there was a whiff of red tape that was very unlike Denham. It had been planned and built around a country house estate in a sober and serious manner, while Denham had been, as it were, thrown recklessly down in towers of concrete by the banks of the River Colne. Denham had the swashbuckling air and the reckless use of space that reminded one, at once, of Hollywood. Pinewood was quietly English. Denham had an aura of magic about it, from the films which had been made there. Pinewood was executive suites. But I managed to keep my Denham caravan.*

All the same, we chose Pinewood for the home of Independent Producers,

---

*Michael hated studio canteens and kept a trailer at the studio where his trusty right hand, Bill Paton, would feed him lunch and tidbits of gossip from the set.

because it seemed to us more practical and more controllable for our team of producers and the films they proposed to make. I often wonder what would have happened if we had chosen Denham: that endless corridor, those huge, concrete barns, the wonderful pattern shop, the laboratories on the hill, the river valley . . . what a challenge they were to a filmmaker, what a playground for giants!

The Archers' new studios were to be Worton Hall and Shepperton. They were both watery studios in the rich valley of the River Thames, west of London. Worton Hall was in Isleworth; Shepperton lay farther upstream on a great curve of the river near Royal Windsor, and no doubt this additional proximity to royalty helped to compensate Alex for the loss of Denham. The area was full of river palaces, and my old studio of Walton-on-Thames was only a mile or two away.

Both Shepperton and Worton Hall had been developed from private estates, like Denham and Pinewood, and the old mansion house was a focal point in all four studios. Worton Hall had been a British film studio since the silent days, and the stages were few and small, with one exception. This was an enormous silent stage, not soundproofed, which stood like a white elephant among the grimy shrubberies. It had been erected by London Films for the elaborate trick shots devised by Ned Mann for the film of H. G. Wells's *Things to Come*, while Denham Studios was still being built in 1935. How it survived the war, when steel was at a premium, only Alex and David Cunynghame could tell. It was about 120 feet square and 60 feet high, perhaps. Since his return from America, Alex had produced two or three black-and-white pictures at Worton Hall, with considerable success, but as he intended to make Shepperton Studios his base, he had the whole immense stage dismantled and carted over to Shepperton, where it was re-erected. It was never soundproofed, and a few years later we used it for *The Tales of Hoffmann*. The entire film was prerecorded with singers and musicians and shot to playback, so it made no difference to us whether the stage was soundproofed or not.

It was part of our deal with Alex that we should bring our own crew with us should they wish to come, and they all did, except Jack Cardiff. His color photography on our last three films had brought him Hollywood offers, and no less a mogul than Darryl F. Zanuck was paging him to direct a Technicolor production of Mary Renault's book *The King Must Die*. (This glorious subject was never made by Twentieth Century–Fox; pity—Zanuck would have been great as the Minotaur.) Hein Heckroth and his art director–collaborator Arthur Lawson were already at work on the first two films we were going to make for Korda, *The Small Back Room* in black and white and *The Elusive Pimpernel* in color. Hein was blatant about his ignorance of everything to do with designing a film, and passed all such questions on to Arthur with the remark "Arthur will know." *The Elusive Pimpernel,* with gorgeous Regency costumes and sets, was, of course, right up his street, but he was quite openly scared at the prospect of a black-and-white realistic film like *The Small Back Room.* I tried to explain the difference to him.

"You see, Hein, when you design a color film, particularly a costume film, and one with music, you have to be always conscious of the audience. Now when I direct a black-and-white film, like *The Small Back Room,* I don't give a damn about the audience. I only care about the camera and me—I am the audience and the camera is me. Do you see?"

"I think I do, Micky. But what is it that makes the difference?"

"I'm not sure. But that's the way it is, and if ever I make a color film as if it were a black-and-white film, I can tell you you'll know the difference."

The company of Archers, which had been training and selecting its members ever since *Colonel Blimp,* was a formidable band, owing allegiance to no one but Powell and Pressburger. Three of them went as far back as *49th Parallel:* Betty Curtis, Joan Page, and Bill Paton. They were my loyal and battle-scarred veterans, but two of them were not coming with us to Shepperton Studios. Betty and Joan had fought beside us all through the war and into the peace, Joan as company secretary, while Betty had entire charge of the script from start to finish, as well as handling my personal correspondence. Now they wanted to be themselves again, and in the general shake-up of our move to Shepperton they saw their chance to part as friends. This was to be expected, but it was an awful wrench.

What you lose on the roundabouts, you gain on the swings.* After service in the Royal Navy, Bill Paton was demobilized and rejoined The Archers. I had missed him sorely. Bill had been my squire, in the chivalrous sense of the word, which I take to mean friend and bodyguard. With Bill standing by my shoulder, I felt safe. Bill would turn to me in the middle of a crowd of five hundred tourists and say, "Yon felly is makin' a nuisance of himself. Will I sort 'im?" Anyone sorted by Bill is not likely to forget the experience. He has the strength of three men and is built like a center-forward. He never shouts and seldom loses his temper. When he does, you remember it.

It is thanks to Bill Paton and to Curtis and Page (and now to Thelma) that I managed to keep all my files, or, as they call it preposterously, my "archive": stories, synopses, treatments, whole scripts and mini-versions of them, production reports, budgets, contracts, correspondence—all the multiple things that belong to film production, that were nursed and handled by Betty and Joan and graduated to Bill's watchful care. Whenever I have thought of

---

*Roundabouts are merry-go-rounds. This traditional English saying means that things eventually even out.

dumping those seventy-five boxes in Loch Morar (the deepest loch in Scotland), or burning them in one magnificent bonfire, I have been stopped from doing it by the thought of my three friends' care and devotion. It is rare for a filmmaker, an independent filmmaker, to preserve his papers: offices change, secretaries change, companies go bust. We producers and directors are Gypsies, moving all over the world, vanishing, reappearing . . . and how can Gypsies preserve records, files, cans of film, and boxes of tapes? Thanks to Betty, Joan, and Bill, I have them all. They have been in some queer places, in considerable danger several times, but now they are safely stored, and Thelma and I are trying to turn this mountain of material into a book, into social history.

I am as old as the film business as we know it. In 1985 we both celebrated our eightieth birthdays. I don't believe that there is anybody else alive who can write this book, so I owe it to my chosen profession.

During the war, The Archers had offices at Dorset House, Baker Street, near the tube station, a large block of modern flats with an entrance on Gloucester Place. The block was considered reasonably bomb-proof and when there was an air-raid warning we had some camp beds, so that we could sleep there, if necessary. We never bothered to furnish it properly or hang pictures or posters—the war was on, and austerity was a way of life—and somehow Betty and Joan made it look efficient and comfortable. We kept these offices on when we moved to Pinewood, for we needed a base in town, but our wartime lease was up and the move to Hyde Park Corner came in very handy. Betty and Joan had always meant to revive their typing business after the war. By now they knew everybody in Denham and Pinewood, and soon they knew everyone at Shepperton. They still typed our scripts, but for a fee. Curtis and Page rode again!

Alex had Carol Reed under contract, as well as Anthony Kimmins, and now he had The Archers. We soon had a taste of what to expect from the postwar Alex, for he started making deals involving us and without consulting us. There is no point in going into all Alex's wheeling and dealing, but there was always a catch in everything you did with him. I had never suspected, during all those months when he was trying to persuade me to remake *The Scarlet Pimpernel*, that when I said yes he put about £100,000 into one of his pockets. He had bought the rights to Baroness Orczy's book when he made the picture with Leslie Howard before the war, and now he made a killing. The accumulated cost was, of course, added to our budget.

The reason that he didn't kick at making *The Small Back Room* was that he had bought an option on all Nigel Balchin's books when he produced *Mine Own Executioner*. *The Small Back Room* was a medium-budget picture, so he probably only pocketed £20,000. Still, every little bit helps. It was part of our deal that Alex should obtain David Niven to play the Pimpernel, but he didn't tell us that in exchange for David and £50,000 Sam Goldwyn got the American market. I wonder who got that £50,000? I always have a mental picture of sums like this scurrying from the balance sheet of one company to another company affiliated with London Films, and finally bolting down some capacious pocket.

Alex was to give us some strange partners. David O. Selznick was working with Carol Reed on *The Third Man* and was looking for a European subject for Jennifer Jones, whom he was parading about Europe at his chariot wheels. Alex had already promised him The Archers and a Mary Webb story of passion in rural Shropshire, either *Precious Bane* or *Gone to Earth*. Need I say that Alex owned all the rights of all the Mary Webb stories, and the moment one of them was filmed, he made another killing?

There was nothing new about this. Many people are in the movie business only for the money, only to make deals, only for the women—only they are not friends of ours. Alex was. We not only admired and liked Alex, we loved him. We had known him as our leader in difficult times, and had admired his coolness in a crisis. We had laughed over his wit and presence of mind. We had told each other of his generosity in giving the credit to others and taking no credit himself. We knew him as a brilliant orchestrator of comedy, an actor's director. He was all that we thought we had most admired in the cinema.

But in those days before the war, we were little men and Alex was a big one. We did not aspire to be great. It was not our scene. We were ingenious, resourceful, inventive, and courageous, but we were not great. Alex was great. I never knew another like him for wit, authority, and charm. I have met great artists in the cinema—not D. W. Griffith, alas!—but I have met Walt Disney, Charlie Chaplin, Alfred Hitchcock, and Fritz Lang. These were all great artists, great filmmakers, but Alex was a great *man;* and although it looked as if it might be difficult to make good pictures with him and his associates, the atmosphere was one of enthusiasm and of great picture making, and a million miles from the bourgeois tantrums of John Davis,* whose tall shadow was falling across his master, Arthur Rank.

*John Davis was managing director of the Rank Organisation in the late forties and was openly hostile to any experimentation or "waste" in film production. He hated *The Red Shoes* and denied it even a normal release in the U.K. It was only saved from oblivion by American exhibitors. John Davis tightened his grip on Rank in the fifties and made it clear to all the independent producers that they would no longer have the artistic freedom they had enjoyed under J. Arthur Rank during the previous decade. Michael and Emeric left the Rank Organisation as a result, ending what Michael called in the first volume of his memoirs "one of the most glorious partnerships in British film history."

≡

Do you know Chesil Bank? It is one of the wonders of the world. It is located on the Dorset Coast. It is a gigantic shingle beach, created by the tides eternally working against the granite wall of Portland Bill. The Bill shelters Weymouth Bay from the southwesterly drift that sweeps up the English Channel. Imagine a dead seabird, a cormorant or a gannet, three or four miles long, lying stretched on the surface of the sea, the long bill pointing toward France. That is the Bill. It has created the marvel of Chesil Bank on the seaward side. This beach, about eight miles long and as thin as the new moon, is not the coast of Dorset—it is the Bank. The coastline crouches behind the wall of the Bank, and is separated from it by great lagoons of brackish water called the Fleet. Only one novelist that I know has ever dramatized this dramatic piece of England—Meade Falkner in his romance, *Moonfleet.*

To see these two sea barriers, the Bill and the Bank, in a sou'westerly gale is an awesome sight. There is nothing nearer to break the force of the Atlantic rollers than Finistère in France, *finis terrae* of the Romans—the end of the Known World. As the waves break upon the immovable Bill they shoot a hundred feet into the air and cut off Portland Town from Weymouth. All this energy has to go somewhere, and failing to break the Bill and flood and destroy the town of Weymouth, the flowing tide sweeps around the throat of the Bill and pounds the stones of Chesil Bank. If you stand at the Weymouth end of the Bank, you stand among huge round boulders, taller than a man, worn smooth with the ceaseless pounding of the sea. There is a continual grinding and crunching noise caused by these giant pebbles shifting. Stand at the other end of the Bank where it ends at Abbotsbury, site of a famous swannery, and here the pebbles are no bigger than your thumbnail. But they are the same pebbles, grinding and ceaselessly smoothing, turning, obeying the will of the tides.

They say that local fishermen, born and brought up in these parts, and maybe not sure of their position on a dark or foggy night, bring their boats in close to the bank if the weather is calm enough. They can tell by the size of the stones what part on the bank they are touching, so regular is the gradation from the huge boulders at the Portland end to the tiny pebbles at the Abbotsbury end. I can believe it. If you stand on the mound of St. Catherine's Chapel and look eastward to the distant, gray, shadowy shape of the Bill, the Bank curves away from beneath your feet to form a perfect crescent, ending at the Bill. This is the stage on which I proposed to play out the defusing of the bomb in *The Small Back Room.*

I first knew Nigel Balchin as the anonymous author of *How to Run a Bassoon Factory,* an undergraduate work, airy, witty, and observant. The next thing that I picked up of his was a love story, *Darkness Falls from the Air*. By now, his personal style was forming and his handling of the lovers was achingly true. After that, I read everything he wrote. But I never thought of filming his books until I read *The Small Back Room*. It was a war story. The hero, with a difference, was Sammy Rice, who had a tin foot and a grudge against the world because of it and because he had a beautiful girl who loved him, he suspected, out of pity. This was at a time when London was full of men in uniform, while Sammy (and his tin foot) were working in an obscure research department of the Ministry of Defence. Sue worked there too, and nobody was supposed to know they were lovers.

The plot turned on the simple premise, whether it is going to be too bad about Sammy—or not. He has a drink problem: scotch. David Farrar and Kathleen Byron had both made personal successes in *Black Narcissus*, and we cast them as Sammy and Sue. The setting was wartime London and everybody had had enough of that, which I might have suspected if I had not been such a fervent admirer of Nigel's book. I was anxious to get my hands on the bomb disposal sequence, which was the high spot of the book and which, I suspected, would not only be the high spot of the film, but one of those cinematic pièces de résistance, so beloved of film directors and film students, and continuously analyzed by film schools as, for instance, the Odessa steps, the trial of Joan of Arc, the hornpipe in *Kean*, the dance of the breadrolls by Chaplin in *The Gold Rush*, the whole of *Le Salaire de la peur* (*The Wages of Fear*), and the Ballet of the Red Shoes. We have our little weaknesses, we film directors. We are inveterate show-offs. We are copycats. We are not content with doing a good job, but always want to go one better than our predecessors. My whirlpool in *I Know Where I'm Going!* had been the definitive whirlpool. When I read the bomb disposal scene in *The Small Back Room* I brushed away at once the author's suggestion of a sandy beach. I saw at once the great curve of Chesil Bank, the waves listlessly breaking on the beach and grinding the pebbles as the undertow retreated, the sinister shape of the bomb, upright in the pebbles like a giant Thermos flask, the Bank itself, where every footstep sent a thousand pebbles rolling. I saw St. Catherine's Chapel on its terraced hill, the only remnant of the great monastery of Abbotsbury. I saw in one composite picture eternal England, with the sea never sleeping, the little group in khaki of the Bomb Disposal Squad, and the tall figure of Colonel Strang against the beautiful lines of St. Catherine's Chapel.

Anthony Bushell had been one of Alex's stable of young actors at Denham before the war. He was tall, slim, truculent, and as blond as any Scandinavian, with the skin stretched tight over his narrow head. I had seen him around at Denham, but I remember him especially at the brief conference that Alex called in his office when Squadron Leader Wright briefed us about the coming Battle of Britain. Tony had worked on Korda's *The Lion Has Wings* as actor, commentator, director. Once that chore was finished he got on his push-bike and cycled down to the Guards Depot in Birdcage Walk in St. James's Park. They took one look at his six feet four, his look of humorous desperation, his blond hair and blue eyes, and his amusing baritone voice, and found him a place without further question. I met him once on Salisbury Plain playing with tanks, and later on I heard that he had been seen commanding a tank in one of the Guards regiments in the invasion of Normandy. He was a great friend of Larry Olivier, and I had heard he had spent several days of his leave with him when Larry was shooting *Henry V*, so I was not surprised when I met him later while Larry was making *Hamlet*. Tony was acting as codirector and associate producer, and I remember a painful hour of rushes at the Odeon Leicester Square, after the performance, when he and Larry insisted on my listening to their various attempts at the speech of the ghost of Hamlet's father. I didn't know what to make of it at the time, but now that I have seen George Lucas's *Star Wars*, and hissed at Darth Vader, I know where George got his voice from.

I was determined to bring Tony back to acting. He had filled out during the war and had become, from a truculent boy, a formidable man. He had taken easily to command and it sat naturally on him. His light blue eyes, unchanging when he was smiling or when he was cursing the daylights out of his men, were disturbing. His steely drawl—"Yeeeesss"—was Colonel Strang to the life. You could feel his cold fury at having to send the best of his young men to almost certain death.

I have said that the main plot of *The Small Back Room* is the love story of Sammy and Sue, but the subplot is the search for an unexploded antipersonnel bomb that the Jerries were dropping. One of these bombs has to be found intact and taken to pieces literally to find out what makes it tick. This search is being conducted by Lt. Stuart, a member of the Bomb Disposal Squad, brilliantly, and nervously, played by Michael Gough. Sammy gets brought into it because one of the best men in his department is Corporal Taylor, a fuse expert, played with an engaging stammer by Cyril Cusack. The main casualties of this fiendish bomb are children, and it is obvious that its shape must be ordinary, and harmless-looking. Stuart is always ringing up at odd times to report a new incident, and coax Sammy to go down with him to crossexamine witnesses. So in the film we jump all about England and Wales, until a bomb is isolated at Chesil Bank, with Colonel Strang glowering down on it from St. Catherine's Chapel.

It really was an ideal story for a film. Sammy Rice, a born loser, gets drunk, quarrels with his girl, and is summoned by Stuart to help him defuse the bomb. By the time he arrives at Abbotsbury, Stuart is dead. There were two bombs dropped about half a mile apart, so one survives. Sammy persuades the bloody-minded Colonel Strang to let him have a go, using Stuart's notes. These are relayed to him by a small, pretty signals officer, who had been in love with Stuart. I persuaded Renée Asherson to play this part. I hand-picked every man on the squad.

Syd Streeter had been working nearly six weeks on constructing the bomb according to the latest patents, and had reconstructed and prepared it in the engineering shop so that each step in the defusing of it could be followed on the screen. The sequence ran about seventeen minutes—the same length, more or less, as the Ballet of the Red Shoes. Seventeen minutes must be the longest time that an audience can hold its breath.

David Farrar and Kathleen Byron created a Sammy and Sue that were as fine as good etchings. Until Harold Pinter came onto the scene, nobody had brought out the extraordinary side of ordinary human beings as well as Nigel Balchin. He knew that there were no ordinary people, and I loved him for it. His people were full of quirks and sudden turns and unexpected decisions. Sammy has a drink problem, for instance, and he always keeps a full bottle of scotch around to remind him and Sue that he mustn't be left alone too long with it. One night she is late; he suffers tortures of temptation for an hour and, when she arrives, storms out with "Thanks for all your help." She runs after him and there follows a gem of a scene, which contains just ten words of dialogue, oh my fellow writers:

SUE: Where are you going, Sammy?
SAMMY: (*No answer.*)
SUE: Woman?
SAMMY: Maybe.
SUE: How about me? (*She takes him by the arm and shepherds him back to the flat.*)

It may be gathered that I liked *The Small Back Room*, that I was pleased with it. And so I was, but it was a failure for all that. The critics said it was the best picture that Powell and Pressburger had ever made. The public stayed away in droves. They refused to accept that it was a love story. It was a war film. And war films were out—O-U-T.

I have said that the critics understood this film and consequently praised it, but there is always a fly in the ointment, and I put it there. There is this sequence when Sammy Rice is waiting for Sue and pining for the one thing that will make him forget his tin foot—scotch. Now, Sammy obviously has a background of breakdowns and lost weekends, and it is probable that Sue is the latest of a long line of women trying to save him from himself. Hein Heckroth and Arthur Lawson came to see me about this sequence, Hein very nervous and taking notes in a book, Arthur calm and precise. He said, "We have come to see you, Michael. How are you going to handle the time element in this sequence? Sammy must have been waiting for Sue for at least two hours. I suppose you'll cut all around the set?"

I said, "How do you mean?" and racked my brains for a solution. Hein said timidly, "I have done some sketches, Micky. Would you like to see them?" I looked at them. They were beautifully done, but it was the usual montage of clocks, photographs of Sue, etc. I said, "That's pretty boring. Let's reduce it to the man, a clock, and the whiskey bottle." Hein brightened up. "How big a clock, Micky?"

"Oh, about as big as a man. It's got to work, of course."

After a brief stir, Arthur made some notes of his own. "How about the whiskey bottles?"

"Oh, different sizes, from life-size to about fifteen feet high."

Hein paused. "Are you serious, Micky?"

I gave him my most innocent stare.

"Well, he has to fight it, doesn't he—push it away and then it towers over him and tries to crush him? Isn't that the idea?"

"The room is very small, Micky," said Arthur reprovingly. "How are you going to introduce a fifteen-foot whiskey bottle into it?"

By now I had the bit between my teeth.

"That's your business. I would suggest building a separate set, just plain white flats. We'll throw shadows on them. Talk to Chris about it."

Chris Challis and Hein got together and worked out some Caligari lighting. Of course, David Farrar loved the idea of fighting off the advances of a fifteen-foot whiskey bottle. We all had great fun shooting it, but then the kissing had to stop. The critics, as one man, and several women, condemned the whiskey-bottle sequence. They hinted at German Expressionism, with sidelong glances at poor Hein, who was certainly not to blame. In the final analysis, they concluded that we were not to be trusted. The Archers had been too clever by half in *A Matter of Life and Death*. They had forced poor David Niven to spout whole verses of English poetry. They had even dragged in Plato, and put words into his mouth that were neither classical nor Greek. *Black Narcissus* was blatant sex . . . that scene with the nun and the lipstick— really!—bad taste. *The Red Shoes* went too far altogether, and had been insolent in its assumption that art was for art's sake, something to die for. With *The Small Back Room* The Archers had made a nice, tidy film, realistic and predictable in a setting familiar to everyone and adapted from a moderately successful English novel that Fleet Street had read. And this for Korda, the arch sophisticate, not for the hitherto uneasy bedfellows of The Archers, Rank, and Davis. And then, just as the critics were prepared to give us 90 out of 100 (for no frustrated filmmaker can give another filmmaker 100 percent praise) we had shown our cloven Continental hoof. We were being unpredictable again. We were untrustworthy. Either Powell was corrupting Pressburger, or Pressburger, Powell. Time would show which. Meanwhile, they would keep their eyes on us.

There are little tragedies in the editing of every film—what David Niven would call face-on-the-cutting-room-floor department—and in *The Small Back Room* the face was Judy Lang's. I had spotted her in the famous little Players Theatre, under the railway arches at Charing Cross Station and facing Villiers Street, where the great Duke of Buckingham, George Villiers, flaunted his crests on the banks of the Thames. The Players was a Victorian music hall, and almost every actor and actress worth their salt had appeared upon the Players' outrageous boards. The chairman of this priceless music hall was, from the beginning, Leonard Sachs, and he was a show in himself. The particular show in question was the annual Christmas Pantomime, and Judy was playing the Principal Boy. She had the legs and knew how to use them, strutting about like a boy and not like a girl in tights. I watched her with considerable interest, as usual when I see raw talent in the making. She had the actress's face. If you want to know what an actress looks like, an actress who has the actress's face, then go to the Garrick Club in London and ask Marius Goring. He will show you the portrait of Peg Woffington there. The members of the Garrick Club adopt certain pictures, and Marius has adopted this one. He's an actor himself, you see, falls in love very easily, and would have out-Garricked Garrick as the partner of the tempestuous Peg.

David Garrick would have approved of Judy Lang. I had a talk with her after the show. She had it—whatever it may be. I decided to give her a break. She was cast as the fanatic ballet fan in the gallery in the opening scenes of *The Red Shoes*.

I did not see her again until we were casting for *The Small Back Room*, when I sent for her. She was acting in the provinces and they had some difficulty finding her. Seeing me, the penny dropped. She said, "Oh—hello!"

I said, "I want you to play this part. Syd, give her the slag-heap sequence." Syd rummaged around for it.

Judy said, "I've read it. I've got a friend in the casting department. It's a very small part, isn't it?"

Syd looked mildly reproving. This was obviously a very forward girl, and Michael was being very chatty, for him. He usually stared at them with those eyes of his. I said, "There's no such thing as a small part in a film. There are long parts and there are short parts, but every part is important, because for that length of time you are carrying the film and you could be alone on the screen."

She nodded. "Do you want me to read it for you?"

"No."

"What do you pay, Michael?"

"What's the part worth, Syd?"

Syd indicated with the point of his pencil a figure on the list of names before him. The figure was £80. "It's only one day's work, Michael, and you said you didn't care what the weather was like, we would shoot anyway."

I said to Judy, "We need you for the whole weekend. Saturday and Sunday. We'll pay you a hundred fifty pounds."

Syd said nothing. She said, "And expenses?"

"What do you call expenses?"

"Twenty quid."

"Done. You get your contract from the casting department."

As a love scene, it had its points.

The slag-heap sequence in the original script is the first time that Sammy is called away from his small back room to do some detective work on the bomb. It took place in the industrial Midlands, and we shot it at Lichfield. Two little boys, brothers, had been playing on a slag heap, found a fascinating object, and the elder one had picked it up and blown himself to bits. Stuart, Sammy, and the mother of the boys, carrying a third child in her arms, bring the little boy who had seen his brother killed to the slag heap in the hope of him remembering what the bomb looked like. The mother is stoical and helpful, and encourages the little boy to speak. When questioned by Stuart, he bursts into tears and runs to his mother. She ruffles his hair and says, "He's a good boy, aren't you, Danny? But he's too young, see?" The men look at each other. They realize they'll have to wait until another child like this is killed before they can make any progress.

Judy wore no makeup and her hair was grimy, but her face was clean and shone like a daisy. She wore a cotton dress of blurred print and bedroom slippers on bare legs. She wore a cheap wedding ring and that was about all. The two men in their stupid wartime clothes made her look more fragile. Stuart wore his long military greatcoat, Sammy his old belted raincoat and soft hat. The children were good and all three actors were top quality. The scene had that poetic quality that only comes by a combination of circumstances. But in the editing, the film seemed overlong and the slag-heap sequence ended up on the cutting-room floor. I wrote to Judy, warning her that the sequence had been dropped and saying, "Better luck next time." She never answered.

I ran into her at the Arts Theatre. She was with Peter Powell. The theatre and the lobby were crowded, but we both knew that the other was there. We met at the bar. We looked at each other. The fish were still biting. She said, "Pity about that scene, wasn't it?"

I nodded. She said, "Remember when you and that cameraman were talking under my window? If I had become your mistress, would you have made me a star?"

I said, "Depends on you. My actresses have to have more on the ball than it takes to fuck your way to stardom."

She said, "So I've heard."

She married Peter Powell and they had four boys. I stopped to see her twenty years later, when she was living in an old mill in Kendal in Westmorland. She and Peter were working with Border Television. The fish were still biting, but it was too late to do anything about it. She had the best of the bargain.

The film may have delighted the critics, but it puzzled our public. Noreen Ackland, Reggie's assistant editor, declared that the love scenes between David Farrar and Kathleen Byron made the public uncomfortable: "They're so real, they make you feel you are spying through a keyhole at the two lovers." There may have been something in it. In the sequence where Sammy Rice isolates and defuses the bomb, a sequence in which the audience is held in suspense for about seventeen minutes, they see the kind of David Farrar that had been promised them by the sexy Mr. Dean of *Black Narcissus.* But for most of the film Sammy is a miserable, complaining, self-destructive failure, and the part required more humor and self-mockery to be written into the script to save Sammy from being a bore. We were to blame for not foreseeing this. It was the same old problem of adapting a film script from a book, particularly when the book is well written. The more that we admired and used Nigel Balchin's mordant psychology, the less the public liked the film, and although Kathleen Byron played Sue beautifully, the public sensed her intelligence and refused to believe that she would waste so much time over Sammy's agonizing. I saw the film through more than thirty years later at the New York retrospective showing of my films, and found this particular movie a cold one. But in 1948, I needed to tell a love story like *The Small Back Room.* I needed to escape from romance into reality. I needed to create the kind of woman that I admire, who keeps the world turning without making a song and dance about it. I needed Sue.

=

Art is the child of sex and religion. This is particularly true in filmmaking, where the director holds the strings of all his puppets, and is answerable to nothing and nobody. It is why the film director has become a legendary twentieth-century character at a time when everything, especially sex and religion, is subject to public analysis. He has the power of a god, a single-minded god. It is why I am writing this book.

The craft is a mystery. Nobody can explain it. Writers on film can list the qualities—supreme confidence, endless patience, excessive energy—but they can't explain how those moving, talking images got onto the screen and excited the audience so. Impressionist painting could not have existed before the nineteenth century. There was no need for it, no demand for it. But when it was recognized, it took over. The twentieth century belongs to film. Once more, this is why I am writing this book.

From my very first film, I was a high priest of the mysteries. I took my authority for granted. Actors and actresses hated me. As for me, I question whether I knew they existed, except as two-dimensional images in the cutting room. Working on quota-quickies* I had no time to teach them film techniques. I was merciless on bad actors, amateur actors, slow actors, or nervous actors. I doubt if I looked on actresses as women at all. I approved of them because they were more efficient than men. They sensed this indifference and were insulted. Most women haven't got time to cultivate a sense of humor. In my first thirty films, I left behind me no broken hearts, but a string of complexes. Then, one after another, I broke my heart for Deborah, was enchanted by that witch Pamela, and met in Kathleen an intelligence as cool as my own.†

I have always had a special respect for Kathleen ever since she pulled a gun on me. It was a revolver, a big one, U.S. Army issue, and it was loaded. A naked woman and a loaded gun are persuasive objects, and I have always thought that I deserved congratulations for talking myself out of that one. There was a blazing honesty about her that I had recognized from the beginning, but that made other people uncomfortable. She was too straight to be an actress, but she was a good one. She had no tricks. She looked straight through a situation with those wonderful eyes of hers and made what she wanted of it. I dreamed up the part of the Angel for her in *A Matter of Life and*

---

*Michael cut his teeth as a director on films that were made very quickly and cheaply (£1 a foot was the average cost) to comply with a 1927 British quota law requiring exhibitors to show a minimum percentage of British-made product, in an attempt to halt the overwhelming tide of American films pouring into Britain. These little films (often barely fifty minutes long) came to be known as "quota-quickies." Many of the twenty-three films Michael directed before he made *The Edge of the World* were quota-quickies.

†Michael had fallen in love with Deborah Kerr, then a young actress at the start of her career, during the making of *The Life and Death of Colonel Blimp*. Pamela Brown was a noted stage actress who appeared in *One of Our Aircraft Is Missing* before she and Michael began a long relationship during *I Know Where I'm Going!*

Death, and in *Black Narcissus* she played the passion-torn nun, Sister Ruth, in a way that made people shift uneasily in their seats. She had a strange beauty that flared and faded while you watched.

Sue, in *The Small Back Room,* might seem a bit of an anticlimax to play after Sister Ruth. But that is only half true. Kathleen is a close-up girl. Like Myrna Loy, the luminous intelligence with which her eyes and mouth were endowed transcended the substance of her scenes with Jack Hawkins and David Farrar. They were in a different world. Only in the brief scene with Michael Gough, an actor of her quality, did I capture the flutter of an angel's wings.

Why didn't I make more pictures with Kathleen Byron, if I thought so highly of her? Because the parts were not there; and I'm not in this business to work for women.

At the Guildhall celebration of the British Film Institute's fiftieth anniversary, thirty-five years later, Thelma suddenly clasped my arm and said, "Look, there's Kathleen Byron!"—and so it was! There was the deep, withdrawn personality and the luminous eyes! There was the voice with the hint of mockery in it. Thelma was more excited than she had been by meeting Moira Shearer and Wendy Hiller in the flesh. She had recognized Kathleen's special quality, then and now, woman to woman.

Chris Challis and I went straight from shooting the final scenes of *The Small Back Room* in black and white to the opening scenes of *The Elusive Pimpernel,* in elusive Technicolor. I had agreed to the new title, but my heart remained unconvinced. Whichever way we sliced it, the film was still a remake of the original book, play, and film. Korda's film had been such a success because it was brilliantly theatrical, was directed with style and wit, and had three big stars in Leslie Howard, Merle Oberon, and Raymond Massey. The big scenes were all studio scenes with one or two shots of a coach bowling along a carriage drive to reassure the audience that there was some action in the picture. It had nothing to do with European filmmaking. It was a Hollywood picture. And it was before the war, when films were a popular form of entertainment with no responsibilities to the future.

I hate remakes, and I have always said so, unless it is the reworking of a classic like *Tartuffe.* It was dishonest of Alex to beguile me into an artistic decision for his financial gain, but I follow his reasoning. He had commissioned *The Red Shoes* from Emeric before the war, had sold the rights to us and pocketed the profit after the war, without ever thinking that we were going to turn it into one of the greatest international successes ever made. He had seen the picture at the press screening, and unlike Arthur Rank and John Davis, had at once realized the box-office possibilities of such a stunning show. I have already related how it was he, and not Arthur Rank, who showed the film privately to the King, the Queen, and their daughters. Naturally he thought, with his clever brain full of a myriad combinations, that we would do the same brilliant transformation job on *Pimpernel*. I followed his piping and fell into the trap.

The French have a word for it. When a film is a failure, they call it a *navet*, a turnip. When the film has color and costume and music and a great deal of money has obviously been spent on it, and it is still a failure, they call it a *super-navet*, a super-turnip. *The Elusive Pimpernel* was a super-super-turnip.

We had great fun making it, this super-turnip, this gilded turnip. There was to be no singing, but music and action throughout. The costumes, both English and French, were to be the most fantastic of a fantastic era. We commissioned Brian Easdale to write the music, Hein Heckroth to do the sets and costumes. They gathered around them all the team that had made *The Red Shoes* and many more.

The original film was studio-made and had virtually no exteriors. "We need fresh air in this story," I proclaimed. Sir Percy had a schooner, the *Daydream*, in which he and his followers cross the Channel to France, and return with it loaded with noble French aristos, snatched from the guillotine. "We need this ship. Find it!"

> Up spoke Bill Paton
> And a salty man was he

"Cocky Mills is the man for the job."

He was right, of course. Bill always is right when it's a question of mice and men. George Mills, known to his friends as "Cocky" Mills, had met The Archers head-on at Ramsgate, at the time we were making *Contraband*. As a deep-sea sailor, a master mariner, a film fan in the Royal Naval Reserve, he had been invaluable to us as liaison. Bill and he had lost touch, and when we started shooting the scenes on Chesil Bank for *The Small Back Room*, who should I see turn up as acting quartermaster to the unit but Cocky Mills, who, being an old hand at scrounging, soon became the most influential man in the company. For the first time since we won the war a film unit was served a hot meal on location, and The Archers' care for their personnel began its legend. George hoped to go with us on *Pimpernel* as location manager, but the unions objected. But there is one thing about the film business—if you're an expert at anything that happens to be of vital importance to the director, all doors that are otherwise closed to you fly open and let you through. It was about this time that I called for the *Daydream*, and with a master's ticket in sail, nobody could dispute George's credentials. He located a two-masted schooner, the *Nellie Bywater*, owner and master Captain Richard England. The Captain describes in his book, *Schoonerman*, how Cocky Mills boarded his ship and signed him up to support David Niven: "He assured me that the film charter would be just a well-paid holiday for us all, and we'd personally meet some of the world's top screen stars and see them at work. 'All we need,' he said, 'is a few shots of your ship sailing off the Breton coast, and off Dover. You'll have a marvelous time!'"

We searched southern England for Regency houses, streets, palaces, crescents. We found wonderful locations on the Marlborough Downs and in Savernake Forest. We sent scouts out especially to find white dusty roads on private estates. Personally, I was more inspired by Arthur Conan Doyle's *Rodney Stone* than I was by Baroness Orczy's cloak-and-dagger book. Conan Doyle's book glorified the eccentric and extravagant men who set the style for the English upper classes for more than a hundred years. They were horsemen, gamblers, connoisseurs, and only afraid of being unfashionable.

Around David Niven I assembled a group of remarkable young men, eccentrics like Beau Brummel, who caught a cold because his man sent him out on a cold morning with a tortoise-shell snuffbox instead of porcelain. I wanted dandies and daredevils, and I found them: Pat Macnee, Dave Hutcheson, Bob Coote, etc. I wanted beautiful young women in every shade of color, women who would have made the painter Romney, the lover of Emma Hamilton, grab for his brushes. I held a special audition for beautiful bosoms for the camera shot in the scene where the Prince is blindfolded but, as he is circled by the ladies, is able to identify them by means I am afraid I cannot disclose for fear of *lèse-majesté*.

I wanted the scenes in France to be shot in France and in the French language. I wanted the French actors to be French. You would think that reasonable, wouldn't you? Above all, I wanted the fascinating Lady Blakeney, who was French in the book, to be a French actress. Here I struck a rock—I was going too far. Maggie Leighton was to play Lady Blakeney, declared Alex! I came down to earth with a bump. Maggie Leighton! She looked like a horse and had cross eyes, always a bad sign in a horse. She wasn't a film actress. She had a breathy, Manchester voice with overtones of Brighton. Ralph, Larry, and John Burrell had picked her out to play the principal female parts in their wonderful comeback season at the Old Vic. She had been comic as the Green Woman in *Peer Gynt*, wilting as Roxane, wispy and droopy in *Uncle Vanya*—why the hell did Alex, apart from the obvious reason, want her to play the fascinating, volatile, fashionable, and perfidious Lady Blakeney?

I was still young enough—I *am* still young enough—to think that the good of the film comes first. Alex waved away my furious objections with the glowing tip of a Corona: "You will enjoy working with her, Micky dear. She is very *spirituelle*." (*Spirituelle* is French. Alex was rubbing salt in the wound.) "David is enchanted with her." That is not what David told *me*.

She was sent to my house in Ilchester Place. She looked as enthusiastic as a Christian martyr baiting a lion. I knew she was impulsive, generous, and foolish, qualities that are all on the right side. We gazed at each other glumly. She looked just like a man to me. She said, "I know I am just about the last person you want to work with, Micky." I couldn't contradict a lady. She faltered those well-worn words, "How do you see the part?"

Whatever I saw, I certainly didn't see *her* in it. I said, "In the theatre, the whole stage lit up when she came on."

"Who?"

"Julia Neilson." Her face changed and she looked interested.

"You mean that you actually saw Fred Terry and Julia Neilson in the play? How wonderful!"

We talked theatre for half an hour and then she went off to report to Alex. I was profoundly depressed. I was about to direct a huge film that I didn't believe in, and starring a horse. Worse, I was leading one of my best friends, David Niven, into this trap. We were all going to work together not for fun, but for the old, dreary producers' reasons that had turned filmmaking into a great yawn. I was responsible to Emeric and to all my people. I was trapped.

Although delighted to be back with The Archers, David was as uneasy as I was. We confided our doubts to each other over the makeup tests. It has to be remembered that David Niven would never—could never—and never did play anybody but himself. His two wonderfully funny books, *The Moon's a Balloon* and *Bring On the Empty Horses,* make this quite clear. His charm, his rugged honesty, and, let's face it, his shrewdness carried him through many a sticky situation. Just before he came back to England to join up in 1940, Samuel Goldwyn had signed him to a long-term contract on the strength of his performance with Ginger Rogers in a delightful comedy, *Bachelor Mother.* Sam never had the slightest idea what David could really do. He proved that by putting him into the romantic part as Merle Oberon's husband in William Wyler's *Wuthering Heights.* David himself knew very well what he could do best, and we discussed this as we sat side by side, gazing into the dressing-room mirror studded with lights, while the makeup man behind us carefully adjusted a new, beautiful wig.

"Micky, old chum, do you really think it's me—the Pimp, I mean?"

"Of course it is. We've written it for you, haven't we?"

"George, how about having the hairline a little bit lower. I don't want to look like the bald-headed woman in the circus, do I? It's all very well, Micky, to say you have written it for me, but it's still the same part, really."

This was true and hard to rebut. I played for time.

"Are you talking about a particular scene, or the part in general?"

"Oh, come on, Micky—you know very well what I mean! It's pure corn, isn't it?"

"What's wrong with that? Doug Fairbanks pinched the whole idea for his *The Mark of Zorro* . . . languid, jokey aristocrat, moving in the best circles, out the door then in the window as the daring, avenging Zorro. It can't miss. It's been great theatre ever since Martin-Harvey played the dual role in *A Tale of Two Cities.*"

"That's just it, you oaf! It's theatre! That costume stuff was all right for Doug and for Larry, Tam Williams, and Miles Mander and all that. They enjoy it and they're good at it. Now I'm not. George! You'll have to do something about my ears!"

"S'awright, Mr. Niven, I'll tape 'em."

"I mean to say, Micky, look at me! Do I look like a cloak swisher to you? I've got the biggest bottom in the world, and I know it. Can you see me popping in and out of windows like Douglas Fairbanks? The idea is ludicrous!"

"Nobody wants you to play it like Doug Fairbanks. You just have to play it in your own way, that's all."

"Yes, that's all. All right, George, let's try the other wig—the one that makes me look like Joan Blondell."

We had many similar conversations. A lot of it was David's way of coming to terms with his director about how to play the part. He was a most conscientious worker. He always knew his lines and he was always running them with any actor who was willing to take the time to go through the scene with him. He was quite sincere in declaring that he was no actor, but he cultivated his personality rigorously. He was always telling stories, inventing characters, trying out jokes. He had a priceless sense of the absurd.

"Micky, old squirt, have you noticed how extras always agree with each other?"

"What do you mean?"

"Well, look at 'em! They nod and smile . . . they like the wine, they like the food, they like each other . . . see how they do it? They never hate the food, they never send for the headwaiter; they just sit there nodding and smiling and agreeing with each other and drinking this dreadful French wine, Château Hogwash, that the prop department dishes out to them, until you say, 'Cut!' "

I opened my eyes and looked. He was right. There they were, nodding and smiling, sedulously avoiding the director's eyes until he should yell, "Cut!"

I yelled, "Cut!"

We had made *The Small Back Room* for London Films, from and in the little Worton Hall Studios. We knew nothing about Shepperton, except that Zoli Korda had shot a lot of the canoe scenes of *Sanders of the River* there on the weedy river overhung with trees that runs through the grounds. The studios had been commandeered throughout the war and were only just restaffing. Alex was moving in with great plans that included us, but we didn't trust

Alex not to interfere with our production, and so we decided to get as far away from Shepperton as we could—to Elstree, the other side of London, in Hertfordshire.

I returned to Elstree after twelve years with no enthusiasm. It had been my first contact with British films and I associated the place with all that I disliked most about them: amateurism, snobbism, insularity, smugness, a lack of friendliness and an almost total lack of information . . . and mud. I shall always associate the name of Elstree with mud. To reach it by train you go to St. Pancras Station, one of the triumphs of Railway Gothic. You take a ticket to Borehamwood, the station and village that serves the studios. There is no wood at Borehamwood, but there is plenty of Boreham. It is not a village, it is a happening. This was all good arable land not many years ago: fields and hedges and pasture sloping up to the high ridge overlooking the Thames Valley, from which during the last war Fighter Command looked down on and protected London. On a clear day you can stand on this ridge, near the house where Stanley Kubrick holes up, and look across London to the Surrey hills. This view and this ridge, which runs for miles, almost redeem this part of Hertfordshire. The actual village of Elstree lies about a mile away along the ridge. It is tiny, and in my day the traffic thundered through it unceasingly. There is a little inn there called The Plough, which has many associations for me with Alfred Hitchcock and others. Why this small and rather charming village had given its name to the vast studio complex a couple of miles away, I don't know.

The shambles that is Borehamwood lines the road between the railway station and the big studios. In 1928 a little group of red-brick buildings stood in a field to the north of the road. In bold letters on the roof was painted IDEAL FILMS. There was something pathetic and yet defiant about this morose statement. The studios had been there some time. But in 1928 times were changing, and soon after I first set foot in Elstree mud, the sign IDEAL FILMS was changed too, first of all to BLATTNER FILMS and then a year or two later to ROCK FILMS. This was not an anticipation of the rock-and-roll era, but the name of Joe Rock, who had financed my *The Edge of the World*. After Joe vanished back to America the studio was taken over by an entrepreneur called Lou Jackson. He was almost too good to be true. He was like a caricature of a B-movie producer, and he knew it and enjoyed it. But he got films made, and it was on a visit to his studio to see my old friend Vernon Sewell that I met David Farrar, who was playing a stunt flyer in a wartime movie that Lou had thrown together and Vernon was directing.

But now, in 1948, all that was past history. The boom was on, and films were being made and stages were being built. The hopeful little studio-born Ideal Films, which had been through so many metamorphoses, had gone, and a vast new studio had arisen on the site. It was new, it was very new. It was not yet finished, but we had our own unit, including our head electrician, Bill Wall, and we moved in anyway. Until Shepperton would be ready it was the only studio available with stages big enough for our musical numbers. Pinewood and Denham were closed to us. We needed a base for our art department to sketch and prepare sets and costumes. Hein and Arthur had to organize all this from zero. The famous theatrical costume firms—Morris Angel, Simons, Bermans, and Nathans—had somehow survived the war, but none of them were big enough to tackle a job like this, which called for hundreds of original costumes. Today, of course, a great firm like Bermans (which has swallowed Simons and then merged with Nathans to become Bermans and Nathans) could costume everybody but the principals at a week's notice. But in 1948 England was still on rationing. Austerity was the cry! We had won the war. We had lost the Empire. Now we must tighten our belts and save Europe. Meekly England submitted. But not The Archers. We thought that the best way to save Europe was to make extravagant, romantic British films. We had already seen the effect on the European countries of *The Red Shoes* and *A Matter of Life and Death.* We were beginning to see it in the U.S.A. Our allies, now our competitors, were staggered to see such wit, such luxury, such invention, bouncing out of this gray, weather-beaten little island. All our people were imbued with the same confidence, the same audacity. We were invincible.

I had already made a quick reconnaissance trip to France and settled on the city of Tours, in the valley of the Loire, to be our base. George Busby was, of course, very much in his element because of his perfect French, and the hotel we stayed at had a restaurant that was many-starred in the *Guide Michelin.* The châteaux of the Loire had suffered very little damage in the fighting. We had swept around them, or over them, and they had been kept in very good order by their owners, who had been forced to stay at home for a change. Châteaux like Chenonceaux and Rigny Ussé were dreams of beauty, their gardens and cascades scrupulously cared for. Of course, these are picture-postcard châteaux, heavily restored, but none the less beautiful for that. But at Amboise you feel you might meet François I round any corner, strolling with Leonardo da Vinci, and as for the Royal Château of Blois, it is not dead, but sleeping.

It was like fairyland after the grim realities of *The Small Back Room,* and we reveled in it. My plan was to keep Percy and his elegant friends always on the move, either on horseback, or at sea on board the *Daydream.* The word went out to Sir Percy's gentlemen that they had to learn to ride a horse, or get left out of the best of the action. Some of them never learned, but they hung on somehow. There was a rumor that I had used dummies on horseback, but that was only the way that some of them rode. I won't deny that there was a certain snobbishness about this on my part, having been, as my readers know, brought up on a horse.

The film opened with a magnificent shot of thirty horsemen, which included all the male members of the cast, cantering along the banks of the Loire. I know there were thirty when they started, but I wouldn't like to say how many of them finished the course. The horses were a mixed bag, too—none of your English thoroughbreds that I would have liked to have seen. We picked them up when and where we could. Most of the horses, of course, had been eaten during the war. We planned to be at Tours for about two weeks and then cross the river and jump north to our other big location sequence at Mont-Saint-Michel, on the coast of Normandy.

Mont-Saint-Michel has to be seen to be believed, and having seen it it is still hard to believe it. Imagine a fortified mountain, crowned by a cathedral, shooting up out of the level sands of an enormous inland bay. At low tide the bay empties and peasants' carts trundle over miles of sand, looking for seaweed and shellfish. They keep a weather eye on their watches, for the sea lurks behind a distant sandbar that holds back the rising tide until, with one final effort, it bursts over the bar and floods the huge basin in a matter of minutes. Then, if your watch has stopped, you may run and pray, but nothing can save you. At high tide the sea surrounds Mont-Saint-Michel and you can only reach it by a stone causeway. At the seaward end of the causeway is a hamlet where you can buy souvenirs and where the famous hotel dispenses its equally famous omelettes made in an iron frying pan held by a four-foot-long handle over an open fire, with a pound of butter frothing in the pan. From here the fortified pathway zigzags up the mountain to the abbey and the church at the summit. No more romantic or dramatic location could possibly be found for the last confrontation between the foppish Englishman, Sir Percy Blakeney, and Citizen Chauvelin, representative of the French Republic.

I would have liked to play Marius Goring as Chauvelin. It would have completed a triptych of memorable performances: the Heavenly Messenger of *A Matter of Life and Death;* Julian, the young composer of the Ballet of the Red Shoes; Chauvelin, the crafty representative of the people's republic. But I felt—and I think Marius felt too—that to play another important part with a French accent would be a mistake and that audiences who had loved him as the gay, foolish young Heavenly Messenger would be disappointed by the sinister aspects of the remorseless Citizen Chauvelin. Then, in *The Red Shoes* Marius had added at least another ten years to his career by playing down to about twenty-six years old as the beloved, and lover, of the glamorous Miss Shearer. He could reasonably hope for a few more juveniles or leading men after creating the impulsive and passionate Julian Craster. Luckily, I had another candidate for the part: Cyril Cusack.

I had not been working for five minutes on the scenes between Sammy Rice and Corporal Taylor in *The Small Back Room* before I realized that here was a great actor. Great acting is compounded not only of personality and imagination, but of vibrations. Sometimes suddenly, sometimes slowly, the director, or the audience, becomes aware that a new element has entered the scene. The words are no longer a screen behind which the author hides, they have become a musical instrument upon which this genius, or this monster, or this witch, plays a fascinating tune. We become aware of height and depth, of human joy and grief that we have never known and never suspected. The director stops thinking about the wardrobe or schedule, or the lunch with an important person, and lets his imagination take wing. For a brief while he is a very happy man. Problems that seemed insoluble vanish. Harmony is created. Other actors discover that they had it in them after all, so contagious is the divine gift of inspiration. And at the end of the day's rehearsal, what does the possessor of this divine gift do? If he is a Continental actor he goes home, eats a good dinner prepared by his wife, goes to bed, and sleeps with her until she brings him a *café* and *croissant* in the morning. If he is English— or Irish, or Welsh, or Scottish—he gets drunk.

Bad actors get drunk too, but they are not so bad in their drunkenness as good actors. This is known as Powell's Law.

Way back at the beginning of the war, either before Larry went to Hollywood or after, I forget which, Vivien Leigh, anxiously supervised by Larry, played Mrs. Dubedat in a revival of GBS's *Doctor's Dilemma*. She had appeared on the stage before, in Sidney Carroll's production of *The Masque of Virtue*, but she had never sustained a big role like this. Larry needn't have worried. Whereas in the other play her looks had carried her through, here her brilliant, witty brain triumphed. I had never cared for Vivien, either as an actress or as a woman. When Pamela told me that she and Vivien were thinking of playing together in Albee's *A Delicate Balance*, I applauded the intention (particularly as Pamela was to play the drunk), but I felt sorry for Vivien—they were not in the same class.

Anyway, I went to the Haymarket out of curiosity and stayed, and was completely bowled over by Cyril Cusack's performance as the selfish painter Dubedat. We met backstage and I told him I hoped we could work together. Shortly after this, I was told that Cyril arrived at the Haymarket Theatre one matinee afternoon with a few whiskeys under his belt. He hadn't eaten. His condition was not observed until he was on in the second act. As can be imagined, the act was a riot. Eventually Vivien stormed off leaving a trail of four-letter words, and the ASM* rang down the curtain. The audience was told that Mr. Cusack was ill, and the performance would be finished with the

*Assistant stage manager.

understudy. Cyril was not a drunk. If Vivien hadn't already been such a big star, I think the incident might have been forgiven or overlooked, and I can't help feeling there was a certain amount of vindictiveness on the part of the young Oliviers. Anyway, Cyril was fired and another actor brought in to take over. Meanwhile, the play went on with the understudy.

It would have broken many an actor, but Cyril is a devout Catholic. He is also made of steel. He returned to Ireland and resumed the unrewarding job of creating an Irish Theatre in Irish. I say unrewarding, because if you do something new and experimental in Ireland the Church comes down on you. On the other hand, if you do something old, tried, and true the critics come down on you. I am always stirring up trouble, so during the war years I tried to get him over to play a small part in *I Know Where I'm Going!,* but there was too much danger of him being press-ganged into the British Army. Emeric had only seen Cyril as Corporal Taylor in *The Small Back Room,* but he shared my opinion of him as an actor of subtlety and power.

So we cast him as Chauvelin, which gave some originality to the cardboard parts, but the more we put into the wooden old play, the more it creaked. No wonder! We were all pulling in different directions. I was directing a musical, David was playing David Niven, Emeric was buying a new house, Cyril was wrestling with a realistic French accent, and Maggie Leighton was giving a rep performance of a breathless Englishwoman, all eyes and mouth.

I made one last attempt to get her off the film. While we were shooting in Tours, a Paris agent sent a young French actress down to see me. She had been working in Hollywood, and had sung "La Marseillaise" in *Casablanca.* She didn't seem to be much of an actress, but she had all the looks that Lady Blakeney ought to have. She was tall, dark, and romantic, with magnificent eyes. She spoke good English with an accent, and I thought I could make something of her natural assets. I sent her over to see Alex, who made her a proposition, all right—but not the one I had in mind. Margaret was too firmly in the saddle. The girl's name was Madeleine LeBeau.

I am sorry to be so unkind about Margaret Leighton—"and besides the wench is dead"—but this total lack of comprehension of the difference between stage and screen acting, between stage and screen personality, has always dogged British films, and continues to do so. It is desirable for a country to have a capital city like London or Paris, where the arts are dominant, where money can be raised, and where the leading writers, actors, and directors can work in theatre and in films simultaneously. In America, the unnatural situation that is created by Hollywood on the West Coast and New York on the East Coast is solved by money. It is not a good solution. To have no money is bad, but to have too much is worse. An artist needs to find his own level.

It seems that it is only France that is able to produce every year, with unfailing regularity, a bunch of attractive, intelligent women who take to the screen like ducks to water. They are, of course, French, which helps a lot, because they have been trained since birth by their equally gifted mothers to look on man as the natural enemy. A Frenchwoman knows her place in the world and sets about organizing it as soon as she can talk. An English girl, when asked her opinion about anything, usually says, "I don't know. What do *you* think?" An American girl quotes *Time* or *Newsweek*. A Frenchwoman (there are no French girls over the age of puberty) has opinions about everything and is prepared to defend them in a thousand well-chosen words.

My master in the movies, Luis Buñuel, loved Frenchwomen; you could see it in his films. He loved their poise, their imagination, their childishness: I don't believe he thought they had a soul. In one of his last films (I think it was *The Discreet Charm of the Bourgeoisie*), he had some excellent actresses in the cast, who moved and walked divinely, and whenever he had nothing else for them to do, he set them walking on French provincial roads. They walked—how they walked!—with nobility, swiftness, and decision. I too could watch Frenchwomen walking forever.

We in England have our lovely women, and I have tried to show you some of them in my films. But since our lovely girls are tall, they are more usually model girls who get snapped up at once by discerning politicians, painters, and athletic-looking City men. This leaves too many holes for little rats and mice to creep into the theatre and cinema. One good thing about Maggie was that she was tall. She was very conscious of this, and instead of letting me handle it in my own way (for the camera can make people tall or short, according to where you place it), she was always stooping with the idea of minimizing her height. I was always picking on her for this. One day, she came on the set with the whole of her lower jaw outlined in dark greasepaint. She looked nervously at me for approval. I said, "Didn't you shave this morning, Margaret?" The camera crew grinned; she looked flustered.

"It's this awful jawline of mine. I thought some shading would improve it."

Chris Challis said cheerfully, "Don't worry, Maggie. I can fix that. What you've done is give yourself a five-o'clock shadow."

The makeup man who had accompanied her onto the set nodded vigorously. I said, "Take her away. Give her a plain makeup and lots of eye makeup. No lips. We'll fix that later on the set."

Poor Maggie! She was never allowed to forget that "five-o'clock shadow." She was stage through and through. Many actors and actresses don't understand the difference between the audience watching you act and the camera watching you think. The film director is to blame here too, of course, for forgetting this simple fact, or, perhaps, for never having known it. I am always unhappy if I can't see both eyes of an actor during an important scene. Words! Words! Actors get drunk on words, and so do directors, to their shame.

We went to see a film last night at Tiburon, halfway between us, at San Quentin, and the Golden Gate. It was a British film and it was full of words. It was full of images too—rich, seductive images. But words poured out of the mouths of the characters as if they had been formed for no other purpose but to speak. I think that the film was clever—it *looked* clever—but I was too confused by the spate of words to be sure of that. After all, it was the director who had written the script and directed this cataract of words, so it was reasonable to suppose that he hadn't known where to stop. The film was a Restoration comedy and was beautiful to look at, but there was too much of everything. It was shot around some stately home in Kent, and I had the impression of being hurried through the rooms and gardens by an impatient guide, shouting facts at me and opening and slamming doors and cupboards. I was like a man in a boat without oars, being whirled along a torrent of words, grabbing helplessly at bushes, sticks, and even reeds in the hope of giving myself time to understand all the words I had just heard, and prepare myself for the new foaming cascades that would tear me away from the bank to which I clung and send me hurtling downstream only half comprehending what was being shouted at me by these Restoration faggots in enormous wigs.

This is not a criticism, it is a report. No doubt this director needed all these words to complete the film. I myself, all these years in movies, have been trying to get rid of words, or at least reduce them to a manageable handful. A film—a good film—does not have the shape of a play, nor of a book. It is more like a saga, a symphony, or a poem. In the early days of silent films we felt this instinctively. Lenin and his film directors had taught us the universal power of image. We imbibed their political statements because of the beauty of the images in *The Battleship Potemkin, The Mother, The General Line, Storm over Asia,* and *October.* These were films! Their directors were concerned that the whole world should understand their message.

I saw a Hollywood film yesterday, January 31, 1984, with a contemporary theme and full of attractive people, talking Hollywood English. The current version is a funny sort of language. An Englishman might possibly understand one word in ten. I can imagine what the old-time film producers would have made of it: "I want to understand what I'm looking at. Take those actors away, wash their mouths out, spray their tonsils, fire the director. I don't want to see what they are saying. I want to hear it. Don't they realize that the British market is thirty-five percent of our European gross?"

The film was shot somewhere in the South, but it might as well have been

Hollywood, for all the Spanish moss hanging on the trees. It has been so overdone in the past that it always looks to me as if the prop man has just nailed it there. Put it down as somewhere in a consumer society. The direction was sympathetic, but remained outside looking in. If I had been an American, I would have been very cross to think that this was the latest modern product of the Hollywood dream factories that had given us, in their day, films like *The Best Years of Our Lives.* This is what talkies and TV have done to the movies. The studio giants have gone, and their pygmy inheritors have taken us back to the 1930s, when two-dimensional images talked, and talked, and talked. And yet there are giants still, creative giants: the men who made *Apocalypse Now, Reds, American Graffiti, Chariots of Fire, Mean Streets . . .* all of them intensely personal films, but with a wild dissimilarity of budgets. It seems as if the film business has to burn itself out every twenty years or so, and start again. It seizes upon each new invention, gobbles it up, and is in its turn gobbled up by the invention: big screen, wide screen, triple screen; the tinted image, the hand-painted image, hand-painted color, Technicolor two-strip, Technicolor three-strip; CinemaScope, Todd-AO, VistaVision—we have had them all, and looking back they seem to moviemakers to have been an enormous waste of time and money. The only invention that has justified itself—and it took years for the camera to regain its mobility—was the talking picture.

In 1948 we had reached one of those watersheds. The decisions that we had to take were, for once, not technical but moral ones. By the end of the war, thanks to the Ministry of Information, we had become accustomed to consultation and approval at a high level of the film we proposed to make. It worked because we respected this higher authority whose brief from Churchill had been to win the war and win the peace. Miraculously the system worked, and important films were made, financed by Arthur Rank, Lady Yule, Two Cities Films, and others. The Americans had nothing like this. Their combat films were an extension of the armed forces, and very remarkable some of them were, particularly when they were directed by filmmakers like John Huston and John Ford. Hollywood made training films and commercial films as part of the war effort. But in England, thanks to *49th Parallel, One of Our Aircraft Is Missing,* Noël Coward's *In Which We Serve,* Ian Dalrymple's *Desert Victory,* a proud and responsible film industry had been born. Thanks to organizing geniuses like John Davis it rested on a sound foundation, and thanks to Independent Producers it had a high reputation before going to the public for money.

I can only speak for myself when I write that the switch for The Archers from wartime idealism to peacetime commercialism was disastrous. Instead of blaming themselves for not finding a market for our films, Rank and Davis blamed us for being too ambitious. I blame myself for deserting to Korda, although what would have happened if I had stayed to fight it out with John, I don't know. He told me one day at a lunch of the Children's Film Foundation, twenty-five years later, that I had said, "Davis must go!" Very possibly I did. I don't see why he bore a grudge against me for it. After all, it was I who went, not he. Probably we should have gone to Hollywood. We had offers enough. But neither Emeric nor I wanted to go. We were proud of what we had done, and we loved the country that had given us the means to do it. We had a wonderful team of collaborators who were devoted to The Archers and when we worked that summer of 1948 on the musical version of *The Elusive Pimpernel* we were confident that we could bring it off, in spite of Alex's little intrigues. But we had not only Alex to deal with. We gradually became conscious of two other powerful figures, whose grotesque shadows were falling across our future plans.

=

In the early years of this century, Samuel Goldfish, born in Warsaw, Poland, emigrated to the United States, changed his name to Samuel Goldwyn, and together with Louis B. Mayer (from Minsk) absorbed the actively producing Metro Company to form Metro-Goldwyn-Mayer—MGM—the famous and fabulous company for which both Rex Ingram and I worked from 1925 to 1927. Goldwyn detested partners and, having assisted at the merger, left the company as soon as possible, although his name remained. It was impossible for Goldwyn and Mayer to be in the same building, let alone the same room. It was the old Metro Company that had produced *The Four Horsemen of the Apocalypse*, the film that had made Rex Ingram a world-famous name, and it was June Mathis, the scenario writer, who brought Ingram to the notice of the Metro Company and later on to Metro-Goldwyn-Mayer. She was the first of many clever women to infiltrate the highest executive positions in the rapidly growing new film business.

Ingram made no secret of his contempt for Mayer's opinions and for his attempts to control Ingram's scripts, and so long as he made successes he got away with it. (Now where have I heard that story before?) Anyway, I heard all about these politics many times during the years that I worked at the Victorine Studios, partly from Frank Scully, and partly from Howard Strickling, who returned to Hollywood and MGM to become Mr. Mayer's personal publicity representative. Frank Scully remained a *Variety* byliner all his life, a completely fearless press man and feature writer who, when the war was over and won, and the Hollywood big shots were high in the saddle again, was responsible for the memorable crack about the return of "the liberated executives of Twentieth Century–Fox: Zanuck from the army and Schenck from jail."

Sam Goldwyn set up his own producing units and eventually released his films through United Artists, which had been set up by D. W. Griffith, Mary Pickford, Douglas Fairbanks, and Charlie Chaplin. UA was formed mainly for distribution purposes and for financing, and it was into this company, before the war, that Alex Korda bought his way, only to find that they had enough product of their own, with the natural consequence that his films became second choice and ended up either as the lower half of a double bill, or on the shelf. The UA studios were in Hollywood, on Santa Monica Boulevard. They later became the Goldwyn Studios. They were a nice handy size. The buildings had some pretentions to style. When I was working with Coppola, and when I got paid, which was not often, I used to walk down to the bank to get my money while it was still in Zoetrope's account, and then stroll on along the boulevard until I came to Goldwyn Studios. The executive offices that form the façade on the street and boulevard (for it was a corner lot) were unpretentious and friendly, in the pink wedding-cake style so beloved in Hollywood's prime. The stucco was pink and fading. Reggie Mills, my editor for so many years, was editing a picture there for Zeffirelli, and Herbert Ross was directing a film musical based upon the BBC production *Pennies from Heaven*. Everybody, including the director, seemed to know what they were doing, but I had my doubts. The stages and services were fine. I hear that Warner Bros. has bought the studios and has already changed the name from Goldwyn Studios to Warner-Hollywood Studios. What barbarians! Goldwyn is one of the great names in films.

For half of our working lives (I mean for those of us in Europe), Sam Goldwyn was a name that spelled quality, like Rolls-Royce. We didn't know him, but we knew his films, and it was obvious that nothing but the best would do for him. At the height of his power and achievement he had the best director (William Wyler), the best lighting cameraman (Gregg Toland), the best editor (Daniel Mandel), and the best of everything. His agents were on the watch all over the world for potential film material and for new actors, actresses, and writers. Anything that spelled quality or box office Sam Goldwyn had to have. He outbid everybody. He bought *Dead End, Dodsworth, The Little Foxes, The Secret Life of Walter Mitty, Wuthering Heights, The Goldwyn Follies*. He filled them with stars and served them up hot. We European gawkers gaped at the smoothness, the quality, the lushness, the realism of these superlative film productions. Actors and actresses who joined his roster were transformed: they had never had material like this before; they had never been like this before. Thanks to Sam Goldwyn we saw Bette Davis, Walter Huston, Fredric March, Barbara Stanwyck, Miriam Hopkins, Herbert Marshall at their very best, at the peak of their achievement. Sam Goldwyn, as far as we were concerned, was the tops.

Some people may say—some people did say—that all that Sam Goldwyn had was money and a clever wife. Frances Howard had certainly been an enchanting actress, and she certainly made him an enchanting wife. Anyone who could live with him that long had to be clever. He never really mastered English, but he bashed it around to such good effect that Goldwynisms became famous the world over. A good specimen is "A verbal contract isn't worth the paper it's written on." He never understood what was wrong about the things he said, but he was delighted that what he said made him famous. As for Frances Goldwyn, she kept her own counsel. And his.

The picture of him that emerges is of a shrewd, power-crazy vulgarian, with an uncanny flair, not uncommon in Eastern European Jews, for the very best in the arts. We shall see what truth there was in this picture.

In the early 1920s, when Samuel Goldwyn and Louis B. Mayer agreed to differ, Lewis J. Selznick, one of the pioneer New York film producers, went broke. But already Hollywood was becoming the most important film center, and his two boys went to California. The elder, Myron, was already smart enough to have realized that if you were an agent in the film business you made twice as much money for half the work. The younger son, David O., was possessed of buckets of adrenaline and he demonstrated his own belief in himself by courting and marrying Irene Mayer, Louis B. Mayer's daughter. Anyone who could deliberately choose Louis B. Mayer as a father-in-law needed all the adrenaline he could command. As a wedding present David O. received a producer's berth at MGM and rose rapidly in the Service, as they write in the obituaries of military gentlemen. There were a lot of dusty properties lying around the MGM story department in those days. David O. picked them up, dusted them off, and remade them. He remade *David Copperfield*. He remade *The Garden of Allah*. He remade *The Prisoner of Zenda*. They were handsomely mounted, well lit, and faithfully followed, without actually comprehending the intentions of the original authors of the books from which the films were taken. These films were carefully stuffed with known names that, if not actually venerated, like Ronald Colman's, were becoming so. This policy resulted in some strange casting: Douglas Fairbanks, Jr., as yet another Rupert of Hentzau—ye gods! But there were occasional felicities: Hugh Williams as Steerforth in *David Copperfield* and of course David Niven as that spritely young officer Fritz von Tarlenheim in *The Prisoner of Zenda.*

It was on this production, Niven relates, that he found himself on horseback in a wood alongside C. Aubrey Smith, the famous old English actor who in the course of time had acquired a face like a map of Central Europe and a voice to match. He was playing Colonel Sapt, the captain of the King's bodyguard. They had been waiting two days, and the horses were restive. C. Aubrey Smith remained calm except for an occasional rumble, as if Mount Etna had cleared its throat. At last Niven ventured, "This seems a rattling good show, sir."

Another rumble came from the lavalike figure beside him, which resolved itself into the words "Dear old play. Wonderful old play. Never fails."

Encouraged, Niven followed this up with: "Ronald Colman was saying the other night this was once a play . . . in the theatre, I mean. Were you ever in it, sir?"

"Played everything but the Queen, dear boy—everything but the Queen." There was a pause, then another rumble.

"Niven!"

"Yes, sir?"

"They have left out one of the best lines."

"Have they, sir?"

"Yes. At the end of the play, when this fellow Rudolf Rassendyl gives up the Queen for the sake of her honor, I'm supposed to clasp his hand and say, 'By God, Rassendyl, you're the finest Elphberg of them all!' Well, it isn't in it—they've cut it out!"

"Really, sir? What a shame."

"Best line in the play. But you watch, Niven. I'll get it in . . . somehow."

David relates that all through the shooting Aubrey Smith was continually buttonholing either the director or the producer or his fellow actors about this line, and sure enough, on the final day of shooting an astonished Ronald Colman found his hands grasped by Colonel Sapt thundering, "By God, Rassendyl, you're the finest Elphberg of them all!"

Whether Colonel Sapt's line remained on the cutting-room floor or not I can't remember, but this priceless anecdote almost justifies David O. in remaking the historic silent film, directed for Metro by Rex Ingram with style, wit, and humor. There were some stylish directors in those early days, but most stylish of all was this twenty-four-year-old graduate of Yale University, with a Northern Irish minister for a father and a mother whom I know nothing about (but I must ask Alice).* Anyway, it is probable that genes had nothing to do with it. Rex was just born at the right time, like me.

Ingram's mythical kingdom of Ruritania was believable. The casting was interesting. Lewis Stone played the dual role of the King and of the English gentleman, Mr. Rassendyl, his distant cousin under the blanket. Alice Terry played the beautiful Princess Flavia with tenderness and humor. Stuart Holmes played Black Michael—he was the blackest of Michaels—with waxed mustaches and a dissolute air. Rupert of Hentzau was played by Ramon Novarro, destined to become one of MGM's greatest stars and to play Ben-Hur in the 1926 version. He was a young Mexican actor, passionate and graceful, highly intelligent, with a genius for mime. This was his first important part,

*Alice Terry, silent film star (*The Four Horsemen of the Apocalypse*, among others) and Rex Ingram's wife. She was still living in Hollywood when Michael wrote this passage.

and I remember how the director introduced this new young actor in a close-up on the stairs in which he paused and flipped a monocle into his eye before surveying the company. Such touches were typical of Ingram and he brought them off with style and wit. He knew how to flatter the audience by assuming that they were as cultivated and appreciative as he was. They responded. In this film the director resembled the conductor of an orchestra, with the added advantage that he is invisible, while the conductor is not.

There was nothing invisible about David O. Selznick. He came to meet the audience beaming, with hands outstretched, like Elmer Gantry. He was certain of his mission, which was to make great films. For him, Great was Big, and this confusion of the two adjectives was to haunt him all his life and prevent him ever becoming Great, although he was certainly Big. He achieved the ultimate in Bigness with his production of Margaret Mitchell's *Gone With the Wind*, but before that he had left his father-in-law's stables and set up for himself down the road as an independent producer. There he had surprised everybody by producing some excellent hard-hitting comedies like *Nothing Sacred*, starring Fredric March and Carole Lombard, and by signing up Alfred Hitchcock and bringing him over from England to direct Daphne du Maurier's *Rebecca*, starring Joan Fontaine and Laurence Olivier. Vivien Leigh accompanied Larry on this trip to Hollywood and in this way met Selznick, which resulted in her being cast as Scarlett O'Hara in *Gone With the Wind*. *Rebecca* was a great success, and, as I have already related, Hitchcock stayed with Selznick through the war, learning the Hollywood game and assembling his forces around him, including stars like Cary Grant, James Stewart, and Ingrid Bergman.

Somewhere about 1943 or 1944 Henry King, one of the great old-timers, directed a film for Fox about Saint Bernadette of Lourdes, from a book entitled *The Song of Bernadette*. The part of the peasant girl who has a vision of the Virgin Mary was played by an actress hitherto unknown, Jennifer Jones. It made her a star overnight. She was one of the most beautiful and talented young creatures that I have ever seen. She had the grace, strength, and agility of an untamed animal, and I never tired of watching her. At the time she rocketed to stardom she appeared to be a teenager, but she had actually been married for four years to an actor, Robert Walker, and had two sons by him. He was a sensitive and intelligent young man in steady demand, and had already been spotted by Hitchcock, who played him in one of his more popular melodramas, *Strangers on a Train*. That film, like *Bernadette*, was in black and white. It must be remembered that at this period most films were in black and white, but Dr. Kalmus and his wife, Natalie, had given us a long lead in England by establishing a Technicolor lab at Heathrow just before the war and were anxious to help us in any way they could to make big films in color.

If you are a filmmaker, you think in black and white or you think in color. The Archers thought in color from *The Thief of Bagdad* onward.

Selznick had also experimented in color with his comedies and, of course, the monumental *Gone With the Wind* had to be in color. Scarlett O'Hara and Rhett Butler were unthinkable in black and white. But big films like the Hitchcock productions of *Rebecca* or *Spellbound* were still being made in black and white, particularly since Hitch thought his stories out in terms of black-and-white images and was uncomfortable in color. His later films never showed a flair for color, and his most commercial film, *Psycho*, was shot in black and white with a television crew.

When David O. first met Jennifer Jones, he went off the deep end. The effect upon this megalomaniac was terrible. Her name was Phyllis Walker at that time, and he created the name of Jennifer Jones for her and then badgered Henry King and Twentieth Century–Fox to cast her in *The Song of Bernadette*, for which she won an Oscar. She triumphed again in *Since You Went Away*, and Selznick started to plan a new production around her. It had to have his greatest male star in it, Gregory Peck. It had to have a great director . . . it had to have *three* great directors. He told her that he would make her the greatest star of the world. His intentions were obvious, but she refused to have anything to do with him. She told him she was happily married and had a family, and I don't suppose he heard a word of it. She was under contract to him, and completely at his mercy as far as work was concerned. Whether she liked it or not, she had to be in this film that he was preparing for her. There was no escape.

It was a tiny story, not much more than an anecdote, but he blew it up until it became almost another *Gone With the Wind*. She was to play a part-Indian girl and Greg the young rancher. It was set in the Southwest, and was a story of lust and dust and rape, and was to be in Technicolor. King Vidor, one of the greatest of early directors, was to direct it. Later, Josef von Sternberg, the one and only Josef von Sternberg, was brought in to advise on the production. After Vidor left the film William Dieterle was brought in to complete it.

It was the most outrageous courtship. Caught in the Hollywood net, the girl struggled desperately to escape the huntsman, but her struggles and appeals for mercy were greeted by an avalanche of presents and another million dollars on the budget of the film. I really believe that David O. added a train wreck to the picture because she had refused him the night before. In the end, of course, he triumphed, and by the time the film stopped rolling, his wife, Irene, had left him and the actress's husband was no longer on the scene.

You might have thought that these Aeschylean results of his passion would have given him pause, but not a bit of it. He had spent millions to put her on a throne of blood for everybody to see. He had made her his mistress. Now she must be his wife. This man was capable of a genuine grand passion. He had possessed her body, now she must possess him, body and soul.

She refused. He insisted. He couldn't understand that he was an object of horror in her eyes. For the next four years, wherever they went, whatever they were doing, he continued to pester her to marry him. He thought of little else day and night. He never let it drop. What a candidate for *La Comédie Humaine*!

The film, of course, was *Duel in the Sun*. I have described how Emeric and I, visiting Hollywood for the first time in 1945 in search of an American girl—who turned out to be Kim Hunter—visited Hitchcock at the Selznick Studios and met David O., who insisted on showing us his favorite sequences from *Duel in the Sun*, which was then in production. It had been an interesting experience to sit with this big boyish man while he acted out his fantasies with the two people on the screen. First he showed us the rape sequence. The young rancher comes into the room where the part-Indian girl is scrubbing the floor. He does the cigarette bit, smoke through the nostrils, the lot, and stands watching her. Conscious of his glance she turns away from him, and the swing of her hips as she works gives him other ideas. He throws away his cigarette, grabs her, and they struggle. I glanced at David O. He was watching the screen intently. He wasn't in the least interested in my reaction. When the rape was over he rang the projectionist and said, "Okay, run the duel sequence." He sat back. This was his favorite bit. We sat, stunned with boredom, while mile after mile of film was unrolled of Jennifer Jones crawling up a mountain with a Winchester rifle, and Gregory Peck crawling down the mountain with another Winchester rife. When they finally opened fire on each other, Emeric whispered to me, "What a pity they didn't shoot the screenwriter."

I thought of the hot splintered rocks under the Arizona sun, Jennifer Jones's bleeding hands, knees, elbows, her face as she dragged herself up the mountain, trying to act, desperately hoping for the director to say, "Cut!" The reel finished abruptly. I said chattily, "Poor girl. You certainly made her work for her living."

The great David O. took a long draw on his cigarette, nodded, and drawled, "Yeah, the poor kid took quite a beating."

Duel in the Sun would have disgraced any B-movie. David O. thought he could disguise this by hiring the best director and throwing in a perfectly gratuitous train wreck, which got a roar of laughter at the press show in London, together with a sunset sequence that must have emptied the Technicolor dye vats for several months. Not content with that, he added a line of dialogue to the sequence, "There's a strange glow in the sky tonight," which brought the house down. All through the film we felt that the producer was trying to pin the word "epic" onto a plot that even Richard Wagner would have scorned to have cluttering up his studio. The final film was a piece of pulp bound in morocco.

All through his life David O. was dogged by this confusion between Bigness and Greatness. He wasn't content to have made a success with Jennifer. Now he wanted to make an epic. Eventually he settled upon a story that could have been told in ten lines, about a girl all of whose problems were solved by a tidal wave. Christopher Miles's beautiful film, *The Virgin and the Gypsy*, from the story by D. H. Lawrence, has a similar construction; so has my own *I Know Where I'm Going!* In the one a dam burst comes roaring down the valley, washing the virgin into bed with the Gypsies; in the other the principals get involved in a giant whirlpool. Both these films were loved by audiences, and I am sure David O. wanted audiences to love *Portrait of Jennie*. But his passion for Bigness, as opposed to Greatness, was too strong for him. He forgot his original intention—of creating a great film that would make Jennifer the biggest star in the Hollywood heavens—and spent all his money on the tidal wave, which was very fine in its way but which crashed down into empty cinemas because the audience, who liked stories and didn't get one, had gone home.

On the evidence, I think we must come to the surprising conclusion that the great David O. Selznick was a big fraud. He was a producer like other Hollywood producers: a packager, a memo writer, a picker of other men's brains—not a creative person at all. When he worked with good craftsmen— Victor Fleming, Alfred Hitchcock, Howard Hawks, Ben Hecht, George Cukor, Carol Reed, Powell and Pressburger—he made good pictures. When he didn't, he didn't. He was a great director of other directors. After seeing their dailies he would send them page after page of criticisms until they threatened to walk out, and frequently did. Actors and actresses refused to perform if he appeared on the set, so he had to sneak in unobserved and hide behind the flats if he wanted to know what was going on. He was a pain in the neck.

We met him again at Elstree in the new half-finished studio where we were preparing *The Elusive Pimpernel*. Emeric and I were inspecting costumes with Hein. *The Red Shoes* gang were in their element. A mixture of fantasy and high romance was their meat, particularly when two cultures clashed: the French Revolution with its republican austerities, and the English Regency with its last long-lingering look back to the eighteenth century. The art department had lined up the sketches on a long corridor, perhaps two hundred feet long, and a lot of the dresses were already completed and being paraded by the actors and actresses of our permanent company, preening themselves, bowing and curtsying to each other, learning how to handle their voluminous skirts and huge hats, and comparing their costumes with the sketches on the walls. It was a charming, busy, inspiring scene, typical of The Archers in their heyday. We expected everybody to contribute what they had and there was always a great deal of laughter and chatter on our set. When I was working I was oblivious of this, and once somebody said to me, "How on earth can you work with all this noise around you?"

I said, "What noise?" and stopped to listen, and by God, he was right. There was a hell of a row. I tugged Syd's sleeve and, when he turned to look at me, said, "Less noise."

Syd blew his whistle and there was an instantaneous shocked silence, which embarrassed everybody, including me. The five-piece orchestra, which I had hired for the rehearsals of the ballroom sequences, kept on playing. I took the microphone and said, "Less noise, please, ladies and gentlemen. Mr. Easdale, please continue to rehearse the gavotte, but *piano, piano.*"

It was into a scene of controlled confusion like this that George Busby, his dark face purple with excitement, introduced David O. Selznick and Jennifer Jones, in that order.

These were two very big fishes to arrive in our little pond. But they didn't see it that way. They had come seeking The Archers, as persistently and reverently as Sir Aurel Stein sought the Dalai Lama, or was it Sven Hedin, another hero of my youth? Our visitors had seen *The Red Shoes* and were overboard about Moira Shearer. What was she doing? Where was she going? Was it true that she had gone back to the "ballay"? They couldn't conceive how, after having been made by us into one of the greatest film stars in the world, she could choose to return to the "ballay," the monastery doors closing softly behind her. And who was this Sadler Wells, anyway? It was beyond David O.'s comprehension that we had no long-term contract with Moira, that she was not "all carved up."

David O. had seen *A Matter of Life and Death.* "I told those boys they were crazy to change the title to *Stairway to Heaven*—it misses the whole point of the title *A Matter of Life and Death*! That's the only possible title for your picture!"

Of course, this inclined us to like him. We stared at this big, boyish man, at this beautiful sensuous woman trailing tragedy like a cloak, an eager woman, innocent and vulnerable. Everybody frankly stared as they walked around with us, looking at the sketches and admiring the costumes on the girls. They were out to woo us and they won. For them, after the scandals of Hollywood and the snide remarks of the Henry Luce press, to work on a big European film, with a partner like Alex Korda and top European filmmakers like Emeric and myself, was a haven after a sea of troubles. They had already been entertained by Alex, who had suggested they come out to see us. They said that Sir Alex said that London Films had a property he thought they should consider. ("Conning-ham . . . what was the name of that wonderful novel about the wild girl and the fox?")* He thought it would be acceptable to all parties, including The Archers. How did we feel about that? We felt fine.

They stayed for lunch. There was no regular studio canteen yet, but The Archers were famous for their food and for their hospitality, and George Busby loved an emergency party. Where he got the caviar and smoked salmon from, I have no idea. George had his methods. David Niven was not on call that day, nor was Cyril Cusack, but Maggie Leighton and Jennifer were introduced and were soon chattering like . . . like two pros. Jennifer had an immense awe of English actresses and particularly of actresses from the legitimate theatre who had worked with Sir Laurence and Sir Ralph. David O. greeted Maggie with badly concealed astonishment when he was introduced to her and told what part she was playing. He expressed regret that we hadn't met before. They had been doing the Grand Tour of Europe and were astonished by Venice and "those doges."

"If only we had come to England earlier, maybe you would have found a spot for Jennifer in your movie," said David, laughing heartily, and glancing from the glowing American nectarine to the paling English tulip drooping upon her stem. At that particular moment, I would have traded all my light fantastic musical comedy ideas for the pleasure of having Jennifer Jones play Lady Blakeney; and I am sure that Chris Challis would have agreed with me. He had deserted his envious camera crew and was drooling over Jennifer, showing her cynex-strips of his makeup tests, which were modeled upon portrait paintings by Romney and Goya. I groaned inwardly. Alex had maneuvered us into making a colored copy of a stagy film from a stagy play with a stagy actress. Thank God for David Niven! With David's help I would be able to establish the light, airy atmosphere that I wanted and that I had so admired in Noël Coward's *Conversation Piece* on the stage.

Too bad, I thought, glancing at the rosy, eager child opposite me. She was obviously a fireball of energy. We could have had some fun with her.

=

All of England is carved up by lady novelists. There is hardly a contour of our sceptred isle that has not fallen captive to some lady's pen. It was all started by Jane Austen, annexing Lyme Regis and Bath. Sheila Kaye-Smith partitioned Sussex with Rudyard Kipling and Hilaire Belloc. In Cornwall lies Du

---

*Korda liked to surround himself with members of the British aristocracy. "Conningham" was the way he pronounced the historic name of Sir David Cunynghame (11th Baronet of Milncraig), who was his production manager and a member of the board of directors of London Films.

Maurier land, a kingdom stout enough to withstand occasional upstarts like Winston Graham. Beatrix Potter has successfully defended the Lake District against Hugh Walpole, and on Wenlock Edge, Mary Webb is the Shropshire lass.

Mary Webb's most famous book is *Precious Bane*. Stanley Baldwin, an ironmaster from the Midlands who happened to be prime minister of England at the time, picked the book up at a friend's house, read it, and spoke favorably of it in an interview on the radio. Such was the confidence of the British public in the 1920s in their prime ministers, particularly when they happened to be millionaires, that the book was sold out within a few days and became a classic. It was found that she had written other novels that had passed completely unnoticed, and they were reprinted too. They had earthy, feminine titles like *Gone to Earth* and *Seven for a Secret*, and they were full of topographical allusions. Mary Webb enthusiasts, book in hand, toiled over the steep hills and valleys of the Welsh Marches, climbing the Wrekin, identifying frowning hills, smiling ponds, and snarling farmhouses. It was this boring trick of tagging human attributes onto inoffensive landscapes that inspired Stella Gibbons to write *Cold Comfort Farm*, a morning glory of a book, in which she gave herself one, two, or three stars, after the pattern of Mr. Baedeker's guides, for any passage of purple prose of which she was particularly proud.

It is amazing to me now, looking back from the heights of 1984, the sun sinking not only over San Quentin but over Hollywood, that we let Alex get away with Mary Webb. Once more, as with *The Scarlet Pimpernel*, he was looking back to his past, before the war, when he had created Denham Studios and made wonderful films for an audience that no longer existed. After the success of *Wuthering Heights* in 1939 he had looked around for another folk drama for Merle Oberon and had bought, or optioned, Mary Webb's *Precious Bane* as a starring vehicle for her and Robert Donat. He had optioned Mary Webb's other books as well. This was a normal precaution for a European producer in those days, for fear that, if he made a success, Hollywood would snap up the other titles and benefit from his acumen. At one time it seemed to me that everyone wanted to make a film of *Precious Bane*. I remember that I was asked to do a test at Denham of a scared young actress called Hazel Court for the Mary Webb film, but who the producer was or whether the film was made I can't remember, or perhaps I never knew. She was a very pretty girl, but very raw when I made the test, and when I met her again at Mar del Plata, when President Perón of Argentina and his wife, Evita, threw a party for the whole of show business, I liked her a lot better. She had filled out and discovered a sense of humor and become very good company.

The reason that all these pretty ladies wanted to play the heroine of *Precious Bane* was because she has a harelip. This sounded very European and avant-garde. This deformity and her despair of ever being desired by the man she loves gives her an excuse for appearing naked before him and other men in a kind of hocus-pocus Gypsy magical scene. This was hot stuff in the 1930s. It never seemed to occur to any of these great producers that the harelip dodge works in a book but would never work well on the screen.

Skip eleven years and enter Powell and Pressburger—fall guys. Alex still has an option on all of Mary Webb's works, and as soon as we take up the option on *Gone to Earth* he picks up the rights at the prewar price and sells them to us, but *not* at the prewar price.

I was a bit wary about Mary Webb. I was not a townsman, for one thing. The Corbetts* and the Powells had their roots in the very counties she was writing about. In the eighties and nineties of the last century my mother and her sisters used to be sent for the long summer holidays to stay in a farmhouse in the Marches called Hollow Fields, and their memories of the Mary Webb country were full of laughter and good stories. Mrs. Webb's view of the countryside was that of a townswoman—outside, looking in. Then my mother had Stella Gibbons on her bookshelves as well as Mary Webb. All together my own feelings about the countryman as a subject for drama were more like those of Marcel Aymé toward his native district of the Jura. He saw his peasants clearly as an extension of their own animals. He drew them with love and humor, and laid on the colors very sparingly. Daumier was his master, as he was mine.

Gone to Earth, titled in France (where it had its greatest success) *La Renarde* (*The Vixen*), is about a girl, Hazel, who has a pet fox. Her mother is dead and she lives with her father, a coffin maker. No Mary Webb character could be a carpenter or cabinetmaker. It had to be coffins. He also plays the harp. Esmond Knight played this bizarre character as if he had played the harp and fashioned coffins all his life. The girl is pursued by two men: the Baptist minister, who is under the impression that he loves her soul, and the squire, who makes no bones about the fact that he wants her body. Hazel is torn this way and that between the two men. Finally, the young minister wins her soul and body, but in a scarlet-coated hunting sequence of rare ferocity she is hunted down by the squire while trying to save her pet fox from the hounds, falls down a mine shaft, and is killed, together with the fox, to the sound of the huntsman's traditional cry when the quarry escapes to his lair: "Gone to earth! Gone to earth!"

The story had just about the right mixture of sex, sadism, and masochism

---

*Michael's relatives on his mother's side were Corbetts and came from Worcestershire.

for David O., who was enthusiastic about it. Jennifer appeared to share his enthusiasm, but I was already beginning to identify with her and I could feel that she was uneasy at certain aspects of the story. However, she said nothing, and when we suggested David Farrar to play Jack Reddin, the squire, she was delighted by the idea. They had both seen *Black Narcissus*, of course, and had made the usual Hollywood mistake of identifying the actor with the part and vice versa. I think that they expected David to play the Squire like a new Gary Cooper, all charm and reticence. Who should play the part of the idealistic young Baptist minister was another matter. We all felt that it should be an English actor, but at this period, so soon after the war, no obvious candidates for stardom had emerged, and after some discussions it was agreed that The Archers would make tests of likely candidates, which we would screen together with Selznick before making the final choice.

I went away from that meeting with a sense of foreboding. The reader has been told the strange and tragic story of David O.'s obsessive passion, but at this time I knew very little of it, only that this couple were runaway lovers from the witch-hunters of Hollywood. Now we were committed to these notorious partners for a whole year. Once more, Alex had spun a glittering web and we had walked into his parlor. *But the story was a good one*—yes, but it was a book. Why did we have to buy Mary Webb when I had the most ingenious screenwriter in the world as a partner? The answer was simple: because Alex owned the rights and at one stroke had unloaded them onto The Archers. True, we had unloaded David Farrar on London Films and they would have to pay his salary for a time, but that was nothing compared with the killing Alex had made. Twice in a row, I had been maneuvered into making a film I didn't want to make, and that I would not have chosen given a free hand. I was betraying my instincts, and no real filmmaker can afford to do that.

David Farrar was delighted. He went out and bought a horse—no double for him! This was typical of David. He was what the Irish call "a darlin' man"—he was too good to be true. I was proud of him because I had pulled him out of B-movies to play Mr. Dean in *Black Narcissus*, and because he had made such a success of the part. On his side he had been grateful and had accepted the part of Sammy Rice in *The Small Back Room* with enthusiasm. When he learned about *The Elusive Pimpernel* he naturally hoped that he would play Sir Percy, for his greatest successes on the stage, touring with his wife, had been in costume parts, and at the time we engaged him for *Black Narcissus* I had been to see him play in one, in a tiny theatre off Tottenham Court Road. He would have played one aspect of Sir Percy very well, but not so well the other. At all events, he would have acted it, which dear David Niven had no intention of doing. I had to explain the Korda-Goldwyn compact, and that David Niven came with the dinner. He took the news with good grace, although I am sure he was bitterly disappointed. It was pleasant to be able to tell him that all of us wanted him to play the part of Squire Jack Reddin, and that his leading lady would be Jennifer Jones.

David Farrar had never been on a horse in his life, so for the first few days of learning to ride he had to eat his breakfast off the mantelpiece. The English saddle is tough on actors who have to learn to ride for an English film. The saddles are hard and girthed high on the withers and the stirrup leathers are usually short. The idea is that you keep on the horse not by using the stirrups, but by pressing into his sides with your knees. My father and our groom, Woodcock, taught me to ride by chanting the following jingle:

> Your head and your heart well up
> Your heels and your hands well down
> Your knees well into your horse's side
> And your elbows into your own.

American actors have an easier job. The long stirrup and the Western saddle make it easy to get into—in fact you can almost step into it. To an Englishman it seems as if the Americans regard the saddle on a horse as a chair, and the horse as the rollers on which it sits. And although David was courageous and handled himself well, my father would have said that he looked like a sack of potatoes on top of a horse. The English horseman is meant to be looked at, admired, and perhaps obeyed. The American horseman is part of the landscape that he owns.

At all events, David Farrar was right to put first things first. Reddin was a Shropshire squire in the 1890s and most of the working day he would have a horse between his legs, like my father. In the winter he would be hunting three days a week, with an occasional extra. One assumes in the film that the pack of hounds has a master and that it might be Jack Reddin, but I made no attempt to establish it either by hearing the hounds baying in their kennels at Undern or by showing Reddin at a meet. Undern, in the film, is a lovely, old moldering pile, and the Reddins are obviously a landed family that has petered out. To a man who is the son and grandson of landed men, the year 1949 was a nostalgic time to be making the film. In England, the sons of county families are always the first to get killed in a war. The big houses are either commandeered or shuttered, and it takes several decades for the countryside to return to—I won't say normal, because after the 1914–18 war a whole century of British culture and quiet living vanished forever, and after the 1939–45 war we have mortgaged the future, let alone the past. Although it was four years after a war that we had won, England in 1949 was still on rationing, horses were still being used around the farm, airfields and their vast perimeters were still occupying valuable farmland, and country folk had learned to be self-sufficient, as they were at the time Mary Webb was writing.

Jennifer was anxious to know about her Shropshire, or Worcestershire, accent and I promised to have an actress study it and make some records for her to listen to. Was I sure I wanted her to play the part with an accent?

"Of course we'm sure!" roared Esmond Knight, who had by now been brought into the discussion. "Yew can't play my daughter with an English accent, gurl!" He looked appraisingly at her long, coltish body. He couldn't really see her, but he got the general idea. When Esmond joined a group of women, he raised their morale several degrees in a matter of minutes. "Yew listen to me, lass, yew'll soon get the hang of it!" Jennifer began to enjoy herself and feel at home with the English actors.

So it was a deal. David O. whisked her away to see the Alhambra, or the Sphinx, or to have another dose of doges, and, in between the other trips, to Vienna, where *The Third Man* was being shot at night by Carol Reed and Orson Welles.

Carol knew how to handle David O.—how to flatter him and how to ignore him. He had worked with egomaniacs like Edgar Wallace and Basil Dean. Carol had charm and an eager way of sharing things with you that was irresistible. And he was tall, like David O., and lean, as David O. was not. Carol and Graham Greene knew exactly what they were doing on the film, and how to keep David O.'s interference to a minimum. David O. told us, giggling self-consciously, "He rings me up at all hours of the day and night to play the zither to me."

"The what?"

"The zither."

"Oh, that Hungarian thing."

"I guess so. Carol says it's the sound of black-market Vienna. Everywhere you go they have these zither players in all the clubs. Carol wants to use it as a theme tune all the way through the film."

"Sounds a good idea."

"I guess so. He calls it the Harry Lime Theme." Harry Lime was the part played by Orson.

I wish that I had been born with Carol's tact and caution. I hate excessively, or love excessively. In either case, a tumble is inevitable. As for tact . . . a bull in a pasture has more tact, but at least I have learned to hold my tongue. Hence this book.

=

I didn't need tact on *The Elusive Pimpernel,* only energy. We worked happily for a week or two among the fairy-tale castles of the Loire. We picnicked in the beautiful valley of the little River Cher. We drank the lovely light white wines of the Loire. We ate a gourmet's dinner every night at the three-star hotel in the square at Tours, or at least the crew did. I had too much respect for my liver. I stayed at Mont Richard, a few miles away on the Cher.

The Cher! Who but the French would call a river and a *département* a darling? I loved the idea, for the Cher is a darling river. It runs through the greenest and loveliest countryside until it joins the Loire, that great stern river that rises six hundred miles away in the high plateau of central France and which has attained a frightening swiftness by the time it tucks the little Cher under its arm and hurries with it to the sea. We once tried to swim in the Loire, and we ended up a string of pink crayfish, holding hands, badly scared, and leaning against the rush of the torrent as we struggled back to the shore. On the surface, the Loire is smooth and shallow, but once you are in the water you feel the weight of this enormous river pressing against you, anxious to sweep you, too, into the Bay of Biscay.

Oh! Those happy days on *Pimpernel!* They are among The Archers' fondest memories. We loved and trusted one another, we played at working, and worked at playing all day and all night, when necessary. We were making a romantic fairy tale at an exciting period of history, with lovely costumes, beautiful women, brave men, and horses. We were happy to be back in France, which we loved, and the French were happy to have us. We lived on the fat of the land.

When we moved north to Normandy and to Mont-Saint-Michel we missed the wines of the Loire but there was plenty of Calvados. The work was harder but we had just as much fun. Frankie and Kevin joined us again.* They had been with us on the Loire for a day or two, and then returned to Paris. Kevin was three, already worried by his elusive father and anxious to keep an eye on him.

To see the tide come in at Mont-Saint-Michel, when it is a spring tide, is a thrilling sight. You look down from a great height onto this huge saucer of sand, and all of a sudden the sea is coming! The little pile of rocks and earth that is in the middle of the saucer suddenly becomes an island. The sound of the tide thundering on the bar outside suddenly stops, and there are great streaks of foam racing across the sand toward the mount. A ring of armed soldiers surrounds the mount, barring Sir Percy Blakeney's way to the sea. Suddenly, they become uneasy. We hear the thunder of the tide. Water is surging around their ankles, around their knees, around their waists! They scramble to safety, helping each other, and in a minute the place where they were standing is six feet underwater. The bay fills, the *Daydream* sails proudly in, picks up the fugitives, and once more the Elusive Pimpernel has tri-

---

*Frankie Reidy, Michael's wife for forty years, and their firstborn son, Kevin.

umphed! It made a rousing finale, but it meant a lot of work, and, above all, it meant a lot of waiting.

The schooner could only stay on top of the tide for half an hour at most, followed by a desperate race back to the open sea. Captain England, for whom the ship was home as well as livelihood, says in his book, *Schoonerman,* "It was an anxious time for me and my family, with only a few inches of water below the schooner's keel, I could feel her smelling the bottom."

It was an anxious time for me, too. The schooner was fifty years old, and if she stranded she might open up. I doubted whether Lloyd's of London, who insured the vessel, would consider the Bay of Mont-Saint-Michel to be "safe, navigable waters." The *Nellie Bywater,* the registered name of Captain England's ship, was later to come to a tragic end, drowning two of her company when she foundered and broke up off Bolt Head in one of the worst storms of this century. In his book Captain England has written a noble account of her foundering, worthy of Joseph Conrad.

We returned to England and completed the *Daydream* sequences off Dover after a spell of contrary weather. Bill Paton was, of course, very much to the fore and spoke mutinously to Captain England. I had felt the audience would like the White Cliffs at this point, but the wind was in the wrong direction and whenever we veered around to show the cliffs we found we were shooting the actors' backs. We tacked to and fro all day and the French actors were sick. Not because they were French, I hasten to add, but because they had had to eat an English packed lunch.

But I think that my greatest triumph on *The Elusive Pimpernel,* and one that will be remembered by other directors (I know that Martin Scorsese particularly admired this visual gag), was the sneezing fireworks sequence. It started as a simple joke. In the scene between Chauvelin and Sir Percy the latter diverts his opponent's attention for a moment and empties the pepper pot into his enemy's snuffbox. From then on it is one long suspense until the hapless Chauvelin, full of triumph, takes a pinch from his box. Obviously a simple suspense gag like this has to be spun out for as long as possible. When the fit of sneezing finally explodes, Sir Percy and his friends deal with Chauvelin easily and make their escape. I decided to prolong the sequence for the audience by giving them a fireworks display. Every time that Chauvelin gave a huge "atishoo!" fireworks exploded in the audience's face. It was a real film gag, and it worked wonders. The audience laughed and laughed and laughed. Each time that there was a new shower of colored fire there was a new outburst of laughter. It worked like a charm. It could have gone on even longer. Green directors, please note.

At Elstree we rejoined Hein and Arthur, who had built most of the sets by now, and we ran everything that we had shot in France. On the whole we were pleased, but Reggie Mills, our editor, agreed with me that we had a lot of work to do to bring the sequence at Mont-Saint-Michel up to The Archers' level. The actors were pleased with the look of things, and we left the next day for the west of England and Bath. Jack Hawkins joined us at this point. He was playing "Prinny," the Prince Regent, later King George IV.

Alex, with his usual eye for talent, had signed Jack Hawkins to a long-term contract. I had never met him until he played Waring in *The Small Back Room.* I knew his stage work and had seen him play the King in *Hamlet.* (I have seen so many *Hamlet*s that I can't remember which one. Could it have been Alec Clunes's *Hamlet* at the Arts Theatre?) Jack was strangely shaped. He was a tall, handsome man, with shoulders so broad and chest so deep that they almost amounted to a deformity. He carried it off well. He gave the impression that he would force the pace a bit in a big role, but on the contrary, his acting was extremely subtle.

I had enjoyed every minute of working with Jack on *The Small Back Room,* and had invited him to make a guest appearance in *Pimpernel.* Although the Prince Regent, so far as the story was concerned, was only along for the ride, Jack accepted the part. We made a test of him in full costume, with the Garter ribbon across his broad chest, admiring his own reflection in an eighteenth-century mirror, and convinced him. Even without padding he seemed twice his size with all the magnificent clothes, wigs, quizzing glasses, jewels, many-tiered coachman's capes, and lacquered canes that Hein and his costume department showered upon him. He made a glorious sun around which our daredevil young men revolved. Each one vied with the others in eccentricity, in simplicity, and in beauty. Robert Coote joined us to play Sir Andrew ffoulkes and brought his own brand of looks and sardonic humor to the group. Altogether, as the vans, generators, coaches, and automobiles started rolling from Elstree to the west of England and the Royal Crescent at Bath, I was not too displeased. Hein's studio settings had worked out splendidly. I mean, we had agreed there would be no moldings and fussy details, and in some cases even the mirrors and the furniture were a painted replica of the real thing. Because of the rich costumes we had kept the colors subdued. Since Rouben Mamoulian, that clever fox, who knew his theatre as well as he knew the movies, had directed *Becky Sharp,* I did not think that there had been such taste and control in a Technicolor picture.

For the past two winters I had been riding regularly in the park each morning. Bill Paton, the eye that never sleeps, would call me with a cup of tea at six-thirty. I said *a* cup of tea, because Frankie refused to admit the existence of such an hour. I shaved and struggled into my riding breeches and boots, my rollneck sweater, my tweed jacket with the tails cut skirted for riding, and my brown bowler hat. I crept out of the house, stepped into the open Bentley without using the low door, and purred my way to Bert Varley's stables in a mews off Queen's Gate. It was still dark, but the dawn was in the sky and Bert and his girls were grooming the horses by lantern light.

Bert was the Lord Mayor's coachman whenever the Lord Mayor's coach was taken out of mothballs. He looked like a drawing by Cruikshank. He could handle horses as easily as you and I handle our wives, and with much less fuss. He had one of those larger-than-life faces, with a nose like a Roman emperor and a mouth chiseled out of some composition resembling granite. To see him exercising his grays and waving his whip in salute to Mr. Watney of the beer family, also out exercising his team and wagonette, was to take you straight back to the eighteenth century. I made him Master of the Horse in our production. Miss Dixon, who also answered to "Dickie," was his head groom, and a smarter one I have never seen.

There used to be a mews at the end of Carlton House Terrace, between the Admiralty Arch and Trafalgar Square. The stables were still in use. They were in three stories, connected by sloping ramps paved with cobblestones. There were about twenty stables to each story. I was quite staggered by the original-ity of the building when we discovered it, and determined that it should be in the film. It was a night scene, and when the lanterns were swinging, the grooms were swearing, the horses slipping and stumbling on the cobbles, the coaches rumbling out of their houses ready to be harnessed up, the noise and confusion were considerable. I was standing thoughtfully in the middle of it all when I felt a tap on my shoulder and, turning, saw Clough Williams-Ellis and his wife, Amabel, dressed for some reception: she in brocade, he in white tie and tails and a short cloak lined with yellow, with his beautiful hair brushed back in a sweep. In the lantern light, and with the shadows of the horses passing thrown across their faces, they fitted perfectly into an eigh-teenth-century picture. They were staying at a friend's house and had taken a shortcut through the mews to discover me there. Why hadn't I come to Portmeirion* since the war, they asked. What was going on here?

I explained. "Ah! The Pimpernel! They seek him here, they seek him there—eh?" They went off with aristocratic disregard for the horseshit, yell-ing, "Good hunting!" through the shouting and stamping of iron hooves on the cobblestones. We were still there at three in the morning when they came back.

There is something about working with horses, those faithful servants of man, that brings the best out of men and women. To be so strong and so

---

*Portmeirion was an architectural extravaganza created by Clough Williams-Ellis on the north coast of Wales. It would later be used as a set for the TV series *The Prisoner*. Michael found seclusion and quiet there when he was working on scripts.

obedient, to wield death in powerful legs and iron shoes, and to be so gentle—surely this is admirable and timeless? The mounted man has always been and will always be a superhuman figure. Even to drive in a dogcart or trap behind a fast-spirited horse is a thrilling experience, while to bowl along in a light, springy carriage behind a matched set of bays was absolute bliss. I wanted to get this feeling, this communication between man and horse, into the film. On the whole I had not been too successful in France, but I thought that back in England, with Bert Varley and his men (and Miss Dixon), we might do better.

Now we were all converging upon the city of Bath, where Lady Grenville's ball was taking place at number 2 Royal Crescent. It was night, and there was a crowd outside awaiting the arrival of the Prince. Carriages were driving up and rolling away, and the crowd were oohing and aahing as the guests mounted the steps and entered the brilliantly lit house. The whole elaborate set piece was for a single gag: Who would arrive last at the reception—the Prince or Sir Percy? Naturally, the star spot was the last arrival, and naturally Sir Percy won with Lady Blakeney on his arm. The numerous costume rehearsals that we had held paid off here, for everybody looked at home in their gorgeous clothes. Jack Hawkins was splendid as "Prinny." My spirits began to rise.

The next day we moved to Savernake Forest, and the next to the Marlborough Downs. That finished the exterior shooting, and not too soon, for the leaves were beginning to turn. On the Downs I had found a dusty white road just wide enough for two carriages. It ran at a gentle slope down to a narrow bridge, just wide enough for one carriage. It was the perfect setting for the scene where Sir Percy forces the Prince to chicken out and pull up his carriage when both of them are racing to be first over the bridge. Bert Varley drove Jack Hawkins, David Niven drove himself, with his manservant beside him on the box. He looked impeccable. He had been coached, in general and in detail, by an old friend of his father, a major-general and a great horseman.

"Hold your hands down, Niven. Do you want to look like a coachman?"

"Might do worse, sir."

"No, no, my boy. You are a gentleman driving his own carriage. Don't try to be anything else. It used to be the fashion then to ape the coachman. My great-great-grandfather was one of the West Wycombe set—dressed like a coachman, swore like a coachman, and smelt like a coachman, by God. He took the stables with him into the ladies' drawing rooms—all right then, matter of fashion. But in this cinematograph show of yours, you are a baronet! Got to behave like one. Now, let's have a look at you. Right-hand glove a bit worn. Hands down—elbows in—good! Brimmed hat just shading the eyes, good! Carriage rug folded and wrapped around the knees, just eight inches above the knees, not an inch more, Niven—good! Now the whip!"

"What about it, sir?"

"Never touch it, my boy. Your horse will do his best for you. He can't do more. Only cads whip a horse when it's doing its best. Well . . . mmmm . . . you'll do."

Bert Varley always mounted me well. Captain was the name of the horse that he always kept for me for the early-morning rides in the park. He was a big, rangy, brown animal with a lovely temper. He was far too good and too fast for Rotten Row. On a cold winter's morning there were very few people out before eight o'clock, and after pacing sedately down the Row and crossing the Serpentine by the bridge as the sun rose behind the Admiralty, I would give him his head and we would thunder down the Row at full speed, directly contrary to park regulations. I never got caught out, though. Sometimes I had a hard job stopping him before we ran into the traffic at Hyde Park Corner. The park was still a royal park then.

I had Bert ship Captain down to Marlborough and I rode him all day in Savernake Forest, and Kevin rode for an hour or two on my saddle bow. Next day Captain and I had several gallops on the Downs while they were setting up the shot. It was a new experience, directing my film from horseback. I hadn't been so thrilled since I charged with the Sussex Regiment on my pony, Fubsy, in 1915.

We had some narrow shaves while shooting the bridge sequence. I quite expected to see somebody's wheel go spinning off across the Downs when the two carriages came roaring along the narrow road neck and neck. Both the actors were splendid, but Bert Varley was magnificent—not a muscle moving in that great face (he was swearing all the time under his breath), his eyes on the road, and when Jack threw his arms round him and brought the carriage to a halt, he said never a word, but you could see by his eyes what he thought of his royal master's lack of nerve. As for David, when his carriage flashed over the bridge ahead of "Prinny's," he just rubbed his nose. Except for some night shots in London, that finished the exteriors. We moved into the studio, settled down, and started the real work; or if you were an Archer, the real fun.

I looked back over what we had done and I was not pleased. I had fallen into the oldest trap in the world: the trap of the picturesque. Even the great Stanley Kubrick fell into it when he made *Barry Lyndon.* It's a particular curse of the British cinema. In black and white cinematography, which is completely unrealistic, this artistic trap does not exist. But in Technicolor, which is supposed to add realism to a film, the jaws of the trap await you round every corner. I looked back over my own color films.

Colonel Blimp had been a studio picture and was well within my own age and experience. *A Matter of Life and Death* was planned as a fantasy in monochrome and Technicolor, and it worked. *Black Narcissus* was a studio picture, planned and controlled, even to the makeup. The off-white habits and cowls of the nuns pulled the key down and added to the color control. Thanks to Jack Cardiff and the others, it was our best color design. *The Red Shoes* was a modern fairy tale in familiar settings, the ballet was pure theatre. It worked. Back to *Pimpernel*. Our progress so far can be expressed in the following equation: actors plus costumes plus twentieth-century landscapes equals colored picture postcards. I was to blame for this, but so was Baroness Orczy, indirectly, I hasten to add. It was the play, with its surefire theatrical situations, and not her book that was giving me trouble. It was amazing how the old play took control. Essentially, Alex had been right in his version to get three stars together and to shoot the whole thing in medium close-up.

For some weeks now Emeric had been working on the script of *Gone to Earth*. He had roughed out an adaptation for my approval and was now working on the first draft of the script. I summoned him from his Hampstead eyrie and he flew to help me. Reggie Mills ran all the material for him. He liked it better than I did. Reassured, I got on with the job. By now, Bob Coote had joined us. David Niven always had to have a chum on every picture that he did, and the character that the chum played had to be called Trubshaw, after a legendary messmate of David's pre-Hollywood army days. Various startled actors had had this honor conferred upon them. But Bob Coote had played Flying Officer Trubshaw in *A Matter of Life and Death*, and had established himself as the definitive Trubshaw. Until *the* Trubshaw himself appeared in a film with David (which he eventually did), Bob Coote was in, and became the Honourable Michael Trubshaw in *Pimpernel*. I offer this explanation to future film historians who are bound to be puzzled by the proliferation of Trubshaws in the casts of David's films.

I have often thought about David's wonderful life, and I thought it over again when the news of his merciful death came late in 1983. For more than a year he had been wasting away from amyotrophic lateral sclerosis, but had never lost his love of life, nor the love of his friends. He came to Hollywood with nothing but his wits, and within a few years, and with the help of Errol Flynn and a few others, he established himself as a promising juvenile actor by the time the war burst upon us. He gave up Hollywood and came back to fight, and marry Primula Rollo, who gave him his two sons. David's tale is that he met Prim by diving into a slit trench on top of her during an attack on the aerodrome where she was stationed.

At the end of the war *A Matter of Life and Death* reestablished him as a charmer of the first order. He returned to Hollywood and his career and lost his lovely wife in a fatal and pointless accident during a Hollywood party. Two years later he met Hjordis and married her. He was not marrying for the sake of his baby boys. It was a true love match for the rest of his life. She matched him in wit and spirit. At the time that we were all working together he was still considered an actor of the playboy type, and not really an actor at all. He was still playing the juvenile, and it looked as if his Hollywood career was toddling to its end. Then Mike Todd played him as Phineas Fogg, the hero of his gloriously corny production of *Around the World in Eighty Days*. From an aging juvenile, David Niven became the friend of all the world. He made success after success. He wrote the delightful books about his life, which sold in the millions. He became a star again, and a star he remained, a beloved shining star, to the end of his life. We were neighbors for many years in the south of France. He was a great friend of the Rainiers, and must have been a godsend to Princess Grace, with his sense of fun in that musical-comedy court. He was generous, prudent, and kind. Meanwhile, in the most friendly and helpful way, he expressed his doubts about my treatment of *The Elusive Pimpernel*, and although he was a distinguished amateur rather than a true professional, he had a fine instinct as an entertainer.

"Micky, old chum," he said, after I had persuaded him to do some particularly outrageous piece of business, or adopt some particularly fantastic disguise in his battle of wits with the foxy Chauvelin, who was being cleverly played by Cyril Cusack, "Are you sure we're on the right track with this Lon Chaney stuff? I don't think my public is going to go for 'Niven, the Man with a Thousand Faces.' "

"They love it when Sherlock Holmes does it," I suggested.

"Well, Basil's such a bloody good actor, who wouldn't?" (David had an extravagant admiration for all his friends who were what he called "real" actors.) "But when I do it I'm more like Douglas Byng." (Douglas Byng was a particularly obnoxious female impersonator in the London nightclubs of the 1930s.) "It just isn't my sort of stuff. Now, Leslie was great at it." (Leslie Howard in the Korda *Pimpernel*.) "Merle told me Alex would come in in the morning and change everything all round with lots of new business and Leslie would do it right off the cuff. Now, I'm not like that. I'm just me. See?"

I did see and I didn't agree. But David was right, and I was wrong. When using disguise to outwit the villain or the hero, the audience must be fooled first if it is going to believe that the other fellow is going to be fooled. When a romantic actor like Leslie Howard played the Pimpernel a sudden glance from his eyes, while playing a comedy scene with Chauvelin, could reveal the danger and importance of the issues behind the jokes and smile, but this sort of acting was not in David's range and he knew it. He was uncomfortable in costume, and he showed it.

Apart from these doubts and fears, the film went gaily and looked gorgeous. The gentlemen were fantastic, elegant, and inventive. They made me feel proud of my countrymen. The ladies were the most charming and bosomy group of lovely women that I have ever worked and played with. All of them, male or female, could dance, fight, and make love, and they did. For a time we all lived and breathed in those magic years at the end of the eighteenth century, the years of Enlightenment when men and women would die for an idea and kill for an insult.

And then one Monday morning we woke up and did *not* go to the studio that morning. It was all over. Bill Paton and I took off for the wilds for a week. It was our custom at the end of a film to have our rucksacks packed and with us, and when the last shot of the film went into the can, Bill would have a hired car waiting, and we would walk straight off the set into the car, then from the car into the night train, or night plane, to wherever we had planned to go, and in the morning we woke up in an entirely new environment and completely surrounded by strangers. We spent the next few days walking, eating, and sleeping, hardly exchanging a word. There was no need of one. By the end of the third day I had completely shaken off the hopes and worries, the success and failures of the current production, and was ready to come back and run the film with Emeric and Reggie Mills and any of The Archers who cared to be present. On *Pimpernel* Reggie had asked for a week to complete the rough cut. I had been shooting hard and fast to a musical playback and he had fallen behind. During the shooting I never saw the sequences that Reggie was cutting unless he asked me to. Or sometimes Noreen* would say to me, "Micky, after the rushes, would you stay behind when the others go? Reggie wants to show you and Emeric something that he's done."

On *Pimpernel* I had seen nothing since I had checked the exteriors, and I was curious to see how it had worked out. The film opened with a revolutionary chorus around the guillotine, and changed swiftly to an action sequence in which a tumbrel full of aristos on their way to the guillotine was intercepted and the occupants whisked away to the north of France and across the Channel. From then on it was the lightest of soufflés, following the lines of the old plot, treating it with affection but refusing to take it seriously, and contrasting scenes of the English aristocracy dancing and gambling with others of the bureaucracy that was taking over France in the name of the people. England and France were not at war yet, at this time in the story, and we made Chauvelin the ambassador to royalist England from republican France. He is coldly received by the Prince Regent, and mockingly by Sir Percy and his friends. Lady Blakeney is a Frenchwoman he is able to threaten and to use, because her brother is a hostage in France. Cyril Cusack made a delightful Chauvelin, his eyes full of malicious superiority, which, being an Irishman,

---

*Noreen Ackland, first assistant film editor and later editor of *Peeping Tom*.

came naturally to him anyway. In his black Directoire costume he looked like a black beetle. There was comedy and drama in the film, but music and dancing were never far away.

As I had suspected, I had undershot the sequences of escape at Mont-Saint-Michel. We needed more close-ups, more action scenes of the tide rushing in and the soldiers struggling with the water, but Hein's and Arthur's costumes and sets, Brian Easdale's musical score, and the color photography of Chris Challis and Freddie Francis were delightful and new. Such colors, such make-ups, such contrasts, had never before been seen in three-strip Technicolor. David was still in England and available for extra scenes and retakes, but before doing them we decided to show the film to Sam Goldwyn in its present state; and as the Mountain was a bit old to come to The Archers, The Archers went to the Mountain.

He hated it. The Mountain, I mean.

I think that he thought we were getting at him by not taking the plot seriously, and he took it as a personal insult. He had admired Korda's prewar film and expected to have a color replica of it starring his own star, David Niven. I suppose that The Archers were among those filmmakers who say to the public at large: "Yes, it's lovely. You like it and we like it too. You don't believe, but you enjoy it. We need you—YOU, the public—to help us put it over." In *The Thief of Bagdad*, with Sabu, I was doing this all the time. In *Colonel Blimp* we did it visually in the duel sequence, where all the suspense was in the preparation and as soon as the duel started we tracked up and went through the roof to show the whole of Berlin under snow. In *A Matter of Life and Death* it was Marius Goring's inspired line of dialogue, "One is starved for Technicolor up there," pointing to Heaven with his cane, that captivated the audience and made all things possible. In *The Red Shoes* there were two worlds again, the world onstage and the world backstage, both of them transitory, both of them illusory, and we and our audience moved from one to the other and back again with great confidence. In *Pimpernel*, we were filming a piece of romantic nonsense: I decided to treat it for what it was and to let the audience in on the joke. A few years later a brilliant director, Richard Lester, did the same thing with *The Three Musketeers* and carried it off in triumph.

We arrived in New York on one of the Cunarders, and went on by airplane to Los Angeles. In those days there were night planes from New York to Hollywood. You left around midnight, and arrived for breakfast in Sodom and Gomorrah. There were bunks on the plane, just like the old railroad sleeping cars, with the added improvement that they were made up for you by lovely stewardesses who wanted to know all about England. You undressed, put on your pajamas, and went to sleep, just like on the *Twentieth-Century Limited.*

I woke early and demanded tea, which was brought to me by the two most charming stewardesses. They sat on my bunk with me and admired the shadow of the Rocky Mountains, cast across the plain by the rising sun, which the covered wagons took weeks to cross in a dozen feature films. I couldn't help thinking that they must have seen this sight before. We were staying at the Beverly Hills Hotel. We shared a comfortable bungalow and Mr. Goldwyn sent his compliments. The show would be that night at eight o'clock. We arrived five minutes late at the Goldwyn Studios.

They had started without us. We were guided to the projection theatre and pushed into the darkened room. Our guillotine chorus was thundering away on the screen. You always feel a fool when introduced into a show in progress, and we were no exception. Nobody moved to help us. Nobody said a word. Dimly we made out in the darkness a few sleeping dinosaurs and murmured apologies, which were unacknowledged, as we stumbled over their legs. Mrs. Goldwyn hoisted herself out of an armchair as big as a twin bed beside that of her husband, and came to meet us and guided us to our seats.

Have you ever arrived late for your wedding? Or for your funeral? We sank into our seats, not daring to look either at the screen or at each other. We had admired, in fact we had revered, Sam Goldwyn. His name had meant top quality to us for all our working lives. We were quite shattered by his rudeness in starting without us. Of course, I realized later that to him and his wife and his Hollywood henchmen the rudeness was not intentional—it was not even noticeable. But we were The Archers, who had written, produced, and directed over the last ten years films that were not only good entertainment, but films that had helped to win the war, films good enough to displease Churchill, films that had built the empire of Arthur Rank, and that had received royal approval many times.

We felt that the whole film industry was humiliated by Sam Goldwyn's unthinking rudeness toward us. For the first time we started to understand the horror of the old Hollywood empire and its moguls. The shock would not have been so great if we had not fought for the privilege of choosing and making our films, and of being consulted every step of the way, script to final release. We sensed, without knowing, that this was the way Goldwyn treated his collaborators once they had signed a long-term contract with him: this was the way he talked and behaved to craftsmen whom we admired to extravagance. He gave them great opportunities, but he took away their power of decision. *What, you say? All these hysterical denunciations? All these accusations because of a simple impoliteness?* Simple! What's simple about slamming the door in someone's face? What's simple about treating a friend as a slave?

I hardly looked at the screen that night. I sat beside Emeric in silence, feeling closer to him than I had ever felt, hating Goldwyn and waiting for the show to be over. The atmosphere was hostile from the start, and we could feel it thicken as the film unspooled. Occasionally someone laughed in spite of himself. Goldwyn and his wife talked together in low tones through the screening. When the lights came up the dinosaurs rose on their hind legs and proved to be human. I never knew who they all were, but they had some nice things to say about the production, and obviously didn't care whether Goldwyn liked it or not. True to form, Sam never looked at us nor addressed us, and he went out while Frances Goldwyn came to us.

"My husband says he is going to talk to Alex. The transport office will contact you in the morning to arrange your flight back to London. I hope you have a safe journey. Good night."

And that was all.

≡

Before returning to Alex with our respective tails between our respective legs we both looked up old friends in Hollywood, and I for one got another reminder about Hollywood and its treatment of its children. I had to perform a duty that was painful and embarrassing to both parties. All the same, I'm glad I did it. I went to see Rex Ingram. That proud genius had been waiting twenty years to make another film.

Frank Scully and Howard Strickling had insisted on a meeting. I hung back. This man was a god, a king, an emperor to me. All three of us had seen him riding the skies in the south of France. We had all been sad witnesses of his decline from a throne in the clouds to a canyon in Hollywood. For me, he had been an inspiration, an ideal. My life had been in movies, and the memory of Rex and Alice Terry, his wife, had inspired me through many a crisis. They were beautiful, they loved each other, they worked together, they played together, they were a living legend for me. And now that they had fallen from their high estate, was I to call upon them with all my laurels upon my head? I knew that Rex had seen *The Red Shoes* and had been lavish in his praise.

"And not one word of envy or regret," Frank said. "He wants to see you, Micky. You must go and see him. You can't not see him."

Howard Strickling joined in with his agreement, stuttering with earnestness as he always did when excited: "M-M-Micky . . . little M-M-Micky . . . you don't know what it would do for Rex. I've told him that you are in Hollywood, and we are going to see him this afternoon. So d-d-don't say n-n-no!"

I gave way. I said I would go. But my heart was like lead.

See how heroes and hero worship transform reality! Learn how men and women live and die! Not in their words and deeds, but in the memories they leave behind them. I joined Rex Ingram and his company at Easter 1925, when he was at the height of his fame and glory. I had my share in Rex's extravagant dreams and thundering mistakes, and returned to England with reluctance in 1928. I am writing these words sixty years later, in 1988 in New York.

We are in the Hollywood Hills. As we are helping Frank and his crutches out of the limousine, three figures are walking down from the ranch house to meet us: a slim, handsome man with jet-black hair, a gold bracelet on his wrist, and a gold chain around his neck—he wears a khaki shirt and slacks; beside him is a lovely woman with auburn hair, dressed in casual good taste, her arm in her husband's; while strolling along a little behind the others is a man I know—darkly good-looking, slightly embarrassed, Gerald Fielding.

All of a sudden my reluctance to meet Rex, my embarrassment, vanishes. The warmth of their welcome, their pride in my accomplishment, is so genuine, so generous. I had worshiped Rex as an artist with high ideals who brought glory and importance to our art. I now accepted all the compliments they showered upon me, for the same reasons. I noted that it didn't make me swell with pride. It made me feel very humble, and very proud. Frank Scully, with his great heart, and Howard Strickling, with his knowledge of the world, had been right. The laurel crown must not be allowed to wither, it must be passed on for the good of the art.

I have a book in front of me. It is a stout book, of 337 pages with faded covers, well bound, published by Knopf. The title is *Mars in the House of Death;* the author is Rex Ingram. It is about bullfighters and bullfighting, and is brilliantly illustrated by Carlos Ruano Llopis. It is a novel, and it is obvious that a great deal of love and care had gone into it to try and make it visual. There is the same respect for the material and for the story that we all loved when we first saw Rex's *Scaramouche, The Prisoner of Zenda,* and *The Four Horsemen of the Apocalypse.* On the flyleaf of the book is scribbled: "Am very proud of you, Micky—more power to you. Keep on showing them. Rex Ingram."*

Howard Strickling told me some years later that he could have got Rex and Louis B. Mayer together, but neither man would make the first move. Mayer would never forgive, nor forget, that Rex had refused to have Mayer's name on the films he made at MGM. And Rex was too proud. He died a few years later.

=

Back at Shepperton Studios, Alex was gloomy.

"Goldwyn won't accept your picture. He says it's not the picture he signed for."

"What does that mean?"

*For the rest of his life, Michael always kept this book close by him.

"He has to pay London Films fifty thousand pounds on approval. He refuses to pay it."

"There's nothing in our contract about approval by Goldwyn."

"That was a separate deal, boys."

"Oh."

"He's sending us a list of the changes he wants made."

"Changes? You mean in the cutting, Alex?"

"Some of them are retakes or extra scenes."

"Who will pay for this?"

"London Films will pay."

"Alex! That's crazy! Who the hell does he think he is? Let's finish the film the way it is and preview it. Then we'll know what needs doing."

Alex cut a cigar with great care, squinted down it, brushed the shreds of tobacco onto the carpet and lit it.

"Have you boys kept anything in your budget for retakes?"

"Of course we have. Do you think we're crazy? Three and a half percent below the line. But I need most of that for my retakes and extra shots on the Mont-Saint-Michel sequence. The picture needs a bang-up finish. We have discussed that already."

But Alex wanted his £50,000.

"Sam is airmailing me a list of changes that he wants. We will discuss them together, Micky and Emeric." He pressed a buzzer.

"Conning-ham, Micky and Emeric will come to see me about *The Elusive Pimpernel* next Thorsday."

Of course, Goldwyn wanted all the old, creaky theatrical scenes restored to the film. Of course, he wanted them played out by David Niven and Maggie Leighton. Of course, he thought there was too much music, dancing, and other frivolities. He wanted a color copy of the old film, and no incidentals. Of course, Alex agreed to whatever he wanted, and of course we had to pay for it with our three and a half percent below the line that George Busby had so carefully husbanded for my extra shots on Mont-Saint-Michel. We should have insisted on there being two versions of the film as we did later on with *Gone to Earth*, but we were so crushed by Goldwyn's attitude toward us, and toward our version of the film, and by Alex's helplessness or unwillingness to help us, that we gave way all along the line. Today we would have duped our own version, but this was 1949.

So whether Alex actually received the fifty thousand smackers from Sam we never actually knew; but I guess that he did, because later on a recut version of *our* recut was presented to the indifferent American public, *and* in *black and white*. A Ph.D. thesis is probably being written about this copy at this moment, and no doubt several archives are fighting for it. But my beautiful, elegant musical, my *Elusive Pimpernel*, is gone forever. It is one of the lost treasures of The Archers. It would take the combined efforts of Superman, Indiana Jones, and Reggie Mills to reconstitute it.*

We reviewed our position. I was seriously alarmed. Emeric rather less so. In the Western world the spokesmen say, "Things are serious, but not hopeless." In Central Europe the spokesmen say, "Things are hopeless, but not serious."

On *The Small Back Room* we had been given a completely free hand, but the picture had flopped at the box office. On *The Elusive Pimpernel* we had refused to go to London Films' new studios at Shepperton, and instead ran our own production at Elstree. We had thought to protect our front by this maneuver, and had been kicked in the rear by Alex and Goldwyn. Result: another flop at the box office, and a blow to our friendship with David Niven.

=

What next? We had agreed to make *Gone to Earth* with David O. and Jennifer, but our experience of partnership with one Hollywood tycoon had not encouraged us to make a partner of another. On the credit side was the fact that David O. was twenty years younger than Sam Goldwyn, and had seen all our pictures since *A Matter of Life and Death* and was mad about them; and we were all mad about Jennifer. He had thought Alex was crazy to want us to remake *The Scarlet Pimpernel* and this, naturally, endeared him to us. We could see that his other coproduction with Alex, *The Third Man*, was going to be a winner. We decided to go ahead with David O. the way that hedgehogs made love: verrry carefully!

For some months, Emeric and I had been leading sedentary lives and had got fat, not to say sleek. We had been editing *Pimpernel*, re-editing *The Small Back Room*, and collaborating on the second draft of the script of Mary Webb's *Gone to Earth*. This script had been sent to David O. for his comments. He was jet-setting around the world with Jennifer, and I think it caught up with him in Hong Kong. He suggested a meeting in Zürich at the Dolder Hotel, and since Emeric's favorite restaurant in the world was the Kronenhalle, we agreed on the rendezvous. "But no lunches!" said Emeric, with a sigh, remembering the Kronenhalle's specialties.

"These tycoons never get up till midday, and have eggs Benedict for brunch. It's safer for you and me to eat nothing. We need to slim and we can make up for it later," he added, recovering his accustomed serenity. Emeric loved the city of Zürich, and the city of Zürich loved Emeric. He was almost

*Martin Scorsese and I are still hopeful that we can unearth a print of the original version in some Hollywood vault.

prepared to approve David O.'s choice of a hotel, but he would have preferred to stay at the Baur-au-Lac. Still, the Dolder was a first-class hotel, and had been used often as a rendezvous by the directors and writers of UFA,* which gave it a pedigree. Also, Emeric's old friend Günther Stapenhorst, an ex–naval officer who turned film producer in Germany and England before the war and spent the whole of the war years in exile in Zürich, still lived there and had business there and Emeric was looking forward to seeing him.

The Dolder can only be described as a Swiss hotel. It is very large, very plain, very comfortable, very clean, and altogether healthy-looking. It stands on the top of a green hill above Zürich and has lots of steps and terraces and balconies and lawns and tennis courts. It is reached by a winding road. It is the sort of place where, before the war, you used to see Continental families of eight or more drinking coffee *mit Schlagobers* and eating cream cakes. By no stretch of the imagination could it be called exciting. To this haven David had brought Jennifer and summoned us, and when we duly reported by telephone he suggested we meet next morning around eleven. Delighted by this unexpected respite, we hailed a taxi and drove to the Kronenhalle, where we were received with cheers by Frau Zumsteg and her girls (the average age of a girl in Frau Zumsteg's establishment is forty-five), ordered two large Pilsen beers, and studied the menu, which we already knew by heart. Emeric ordered classical boiled beef with grated horseradish and dumplings; I ordered roast venison with cream sauce. The memory of Samuel Goldwyn's hospitality was fading.

It was a beautiful sunny morning when we all foregathered on the terrace of the Dolder. David had a rolled-up copy of the script in a side pocket of his jacket, took it out, and threw it on the table. Jennifer said, "Hello, boys!" David said, "I don't know how you boys generally work, but when I start a script conference, I like to go through to the end and finish it. It is the only way to keep a clear line on the story and get some idea of your length. Okay?"

We said, "Okay."

He searched in his other jacket pocket. It seemed to be full of pills, bottles and boxes of little pills . . . aspirin, amphetamine, Benzedrine . . . you name it. He selected two of them and swallowed them with a glass of orange juice, then said, "Emeric, you're the boss. Let's get the ball rolling."

Jennifer opened a copy of *Time* magazine. Emeric produced a small piece of paper and started to unfold it. Three hours later we got about halfway

*Universum Film Aktien was formed in 1917 when the German government forced most German film companies into a consortium that monopolized filmmaking until the late twenties. UFA became the leading European producer of large-scale, artistically ambitious films, such as Fritz Lang's *Die Nibelungen* and *Metropolis*. Many of its leading directors—Lubitsch, Murnau, Lang—went to Hollywood.

through the script without any serious disagreement, and David O. was looking rather faint. Jennifer had vanished, saying, "Guess I'll have our driver show me the town, David."

We were relaxed. We had dined well the night before, had had an English breakfast that morning, and were looking forward to our dinner that night at the Kronenhalle. Another half hour passed. A weak voice addressed us: "Don't you two guys ever eat lunch?"

Emeric said, "Not usually when we're working. Are you hungry, David? Do you want to stop?"

He shook his head and took a sniff of Benzedrine. At half past three a yawning, blinking David O. Selznick grumbled, "Guess I'll take a rest. Done enough for today. What do you say, fellas?"

We fellas said, "Okay."

"I like that baptism sequence, Micky." This was a scene at Lordshill Chapel on God's Little Mountain in which Jennifer is totally immersed and baptized according to the simple Baptist rites by the minister, her future husband.

"Say, we better start thinking about that minister-lover of hers. Any ideas?"

I said that we proposed to test James Donald, Cyril Cusack, and Paul Scofield, and would like Jennifer and David Farrar to read their own lines when we made the tests. Jennifer had returned from her tour of the lake and was lying in the sunshine with her eyes closed.

"What do you say, honey? Micky says we should do the tests in about two weeks' time. We could go to Istanbul first, honey."

"I don't know, David. You decide," Honey answered, without opening her eyes.

"Or we could go to Tangiers, honey," pursued David O. "Alex says Tangiers is great. Just so long as we're back in London in time for the tests. We'll talk it over tonight, baby."

"Can't we go to Paris, David? I like the shops in Paris."

"Oh, baby! You don't want to go to Paris again. Tangiers has bazaars that can beat anything in Paris, Alex says. And everything's duty-free to Americans. I'll tell you what, honey, we can go to Tangiers tomorrow and then spend a week in Paris shopping before we go to London for Micky's and Emeric's tests. How would that be, honey?"

"I don't know, David. I'm just tired of packing and unpacking."

It seemed a pity to cut in on this duet, but it appeared to us that the main purpose of the meeting at the Dolder was being overlooked.

"What time in the morning? We'd better meet early, if you are flying out tomorrow. We've still got half the script to go over. We want to suggest some cuts to you."

"Oh, gosh, boys. We can do that when we come to London to do the tests.

Once Jennifer gets started on the film there'll be no more holidays, honey. Jennifer is crazy about Europe, aren't you, baby?''

Baby murmured something.

"I like the way the script is going. We're going to have a great picture. I love that baptism scene. He takes you right down into the water, honey, and ducks you under. You'll be crazy about it. Well, so long, boys. Give my regards to Alex.''

I have tried, as well as I can, to give the flavor of our conversations and relations with David O. and Jennifer J. Just as we were astonished to find Samuel Goldwyn such a hog, so we were amazed to find David O. so innocent. Of course, at this time when we were planning together to make *Gone to Earth* he was a man madly in love. Not many great and powerful men are capable of such a tragic passion as David had for Jennifer. For big, rich, and powerful David O. was. But he wanted desperately to make the greatest film that had ever been made, and he wanted desperately to be liked: two things which made him a child in the hands of men like Sam Goldwyn and Louis B. Mayer, his father-in-law. They neither wanted to be liked, nor expected to be. They were tyrants, and liked to be tyrants. No doubt in Hollywood David O. was as big a tyrant as they were, but in Europe he felt able to relax, probably for the first time in his working life. He was a little out of his depth and that excited him. He liked the unpredictable quality in his relations with the group around Alex. In return we liked him. We were tolerant about his big-boyish enthusiasms and we were sympathetic about his infatuation with Jennifer. At this time, I had no knowledge of the tragic undertones of the love affair. There were no basic disagreements between us about the adaptation from book to film, and the general line of the script. We sighed with relief. We had a wonderful cast of character actors, including Esmond Knight, Hugh Griffith, Edward Chapman, Bartlett Mullins, and George Cole, and there were only two important parts left to be cast: the Baptist minister, Edward, and his mother.

I had had my eye on James Donald for some time. He was lean, all intelligence, knobbly, with a vein of humor and a gift for making enemies. I noticed him particularly in the production of Jean Cocteau's play *The Eagle Has Two Heads* at the Lyric, Hammersmith. Most people will remember him in the role of the army doctor in *The Bridge on the River Kwai*, the one who at the end of the film, when the bridge is blown up, has a brief close-up from David Lean saying, "Madness! Madness!" He was secretive and detached and rude, and I liked him. No doubt there were points of resemblance between us. I thought that his secretiveness and his humor would give a double dimension to the film: to play Edward straight was unthinkable.

Cyril Cusack was the outsider among the three starters. First of all, he was a bit old for the innocent Edward. Then, he had only character parts to show:

the young Irish gunman in *Odd Man Out*, Corporal Taylor in *The Small Back Room*, Citizen Chauvelin in *The Elusive Pimpernel*. His experience with the Abbey and the Gate theatres in Dublin would mean very little to David O., and although he had given a superb performance as Dubedat with Vivien Leigh in *The Doctor's Dilemma*, there was no point in raking that one up. No, I decided, he would have to play Edward as a saint—and saints are hard to handle.

Paul Scofield I have loved and admired all my life. I've always wanted to work with him, but never did, and now never shall. He was the most unusual of my choices, but it was the most perceptive. He has had a great career, has played many of the parts that he wanted to play, but I think that if he had played Edward in *Gone to Earth*, and Matthew in William Sansom's *The Loving Eye*, he would have become less remote to the average man and woman, and the public would have understood him better and loved him more.

He was my favorite for the part, but I was determined to leave the final decision to David O. I didn't want any major squabbles or recriminations at the end of the picture. I had learned a good deal about Paul Scofield from Pamela. They had been in Charles Morgan's play *The River Line* together, and of course in the great season with John Gielgud at the Lyric, Hammersmith, when the two younger actors made their names and reputations forever in Otway's *Venice Preserved*. I worked hard at the tests and played no favorites, but I must admit that I kept Paul's test until the last. When the lights went up there was a silence for about ten seconds. Then David said in a low mysterious tone to me, "Is he queer?"

I explained that Paul was not only not queer, but that he was married to a beautiful actress who had given up her career to devote her life to him and their children. David shook his head in disbelief. Exit Paul.

James Donald gave a beautifully paced performance: brittle, thoughtful, a Darcy out of *Pride and Prejudice*. They admired him. David thought he was "too strong" for the part, Jennifer "too modern." I thought it would have been interesting to see such brains and fire up against the brawn of Jack Reddin. Finally, it was James's intelligence that lost him the part.

There remained Cyril Cusack. He was short in stature opposite the tall Jennifer, and "a little old-fashioned-looking" according to David O. But the quality of the man and the intensity of Cyril's acting drew David. He asked to see all three tests again, shook his head over Paul Scofield, definitely dropped James Donald, and, after seeing Cyril's magnetic performance once more, said reluctantly, "Well, I guess it's him."

I chose Sybil Thorndike to play Edward's mother. And that completed the cast.

For me, making *Gone to Earth* was as happy an experience as a return to childhood. Although I have announced myself sturdily as a Man of Kent, which means that I was born east of the River Medway, I was undeniably Worcestershire on both sides, with a touch of the Welsh in my father's blood. It was easy and natural for me to fall into the speech of my ancestors, with its broad vowels and unexpected crescendos. I was determined that this should be a genuine regional film, not out of respect for Mary Webb, but because I felt this was the way to do it. I planned to make nearly the whole film on location in the Shires, shooting well into the autumn for the hunting scenes and hunting skies, and leaving only a week or two to pick up in the studio as the winter came on. We were using only local people for the crowd scenes and small parts. We brought hundreds of costumes with us and everybody turned out their father's and grandfather's wardrobes to bring in props and costumes for the film. We hired a mothballed aerodrome not far from Shrewsbury, and used the empty hangars like a film studio. We brought chargehands* and master craftsmen from Shepperton, and used local crafts-men and -women to build the sets and staff the wardrobe and costume department. There were problems over plumbing and heating and feeding such a large expedition, but we were used to that and brought in locals to cope with it. The Archers, led and stimulated by the old hands and pioneers Bill Paton, Syd Streeter, George Busby, and Chris Challis, encouraged people to cope for themselves. I have always found that this makes for a happier unit or expedition. When any of my people come to me with vague or specific complaints, I say to them, "Well, what are you going to do about it? Would you like to go home?" I have always found that minor obstacles vanish under this treatment.

Kevin was rising four in 1949, and had decided that he wanted to have his birthday on location. He brought his mother, who approved of Jennifer but was stunned by her innocence—or do I mean her ignorance? Cyril brought his actress wife, Maureen, and their son Paul, who was a bit of a hell-raiser like his dad, so it was quite a family party. Jennifer brought David O., but he didn't stay long. He cast himself as Number One in any setup, and so far as The Archers were concerned he was Number Three. We planned to cut as we shot, according to Reggie Mills's usual custom. As David O. naturally wanted to see the uncut rushes, we ordered two prints of everything, one set of rushes uncut to be held at Shepperton whenever David O. jetted in. He had okayed the script; so had Alex. Personally, I thought it made too good a read. I could hear the crackle of the pages turning. But I thought Jennifer and I and particularly Esmond Knight could handle it.

By the middle of August everything was ready. The rest of the actors moved

_____

*An old-fashioned name for foremen.

up. David Farrar (and his horse) had been there a week or two, galloping around the countryside in costume, contributing a new legend to the local folklore or a verse or two to Mr. Housman's *A Shropshire Lad*. In early August we were off.

Why is it that legend is more potent than reality at stirring the emotions? Why do the songs and tales of our fathers and mothers and of their fathers and mothers touch our imagination more than our own personal experience as children? When I agreed to make *A Canterbury Tale* I expected that it would be a far more personal film than it turned out to be. I was working, creating a story in the county I was born in, the "garden of England," a chalky country of bare downs and shallow valleys, of chestnut woods and little chuckling streams, of slowly turning water- and windmills, and white-capped oasthouses with the bittersweet smell of hops drying in the kiln. All this I knew from my childhood, yet somehow I failed to get it on the screen. No doubt that was because the principal characters in the story were all strangers to my countryside. They were intruders—well-meaning, but still intruders—whereas in *Gone to Earth* the characters belonged to the Shropshire and Worcestershire countryside and to me. When Esmond Knight roared, "Drop that dratted fox, gurl!" or "Put 'un in coffin!" it was the very tone and accent of my father's bailiff, Joe Wood, whom he brought with him from Worcestershire to Kent. When that great Welsh actor Hugh Griffith announces in the tone of a minor prophet, "A mistress at Undern! Never will I!" I hear the power and the instinctive rhythm of the Welsh preacher who was a great friend of my Powell grandfather. All around us, from our crowd of locals, from our artists, and from the onlookers, I was being reminded of my mother's tales and of my childhood visits to Worcestershire. Even the landscape, with its abrupt changes from civilization to savagery, contributed to the story and helped the actors. I think it was, perhaps, because the story and my own feeling for the countryside were both so intensely regional that the French public liked the film so much. France is a very regional country, with a marked difference in the flavor of each region, which writers like Aymé, Proust, and Mauriac loved to evoke. Me too.

We started in Much Wenlock with Jennifer visiting the little market town as if it were Paris. She wore long, black boots laced halfway up the calf, and a worn green cotton dress and a straw hat. She looked ravishing. She had lost several pounds for the part, and had had corsets specially designed to pinch her in and to push her out. She knew where the camera was very well, and she also knew that the camera tends to exaggerate and enlarge, and that a big girl like she was, well made with big bones, can never appear too slim; so she cursed and swore and, abetted by me, insisted upon the wardrobe mistress pulling the corset tighter and tighter until her body moved within the dress like a panther in its skin. This sounds obvious, but I was delighted by her professional attitude to the part. Too many English actresses wander into a part in a historical film wearing the lightest of modern underwear and think that they get away with it. Let me tell them here and now that they don't! In playing a costume part the first thing to do is to study the portraits of the period and then to start constraining your body, altering its sense of balance and movement. The world has been shaped by the way that men look at the shape of women, and if you think that over you see that it must be true. Jennifer had had good teachers in Hollywood, but this approach of hers to the physical side of the part was entirely her own, and it is one of the reasons why I think she could have become a great actress in any medium in which she chose to venture her heart and brain and body.

The weather was great, with high clouds sailing and casting shadows over The Wrekin, and small clouds that ran like rabbits across the short grass and vanished into rabbit holes. We moved over to Church Stretton and Craven Arms, in the Welsh Marches, and made them our base for a week or two. We were shooting sequences of our principals and I had planned it this way so Jennifer could get acclimatized before we tackled the big sequences. I needn't have worried. From the moment that she arrived she threw her shoes away and went barefoot over the Welsh mountains. She had long toes, good for gripping, and the soles of her feet were like tanned buckskin. Whenever she wasn't wanted she would be off on the hill with Foxy on a lead and Bill Paton carrying her shoes. She gave assistant directors a hard time, but I approved everything that she did. She never gossiped or talked personalities, but asked interminable questions about everything she saw, felt, and smelled. She wanted to know everything that Hazel, who had been born and bred in that countryside, would know. The unit stayed at a big spa hotel, which was just getting into its stride again after being requisitioned for the duration of the war. I recommend it, if you can find it.

Personally I stayed in a Shropshire farmhouse that was back in the hills. After Frankie and Kevin went home I stayed on there alone. It suited my mood. Bill Paton stayed at the big hotel with "the boys," and he would report to me all the scandal the next day. I drove up to the farm in the Bentley. There were two gates to open and close before you arrived at the farmhouse. They always left a lamp for me in the hall, as they retired early. I don't remember that there was any electricity in the house, and the only running water was in the kitchen. It was immensely comfortable. The walls were thick and the windows deep, the ceilings high. I had a big bedroom and a big bed and an oil lamp and used to work on the script when I wasn't dozing and dreaming. An old farmhouse like these Shropshire ones responds to every mood of the weather, but I never felt more protected than when the wind was roaring down the chimneys and threatening to take tiles off the roof. I hardly ever saw any of my hosts. They went to bed early and rose in the dark, but all the farm dogs knew me and never made a sound when I came in, except for the watchdog, who gave a token bark to show that he was awake.

David O. appeared and disappeared every weekend. Sometimes we arranged things so that Jennifer could be free on Friday (I mean free of us) and then he would hire a private plane to whisk her to Vienna or Stockholm or Rome. They had learned by now that all European capital cities are not necessarily within an hour's flight of London and that, since the flights were made over land for the most part, they were subject to the vagaries of weather. *The Third Man* was out and a huge success, and everybody was buying zithers. David O. and Jennifer attended several gala premieres. Jennifer spoke little of these raids on Europe, but Chris Challis reported that in a conversation with him she had complained that there were too many foreigners in Europe, all talking different languages. Why couldn't they speak English, like we do in America? Chris, being Chris, agreed and added with a perfectly straight face that he was in favor of foreigners not only being made to learn English, but also being made to eat proper English food, like boarding-house mutton and fish and chips, instead of the foreign messes to which they were accustomed.

David O. seemed to like what he saw of the rushes, and occasionally sent me long cables about them, which Bill read and then put carefully in a drawer. We were more or less up to schedule, which is about all you can ever say on a location film. Hein and Arthur were furiously building sets in their airplane hangar, and it was time to shift our quarters to Shrewsbury. It was on the water meadows nearby that we planned to stage the point-to-point horse races for the scene where Jack Reddin spots Hazel among the crowd of onlookers and rides out of the race in pursuit of her. We were all within easy reach of the house we called "Undern," and of the aerodrome that was to be our studio and where we would film the fairground sequences and the public-house sequences. It was the end of September, my birthday, the evenings were drawing in, and ten days would see us back in Shepperton.

Up till now we had seen comparatively little of David O. He had his spies, of course, who kept him informed of everything Jennifer did or said, but they were not too obvious and she ignored them. When David O. appeared, it was usually with an apology and with some remark like, "Say, I saw the scenes at Undern yesterday. That ball gown looks great on Jennifer."

He would be around for a while and we would hear the usual conversation going on between them: "Honey, how would you like to go to Casablanca?"

"Well, I don't know, David, I didn't much care for it in the film."

" 'Time goes by,' honey?"

Then they would both sing a little bit, then: "Where is Casablanca, David?"

"What does that matter, honey? It sounds like it would be fun to go."

"But where is it, David?"

"In Africa, honey. Not black Africa . . . Ayrabs. It's in Morocco. They've got a king there and a casino. It sounds great. If Micky and Emeric can spare you, we could go down Friday maybe, or even Thursday."

"Well, all right. If it's Ayrabs. There won't be any of those beetles, will there—that have that rear end over their back that sting you?"

Jennifer never spoke about these expeditions. Occasionally I would ask her some question, while we were waiting for a setup, about the people and places that she was visiting for the first time, and she would answer that Copenhagen was "kind of cute," or that Stromboli was "cute."

"Stromboli is a real live volcano, Micky. I never knew that. It threw up while we were there."

But such items of interest were rare and she never volunteered anything on her own account. Nor did she ever quote David O. She went through the film as if she were the real Hazel playing herself. She never tired of talking to the local people and picking out their accent and their words for everything. She was insatiable at asking questions, and from the beginning she was tireless in her attentions to Foxy and all the other Foxies, taking them for a walk, nursing them in her lap all day, calling to them by name, "Foxy, Foxy, come 'ere, come 'ere," with a sympathy and identification for the animals that received open praise from the property man and from Jean Knight, the animal handler.

Those of you who have seen or read about *I Know Where I'm Going!* will remember Captain Knight, the owner and trainer of a golden eagle named Mr. Ramshaw that appears in the film together with its owner. Captain Knight was the uncle of Esmond Knight, and Jean Knight was his daughter and Esmond's cousin. In the book of *Gone to Earth* the tame fox that Hazel calls Foxy symbolizes Hazel's own wildness and contempt for convention. It is the only creature that she loves and that loves her. They are inseparable, and when they die, they die together. It can be imagined what importance I gave to the finding and training of a pet fox, and since Esmond was in on all our early discussions about the film, which was the kind of subject that was very near to his own heart, it will be no surprise that Captain Knight and Jean Knight were almost the first people to be on the payroll, with a brief to find not only one tame fox, but three, if possible, for I already had visions of our Foxy in the film being gobbled up by the hounds before she had started playing her part. No insurance company was going to insure a fox against *that*.

Captain Knight and his daughter found one tame fox easily enough, two with great difficulty and many doubts, but reported that three seemed impossible, and they suggested that instead they should train and hold in support two or three corgis, a foxy-looking little dog with a low wheelbase, much favored by our gracious Queen. They would make a very passable double for a fox, provided that a fox's brush were first attached to the corgi's short and stumpy tail. The proposal was greeted with enthusiasm by me, but not by the corgis. They behaved beautifully, came and went at the word of command, and submitted to being handled by Jennifer in a most cooperative way. But when they found themselves held between the property man's knees while a fox's brush was taped to what other people might call a short, stumpy tail but which was, after all, *their* tail, down it went like a railroad signal and no amount of persuasion could encourage them to lift the hated fox's brush from the dust in which it trailed. It only added to their acute embarrassment that there was a great deal of laughter over the attempt, but not from Jennifer, who was on the side of all animals and wild things and snatched them up and cuddled them to her, and said she knew exactly how they felt and that we were to stop laughing at them, because animals hate being laughed at. Which is true. Even the cat who walks by himself, and for whom all places are alike, doesn't relish you seeing him being chased for a joke by the household dog, nor does he enjoy being jeered at for missing a pounce on a bird.

As to corgi and fox, there is a marked difference of size between the two animals, and it would take a small corgi to make a large fox. The corgi is short, square, and muscular, like Emeric, the fox lean and wary, like me. To add to Captain Knight's worries, Jennifer had to run carrying the fox at high speed in the final sequence of the film, when she is hunted down by the pack, an experience alarming enough for the actress, but doubly alarming for the fox.

Although Jennifer and I had become comrades in work at all hours, and in some of those barefoot scrambles over the hills, we seldom saw each other out of working hours. She never came to see the rushes, or dailies, as you Americans call them. I relied upon Bill Paton to alert me if anything was going wrong. He had reported that when David O. was not with us, Jennifer always ate at the table with the other actors and seemed cheerful and homey. There was always a great deal of laughter, he reported. She was a nice, friendly girl, was his opinion, and not like some we'd had.

It was time to go into our improvised studio and shoot the fairground scenes, in which both Squire Reddin and Parson Edward are claimants for the hand of Hazel, overseen by Esmond Knight as the coffin maker, Hazel's father. They were important and difficult scenes and the whole emotional weight of the film turned upon them, so I was persuaded to make an unwise decision: to shoot them at night. Our makeshift studios were not soundproofed, of course, and there was bound to be a lot of interference during the daytime from sightseers and from extraneous noise, so I reluctantly agreed.

I hate night work. Performing at night is all very well for actors who come from the theatre and who are used to calling up and concentrating their emotions for a few hours and in an unnatural time and place. But for a movie crew, who have to prepare as well as they can for the surprises of the night, night work is not to be recommended, even to the most enthusiastic of young directors. Union regulations insist that you have to break several times during the night for snacks or even full meals, with the result that you never get more than half of what you wanted to; and rehearsals of scenes that went very well in the afternoon take on a very different color at night.

It was autumn and getting cold o' nights. Everybody was grumpy. Chris Challis complained that he hadn't got the lights that he had ordered and Bill Wall was assuring him that he had more than enough—"if you know where to put 'em, Chris"—and certainly more than Georges Perinal had used in *Colonel Blimp.* The wardrobe ladies were snapping at everybody and there were not sufficient work lights around for everyone to find their way and do their job. The electricians were running out more and more cables for people to trip over. It was a scene of organized confusion.

The two leading men were both edgy. They had been in full costume and makeup since six o'clock and it was now about midnight. Esmond was in full flight, as usual, roaring jokes, running lines, and drinking the local cider. It was the real stuff, and a couple of pints of it could set your head spinning—not Esmond's. The scene in which he tells Reddin that he has come too late to ask for Hazel had gone pretty well, and Esmond felt entitled to another pint from the indulgent property man. All this while Jennifer had been waiting to come on, sitting in the bar of the pub set chatting to the extras and sipping her mug. It was a convenient shelter out of the mainstream of events, although within view, and the actors and makeup people had been gravitating there in between setups.

Suddenly I burst in, followed by the crew, and started to set up the scene in the pub, placing people and rehearsing as I went along. I told my assistant to warn Jennifer and he came back to me with a scared face.

"She says she can't."

"What do you mean, she can't?"

"That's what she said, Micky."

"You don't think she's ill?" I went over to her. She wasn't ill. She was drunk.

She looked at me and giggled. She had a half-empty pint pot in her hand and took a swig from it. She held it out to me.

"Have a drink, Micky. Go on! It's only cider. Esmond and the boys . . . all been drinking it." I took it and tasted it. It was the real stuff all right.

"How much has she had?" I said to the scared barman. He was a local extra.

"Quite a bit."

I held on to her mug, but she grabbed another and was doing the Anna Christie bit, slumped across the table. "Well, what are you and Mr. Fucking Selznick going to do about it?"

It was not the Jennifer we knew, the eager and nervous girl. It was a tragic woman speaking. She went on, "Don't try to play the director with me, Micky. You don't know what it's all about, but I do. How would you like to be murdered? Murdered every night and lie there waiting for it? What do I care about you and your picture? Screw you! And screw your picture and screw . . . Mr. . . . Mr. Selznick, the greatest producer in the world . . . the . . ."

Here there followed a stream of filthy phrases and words of abuse, most of which were new to me at that time. I beckoned to Syd and said, "Get one of the hired cars outside the door, put some rugs in it, and a bucket, and help me to get Jennifer into it."

I looked at the scared faces all round me and said to Chris, "Get your lights set up and then call a break for supper." He nodded.

Jennifer went quite quietly between the two of us, muttering earthy obscenities in a conversational tone all the way to the car. As soon as she got in, she was sick. I held her head over the bucket and said to Syd, "Get some towels." He got them. I said to the driver, "Have you got plenty of gas?" He nodded. I said, "Drive us up to the perimeter of the aerodrome and then drive us round and round until she sobers up. I'll tell you when to stop."

He nodded. He knew the drill. For an hour he drove us round and round in that provincial hired car with its smell of mothballs, faded upholstery, and tarnished leather. It even had a speaking tube to the driver. The bucket came with us. It was an hour I would like to forget.

Out it all came.

She hated him. He had forced himself into her life uninvited, been repulsed again and again, had broken her marriage, destroyed her husband, alienated her children, and was such an appalling egoist that he believed that his attentions could compensate for all the harm he had done. He had enslaved her with a contract that promised to make her the greatest star in the world, without the least knowledge of how to do it, and was expecting other people to do it for him. He was dragging her about Europe as if she were the captive of his bow and spear, and everyone assumed that she was madly in love with him. She hated him. But worst of all, he had decided that they must be married: not because he wanted to give her children a stepfather, not because he wanted a child himself from her, but because he wanted to show the whole of show business that he was not like other men. He had brought her to

Europe to take her away from her family and friends. He took her with him everywhere. Whenever they were alone he kept on asking her to marry him. He never let up. He had long since ceased to ask himself why she refused him; he no longer thought about her. It had become an obsession. She dreaded each moment that they were left alone. The only peace that she had had been on *Gone to Earth*. We were all so kind and she loved everybody and she loved Foxy and it wasn't like being on a film at all. But in three weeks the film would be over and then what would she do? She wished she could jump down a hole in the ground like the girl in the film. She wished she could escape—run away—but there was no escape, none, none, none! None of us could understand what her life was like. Nobody could understand what it was like living with a man like David.

I covered her up with rugs. She went to sleep on my shoulder. When her breathing became more regular I told the driver to take us in. Syd and George Busby were waiting for us. They said that David O. had telephoned from Vienna. He had good information, I thought. I said to my friends, "Let's all go home."

≡

I went to see Mrs. Norton Simon the other day. I am writing this in 1984, and I say "the other day," but time moves fast when one is old, and I find that it is already six years since I was driven to the house on Malibu Beach where she lived with her husband, the art collector Norton Simon. The large house sprawled on the beach at different levels, and on the west side only enormous plate-glass windows kept out the sound of the Pacific rollers as they broke on the sand, to all appearances only fifty yards away. The frontage of the house on the east side was on the street, and gave nothing away. When I rang the bell a tall guard eventually opened the door, and behind him there was another guard, even taller, standing watchfully in the hall. I gave them my coat and hat. I am the only person in Los Angeles who wears a hat, and quite possibly the only one who wears a coat. Los Angelenos sprint from the door of the limousine into the house, or from the restaurant to the limousine.

I was shown into an enormous room full of wonders. I had been prepared for this by my visit to the Norton Simon Museum at Pasadena, with its rich and varied collection. In his own house Norton Simon gave favored place to sculptures and images, and there were splendid examples of both, carefully lit. The effect was theatrical, but it was also intimate and friendly. Partly this was due to the lighting, and to the great glass wall that kept the restless Pacific Ocean at bay; partly it was the exotic trees and plants that created splashes of greenery in the enormous room and changed the perspective as one moved. Norton Simon came to meet me. He was slender, quiet-voiced, not very tall, and made me feel at home.

"Jennifer knows that you are here. She'll join us presently."

I strolled about with him for nearly half an hour, sounding him out, talking art. He had taken up art collecting fairly late in life, but had already been everywhere, seen everything, knew everybody. I admired the Cambodian figures, the Greek sculptures—suddenly the most beautiful figure of all was holding me in her arms.

"I consider it a compliment, Jennifer," I said, "that it took you half an hour to pluck up your courage to meet your director again. If I was still your director I would look at your face"—she had made it up an inch thick—"and say, go and take it off! I don't want paint, I want a woman. And you were the most beautiful woman that I ever worked with."

She laughed in triumph and said to her husband, "See what a good picker you are?" But she kept her war paint on.

The dinner was simple and good, like everything in that house. I was the only guest and she talked about David O. without rancor.

"Why is it, Micky, that young men are cute and old men are cute, but middle-aged men are bores?"

"All compromises are bores, Jennifer."

David had died in 1965. Heart failure.

"At least he had a heart," I said. "Not like Sam Goldwyn." I told her the story of our terrible night at the Goldwyn Studios. She laughed and laughed.

"I can just see you and Emeric."

Norton Simon stifled a yawn and offered me a dram of malt whiskey. It tasted like Glen Morangie, one of the great malts. It was obviously meant to speed the parting guest and to remind me that I was no longer a youngster of forty-four. One of the guards drove me back to my bedsit* in Hollywood, a princely gesture, for my taxi to Malibu had cost me $26. I asked him about the houses on the beach. Weren't they built too close to the not-so-Pacific Ocean? It depended upon the reefs and upon the tidal currents, he answered. But houses were often damaged and sometimes washed away. Didn't this discourage people from rebuilding?

"No. This is California," he reminded me. If he might on any day see his Khmer Buddhas and marble Medusas rolling out to sea, why did Mr. Norton Simon risk them there?

"He likes having his things around him. And he says they are as safe there as anywhere else. Good night, sir."

*Bedroom/sitting room. At this time, after being rediscovered and brought to America, Michael was asked by Francis Ford Coppola to become "senior director in residence" at the short-lived Zoetrope Studios in Hollywood. Michael did not reveal that after years of failure to get his projects off the ground, he could not afford a car. He lived quite happily within walking distance of the studio, in a slightly run-down apartment with no telephone, television, or radio.

He had dropped me as requested on the corner of Melrose and Vine. There was a street telephone there that I used, for I had no telephone in my apartment. I was the only man in Hollywood to have no telephone.

Lem Dobbs was awake.*

"You'll never guess where I've been."

"Where?"

"To see Jennifer Jones."

"*Gone to Earth!*"

"What are you doing—working?"

"Just finished a new script."

"What's the title?"

"*Ohio River.*"

"That's a lousy title. Why don't you consult me before you pick a title? What are you doing now?"

"Starting another one."

"Tonight?"

"Tonight."

"What's the title?"

"*The Ghost Hunter.*"

"Swell." He squared off *Ohio River*, inserted a new piece of paper in his typewriter, and started to type.

"Good night."

"Good night."

I turned down Waring Avenue, thinking of David and Jennifer. He had appeared soon after Jennifer's cider binge, but he never mentioned it to me. No doubt he had had several versions of the incident from members of the company, but my prompt maneuver in bundling her into the car and keeping her isolated where no one could hear her had stymied gossip, and a few days later we were back in the less intoxicating environment of Shepperton Studios.

≡

The script was working out all right, and everyone was very pleased; but I was uneasy. There was no humor in Mary Webb. Nothing unexpected, and therefore no life. Unlike Thomas Hardy, whose sudden poetic passages can be swallowed whole, Mary Webb's range is limited by the garden gate.

*As a boy, Lem Dobbs played the part of an electronic whiz kid in the last film Michael and Emeric worked on together, *The Boy Who Turned Yellow*, which was made for the Children's Film Foundation. His father, the painter R. B. Kitaj, is a huge fan of The Archers, and claims that after seeing *The Red Shoes* he decided to devote his life to art.

David Farrar had the most difficult part to play. He had the guns for it: muscle, masculine beauty. They had all served him well in the past, but he was a kind and compassionate man, and there was no shred of kindness in the makeup of Jack Reddin: the squire was vulnerable, yes, but vulnerable in the way that a spoiled child is vulnerable when he can't get what he wants, like my father. When I hazard a remark that David Farrar was having a bit of a struggle with the part, I'm being unfair. In the exteriors his part was limited to thundering about on horseback chasing the girls, and this he had done very efficiently. It was only in the last few days that he and Cyril and Jennifer had come face to face in the fairground scene, and everyone felt the better for it. The subtle Cyril, who had realized that the way to play his part was to keep still and have lots of close-ups, had been scoring points all along the line, and it was a relief to enjoy a bit of conflict between the two men. Their big scenes together, and with Hazel, would take place in the studio, and I wasn't worried about that but about the climate of the film as a whole. It seemed to me that I smelled a novel, not a film. Once again I asked myself, why are we doing this? We were The Archers. Our films were "Written, Produced and Directed by Michael Powell and Emeric Pressburger." Out of thirteen consecutive films The Archers had eleven on target. They are playing now, more than forty years later. They will play as long as the negatives last.

We had needed a change, and we had gone back to Korda because we had nothing but dazzling memories of Alex, and because he promised us the same independence that was originally given us by Arthur Rank. Instead of sticking to our guns and writing our own stories and scripts, we had fallen into Korda's web. He had used our new, dearly acquired reputation to make deals that benefited him and his companies and left us with partners like Goldwyn and Selznick. He had coated his web with sugary promises and we had got stuck with them.

Back in London, with a few hours every day that we could call our own, Emeric and I talked this over together. He was not as worried as I was. For one thing, he was more used than I was to the vagaries and tyrannies of a big studio, with production heads like Erich Pommer at UFA, and Alex Korda. A big company is used to a percentage of failures among the hits and vice versa: it writes them off. But I didn't regard myself as working for Alex—not even with Alex. I had this passion for independence, which I had always had and which had been stimulated by the war. I had found the ideal creative partner and I was not prepared to take one step backward from that position. My mother would have recognized my expression when I made this declaration to Emeric. The boy is father to the man.

We had a five-picture contract with London Films, of which we had made two (*The Small Back Room* had been a sprat to catch the mackerel, for we were still working for Rank at that time). It was a very advantageous contract. It not only paid us better fees than we had ever had in our lives, but also paid retaining fees to our creative partners like Hein and Chris and the others. In filmmaking this is a rare and sought-after privilege, and we had built up our unit since the war until it was the best in the world. Even Technicolor in Hollywood could not explain our success: why our color was superior to all others. Their people said that it must be the London water. It had never occurred to them it was because we had half a dozen painters on our staff. Our two cameramen, Jack Cardiff and Chris Challis, had been apprentices in the Technicolor laboratory before the war. We had continuity, that rare and evanescent thing, and I dreaded to see us lose it. I talked passionately about colored picture postcards, and said that I intended to do more work in the theatre if I couldn't get more interesting films to make. Emeric looked thoughtful.

Ever since I had seen the Group Theatre's production of Clifford Odets's *Golden Boy*, I had been madly envious of the legitimate stage. Here was a living, breathing slice of life, starting quite arbitrarily in the middle of people's lives and finishing just as arbitrarily, leaving you with the sense that life was going on. The actors weren't acting it, they were living it. There were no sets to speak of: a prop, an offstage noise, a lighting effect, a cue to change the scene, a shift in time worked as surely and as clearly as the most elaborate stage machinery. The director cut from one scene to another as boldly and as accurately as in a film. A word, a gesture, a slam of the door, and—bingo— you were somewhere else.

"They have beaten us at our own game," I thought jealously. "And at a hundredth part of the cost of one of our films."

Hein looked startled when I first broached the subject with him and Arthur in the middle of an art department conference. Then he looked guilty.

"I gave you your chance on *The Red Shoes*," I said, "and we shook all the traditionalists to their concrete foundations. What's so special about naturalism? I've been fighting it for years. The only art director that ever understood me was David Rawnsley.* He was just as practical as Arthur here." It was Arthur's turn now to look self-conscious.

"After all, he and Syd Streeter practically single-handed built the submarine for *49th Parallel*. And, when we had to make *One of Our Aircraft Is*

*Art director on *49th Parallel* and *One of Our Aircraft Is Missing*. Rawnsley was supported by Michael in his efforts to develop what he called "The Independent Frame," which aimed to use the very latest techniques of back projection and model work so that films could be made quickly and cheaply entirely within the studio. Francis Coppola has long been intrigued by this idea, and updated it for Zoetrope's *One from the Heart*.

Missing with John Corfield on a shoestring, and we had to take six actors across Holland and back to England . . . Jesus! . . . there must have been about forty sets, of which at least half were on-the-spot improvisations, effects of light and shade, cooked up by Ronnie Neame and David and me, and not only perfectly satisfying to the public—it was a damn sight more satisfying to us. Realism is one thing and naturalism is another. I hate naturalism. I hate it when we have a simulated exterior scene in the studio, and I see prop men bringing in great branches of living trees, covered with leaves, which wither under the light and are thrown out the next day." Hein was puzzled.

"Excuse me, Micky," he said, "but we are dealing here in this film with anthropomorphism, no?"

"Yes."

"So what is wrong with our sets? You don't like them?"

"They don't say anything."

"Say? They say what is there!"

Arthur intervened: "What do you want, Michael?"

"What isn't there."

They looked despairingly at each other. They both understood, dimly, what I was bellyaching about, what I was asking for, but the traditions of the film business were too strong for them. One of the key words of the film establishment is the word "established." Example: "We have established the exterior of this house," and that means the interior must conform with it. Measurements will be made by some assistant art director, photographs will be taken, and eventually a four-walled set will arrive in the studio. They will even put a ceiling on it if you don't keep a sharp lookout. The fact that it may be impossible to create the atmosphere that you have in mind, or to set the actors about their business in it, is nothing to do with the stage carpenter. It's the same as with a script that is based on a novel. The analogy is perfect. The novelist has "established" the place, the time, and the characters, and try how he may, the director cannot break out of the mold. I felt the walls of Undern in the film closing around me. I feared that my actors would never rise above the psychological level of an obscure nature-poetess. Mary Webb was a good storyteller, but she was no Brontë, breathing fire and brimstone into her characters' veins.

Hein and Arthur did their best to give me what I was groping after, but it wasn't until our next film, with its complete departure from all convention, that we were able to show the world that *The Red Shoes* was not a flash in the pan but was part of a general statement about the art of the cinema that had never ceased to gain disciples and acceptance since *The Cabinet of Dr. Caligari* in 1920.

1920! Sixty-nine years ago, for I am writing these words in 1989. I had been climbing steadily in comprehension and in determination ever since 1925. I was a long way from the top, but I thought I could make it. I had no inkling that there was to be no top! It was as if Hillary and Tenzing had left Camp 4 at daylight, with the snow in perfect condition, only to find that there was no summit. What I had taken for the top was only a high ridge, with a deep valley beyond it, and television at the bottom of it—a dangerous valley, full of avalanches, and deep crevasses, and the end of film as I knew it.

Syd stayed behind in Shropshire when we went down to Shepperton to finish the film. Reggie Mills had asked for more coverage on the hunting scenes, and they needed good organization as well as good handling. It took weeks and weeks, but Syd is a sticker, and had the master of the Wheatland Hunt jumping to his orders.

David O. was anxious to get away. Jennifer had become a different girl since her breakout in the pub. She had got the whole thing off her chest and it had done her good. She changed arrangements, broke appointments, and became very friendly with the crew. An English crew, if they like you, can be friendly without being familiar, and she enjoyed that. She gained in confidence, remembered that she wasn't a Babylonian slave, and made some decisions of her own. One day when she wasn't on call she disappeared from the studio, and David O. was all for calling in Scotland Yard. When I got home that evening I found Jennifer sitting with Frankie before a blazing fire, while Cyril walked up and down trying to look romantic. I'm sure that Jennifer would have run off with him, or anybody, at the drop of a hat. She turned up at the studio a day or two later, without a word of explanation, to finish the film. No wonder David O. was a bit jittery. She had turned the tables on him, and he was not used to it.

We ran the rough cut and nobody liked it much, except Alex. Jennifer was splendid. We could do a lot to it, but it would take us about eight weeks to record music and effects, approve the final cut, and do the mix. David urged us to get on with it, and took off with Jennifer to America, I think. We suspected that our lovely film was not Great, or even Big, by Selznick's standards. Eight weeks later we ran the show copy for him. Alex had seen it already. When the lights went on there was a pause while he took a Benzedrine. Then he said, "I'm not satisfied with your cut, boys. I am going to take this picture over."

Emeric and I looked at each other. Then I said, "Aren't you taking on rather more than you can chew, David?"

He gave me a look. He was quite calm. He said, "Has Alex seen the film?"

"Yes."

"What does he think?"

"He liked it."

"I'm going to see him."

"Go ahead." I dialed David Cunynghame.

"David Selznick is with us. He's seen the film. He wants to see Alex." A pause. Then Cunynghame's voice: "Alex has Sir Robert Vansittart with him, but he'll come out."

Cunynghame's office was adjacent to Alex's, and he meant he would see him there. David heaved himself up.

"Where will you be?"

"In our office."

"See you there in half an hour." He went.

Syd and George, Chris and Brian, looked at us despairingly. None of them had been complimented by this monster for their wonderful work on the film. I said, "Don't worry, boys. Come on, Emeric." We went to our office. It was on the second or third floor of the building on Hyde Park Corner, and we hardly ever used it except for interviews. London Films had bought it not for our convenience, but for the address. David O. was back with us in ten minutes. He looked almost genial.

"It seems that The Archers are the producers on the film, not London Films, and not Alex."

"And not you."

"My contract is concerned only with the American rights of the film."

"Correct. You can do what you like with the film in America, but we hope that you won't."

A long pause while David O. looked out of the window. Then: "I'm going to sue you two boys."

"On what grounds?"

"Deviations from the script."

My heart jumped. Emeric looked amused: "David, you know that is nonsense."

"That's what I'm going to do."

"You can't possibly win."

"We'll see. So long, boys. See you in court."

His tone was perfectly detached. He was neither friend nor enemy. He was used to getting his own way.

=

David O. will always be remembered for his memos. He was the definitive memo writer. A selection of them was collected and published in a book of 508 pages, plus an index. It has a straight-faced introduction by S. N. Behrman. You start yawning as soon as you open it. He wrote these memos to all his directors. He wrote them to me. I never read them. They accumulated in some pigeonhole until Bill Paton cleared out the mess. I reasoned that David O. wouldn't expect an answer once he had got them off his chest, and if I read them I would only be annoyed, so both of us were happy. Emeric read them, and then went back to reading *Time* and *Life*.

The suit that David brought against The Archers was thrown out of court, as Emeric had told him it would be, and a few weeks later the film opened at the Rialto Cinema in Coventry Street, just off Piccadilly Circus. It is now shuttered. It had a good position, but it was a small, old-fashioned hall. It was the only West End cinema that Alex owned. The others were tied up to one or another of the big distributors and the rest were part of the Rank empire. Rank had the pick of all the big American films coming in, because he had the best theatres, and he was not inclined to give London Films a break, especially when Alex was stealing all his directors.

Our film was not a success. It was praised for its beauty and atmosphere by the critics, but apparently it was not what the public wanted to see. A week or two later Alex invited me to dinner in the Penthouse at Mr. Claridge's hotel. His brother, Vincent, whom I loved, was there too. It was evidently a Conference of the Powers. Alex could be a charming host, and that night he was more charming than ever. Not a word was said about *Gone to Earth,* or what we would do next, until coffee. Even then, although both the Kordas had liked *Gone to Earth,* we didn't waste much time over it. The foreign sales were going well and did we know that David O., now that he had a copy of the film and a negative for America, was asking all the top directors in turn to see the film and tell him what was wrong with it? King Vidor, William Wyler, Josef von Sternberg, all to a man had admired the film, finding its atmosphere fascinating. When pressed by Selznick they had said there was nothing wrong with it, and refused to have anything to do with retakes. But Rouben Mamoulian needed the work and had no such scruples. He was a professional.

"Poor Mamoulian," I said. "He's a great director, but he'll never survive that tidal wave of memos. What is it that David wants, anyway?"

"Sex," said Emeric solemnly.

"You're not serious! Why, the film reeks of sex."

"Not his kind of sex," explained the sex expert. "Do you remember, Michael, how David made us sit through all those interminable scenes in *Duel in the Sun,* when Jennifer's knees were being ripped to shreds as she crawled up the mountain with a Winchester in her hands? He is trying to recapture those emotions. He is a little boy. He hoped that you would do this for him, and when you didn't, he runs to other directors to do it for him."

"With two Winchesters?" I suggested.

"Something of the sort."

The conversation turned to Moira Shearer. Alex was obsessed by her career, or rather by the way she was handling it. He simply could not understand, any more than David O. could, how a young, unknown dancer with spectacular good looks, who had become one of the greatest stars in the world on the strength of her performance in one film, should elect to turn down all other offers and go back to the ballet. The mystique of ballet baffled him. He had decided that classical ballet bored him, and that the men were a lot of poofs. Even now, he couldn't understand the international success of *The Red Shoes*. But he understood what the box office told him. I think that he felt partly responsible for our success, and of course he implied as much to his influential friends. After all, who but he had started the Red Shoes dancing when he commissioned Emeric to write the script at Denham before the war? He would kick himself until the day of his death for letting a property like *The Red Shoes* slip through his fingers for a mere £20,000. But even more incomprehensible to him was the failure of The Archers to secure options on Miss Shearer's future services. It was useless to tell him that Moira was a dedicated ballet dancer who, on returning to the ballet, had described *The Red Shoes* as a prostitution of her art and had stated that she had no intention of making any more films. He pooh-poohed the statement, and talked about human nature as if he were Lermontov in the film. We would see what would happen when Hollywood got to work on her, "wouldn't we, Vincent?"

Vincent was sitting opposite me, crumbling bread. He smiled and nodded to me. We had always been friends since those days at Denham before the war, with Connie Veidt and Vincent's dog, Nuisance—alas, no longer with us. Alex chose and lit another Corona: "We would see." Sam Goldwyn had been looking for years for a girl to play the heroine of Hans Christian Andersen's fairy tales. The actress not only had to play the love of the writer's life, but she had to dance like a snowflake, swim like a mermaid, and look like a princess. Danny Kaye was to play Hans Christian Andersen. Here, at last, was just the right girl. Did we think that Moira would turn down the kind of offer that Sam Goldwyn would make, or the chance of working with a performer as good as Danny Kaye? Did we think that?

I looked across at Emeric. It seemed as good an occasion as any other to stick our neck out. He nodded and said, "Alex! We went to see Sir Thomas Beecham the other day."

"Where? At Covent Garden?"

"No. At the Waldorf. Michael says that he always stays there."

I nodded. "They give him a suite with a piano and make him a good price. It's handy for the Garden."

Vincent looked interested. "Where is the Waldorf?"

"Round the corner from Bow Street." Vincent nodded. Every foreigner who came to England before the war knew Bow Street police station.

"What did Tommy want? Has he got any new stories?" said Alex. Sir Thomas was a famous raconteur and Alex had met him at the Beefsteak Club with Winston Churchill. They were both members.

Emeric continued as our spokesman: "He wants us to make the film of an opera, Alex." The ash dropped from Alex's cigar. Emeric continued undaunted. "He would conduct the score and find the singers. We would film it." There was a silence. Vincent crumbled some more bread and smiled sweetly at me. A smoke ring wobbled in the air above Alex's head, lending him temporarily a saintlike appearance.

"What did you say to him?"

"We asked him what opera he would suggest."

"And what did the old boy say?"

"*Carmen, La Bohème* . . . but Michael said that they would be filmed operas, not films."

Vincent joined in: "The story *Carmen* by Prosper Mérimée would make a wonderful film, Micky. It has been filmed already."

"I know, Vincent. I worked on one of the silent versions twenty-five years ago in the south of France. I was shooting the stills."

Alex looked at me suspiciously. "They are not bad ideas, Micky—*Carmen* and *La Bohème*. They are famous operas and good stories. Murger and Mérimée are wonderful writers. You could take what you want of the music of the operas and Emeric could dramatize the story. It's not at all a bad idea."

Vincent nodded and started to hum "Che gelida manina." I decided that things had gone far enough.

"I think it's a rotten idea, Alex. That's just what I don't want to do: take a few arias and choruses from the opera and make a film which is half opera and half stage drama. Why do you think that the Ballet of the Red Shoes was such a success? Because the music was composed first. The action of the ballet sprang from the music. The music was the master. Do you remember how Lermontov always used to say nothing mattered but the music?"

Alex winced. There was no love lost between Alex and Anton Walbrook. "You would record the opera first, bar by bar, and then make a film to it, bar by bar?"

"If the opera were a suitable one. There are operas and operas, you know. The best way would be to commission one."

Vincent poured himself a large brandy.

"What did Sir Thomas say, Micky, when you turned down both *Carmen* and *La Bohème*?"

"He suggested *The Tales of Hoffmann*."

Alex, who had the usual smattering of culture of an ambitious Central European journalist, looked across at Vincent, who nodded approval.

"Offenbach."

Alex brightened. Offenbach was box office. Offenbach was the can-can. With growing enthusiasm, Vincent made the longest speech that I had ever heard him make in his life.

"Hoffmann's *Erzählungen*! . . . Hoffmann's *Tales* . . . Alex, you know them. We all know them since we were"—he held his hand about two feet off the ground—"and it is he, Hoffmann, the writer, the hero of his own tale"—he waved his arms—"the opera is about. There is a prologue in a beer hall, where Hoffmann tells his fellow students the story of his three loves. Then, there are three acts, each one with a different love, each one with a different girl. At the end of his stories he is drunk and when his first love comes to see him he has—what you say—passed out. And she goes off with another boy—his rival always."

Alex was listening attentively.

"Three loves? There are good parts for three girls?"

"Of course, Alex. They are marvelous parts. The first one is a beautiful dancer, who turns out to be a marionette; the second is a—what you say—courtesan in Venezia; the third girl is a great opera singer, a great artist . . . no?"

Up till now, neither Emeric nor I had said a word. It was all being done for us. Alex mused, "A dancing doll, a whore from Venice, and an opera singer! Did you two boys think about casting?"

"You remember Tcherina—Ludmilla Tcherina—who played the Russian ballerina in *The Red Shoes*?" I said. "She was a bit fat and young then, but she's taken off a few pounds and is in wonderful form. She'd be good for what's-her-name . . . er . . . Giulietta."

"And we thought of Ann Ayars, the American actress, for the girl in the third act," said Emeric. "It's the best music, and she's an opera singer as well as an actress." Alex nodded.

"And the doll? What a pity that we cannot get Moira Shearer for the dancing doll." Emeric looked at me, and I nodded. He said calmly, "But we can, Alex. She is free and she wants to do it."

The events that preceded this carefully calculated depth charge were as follows. When Sir Thomas Beecham failed to sell me the two grand operas that he wanted to conduct, he asked me to explain my objections. I explained that I was going to make a film, and a film moves. A film didn't necessarily have to move out of doors and in again, but it had to move, and if the best music in the opera is a static scene—a love scene, or a death scene—the film will stop moving and the audience will start leaving. I expected Sir Thomas to be impatient, but he wasn't. He listened closely to my amateurish and most unmusical statements, then said, "You're the director. I'm only the conductor. What do you say to *The Tales of Hoffmann*?"

Stopped in midstream, I gaped. I had nothing to say. I had a copy of

Hoffmann's *Tales* in my library, not a very good translation, and I had never seen the opera. Emeric knew it well, and had often played it in the orchestra in his student days. Lady Beecham walked over to the piano and started to look through a pile of scores. Tommy walked over too, and without looking at us, sat down and started to play, with a sure and dynamic touch, the Barcarolle from Act 2, the Venetian scene. Although the tune has been overperformed, a thrill ran up my spine. It was irresistible. By this time his wife had the score open at the overture and he dashed into it, playing it with great fire and vigor. She turned the pages. We were all very excited. Would he, we asked, consent to come to the studio and play through the whole opera on the piano? He could expound, explain, sing all the parts, if he wanted to.

"He usually does, anyway, when he's conducting," said Lady Beecham, and a few days later he came to the studio and gave us an unparalleled performance. We had laid on a recording studio with chairs, potted palms, and a grand piano. The potted palms were the propman's idea.

"All these old musical gents like 'em. They always have 'em up on the platform when they give a show." Harry had obviously been to Bournemouth for his holiday.

"What about the old girl, Lady Beecham? He's a knight, isn't he?"

"A baronet."

"Cor! A baronetess. It'll have to be roses."

"Can we run to roses, George?"

"I think so, Michael."

Harry saw the chance of a profitable little deal.

"What can I go to, George?"

"A fiver."

"Oh, come on, George! Don't be stingy. Make it a tenner."

"Eight quid."

"Done."

The audience favored with an invitation was select: myself and Emeric, Hein and Arthur, George and Syd, Reggie Mills, Brian Easdale, by special invitation; Fred Lewis, our musical director and assistant conductor, a stills photographer, two recording engineers, and Harry, the propman aforesaid.

We had ordered half a dozen copies of the score in the authorized English version. Emeric and I had skimmed through the libretto together with a great deal of laughter and some horror. English translations of Continental operas vary between the incredible and the impossible. The translators have noticed that nobody listens to the words in opera, and they put down anything that is singable. These particular translators were masters of the inverted phrase. We had already decided we would have to have a new translation, and I had spoken to Dennis Arundell. Emeric and I had our two copies and there was a rush for the others. Hein, of course, knew the opera, and had done the costumes for a production in Germany before the war.

Sir Thomas arrived on time, accompanied by Lady Beecham and the business manager of the London Philharmonic. The property roses were presented ("I'll put them in water, m'lady!") and I introduced everybody. Beecham nodded and said, "Well, let's get started, what!" stepping briskly to the piano. Fred Lewis murmured something about the piano having been tuned that morning, but without waiting for that assurance, the Baronet launched into the overture, Lady Beecham turning the pages.

He announced, "End of overture!" and then went straight into the recitativo, humming, and occasionally singing, important phrases. He stopped before the scene in the beer cellar.

"Any comments?"

I said, "Yes. The overture is fine. We can handle that. And, of course, the love theme is important, but it's too early in the film for so much singing."

Sir Thomas was unperturbed.

"What do you suggest?"

Hein and Arthur looked at me like two hounds ready to slip their leashes. I said, "Emeric and I have discussed this in detail, but the general idea would be to make a recording of the opera with singers and then, using this recording as a playback, shoot the film with dancers."

There was a pause while everyone digested this idea. Hein's and Arthur's tails were positively wagging. Sir Thomas said, "Hmmm. So your film would be a three-act ballet—with voices?"

"Not exactly a ballet," I said. "There are whole sequences in all three acts that are full of action and drama—"

"—and not exactly an opera," said Emeric, "for Hoffmann is an acting part as well as a singing part, and we have three different heroines. It's more like a film than an opera."

"And not exactly a film in which the director can do what he likes," retorted Sir Thomas, grinning, "but an opera which I shall cast, I shall conduct, and I shall record."

I said, "Exactly."

Lady Beecham, anxious to show that she was hip, said, "Shall you use ballet dancers in the film—I mean, classical dancers—or would you use modern dancing like *Meet Me in St. Louis?*"

I said firmly, "Classical dancing. Classical dancers can dance anything and everything. We proved that in *The Red Shoes.*"

Sir Thomas said, "By Jove, what about that girl . . . who danced in your ballet . . . Norma Shearer?"

A shudder ran round the assembled Archers.

"Moira Shearer, Sir Thomas," prompted George Busby, reverently.

"Yes, that's what I said. Moira Shearer. She could dance Olympia on her head. Olympia's a doll, a singing doll. You could easily make her a dancing doll too. Look here! I'll tell you what I'll do. I see your point about the recitativo. Too early for that sort of thing in a film. We'll drop the voice and make a new orchestration of the tune."

"Who will do the orchestration?"

"I will do the orchestration. You can have dancing or photography or anything you like."

"We'll have a ballet," I shouted. "And then the beer-hall chorus would introduce Hoffmann and his fellow students, and put the audience into the right mood for a singing film."

Hein was making notes. The others were turning the pages of their scores, trying to locate the exact passages in question. Sir Thomas and Lady Beecham had their heads together, while he strummed on the piano.

"How long would you want this ballet scene between the overture and the beer-hall scene?" he inquired.

"It's up to you. About five minutes, I should think." (The Dragonfly Ballet that is in the film runs about seven minutes. It is danced by dear, dead Edmond Audran and Moira, and is one of the most unforgettable things in the film. This is how we found the music for it.)

Emeric said, "Aren't you afraid what the critics will say, Sir Thomas, if we alter the opening of the opera?"

"You leave the critics to me, Mr. Pressburger" was the only satisfaction he got. Sir Thomas was evidently not only determined to do the film, but was going to be a collaborator in a million.

Syd whispered, "Do you think we might be able to get Moira, Michael?"

I said, "I don't see why not. Bill! Find out where Bobby Helpmann* is and tell him I want to talk to him tonight. Have you got his home number?"

"I have." Bill vanished.

"Well, shall we get on?" barked Sir Thomas and launched into the beer-hall chorus. When he came to "Sing Us the Song of the Rat" he paused: "What about Kleinzach, gentlemen? In or out?"

"What do you think?"

"It's often cut in performance. I'll play it for you." He was particularly good on the choruses:

> And his knees cracked together
> and went click-clack.

---

*Principal dancer of the Sadler's Wells Ballet and an actor as well as a choreographer. He played the part of Ivan Boleslavsky, Moira Shearer's dancing partner, in *The Red Shoes*.

Click-clack.
Click-clack . . . for
that—for that's Kleinzach.

Everyone could follow this in the score, so they liked it. With a final "crick-crack" Sir Thomas paused again. "Mr. Powell? Mr. Pressburger? In or out?"

"What do you think, Michael?" I gave the thumbs-up sign. Hein shouted, "Micky, I have an idea! We will have beer mugs!"

"Well, of course, it's a beer cellar."

"Yes, yes, but for Kleinzach—we will have beer mugs! So! And the beer mugs come alive and we make a ballet!" He showed the sketch he was scribbling. Certainly Kleinzach and his stomach "like a sack" fitted neatly into a beer mug.

"Gentlemen, in or out?"

"In!"

"Good." He played the rest of the scene. When Hoffmann says, "I'll tell you the story of my three loves," and Nicklaus sings, "Begin, then!" I interrupted. "Sir Thomas, I don't understand about Nicklaus. Is it a boy or a girl?"

"It's a boy. A fellow student, a friend."

"But it's a mezzo-soprano part."

"Yes. It's a girl in boy's clothing."

"But is it a girl?"

"No, it's a boy. A young man. Hoffmann's muse, if you like."

"Yes, I like that."

The idea of an androgynous being accompanying a Gothic-style hero in his amatory adventures appealed to me. Pamela's rich, auburn hair, round head, and great eyes swam into my consciousness.

Sir Thomas was already into Act 2, singing all the parts and dashing off short descriptions of the action as well. Act 2 is set in Venice and opens with the famous Barcarolle. At least half of his little audience had never connected the familiar tune with *The Tales of Hoffmann*, and there was a ripple of excitement as they heard the first notes. Some of them found the passage in the score and read the appalling lyrics with the same disbelief that Emeric and I had had. Hein and Arthur had been whispering together for some time, with one ear to the piano. Suddenly, Hein erupted, shaking with excitement.

"Micky! We have a marvelous idea! We have a different color for each act, a dominant color to suit the music! For the first act, so light and young, and full of sunshine: yellow! For the second act in Venice: of course it must be red—Venetian red. And for the third act—"

A firm voice interrupted him: "Blue!"

"Of course, the classical color. Thank you, Emeric." Hein galloped back to Arthur and whispered furiously.

Sir Thomas cast one of his looks in Hein's direction and announced, "Aria by Hoffmann: the usual stuff—wine, women, and song. What do you suggest?"

"Just a moment, Sir Thomas!" I said. "The Barcarolle . . . is it an overture?"

"Make it whatever you like."

Emeric was reading the libretto. "Music playing . . . gondolas gently swaying . . . it sounds like the Grand Canal, doesn't it, Michael?"

"Yes."

"We could have gondolas, many gondolas, and Giulietta, the courtesan whom Hoffmann desires, arriving in one. It could be a lovely opening. I had an idea just now, when the doll is pulled to pieces at the end of Act 1. When her head is pulled off," he added with relish, "we could have a spring which springs out of her neck. *Ping!* So! And then we cut close to the spring which is still trembling and it becomes the ripples in the water of the Grand Canal."

Chris Challis was delighted. "That's a great idea, Emeric."

Sir Thomas was impatient. He struck a chord on the piano and went into a rollicking tune.

"What do you suggest, Mr. Powell?"

"An orgy!" There was general approval of this. There's nothing like a good orgy for uniting public opinion.

"An orgy would be a good idea, Michael," said Arthur, who had never been near one in his life.

"A very good idea," said Hein, whose thoughts and private life, when he could avoid Ada's eye, were one long orgy. We pressed on.

"Who is this Dapertutto, Michael?" inquired George Busby.

"He's pimping for Giulietta. He sees that Hoffmann is rich and foolish and he wants Giulietta to take him for a ride."

Syd had been looking at the synopsis of the score.

"And Schlemil?"

"He's fucking Giulietta, but is running out of money," explained Hein, with charming directness. He had been there himself.

"This looks like being a lively film," was George's comment, "not like an opera at all."

The music for this act is wonderfully dramatic and sensual. As I began to realize that there was an undercurrent of black magic running through the music, and that Dapertutto was not just the villain but a magician, I remembered other great European films full of magic and fantasy and my imagination took wings. I could see a great Venetian palace full of burning candles of all colors. Giulietta would see Dapertutto first of all in a great mirror and then the magician would walk out of the mirror into her arms. Taking the colored wax of the burning candles in his fingers, he would mold them into fantastic gems to bribe Giulietta. He would dangle necklaces in front of her eyes, one moment lumps of colored wax, the next moment flashing jewels, until she cried out, "I'll make Hoffmann pay!"

Nicklaus is especially moving in this act. Later on, when Pamela played the part, she made you feel all the tenderness and despair that a young man has for a man somewhat his senior whom he admires. When she cried "Come, let us away, or you'll lose your soul!" the atmosphere of terror and bewilderment thickened around Hoffmann, and her despair when Schlemil challenges Hoffmann to a duel was miming at its most intense. In the film I played her against the palace wall, stippled red, where a great face was carved with an open mouth. A gauze curtain hung over the face and rippled so that the mouth seemed to move. This act was full of striking images, some of which occurred to us at the moment of shooting. In one scene, Tcherina as Giulietta descends a staircase made of naked bodies of her despairing lovers, and deliberately steps on the mouth of one of them. The duel, a duel with rapiers, in which Hoffmann kills Schlemil, is all over in twenty seconds, but what doom-laden seconds they are. Finally, stripped and penniless, Hoffmann stands shivering on the edge of the Grand Canal, while Giulietta floats away in her gondola and in the arms of Dapertutto . . . "and so the music ends."

As the last note of the Barcarolle was played by Sir Thomas at the end of the act, the whole room burst into applause. He bowed and smiled. "Any comments, gentlemen?"

Chris shouted out, "What a film, what a film this is going to be!"

After Olympia and Giulietta in Acts 1 and 2, it might be expected that Act 3 would be a letdown, but it wasn't. The first two acts are theatrically superb, but Act 3 has the finest music and the noblest themes—Hoffmann's love for Antonia, and for the sacred flame that is in the voice of the dying soprano. When we finally made the film in the studio, Act 3 was the favorite act of the electricians, those penetrating critics who observe what is going on in and outside of the lamps. Sir Thomas was at his best in this act. He was tender and moving in the love music. He flung out illuminating remarks about those strange characters, Dr. Miracle and Antonia's father, Crespel. He played it and sang it with such sympathy that I was enthralled and I have remained in love with the music of Act 3 ever since. He led us with great ardor up to the climax, and when Antonia hit her top note and fell dead it was a genuine shock for us and we all sat staring at each other. Sir Thomas knew that we were sold, and he turned on his piano stool and faced us beaming. I almost heard the swish of the curtain falling! I ventured, "Is that the end?"

"It can be. It usually is. What do you suggest?"

"Can we go back to the beer cellar?"

"You can, you certainly can. It'll need a linking passage, quite a long one. We don't have to invent anything," said Sir Thomas generously. "There's plenty of music. We can do what we like."

Emeric said carefully, "I think, Sir Thomas, that for our audiences we would need to explain to them what we have seen. A sort of summing up. Is that possible?"

"Perfectly possible. You decide what you want to show your people, and I'll find the music for it."

"And then back to the beer cellar for a finale?"

"And then back to the beer cellar. Yes. And a good rousing playout!"

I had already decided those last eight bars of the opera should be played over a shot of Sir Thomas conducting. After the performance he had given us, no other end was possible.

The American premiere of our production of *The Tales of Hoffmann* was held at the Met. When Sir Thomas flashed onto the big screen, conducting with all his well-known assurance and verve, with his white pointed beard, his white tie and tails, boutonnière, there was a spontaneous outburst of clapping. I had prepared for this and had added an extra shot of a rubber stamp being stamped on the script. It said simply MADE IN ENGLAND. The audience loved it. This was only just, because Sir Thomas was the deus ex machina of the production.

That night, after he had given us his private performance, we spoke to Bobby Helpmann and we spoke to Moira, for the prospect of working again together with our *Red Shoes* collaborators was almost too exciting to be true. Edmond Audran and his wife Ludmilla Tcherina—known to us as Monique, her French name—were on tour. We had scouts out for them. Léonide Massine was somewhere in Europe with his family. The call went out for him. We had decided to keep the cast as small as possible. All the principals would play several different parts. Although the main plan for the film was to record it with singers and shoot it with dancers, both Emeric and I had decided that Hoffmann would be best played by an actor who could sing well enough to satisfy Sir Thomas and act well enough to satisfy our three different leading ladies, as well as ourselves. Did such a paragon exist? Sir Thomas said, yes, and he would find out right away through his agents whether he was available. He was an American. His name was Robert Rounseville.

Both Bobby and Moira were very busy. The Sadler's Wells Ballet of legendary fame was very soon to become the Royal Ballet and take over the Royal Opera House at Covent Garden for their home. World tours and whirlwind performances by the leading dancers were being planned by Ninette de Valois, after the success of the American tours. But Bobby and Moira were no longer the meek instruments of her policy. They had tasted blood when *The Red Shoes* became a world success. Bobby was preparing to make *Hamlet* on the stage, and both of them were ready to make another film, provided it was with The Archers. They thought that in two months' time they might arrange to be free for the film. We could hardly believe our good luck.

I could hardly believe mine. After leaving Rank and joining Alex, I had guessed wrong three times. It was no use blaming the mistakes on other people. I had agreed to make the films, I had made them, and that was that: two years out of our unique collaboration, making films of other writers' stories, when we could choose to make anything we liked. We could have stayed with Rank and handled things more cleverly. We could have accepted one of our American offers and made some money for ourselves and our families for the first times in our lives. Instead, we had fallen for Alex and his maneuvers. Now, just when I had decided that we must escape him at all costs, before he persuaded me to do *The Three Musketeers* or *The Adventures of Sherlock Holmes*, there had fallen into my hands the perfect combination of music, story, mime, singing, and dancing: a love story—no, *three* love stories, or was it four? I had lost count, I couldn't remember! At last I had, almost within my grasp, the perfect combination of all the theatrical arts, the sort of film that ordinarily I would never have persuaded Alex to back, because there was nothing in it for him. It was beyond his comprehension. Unless, of course, there was a magic password that would unlock that door to his self-interest . . . but we knew that password: two words! And it was right that we should know them because we had made them famous, so that Emeric was able to reply that night at dinner in the Penthouse at Claridge's, "Moira Shearer? But we have spoken to Moira, Alex, and she wants to do it."

=

We started rehearsals for the picture on July 1, 1950. We were virtually making a silent film. My life and work had come full circle. I was never more happy. There is a photograph of me at that time, leaping down the staircase of Giulietta's palace in Act 2, which Monk Gibbon included in his book on *The Tales of Hoffmann,* and entitled, "The young lighthearted master of the sound waves." It was never any use trying to explain the meaning of technical terms to Monk. The borrowing from Matthew Arnold should really have been attached to Sir Thomas, who was the youngest of us all. We had given him carte blanche to find his singers. In a remarkably short time he had assembled them, working in close collaboration with us. Robert Rounseville had been found, signed, and expressed to England to sit at Sir Thomas's feet while he studied the part. Ann Ayars, who was putting on weight, as a proper singer should, had agreed to play and sing Antonia. She was finishing a film for MGM. These two, Rounseville and Ayars, were the only two members of the cast who both sang and acted their parts in the finished film. The production came together with surprising rapidity. We had a target date because of Moira's and Bobby's commitments and that helped to rush things along. We reunited from *The Red Shoes* Léonide Massine, Bobby Helpmann, Ludmilla Tcherina (Monique Audran), and Moira Shearer, and we added Mogens Wieth, Philip Leaver, and Pamela Brown.

Léonide was to play three parts in the film: the sly, sophisticated Shopkeeper, who makes a fool of Hoffmann by pretending that the Doll is his daughter; Schlemil, the doomed lover of Giulietta, who is killed by Hoffmann in a duel with rapiers; and Frantz, the gardener, in Act 3. As the Shopkeeper, Léonide wore a silver wig, an enormous bow tie, and was rouged to the eyelids. Alex would have written him off as a poof at once. He was never still for a moment: dancing, singing, and miming. As Schlemil he wore a black and silver uniform, with black hair plastered down over his forehead and huge tragic eyes. As Frantz, the gardener, he was a gay little grasshopper man in clothes so bleached by the weather that he looked like a terra-cotta figure.

Since he knew very well which parts Massine would grab for himself, Bobby Helpmann had made a clean sweep of all the villains in the film: the Rat, the Toymaker, the Magician, Dr. Miracle, and finally as a reward for his astounding versatility and malicious humor, we invented the transformation scene, in which he takes off all his makeups, one after the other, each face revealing that he has been the evil genius behind all Hoffmann's misfortunes. I thought, and still think, that this beautifully economical scene contains all that I could ever say about film illusion. Heavens! What talent we had in that film! The towering figure of Mogens Wieth, the young Danish actor, as Antonia's father, urging his daughter on to greater heights before she dies, strikes the true note of Gothic fantasy and horror.

And then, Pamela.

I have waited until now to write of Pamela Brown, and if I don't I shall bust. When I told Frankie that I was thinking of playing Pamela as the boy-girl, girl-boy Nicklaus in *Hoffmann*, she said, "Hmmm . . . well, I suppose there's nothing deader than a dead love." In this she was wrong. It was six years since that passionate winter of 1944, and she had dismissed Pamela from her calculations, although she knew very well I had seen her from time to time. Frankie always knew everything. She also knew how to keep her mouth shut. In fact, if I had only been the perfect husband, she would have been the perfect wife.

She also said, "I always thought there was a touch of the lesbian in Pamela." In this she was right. All actors are continually experimenting and inventing with their hormones, their male and female genes, and a few have the luck to be evenly balanced between their sexual drives. Pamela was one of these. She was a witch. Women adored her, men feared her, and for the same reason—she fascinated them. She was an invalid all her life, although she had chosen one of the most exacting professions that a woman can choose and she soon reached the top. When she was sixteen arthritis claimed her, twisting her fingers and maiming her feet. Nothing daunted, she recovered and resumed her career. When I gave her the part of the Dutch schoolmistress in *One of Our Aircraft Is Missing* she could barely walk, and sharp-eyed critics, noting her limp, may have thought she was overdoing her characterization.

A year later, when she was playing the leading part in the London production of *Claudia* and was already a name on the West End stage, she was again struck down by the monster arthritis, and it was whispered that she would never walk again. Dangerous drugs were used, she recovered, and was able to join The Archers to play Catriona in *I Know Where I'm Going!* By now John Gielgud, admiring the speed of speech and intelligence that matched his own, had taken her twice with him to America on short tours, on one of which she gave a stunning performance as Gwendolen in *The Importance of Being Earnest*. Now, at the time we were making *Hoffmann*, she was co-starring with Gielgud in Christopher Fry's play *The Lady's Not for Burning*. The witch—twisted, tortured, unstoppable—had arrived.

Since Frankie had chosen to decide that Pamela was a lesbian, I considered that I had permission to go ahead. John Gielgud was shortly going to take *The Lady* to New York with the original London cast, the only exception being Richard Burton, who was playing the juvenile and was now going to Stratford to play *Henry V*. But it looked as if the limited times Pamela could give us could be fitted into Moira's and Bobby's dates. It was a tight squeeze, but we managed it.

Pamela's marriage with Peter Copley, a mutual friend of all concerned, was going two different ways, and Pamela had acquired a new protector who was also her business manager. He provided some light relief, but he couldn't understand, or rather he thought he did understand, why I wanted to play Pamela as a bisexual student in an opera. But the money was all right, and his actress would be co-starring with Moira Shearer, so he signed on that dotted line. But he had no intention of chancing his luck, so every morning at 8:00 A.M. he would deliver Pamela to the makeup department at the studio, and every evening at 6:15 P.M. he would arrive in his sports car and whisk her away, watched with sardonic amusement by Bill Wall, who was a chum of Pamela's.

"He's really worried about losing his meal ticket, guv'nor," said Bill Wall. "Why don't you give him a run for his money? We'll keep the polisher in conversation while you slip out the back way."

I was really flattered. Of course, all the crew knew that Pamela and I had some mysterious relationship, and they were equally intrigued by the part of Nicklaus, especially Bill Wall.

"Look here, Pamela," he said, "when you're acting old Nicklaus, do you feel like a boy or like a girl?"

"It depends, Bill. Sometimes one and sometimes the other."

"Cor, having it both ways, eh!"

On stage Pamela and I had a very formal relationship, but in the waits I would catch her sometimes looking at me with those enormous eyes and would lose myself in their depths. She made a splendid Nicklaus. Even Emeric, who didn't like intelligent women and considered Pamela to be hideously ugly, admitted that. And Laurence Olivier was so impressed by her handling of the role, and feeling the need of an onlooker for his lonely, monstrous Richard III, that he wrote the nonspeaking part of Jane Shore, Richard's mistress, into his film and chose Pamela to play it. He didn't think she was hideous. He, like me, had seen a few portraits in museums, and seen that wonderful, mysterious face—those eyes, that mouth, those shoulders—appearing again and again throughout the centuries. We didn't think a woman's brains were given to her only to figure out what a man would do next. Our kind of woman knew what a man would do before he did it.

One morning, while preparations were in full swing, Alex learned quite casually that I had never seen the opera on the stage. He blew up.

"Imre! Micky has never seen *Hoffmann* on the stage! Are you both mad? How do you think that he can direct the film if he has never *seen* the opera?! Have *you* ever seen it?"

"Yes, Alex, in Prague. I was playing second fiddle in the orchestra, but you don't see much from there."

I assumed my most innocent expression.

"Why should I want to see someone else's production, Alex, when I have the music? As for the words, Dennis Arundell has written a new libretto for us. Why should I want to see somebody else's production?"

Alex snorted and dropped the subject, but a few days later Cunynghame told us that there was a production of *Hoffmann* in the current season at the Vienna Opera, and that Alex wished us both to see it. It was in repertory, of course, but a date had been arranged with the intendant, and rooms booked for us at the Hotel Statler. We would fly down to Vienna on a plane that would get us there in good time for the theatre. We were booked back the next day. This was holding our noses to the grindstone with a vengeance, but Vienna at that time was split up into four zones run by four military powers, Russian, French, English, and American, and Emeric was curious to see how it worked. We agreed to go.

It was winter and there was bad weather all over Europe. Our plane was late leaving, and when we arrived over Vienna there was a snowstorm raging. We spent about forty minutes looking for a hole in the clouds, and then landed in the Russian zone. I figured that we had already missed the first act. Getting passes from the Russian zone to the British zone was quite an experience, and by the time we arrived at the opera house there was nothing much left of the third act but the final aria. Scouts were on the lookout for us: "This way! This way!" We were hurried through emergency doors, down corridors, up steps and down steps: "Schnell! Schnell!" Finally a door was flung open and we panted into the imperial box, just as Antonia reached for a high C-flat (I noticed she was a bit flat), gave one piercing shriek on the stage, and fell dead. The audience, which had been somewhat startled by our jack-in-the-box appearance, burst into loud applause and the curtain came down. That was the only time I ever saw a performance of *The Tales of Hoffmann* on the stage.*

Back in London, Sir Thomas and his Royal Philharmonic Orchestra had already rehearsed, performed, and recorded our version of the opera. The sound department pounced upon the recording and broke it down into workable playback sections in consultation with Reggie Mills. I had made it clear from the beginning, and kept on repeating it, that I wanted a performance, *not* a recording! This meant singers who were actors, like Murray Dickie, or actors who were singers, like the bass Bruce Dargavel. Tommy found us glorious artists like Monica Sinclair, who was both actress and singer. Ann Ayars proved to be more singer than actor, which was as it should be. Robert Rounseville, as Hoffmann, was a fine, manly tenor, good in action, but in love scenes about as pliable as the Eiffel Tower. I didn't attempt to change him. I let him play it his way. After all, the Eiffel Tower has its admirers, and in the opera things happen *to* Hoffmann. He doesn't have to dish it out.

Since everyone was playing more than one part, or at any rate more than one characterization, there had been a good deal of jockeying for a place. Bobby, of course, had been determined to play the Toymaker, particularly when he learned that it was a basso part and that Bruce Dargavel was to sing it. After the years in the ballet, Bobby adored using his own voice, and he sang away like mad during shooting, even though it would never be heard. His Toymaker, Dr. Coppelius, was the best slapstick performance I had seen since the great Ford Sterling, Captain of the Keystone Cops. I had always admired Bobby's invention and his acting when nobody else did, and it was a joy for me now to see him gobble up, one after another, these meaty parts. And, of

*This trip to Vienna later inspired Emeric Pressburger to set The Archers' film *Oh . . . Rosalinda!!* in Vienna after World War II, when it was still governed by the four Allied powers: the United States, the Soviet Union, Britain, and France.

course, he and Massine made perfect foils for each other, each one trying to top the other's performance. There was still the same jealousy between the two great artists who had contributed so much to the success of *The Red Shoes*, and I exploited it.

I don't think that I have mentioned Alan Carter, who with his then wife, Joan Harris, had been a member of the ballet company we formed for *The Red Shoes* and who had assisted Bobby Helpmann as choreographer on the film. He had been valuable on that film, but on this one he was invaluable. He was assistant choreographer throughout the rehearsals and the shooting, and he created most of the puppet dances. He appears briefly in *The Tales of Hoffmann* as the cashier at the bank, who refuses to cash the check presented by Dr. Coppelius. Alan went on to a European career.

I have left Moira to the last, just as I presented Sir Thomas Beecham first; and there is a good theatrical precedent for this, which says in its wisdom: "If you can't get to the top of the bill, the next best place is the bottom." So far as Sir Thomas goes, I have tried my best and used all my box of tricks to paint an accurate picture of this great little man, this artist, this wit, this generous patron of the arts. Now—here goes for Moira.

I had better begin at the end. Moira and I have had the most perfect relationship that can be imagined between two creative artists: it is based not upon love, but upon suspicion and fear. For the past two years, every producer in Hollywood had been trying to sign "that redheaded dancer" in *The Red Shoes* to a long-term contract. Alex too, of course. Even Arthur Rank and John Davis, suspecting that they had made not a mistake, but a slight error of judgment, made Moira some derisory offer. All these offers, derisory or not— and some of them were very handsome offers indeed—were politely turned down by Moira and her agent, and pigeonholed. He must have been a patient man, but if he had the right temperament, he must have enjoyed himself. It is not every day that one is able to turn down an offer from Louis B. Mayer. But Moira had the best legs and hardest head in two hemispheres, and to be the greatest ballet dancer in the world is not a small ambition.

Came *The Tales of Hoffmann*. When Bobby Helpmann telephoned her that night, she made a quick decision. She turned it down flat. I can understand that she was frightened. Coming out of the blue, the offer was too sudden, too good. And there were no strings attached to it. It was made by people whom I won't say she trusted, but who had artistic standards not dissimilar from her own. She had refused such an offer from them once before, when *The Red Shoes* was in the offing, and Bobby had told her she was missing a great chance. She had been wrong then—or had she? She had changed her mind and accepted the offer. She had been right to do so—or had she? Her steady climb in her chosen profession had been interrupted. Her success as a film actress had made other dancers jealous. She had ignored all this and had shown rare spirit in the way she stuck to her goal. The glittering prize of prima ballerina of the Royal Ballet, which Miss de Valois was reserving for Margot Fonteyn, was out of her reach. It was still her ultimate ambition. And the ultimate ambition of a Scot, whether male or female, is a fearsome thing. All these thoughts must have crowded into the brain behind those clear, blue eyes and that flaming crown of hair. She couldn't face a decision.

Bobby Helpmann, who adored intrigue and was building himself up to be the Talleyrand of London's West End, said, "Quite right, my dear Moira. It's what I expected you to say. See you tomorrow at class!"

The next day she went to see the Sadler's Wells librarian and archivist. What for? To consult the score of *The Tales of Hoffmann*, goofy! Do you think that a Scot is going to rush into Charing Cross Road and *buy* a secondhand copy, when she can borrow one for free? Anyway, she was too late. Bobby Helpmann had already borrowed it. He reported to us, "She likes the part, of course. Olympia should be played by a dancer, anyway. But she's not too keen, between you and me, on appearing in Act One only. What else can you offer her?"

"We have been talking about that with Tommy Beecham. We've got plenty of music. We can bring Moira in at the beginning and end of the film as Hoffmann's latest and purest love, whom he loses, of course. Then there's the Kleinzach Ballet. It's only three minutes, but good fairy-tale stuff. But the best part is Sir Thomas's rearrangement of the love scene as a ballet of about six minutes. It should be a pas de deux. If Monique plays Giulietta, we could do a deal with Edmond Audran to be Moira's partner in the pas de deux. He'll be coming over with Monique anyway. Would Moira agree to Edmond?"

"I don't see why not. He's a big, strong chap. Moira's not lightweight, you know. She hasn't got an ounce of fat on her, but she's tall and she's got big bones. But if Edmond can lift Monique, he can lift Moira."

We wanted her for two weeks' rehearsal and two weeks' shooting guaranteed; after that pro rata. Her agent asked a pretty penny. We agreed, and he wished he'd asked ten times as much. Two days before the famous Penthouse dinner with Alex she said, "Yes." Three days later she said, "No." We had committed to Alex, and he to us. What to do about it?

"Remember *The Red Shoes?*" said Emeric. "She doesn't know what she wants, but we must keep up the pressure. She cannot turn down all that money for two weeks' work. There is something that she is unhappy about. We must find it."

Bobby was doing his utmost. She still wouldn't say yes. Emeric was right. There was something missing. Alex was getting alarmed. We were in for fifty thousand quid already. And for another thing, he wanted to have options on Moira for other pictures for London Films, not for The Archers.

"Well, Micky? Well, Emeric? Is she going to do it or not?"

"She'll do it, Alex. We're having talks with her and meetings every day."

"Then, why will she not say so?"

The starting date was only four weeks away, all the other actors and dancers were signed. Sir Thomas had started rehearsals with his singers. Emeric came to me.

"Michael. I am a fool and you are a fool."

"When did you discover that?"

Emeric was shaking. "She doesn't trust Bobby Helpmann. She thinks he will have too much to do with his own parts. She would feel safe if Frederick Ashton was the choreographer, but she can't say so."

I whistled. "Freddie Ashton? How do you know we can get him?"

"Michael! These marvelous people, they work for peanuts—of course we can get him!"

I thought about it. I could have kicked myself.

"Of course, you're right! Bobby's wonderful but—Ashton is Ashton. Do you think Ninette will let him work for us full-time?" Emeric snapped his fingers.

Twenty-four hours later I was in the middle of a costume parade. Emeric telephoned.

"Michael! We have got Frederick Ashton!"

"For the whole picture?"

"For the whole picture."

"Shall I tell Alex?"

"No, no, don't tell him anything!"

Another twenty-four hours ached by. I was down at the big silent stage at the corner of the lot in which we were going to make the whole of the film. It was not soundproofed, but then we didn't need it. We were shooting everything with playback.* I was standing with Hein and Arthur in the middle of this vast building, pacing out the acting area for the set. The fireman called from the entrance door: "Micky . . . Hi . . . Micky! Your partner wants you on the phone!"

"Tell him I'm coming!"

I ran over and picked up the phone and said, "It's a good thing you telephoned. I saw Alex at lunchtime. He's—"

"Michael, we have got Moira!"

"Are you sure?"

"When she heard that Frederick Ashton was to do the choreography, she said, 'That makes all the difference.' "

---

*The score for The Tales of Hoffmann had been prerecorded, and during filming the soundtrack was played over a loudspeaker and the actors mimed the lyrics and danced in synchronization to the music.

"That redheaded bitch."

"Michael, do you want to make this picture or not?"

"I do."

"Then wait for me. Let us tell Alex together."

But wasn't that clever of Moira?

≡

What shall I say about Sir Frederick Ashton, member of the Order of Merit, Companion of Honour, Knight, Commander of the British Empire, etc., a guide, philosopher, and friend to God knows how many dancers, writers, composers, and designers, and to at least one film director. The fact that he let me direct him and teach him the tricks of silent-film slapstick is one of my happiest memories. Fred Ashton's discipline and authority with the dancers and actors was complete, and he was a wonderful mime himself, as anyone will know who has seen his outrageous performance as one of the ugly sisters (Bobby Helpmann the other one) in the Royal Ballet production of *Cinderella*. But it was as teacher and choreographer that he excelled. It was not only the purity of his line but the purity of his thought, and his output was immense and always of the highest quality. He went back to Arnold Haskell and the Camargo Society, the joint godfathers of British ballet; and it isn't generally known that when he came from Peru as an aspiring young dancer, he and Bobby Helpmann both had lessons from Léonide Massine.

"He made us put down our money, first," remembered Bobby bitterly.

Besides choreographing major pieces for Moira—the Doll Dance and the Dragonfly Ballet—Fred mimed Kleinzach, the hunchback dwarf in love with Beauty, and Cochenille, the puppet master who is revealed in the end to be a puppet himself (the film was full of instant ideas like this, thrown out at white heat, and instantly adopted by everybody). I asked him—it was at the memorial service for Bobby Helpmann at St. Paul's Church in the Garden*—what it felt like to choreograph two termagants like Massine and Bobby, as well as dance his own part in the threesome. He murmured, "They were always fighting, of course, for the best position. When I had them both happy, I used to say to Bobby, 'Where am I going to be?' And he would answer, 'There, with your back to the camera!' "

Dear Fred!

So now we were complete, and music rehearsals were in full swing—but Alex was still worried. We had been rather naughty about the script. Executives and distributors who are not directly concerned with the day-to-day progress of a film in which they have a vital interest tend to rely upon the

*Helpmann died in 1986.

script or screenplay for their information, that is, in the early stages. The average length of a script is between ninety and one hundred and twenty quarto pages, and although it cannot be read for entertainment (even an Archers script is not literature), it can certainly be read, and provide plenty of information.

I was determined that my conception of a composed film should not be undermined, and I didn't much care whether it was understood or not. All our technicians knew what I wanted, and how to get it, and we had daily meetings. By this time they were all experts at reading a score—this score at any rate—and were glib about referring to "page thirty-nine, bar sixteen" in the music for a particular effect or change of scene. The Archers' script, for we had a script, consisted of about seventeen pages instead of the one hundred and twenty that Alex and Cunynghame would have liked to see on their desks. Brief, clear narrative directions were followed by a reference to the page in the score and the bar in the music. This was all very well, and Alex had to agree grumpily that the system appeared to be working in all departments, but the sort of thing that drove him mad was the choruses. He had several recordings of the opera brought to him and sat listening, reasonably satisfied, to Act 1 until he came to the choruses. These were big and elaborate, and had been recorded by Sir Thomas with the BBC Opera Company. Alex would send for Emeric and would throw up his hands in despair: "Imre! What is Micky doing about these choruses? There is nothing in the budget for them!"

"Don't worry, Alex. He will do them with puppets."

"Puppets? What does he mean? We cannot hold the film up while he has puppets standing around singing? It could be very expensive."

"They won't be standing, Alex, they'll be dancing."

"Dancing!"

"It's really quite simple, Alex, Michael says. There will be dancers who are puppets and puppets who are dancers. He has talked it over with Hein, and they are not worried."

"I am worried, Imre."

Except for these puppet choruses, which had to be filmed when the rest of the shooting was over, we made the film in nine weeks: that is to say in forty-five working days. It was a composed film, you see. We all knew what we were doing, and why we were doing it, and the music told us how to do it. Rehearsals had been intensive and took two weeks. There was a break of two weeks after the main shooting and then we all came back into the studio to do the puppet sequences, which had so much exercised Alex's imagination, and pickup shots. And the film was a delight. It dares everything and never falters. We were a law unto ourselves. Problems cropped up every day, and were solved, either on the spur of the moment or in an instant conference. For instance, George Busby would say to me, "Moira says that she can't dance and sing at the same time, even though it's someone else's voice. She says it will spoil her breathing."

"What does Freddie Ashton say?"

"He says that she's right to be nervous, but he thinks she can do it."

"Tell her that we're worried about her breathing, and that she doesn't have to sing the Doll's part if she doesn't want to."

George was beginning to know Moira too. He smiled, and went back to the rehearsal room. Two or three days later, he came to me again. "She says that it's very difficult technically, but she'll do it."

"Good. Is she happy with Edmond as a partner?"

"Oh, she seems to be. I think Edmond finds her a bit . . . well . . . standoffish. You know, Michael, dancers are extraordinary creatures. Not at all like actors. They are more like athletes. You know what a delightful fellow Edmond is, and how madly in love with Monique he is, and Monique with him. I don't think Moira thinks about Edmond as a man at all. He's just a catcher."

"Like in baseball?"

"Exactly."

On another occasion, it would be Reggie Mills: "Michael, I have told David Cunynghame that if Alex wants to see our rushes every day, he will have to see them silent."

"Oh, will he?"

"So will you."

I looked at this gentle bear who was growling at me. "Yes, I suppose so."

"You agreed that we wouldn't record any guide tracks, and that means the rushes will be silent."

"Yes, I suppose it does. But it's going to upset the actors, not hearing a soundtrack. Especially Bobby Helpmann. He really believes that he can sing as well as Bruce Dargavel."

"He's got better timing than Bruce Dargavel. Bruce has a lovely voice, but he suffers from creeping sync."

"Ugh! Is it curable?"

"Not really, but Bobby Helpmann and I will fix it between us."

"I remember that on *The Red Shoes* you said that no dancer was ever in sync. Isn't it better with singers conducted by Sir Thomas?"

"Worse. What shall I tell Cunynghame?"

"Don't tell him anything. Recording a guide track would slow all of us up. We'll tell Alex that we'll have a special little show for him every other week or so—him and the actors. He'll like that."

=

I have said that we were a law unto ourselves, and we had our own kingdom quite separate from the rest of Shepperton Studios. I have mentioned already how, as soon as Alex had bought Worton Hall Studios, London Films had the big silent stage taken down and re-erected in the grounds of Shepperton Studios. It was intended for big effects sequences and process shots and could be flooded. It had the bare minimum of services, and we had to lay on extra cables for the lighting, but it was ideal for our purposes. It was just the kind of logistical problem that Syd Streeter reveled in. Outside the stage he built a neat row of five bungalows for the stars. They had all the latest niceties, and the telephone was laid on to each one. The actors were delighted with them and established, at once, a little village full of laughter and gossip. On the other flank, Syd brought up trailers and established offices for the telephone switchboard. Inside the huge buildings, he had ample room for makeup and wardrobe and every service for the production. I had agreed with Hein that the acting area would be in the center of this great box, and that we would build a huge cyclorama that would go two thirds of the way around the stage and be a permanent backing. The central acting area would have circular curtain rails enclosing the whole space, and in several depths. On these rails would hang the gauze curtains—yellow, Venetian red, and blue—that gave the color tone to each of the three acts. Within this gauze-enclosed circus anything could happen. It was all worked out on the drawing board, and we could change the scene in a few minutes. There was literally no waiting. It was like an ideal opera production on a huge opera stage. Even the most massive props were mounted on castors and were wheeled in by a few men under Hein's supervision. I worked with a score in my hand most of the time to make sure that there were no holes left in the action, and the crew were astonished at the speed with which we worked. It was wonderful to be released from the tyranny of sound, and the constant yells of "SILENCE! . . . QUIET!" etc. There was a great deal of laughter and joking. There was a wonderful feeling of creative comradeship. When we went to the studio canteen for lunch, people working on other films used to look at us in wonder. We all seemed so happy.

There were none so happy as Pamela and I. She was giving eight performances a week in *The Lady's Not for Burning*, but her watchdog still continued to watch her.

"Your old man ain't half fond of yer, Pamela," Bill Wall would say. "What does he do with yer weekends? Take you out on a leash?"

Pamela would smile her most enigmatic smile. She was fond of Bill. So was Monique, whose appearance on the set in black tights had caused several electricians to fall off the spot rail. After observing her closely for a few days and deciding that she was a good sport, Bill got hold of some of the wire mesh that we used for diffusing the lights and that when torn apart exactly resembled the sound of fabric ripping. He then persuaded Monique and Freddie Ashton to rehearse some high kicks in the middle of the set, and at the highest kick, he ripped the steel mesh apart in perfect sync with her movement. It couldn't have been better done. Monique screamed aloud; then realizing the trick that had been played upon her, snatched up an enormous candlestick and chased Bill all round the stage, both of them roaring with laughter, brandishing her candlestick and calling him every filthy name she could think of in three languages. Bill wouldn't have dared do that with Moira. Such goings-on in the Temple of her Art would have been greeted with a puzzled smile.

Although Pamela and I were devoted to each other then, and until her death, it was a love far more spiritual than carnal. We completed each other. That was all. I sometimes felt that I was wandering about in a huge, empty building with a symphony orchestra playing somewhere, or in a maze with a storm raging and statues toppling, or in a forest so illimitable and quiet that I could hear a pinecone fall. Pamela was a dreamer, too, and sometimes, among a crowd of other people, we would catch each other's eye and be no longer alone. This was our secret.

We had only one intimate moment on *The Tales of Hoffmann* and that was on the set of the beer cellar, when Hein was painting her with gold leaf as the Muse of Hoffmann. He had crowned her with golden laurels and swathed her in the lightest of golden drapes. Now her body had to be painted, and Hein would allow no one to do it but himself. The makeup girls surrounded him, criticizing him or cheering him on. My idea had been to turn the faithful Nicklaus, Hoffmann's student friend, into a golden Muse who accompanied him on all his adventures, without him ever guessing who she was. It was to be the apotheosis of Nicklaus, and to explain his/her presence with Hoffmann throughout the film. There is an aria at the end of the opera that is optional. I asked Sir Thomas to make a point of recording it. Hein was as enthusiastic as I was, but alas, Emeric would have none of it. In our collaboration, whenever I became mystic, he became nervous. He had disapproved of the unspoken link between Torquil and Catriona in *I Know Where I'm Going!*, and he was not going to stand for any hanky-panky (an obscure Hungarian phrase) on my part over Hoffmann and Nicklaus. I shot it but we never used it, and as the film was already very long I had to give way.

While Hein, with great delight and the softest of brushes, was touching up Pamela's breasts, I stood beside this golden, breathing, sensuous statue and talked to her. The set boiled around us, but we were so used to it that we heard nothing. We were isolated in the two spotlights placed by Chris at

Hein's requests, while he put highlights on Pamela's torso. She said, "Do you remember Corryvreckan?"*

I too was in the whirlpool, and I said, "Yes."

She said, "Are you still sorry that we didn't get drowned?"

I shook my head.

"Pamela!" said Hein. "Please turn a little. I want to get a highlight on your left tit."

"Yes, Hein, dear," she said, and obliged him.

A few weeks later she and John Gielgud took their play to New York and took the town by storm. New Yorkers had never seen such acting, nor such teamwork. She wrote that it looked like running a year, maybe two.

===

It was on *The Tales of Hoffmann* that I fell in love again, this time with Massine.

I think that it had really been at first sight, when we met on *The Red Shoes* in that Kensington flat. I shall always remember that monkish (and monkey-ish) face, looking inquiringly and politely into mine. For me, he wasn't just the famous Massine, one of the world's great mimes, one of the great choreographers; he *was* ballet, and for me that meant painters like Derain and Picasso, musicians like Stravinsky and Satie. Massine had been in the forefront of every modern movement in art. He had turned from modern to classical music and made full-length ballets out of symphonies and above all, he was the creator and dancer of such masterpieces as *La Boutique Fantasque, Le Beau Danube,* and *Le Tricorne.* I'm sure that his heart was beating as fast as mine, but we had both been as grave as judges.

We had chatted in French and in an English that was Massine's own personal invention. It was a mixture of all the European languages, rendered into basic English, but retaining their original pronunciation—an *omelette aux fines verbes.* Emeric, who was getting very proud of his idiomatic English (he wrote always with three muses at his elbow: *Roget's Thesaurus, The Oxford Book of Quotations,* and me), was a bit doubtful whether anyone would understand the dialogue he had written for Ljubov in the script as rendered by Massine, and suggested that we make a test of him in a dialogue scene before we signed him up. I agreed readily enough. Massine acted with his voice as well as his whole body, and I knew that he had trained as an actor in Moscow and had already been selected to play Romeo in a new production

---

*Corryvreckan is the name given the tidal race off the Scottish island of Scarba, which produces the whirlpool featured in *I Know Where I'm Going!* By lashing himself to the mast of a motorboat, Michael managed to film the whirlpool forming, which was later combined with special-effects footage created in the studio. Pamela accompanied him on the dangerous boat ride.

on the stage there, when Diaghilev arrived and bore him off to Paris to appear as the biblical character of Joseph in *The Legend of Joseph*, the part that had been created by Diaghilev for Nijinsky before the latter's marriage lost him the light of Diaghilev's countenance.

I selected the scene from *The Red Shoes* script in which Lermontov tells Ljubov, who is working alone on the empty stage at night, that all the choreography he has done can be scrapped, because he, Lermontov, has fired the composer. At this news Ljubov blows up and offers his resignation, which is accepted, to his horror. The test was a complete success. As predicted by Emeric, you could only understand one word in four, but it didn't matter. I shot it in the empty studio with the big spotlight outlining the scene from the back rail, and a little bit of front light, just to fill in the slender dancing figure in the huge, empty stage, calling out to the electrician, *"Spotlight sur moi! Toujours sur moi!"*

It was pure magic, even before Lermontov made his entrance. At the end of Lermontov's exit line accepting Ljubov's resignation, the little figure that had been so strong and dramatic a moment before suddenly crumpled, like a dog that has been kicked by his master. I led the applause and said to Jack Cardiff, "Okay, Jack, print it and then go home." Emeric was as moved as everybody else.

I don't socialize much during the shooting of a film, and I hate studio canteens. Bill and I always had a caravan or mobile home where we could cook our own lunch. While doling out the vegetables, or spooning out the rice pudding, Bill gave me the latest gossip. So my contact with Léonide on *The Red Shoes* was strictly professional, and I hardly knew more about him at the end of the film than I had at the beginning. Of course, his family had been down to the studio several times, but I never talked to visitors.

On *The Tales of Hoffmann* things were different, and during the two-week rehearsal period there was ample time to get to know each other. It was the first time that I noticed that his strictly professional attitude toward the dancers, perfectly polite but distant and almost severe, was inspired by his feeling that he and Balanchine, and perhaps Marie Rambert, were the aristocrats of the Russian Imperial Ballet tradition and bearers of the sacred flame. This correct attitude was particularly noticeable toward Bobby Helpmann, who openly jeered at it and was continually sending it up. To Moira and Monique, Massine was polite but distant. They were both slightly intrigued by this, for Massine was a notable ladies' man. With Freddie Ashton he was formal and polite, like a brain specialist consulting another brain specialist. But with the actors—Pamela, for instance—I noticed, to my astonishment, that he was a totally different being, joking, laughing, and gossiping with the friendliness and high spirits that I have always loved in Russian artists.

In the course of these rehearsals he mentioned the three tiny islands that he owned off the coast of Italy. The nearest fishing port was Positano, in the Gulf of Salerno. The islands lie about a mile off shore. The locals call them The Galli. Others, and particularly romantic classical scholars, insist that they are the Sirenusi, the Islands of the Sirens, who lured with their singing many a bold sailor to a happy death in their arms. It could be nowhere else, the scholars assert. It was here that Odysseus stopped the ears of his crew with wax, had himself tied to the mast of the ship, and brought her close to the rock so that he could hear the Sirens' song himself. It was here that one of the crew, pulling the wax from his ears, leapt overboard and was dragged down by the Sirens to their sea cave under the island, and drowned. It was here that Massine came with Diaghilev long years ago and, possessed of money for the first time in his life, was encouraged to buy the islands by his friend.

"The islands are for sale. I have asked about the price. A few thousand lire will buy them, Léonide. You will never regret it. Everyone should have an island. You can come here for your holidays, and when you are rich and famous, you can build a house here and invite me to stay with you. Buy them, Léonide. I will give you the money."

As I listened to Léonide, I could hear Diaghilev's lofty tone. He lies buried on an island himself, in the lagoon of Venice, the island of San Michele. He died on the Lido that he loved, and a procession of black-draped gondolas bore him across the water to his last resting place. It must have been like a picture by Böcklin. As the gondolier leaned on his oar, surely the great head in the glass coffin nodded to Serge Lifar in approval: "Serge! Thank you. How lucky I am to have a devoted friend to bury me so romantically and with such good taste. Thank God, I've always lived beyond my means."

Léonide bought the three tiny islands. Apparently there was a fishing cabin on one of them, and the ruins of an old tower. Over the next thirty years, he paid an occasional visit. The islands stayed much as they were. He had no money to spend on them, and what money he did have went to a fisherman in Positano, who kept an eye on them, and whose boat carried Massine and his companions out to the islands when they came to picnic. Standing there, if only for a few hours, he could feel how wise Diaghilev's advice had been. He was famous and successful in the career that Diaghilev had chosen for him, but he was a Gypsy—a Gypsy who lived in five-star hotels. Here, on his island, he was king. The Mediterranean, which has cradled and drowned so many famous men and women, washed the rocks at his feet. To the north, he faced the towering coast above Positano. To the west, he could see the Isle of Capri and, on a clear day, the rocks that masked the entrance to the Blue Grotto. To the east was the great Gulf of Salerno, where bloody fighting took place during the last war.

Massine was in America during the war. In 1947, when he came back to

London with Tania and the two children, he was still king of his island, but of very little else. *The Red Shoes* changed all that. Of course I knew nothing about his situation, financial or otherwise, when I dropped £10,000 into his lap, and equally, of course, not a muscle of that face moved as a compliment. But although he appeared to remain entirely in control of himself when I said goodbye, he was actually dancing a fandango. At last he could build a house, build a water cistern, restore the ruined tower, buy a motorboat, buy a fisherman, and throw an enormous party. He couldn't have known at that time that I would have enjoyed, as much as he, the way things had turned out, the way the wheel had turned full circle.

Thirty-five years earlier Diaghilev, his mentor and sponsor, had, with a casual gesture, thrown in the islands as a gift. Massine had enslaved his heart and mind and body in the creation of ballets that the great Sergei approved, or would have approved. They had gone separate ways. His master had died, yet he still struggled on. He had created a unique position for himself in the history of art and the history of ballet. He had kept his integrity, but he had no money. Now, just when he needed it, out of the blue the money dropped into his hands, as if it were from the hands of Diaghilev himself, for if Diaghilev and Nijinsky had not lived and loved, if Stravinsky had never composed, nor Karsavina danced, there would have been no Lermontov and no Vicky and no *Red Shoes*.

Two years and a half had passed since then, and now, at last, I learned about Massine's islands. He produced a battered photo album, and showed me snapshots of two European gentlemen in the stiff clothes, high-starched collars, hat, stick, and gloves of the period, that particularly ugly period before the 1914 war, one of them fat, the other desperately thin, one of them middle-aged, the other desperately young, standing woodenly in various positions on the islet. Massine turned the pages of the album, and I saw what transformations had occurred since I took Sergei Diaghilev's place for Massine as a Maecenas. Timidly, he proposed a visit one day, and I carelessly agreed, never thinking for a moment that the invitation would outlast the shooting schedule. But he brought it up again, six weeks later.

"Frankie too, and Kevin," he insisted. "Tania and the children are on the island already. I shall drive down. I have many things to bring. Frankie and Kevin can come with me. You fly out to Naples, Micky, as soon as you can."

The idea was tempting.

"When do you go, Léonide?"

"As soon as you let me."

We were nearly through shooting. There were only the puppet sequences left to do, and Alex was still bleating, "What does Micky mean by saying that he will use puppets?"

The answer was relatively simple, but difficult to explain. Fortunately Hein and Arthur and Alan Carter knew what I meant, when I asked for puppets that looked like human beings, and human beings that acted like puppets. But the whole production had been made at such a pace, and there were so many props that had been literally conjured out of Hein's imagination, that the art department needed a week or two to prepare for the puppets. We gave them the two weeks that they wanted, and I got my holiday.

Naples hit me with a blast like a furnace. It was midsummer. Vesuvius was uneasy, and there was a pall of smoke over the volcano. A huge, shining American automobile was waiting for me at the airport, with Frankie and Kevin lost somewhere in the interior. The driver of this chilling machine was a fisherman from Positano and wore rope-soled sandals, blue jeans, and an American sailor's hat. We roared up from sea level to the escarpment above Positano.

Frankie described their journey down from London in matter-of-fact tones. It appears that Massine was one of those drivers who once they get into a huge, automatic car are unable to stop for anything except fuel. I forget where and how they picked up the huge car, but it was filled with household stores, garden furniture, gadgets, and bedding.

"Make yourselves comfortable, Frankie," said Léonide, leaping into the driver's seat and slamming the door with a noise like the door of the National Safe Deposit closing. He switched on the radio full-blast.

"There is air-conditioning! Make yourselves comfortable, so that you can sleep!"

"Where do we stop tonight?" screamed Frankie.

"Stop? We don't stop! We must be in Italy for breakfast!"

"And Rome for lunch?" quavered Frankie and Kevin, hopefully. They had eaten the sandwiches, and were starting on the chocolate.

"Rome? We do not go to Rome! We go to Naples. We must be at Positano by about four o'clock. The boat is waiting for us."

Further conversation was impossible. The postwar traffic, mostly ex–army vehicles, thundering up and down Italy on roads that had been knocked to pieces in the war, and then patched, was horrendous and extremely danger-ous. Most of them had their horns blaring for the whole time. So did Léonide. After dark it was even worse. Everybody had their headlights full on and drove on the crown of the road. Léonide seemed tireless. He was also an excellent driver. After one or two glimpses of what lay far below and ahead, Frankie and Kevin gave up and fell asleep. They woke up with a bad taste in their mouths as the sun rose over the Abruzzi. There were one or two stops for evil-smelling petrol and worse-smelling coffee, both liquids taken at high speed. Occasionally Léonide screamed some unintelligible remark over his shoulder, but most of the time he was driving. He made up for it with some of his beautiful smiles, which sent Frankie off to sleep again. Kevin was endlessly patient, as he always is. No wonder, with such a family.

The roads south of Rome were full of dust and holes, and Frankie swore that most of the time they were airborne. By 4:00 P.M. they were no longer interested in their destination, or their nourishment. But they *were* at Positano. The hairpin bends down from the top of the cliff to the port below made Kevin sick, and he returned most of the sandwiches and chocolate to their previous owner. Léonide was already screaming and gesturing like a true Neapolitan, and speaking the local dialect like a native.

"Come, come," he said, mopping up Kevin's vomit with one hand and passing out supplies for the island with the other, "Tania will be expecting us! The children are crazy to meet Kevin!" Kevin murmured politely that he was equally crazy.

At this point in her narrative Scheherazade saw the approach of dawn and fell discreetly silent for, in other words, we three had arrived at the harbor of Positano, and Léonide was there to meet us in a brand-new high-speed motorboat. He pointed to some rocks about a mile out: "The Galli." One of the local men came with us. He and Frankie were instantly buddies. Her warm, blond beauty attracted attention everywhere, but particularly in a place like Positano, where everyone is burned black like an African. Léonide, obviously bursting with pride over his new acquisition, took us out of the harbor sedately, then opened the throttle and with a roar the sea monster shot away. The rocks rushed to meet us, and suddenly we were coming into a natural harbor with a flight of stone steps leading up through the rocks. A band of workmen were waiting there to go back to Positano at the end of the day's work, and the two children, Lorca and young Tania, were racing down to meet us. Lorca was a couple of years older than Kevin, Tania about the same age. Léonide plunged into a conversation with the foreman, and we shouldered our bags and went up the steps.

The Galli are tops of a submerged mountain, and the sea around them is very deep. Only one of them has ever been inhabited, the one with the ruined tower. I suppose it is about two hundred yards square. There is no water, as on Capri, and today a waterboat from Naples comes and fills their cisterns. Only a few years ago they depended entirely upon rainwater and these catchments are still in use to supply the garden. The workmen who were taking our boat back to the mainland had just finished building a magnificent new cistern for fresh water, blasted and dug out of the rock. It must have held about ten thousand liters and we could tell from the pride on Léonide's face what it meant to him. He had clung precariously to this almost barren rock for more than thirty years, and now he was not only able to spend the summer there with his family, but could invite honored guests as well. The dilapidated fishing hut had vanished, with its smoke-blackened walls, and instead there was a charming cottage with terraces and guest rooms. And all this had been paid for by *The Red Shoes* and *The Tales of Hoffmann*. Léonide made this clear with every look and gesture, and I was overwhelmed by the justice of it all. To earn the lasting gratitude of a man or woman you have always regarded as a great artist is a precious thing.*

Of the other two islets, one, the smaller, was barren. The other, the largest of the three, was very rocky, surrounded with reefs, and supported a population of goats. It was a mystery how they existed, but even the most unsophisticated goat can scrape a living where an independent film producer, living on hopes of a percentage of the distributor's gross, would starve to death. He can't eat his film, but a goat can.

It was a glorious holiday. On an island there is always something to do, and on a small one you never stop doing. There was no end to Léonide's plans for his beloved island. He even talked of installing plumbing, which everyone thought was going a bit too far. The ruined tower was to be restored, and a library placed in it. A harbor for the motorboat was to be blasted out of the rocks. The foreman of the works came every day for consultations and to draw plans in the sparse dirt of the garden, which they both studied with wrinkled brows and much disputation.

Marketing was a constant problem, and there were always sudden rushes to Positano and back for some essential tool or item for the kitchen. Every morning, after breakfast, the two children attended class with Léonide, armed with the usual ballet master's cane to point out the lack of beauty in his pupils' arms and legs. Lorca, who would rather be playing with Kevin, submitted to this artistic discipline with a bad grace, and it must be admitted that Léonide's comments were somewhat hard to bear. But that's how great dancers are made. I had my 16mm Kodak camera with me, the one that you see in *Peeping Tom*, and I recorded it all: the goats, the terraces, the dancing classes, Frankie rising from the sea like a Siren, the children treading out the grapes to make our own wine, all for posterity. To see Léonide with his family in his little kingdom was a revelation. Our friendship, which had been based upon our work together, became a true and lasting one. He was full of mischief and thoughtfulness and kindness. I learned to love him. Frankie too.

I had promised to be back in Shepperton at the end of the two weeks, but we were all having such a good time that Léonide persuaded Frankie to stay. Kevin and Lorca were bosom friends. I was to propel myself to London, shoot my puppets, and return. Tania pressed into my hand a long list of

*Massine's islands later passed to the ownership of Rudolf Nureyev.

things to bring back with me, which she now considered were indispensable, and I was off!

≡

At the studios, everything was ready. It took only a few days to shoot the missing scenes. The puppets, costumes, wigs, and makeup were enchanting. The puppet-dancers were, of course, full-sized men and women, and the real puppets were about eighteen inches high. Both identical groups were worked by strings from above in the flies. When you cut from one to the other it was impossible to tell the difference, except that, maybe, the real dancers were more puppetlike than the real puppets. I took shots of Freddie Ashton working the puppets from above in the character of Cochenille, and at the end of the whole enchanting sequence I had him hoisted up on the wires too, to show that he was a puppet as well.

Reggie Mills had the picture rough-cut, and as fast as I shot the puppet sequences he dropped them into the film, and suddenly Act 1 was ready and we could run it. It was stunning! Thanks to Offenbach it had a style and an elegance that I have never seen in a film musical, before or since. And the special ballets that had been composed for Moira were triumphs. We had shot the Dragonfly Ballet with Moira and Edmond in a few hours. I think that there were about seven camera positions in the whole composition. These two tall and beautiful human beings, in their fantastic makeups and costumes, loving, mating, and dying, are to me the most unforgettable images that I have ever created. And the show as a whole for the big screen—it worked. How it worked! And the erotic splendors of Act 2, with Tcherina's urchin sensuality! And Act 3, with its cool beauty and its gorgeous music! And then the reprise of Moira's pas de deux with Edmond, taken from half a dozen different camera angles at once! And the unmasking of Bobby as he took off mask after mask, and face after face, until you were no longer sure which was the mask and which was the face! And the last scene in the beer hall, where, alas and alas! I let my arm be twisted until I agreed to drop the transformation of Nicklaus from student into Muse. What a show, what a film! What music! What singing! For me it was the culmination of everything I wanted to do and show the audience. Perhaps I should never have made another film.

I was anxious to get away, to fly back to the islands and to Frankie. We were in love again. It was seventeen years since we had first met and gone mad about each other, telephoning at all hours in the most un-English way, she praying to God every night that I would ask her to marry me, I bewildered by a passion stronger than my love for films, meeting and playing with the large, sport-loving family of the Reidys, strongly Catholic, suspicious of intruders, guarded and guided by the traditions of the professional class to which their parents belonged, a challenge to the footloose Gypsy that I had become. It had taken me three years to disentangle myself from the disastrous marriage, which was not a marriage,* and was not even consummated, but which I had contracted years before. By then we were on Foula† together. Our love had cooled into friendship. I was poorer in money than I had ever been, and was thinking of emigrating to Hollywood. Came the war and my big chance. While the bombs were falling on London there were no more thoughts of marriage. Frankie had found herself in nursing and in leadership. I had become a famous man. We still saw as much of each other as ever. We called ourselves engaged—but to what, and to whom? Enter Deborah.

What a fight that was! When I looked back on it, seven years later, it seemed a miracle that I had been able to decide on one of them. I loved them both. I wanted to marry them both. They were both my ideals—physical, spiritual, and imaginary. I wanted to possess them completely, both of them, but they both made it plain that there was no chance of that. When I married Frankie, I tore myself apart. Half of me, the Deborah half, had been butchered and skewered and exposed, raw and bleeding, in the Hollywood marketplace. The other half of me had missed the bus. When we were married—and it was what we both wanted—I was thirty-eight and Frankie thirty-four. Small wonder that for two years I was projecting Deborah on other actresses. It was a humiliating puzzle for Frankie to solve. She had won, but she had lost. She tried to make me jealous of other men, but of course that doesn't work with a man possessed by movies as I was. It was two years before Kevin was born.

Five years had passed since then. Years of love and jealousy, patience and recriminations, unhappiness and joy. Kevin, who had been splendidly brought up by Bill and Myrtle‡ through all the storms and whirlwinds of our domestic and professional life, was already showing himself to be a potential head of the family. Brief holidays fanned the smoky fire of our physical love for each other. On Massine's island it had burst into flame.

*In 1927, while working under the direction of Harry Lachman in the south of France, Michael impetuously entered into what he called "my idiot marriage." In *A Life in Movies* he says: "She was beautiful, young, strong, healthy, American—and just about the last person to be made happy by me, and vice versa. In 1927 I was slim, arrogant, intelligent, foolish, shy, cocksure, dreamy and irritating to any sensible woman who had her fortune to make and a family to plan. Today I am no longer slim."

†Foula is the island off Scotland where in 1936 Michael made his first important film, *The Edge of the World.* He had asked Frankie to join him on the remote Shetland island to play a small part in the film. Her beauty dazzled the islanders and crew, which made Michael more than a little grumpy.

‡Bill Paton's wife, Myrtle, was a nurse and the daughter of Neville Horton, whose woodworking shop in Kent was an important location in *A Canterbury Tale.* She and Bill met during the making of that film.

There is magic in all microcosms. I have always loved islands, and Massine's island will always be for me the most magic of them all. Nine months later, when I was in a transcontinental aircraft, descending through a snowstorm on Newark Airport—surely one of the more unpromising situations of this life—I was scribbling a little poem to my son, Columba, and his mother, which began with the lines:

> How should he not be remarkable?
> He was conceived on the island where the Sirens sang.

And, unlike most legends, it was the truth. And the legend had become alive because of *The Tales of Hoffmann*.

Thrilled and excited by my news of the beauty and invention of our film, Léonide had decided to throw a party on the island that would show the people of Positano, once and for all, who was boss! From there it was only a step to my declaration that a party was not enough. We must reenact the tale of Odysseus and his boat crew and the Sirens' song that drove Odysseus mad, and I would shoot the whole performance in 16mm glorious Kodachrome. The Sirens of course had to be naked, and volunteers were called for. Frankie, who had nothing to hide, agreed with enthusiasm. The two Tanias cried off, little Tania because of her youth, big Tania because she was—big. Léonide had been warning her for years that she had a weight problem, and here on the island she was on a diet, so nobody could understand why she continually put on weight. She swore that she kept to the diet, but under cross-examination it became clear that she ate the children's food as well as her own. In view of the shortage of naked volunteers, I said that I would overlook her avoirdupois. After all, there must have been fat Sirens as well as thin ones! But she was too shy, and the success of the show would all depend on Frankie.

Léonide was to direct, I was to be his cameraman. He took up his job with enthusiasm, and in no time had a boat and a boat's crew lined up, and a potential and bearded Odysseus. There was to be a feast, of course, and the fountains would run with wine. One of the goats from the other island was to be slaughtered and roasted whole. But when the tenderhearted women saw the respected father of a family bound and carried down the rocks of the other island, while his wife and progeny followed him, bleating their dismay, they pleaded for his life and it was graciously granted by the ferocious butchers. I saw him with my own eyes unbound and leaping to rejoin his family. But when the feast was in full flow, and barbecued goat cooked with herbs was the pièce de résistance, nobody asked awkward questions, and I fear that Léonide had turned thumbs down on Father Goat while the women were having their siesta.

If you could have seen our bearded Odysseus with vine leaves wreathed around his ample locks! If you could have seen our bronzed and grinning boat's crew! If you could have seen Frankie as a seductive Siren, rising out of the water! If you could have seen a member of the crew cast off his earplugs and leap into the water in understandable excitement, you would have applauded, as the Massine family did, when I showed them the film in Paris some years later. If you could have tasted that tender herb-scented goat meat, and the red wine trodden out by Lorca's dirty feet! And the number of times that Frankie was urged by the boat's crew to take a stroll along to the ruined tower! And the number of times that she refused to go! That reel of precious film is, unfortunately, one of the few records in my kaleidoscopic life that is not in my own personal archive. Léonide naturally kept the reel as part of his family archive, and I never had the sense to ask him to have a copy made. A pity, for if my son Columba could see it, it might explain to him some of the contradictory elements in his character.

When Alex first saw the fine cut of The Tales of Hoffmann he was lavish in his praise. He said that I was the greatest technician that he had ever known, and I accepted the compliment for what it was worth, which was not very much. It was true that Hoffmann is a Pandora's box of a movie. From the weathercocks and the musical boxes of the overture, to the final shot of Sir Thomas conducting the last few bars of the opera, there is a visual surprise about every ten seconds. It's all there in the music. Sir Thomas conducted and we followed. Our art department was inspired by Hein. The prop department was like Aladdin's Cave. We had a brilliantly inventive staff of painters and sculptors and prop-makers, and they all contributed to it. There was no limit to our inventions, or to our fun. I would arrive on the set, rehearse the scene, line up the shot, say carelessly, "What a pity that we haven't got this and this, or that and that." Hein would suddenly materialize on the set, accompanied by his gang. "Stop, Micky. I hear you are not satisfied. I have another set ready over there. Please shoot it instead, and tomorrow you'll have this one the way you want it."

As for Sir Thomas, I don't think he ever said he was satisfied with our production of The Tales of Hoffmann. "Not too displeased" was probably the nearest he got to it. He was a generous collaborator. He knew that a film was a film, and he didn't expect to get everything his own way: a very liberal man, a great artist, and a great leader of a great orchestra.

I don't know whether Robert Rounseville is alive or dead, and I expect he's in much the same position as regards me. He was a brave man to take on the acting as well as the singing, but he didn't know how brave he was until he found himself holding a vibrant Tcherina in his arms. Acting an opera in a film is a different job from singing an opera on the stage. Tcherina, when going full steam as Giulietta, was like a throbbing, pulsating dynamo. I know, because I took her in my arms during the rehearsal of the big seduction scene and nearly dropped her! Robert was a sturdy, everyday American type: not very good-looking, but not bad-looking either. He sang the part delightfully. He had the rare gift of being able to sing full out and still look quite attractive. I had taken Beecham's word for it that he could play as well as sing the part. I was not disappointed. Of course, his Hoffmann was not a demon-haunted, demon-possessed Hoffmann, but was more like Voltaire's Candide. There was something attractive about this reading of the character, and it worked with his personality. In fact, Robert later created the part of Candide in the Bernstein musical. Robert! If you ever read these lines, know that I think of you often with affection.

Up until 1951, The Archers seemed to have charmed lives. We both had beautiful wives. Emeric had a daughter, Angela. I had a son, Kevin, and Frankie had a bun in the oven. We were taking steps to get free of Korda, and we had made a wonderful film of *The Tales of Hoffmann.* But Emeric's marriage was breaking up, and suddenly tragedy hit our little group. Monique was telephoning from Lyons: "Oh, Micky, Micky, Micky . . . *Edmond est mort . . .*"

Edmond dead? Killed in a road accident in Lyons.

Edmond killed! That splendid body crushed and broken. That beautiful head and neck lifeless. The perfect marriage broken in a moment. Monique was telephoning from the hospital in Lyons. He had never regained consciousness. His injuries were terrible. She had held his hand and he had died. He was driving back from Barcelona in his little car, on the way to Paris, and the accident had taken place in the city. After you pass under the railway arch, there was a deathly crossroads in those days, badly signposted, badly lit, and he must have thought that there was nobody about. The other vehicle hit him broadside on. It was three in the morning.

They had been working on different films, Edmond in Monte Carlo and Monique in Barcelona. He had driven to Barcelona to spend the weekend with his wife, and had left her on Sunday evening. He had to be in Paris at the studio at noon on Monday. Monique was crying her heart out. She had turned instinctively to us, their closest friends, their guardians and benefactors. They had been riding the crest of the wave of beauty, youth, and notoriety. Money was pouring in. Offers were pouring in. They were out every night. They were spending as fast as they earned. They were *le tout Paris.*

Edmond's family, the Audrans, were a theatrical family, and they were proud of their name. One of Edmond's uncles, or great-uncles, had been a famous actor-playwright. Monique had no relatives except her mother. Her father, a Russian general, had answered the last roll call. (Why is it that all White Russians are generals?) Edmond was to be buried in Paris, and a friend of the family was seeing to all the arrangements. We said we would come at once to Paris and return with Monique to Barcelona for, widowed or not, she would have to finish the film, and they were shooting around her.

When people in show business die, they usually leave problems behind them. They are famous, they have many admirers, they leave nothing but debts. Money has to be found to bury them in the right sort of style, and by that I mean that the money has to be found. It is not cheap to be buried in Paris. There was to be a service at the actors' church, L'Église des Grands Augustins, and then at the cemetery of Père Lachaise. Edmond's business friends were at their wits' end to find enough money, and we all chipped in. They told us that the two youngsters had saved enough money for an emergency, but when they searched for it, it seemed to have disappeared. They shrugged their shoulders. "The old women," they said, "they are always on the watch, and the first thing they do is get their hands on the cash."

It was a painful three days. Frankie and I are not experienced Parisians. When she was a model girl, she was brought to Paris by Chanel and put up in a little hotel in the rue François 1er, the Hotel San Regis. It was a tiny hotel, but very comfortable, and connected with the famous restaurant on the quai, La Tour d'Argent. The director of both establishments was Claude Terrail, a character. We stayed there in a ridiculous room and bath, all tapestry and mirrors, and we have stayed there ever since. They had a wonderful group of concièrges, both for day and for night, led by Charles, the chief concièrge. Like all good concièrges, they knew everything and volunteered nothing.

Well, we buried Edmond and returned with Monique to Barcelona, and her mother came too. She was not Russian but French, and Monique must have got her good looks from her father. Her mother had a hearty appetite. She was not a snappy dresser. She was quite frank about her reasons for accompanying Monique back to Barcelona: it was where the money was. Someone had to handle Monique's affairs, and it had better be her. Gradually, it dawned upon us that we were regarded by her as dangerous rivals. We had asked Monique to return with us to England when the film was over, saying we would put her up for a few months and find an agent, and so on. These perfidious plans had not escaped the attention of Mama and she was inclined to be hysterical about them, because they did not include her. On one occasion she hurled open the window and threatened to jump out of it. Frankie, without raising her eyes from her book, said, "*Allez-y*" ("Go ahead"). She didn't jump.

=

At the end of this year, The Archers, although presenting a bold front, were in disarray. For the first time we two, not as a team, started to look for subjects that pleased us personally, to lay at our partner's feet, anxious to please but not quite sure of ourselves, in the way that a spaniel brings a recently decapitated chicken to the feet of his master and looks for approval. Emeric suggested a film of the life of Richard Strauss, of whom I knew little, either of the man or of his music. I hardly greeted it with cheers. Then he came up with a very different project, which I greeted with enthusiasm. Neither of us knew that in it lay the seed of our future destruction.

It was a war story, but a very unusual one. After the airborne invasion of Crete by the Germans in 1941, the greatest paratroop action of the war, Hitler decided to hold the island and appointed one of his most experienced generals, General Kreipe, to command the defending force. Kreipe proceeded to fortify the harbors and to build runways, and when the Cretans sabotaged these programs there were severe reprisals on the civilian population. The British replied by sending in from Cairo individual officers who took to the mountains, became guerrillas, and began harassing the Germans, the sort of mission that every young army officer dreams of being given. Some of them had been working on archaeological digs for the universities before the war (like T. E. Lawrence in World War I), some on the colossal restoration of Knossos by Sir Arthur Evans, and they spoke good demotic Greek already. Others, with a gift for languages, posed as islanders with remarkable success. They climaxed their operation by planning and executing the kidnapping of General Kreipe, the German commander-in-chief, taking him right across the rugged island to the harborless south coast, where a British navy launch dashed in by night and took them all off to Cairo.

Emeric and I were conundrums to ourselves, let alone to others. People seeing me jumping about, climbing cliffs, and killing actors naturally concluded that Emeric was the sedentary member of the team. Not a bit of it! Emeric was an athlete when young—a runner. I hate all sports. Emeric had to know what was going on, and worried for hours when he missed the six o'clock news. I couldn't have cared less what had happened, so long as they didn't tell me about it. Emeric was a subscriber to *Time*, I to the *Times Literary Supplement*, and to *Variety*, for the newest twist in the language. It was in *Time* that Emeric read of the book by W. Stanley Moss, *Ill Met by Moonlight*. Moss was one of the officers involved in the kidnapping of General Kreipe. The other was Lt. Patrick Leigh-Fermor.

Something clicked in my head. I had read in the *Cornhill Magazine* a remarkable piece of writing by one Patrick Leigh-Fermor entitled *A Time to Keep Silence*. No sweeter prose had been written since Laurence Sterne, another Irishman. He had described how, with a literary work in progress, he had obtained, without funds or influence, a comfortable cell in a French monastery for the winter, and how it had taken him many days and sleepless nights to familiarize himself with the severe routine of the monks, who only allowed themselves five hours to sleep, and how he suddenly started to sleep more and more hours until, for a period, he was sleeping nearly nineteen hours a day. (I read this to Frankie who was carrying Columba: "Nineteen hours, and nobody to disturb you! Lucky bastard!") Then, suddenly, he felt as light as air, and he was into the routine of the monastery. From then on, five hours' sleep was enough. He worked happily all the winter, and emerged with his typescript completed in the spring. I was astounded at his writing. Nobody that I knew, except Kenneth Clark, was writing such good English in that year of grace 1950. Stanley Moss had written a good, straightforward report on the Cretan operation, but this man was an artist. We investigated. Moss was in America, but Patrick Leigh-Fermor was in Greece, and could be got hold of through the British embassy. Emeric was very keen to buy the rights to Moss's book and there didn't seem any harm in it, so I told him to go ahead. Myself, I would get in touch with Leigh-Fermor (I had already found out that his friends called him "Paddy"), arrange to meet him, wherever he might be, go to Crete, and walk over the ground myself.

Paddy Leigh-Fermor was found. He was in Athens, staying with the British ambassador and his wife. I advised him of my coming, packed a few things, and flew out next day. It was Thursday, January 25, 1951. I was entering a new world.

In those days, it took all day to fly from London to Athens in winter, if you were lucky. The last time that I had done it, the year before the war, I went by flying boat, with a stop off at Syracuse for the night. When I arrived I contacted the embassy and was told Paddy would meet me the next day at the Tavern of the Seven Brothers. Each brother had his own cask of wine, all of them different, with his name painted on it. Paddy introduced me to retsina. It is wine with resin in it. Ballet dancers rub their feet in resin, some people drink it. It's a free world.

Paddy was Anglo-Irish. He had no accent, but the quickness, the hardness, was not English. He had eyes set deep in his head, and he was very sure of himself. His smile, his politeness, his sociability, is a guard while he's inspecting you. He found it amusing that Moss had written a book about the kidnapping of General Kreipe, amusing but rather irritating.

"He was only with us a few weeks!"

He started to talk about Crete, and his love for the island burst out of the clouds and irradiated the whole adventure for me: they were wonderful people. The women, particularly, were wonderful. Cretans had saved his life many times at the risk of their own, at the risk of the whole village. Did I know Crete? . . . no? . . . then I was in for a treat! He would draw me a map. He would tell me where to go, and he would send messages to old friends. We ate some meat, a chunk of pork with green vegetables, then very hard cheese. The wine was good. I produced my sheath knife to deal with the cheese and it was admired. Where did it come from? Kabul? Really? Could he touch it? He breathed on the steel, and rubbed it with his fingers.

"Good."

What were my plans? The general's private residence was in the Villa Ariadne, which Arthur Evans had built himself during the dig at Knossos. It was up in the hills, and quite a drive from the general's headquarters. They had nabbed him on the way. That was at the eastern end of the island. The nearest town was Heraklion, where there was a good harbor. I told him that I proposed to survey the terrain of the snatch, find a guide, and walk back to Heraklion by the hills. Then, I would walk with my guide up and over the high island, down to the sea the way the general went. I would find a boat, sail along the coast, cross over the island once more, and come down into Khania, the port at the western end of the island. Crete is a long, high island, about one hundred and fifty miles long and eight or nine thousand feet high. Paddy looked doubtfully at me, obviously thinking I was a bit of a lightweight, but he approved the plan.

We decided we liked each other. From the way he talked about Crete and the war years, I could see that this had been a turning point in his life and would shape his whole career. He was a brilliant storyteller and entertainer, but I had read his fastidious prose and I knew that he was an artist. If he ever wrote about the snatch of General Kreipe it would be far in the future. For Moss, it had been a lark in the dark, a piece of swash and buckle that he had enjoyed without actually knowing what was going on. For Paddy, it was one of many exploits during three years of occupation by a ruthless, heavily armed enemy of a people defending their homes, their wives, their children, with sticks and stones and knives. Every Cretan man had a gun and could use it, but to be caught with a gun was death.

Paddy was a heroic figure to the Greeks. He had grown into it and he knew it. Stanley Moss's story was entertainment, and would be enjoyed by everyone who liked a thriller, but there was far more to it than that. Paddy's war had been a personal war: hand-to-hand combat, treacheries, and heroism. The Cretans had never surrendered, and had fought back as sullenly and as silently as the Highlanders at Culloden. His admiration for their exploits was outspoken. He played down his own. He had given them his love and his blood, and they had given theirs in return. It was very touching.

With these thoughts in my mind, I hardly noticed that he was beguiling me into a tour of the lower depths of Athens. Apparently this could only be accomplished by visiting half a dozen cafés. We ate very little and drank a great deal, small glasses of wine and smaller ones of ouzo, with carafes of water and saucers of little things to eat, usually hard and repellent. Everywhere Paddy had friends. Everywhere, he was greeted as Michali! By this name he was known throughout the war, and is now known throughout Greece. Except for Lord Byron, I don't think that any foreigner has captured the love and imagination of the Greeks so much as Major Patrick Leigh-Fermor.

We were now in the Plaka, the quarter around and below and beneath the Acropolis of Athens. The red earth came bulging out between the paving stones and sidewalks, when there were any, and the taverns had earth floors. One of them was a Cretan tavern, and Paddy got a boisterous welcome. Someone was playing a bouzouki, or whatever they call it. They started singing an interminable song, each man capping the other with a verse, arms flung out, fingers pointing, eyes flashing, as the point of the joke was made. Paddy was very good at this. A man who was leaving the tavern with some friends sent a bottle "from the Amali valley" to our table, but we never knew who he was. We nibbled bits of sausage and tiny black olives.

It was half past two, and a full moon, as we wandered along under the towering walls of the Acropolis, and anything seemed possible. I had never seen the Acropolis by moonlight. Pot-valiant, I suggested that we storm it. The road up to it was closed and the gate guarded by soldiers, but the cliffs looked possible on the north side. Paddy took off his shoes (he probably had goat feet), I kept mine on. After about one hundred feet of scrambling, and some beastly bushes that pulled out of the crevices in the rock when you put your weight on them, we arrived in the Propylaea, the beautiful porch to the main temple. This was voted for by the Athenians out of public funds and ended up costing God knows how many drachmas, beggaring the state for a year, and cheap at the price, the Athenians said. It was delightful to have the place to ourselves. We strolled up and down talking, while the million lights of Athens twinkled below us.

"Let's go into the Acropolis."

Athene's little owls were crying as they hunted mice over the vast marble pavements. We heard voices, and the quick steps of soldiers.

"Sit down in the shadow," said Paddy. "In the bright moonlight they can't see us." Years of hunting and being hunted, years of narrow shaves were in these simple words. Two armed soldiers passed us without seeing us, about fifty feet away. They returned after a while, smoking and at ease, and went on down to the guardhouse.

"It won't be so easy going down the cliff," I said. The night air must have sobered me a little. Luckily, we didn't have to go down the cliff. We were arrested before we got there. In the guardhouse the sergeant took a serious view of the escapade; that's what sergeants are for. Paddy passed round cigarettes and asked to see the officer in charge. We were searched for guns or bombs. Neither of us had our passports. Eventually the officer arrived.

"Michali!" He was a Cretan.

Lots more cigarettes passed round, and lots more talk. Finally, smoking, talking, and shaking everybody by the hand, even the sergeant, we adjourned to a local tavern that was still open. We drank to the eternal friendship between Britain and Greece. We drank to Lord Byron. We drank to John Murray, Paddy's publisher, as well as Byron's ("Murray, my Murray"). We drank to Major Patrick Leigh-Fermor, DSO.* We even drank to General Kreipe.

I awoke early, with a splitting headache, and lay thinking. Paddy had telephoned to his Cretan friends the day before, telling them that a crazy film director was flying from London to Athens to discuss a film about the kidnapping of General Kreipe, and that I might want to come on to Crete. I decided to go, and set in motion a train of events that none of us could have foreseen.

=

Between the wars, and even before World War I, Arthur Evans, the archaeologist, had made the names of King Minos and his palace at Knossos a magnet for all amateur archaeologists. Knossos, having no vowel between "k" and "n," was particularly popular with crossword fans. The fact that in classical legends Crete was the home of the Minotaur—a terrifying figure, half-bull, half-man—and of the labyrinth that the Minotaur haunted made the new discoveries even more attractive. The legend of Icarus, the first man to fly—with wings made by his father, Daedalus—appealed to everyone. Money poured in from public and private sources. A huge program of digging and reconstruction was planned by Arthur Evans, who lived in a cottage on the site. It was given the name of Villa Ariadne, and as more and more discoveries were made, it was necessary to go at the excavations day and night and a caretaker was put in charge. This was the father of Mikis Akoumaniakis.

When it was the turn of Greece to submit to Hitler's blitzkrieg, General Kreipe, one of the Führer's most trusted generals, was winkled out of the Russian front and put in command of the fortress of Crete. Thanks to the British navy, thousands of Allied troops retreated across the island to the southern shore and were taken off by fast naval craft and escorted to Cairo. Plans were at once started for a counteroffensive, and volunteers were asked to return to the island. Preference was given to Greek-speaking young men.

*Distinguished Service Order: British naval, military, and R.A.F. order instituted by Queen Victoria in 1886. Officers can be nominated only after their names have appeared in dispatches for "meritorious or distinguished service in the field or before the enemy."

One of the first British officers to volunteer was Lieutenant Patrick Leigh-Fermor.

Paddy was parachuted into the mountains at the eastern end of Crete early in 1942. Other volunteers joined him, and regular drops of airborne supplies were arranged. Gradually, the separate commands of these guerrilla fighters established communication through Cretan runners—it was too dangerous to use radio communication. Soon they were coming and going almost as they pleased, so long as they kept to the mountains. Offensive action against the German invaders was mooted and planned. In the valleys and the coast towns, the Germans as a whole were at pains to make friends of the islanders.

Meanwhile, General Kreipe had taken up his abode in the Villa Ariadne. He little knew that every movement he made was watched and plotted and planned for by the son of the caretaker of Knossos. At the time of the snatch Mikis was a reckless boy in his twenties. He was seven years older now, was married, a father, and a successful export-import merchant. He had made it clear to Paddy that he hadn't much time for me, but he came to meet me at the airport. Paddy saw to that. We had flown in low clouds from Piraeus to the airport at Heraklion. We burst out into sunshine when we were about ten miles from Crete. It was a stunning introduction to the island. Its great length, the height of its mountains, and its narrow, formidable shape, thrusting up out of Homer's wine-dark sea, were impressive.

We were about fifteen passengers in the little aircraft. Our pilot came straight in and landed and bumped to a stop. I took care to come out last. I was traveling light—rucksack and briefcase—and I was wearing the kilt, the Irish saffron kilt that I reserve for little expeditions like this. There is nothing like the kilt for tramping through the hills, and for silencing conversation. Mikis's jaw dropped, and I had to introduce myself.

We were halfway to Heraklion before he recovered. When he did, he was quite helpful. He had a room for me at the hotel, which was right by his hardware store. He said that the next day we would visit Knossos and the Villa Ariadne. I nodded curtly and barked, "Good." They still talk in Heraklion about that Scottish general who tramped all over the island and was a friend of Mikis Akoumaniakis.

Mikis led the way into his favorite café. I spread out my map of Crete and over a bottle of wine we discussed the plan of my itinerary, while the café gradually filled up with curious faces and flapping ears and Mikis changed from a captain of industry to an excited small boy, chattering away about this reckless adventure, in which he had played an important part.

The next day he drove me out to Knossos, and *I* became the excited small boy. I suppose that no tale is better known, nor more beloved, than the story of Theseus and Ariadne, of the Minotaur and the labyrinth. My friend Michael

Ayrton, sculptor, painter, and writer extraordinary, was obsessed and haunted by this monster, this demigod. He drew him many times, and modeled him life-size in bronze. As for Ariadne, the daughter of King Minos—Ariadne, the young princess, whose ball of twine brought the two lovers safely out of the labyrinth—wasn't she the perfect heroine? Wasn't she the perfect wife for a hero? And when he abandoned her on the island of Naxos could any of us forgive that coward, that cad, that sneak, Theseus? Perhaps there was a modern Ariadne and a twentieth-century Theseus waiting to be discovered by our film.

Don't tell me that with all these stories of hairbreadth escapes and comic inventions there were not kisses in the dark, too? No cowardly heroes, no heroic princesses, no lust for Pasiphaë? There is always this problem with a true story, because the true story is never told. If the film were to be a success, we would have to color truth with invention; if the principals would not talk, we would have to put words in their mouths. Some of these thoughts I communicated to Mikis, who looked at me askance. Was this mad film director about to make him the hero of some torrid drama, a Cretan Iago to Paddy Leigh-Fermor's Othello? What would his wife say? I answered that she would love it.

He dropped me at his parents' house and hurried back to his shop, saying that he would return after lunch and take me to the scene of the Kraut-napping. I sat among the ruins and wrote up my diary. At first sight, the palace of King Minos looked like a derelict station. It had been part of Arthur Evans's scheme of reconstruction, as he uncovered the corridors and staircase and rooms of the palace, to cast new pillars and large chunks of walls in concrete, and paint them to match the ruins. This bold use of modern materials among the beautiful relics of the Minoan civilization made one a little uneasy, but once I penetrated the underground rooms of the palace and saw the frescoes of the bull-leapers, which Mary Renault had made so familiar to us, all criticism was stifled and I longed to bring the Minoan color and elegance into our film. Cecil B. DeMille would have made no bones about it. His exhausted hero, after fighting off a thousand enemies, would have fallen into a deep sleep and dreamed that he was Theseus and General Kreipe the Minotaur. Something like that was needed, I thought.

Some years later, when her book came out, I wrote to Mary Renault, whose home was in South Africa, for an option on the film rights. She answered in some distress that she would have loved The Archers to make the film, but unfortunately she had sold the rights to Twentieth Century–Fox. However, she added, Jack Cardiff would direct it. What a pity I had written by sea mail, not airmail, she said. Worse was to follow. Darryl F. Zanuck trumpeted the news that he would personally produce The King Must Die and that it would be Twentieth Century–Fox's film of the year. That fixed it. Research and preparations went into high gear: designs, costumes, props, and even bulls. Poor Jack Cardiff was swamped with advice that he didn't need. He had to fight for the book every step of the way, and in the end the film was never made. The accumulated cost of preparing the film left no money to make it.

I heard a voice calling me. "Michali! Mr. Powell!" Mikis had returned. He had decided to be helpful. Perhaps he had been talking to Paddy again or, more probably, with his wife. Anyway, he drove me to the scene of the ambush. It was only a mile or two up the road. My incorrigible imagination had pictured a dramatic location—a bridge over a foaming stream, or a narrow defile between towering rocks. Nothing of the sort. It was an ordinary, run-of-the-mill road: open, treeless, descending the mountain on a gentle gradient, with the whole of eastern Crete as a backdrop.

The road made a wide curve at this point, to cross the ditch where Paddy and Bill Moss were hiding. Mikis was stationed about two hundred yards up the road, with a flashlight to signal when the general's car was coming. It all went like television. Our two maniacs, dressed in German uniforms, appeared on the road and signaled the car to stop. The German driver, Emil, whom they all knew, obeyed, as they knew he would. When he returned to Crete after the war as a tourist, they had many a merry laugh over Emil's gullibility in the café next to Mikis's shop.

When the car stopped, Paddy and Bill piled in, seized the general, pushed him down on the floor, and sat on him. Mikis, also dressed in German uniform, took the wheel and drove the car hellbent for leather straight down through all the checkpoints, the bewildered German sentinels saluting and about-turning as the car with the flag flashed by. It was the cook at the Villa Ariadne who finally raised the alarm, because she was afraid the general's dinner was getting cold. But by that time they had driven right through Heraklion and out the other side, ditched the car, and taken to the hills, the general willy-nilly marching with them. He had tried, at first, a policy of noncooperation with his captors, but a few pricks from a fifteen-inch Cretan dagger made him change his mind. Within half an hour they were at the first rendezvous, where a band of local partisans was waiting. Their delight at seeing the German general a prisoner was outspoken and extremely danger- ous. Those who had suffered from the occupation were all for cutting his throat. Knives and pistols were brandished and the general was surrounded by steel. It took Paddy at least three cigarettes before he could convince them that the general was more valuable alive than dead, that the sweetest part of the scheme was passing him from hand to hand across the island and getting him away to Cairo from German-occupied Crete. Hitler would dance with rage! Throughout the discussion, the general said not a word. The night was clear, and as soon as there was enough light to see, they started on their march across the island. From now on, they were never out of sight of friends. Mikis returned to Knossos by a path through the hills. He had not been missed. There were Germans everywhere. The island was buzzing like a beehive.

So far, so good. Mikis had told his story well. But once the general had been snatched, didn't the film then become just an ordinary chase picture, if one stuck to the facts? Of course, there would always be plenty of suspense, and it was easy to see there would be close shaves—there always are in this kind of picture. But that was not good enough for The Archers, nor for Crete. Where were the human stories, the agonies, the betrayals, the love affairs? Paddy had hinted at them, and had told me that I must know the island and the islanders better before Emeric and I wrote the script. He wanted me particularly to visit the western part of the island and meet the Paterakis brothers—all seven of them—and their mother. If I met the Paterakis family, I would begin to understand Crete.

I telephoned Frankie. Columba was anxious to be born. According to Frankie he was sitting up and scoring goal after goal with his feet. The doctor said about the middle of March. I decided I had a few days to spare, and would start by visiting the eastern end of the island, where Paddy was paradropped to start his long love affair with Crete. For the next ten days I was constantly on the move, sometimes in the local buses but mostly on my flat feet. I made friends, right and left and Communist. In Nik Androulakis, who had been with Paddy in the early days, I found a guide, a philosopher, and a friend. Under his guidance I walked all day and danced all night.

I have never seen such stones as in Crete. The paths are not only stones, but rocks, and not only rocks, but boulders. It is like walking in the bed of a torrent. Occasionally, some earth binds the rocks together, but this happens so seldom that you accept it as an oversight on the part of nature. Every step is a problem. Every rock and boulder is worn smooth, and I had nailed boots. Nik was shod with synthetic rubber, but it wouldn't have made any difference to him. He never had to think where to place his feet. They placed themselves. So when I write, in future, that I walked and I climbed, you must take for granted that I also hopped, skidded, slipped, scraped, slithered, leapt, fell, and rose again, to fall again. I shall always remember Nik stopping at the top of a mountain path—there is, thank God, a top to every path—in a sheep pasture in the high mountains, and pointing to a well that collected the water from Mount Dikhti, saying, "Here, Michali drank!"

It was a classical statement. I appreciated its terseness. Here Lt. Leigh-Fermor had made the daring paradrop into the mountains above Asithi that had started the organized Cretan resistance to the German occupation. Here in Tapais, in Katharo, in Asithi, fires were lit night after night, and always in a different place, to guide the RAF to their drops of parcels containing warm clothes, ammunition, food, and whiskey. Here Nik and his friends had had many a close call. It was here that the Cretan runners were first recruited and enlisted: men, women, and children who carried verbal messages between the resistance fighters at the risk of their own lives, a network of spies on the Germans, which extended all over the island. It was here, in the intoxicating freedom of the high mountains, that the great coup, the capture of General Kreipe, was planned and carried out. Small wonder, then, that Major Patrick Leigh-Fermor had become a folk hero.

I returned to Heraklion and Mikis Akoumaniakis. He was resigned to my importunity and confounded by my energy. He submitted meekly to my command and demands. I was now going to take the road the general took and vanish into Sphakia, the region of high mountains and tall men. It was the particular territory of Captain Xan Fielding, that friend of my youth, of the far-off sunset days of the Victorine Studios in Nice, and the Château Fielding. Xan is romantic in thought and in deed, and he ran away with the Marchioness of Bath. I remember one evening on the steps of the Travellers' Club, when parting from Xan, a taxi drew up and a beautiful, haunted face looked out of the window. Xan ran down and got into the cab, and they drove off together. It was like a scene in a fairy tale.

It took me several days to cross the island by following the road the general took. It meant climbing out to the central plateau, which is about three or four thousand feet high, and then coming down to the sea on the south coast, through the famous gorge of Kallikratis. It was like following the steps of Odysseus. Everywhere Paddy had friends and admirers. I met Papa Janni, the priest of Alones, whose house had been one of the centers of Cretan resistance. He fed me and sheltered me, as he had done countless others. I call it a house, but it was half a cave and half a barn, and Alones lies at the head of a narrow valley under a huge cliff. With eggs and lemon and rice and a protesting chicken, Papa Janni concocted the famous Cretan soup. The chicken is reduced to rubber, but the soup is the food of the gods.

He had two sons, one of whom was my guide. Another son had been captured, tortured, and shot by the Germans. Leigh-Fermor had told me that he met Papa Janni soon after this tragic happening, in a shepherd's hut on the height of the pass to Kallikratis. He had tried to tell Papa Janni how deeply sorry all the British in the mountains felt for him and for this boy who had died in their service, and he had never forgotten the Greek priest's courage and resignation and determination to go on with the struggle, even if he, his family, and his whole village were to be wiped out.

From Alones onward everyone was armed to the teeth: they slept in a nest of knives, revolvers, rifles, and ammunition. Rifles and bandoliers full of bullets hung about like sausages, near the fire or over a lamp. Sometimes I had guides, and sometimes I had none. Sometimes I was on the right path, and sometimes on the wrong one. Sometimes we had mules, and sometimes we didn't. The guides were usually reluctant and sullen boys. I ate so many eggs in olive oil that I started to crow. Mostly the weather was fine, cold winter weather, but there was one storm with ice and snow on the top of the highest pass that I shall not forget in a hurry.

How often the British guerrillas must have seen the intense blue of the sea, matched against the white blue of the sky from their eyries as they looked out, their eyes reddened with smoke from hidden fires, and their bodies crawling with lice, but their hearts high and their faith enduring.

My last guide on my way to the sea was George Papadosifos. He had been in America for twenty years, and had come back to Crete to marry a young wife. George took long strides and so did I. We crossed the central plateau and plunged into a long and gloomy gorge. For nearly a mile it ran straight through the mountain wall, just wide enough for the path and the stream, never varying in depth or width. The rising sun struck the peaks, but in the gorge it was still night. George broke his silence: "I was readin' in a book . . . I read lots of books . . . about the war of 1866 . . . you know, the war between the Turks and the Greeks? Well, the Turks set out to march down this here gorge to the sea . . . they marched, see? Thousands of them, and the Greeks they knew the paths, the paths above, see?" He pointed a bony finger to the gigantic red walls above us. "And they got up there, all along, without them Turks knowing, and when they got here, just here, where you and me are, they started firing from the cliffs, and they killed thousands of them . . . yessir. Right here in the Gorge of Kallikratis. It's all there in that book."

As we stumbled down, I glanced up occasionally at the black clouds overhead, and then ahead of us at the high threatening walls of the pass. The gap between them was widening, and suddenly I saw ahead a patch of blue.

"Thalassa! Thalassa!" I cried, remembering my schooldays, and Xenophon's *March of the Ten Thousand*.

"Yes," said George. "Him the sea."

The port of Horasphakion had suffered terribly in the bombardments. At the old fort above the beach the Germans had executed the mayor of the town and twenty-six other men, shooting them three at a time and throwing the bodies in a hollow in the rocks. Then they poured petrol over the bodies and burned them, so that the smell hung over the town for days. This was reprisal for taking the side of the British. A few scattered wooden crosses mark the spot today, but it needs no mark in the memories of Cretans. I remember that the British army blew men from guns at the time of the Indian mutiny.

≡

My destination was west, to the port of Souiya, where a rough road, built by the Venetians three hundred years ago, winds up into the mountains to the town of Koustérako, the home of the Paterakis family—a mother and seven sons, blood brothers of Paddy and Xan Fielding, a family of shepherds who had dedicated themselves to the Cretan resistance. You will remember that it was at the Tavern of the Seven Brothers that Paddy and I first met. Paddy had insisted that, whomever else I met, I should meet the Paterakis clan, particularly Manoli, who had participated in the kidnapping of General Kreipe, and the family had achieved for me an almost mythical quality.

The village of Koustérako had been destroyed by the Germans. Most of the people took to the mountains and survived, hiding in the hills and caves for the whole summer. The men took to arms, killed many Germans, and were killed in turn. The father of the Paterakis clan was executed, as were many others. In 1944, as the last German left the valley, the people started to rebuild. Manoli remained in the British army until 1947, faithful to Michali. He went with Paddy to Greece, and finally to Athens in the work of reconstruction. But in 1947 he came back to tend his sheep.

A Paterakis relative had been sent to guide me and we climbed steeply up to Koustérako, my heart as high as the village. About twenty men were sitting outside one of the cafés under a vine, in the last rays of the setting sun. They all stared at my lone arrival, for I had gone ahead of my guide. One of the men advanced doubtfully to meet me, out to the open space. I advanced slowly to meet him, and, like strange dogs, we eyed each other. I said good evening, I was looking for Manoli Paterakis. I mustered all my forces and described who I was, and by what route I had come. It sounded a long way, even to me.

My Paterakis guide arrived with the mules and beckoned to me, and we went to his house. An old lady in Cretan black came in. She had a strong, humorous face and a quiet voice: this was the mother of the seven Paterakis boys. Presently a slim man, with a fair, apostolic beard, came limping in. He had the Paterakis eyes, tender, humorous, imaginative. This was Vardis Paterakis. Leigh-Fermor knew him when I described his limp: he has seven machine-gun bullets in his leg. At supper appeared another brother, dark and dashing, the handsomest young man I saw in Crete. This was Andoni. I called him Adonis, and he became my friend.

We had a wonderful supper. The food was good, but the company was better. The large family loved one another and were always laughing and making jokes. There was Irish stew, real Irish stew, with heaps of potatoes and mountains of onions. Next came a plate of fish, flat and bony, like flounders, but fresh from the sea. Adonis was the fisherman.

"How did you catch them? Net? A line?"

He made a gesture of contempt. "Dynamite!" He illustrated lighting the fuse, hurling it in—pause: "*Boum!* Plenty fish!"

The mother came in, carrying a plate of stewed small bones to add to the feast. She was greeted with shouts of "Meetera!" and she was made to sit down and drink a glass of wine. She sat down with reluctance: the wine she drank in one smooth swallow. She sat on, making dry jokes that set the whole table laughing. Her sons adored her. Easygoing, happy, natural households like this may not be rare in Crete, but this was the only one I saw. I felt as if I had been a friend for years.

The fair brother now announced that he was going to get Manoli. He stuffed bread and personal things into his woolen bag and, with a final smile, went limping down the hill. I didn't know it, but he was going to take Manoli's place with the sheep so that he could come back to the village. I begged to go with him—I would have liked to stay in a shepherd hut and beg a cloak like Ulysses, and eat cheese and drink sheep's milk—but he would have none of it. It was a rough journey, and rougher when you got there: it was no good telling him that was what I wanted. He waved, and was off.

Adonis and I went down to the café, not the one where I had been received but another. There were Communists in the other café, Adonis assured me.

"All of them?"

"No. Two or three. But they go there and then if you meet them they may start an argument, and if they start talking Communism, you kill them. So it's better to go to the other café and play backgammon and hear the news from Korea at ten P.M."

All the same, it was strange to pass this café—all the dogs yelled and a man opened the door and looked out—and realize that even in this small village there were two ideological camps.

As we strolled back to the house, Adonis stopped and looked through the olive leaves. He laughed, "Brother Manoli!"

In a minute we were shaking hands and I was studying the wiry figure, the narrow eyes, the hooked, narrow Cretan nose, the quick nervous gestures, the breathless English, and the worn old khaki beret and battle dress. The Meetera beamed over all. She already had a hot meal going for her beloved eldest son. Manoli wanted to know a hundred things about his friend "Michali." I told him all I could, and he told me many things.

I never saw a more united or more lovable family. They conquered all my private doubts about the subject. My one thought was to return home and let Emeric read my diary and see my photographs of the people.

On my last evening, I walked up to the church with Adonis, to see his father's grave. The path was shady with olives and women passed us coming down with their tall water pots. In the wide mouth they had stuffed a handful of a prickly herb to serve as a filter. We drank at the fountain. I plunged my heated face in the spring. The white houses shone through the twisted trees, and there was no sound but the falling water.

The next night I was in Heraklion, and the next night in London.

=

The Tales of Hoffmann was to have its world premiere at the Met in New York, and Robert Dowling and Ilya Lopert* were calling for The Archers to be there. But the Ides of March had come and gone and Columba was still refusing to be born. His mother was exhausted and her doctor was talking of a birth by cesarean section. The two events were running neck and neck. I was being bombarded by requests from London Films and our American distributors to go to New York as quickly as possible, bringing Emeric Pressburger, Hein Heckroth, and Ludmilla Tcherina in tow, for prepublicity radio interviews, television interviews, the lot. There were only a few days to go before the gala premiere, and the publicity people were going bananas. They all, or nearly all, knew the situation with Frankie, but they went on bombarding me with cables and telephone calls just the same, and even sent a woman to spy on us at the nursing home. To my disgust and fury, Alex added his voice to the chorus: "Micky, dear, I quite understand your feelings. But I have seen the doctor's report, and there is no need for anxiety. Our partners in New York are getting seriously worried. Robert Dowling has bought out the Met for the gala premiere. You can't let him down."

I refused point-blank to go. The doctor called in a second opinion and they decided to operate. Frankie was visibly weaker. The surgeon was a woman, a good technician, and the operation went well. I was so bewildered from standing siege and sleeping on sofas that I believe the publicity department knew about the baby before I did. I was allowed to see Frankie. She whispered, "Go to New York, Mikibum. It's a lovely picture and you ought to be there." After a while, she said, "*AMOLAD†* was Kevin's picture. *Hoffmann* will be Columba's." I nodded. I had a look at the cause of all the trouble. He looked splendid.

Bill was waiting in the hall.

"You'll need all your time."

We got into the limousine and someone from the publicity department briefed me with all I had to do and say on the other side. I said nothing. I was disgusted with them all. Alex most of all.

*American distributors of *The Tales of Hoffmann*.
†*A Matter of Life and Death.* The Archers loved to refer to their longer film titles by abbreviations like these, which had an amusing sound when pronounced.

At the airport Emeric, Monique, and Hein were waiting in a private sitting room. They were waiting for me, the plane was waiting for us. God knows how Alex and London Films managed those things. Emeric said, "We heard it was a boy." Monique cried all over me. Hein said nothing, but squeezed my hand. The limousine took us out to a passenger plane standing on the tarmac, ready to leave and full of resentful passengers—all part of the London Films service. As soon as we sank into our first-class seats the plane took off rather pointedly.

On the other side we were diverted from La Guardia to Newark Airport by a snowstorm.

The plane landed with a bump. One of those big limousines and a little crowd of people were there to meet us, among them Ray* and Dorothy Massey. It was a friendly gesture on such a night. The young publicity man said with enthusiasm, "We are taking you direct to Washington, Mr. Powell, where they have the interviews all set up in the CBS studios." Washington was five hours' drive.

Ray said, "Dorothy was hoping you would stay with us and see our new house."

I said, "I'd love to."

Emeric said gravely, "Michael, I understand how you feel, but you should not do this."

I said to the Masseys, "Let's go."

They whisked me away to their farm in Norwalk, Connecticut. Ray and I were discussing doing a play together in London, the severest test humanity has yet devised for friendship. Dorothy proved to be the kind of hostess who puts all the latest books in your room and your favorite candies by your bedside. There! It's out . . . I admit it . . . I'm a candy freak. There were also cats that slept on your bed, and huge dogs stretched out by the fire that sighed in their sleep and blew the fire out.

Emeric and the others were having a big brunch next morning at the St. Regis Hotel when Ray dropped me there. Emeric was wading through scrambled eggs and kippers.

---

*Raymond Massey is best known for his work in American films, but it was as a Canadian that Michael came to know and love him. Massey enlisted in the Canadian army during World War II, but was allowed out briefly to appear in 49th Parallel, playing a Canadian soldier in a life-and-death struggle with a Nazi soldier at the border between Canada and the United States. Massey's brother, Vincent, was the Canadian High Commissioner in London during the war, and it is his voice you hear during the prologue to 49th Parallel. Michael stayed close to the Massey family after the war and considered emigrating to Canada. When he couldn't convince Emeric to join him, he abandoned the idea. Raymond Massey went on to appear in A Matter of Life and Death and in The Hanging Judge, one of the two stage plays Michael directed. Later, he and his son Daniel Massey were in Michael's The Queen's Guards. His daughter, Anna Massey, would play the female lead in Peeping Tom.

"Good morning, Michael. How is Columbo?"

". . . ba."

"I beg your pardon?"

". . . ba. Columba . . . ba . . . a . . ."

"Columba."

"You've got it. He was an Irish prince. He converted the Scots. He operated from an offshore base on the island of Iona."

"I remember now. We went there when we were looking for locations on *I Know Where I'm Going!* . . . Colum*bah*."

"Not Colum*bah*—Colum*ba*!"

Hein approached us warily. "What are you two gentlemen 'baaaing' about?"

"About my son, Columba."

"Is that his name—Columbus?"

"Not Columbus! Columba! It's an Irish name."

"Good. I will try to remember. How is he?"

"Very well."

"And his mother?"

"Very relieved. How have you been getting on?"

"Micky, I have been on thirteen talk shows on television, and I have had twenty telephone calls from old friends, all of them asking me to lend them money. It's a wonderful thing, this television."

After breakfast, we walked across town to the Met, to see how preparations for the gala premiere were going on. Inside, a huge screen had been erected on the stage, within the arch of the proscenium, and a rehearsal of the print was already going on. A projection box had been installed in the middle of the circle. Technicians were checking the density of the color print against the long throw from the back of the auditorium. We decided we were in safe hands. Hein vanished to supervise the decoration of the foyer.

"Let's have lunch at Reuben's," said Emeric.

The first night of *The Tales of Hoffmann* at the Metropolitan Opera in New York was a grand and glittering affair. All the regulars turned out: Rockefellers, Vanderbilts, Morgans, and other historic names. There were not a few tiaras. The Diamond Horseshoe glittered with, well, with diamonds. All of showbiz was there, to see what we had done for Moira Shearer, and confident that she would be there too. They were to be disappointed, but their disappointment changed to enthusiasm when they saw Monique arriving on my arm. We had hired the jewels and furs, and she had been working all day on her makeup and hair. She made a late entry, of course, and she filled the auditorium when she took her place in the box that had been allocated to us. The whole audience rose to its feet to case her.

To my amazement, she had been placed in the second row of chairs, while

Mrs. Ilya Lopert sat squarely in front of her. I was not going to have this, and said so, but I had to threaten to walk out of the theatre before I got her to change places with Monique. Mrs. Lopert, too, had spent all day on her appearance, and her off-the-shoulder gown left little to be desired, or imagined, but the particular shade of lemon red that she had chosen for her hair was too striking to be allowed too near to the star of Act 2.

From the opening shots of the weather vanes to the final chorus in the beer cellar, the audience was stunned by the virtuosity of our production. They had never expected to see anything like the Dance of the Dragonflies between Moira and Edmond, or the Doll Dance by Shearer in Act 1. Monique as Giulietta had everybody turning their opera glasses on the box where she was sitting, outwardly unconscious of the sensation she was causing. Again and again, you could feel those wonderful waves of enthusiasm and admiration, which are usually only awakened in a live audience by a live performance.

The emotion was so strong, and so pent up, that when finally, on the first note of the last eight bars, Sir Thomas Beecham, Bart.,* conducting his own orchestra, appeared on the screen, there was a roar of welcome and clapping started. The clapping and the cheering went on while he completed his task, put down his baton, and picked up the rubber stamp on his podium. The clapping started to die down, but when they saw him stamp his copy of the score MADE IN ENGLAND, there was a roar of laughter, and the clapping was redoubled. They loved the cheek of it.

We were all invited by Robert Dowling after the show to go to a hotel he owned, the Carlyle, where a party had been laid on. But the photographers were busy with Tcherina, and people lingered, talking together and hailing acquaintances, as people do after a successful big show. I walked away from it with Murray Silverstone, who had been head of United Artists in the early 1930s when Jerry Jackson and I were making our quota quickies and who had always been kind to me. There was a lunch table reserved for the UA executives in those days, in the Trocadero on Shaftesbury Avenue, and I sometimes joined them there, where I was the only hungry one. He was going home to his apartment on the West Side, and we walked together, in friendly silence. He had loved the film. We were in a part of New York that was mostly warehouses, and there was hardly anybody about. He looked at me with his large, luminous eyes, which were his best feature.

"Micky, I wish it were possible to make films like that . . . I mean . . ."

He paused, and I realized that I had stirred him profoundly. Was this the Murray Silverstone who said to me so many years ago, "See the films that I have to sell for United Artists? Not likely. If I saw them, I couldn't sell them."

*Short for baronet.

He was trying to tell me how much he admired my making the film, and how sorry he was that it wouldn't make a cent. I reassured him.

"The film will do all right, Murray. It'll get its costs back."

"What did it cost?"

I told him.

He looked relieved at once. "Oh, really! I thought it had cost five times as much." He was visibly cheered up. "Oh, then you'll be all right. Ilya's a good salesman. Good night, Micky. Let's meet some time when you're in New York."

But we never met again.

I took a taxi across to the Carlyle, which is on Madison Avenue at Seventy-sixth Street. It was intimate and luxurious, and Robert Dowling knew how to throw a party. I was delighted to see that Monique was having the time of her life. I had been afraid that seeing Edmond on the screen would be too much for her. But that was all past and gone—not gone, but part of the past, and waiting to be turned into something else. Emeric, who usually likes parties, was bored, and I had caught Mrs. Ilya Lopert's baleful eye on me, so we decided we were for bed. It was only a step to the St. Regis.

There was a letter in my pigeonhole addressed to Messrs. Powell and Pressburger. I let Emeric open it. He liked opening things. The envelope and the notepaper were yellow and covered with designs from the Barnum and Bailey circus. There was a legend: "The Greatest Show on Earth." The letter read:

Dear Messrs. Powell and Pressburger:

Recently I had the belated pleasure of seeing your picture "Tales of Hoffman" [sic]. Perhaps you will not mind my writing you a fan letter about it.

From my earliest theatre going days I have been a lover of Grand Opera. The physical drawbacks of the average operatic presentation have often bothered me—in fact it is hard for me to remember a production which did not make heavy demands on the imagination. The only satisfactory frame of mind to bring to the theatre was to say to oneself, "Well, you can't have everything."

Your production of "Tales of Hoffman" has proven that you *can* have everything. For the first time in my life I was treated to Grand Opera where the beauty, power and scope of the music was equally matched by the visual presentation.

I thank you for outstanding courage and artistry in bringing to us Grand Opera as it existed until now, only in the minds of those who created it.

Sincerely,
Cecil B. DeMille

We looked at each other. Cecil B. DeMille! . . . the great C.B.! . . . the greatest showman of them all, whose productions were a legend, who had made more stars than there are on the American flag! We had revered him since we were schoolboys, and now he was addressing us as colleagues. Back in London we had the letter framed and it hung in our office until our partnership broke up.

One more tale of *Hoffmann:* we all went to Cannes, Columba too, seven weeks old—his first film festival. Although both the Italians and the French had good pictures in the festival in competition, *The Tales of Hoffmann* was the favorite for the Grand Prix. Emeric was staying at the Carlton Hotel on the Croisette. Frankie and I and Columba were staying at La Pax Hotel, on the hill at Mougins behind Cannes. Mougins is a charming village where they play *boules* all day and half the night. It looks down upon Cannes and the fury of the festival. Alex, of course, had chartered a luxury yacht, and was wheeling and dealing. Suddenly our peace at Mougins was shattered. I seem to remember Emeric and Alex pinning me against a wall, while Frankie, with Columba in her arms, listened with horror and disbelief as they urged me to drop Act 3 altogether out of the film. If I would do that, then we were sure of getting the Grand Prix. Otherwise, we would be given a Special Jury Prize "for color and general artistry," and the Grand Prix would go to the Italians, whose turn it was to win that year. Cut Act 3!? . . . of course I said no.

Alex was furious. "Agree now—we can put it back later!"

I should explain that the film had only been seen by the committee, and by various interested parties at this point. It had not been seen by the public and in competition. Of course, Alex's suggestion was outrageous film politics, and no doubt from that point of view he was right, but the way that he made this incredible demand, and the obvious fact that he had someone lined up with a pair of scissors, ready to do the job on my film, was too much for me. We'd be the laughingstock of Europe, I snarled. What about Beecham? What about Offenbach? Finally Alex gave up and said, "Come on, Imre," and was gone back to his yacht. Emeric said, "I'm sorry, Michael," and followed him.

Frankie had gathered enough of the argument to be outraged and shaking with fury. "How dare they come and ask you to do a thing like that, after all your work . . . your beautiful film!"

Columba, who felt he hadn't been getting enough attention for several minutes, googled. And that's the inside story of why *The Tales of Hoffmann* did not get the Grand Prix du Festival that year.

TWO

Nineteen fifty-two was the year of destiny for Emeric and me. I was profoundly discouraged by the results of our return to Alex, and the shenanigans at Cannes really took the cake. We had written into our contracts with Alex the same safeguards that we had had with Rank, but it was becoming obvious that once Alex had our films in his basket of goodies, he could, and would, do what he liked with them until London Films had got their investment back. With Rank and Davis, ours was a true partnership, and still is. With Goldwyn, Selznick, and Korda we were dealing not with partners but with predators. Of the three of them, Alex was the only real filmmaker. The films that he directed himself are delightful and full of humor. But when it came to making deals, Alex was as tough as the others. The three men were real independent producers: ruthless, dangerous, alert, their hands in everyone's pockets. Alone of the three Alex inspired affection. He robbed us while we loved him, and then he had such a lovely sense of humor.

I remember one evening at dinner, a week before shooting *Hoffmann*, when Alex got quite heated about our script. He said that nobody could understand it. We said it was perfectly plain to anybody that knew the score or had heard the records. He said he had tried and failed, even after playing the records, but on the sleeve . . .

"But boys, wait a minute . . . on the record jacket is an excellent description of the plot of the opera! You would do well to read it, Imre, and do a little rewriting."

We said, "Prove it."

Alex's valet summoned Alex's driver, who was sent to the office of London Films to bring the sleeve back. We had all forgotten about him when he reappeared with it. Alex, who had reached the brandy stage of the dinner, took the sleeve in his hand, gave us a severe look, and said, "Now, you boys listen to this!"

I don't know if you, my readers (if there are any), have ever bothered to read the synopsis of an opera printed on its record sleeve, but if you want to enjoy the opera, don't. Alex started out confidently enough, then gradually realized how ridiculous it sounded. We were all laughing. His voice got slower and slower, and as he read, "Hoffmann takes off his glasses and realizes that Olympia is a doll . . ." he burst out laughing, too, and threw the sleeve into the corner of the room, saying, "You can laugh, Micky and Emeric, but I tell you that nobody will understand your film—nobody!"

Perhaps that is the great triumph of *The Tales of Hoffmann.* Nobody understands it, but everyone loves it.

Emeric was more philosophical about Alex than I was. Of course he understood him better, but he was more subtle than I and had no illusions. I started a film intending it to be the best of its kind; Emeric started a film thinking, "Well, you can't win them all." But when, after *The Tales of Hoffmann,* I declared that we must be our own masters again, he made no objection. By our contract with Alex we had two more films to make, and Christopher Mann pointed out to us that this meant giving up a great deal of money and that it might even cost us money to break the contract with London Films. But when I stood firm, Emeric did too. A writer has an advantage over a director: a writer lives by his wits, a director by his guts. *49th Parallel* proved that. We depended upon each other completely. When we formed the company of The Archers to make films together and I told Christopher Mann that I was going to make Emeric an equal partner, he told me that I was mad, when I had just won by my own efforts the coveted title "Produced and Directed by Michael Powell," to give away 50 percent of the equity when I could have kept the lot. But I knew what I was doing. I had seen Imre's mettle, and an equal partnership was necessary for both of us.

Perhaps it was only necessary for the war. We looked on ourselves as combatants, with a wider vision than the average soldier. We took our responsibilities seriously and several times contradicted our superiors when we thought we had a good case. Emeric was so valuable because his position was so precarious. Throughout the war he was an enemy alien in England, and all that that implied. Not for a fraction of a second were his decisions activated by fear.

When the crunch came over *The Red Shoes* and Arthur Rank and John Davis decided that they couldn't afford us, it was unthinkable that we should split up, and inevitable that we should go to Alex. We had allowed ourselves to be tempted by Alex and then outmaneuvered. Out of the four shots that we had made at the target under his banner, two were outers, one was a clean miss, and only one was in the gold—and that one, *The Tales of Hoffmann*, although an artistic success, which would stand as a landmark for the rest of the century, would never do much more than recover its costs.

I was getting hard to handle. I couldn't face another tussle with Alex over some London Films property he wanted to offload. Any moment now he would be trying to mate Powell and Pressburger with Gilbert and Sullivan. Emeric seemed to go along with this. We had no plans, no offers. We had lost the urge. We could have gone to America, where several multiple-picture deals were offered to us, but what once would have seemed to both of us an exciting adventure no longer appealed. I was anxious to do some more theatre, and Emeric planned to drive his new Bentley around all the three-star restaurants in the French *Guide Michelin.* We didn't make another film, either together or singly, for three years, and then it was Emeric who took the lead.

Where, oh where, had the panache, the truculence, the confidence of The Archers gone to? True, it was a bold gesture to buy out of our contract, to throw Alex's money in his face, but it didn't look like that to the rest of the world, and frankly it didn't look like that to us. After years of being looked upon as Denham men, and then Arthur Rank's boys, and then Alex Korda's elite, we were homeless, naked, shivering, indecisive. Our friends and comrades were still held together by contracts that guaranteed them thirty-two weeks of work with The Archers during the year, but they had already reluctantly begun to transfer their loyalties to other filmmakers while waiting for us to make up our collective minds. It would have been a natural time for the two Archers to disband, to separate and go it alone, but we ourselves had not arrived at that point. We had been through so much together, we could read each other's minds. Such harmony, and such discord, is not enjoyed by two partners every day.

When I look back at this period, at this long pause in creative production after ten years of frenzied activity, I am amazed at the indecision of our partnership, at our lack of direction. It was to last three years, from 1950 to 1953, from *The Tales of Hoffmann* to *Oh . . . Rosalinda!!*—from opera to operetta. What had my ambitions brought us to? A reputation for unpredictability.

For example: *49th Parallel,* an adventure film filled with starry names, followed immediately by *One of Our Aircraft Is Missing*, an adventure film with not one star name in the cast. Or, to take another example, *The Red Shoes*, an art film to slay all other art films, immediately followed by *The Small Back Room*, a piece of black-and-white gritty realism, and a war story to boot.

Then, we were pretentious, ransacking the classics and *The Oxford Book of English Verse* to show off our superior education. Who would ever forget, or forgive, Abraham Sofaer as the heavenly Lord Chief Justice in *AMOLAD*, quoting Sir Walter Scott! And what was all this stuff about chess and chess champions? Was it subtle Soviet propaganda—a putdown of honest chaps who like an honest game of darts in the pub?

Then, at a time when all Englishmen had to pull together, were we not being overtly Continental with David Farrar in the Expressionist sequence with the whiskey bottle in *The Small Back Room*—eh?! What about that! And Eric Portman pouring glue on nice girls' hair in *A Canterbury Tale*—in the blackout! It was generally agreed that we were dangerously arty, bringing music, singing, and dancing into our films when the true Briton was enjoying, and I mean enjoying, currency control, food rationing, full austerity, the lot. You who read this book will know where and how the decisions were arrived at to make these films. But I can see that, from the public's point of view, The Archers were pretty hard to put into any category. Still, members of the public have told me that they didn't mind that. Martin Scorsese, for instance, has told me that when he was a boy waiting for the *Million Dollar Movie* to come up on TV and saw the target on the screen and the arrow thud into it, he knew something unexpected was coming, some piece of real film magic, and that was good enough for him. But from the critics' point of view it must have been a nightmare. No wonder that when they got me alone and out on a limb with *Peeping Tom*, they gleefully sawed off the limb and jumped up and down on the corpse. So, it was Powell all the time, eh? We suspected Emeric Pressburger with his Continental background, but now we know it was Powell, the sadist, who poured glue on girls' hair, or splashed buckets of blood all over Moira Shearer lying on the railroad tracks, when she should have been allowed to die neatly and tidily, like a British ballerina. Let's go get him!

And did they? Sure they did. But that is another story.

=

In these years of indecision, many things happened. I produced and directed two plays: the first one an honorable artistic failure—everyone who saw it liked it, but nobody went to see it; and the second a commercial failure—a potential success, but the nut was too heavy. Neither of them was turned into a film, either by me or by anyone else. Emeric and I wrote two full-length shooting scripts, *The Golden Years* and *Salt of the Earth*. Neither of them was ever produced. We started work on *Ondine*, with Audrey Hepburn and Mel Ferrer, and abandoned it. We both traveled. I went round the world. We visited the new state of Israel in 1953. We wrote, produced, and directed a film, an English adaptation and translation of Johann Strauss's *Die Fleder-maus*, entitled *Oh . . . Rosalinda!!,* with an all-star cast: Anton Walbrook, Michael Redgrave, Mel Ferrer, Dennis Price, Anneliese Rothenberger, and Ludmilla Tcherina. We might as well have stayed at home for all the good it did us or our public. At least the actors got paid.

We did the craziest things, found ourselves in ridiculous situations. Who would have thought that I, on behalf of Powell and Pressburger, those magical mystery British producers, would ever fly to Phoenix, Arizona, to confer with Harry Cohn, the rough-hewn president of Columbia Pictures, no less, and, having refused to make *Lawrence of Arabia* for him, would try to sell him the life of Richard Strauss, of all people, a classical composer, a modernist, a German, and a rumored neo-Nazi? Naturally, Harry Cohn said, "Let me see an outline."

And need I say that these two lambs were so sure of themselves and so besotted with the idea of their independence and their cleverness that they decided to write not a treatment, but a full shooting script at their own cost, instead of getting their host drunk over dinner and persuading him to commission it? Result: six months' work down the drain, and another row of scripts on the shelf.

Who would have thought that Powell, an Englishman, a pillar of both church and state, a scholar of Canterbury, who knows King James's Bible by heart, would be able to persuade Emeric Pressburger, a Hungarian Jew, and Simon Marks and Israel Sieff, his partner in Marks and Spencer,* and Arthur Krim of United Artists that there was a magnificent film in Chaim Weizmann's autobiography, *Trial and Error.* (But I am forgetting to mention my greatest supporter, Meyer Weisgal, fund-raiser extraordinary to the Zionist movement, who not only talked but thought zillions, and who was our host in Israel, together with his daughter, Helen, and saw nothing extraordinary in the sight of an English Protestant trying to persuade four convinced Zionists that the life of Weizmann would be a smash hit in England and the U.S.A.) This in 1953, when Israel was facing enemies on all sides, when the best-informed commentators wouldn't have given even money on her survival. This was the time, I argued, to make the film. Even Frankie was incredulous: "You're a Welsh Jew. I always knew it."

The point is that I did convince them and they all put up £10,000 for a location trip to Israel, plus a shooting script. But all that came out of it was my diary, illustrated by Hein and called *A Journey Through Israel, May–July 1953,* and a film that I shot in 16mm Kodachrome that has a historical interest and that I gave to the Weizmann Institute at Rehovot. Who would

*A large chain of stores in Britain.

have imagined . . . but I can hear your irritable voice crying, *"Stop! Stop! Aren't we going to hear any more about these scripts, even though you didn't film them?"*

To which I answer, "Maybe yes, maybe no. Maybe later. Who is getting this off his chest, you or me?"

Who could have imagined that I would drop in on Alfred Lunt's production of the play *Ondine* on Broadway, starring Audrey Hepburn and Mel Ferrer—a smash hit, with the whole town talking about their love affair and that they were planning to run away together—and be so moved by the production of Jean Giraudoux's comedy that I went round back to see the two stars and somehow forced my way through the stage door (no mean feat on Broadway, as you will remember from my first attempt at being a stage-door John),* and convinced them that night that they must come to England as soon as possible, and make a film of the play with Powell and Pressburger? And that our respective agents—theirs had been a lightweight boxer in his time, name of Kurt Frings—would get the two lovers to England in time for Mel Ferrer to join the cast of *Oh . . . Rosalinda!!*, solving their immediate financial problems? And that four months later, when production preparation was in full swing, and when Hein Heckroth was already designing the sets and costumes for *Ondine*, and we were writing the script, that Mel Ferrer would disrupt the whole thing by bringing in his own choice of designer and director so that we abruptly walked out of the deal, to the dismay of the lightweight boxer, and of Paramount, which was picking up the tab, leaving the two stars in such an embarrassing position that they had to go to Rome to make *War and Peace* with King Vidor?

And who could have guessed that our sudden freedom from *Ondine*, a sacrifice that I shall always regret, made it possible for us to accept the invitation from President Perón and his legendary mate, Evita, to attend the huge Festival of the Arts that was being organized at Mar del Plata in Argentina? And that Emeric would have said to me, "Don't let's go, unless we can turn it to good account. How about the pursuit of the *Graf Spee* and her destruction by her own captain in the early days of the war? Stapi† says it would make a fabulous naval picture, and just our cup of tea?" . . . and that it would lead to our making, with Rank and Davis once more, our most successful film commercially, *The Battle of the River Plate*? Also our greatest

---

*The Archers had considered Betty Field for the part of the American girl June in *A Matter of Life and Death*. When Michael tried to meet her by going to the stage door of a play she was in in New York (a common way for producers to meet actors in London), he was rudely treated by the doorkeeper and left without meeting Miss Field.

†Emeric's nickname for his close friend Günther Stapenhorst.

mistake in titling our films, because the Americans always think the River Plate is the River Platte, and consequently that the film is a western, and that the German pocket battleship *Graf Spee* has somehow wormed its way into the cast.

And fate must have smiled when, by John Davis's astute maneuvering in 1956, *The Battle of the River Plate* was selected as the tenth Royal Command Performance, this time before Her Majesty Queen Elizabeth II, who had been a teenager at the time we all met for the first Royal Command Performance in 1946 of *A Matter of Life and Death.* And who could have foreseen that this healing of the breach with the Rank Organisation would lead to our agreeing to make another film for them, based upon the book by Stanley Moss, *Ill Met by Moonlight,* and that it would lead to a final rupture with John Davis and the breakup of The Archers, and the end of our partnership?

But what am I doing, what am I saying—what a rhetorical outburst! Let's go back to the beginning. My life isn't over yet. How shall I start . . . how shall I end . . . ah, indeed, how shall I end? I am in my eighties now, and swimming strongly, and the horizon seems as far away as ever. But I notice that I am getting slower and stiffer with my strokes, and maybe Steven Spielberg is waiting for me out there with his hungry jaws . . . brrrrr! I hope that I shall never know. My readers will tell me when they join me. *"Didn't you know?"* they will say. *"You know how clumsy you once were . . . you did a double somersault down those awful stairs at Lee Cottages trying to avoid stepping on Sundance the cat, and broke your neck."*

≡

In the palmy days before World War II, before Rank and his gong, and Korda's Big Ben, before Hitler and the fatal year of 1933, before Erich Pommer and the great UFA Studios in Berlin, and the great days of the German cinema—yea, even before silent films learned to talk—Emeric Pressburger was a good trencherman. If as a student you have starved in Budapest, in Prague, in Stuttgart, and in Berlin as a freelance journalist, if you have read all the newspapers, and met all your friends in your favorite café, all for the price of one small cup of coffee, if you have become an adept at writing short stories on the back of post-office telegraph forms, while for sleeping there were park benches and railway stations, you have learned to keep a very tight belt indeed. But once Emeric had broken through the magic ring that surrounded the UFA story department, he never looked back: he was in, he was eating, and although at first he slept in dressing rooms instead of railway stations, he soon had a room of his own, with a larder and three meals a day, not counting snacks. His gastronomic horizon soon widened under the leadership of Reinhold Schünzel, writer, director, and actor.

Emeric found himself installed in a suite at the Hôtel de Paris, Monte Carlo. Out of the tall French windows, Pressburger stepped onto a balcony and looked down on a landscape later immortalized by him in *The Red Shoes*. The telephone rang. It was Schünzel.

"That you, Pressburger? It's too fine a morning for work. I've ordered a car, and we'll have lunch at the Réserve de Beaulieu. We can talk about your script while we eat. Then you can work on the script, while I go to the casino."

This would go on for three weeks, after which they returned to the studio in Germany, very pleased with themselves, and with the script of a comedy to be made in Berlin in the winter, and Emeric a convert to garlic in the *soupe de poisson*. Small wonder, then, that Emeric took his gastronomic adventures seriously, and later renewed contacts with his beloved France and Monte Carlo with enthusiasm when we made *The Red Shoes* in 1947. From then on, every year saw a Pressburger gastronomic tour of France (supported willy-nilly by Wendy and Angela) being planned and achieved. It usually culminated with a few weeks at Monte Carlo Plage. But after 1950 he came alone.

If you are a lover of good food, *un bec fin* (the highest praise that one French gastronome can pay to another), you will insist on hearing more about Emeric's gastronomic tour of France. The pilgrimage to Santiago de Compostela had nothing on it, the way Emeric planned. For days before his departure, the floor of his study was strewn with maps ("Tread softly on my maps"), and the occasional tables were loaded with cookbooks, guidebooks, and the indispensable works of the great Samuel Chamberlain, finest of gourmets and most urbane of guides. Schedules were planned, replanned, and discarded. The critical advice of friends, frequently knowledgeable, was accepted in principle and ignored in practice: only Emeric Pressburger can plan for Emeric Pressburger.

One morning, all is ready. The gray four-and-a-quarter-liter Rolls Bentley limousine stands in the drive at 72 Redington Road in the heights of Hampstead. Emeric appears in his camel-hair coat, no hat, putting on his gloves. Nobody else appears, for the very good reason that it is quarter past four in the morning. He climbs in and touches the starter. An almost inaudible *clunk* is followed by an acquiescent purr, and this formidable mass of steel and glass rolls down into Redington Road and disappears down the hill.

Question: Why the unfriendly hour?

Answer: Because Emeric is never late.

When Dilys Powell, in her column in the *Sunday Times*, inadvertently referred to him as "the late Emeric Pressburger," Emeric wrote her:

Dear Dilys,
  I am often early, but never late.

This morning he is on schedule. He is going to Southampton to take ship for Cherbourg.

Question: Why the northwestern route down the Cherbourg peninsula? This is not gourmet country. This is farming country, which supplies the gourmand Parisians with their beef, pork, mutton, eggs, and apples. True, but there is one little Pressburger *hôtel-restaurant*, managed and presided over by its owner in the great French bourgeois tradition, and whose charming wife cooks the great Norman dishes as only a Norman's wife can. It is the sort of inn where your name is always known on arrival, where a squat bottle of Calvados is already standing by your bed. Calvados? Apple brandy, a fiery, golden drink, known to Americans as applejack.

So you see, there is method in Emeric's madness. This little inn is his first stop on his arrival in France, and his last stop on leaving that country of fifty million hedonists. What better preparation for an early-morning start than *langoustes à l'armoricaine* of Madame Mère, preceded by *artichauts sauce hollandaise*, and terminated by a *soufflé crème de menthe*, a choice of ten cheeses and fruit, accompanied—*arrosé*—by champagne from Epernay, a Muscadet from the north bank of the Loire, chilled until your teeth rattle, and crowned with an enormous *ballon* of brandy from the *patron*'s own cellar—and all this merely a stepping-stone to an early start next morning, for at six o'clock Emeric must leave. *En avant*, Pressburger!

By half past eleven, he must be sipping his *apéritif* on the terrace of the hotel on the banks of the Loire, five-star and God-knows-how-many-spoons-and-forks in the *Guide Michelin* of that year, with one of the best kitchens in the West, and where he has already ordered his luncheon: a *Chateaubriand sauce béarnaise*, swiftly followed by an enormous *meringue crème Chantilly*, which is a speciality of the house—a simple, serious, classical meal, to be digested *en route*, for he must leave at 2:15 P.M. exactly if he is to dine and sleep at the famous Château de la Caze, in the Gorges du Tarn, deep in the limestone caves of the Roquefort cheese country, followed next morning by a late start, 8:00 A.M., for he only has to go two hundred miles for lunch on the banks of the Rhône . . . and so on . . . get the idea?

Yes, yes, you say—your friend must have had a constitution of iron . . . yes, yes, you say—but was your friend and partner so dedicated to the joys of the table that he had no time for the joys of the bed? An artist like him must surely know that pleasure shared is pleasure doubled? Surely, he must always have felt the need of a companion to join in the congratulatory murmurs that a fat truite aux amandes, *a superb* paté maison, *a succulent* civet de lièvre, *flanked with buttered noodles and accompanied by a youngish Châteauneuf-du-Pape must inspire.* But here you touch on one of the great mysteries.

The world of the great gastronomes in the 1950s and 1960s was small, and the true believers tended to know each other by sight, although few had time for more than a hurried wave of the hand as they scrambled into their Mercedes-Benzes, their Rolls-Royces, their Bentleys, and their Citroëns, their gastric juices already preparing for the next shock of surprise or pleasure. According to the reports of these pioneers, Emeric was always accompanied by a female companion. But where, when, and how she materialized, and how she managed to make her presence felt among the other *plats du jour*, can be only a matter of conjecture. Certainly, he left Hampstead unaccompanied. Certainly, he met me in Paris or Monte Carlo as arranged, and alone. He was alone when he returned to Hampstead, noticeably sleeker. Where did they come from, where did they go, these heroic ladies? No lady worth her salt would consent to compete for more than three days with these other *spécialités de la maison* (or with the menu). How was this heroic relay race organized? Only Emeric knows, and Emeric ain't telling.

But on this occasion, with *The Tales of Hoffmann* in the can, with my refusal to work any longer with Alex, and with no Archers production in sight for 1951, or even 1952, and with his partner proclaiming that he wanted to do more theatre and art films for the new medium of television, or take a year off and go around the world, Emeric felt the need of a less moody partner. He crossed the frontier from France into Switzerland and drove to Zürich, where he had already arranged to meet Günther Stapenhorst for lunch at the Kronenhalle. It's a toss-up which of the two events had most priority for Emeric. Excepting only the restaurant La Cabaña in Buenos Aires, the Kronenhalle in Zürich, as we know, was Emeric's favorite restaurant in all the world. Frau Zumsteg's boiled beef, her *Leberknödel*, her unmatchable *Hasenrücken*, brought tears to the eyes and water to the mouth of Central European gastronomes. Her son, on the other hand, was a connoisseur of art, and generously allowed his latest acquisitions to be displayed on the walls of the restaurant—a gesture not altogether approved of by his mother, for what need was there of a rich dessert with Kandinsky sharing the main dish with you, and Munch peering over your shoulder while you sat in your window-seat and were served dumplings by Klara, who was as indispensable to regulars of the Kronenhalle as La Goulue to the habitués of the Moulin Rouge.

On an important occasion, such as two old friends and clients lunching together, Frau Zumsteg came stumping out of the kitchen, leaning heavily on her stout walking stick and beaming through her spectacles. News had to be exchanged, toasts had to be drunk before the two great men could get down to business. Perhaps this is the moment and the place to explain who Stapi was, and why he, a German of Germans, should be so much at home in Switzerland, and should hold such a high position in the esteem of such notable connoisseurs of mice and men as Frau Zumsteg and Emeric Pressburger.

I have often thought how different my life in movies would have been if I had met and worked with Stapi in the 1920s and 1930s. In that fateful year, 1933, he was an established film producer and I was a formidable technician. We would have made a good team together. He was older than me, and a student of the art of the possible. He was patient, long-sighted, and cunning. He had hosts of friends and no enemies. It is interesting that, according to his daughter Marga's account, he was a dedicated gambler, not a big gambler, but one who seldom got up from the tables a loser. He liked to say, "I am a sly fox," and chuckle as he looked at you with his blue, innocent eyes. He interested me, and puzzled me, but I didn't think much of his choice of subjects, and in the end it was Korda who gave me my chance. But above all he was a man, and a man of honor, a rarity in a business that is overproductive of monsters and crooks.

Stapi was tall and polite and built like a Friesian bull, with curly hair and blue eyes. He served in the German Imperial Navy during World War I, and intended to make the navy his career. The defeat of Germany, and the consequent cutting of the navy by two thirds, forced him to change his plans. He was thirty-four. He decided that he was a merchant adventurer, and that the new revolutionary government of Russia was likely to be a good customer for an enterprising buccaneer. He got the backing of an old shipping firm, put in his own savings and his wife's (he was already married to Charlotte), and chartered a stout, speedy vessel. In the early days of the revolution a piece of private enterprise like this was perfectly possible, and for two or three years Stapi's business boomed. He and Charlotte had an apartment in Leningrad, and their family, two boys and a girl, was on the way. He learned only enough Russian to read the newspaper. The whole episode had a distinctly adventurous air.

Stapi bought carpets, furniture, gold, silver, and jewels from the disenfranchised middle class and aristocrats, and sold them at enormous profits in the European market. Russian customs officers were royally entertained and trained to look the other way. Eventually these trading activities came under the scrutiny of the new authorities, and it was hinted to Stapi that he was persona non grata. The apartment was disposed of, and the furniture, carpets, and pictures were dispatched by the Trans-Siberian Railway to Berlin. They all arrived in Germany, via Japan, several years later, rather travel-worn but intact.

Back in Germany, Stapi looked around and decided that the film business was going to be a growth industry in Germany. He moved the family to Berlin, met a partner, and together they founded a production, distribution, and exhibition company. They even bought a cinema. Stapi used to go down every day to see the films projected, but mainly to collect his share of the box-office receipts. He and his partner even produced a couple of films with young inexperienced actors like Conrad Veidt and Werner Krauss. Stapi had found his métier.

Me too. It was 1925, and I had just joined Rex Ingram and Metro-Goldwyn in the south of France. Three years later I was back in England shooting stills for Alfred Hitchcock. The inevitable had happened to Stapi. His partner defaulted and left him all the debts to pay. Stapi said philosophically to his family, "I have bought my experience." In time he paid all the debts back.

He was now working for UFA as head of a production group making six films a year. Erich Pommer headed the other group. I was a director in England, making quota-quickies. German films by now were famous all over the world. Now that films talked, most European producers were making every film in three versions: German, French, and English. Stapi had made many trips to England and had made many friends there. It was a time to make friends. It was 1932. The inevitable caught up with Stapi once more: Hitler became chancellor. Stapi was not a Jew, nor was his wife. But he was not a Nazi either. He moved his family to London and made some productions for Gaumont-British. It was 1934. I was preparing to make *The Edge of the World*, my first important film. Stapi joined Alexander Korda, and in 1938 produced *The Challenge*, a film about the ascent of the Matterhorn, starring Luis Trenker with a script by Emeric Pressburger. By then Korda had seen *The Edge of the World* and given me a year's contract. He assigned me to direct *The Spy in Black*, to star Conrad Veidt in the leading role. Emeric got the job of adapting the script, and in fact rewriting it. It was our first picture together, and a smash hit.

In 1939 came the war. Emeric and I were both working full out on propaganda films. Stapi was unwilling to return to Nazi Germany, and equally unwilling to stay in a country that was at war with his country. He handed the keys of his house to Emeric, and the family saw the war out in neutral Switzerland. Stapi was penniless, but his credit was good, and within a year he was producing films for Gloria Films. He and Charlotte were able to make a home for the family in Zürich, but being German citizens the boys were called up. After the war the family were reunited, and Emeric solemnly handed back the keys of Stapi's house in London. He had carefully stored the silver and other valuables in the vaults of the Bank of England, under the Thames.

Stapi remained a German citizen after the war, with the status of one who lives abroad. Gradually he built up two companies, the one in Switzerland, and Carlton Films in Munich. By the time that Emeric came to him in Zürich for advice, Stapi was ready for him. Business was booming, his two sons, Klaus and Fritz, were working for him, and his daughter, Marga, ran the distribution office in Vienna. Stapi owned, or had acquired, the copyrights of a number of films that had been big successes before the war, and remade them. He knew the importance of announcing a big program of film production so that the success of one film would cover the failure of another. At first he had nothing but successes. The public came in droves, but Stapi's real money-making films were what he called "my little perversions": Viennese operettas—Lehár, Strauss, junior and senior. They never failed to please the simple German, and the not so simple Bavarian too: *White Horse Inn, Countess Maritza, The Last Waltz, Roses for Bettina,* etc., etc. They swallowed them wholesale and screamed for more, so it was natural that Stapi should say to Emeric, "Would Michael consider making an operetta?" and for Emeric to reply, "I'll try."

This was in a private projection theatre in Munich, where they were running a print of *Das Doppelte Löttchen,* which had just won for Stapi the award of best German picture of the year. The title, literally translated from the German, means "twice times Lottie," a pun that Emeric immediately translated into the English title *Twice Upon a Time.* The director, Josef von Baky, was there, and also Erich Kästner, the author of the original story and screenplay. He had been a friend of Emeric's since the UFA days, when they both worked together with Billy Wilder on the production of *Emil and the Detectives.* He had an understanding of children's minds and imagination that was very similar to Emeric's.

When the lights came up and after congratulations all around, Emeric announced his intention of approaching Alex and London Films to finance an English-language coproduction of the film. He was sure it would do well in the English and American markets, and the others were not slow to be convinced. A great deal of the original production could be used in the English version.

"But would Michael agree to make an English version of a film that already has the stamp of another director's style on it?" asked Stapi.

Emeric's blood was up, however. "Perhaps not," he said, "but I would."

Idiot! He was walking into a trap. In due course, Alex ran the film and seemed as charmed with it as Emeric had been, and the deal was agreed. In this way Emeric Pressburger, director, peeped shyly at the world, to the confusion of all subsequent critics and film historians.

The story? Sorry, I forgot I hadn't let you in on it. Lottie is the daughter of a soprano, a star of the opera. She lives with her mother. She has never known her father, who lives and works in America. She is about nine years old. She goes to boarding school and stays with her mother in the holidays, but in summer she goes to summer camp. The film opens there, in the camp. Suddenly Lottie comes face to face with her double. The shock for both little girls is considerable, and at first they treat each other as enemies. After all, what could be more cruel and embarrassing for a little girl than to find that she is not unique. Then they find out that they were both born on the same day, and the same hour, and this brings them together. Obviously each girl is one half of a pair of twins. There is a mystery here to be solved, and obviously a direct question to Lottie's mama is not going to solve it. They have to be clever, and little girls are clever, even smart.

So one of the little girls can bring a father to help solve the problem, and the other brings a mother—obviously there was a divorce: When and where? They find out. They also find out that their parents are both artists—the father a famous conductor. It is clever of Kästner that he doesn't try to solve the problem for the audience, nor pick a solution from the idiotic grown-ups who have caused this confusion. He treats the little girls with the attention and seriousness that such detective work demands, and of course there is a happy ending, with a remarriage, and the whole family reunited.

Now, can you blame Emeric for falling for this piece of schmaltz? I can. I don't remember that he ever actually broke the news to me of his usurpation of my director's chair, for of course Imre would be working on the floor for the first time with the company of Archers. When Chris Challis heard that Emeric was directing our next picture for Alex, he doubled up laughing.

"Emeric directing? I don't believe it!"

But, of course, they all gave him of their best.

If Emeric did tell me, I probably said, "Oh," or some equally helpful remark. Later, feeling my contribution to be inadequate, I might have added, "Sounds as if it might be fun."

Alex gave his strong support, and the film went into production in the summer of 1951. They advertised for twins to play in the film and got two hundred pairs, all of whom gathered one day at Shepperton Studios for the final reading out. There must have been some murderous incidents, if not between the twins then between their anxious mothers. But in the end the right pair of twins turned up. I never saw the final film, any more than Emeric ever saw *Peeping Tom*. The Archers were like that. On their first meeting they had recognized each other's quality. They were predestined collaborators, like Gilbert and Sullivan, like Rodgers and Hammerstein, Verdi and Piave, Beaumont and Fletcher, like Hofmannsthal and Strauss—lucky the collaborator who finds his rightful partner. It's like a marriage without sex. He will be continually rediscovering himself. His thoughts will be continually turning upward and outward, never inward . . . like Shakespeare and . . .

My prayers rise up, my thoughts remain below.
Words without thought, never to heaven go.

. . . who was Shakespeare's collaborator? Shakespeare had been in the wars
in the Low Countries; we are pretty sure of that. He had seen and taken part
in battles, murder, and sudden death, in triumph and disaster, in love and
friendship. Who was this collaborator, who with every word could start
Shakespeare's blood racing, whose slight shake of head, whose every gesture
told him that he had gone too far, or not far enough? Who was it who put
the finishing touch to lines like:

Mad in pursuit, and in possession so,
Past reason hunted and past reason hated.

Who was it who inspired him to write that wonderful prayer, "O God of
Battles!, steel my soldiers' hearts"? Perhaps some companion of the Flemish
wars, some recluse living in retirement and obscurity—like the noble Roman
invented by Thornton Wilder in *The Ides of March:* mutilated, helpless, but
with his head buzzing with golden thoughts; tongueless, eyeless, but an
inspiration to Caesar, the great soldier and the wily politician?

Do I claim too much for them, these collaborators, these entertainers, these
lovers of ideas, these chasers of shadows? I don't think I do. I had no illusions
which of the two of us had the finer mind. He was subtle, I was quick. Emeric
used to say to me that when he started to expound a new idea, I would come
to it, meet it, appropriate it, make it work, and by the time he had finished
explaining it I would be coming to him, explaining it, improving it, and
introducing it as my own. There had never been a break in our love and trust
and belief in each other for nearly thirteen years. Although Emeric's escapade
seemed to threaten the famous partnership, it saved it for a few more years.

=

Meanwhile, I had turned to the theatre, the legitimate theatre, which had
always fascinated me, for I felt that I could never understand actors and the
way that they set about their work unless I too worked in the theatre, and
with Pamela in New York, and Deborah in Hollywood, a very different face,
voice, and spirit had entered the scene.

She died yesterday, November 17, 1986. In the obituary column of the
London *Times,* I read:

Miss Siobhán McKenna, actress and scholar, died in Dublin yesterday at the
age of 63. Her most famous role was as Shaw's Saint Joan (Arts, 1954),

though she was also memorable in Synge, Sean O'Casey and Chekhov. She was born in Belfast on May 24, 1923, but when she was still young, the family moved to Galway, and she was educated at St Louis Convent, Mona-han, and University College, Galway, where her father held the chair in mathematics. She herself took a first in English, French and Irish literature. Gaelic was the only language she spoke at home until she went to school. As she grew up she became involved in the Gaelic theatre. Her first stage appearances were in Irish language versions of European classics at Gal-way's An Taibhdhearc. She played a Gaelic Lady Macbeth and roles in O'Casey and Eugene O'Neill, as well as translating Shaw's *Saint Joan* to create for herself the title role in Gaelic, and J. M. Barrie's *Mary Rose*. In 1943 she went to Dublin, and for the next few years appeared at the Abbey Theatre, where she played English language parts, but also got the chance to tour in a number of Gaelic ones. In 1947 she made her first appearance on the London stage as Nora Fintry in *The White Steed*, at the Embassy and White-hall theatres. From then onwards she was busy for a while in Britain. In London her roles included Regina in *Ghosts*, at the Embassy in 1951, and the title role in *Héloise* in. . . .

I stopped reading.

I first saw Siobhán in Ireland on the stage of the Gaelic Theatre in an Irish domestic comedy by Walter Macken. Most of the cast were ripe in age, as they usually are in a Dublin play, because there are not enough parts to go around. But it wasn't her youth that attracted me. She had it. She had it, unmistaka-bly. She had black hair and brown eyes, and was built like a peasant. I was still thinking about making *Paddy the Cope*,* and knew that I would have to have this girl with me.

I don't remember that we met then, but of course she knew that I was in front. She probably stuck her nose in the air at the news. She came from Galway, spoke the Gaelic, was a passionate Irish patriot and fierce partisan of the Irish theatre. A while later she married Dennis O'Dea, a tall, handsome Irishman whose one great love in life was fishing. I'm not sure whether he or Walter Macken played the lead when I saw Siobhán for the first time. Dennis made a great impression in Carol Reed's film *Odd Man Out*. He played the

---

*Michael dreamed of making a film about an Irish peasant from Dungloe in County Donegal who became known as Paddy the Cope. In 1903 Paddy founded a farmers' cooperative that bought seeds, fertilizer, and tools directly from big firms, thereby avoiding the ruinous prices of greedy local shopkeepers. Paddy so incensed the middlemen that they got him tried and sent to jail on trumped-up charges, but the prisoner governor refused to accept Paddy, who returned home in triumph. The cooperative movement, meanwhle, flourished and spread throughout Ireland. Michael and Frankie rode across Ireland on horseback as part of the research for the film.

Dublin police officer. He was a great screen personality, and could have had a great career in films, but his thoughts always seemed elsewhere—possibly with the fish.

The next time I saw Siobhán, she was playing Pegeen Mike in *The Playboy of the Western World*. I forget who was playing Christy, but it might have been Cyril Cusack. Every Irish actress starts her career with the intention of playing Pegeen Mike, and every Irish actress is usually wrong, but Siobhán stood like a red-petticoated rock upon the stage. She was great. By this time, she had attracted attention in London and New York and she came to London to make a screen test for *Hungry Hill*. She told the wardrobe mistress that she knew me, and that I had promised her a part in an Irish film, if I made it. To this, the woman replied with an enigmatic look, "Yes, he likes the quiet ones."

During the next year or two, Siobhán toured America with an Irish company, appeared on Broadway and in London, and was quite well known by the time I was ready to produce *Héloise*. I think that she had only appeared in the plays of Synge and O'Casey, and was in danger of being tabbed as an Irish actress. To be identified with Pegeen Mike in *Playboy*, or with Juno in O'Casey's *Juno and the Paycock*, has stunted many a promising career.

It was the late summer of 1951, and we started rehearsals in the empty house at number 2 Ilchester Place. It was empty, and it looked very airy and very big without all the furniture in it, because Frankie had decided it was too big for us.

"There are too many windows," she said, with a toss of her head. I think what really worried her was that she thought that we would be a family upstairs and downstairs. The house had been designed for a neo-Georgian family in the 1920s—ground floor: kitchen, master's library, big salon, garden, etc.; second floor: master bedrooms and guest bedrooms, and a big, sunny room that was the nursery; top floor: the apartment of Bill and Myrtle. To me, being a country boy, this was a normal arrangement, although it was rather grand, and we had more space than we needed. But Frankie had been brought up in a large family and she missed the ruck and tumble of everyone living together. She was right, of course. Frankie always was right.

She didn't have to go more than one hundred yards around the corner of Abbotsbury Road into Melbury Road to find what she wanted at number 8. It was a Norman Shaw house, and you can get a rough idea of what it looked like from the scenes in the film *Peeping Tom*. First and foremost, it was a Victorian painter's house. It had high windows everywhere, sash windows and lattice windows, letting in lots of light. There was a big bay window in the back looking over the garden, and the room that was later to be my library and workroom had ceilings sixteen feet high, which I had painted in Pompeian red by Keith, master painter at Denham.

The chimneys of the house were very tall and built of brick and full of invention in their shape. There were big fire grates and splendid mantelpieces. The whole house was on the point of being divided into five separate apartments, and Frankie's intervention came at exactly the right time and improved the builder's imagination. I brought in Syd Streeter, and Syd brought in Bill Leather, his chief of construction at the studio, and they worked wonders. Frankie took the whole ground floor and the garden and made two flats out of it: a separate flat for Bill and Myrtle, with a separate entrance on the garden, and a big flat for us and the two children. When you came down to it, there were only three big rooms, with the usual kitchen and bathroom. She had got what she wanted. We were all on top of one another, and it made for a united family, and gave Bill and Myrtle an independent home of their own.

We lived there for more than twenty years, except for one brief interval when, believe it or not, we returned to number 2 Ilchester Place in order to sell it. This was before London became the new Mecca for the oil-rich Arabs and the dollar-rich Americans. The British were still sermonizing one another about paying for the war, etc.—as if one can ever pay for one's mistakes. It was no time to sell a large, handsome, empty leasehold house, and it stood for six months until Frankie had the bright idea of moving back.

"It's easier to sell a house with people in it." And she was right, for within three or four months, the house was sold to a Canadian corporation and a neighborly family of Fraser-Bruces moved in. The rest of the lease was about thirty years, and I think the asking price was about £10,000. We would have been better advised to let it, but we were still short of money, and needed it to buy the lease for Melbury Road.

From this vantage point of 1990, it is odd to look back and realize what terrible businessmen Emeric and I were. Of course, I am an equally terrible businessman now, but at least I know it. By the time we left Rank our films were beginning to make fortunes for distributors and theatre owners all over the world, and we were buying our houses in London on mortgage! By the time we left Alex, The Red Shoes had been included by Variety in their listing of the fifty all-time highest-grossing films, the Golden Fifty, and we were scratching to find money for our rates.* We had a very good agent, in fact the best, but he was not a business manager. His horizon was limited to the 10 percent he gained from our earnings, wherever and however they might be earned. We had very good lawyers, but it was not their job, unless we asked them, to advise us to invest in property or properties, and we never asked them. We both of us behaved as if living in a mortgaged house, on a leasehold property, was the summit of human happiness. Perhaps it is. We were happy for a time.

*Property taxes.

It was in this environment, and during one of the periods between moving from the house to the apartment, or from the apartment to the house, that I started rehearsals for *Héloise*. James Forsyth had been nursed by the Old Vic as a baby dramatist, and they had produced at least one of his plays, the one about François Villon. Christopher Fry, with his BBC productions, had opened the door to the English verse dramatists, and the success of *The Lady's Not for Burning* had thrown it wide open. Its success had been dazzling. It was first produced by Alec Clunes, at his little Arts Theatre, with himself playing the part of the soldiering soldier of fortune, later played by John Gielgud. It was at once seen as a star vehicle, was bought by H. M. Tennent,* and with John and Pamela in the leading parts it ran for three years in London. Of course, all the scholars and medievalists in universities ferreted out their rejected playscripts, typed them up fresh, and sent them in again. But Christopher Fry was a hard man to follow.

The trend interested me, and I had almost commissioned from James Forsyth a play called *Red Queen and White Queen* around the time he brought me the first draft of *Héloise*. The love story of Héloise and Abelard had always fascinated me and Pamela as the greatest of love stories. But Pamela was the toast of New York, and Deborah was stuck in Hollywood, where they persisted in playing her in ladylike parts that gave her no chance for real acting. I decided to do James's play with Siobhán.

Immediately I made a fatal mistake in casting. When Walter Macken first hit London town it was at the Lyric Theatre, Hammersmith, playing the leading part in his own play, *Galway Handicap*. It was a roistering Irish play, and he made a personal success of his own performance. He was a good writer. It was in a play of his, you will remember, that I had first seen Siobhán act in Dublin. The critics liked him, and it seemed that a new popular voice from Ireland was being heard. And mercy of mercies, he hadn't yet come under the ban of the Church. I decided that a flame could be ignited by the conjunction of these two Irish Catholics, Walter and Siobhán. But it wasn't a flame, it turned out to be a damp squib.

The best way to describe my nonsuccess with James Forsyth's play is to report a conversation I had with my old friend Nino Cauvin, of the Restaurant de l'Étoile, after he and his wife, Lola, had seen the play.

"Did you like it?"

"Very much. Michael, may I ask you a question?"

"Go ahead."

"What makes you think the English will come to see a play about religion and God?"

*H. M. Tennent Ltd. was the dominant theatrical producing entity in Britain from the mid-thirties until the mid-sixties.

I stared at him aghast. Such a thought had never entered my head.

Another visitor was Godfrey Tearle, dating a teenager, Miss Jill Bennett.

"Michael, I liked the scene between Nigel Green and Miss McKenna. Jill did too, didn't you, Jill?" Jill nodded, a girl of few words. Godfrey meant the furious scene between an emissary of the Church and Héloïse on the pavement of Notre Dame. Nigel Green, with his great face and towering figure, would soon make a name for himself in movies. Who could ever forget him in *Zulu?* He was an almost mythical figure, like Harry Andrews and Victor McLaglen, and later John Wayne, all of them genuine and generous artists. Among other men they were like Norse gods, mythical, large, and gentle, suddenly exploding into rage and performing fabulous feats of strength. But Nigel was a good actor, and this scene in *Héloïse* was a beauty, and he made the most of it. Godfrey knew quality when he saw it: "They were like two great hooded crows with their dander up, circling around each other, screaming and jabbing, their wings fluttering, their tongues hissing menaces. First-rate!"

But Nino was right. Nobody came.

Héloïse was dead. But Siobhán and Michael were very much alive. They were in despair. They loved, but it wasn't carnal love. It was the love of Pygmalion for Galatea, of an artist for his ideal, of a dog for his master, of a pagan and a nun. But the nun was a married nun, with a three-year-old son, and a full chorus of Irish-speaking relatives: father, mother, confessor, and every last member of An Taibhdhearc, the famous Irish-speaking theatre of Galway town, without mentioning the shinty,* of which Siobhán had been captain and center forward, and the local schools and colleges, who took pride in each one of her triumphs. All that was needed was a good dramatic libretto, two acts, and music by Poulenc.

All this emotion, pent up in her heart and brain, was poured out to me on paper by Siobhán:

"Hasn't Frankie introduced you to Catholicism? It is the *only* true faith. Protestantism does not mean a thing. Where *are* its people? Its Saints? Anyone I admire has been Catholic, even Shakespeare, except Milton of course, and he was selfish lecherous and unlovable in real life. But I wish I were born a Canterbury Protestant.

"My Mother's uncle is a Bishop. My father's brother a monseignor (next door to a bishop). His Sister, a head of a convent in Cork (she is a pet). She asked me when I was captaining the hockey team in the intercollege games

*A raucous variation of hockey played in Scotland, Northern England, and Ireland. From the seventeenth-century *shinney,* the cry used in the game: "shin ye" or "shin you."

if I had a boy. I stuck my nose in the air and said: 'Don't be silly.' She replied: 'Oh, what a pity. If I were not mad about Our Lord, I'd have to be mad about someone.' I was shattered."

"I was born—very likely because of my mother—very near to God. As you say, I always knew everything, realised and appreciated everything without practical thought or experience. I loved only God. Some day I shall tell you of the way I loved Him. He was completely real and always present with me. I talked to Him all day long and told him everything, just as one can do with a nice husband (what a horrible word for what should be a good thing; a house band. In Gaelic it is *fear céile*, a man who is with you. With you—not necessarily resident—*with* is the operative word e.g. 'are you with me ar agin me?'). Old Irish is full of humanism and naturalism. There is an old slogan that a country without its own language is dead. That is what is wrong with us in Ireland. The British, being very clever colonists, recognised the two strengths of Ireland—her faith and her language. Ireland's heroic clinging to her faith is enough proof positive that Catholicism is the true faith. At that time you could retain a farm or buy a small kingdom with your soul; but they wisely preferred their souls, except for a few unhappy 'jumpers'. Britain tried very hard, but failed to stamp out Catholicism. She succeeded incredibly well where the language was concerned. Irish has vanished from the far greater part of Ireland in a very short space of time. That is still inexplicable except partly, which seems insufficient reason. England knew Ireland's desire (in those days) for scholarship, so she built schools, and punished any child cruelly (literally) if it spoke its own language. And so was spoiled and destroyed the inherent and traditional nature and human-ness of the Irish.

"Catholic faith was saved not by nattering priests on nattering subjects such as morals or behaviour, but through the Mass, the greatest heroic adventure in our history. People went voluntarily over miles of spied on hills to the lonely hills to hear Mass said with a Rock as altar. All was because of Faith, voluntary Faith. No one then was compelled to hear Mass under pain of mortal sin; so they went and their faith remained wonderfully alive. If for no other reason but in respect and honour to them I shall always be a Catholic. But today in Ireland there are too many commandments and too few voluntary heroes. That is why I say there is bound to be a Revolution in Ireland soon. It is important that the Match is a good match; not a match which destroys, but one which rekindles. My spelling is rocky. But my heart is sound. Or is it rocky? I don't know.

"Dear Canterbury protestant, I love the pilgrim soul in you and would not wish to change it. That was the first time you were angry—in a Soho Restaurant (near the church) and you said you took your religion from nobody. Neither do I. But I am not angry about it. Dennis is righteous about his faith (sincerely so I think) but unspiritual (I think) but one never knows anyone else's soul: which is wonderful because it means no two are ever one; that the right to remain individual is true and natural. D. said I did not love him as much because I was never jealous. He may have been right— although I do not think so. You may be right about my not being in love at all. Do you want to be right? Men love being right. I am always wrong about tickets, dates, days but it is never a humiliation to admit it because I am sometimes surprised pleasantly by being right. So you cannot expect me to deny my faith. I could with a great regret deny my friends, my country and my beliefs in my duty towards Gaelic things, the language and the theatre, but I'd be bound to turn to Belfast as a substitute. But my faith and my family have always meant everything that lasts to me. So you must treat them with respect."

. . . From the moment she made her entrance, barefoot, in a tattered red flannel dress, she held the audience spellbound. An Irish girl was, anyway, an inspired piece of casting for the Maid of Lorraine. But in addition she brought to the part both the necessary peasant qualities, earthly and humorous, and the lofty vision of Shaw's anachronistically Protestant saint. She herself said that Joan's character was merely a reflection of her own, and it was always her favourite role.

The truth was that the role of Saint Joan chose Siobhán, not Siobhán the role.

≡

I decided to go around the world. I have never really believed it was round, and now was the time to prove it. When we were at Cannes for *Hoffmann,* Ludmilla Tcherina and I had been invited to go to Tokyo by Mr. and Mrs. Kawakita, whose firm, Toho Films, was distributing *Hoffmann* in Japan. I decided to accept the invitation. I was collecting men, women, and materials for a group of art films, of varying lengths, to be labeled *Powell's Tales.* I had the nucleus all ready, and I didn't see how any television producer could resist them. I had set my sights on a new name, one William Paley, who was chairman of the Columbia Broadcasting System in New York. My friend Arthur Loew (our friendship dated back to Rex Ingram in Nice in the 1920s) had succeeded his father as president of Loews, Inc., one of the giants in New York and Hollywood films. He promised to "get the ear" of Bill Paley. I had a vague picture in my mind of these titans sitting in conclaves around a huge table in New York. It was not very far from the truth. I aimed at about twenty hours of entertainment. I wanted to be able to say to these magi, "Sirs, here are twenty hours of entertainment, of art, by the most famous artists in the world: painters, sculptors, dancers, actors, musicians, composers, architects, and poets. Some of the tales are only five minutes long, others run for two hours. Some of the five-minute shows may represent an investment of a million dollars, some of the one-hour and two-hour shows may represent the same investment—what does it matter? The point is to make art, and to say to the public: 'Here is the very best in art. We can afford it, and you shall have it.' "

Happy in this innocent concept, I had started industriously to collect a few goodies. Also I thought, not unreasonably, that I could pick up a few tales and the art and artists that accompanied them, in countries like Japan, Korea, Borneo, Ceylon, India, Persia, and Egypt, in my travels.

The year started well, on Wednesday, January 2, 1952, with a meeting with Dylan Thomas in Soho at the York Minster. He was round, thirtyish, pugnacious, with good eyes and a hilarious nose. He told me he lived in London in the winter, in Camden Town, and was shortly going to America. In summer he had a house, the Boat House at Laugharne in South Wales. I told him that ever since I bought his first book, *Eighteen Poems*, I considered him the best poet writing in English today. He blinked. I explained my plan for *Powell's Tales*. He caught fire instantly: "Of course, every story has to have its own length!"

There spoke a poet, a craftsman. Poets, painters, and composers of music— these are the people to make films. They have some idea of form, they welcome the discipline of the craft. I said that I had thought that he would be the right man to write a screenplay of *The Odyssey*, and I would match him with Orson Welles as Odysseus. His eyes grew rounder than ever.

"You had better talk to Louis MacNeice."

"Why?"

"He has a classical education. He is a great scholar, and a poet too."

"My dear Dylan, don't talk nonsense. How much classical education did Homer have? And you are a much better poet than Louis MacNeice."

His face cleared. "That's true."

We heard no more of MacNeice. Dylan told me that he was booked on January 15 on the *Queen Mary* to go to America on a lecture tour, doing readings from his poems and other poets, and recordings for Caedmon. It was an appointment in Samarra.

On the same day I finished reading *Diarmuid and Graunia*. It is an Irish reworking of the tale of Launcelot and Guinevere—but what a beautiful, simple tale it is, when you strip it of Tennysonian images, Pre-Raphaelite robes, and shining armor! What a wonderful image when Finn is hot on the trail of the lovers, one day ahead of him, finding and seeing the forms of their two bodies where they slept together in the heather, and then at last, the third and fatal night, when there is only one form in the heather.

I was for Paris in pursuit of my *Tales*, so I went to call on Hein at his studio in the Pheasantry in Chelsea, to cheer him up with promises of working together again. But he was working on *Gilbert and Sullivan* for Alex, and was beyond cheering. Only Alex could have conceived a misalliance such as Hein Heckroth, the Gothic, romantic artist, with the very English entertainers typified by W. S. Gilbert and Arthur Sullivan: Frank Launder and Sidney Gilliat. Unique in their own fields, together they were arguing from different premises, as Sydney Smith is said to have remarked on observing two ladies shouting at each other from opposite windows across an Edinburgh street.

Ada told me that Hein had tried to escape from the film by being sick and taking to his bed, with the result that next morning Sir Alexander Korda in person was on the doorstep, saying that he would see Hein never worked in films again unless he reported for work.

"You must mean Vincent Korda! Alex is too clever to appear himself."

Hein groaned.

"No, Micky, it was Sir Alex. I had to go back. What the hell am I doing, Micky, designing this bloody Gilbert and this bloody Sullivan. Rescue me, Micky! Rescue me from the bourgeoisie!"

I promised him that when I came back from Japan, he should choose his own *Tales*.

"What shall I bring you from Japan?"

"Brushes . . . paintbrushes . . . the Japanese make the best."

The next day I was in Paris on board Jan de Hartog's Dutch barge. He had sailed her from Holland along the coast to the mouth of the Seine, and then up it, finally coming to a mooring on the quays at the Place de la Concorde. His plays were running in translation in Paris, he was writing a film, he was the new Shakespeare. His particular *Tale* for me was to be *The Sea Mouse*, adapted from his book *The Lost Sea*, all about a cabin boy on board the ships in the Zuider Zee before Holland built the dikes and turned the sea into land. Captain Jan was roaring and laying about him as usual, pretending he didn't enjoy his notoriety. Angie, his wife at the time, made a great pigs' knuckle soup. I was running a feverish cold, and it cured it.

I went to the Port Saint-Martin to see the production of *The Three Mus-keteers*, staring Reggiani. I really came to see the costumes, which were by Jean-Dennis Malcies. The costumes were extravagant, the pace was terrific, but the whole thing was too much of a joke. There was nothing for me.

The next morning I had breakfast with Massine, at his house on the river near the Bois de Boulogne. We had agreed to do a story from *The Thousand and One Nights*, decor by Matisse, but none of us could decide on the story. While I was with Léonide, Matisse himself came on the phone from Nice, and I said I would be calling on him in a few days' time. The garden of Massine's house sloped down to the river, and it was here that the perambulator ran away with the two children of Isadora Duncan and drowned them in the Seine.

That evening, I found myself sitting for four hours through Jean-Paul Sartre's *Le Diable et le Bon Dieu*. The first act was about an hour and a half. Pierre Brasseur bestrode the stage like a colossus. The two girls, both of them good actresses, couldn't get a word in. There were two intervals of twenty minutes each. We all went out to have supper on Jan's barge, Pierre Brasseur still talking. I seem to remember there was a brawl, and somebody fell in the Seine.

I think that Sartre is a great man of the theatre, and every word he writes is speakable. But half the point of the play is its length, and in translation into English it would never do, however much the leading actors of London and New York wanted to play Brasseur's part. I had already picked Sartre's *Huis Clos*, his classic one-acter, as one of my *Tales*, and had started to translate it myself, feeling I couldn't trust anybody else to do it. Unfortunately in English I couldn't call it *Dead End*, because of the Dead End Kids. *Continuous Performance*, perhaps . . . or *This Is Where We Came In* . . . I'm interrupted here by Thelma, who points out that the one-acter is known all over the English-speaking world as *No Exit*.

The Hôtel San Regis, where I was staying, was only five minutes away from Jan's barge, so leaving the two lions, French and Dutch, roaring (Dutch is a roaring language), I walked home to bed, for I had an appointment with Orson Welles in the morning. The night concièrge assured me that M. Welles had arrived and immediately gone out. A pity he couldn't have joined us on Jan's barge. Jan, Brasseur, Orson—they would have torn the boat apart.

Orson was down before me in the morning, and eating an enormous breakfast, one course of which was eight boiled eggs, shelled and beaten up with ground black pepper, sea salt, and butter in a bowl. We discussed *The Odyssey*. At first enthusiastic, I felt his interest cool when he realized that I didn't want to film the whole *Odyssey* but only one episode as one of my *Tales*. Orson himself would direct the *Tale* and play that crafty man, Odysseus. I offered him Circe's isle, where men were turned into animals. I sang the Sirens' song . . . didn't he fancy being tied to a mast? I described the wonderful scene after the shipwreck, when the hero emerges naked as a god, his limbs cut and bleeding from the sharp rocks, with only seaweed to hide his noble parts and great muscles from the eyes of the Princess Nausicaa and her maidens. I thought this would get him, but it didn't. He wanted *The Odyssey*, and nothing but *The Odyssey*. We parted friends. He vanished into Europe, and I didn't hear from him again until we were casting *Die Fledermaus*.

Alice, my father's housekeeper, rang me from Cap Ferrat. Pop was not well, and wanted to see me. I flew down to Nice and took a taxi to the Voile d'Or.* He had had a slight stroke. He was quite recovered and talked big about driving me along the coast to Valescure, where he used to play golf in the old days. He was in despair at being told that he must never play golf again. It was cold, blowing weather, and the golf hotel was empty. We walked over the course morning and evening, and he told me mighty tales of defeats and victories on various holes. The bookshelves at the hotel were full of Tauchnitz volumes, and I found Synge's *The Aran Islands* among them. It's a rare book to find like that, and I took it as an omen. I skimmed through the book. It was a paperback. At home I have the original edition, with the drawings by Jack B. Yeats. There was a story of a woman who died, was buried, and reappeared the next night, suckled her baby, ate potatoes and milk, and vanished. The fairies had put some old thing in her coffin, and taken her to be one of them. I liked very much "some old thing," and I liked the way she was rescued by her husband. What a tale! Synge is a witch. No wonder he died young.

A day or two later I went to see Matisse at Cimiez, the town above Nice. It used to be one big palace hotel after the other before the wars, and all the invalids and semi-invalids of Europe used to winter there in palatial suites. The suites were now gaunt apartments, and Matisse was ending his days in one of them. The Regina Palace was like the Vatican, vast echoing halls, acres of marble. At last I arrived at the third floor, Block B. There was an ordinary bell, with an ordinary card, and an extraordinary Henri Matisse. A beautiful young woman appeared, opened the door, and another beautiful woman appeared before she could speak. She beckoned. "He's expecting you."

Matisse was sitting up in bed, cutting out a shape with scissors. Yet another young woman, very young this time, with lovely transparent skin and a good body, was standing by the bed, waiting for the cutout. Matisse handed it to her. The wall was covered with a large color composition, and she placed the new piece where directed. Matisse was in the act of designing a stained-glass window. He looked very much as I remembered him, but the beard was much shorter. His sight and hearing were as good as ever. One of the girls drew me aside. Would I like to see the master's latest work? We went into the next room, a very large one. On the wall was a large design, with a very black Negress at the center of the composition. She indicated, "On dirait déjà Les Mille et Une Nuits."

*While in the army in France during World War I, Michael's father bought the lease of a small hotel at Saint-Jean-Cap-Ferrat with winnings from the casino at Monte Carlo. Attracted to life on the Riviera, he abandoned his family in England and spent the rest of his life running the hotel, which he named La Voile d'Or. It was during a summer visit to his father in 1925 that Michael got the chance to meet and work with an American film crew shooting at the Victorine Studios in Nice. The director of the film, Rex Ingram, inspired Michael to become a director himself.

Obviously, Henri Matisse's acolytes were very keen on motion pictures. While Matisse worked we chatted and reached some sort of an agreement. I was deeply moved. What a picture to retain for oneself of the master. There he was, eighty years old-young, happy, interested, saying, "Pourquoi pas? On verra ça. Nous ferons un coup, si c'est possible," surrounded by adoring young women . . . how happy a man an artist is.

I couldn't help contrasting this happy child of eighty with my father, who still had some years to go, and who was in despair at being forbidden to play golf. A materialist is always near to despair without knowing it.

I picked up my father at the Cercle Artistique in Nice, and we drove back to Cap Ferrat. My father was a great reader of romances—not novels, but stories of wild adventures and exotic countries, like *King Solomon's Mines*. So when I confessed that I had no particular project in mind, apart from my *Tales*, he put a copy of *The Needle-Watcher* in my hand and said, "There you are, Mick. I always thought this would make a rattling good film. Take it along with you, and don't bother to return it."

It was by Richard Blaker and was the story of An-jin the Needle-Watcher: Will Adams, the British pilot from the Medway in Kent, who became a friend of the great Shogun Ieyasu, who gave him swords and made him the only British samurai. I thanked my father and put it in my briefcase. I fancy that he had been a bit alarmed by all my talk about art with a capital A, and thought that a good stiffener of romance would be more likely to bring home the bacon.

There were letters waiting at the hotel, one from Graham Sutherland in reply to mine, which had found him at Villefranche, where he lived with his wife—another of my *Tale*-tellers. The other letter was from John Piper. Both of them were painting for exhibitions, but both were interested in my *Tales*.

I called on Sutherland the next day. He was out, but his wife was in. They had an apartment three stories up in the middle of the town. His wife was delightful. Graham was going to see somebody off at the airport tomorrow, when I was going, so I might see him there. It was their lawyer that he was seeing off, Wilfred Evill. I had heard of him. He had been there ten days, collecting canvases and stopping Sutherland from working.

"Why not paint him?" I suggested.

She said, "Lawyers are not a good subject. Besides, Graham is on the point of changing."

"To what?"

"That's just it—he doesn't know. It's nearly driven him mad having a lawyer here."

I thanked her and went down the steep, dark stairs. She shouted down the well, "I shall tell him a gentleman in a red waistcoat. I don't know your name, do I, Waistcoat?"

I shouted it back, but I doubt whether she heard me, and I would rather be a stranger robin anyway.

My father and Joseph drove me to the airport the next day. I recognized a man of medium height, compact, with a brown humorous face and strong hands, and said, "You must be Sutherland."

"And you must be Michael Powell."

We talked for a while. His lawyer, a huge old man, was buying mimosa. Sutherland was enthusiastic about my *Tales*. He had always wanted to make a tense murder mystery in the reeds at the mouth of the River Var.

"There are passages through the reeds like a cathedral."

I said that I would ask Simenon to write it for him.

"He's very big, your lawyer."

"Monolithic."

Back in London, Columba was ten months old and Frankie said he had missed me, perhaps because it was only now that she realized that I really was going round the world. She also reported with some pride that when Kevin was playing with his little brother on the floor and blocking his movements, Columba just simply bit him, much to Kevin's surprise and outrage, for he loved his little brother and, being an optimist, expected to be loved in return. Frankie also had news of Monique.

If you cast your mind back a century or two, you will remember Robert Taylor, one of the brightest stars in the MGM constellation. He was beautiful, unlike Wallace Beery, and innocent, unlike William Powell. He played kings and outlaws. He was the Yank in *A Yank at Oxford*. He was the soldier in *Waterloo Bridge*. He had dark hair, fine eyes, and all the girls wanted to mother him, and all the mothers wanted to sleep with him. He was box office, and here he was sitting at the bar at Lay-zay in Park Lane, London W.1. I don't know how you spell Lay-zay, but that is what we all called John Mills's lovely bar and restaurant, Les Ambassadeurs: Les A.—get it? And this was the big, six-foot-three John Mills, gambler and connoisseur, not little Johnnie Mills, one of the best actors we have ever had in England, but who is so small that when they couldn't find a *pissoir* in a Paris bar and all had to pee in the washbasin, somebody had to lift Johnnie up so that he could do it too. But I digress. Back to Robert Taylor and Les A.

I introduced myself, and we were soon deep in Culver City gossip. Monique arrived. Her apartment was only a few hundred yards away in Curzon Street, so she had walked. She wore black, no jewelry, and looked stunning. Since Edmond's death she had lost a lot of weight, but not those curves. She pinpointed Robert Taylor at once, but said nothing. I kissed her on both cheeks and introduced her: "Madame Ludmilla Tcherina, who . . . etc."

There was a burst of flame and Robert stood carbonized, like those figures in Pompeii or Herculaneum that stood for two thousand years when the two cities were destroyed and then collapsed into a heap of ashes on being touched. Monique gave him the wide eyes.

"You are Robert Tyler, no?"

The ashen figure mumbled something and we all had dinner together. Frankie joined us, thus supplying the answer to a hundred questions that were overcrowding the brain behind that manly façade. He kept on looking at Monique with his mouth half open,

> . . . like stout Cortez,
> When with eagle eyes
> He star'd at the Pacific.

He just couldn't believe his luck. It must be remembered that Monique was then, as she is now, one of the most beautiful, elegant, and desirable women in Europe, while behind those beautiful breasts beats the warm heart of a friendly puppy.

The dinner over, he stammered a request to see her home, or take her to a nightclub, perhaps? A little yawn was stifled.

"Not tonight. I am tired. Another night perhaps."

Frankie and I exchanged a look, a nod. Monique was going to be off our hands for some time. All four of us walked down to her apartment block, into which she then vanished after kisses all round and allowing her hand to be kissed by her stuttering swain.

Robert was making one of those strenuous movies. Perhaps it was *Ivanhoe.* Anyway, our old friend George Sanders always played the heavy. They were planned and designed by Uncle Alfred, who was now head of the MGM art department, and directed by a competent hack from Hollywood. They rumbled off the assembly line, these historical romances, heavy, gleaming, and spectacular, like the Intercontinental Express. And like the Intercontinental Express, they were a little bit slow. This meant that Robert's days were occupied, but his nights were free—if you can call it freedom to be called every morning at 5:00 A.M., ready made-up and in full armor at 9:00. Monique gave us a blow-by-blow account of the courtship. They dined together every night, but the problem was going to be to keep him awake long enough. Frankie was fond of Monique, partly because of Edmond. I hazarded a guess that Monique was ready to work again, and might possibly be thinking of a Hollywood career. But Frankie said no.

"A little love affair would do her good, I don't say it wouldn't. But she is a peasant at heart, and what she is looking for now is security—and love—and a man who can give her both these things. She's flattered now, and enjoys being made a fuss of, but you'll see, she'll marry another Frenchman."

"Why a Frenchman?"

"Because of the language, and because of Paris. If you were an artist and a woman, wouldn't you choose Paris? I would. The man she marries must be rich, very rich."

Frankie knew. She really worked at being a woman. Appearances meant nothing to her. Instinct was in everything she did or said. All of the things that she prophesied came to pass. It mustn't be supposed that she strung all these apothegms together in one connected and coherent speech. That was not Frankie's way. It was a word here, or a sentence there. But she was always right.

As for Robert, he proved to be a martyr to lumbago—you heard me, lumbago. No, not plumbago—that's um, well, whatever it is. Lumbago gets you in the lumbar region, after you and George Sanders have been jousting all day, whanging away at one another with seven-foot swords in full armor. The great day came, or rather the great night. There was dinner in the private suite. There was the gleam of diamonds—and then lumbago struck! It was tragic. It was comic. Monique couldn't stop giggling. As he was in great pain, Robert was furious. Then he saw the joke and started laughing, and they ended up rolling about the floor, roaring with laughter. Monique put him to bed with a heating pad on his lumbar region, and let herself out.

Robert's romance was over, but he had got himself a nurse, and a week later Frankie's words began to come true. Monique had to go to Paris to sign some papers, and Raymond Roi appeared upon the horizon.

＝

Vincent Massey, Raymond Massey's brother, was in town to see his tailor. He had just been appointed Governor-General of Canada, and had to have a Court uniform to be sworn in. He was a small man, with the heart of a lion. The head cutter of Lesley and Roberts was Mr. Robinson, and he was a character. A taste for tailors makes the whole world kin. Robinson was my tailor too. He had been with the firm from the beginning, as an apprentice. He was a very spry, rather dapper Cockney Jew. His hair and mustache curled inquisitively, to set off his bright eyes and inquiring nose. He loved to tell stories, and he told them very well. He was an artist, he was imaginative.

Robbie had cut for the Massey brothers since they were at Balliol, and now Vincent was to succeed Lord Tweedsmuir as Governor-General of Canada. It was February 1, 1952. I had sauntered down to Hanover Square that morning, carrying a parcel of tweed that I had ordered from the Isle of Skye. I hoped Robbie would approve of the tweed, which was a lovely green color, and would feel inspired to make me an Inverness cape, a garment I had always wanted, but Robbie was too excited that morning to give me the service I was used to from him.

"You must see Mr. Vincent Massey, sir!"

"I have, Robbie. I missed you at the house, but I heard all about your visit."

"There, sir . . . wasn't that a miracle! I never heard of such a thing . . . not an inch to alter!"

Susan Tweedsmuir, writing to Vincent to congratulate him, had suggested that John Buchan's official uniform would fit Vincent, and begged him to accept it as a present. It came in tin boxes, rich with embroidery and stiff with epaulettes, and crowned by a cocked hat, adorned with nodding plumes. We had had a dress rehearsal the evening before, when the chief admiration of the ladies was reserved for the wonderful tin boxes in which the pieces of the uniform were contained. And when Robbie came to mark it for alterations— lo!—it fitted Vincent so perfectly that not one thing remained to be done. We all, not the least Robbie, felt that it was a happy augury for the new Governor-General. Robbie went on and on. He was convinced that it was a unique occurrence in the history of court tailoring.

On that same memorable evening, Vincent recommended that I add the drama *Icaro*, by Lauro de Bosis, to my *Tales*. *Yes, that's all very well*, you say, *but what happened to the Inverness cape? Did he approve of the tweed, or not?* Yes. Eventually, I won him over, and we lined the cape with Irish saffron tweed. Thirty-five years later, I still wear it every winter. When the leaves of the horse chestnuts at the top of the garden start to fall, my Inverness cape is brought out, inspected for moth holes, brushed, cleaned by hand if necessary, and worn until the swallows return in the spring. Its comforting warmth envelops me, and as I strike my stick on the ground to test its frostiness, Robbie's mischievous Cockney face, with those large, luminous, Jewish eyes, appears before me, and I remember his voice saying, "Did I ever tell you 'ow I had to fit the Marquess of Ripon with his riding breeches, sir? I didn't? Well, you know riding breeches have to be fitted on an 'orse"—Robbie meant a wooden horse, of course—"and his lordship wouldn't come into the show-room to be fitted, so someone had to take the 'orse to 'im. I was the youngest apprentice, fourteen years old, and hadn't got me growth yet, so, of course, I was the one to do it.

" 'How'm I to take the old bastard his 'orse?' I asked the head cutter.

" 'In a barrow,' he said, 'a wheelbarrow.'

"Had to go down to the mews and borrow one, clean all the horseshit out of it, and put the 'orse in it. At the shop, they were all taking the mickey out of me. I was near crying, but I didn't show it.

" 'White's Club,' says the cutter, which means I have to wheel the 'orse

down Bond Street, across Piccadilly, and down St. James's, and all the apprentices and the cabbies laughin'. Cor . . . I'll never forget it. And when I get to
White's, the head porter complains that I smells of horseshit."

Dear, wonderful Robbie—if Charles Dickens could have met you, he would
have jumped for joy.

=

I came back to Melbury Road to find Hugh French waiting for me. Hugh was
one of my boys, an actor I believed in, but who hadn't yet made the grade.
Patrick Macnee was another. Hugh was a good actor, but his heart wasn't in
it. He described himself as the poor man's David Niven. His destiny was surely
Hollywood, but not as an actor—as an agent. Hugh was the nephew of
Harold French, who had played the title role in one of my early quota-
quickies, *Star Reporter.* He was an excellent director of comedy, and I learned
a lot about speed and timing from him. When the war came, and I was
banging around Canada directing *49th Parallel,* he got his chance and became a film director on one of those wartime films about Norwegian resistance and heavy water. Deborah Kerr was in it, and he nearly succeeded in
stealing her away from me—nearly, but not quite.

So it was Harold's nephew who brought me an invitation from Hughie
Green, a showbiz personality with more than one string to his bow. He was
a ferry pilot, and was flying a Dakota over the Greenland icecap to New York.
He suggested I come as passenger for the experience. Hughie was a pilot with
many thousands of flying hours to his credit, and at this time, so soon after
the war, with so many aircraft changing hands, ferry pilots were earning big
money and were in great demand. The home port of the aircraft in question
was Bombay, where she had belonged to a Parsi businessman. The plane had
one memorable feature: an iron lung fixed up inside. The original owner had
poor health. He had now sold the plane to a Greek businessman with aspira-
tions to be a theatrical producer. With a name like Toni Couloucoundis, he
could hardly fail to achieve this. He was flying with the aircraft to New York.
Space was limited because of the iron lung, but there was room for me if I
were traveling light. I had only to say the word. I said it.

My son Kevin was now rising seven, and had been my self-constituted
guardian and adviser ever since the epic drive from London to Positano had
revealed to him the horrors of modern travel. He had followed me all over
Europe, picking up scripts, hats, and coats abandoned by their absentminded
owner. He saw to it that I was in time for trains, planes, and ships. When he
heard that I planned to go around the world without him he was worried.
When he heard of this new plan he was seriously disturbed.

"Daddy, are you really going to fly over the Greenland icecap in a private
aircraft?"

"Looks like it."

"I've been looking at the globe in the library . . . the one with Captain Cook's voyages on it. . . . Daddy!"

"Yes?"

"Would you mind telling me your route?"

"Oh . . . Prestwick . . . that's in Scotland, near Glasgow . . . Keflavík, that's Iceland . . . Greenland, Bluie West One, that's an American army post, like Keflavík . . . then Goose Bay in Labrador, that's Canada . . . Moncton . . . Dorval, and down the Hudson River to New York."

"La Guardia Airport, Daddy?"

"No, they've got a new one now. It's called Idlewild—somewhere out in the marshes . . ."

All of a sudden Hughie Green was on the telephone. "Michael? . . . Hughie . . . we leave on Saturday at nine o'clock from Croydon."

"Croydon! It's not much bigger than a cricket pitch!"

It was from Croydon that those great, lumbering aircraft of British Imperial Airways, with names like *Hannibal* and *Hamilcar*, got airborne . . . Why, it was a grass runway! . . . but aloud I said meekly, "Okay."

"Daddy!"

"M-m-m?"

"You've got thirteen pieces of baggage."

Bill had packed everything.

"Have I got thirteen pieces of luggage, Bill?"

"Aye."

"There can't be!"

"There are, Daddy. I've counted them:

      two suitcases
      a shoe case
      an overnight bag
      a last-minute bag
      an accessory bag
      two briefcases
      a file case
      a case of books
      a box full of Staffordshire pottery
      a box with a dozen Wexford wineglasses
      a cardboard tube with sketch plans for the decor
        for the play *Hanging Judge*
      and a camera bag."

"Well, we'll have to smuggle them on, somehow."

Saturday dawned. At the last minute, Hugh French decided to go with us. He telephoned Hughie Green, who was not encouraging: overweight already. But Hugh persisted, and went to get some shirts from the cleaner's. Kevin, game to the last, went with us to Croydon.

There was the aircraft: a silver Dakota, with a red stripe! To Kevin's intense excitement, we drove right up to it. There certainly wasn't much room for passengers. The famous iron lung took up half of the space, and four comfortable chairs had been rooted out to make room for an extra petrol tank. By the time the chairs had been piled in again as freight, there was even less room. Hugh French's chances began to look pretty slim.

Hughie Green appeared, tall, bony, blond, and imperturbable, with a faint aura of recklessness about him. He taxied the Dakota out to the runway, and Bill, Kevin, and I loaded up, feverishly hoping that nobody could count up to thirteen. And now, here was poor Hugh French, with his shirts over his arm, being refused a passage! We all pleaded for him, but Hughie was adamant: "Too many people already. We'd never get off the ground. All aboard!"

Kevin rushed into my arms and kissed me goodbye, manfully suppressing tears, grabbed Bill, hung on to his hand, and they both waved. Bill's hat was blown off as Hughie, treating the machine like a motorbike, taxied to the beginning of the runway. He wheeled around sharply, and started to rev up the engine, until the roar of the motors drowned every other sound. The aircraft rattled and banged, and our teeth chattered. All of a sudden Hughie slammed in the clutch, and we shot forward and upward, doing an almost vertical takeoff, clearing the end of the runway and somebody's garden fence by fifty yards. Yippee! Prestwick, here we come!

In the winter of 1952, Irish Shannon and Scottish Prestwick were important international airports. We were supposed to refuel at Prestwick and press on to Keflavík in Iceland. In actuality, we were becalmed in bonnie Scotland for four days and nights. Hughie explained, "There's ground fog over Iceland, and supercool water droplets."

"What on earth are they?"

"Large drops of water that turn into ice as soon as we go down, and mushroom out on us. In less than a minute, we can be carrying a ton of ice on our wings."

"What then?"

"If we don't ditch, and miss the runway on the landing, we might be too heavy to get up again."

Iceland would be only a stepping-stone for us. The long haul was over the icecap to Bluie. The Yanks had established, and were running, Keflavík and Bluie West One in Greenland as part of their Distant Early Warning system—

the DEW Line. Luckily for all of us, there was room at the inn. I lay on my bed and read. Guy Bolton had sent me a translation he had made of a play called *Anastasia*, by a French woman writer, Marcelle Maurette. It was first-rate. What a part for Jennifer Jones! Then I read *Icaro*, by Lauro de Bosis, the Italian poet who learned to fly, flew over Rome in the afternoon scattering anti-Fascist leaflets, and was shot down by Fascist planes into the Tyrrhenian Sea. I chalked it up as another of my *Tales*.

The next morning we all went down to the Met Office. We looked at the long, straight lines of our approach to Iceland, then at the lowering circle of fog sketched on the big map, pushed up by the wavy warm currents from the southwest, then at the board with signs and figures scribbled in chalk against a list of names, beautiful names: Dorval, Stevenville, Goose, Keflavík, Moncton, New York. The men in shirtsleeves were quietly drawing lines over the clean maps of the North Atlantic, from Gibraltar to Montreal. This large-spread, quiet activity, this awareness of winds and temperatures over a great and tempestuous area, reminded me of Nelson's brooding eye during the months before Trafalgar.

We all began to realize that we were not going to get away that day either, and everybody rushed to telephone their offices. I phoned Kevin. Frankie said, "If you've time to spare, travel by air."

Next morning, conditions were worse . . . we were not going. We waited. At eleven, we were going . . . definitely. We all packed, and gave up our rooms. At noon, the ceiling was right down over our destination . . . we didn't go. There was a scramble for beds. But the waiting ferry pilots were cheering up. The American captain of the Lodestar said good night at eight o'clock, and went to bed. He was going to be up at 2:00 A.M. Visibility was improving every hour.

Suddenly, it was daylight, and in a flurry of men and machines, we were airborne at 7:30. The cloud ceiling was at fifteen hundred feet, and as we burst through we saw only the high tops of the Highlands, sticking out like thumbs in a giant's pudding . . . there were the Paps of Jura, modestly unveiling . . . the lone peak was Cruachan, and the other one . . . no . . . yes . . . yes, it was Ben Nevis.

The cloud smothered everything. We headed out over the sea, over the islands of St. Kilda, alas invisible below us. We droned on for two hours, and then . . . there was the front, the great wall of fog ten thousand feet high, which was thrown up by the meeting of human warmth with Arctic cold. Everyone feared the front. It stretched across the top of the world, like a huge, invisible frontier, anything from ten thousand to twenty thousand feet high. We droned along the edge for two hours, then suddenly burst out, and there ahead was a formidable coastline of mountains streaked with snow: Iceland!

The big snowcap and glacier to the east had the sun full on it. Through the glasses I could see the tortured flanks of the mountains, the red rocks, and the gleam of glaciers. This was Mount Hecla, whose gaping mouth was reputed by the ancients to be the gate of Hades. We circled round and round, and now we were over the land and over Keflavík.

We could see the red-roofed buildings beside the sea. Hughie was awaiting permission to land, and I joined him and his copilot, Neville, in the bows. Attention was riveted on the landing strip, when suddenly there was a scuffle aft. When you are a small crew you become very conscious of each other. Toni appeared from the iron lung accompanied by someone else—but there was no one else! But there was. We had a stowaway on board, a girl, for Christ's sake! They don't have cabin boys anymore. We all knew her. She had been at all the parties in Prestwick. She was a Brenda, a Paula, or a Mona— that sort of girl. What did we want with a stowaway?

Hughie, intent on landing, snapped, "We'll dump her in Iceland."

"They won't let her land without papers," said Neville.

Toni Couloucoundis contented himself with "Oh, you awful girl!"

But the stowaway was tough. "I want to go to America," she said. "You'll have to take me with you, won't you?"

"Hello, Dakota? You may land now, Captain. Circle out to sea, and come in on the beam. Please have all your papers, and those of your party, ready for inspection."

An hour later, we were on our way to Greenland, stowaway included. She knew her stuff, all right. It was probably not the first time. At Keflavík, Hughie had been refused permission to dump her.

"Sorry, Captain, you'll have to take her back to Prestwick, or on with you."

"Why me? It'll be dark before we get to Bluie. How do I know they'll let us land with a stowaway on board?"

"That's your business, Captain. Good luck." Then a change of tone. "Don't worry, Captain. She's not a bad-looking dame. They'll let her land at Bluie, all right. Dames are in short supply at Bluie. There's always room for a new piece of tail."

We had landed at Keflavík in a sudden snowstorm, the landscape glittering with light, ahead of us a green-gold curtain of sunlight with a black hill looming in the middle of it. We were now in a United States army vehicle, and were at once in America. Everything proceeded at a slow, easy tempo, and with vast efficiency. All our documents were ready for us, and within half an hour we were eating a typical American meal in the canteen—slices of ham covered in syrup, canned asparagus, a heap of something sweet, tinned peaches, coffee: $1.20. Poor Hugh French! Why didn't I think of stowing him away in the iron lung?

Hughie was champing at the bit. As we trooped out into the hall we were accosted by a vast, shapeless figure wearing a red-peaked cap and looking like a crazed baseball player. However, I recognized the crumpled face and blue eyes: it was our friend from Prestwick, the captain of the Lodestar, in working dress. He would be leaving before us.

"I'll keep drinks waiting for you at the canteen at Bluie. We are next, and then two Doves."

An army officer, lounging in the doorway, said, "You bound for Canada?"

"New York."

"So what's your speed?"

"One-sixty."

"So what are those cute little aircraft behind you?"

"De Havilland Doves."

"And what speed do they do?"

"Two hundred."

"Are you kind of mothering them?"

"Looks like it."

As we taxied out the Doves were right behind us, and when we took off, they took off. It was instructive to watch the stowaway, no longer a stowaway but a listed passenger, unheralded, unsung but accepted. Of course, half her job was done for her by being the only woman on board. She set her sights on Hughie, not only as the captain of the aircraft, but as a showbiz personality and an actor. In no time she was up in the nose beside Hughie, asking dumb questions and getting first condescending, then friendly, answers. The copilot had no opinion of his own, and followed his captain's lead. The girl was a two-legger, approved by the skipper, and that was good enough for him. Toni Couloucoundis was busy drawing up statements for the girl to sign. He didn't intend to be responsible for a stowaway in New York, and I didn't blame him. I wrote up my diary, and waited for her to come to me. She cast several glances in my direction, but I didn't see her. Finally, she picked her way through and around the crowded aircraft to my side.

"What are you writing?"

"Diary."

"About the flight?"

"About you."

She tittered. "Little me. It was a crazy thing to do, wasn't it? But I've never been to New York."

"You're not there, yet. Maybe they won't let you land."

"They will. You'll see."

The calm certainty of her trust in the power of sex made me laugh in spite of myself.

"You're a tramp."

"Yes, I'm a tramp. See you."

She picked her way over to Toni Couloucoundis. After all, he was the owner.

It was clear over the Greenland icecap. We were going over the top of the world at ten thousand feet. To the north a narrow line appeared. It broadened until it filled the whole horizon. The pack ice! We passengers strained our eyes ahead, and saw sharp-toothed mountains rising out of what looked like a bank of clouds. Below us, the open water had gone. We were flying over a world of ice. Then we could see that the cloud out of which the mountains rose was not cloud, but ice. Central Greenland is a great dome of ice thousands of feet thick. The jagged mountains that rise up out of it are seven thousand to nine thousand feet high.

We sailed on for an hour over this beautiful and terrible landscape. There was not a cloud in the sky, and a low sun threw fantastic shadows at these giant peaks, across the ice dome. At one point, a great master peak soared up to only a few hundred feet below us. Then we were over the top and a huge fjord opened up. This was what Hughie had been looking for. We followed it down until it led us to open water, fed by huge glaciers. Hughie took a great sweep around with the aircraft, over ghastly hills and terrible crevasses. Then, with the regal assurance of a golden eagle coming down to his eyrie, he descended, thousand feet after thousand feet, our ears crackling and our eyes dazzling, until we were between the cliffs and rushing over black water. Broken ice appeared and then the runway, and we were landing with scarcely a bump—and there was the Lodestar ahead of us, waiting for us, while behind us the two Doves landed primly and followed us until they swung around and came to a halt, primping their feathers.

Apparently, the official name for Bluie West One was Narsarssuak Air Base, U.S. Army.

We saw a sign, "Hotel Gink," and went in. Everyone was welcome, especially our stowaway. There was a mixture of civilian and service personnel. Everyone was friendly. Unlike a British air base, nobody looked at you as if a civilian were the lowest form of human life. You were just a newcomer to be welcomed and questioned in the friendly manner with which Americans question each other. Dinner was seventy-two cents: clam chowder, roast pork, mashed potatoes, turnips and succotash, masses of soggy vegetables piled up on your plate, followed by tinned fruit and cawfee. Drinks at the bar were thirty cents. Hughie planted the stowaway on a stool at the bar and said to the barman, "Fill her up."

She soon had a crowd around her. The movie theatre was showing Burt Lancaster in *Ten Tall Men*. There was quite a queue to take the stowaway outside to see the aurora borealis. It was cold outside—20 degrees below.

We stayed at Bluie three days and nights, prisoners of the front. Everyone was furious, except our stowaway. She was having a whale of a time. Once you had walked up the road to married quarters, and down the road to the jetty, there was not much to do at Bluie except date our stowaway. There was an Eskimo village on the other side of the fjord, but all contact with the Eskimo was strictly forbidden, and enforced by a representative of the Danish government. This was not for moral or immoral reasons, but just plain precautions for health. Greenland is so completely germ-free that a visitor coming from outside with just a common cold could decimate a community. I had encountered the same problem on the island of Foula, in the Shetlands, when I made *The Edge of the World.* The islanders called it "the boat cold," and were cautious about too close a contact with casual visitors.

However, the captain of the Lodestar became a pal. We would go fishing for trout in the river, with an ax to cut holes in the ice, or for cod off the end of the jetty. He had been a ferry pilot during the war and now had been called up again at short notice. He had flown eleven thousand hours. His face was crumpled, because he had lost all his teeth from malaria, contracted in the Pacific in 1942.

All the ferry pilots were getting restive. The reports from Goose, in Labrador, were discouraging. They were having everything thrown at them: snow, ice, wind. Finally one of the Doves decided to try and make Goose. It flew off at about 1500. The pilot had invited our stowaway to go with him, but she had refused, deciding there was safety in numbers. The old hands were worried. We were all getting jumpy.

The next day was Saturday, March 1. If you've time to spare, travel by air. I got up early and went down. The captain of the Lodestar was going down to the Met Office, and gave me a lift in his jeep.

"The Dove didn't make it," he observed with his eyes on the road.

"Where?"

"Oh . . . Goose. Guess she was iced up. That runway is too short."

"Did they get away with it?"

"Don't know. But Goose has wired up for their names and next of kin."

The sun had gone in, and the wind was blowing in fierce gusts. I thought sadly of the poor Dove, its wings iced up, nipping into Goose in the dark, circling, calling, crashing, burning.

At breakfast, nobody said anything but our stowaway.

"To think that I nearly went with him. Such a nice boy, too."

A stout trencherwoman, she could eat nothing.

Walking back to the recreation hut, the wind was so strong that we could let ourselves be blown along over the icy ground. It came off the icecap, and was cold enough to strike through my duffel coat and three sweaters. Even

Greenland could hardly keep this up and Hughie said it would be followed by a calm, and we would all get off the next day.

Hughie was right. We flew south down the fjord, and I got another clear look back at the extraordinary Greenland icecap, a fearful sight with the peaks of suffocated mountains struggling to get out of the domes of ice—an inspiration to any poet, a Milton or a Coleridge. I felt vast phrases burgeoning within me. I might have missed my appointment with Mr. William S. Paley, but I had seen the Greenland icecap, and followed the path to the Vikings who discovered America.

Soon we were flying over the barrens, lakes, and forests. Labrador has trees, Greenland none. Then we were over Goose Bay and coming in to land. It was impressive to think how men had worked out this air and sea route and now flew daily, and with confidence, over certain death. The Lodestar landed right behind us at Goose, and we all saw the wreckage of the Dove. Both pilot and copilot were killed. Nobody said much about it. They lived with it.

Nobody wanted our stowaway at Goose, and nobody wanted her at Dorval. They grinned at Hughie: "She's yours, Captain. Take her on to New York."

Her manner was more confident than ever. Cheek can take you a long way. We flew over the Catskills and down the Hudson, along the Palisades, and over the George Washington Bridge, past the towers of New York, over the Battery and over the islands, over the marshes and out to sea, and there was the new port of Idlewild, half sea and half land, for the whole airport had been reclaimed from the marshes. We circled like a weary duck and settled down on the runway, with a fierce crosswind blowing but with good visibility, and none of the snow blizzards we were threatened with.

The date: Monday, March 3; time out of Bombay, twenty-eight days; 8,500 miles, no navigator, only one crew, and an anxious owner on board. Not a bump, not a jar, nor a mistaken judgment the whole trip. I put my hat on, took it off to Captain Green.

The immigration officer, after some badinage, gave our stowaway a week to see the sights, and then go home.

"And mind she does go home, Captain. We hold you responsible."

Then, to the girl, "What are you doing tonight, beautiful?"

≡

We finally left the field with all our baggage in two taxis. I dropped Hughie, Toni, the copilot, and the unrepentant stowaway at the Paramount Hotel, then went on to the St. Regis. Salvador Dalí was seated in his usual chair in the lobby, balancing an elegant cane in his right hand, a long cigarette holder and an even longer cigarette in his left, his mustache two needlepoints.

"Bonjour, maître."

"Bonjour, Miguel. Tu as bonne mien."

"Tu crois?"

I signed on and went up to my room, counted the pieces of baggage, and tipped the porter. I sat on my bed, and a great weariness swept over me. I lay back, went to sleep, and woke at half past seven the next morning. I ordered a full St. Regis breakfast and had a shower. The breakfast arrived with a clatter of lids like a Bren carrier, and proved to be stone cold. I remembered that I was in New York. The telephone rang.

"Micky? . . . Ray. Welcome to New York. Dorothy sends her love. We have an appointment at the Chrysler Building to meet Walter P. Chrysler, Jr."

The Chrysler Building stands at Lexington and Forty-third Street, the St. Regis at Fifty-fifth and Fifth. I hurried down Fifth Avenue, against a stream of New Yorkers heading for their midmorning coffee at Schrafft's. It was a bright, windy morning in March. Several citizens passed remarks about my London bowler hat and my malacca cane. I turned east on Forty-third Street. I had never had a good look at the Chrysler Building before, and it was impressive. So was the Art Deco revolving door. The whoop of a whooping crane caused every head to turn to where Ray stood, towering over the crowd and flapping his wings.*

Ray was escorted by the chief of the Chrysler police, and a formidable couple they made. The guard unlocked the door of a private elevator, and we were whisked up to the fourth floor. More locking and unlocking and we found ourselves in the sort of salon you would expect to find in a French château, the walls lined with paintings of a decidedly mixed quality. I saw one Matisse that I knew, and nodded to it with familiarity.

"Mr. Chrysler will join you gentlemen shortly," said the guard. A colored maid brought coffee.

"Explain," I said.

"It's *The Hanging Judge*," said Ray.

The coin dropped. In the spring, when we had come over for *Hoffmann*, Ray had told me that he was writing a play for production in London, and that he wanted me to direct it in the summer.

"It's *The Hound of the Baskervilles*," he had roared enthusiastically. "I always wanted to do it. We'll have loudspeakers all over the theatre. Gee, I can hear the howling of that hound at the beginning and end of each act."

---

*Michael writes of Massey in the first volume of his autobiography: " . . . only his friends knew his cavernous laugh and the enthusiasm with which he tangled up his sentences when carried away on the wings of his imagination. When he started the inevitable whooping and crowing with excitement, so that his words and phrases became unintelligible, Dorothy would say: 'Whoops! There he goes again.' "

I could see that Ray wanted to play Sherlock Holmes—who wouldn't?—and decided to kill it once and for all.

"There's no part for you in *The Hound of the Baskervilles*," I said firmly.

"I thought, perhaps, Holmes?" he faltered.

I was brutal: "You're too old. Every actor who ever plays the part is too old. Watson was a young medical man, who had knocked about the world like Conan Doyle himself, and Holmes was in his thirties, and in the peak of condition."

I was talking myself out of several million dollars, but art is art. Ray had then brought up his reserves, and suggested *Hanging Judge*. I read the book in bed. It was by Bruce Hamilton, brother of Patrick Hamilton, the author of *Rope, Hangover Square*, and *Gaslight*. They were both good storytellers, but there the likeness ended. Patrick was a dramatist and a master of the cat-and-mouse situation, while Bruce was a novelist who had tumbled on a good dramatic idea. The chief character was one of Her Majesty's judges who was leading a double life. Hardly original, I said to myself, but press on! To his brother judges, he is an admirable judge but a bit too fond of the cap and the rope.* His life is an open book. When not on circuit he lives at his London club. He spends his holidays abroad. Weekends he stays at his sister's cottage in the country. The telephone is ex-directory.† In his well-ordered life he has overlooked only one detail. In *Who's Who at the Bar*, Sir George is listed as the only child of his father. He has no brothers or sisters.

At his club Sir George is tolerated and respected. The Home Secretary, who is also a member of the club, may perhaps feel a bit queasy to hear Sir George order a double scramble of eggs on the morning of one of his hangings. But then the Home Secretary doesn't believe in capital punishment.

I yawned and riffled the pages. Of course, Sir George has a mistress in his country cottage, and of course Sir George is accused of a murder that he didn't commit, and after a protracted trial by jury he is condemned to hang by the neck until he is dead. So far, this was a simple Balzacian tragedy; but now came the twist. The judge's mistress joins forces with his greatest enemy at the club to prove that he has been unjustly condemned. At the last minute they discover the truth and get a reprieve from the Home Secretary, but they arrive too late at the prison and the judge is hanged.

A door in the books opened and Walter Chrysler came in. He was short, dark, and chunky with beautiful eyes, and I found him attractive. He asked my opinion of the Matisse, and was pleased when I said it was a good one and

*In the days when England still had the death penalty, the judge would don a special cap when he sentenced someone to death by hanging.
†Unlisted.

that I knew the master. He liked the idea of producing a play in London. What did I think of Ray's alternative subject, *Hanging Judge*? I said I liked it better than Sherlock Holmes. Ray was already working on a draft of the play, and I would be back in London at the beginning of April, when we would decide to go ahead or not. I was asked what it would cost and I said I hadn't the remotest idea, but that plays with murder trials in them were always expensive—too big a cast.

Ray rushed back to Norwalk to write the play, and I rang the office for Loews, Incorporated. Arthur Loew came on the phone: "I was hoping you'd show up. Come and have lunch at the office. We can meet Bill Paley together."

The fabulous offices of Loews, Inc., were in Times Square, all brass and glass and elevators. The presidential office was . . . well, presidential. There were some nice things to see while you waited. Arthur was a bit of a connoisseur, and a millionaire, which always helps, and he had some pretty pictures and a lot of Central American art, some of it genuine.

We rang Bill Paley at CBS. He was in Jamaica. Arthur exploded. "Goddamn it! . . . How does he do it? . . . He's never in his office! Look at me! I can't call my soul my own since I became president, and he takes a vacation whenever he feels like it!"

He hesitated and looked at me. "What do you want to do?"

I shrugged. "Stick around for a bit. When do they expect him back?"

Arthur spoke to the secretary.

"She thinks a week."

"Okay. The Hollywood awards aren't for two weeks, yet. I've got plenty of people to see—you for a start."

He grinned. "Don't try to sell *me* your art for art's sake program. Loews is in the business of art to make money."

I pointed to a picture of some apples on his wall.

"Arthur, do you think that Cézanne painted that picture for money? He painted it because he was loving it and looking at it, because apples were good, and good to eat, because he had a problem in the relation of the apples with the dish and with the background." He was listening. "What did you pay for it?"

He grimaced. "Six figures."

"Six big figures?"

He nodded.

"Cézanne's agent got him three thousand francs for the painting, among a bunch of others. The agent and Cézanne were happy. Are you happy?"

He laughed out loud. "Very happy."

"And yet you say there is no money in art, Arthur."

"I was talking about films."

"And I am talking about art. All art is one, Arthur—one. We must give the public of our best, or else we die. We who love art, but are not great artists, have a responsibility to the audience. How many years did people look at that little yellow chair of Van Gogh's, and wonder why he painted it? It's only an ugly little chair, they said, and now, a hundred years later, it is *the* chair—the chair of chairs—because the man who painted it didn't cheat. Arthur, would you describe *The Red Shoes* and *The Tales of Hoffmann* as works of art?"

He had stopped smiling. "Yes, I would."

"Are they going to make money?"

"Yes, a lot of money."

"And yet, in both films the theme was that art was worth dying for. Emeric and I, and all those artists we got together on the two films, believed this, and we made the public believe it too. That is why I want to give them the best. Ninety-nine percent of the best creative artists in the world—composers, painters, sculptors, actors, singers, writers—never get to the great film public, because there is no way for them to do it. I want to open this way for them. Dylan Thomas said to me, 'Every story has to have its own length!' That's an artist speaking. I am in touch with all these artists. I can bring you and Bill Paley twenty hours of the most wonderful entertainment in the world, and *you* don't want to talk about art!"

The buzzer rang. A silvery voice: "Shall we bring the lunch in, Mr. Loew?"

"Yes, of course."

They wheeled it in. It was caviar, beluga *gros grain*, that beautiful gray caviar—not blackfish roe. We helped ourselves.

"At least you are an artist to your stomach, Arthur."

He gave me a sidelong look. "I'm looking forward to seeing you tangle with Bill Paley. From what I hear, you may get a surprise or two."

"Possibly. In England, the moviemakers look upon television as the great enemy. Have you heard of FIDO?"

"Fido?"

"Yes. The Film Industry Defence Organisation: FIDO. Bow-wow! The idea is to persuade independent producers not to sell their films to television, but to FIDO. Bow-wow!"

"Where does the money come from?"

"From distributors and exhibitors."

"That's like trying to hold back Niagara with a Band-Aid."

"You ain't whistling Dixie. Of course, the smart producers took FIDO money and sold their films to television anyway."

"Ha, ha!"

"Precisely. But I have a sneaking feeling that television will become not the great enemy of the movies, but our biggest market, and our greatest friend. All art is one, Arthur—one."

This period, 1950 to 1955, was to prove one of the great watersheds of the entertainment business, and most of the water came from the eyes of the exhibitors. Historically speaking, the first watershed had been the formation of the United Artists Corporation, in the peak days of the silent film, when power and finance were in the hands of the creative artists. Their reign was short but influential. Their names spelled quality, something to aim at and be proud of.

The second watershed was the coming of radio: sound without picture.

The third, the coming of the talking film: sound *and* pictures, when power passed to the great new entertainment corporations.

The war halted any further exploitation of the artists, but then came the fourth and greatest watershed: the coming of television, and all that that implies. The struggle goes on yet. Art is no longer important. Money talks. It talks the language of the businessman, and the businessman is not the most entertaining of conversationalists. The aim is no longer to entertain, but to make money. The artist works all his life in pursuit of an ideal, and thinks his life well spent. Ditto the businessman who invented the Xerox machine.

"Every story has to have its own length!"—this dictum of Dylan's rang in my head. I sat down in my hotel room and read two lists—Powell's *Films* and Powell's *Tales*. The films were assumed to be of conventional length, i.e., from ninety minutes to one hundred and ten minutes—long enough to be the main feature of a program, and short enough to stop the male members of the audience from sliding out to the toilet. Here they are, on that morning in March 1952:

1. *The Promotion of the Admiral*, starring Bette Davis, Gregory Peck, and Roger Livesey, based upon a short story by Morley Roberts, about the shanghaiing of an English admiral onto an American ship at a time when Yankee skippers used to race one another around the Horn from San Francisco to Boston.
2. *Trial and Error*, the autobiography of Chaim Weizmann, organic chemist and the first president of Israel.
3. *The Golden Years*, the autobiography of Richard Strauss, with *Salome* and *Der Rosenkavalier* as the high spots.
4. *1984*, by George Orwell.
5. *The Reason Why*, by Cecil Woodham-Smith, a new look at the Charge of the Light Brigade, with a script by John Whiting, based on Woodham-Smith's best-selling book, starring Rex Harrison as Lord Cardigan and James Mason as Lord Lucan.

6. *All Passion Spent*, by Victoria Sackville-West, in which Deborah Kerr would play a woman at nineteen, and the same woman at ninety.

7. *Columba*, by Prosper Mérimée, the author of *Carmen;* an English family doing the Grand Tour gets mixed up with blood feuds in Corsica.

8. *The Loving Eye*, by William Sansom, a back-garden romance.

9. *The Edwardians*, by Victoria Sackville-West; the heir to a great position, and to great possessions in Edwardian England, decides to opt out, with the encouragement of a famous explorer, starring Paul Scofield and Robert Mitchum.

10. *Anastasia*, by Marcelle Maurette; the resurrection of the tsar of Russia's long-lost daughter, believed murdered by the Bolsheviks; to star Jennifer Jones.

11. *The Rise and Fall of the British Nanny*, inspired by and adapted from the book by Jonathan Gathorne-Hardy; with the British nanny fell the British Empire.

12. *Alone*, to be shot entirely in the Antarctic, based on the book by Admiral Byrd, who spent the whole of the winter in Antarctica; to star Gary Cooper and five thousand penguins; script by Thornton Wilder.

These were all feature films of varying lengths. *Powell's Tales*, as distinct from *Films*, follow:

1. *The Odyssey* by Homer, libretto by Dylan Thomas, music by Stravinsky, decor and costumes by Hein Heckroth, to star Orson Welles. Two possible choices as subject: the song of the Sirens, or the love affair between the shipwrecked hero, Odysseus, and the king's daughter, Nausicaa. Length: about forty minutes. (I put these two tales at the top of the list, because they seemed to me to be highly charged, even for morons.)

2. *The Lotus of the Moon*, a Hindu love story of two immortal beings, by F. W. Bain, a tale of love that goes beyond death. About an hour. Music by Brian Easdale (composer of *The Red Shoes* and *Black Narcissus*), with an Oriental cast of actors and singers.

3. Léonide Massine's *Tales from the Arabian Nights*, decor and costumes by Henri Matisse, music by Rimsky-Korsakov and Mussorgsky. Each tale would be approximately forty minutes.

4. Graham Sutherland designs and directs *The Reeds, a Mystery*, a detective story laid in the south of France, written by Simenon.

5. A Lafcadio Hearn ghost story of Japan, directed by the Japanese director Akira Kurosawa. Length: about an hour and a half.

6. *Casanova's Homecoming*, an erotic fable by Arthur Schnitzler, to star Jean-Paul Belmondo.

7. *Tam O'Shanter* by Robert Burns, a Scottish ballad and ballet, with John Laurie as narrator of the poem, and Moira Shearer as Maggie.
8. *The Gentleman from America*, by Michael Arlen, a horrifying fable of cruelty and madness.
9. *In Bezhin Meadow*, from Turgenev's *Sportsman's Sketches;* tales told by boys in the animal corral at night. About two hours.
10. *The Murder of Christopher Marlowe*, an Elizabethan murder mystery, to star John Gielgud as Chris Marlowe, suggested by the book *The Death of Christopher Marlowe* by Professor J. Leslie Hotson, who also wrote *The First Night of Twelfth Night.*
11. *Gabriel Grub*, a ghost story by Dickens, to star Robert Helpmann, Alec Guinness, and Peter Ustinov.

There were lots more stories, and there still are, I'm glad to say. You directors, actors, writers, choreographers, and composers, who are always looking for a story, help yourselves.

While waiting for William S. Paley, I was playgoing and filmgoing. The best of the new plays was *The Shrike;* the best of the new films was *Rashomon.*

Rashomon was a sensation. It was like when *The Graduate* hit town sixteen years later. All we directors and actors, who thought we knew something about acting and directing, suddenly discovered that we knew nothing, and that a trip to the Little Carnegie movie theatre was a must. Suddenly, Japan was the in thing. On Fifty-seventh Street you heard nothing but Japanese: "Kurosava . . . Kurosawa . . . Akira Kurosawa," the in people trying to get their tongues around Japanese: "Mimune . . . Mifune . . . Toshiro Mifune . . . Towa . . . Toho . . . Teehee."

I joined the worshipers at the Little Carnegie shrine, and kissed the feet of this great director. Never had film as an art asserted itself and made its point more clearly. It was only seven years since Hiroshima, and suddenly all war memories and race prejudices were swept away, and everyone was talking about, and going to see, a simple murder mystery in simple black and white, obviously made with the slenderest of means, with no attempt at naturalism, but, on the contrary, elegant, formalized acting by all three principals, direction by a demon, a conjurer, a choreographer, and, quite obviously, a film buff who had seen everything, and who had no doubt that he could do better.

The story? There was no story, only a situation. But Kurosawa had us in the hollow of his hand. Every image, every twist in the plot revealed a master. His opening sequence in the pouring rain, the oldest gag in the world, riveted our attention. It was as if the same story had never been used before by unscrupulous movie directors: the beautiful, impassive, untouchable lady; the monosyllabic, narrow-headed nobleman, her husband; and their guide, their betrayer, in this story of rape and murder and mystery. There is nothing new about the story—but oh, the art with which it is unfolded, the skill with which it is handled! I came out walking on air.

And I was going to Japan! I would be there in ten days' time. With luck, I would meet this magician, and he would take me to meet Isamu Noguchi, the great architect and designer, who was obviously born to design one of my *Tales* . . . and then . . . and then . . .

I went that same day to the legitimate theatre, to see *The Shrike*, and was bowled over once again—by the integrity of the production and the performances by José Ferrer and his co-star Judith Evelyn. It was a classic production: one set and a small cast. Of course, I had heard all about this Puerto Rican actor, whose performance as D'Artagnan in his own production of *The Three Musketeers* had made him a star. Besides *The Shrike* he had two other productions running: Jan de Hartog's *The Four Poster*, starring—wait for it—Hume Cronyn and Jessica Tandy, and the all-male play *Stalag 17*; both long-running hits. And now here he was in full control, directing, producing, and starring in *The Shrike*. The shrike is a butcherbird that likes to display its victims impaled upon sharp thorns, so you can imagine that it was pretty powerful stuff that I was seeing that afternoon, and Joe knew that I was in front. We went round. Did I say "we"? Yes. Pamela was with me.

The Lady's Not for Burning was the talk of the town, but they had their matinee on a different day from *The Shrike*, and I had snatched Pamela from the Algonquin, where she was staying. Then I made a terrible mistake. I went to see Audrey Hepburn in the play of *Gigi*, not the film. Still, to have seen the film of *Gigi* first would have been an even more terrible mistake. It might have put me off showbiz altogether. There was nothing wrong with the star—she was delightful. And it wasn't the desperate attempts by the producer and the cast to be witty, smutty, and French. It was the tone that would have infuriated Colette, that and the overacting. The play was drawing a weird audience that saw a double entendre in every line of dialogue; perhaps there is—but I can't stand Colette. At least the show had given the girl the chance to show how she could handle herself onstage and show whether she had humor and courage and imagination and guts, and in all these things she came to meet the audience fairly and squarely and didn't let them down.

At that time, The Archers had no idea of making a film with Audrey Hepburn. She had appeared in several films in England, including *Secret People* directed by Thorold Dickinson. Audrey had flair and intelligence and Continental elegance allied with simplicity, and a natural feeling for form. She was the right shape for that year. But at the time she came on the market The Archers were working out their own destiny, and The Archers never fell into that old film trap of signing up the star first and then looking for a story.

Emeric and I were, certainly, looking for a story that we both liked, but that didn't include Audrey Hepburn. When America snapped her up we said to each other, There's another good girl gone to the Yanks.

Her first American picture, *Roman Holiday*, directed by William Wyler, made her a star, and Gregory Peck, who co-starred with her and played the American journalist, was transformed. His shoulders, bowed by the weight of all the Hollywood leading ladies he had had to support, straightened; the years dropped off him. The story was the best kind of Hollywood fairy tale, the kind that the great Ernst Lubitsch used to delight us with, the kind that Emeric used to write, the kind of screenplay that is scribbled on a coffee table between one espresso and the next. But Wyler and Audrey were both Continentals, and knew how to handle such airy nothings; she was half Dutch, he from Alsace. Good taste and good manners were not wasted on them. The public loved them and took them to their hearts.

I was preparing to leave for Hollywood, where I had arranged to meet Stravinsky. He had a house somewhere off Sunset Boulevard. I had no idea how the great maestro would receive me, but I tried to find out from Robert Rounseville.

"Robert," I said, "how did you enjoy being conducted by Stravinsky?"

We were walking up Seventh Avenue. He groaned and flung his arms about. Robert had created the title role in *The Rake's Progress* at Venice the year before.

"The old boy only conducted on the first night, and it was the only unhappy performance. All those lovely Mozartian recitativos that he had written—I begged him to take them parlando! He conducted them as if he was giving a lesson in geometry: one, two, three, four . . ."

Robert slashed a tolerable tetrahedron out of the air and several passersby dodged, until they realized that we were passing Carnegie Hall and that Robert was a musician, a licensed lunatic. One even asked for his autograph.

Time was getting short: On Thursday of that week were the Academy Awards in Hollywood, and Monique and I had to be there, and after that, en route for Japan and Mr. and Mrs. Kawakita. Yet still no certain news of William S. Paley. He had escaped from me to Jamaica, and now he was in London—or Paris—with Edward R. Murrow. Arthur Loew was apologetic: "If only you'd come sooner!" He would have added, "Instead of pissing your time away at the North Pole with a lot of polar bears," but he was too polite to say so.

We were at a party very high up on Riverside Drive, round about Columbia University. There were few white faces. The atmosphere was cool and cultured. I sensed a love of the arts, and a political awareness absent until now from any party I had been to in New York. An outstanding personality, and a good talker, was John Henry Faulk, whose ideas were liberal, explosive, and original. I gathered that he had a radio hour—or was it a television hour? He was talking at a great rate about T. H. White's book *The Goshawk*, which I had already decided to add to my group of *Tales*. He went wild with excitement and smashed several glasses when I mentioned it. A young girl, about seventeen, played the piano very well, and after theatre time Canada Lee arrived in a great fuss and bother. Arthur dropped me off at the St. Regis at three o'clock in the morning, and even Salvador Dalí had gone to bed.

The next day was St. Patrick's Day. I don't like watching parades, any more than I like watching sports. Film directors are super-egotists; they don't like one another's shows. The brass bands woke me up. Everyone was out on the streets, and if you weren't wearing a shamrock-green sash and marching in the parade, you were nobody. Fortunately I had two invitations, the first one for luncheon with Arthur W. Kelly and his whole office staff. For some obscure reason the food was Italian. Miss Ramsay, Arthur's secretary, made several risqué jokes and Arthur sang a verse of "The Wearing of the Green"—

> They're hanging men and women
> For the wearing of the green. . . .

—and I protested that he was being anti-British, and a good time was had by all. United Artists didn't get much from its wage slaves that afternoon. Arthur dictated a letter to Harry Crocker at the Chaplin Studio, and another to Chaplin himself, and told me that I was expected to dinner at Chaplin's house and that I would find an invitation waiting for me at the Beverly Hills Hotel, where Monique was about to be installed. Arthur was a great host, and a great friend.

The other party was not a New York party at all. It was a Hollywood party that got lost in New York. Hollywood people, who consider themselves ten feet tall, become surprised and embarrassed midgets in New York. The discovery that they belong to the human race is almost too much for them. They are so used to acting out their emotions in public that they think the only thing to do is to have a quarrel, or a lover, so it was Jennifer Jones ringing me up and insisting that I come and meet her great, best friend, Joseph Cotten: "You two were just made for each other. I want you to be friends."

Joseph Cotten proved to be witty, sophisticated, cynical, debonair, and funny, all of them qualities of which his film personality is noticeably devoid. We got on well, and Jennifer was in seventh heaven. I kept on saying to myself, "Why hasn't this delightful man made more films?" and then realized that he had, and that I had seen them, and that he had made as much impression as a hole in the screen. Could this be because Orson Welles had given him such a rocketing send-off—first with the WPA, and then with

Citizen Kane—so that he had nothing more to give, except his natural charm? That he had in abundance, and I was glad to know that Jennifer had such a good friend who was in touch with reality.

We were in a Park Avenue apartment somewhere, and the next arrivals were David O. and Gene Tierney. She wandered about looking at the pictures—it was David's apartment, so there were some good ones—and she was quite a picture herself. But she didn't speak. There was a buffet that nobody ate, and fashionable drink like tequila and akvavit. A young man arrived who was in love with Miss Tierney, and who was inclined to be a bit excited about it. She suggested we go to her apartment "in the Nineties." Outside on the street it was bitterly cold. Jennifer suddenly grabbed my arm and said, "Let's walk," and took me off at a great rate up the avenue. The others tagged along, and there was a limousine and a chauffeur tagging along as well. I think that Jennifer was trying to recapture some of the comradeship that we had all shared on *Gone to Earth*, and she asked about members of the crew, and dear Esmond Knight . . . and how was Foxy?

The others started yelling, and we stopped and waited, and they came up and we all got into the limousine and went to Miss Tierney's flat. We didn't stay long. It was plain that the desperate young man wanted Miss Tierney for himself and was prepared to get tough about it. She, meanwhile, had disappeared.

Back in the street, Jennifer seized David O.'s arm this time, and marched him off at a great rate, feebly protesting. Joe Cotten and his wife were staying at the St. Regis, so we went back together in a cab. His wife was blond, fat, smart, and intelligent. They had an apartment at the St. Regis, so I went up with them and we all started to drink whiskey. Joe's wife went to bed, and I listened to Joe telling tale after tale, drinking enormous whiskeys, until about five o'clock, when we decided to call it a night. A typical end of a typical Hollywood party, where they have to be ready, made-up on the set, at 9:00 A.M.

But where, oh where, was Bill Paley? In Rome, of course. No self-respecting executive could be anywhere else, in the spring.

I had one last glimpse of Arthur Loew. He patted my shoulder.

"So long, Micky. If only you'd been here a bit sooner. I had it all set up for you. What are you doing for lunch?"

I said firmly that I was lunching with Mike Todd at the "21" Club. I saw Hugh French, Hughie Green, and the stowaway. They were seated at the bar and they all waved.

"Friends of yours, Colonel?" inquired Jack Schindler.

"Acquaintances," I said, reprovingly. "We all met in a bar at the North Pole."

Mike Todd was running the Aquacade at Jones Beach: girls in G-strings, with tons of falling water. He had black hair and blue eyes, but that wasn't what made him look so formidable. It was the look of the hungry impresario, the look that Napoleon had. He tried to sell me the Aquacade, but I wasn't having even a piece of it.

=

In Hollywood I was met at the airport by another gigantic limousine, from the William Morris Agency. The driver was a square, weather-beaten man, a Dane.

"Call me Ferd, Mr. Powell. I met your Mr. Mann the other morning. How was your trip?"

"Swell."

"Mr. Mann, he had it very stormy, and there was floods that morning too. You can see the mud yet on the road."

Poor Chris, as carefully clean as a cat. He should never have left his handsome office, with the windows looking down on the Marble Arch, and he hardly ever did. At a busy crossroads near the MGM Studios we were stopped by a huge traffic cop, with an even bigger revolver.

"Hello, John," said Ferd.

"Hello, Ferd," said John.

"This is Mr. Michael Powell. He's one of the top British film directors."

"You don't say?"

A vast hand came through the window, and I was shaken by it.

"Welcome to L.A., Mr. Powell."

At the Beverly Hills Hotel I had a room in a bungalow in the garden. It wasn't ready for me, so I went down to the coffee shop for breakfast. Like all American coffee shops, it was spotlessly clean and the food was crisp and fresh and tasted of nothing, unlike the girls behind the counter, who were very tasty. So was my garden room, fresh and white, with green stripes and white muslin curtains: Kate Greenaway superimposed on Death Valley.

Midmorning, Greta Peck arrived to take me to the Twentieth Century–Fox Studios. She was tasty, too; Scandinavian, I fancy. She was small, blond, with a saucy, turned-up nose. She sat in the middle of a mass of machinery that, like all these California ladies, she maneuvered with ease, never raising her voice above conversational level. At the studio, on Stage 15, they were shooting a scene in Paris, France. The two actors were outside a taxidermist's shop, and the Paris street scene was reflected in the windows from a back-projection screen. Henry King, one of the great silent film directors—tall, thin, bony, and battered, in a gray suit and hat—was directing. His long arms hung nervously at his sides. He was having trouble with the stand-in, who had the elasticity of a block of teak.

"Greg, stick around," said Henry King. "I'd like to get this shot before lunch."

I whispered to Greta Peck, "Who is Greg's leading lady?"

She said, "Ava Gardner."

"Will I see her? Is she on the set?"

She gave me a look, and indicated the cigar-store Indian.

"That's our Ava."

They shot the scene, and Greg came over, shook hands, and kissed his wife. He was tall and slender, but the wardrobe had padded his shoulders until he looked almost deformed. Everything at Twentieth Century–Fox was like that. Hitchcock told me, in his plummiest voice, "The first thing Darryl Zanuck asked me was 'Do you play polo?' " Hitch's disgust was profound: "I ask you!"

It was compulsory to eat in the canteen, and on the walls there was an enormous mural of all the stars and chief executives, but culminating in an enormous head of Darryl himself, glaring down aggressively at the multitude like one of the wild animals he loved to hunt and shoot.

Gregory Peck had melancholy in his hands and face, and one could sense that he had a hot temper. It was our first real talk, and it went well. He wanted to escape from Hollywood and make some films in Europe and in England. He wanted to do more theatre, and was a friend of the Masseys. He told me about a theatre group at La Jolla, down the coast toward San Diego, where legitimate actors tried out legitimate plays, and I told him about London, where it was possible for an actor to work in a film and a play at the same time. His favorite classical play, and part, was *Tamburlaine.* Christopher Marlowe, as a dramatist, is not a favorite of mine, but cut into short, blood-stained chunks, he serves, and since I had seen Tyrone Guthrie's Old Vic production I was able to keep my end up, and add *Tamburlaine,* starring Gregory Peck, to my *Tales.*

I had an appointment for tea with Stravinsky, and I persuaded Mrs. Peck to drop me off on South Beverly Drive so that I could walk to the composer's house, which was in some canyon. She tried to persuade me not to—nobody walks in Hollywood, particularly in Beverly Hills—but with firmness I won my point, and she put me down between an enormous castle and a Tudor farmhouse. I strolled along with delight between the forty-seven varieties of architecture that lined the drive. Here were the Elizabethan mansions, the houses that looked suspiciously upon the intruder through latticed windows, the copies of Versailles, the Moorish palaces, the simple thatched cottages with fourteen rooms and five baths, the red-brick William and Mary residences with tall, red chimney stacks reaching to the sky, and the usual modern constructions, all steel and glass, that faced each other across the drive, itself lined with slender palm trees, thirty feet high and naked as chorus girls, and with tufts of leaves at their tops. I turned into Sunset Boulevard. On the drive there had been broad sidewalks, but here there were none. The commuter traffic hadn't started yet, but I was continually forced to take refuge in a rhododendron bush.

Fortunately Stravinsky's particular canyon was not far and his house only a short way up it. It was modest enough, half brick, half timber. A son-in-law in a checked shirt let me in and went to find the maestro. There were people talking, humming, singing all over the house, quite unself-consciously. It was like a musical beehive. There were framed photographs on all the tables. I recognized a few of the faces, but there was no mistake about one of them. A photograph from a newspaper had been torn out and encased in a silver frame, and stood in a place of honor: it was Dylan Thomas. Marveling, I picked it up. Yes, there was the bull neck, the curly hair, the enchanter's eyes, the pugnacious nose, the dreaming lips that had said to me in a tone that brooked no argument, "Every story has to have its own length!"

A door opened, and Stravinsky came in. Robert Rounseville was right. This musical genius, this passionate and romantic Russian, this pure intellect, looked like a professor of mathematics, or like one of the human-sized insects in the Čapek brothers' *The Insect Play*. When serious, he was formidable, because he was so very, very serious. Diaghilev, who admired him greatly, also feared him. I think the only person who didn't fear him was Cocteau, that bright and dazzling butterfly of the arts. I held out my right hand to him, still holding the silver frame in my left hand. He looked enquiringly at it. I said, "Cher maître, I have come to ask you to collaborate with Dylan Thomas on a film."

The next two hours passed like a dream, laced with Haig's Dimple Scotch, and with Teachers Highland Cream when the Haig gave out. Stravinsky's wife joined us, a vital and charming woman of about forty-five. Students joined us, listened as we talked, went out, appeared and disappeared. Pot-valiant with whiskey, I talked about *The Odyssey* and how Dylan had suggested to me that he was no classical poet. At once, the master seized and developed my suggestion.

"It must be Nausicaa and her maidens washing the linen, when the hero appears, naked like a God! The girls must bring the linen to be washed at the fountain—"

"And dance upon the linen!" I suggested boldly.

He seized on the idea: "Of course, of course. We must have a dance, and a hymn . . . a hymn—we must have a hymn . . . what did you say, Michael . . . forty minutes?"

"Yes, forty minutes should be about right, but we must see what Dylan says."

"I will ask him here. We have no room, but I'll build an extra room on for him. He shall have a room in the garden, and we shall all work together . . . that's the only way . . . every story has to have its own length, eh? . . . and so, this wonderful boy thinks he is no classical poet? But we know better, don't we? What about: 'Where once the mermen through your ice / Pushed up their hair—' "

" 'The dry wind steers through salt and root,' " I joined in, capping him. " 'Where once your green knots sank their splices / Into the tided cord, / There goes the great unraveller. . . .' "

We continued to quote and misquote. The Haig helped me, the Teachers Stravinsky, until the end of the salt-stained solace. Stravinsky smacked his lips over "the dolphined sea."

"No classical poet he, eh?"

They had all Dylan's poems, books, recordings, and Stravinsky knew them all and handled them all as he talked. We talked of many things: of art, of materialism, of Stravinsky . . . of cabbages and kings. The maestro said many memorable things.

"If you love materialism, that's all right. If you pursue materialism, without love, that's all wrong; that's the difference between Lenin and Stalin. I like Karl Marx as an historian—it is as a philosopher he does the harm."

He knocked back a double whiskey and put the glass down.

"I can say some things complete, with all the organs, blood, brain, and heart and legs in forty-seven seconds . . ."

Talking of legs, I was not too steady on my own. They wanted to drive me back to the hotel, but I insisted on walking, so of course I got picked up by the police almost at once. The Beverly Hills cops are skeptical and unimpressed by anything and anybody. The dialogue went like this.

"Hey, you—where are you going?"

With dignity: "The Beverly Hiccup Hotel."

"Who are you, what's your name?"

"My name is Michael Powell. I am an English film director. I have just been visiting Mr. Stravinsky."

"Oh yeah? Get in!" They whirled around and took me back to where I came from.

"Are you Stravinsky?"

"I'm his son-in-law."

"This English guy says he's a friend of your pop's. Is that correct? He's been hitting the bottle."

"It's quite all right, officer. He's an English film director."

"That's what he says. William Powell, he said his name was."

"Michael Powell," with dignity.

"What's he been doing?"

"Jaywalkin'. Don't worry, bud. We'll take him home."

Screech of brakes, blare of siren, and I'm driven back to the Beverly Hills Hotel, which is not at all surprised.

Seven P.M., nearly dark, and Alma Hitchcock is coming to fetch me for dinner with Hitch. Hollywood is a town where things happen to you if you are single and male. If you are single and female, even more things happen to you, or so I'm told. I'm describing this trip of mine in detail because it is so typical of so many others, which I don't intend to describe. O. Henry, when telling his neat stories of New York, called it "Bagdad on the Subway." What would he call Hollywood, I wondered, "Babylon on the Freeway"?

Hitch was off-balance—neuritis. He'd had it for nearly half a year, and it was souring his life. He had won too much independence for himself, too much responsibility for his choice of paths through the Hollywood jungle. They were narrow and dangerous trails, and one never knew where they led; sometimes nowhere, sometimes to the open country, where he was a master among masters, and all the time invisible. But near, he could hear the crashing of great beasts, their sudden roar as they charged, and their snarls as they fought and tore over the quivering flesh of their victim.

For make no mistake, these Hollywood monsters didn't want Hitch to succeed. They don't want any artist to succeed on his own. They fear the creative talent. Possessing none, they claim the power of money. Possessing the money, they claim the credit, too. It was in this twilight world that Hitch was preparing and making his films. He had thought he could play the Hollywood game as well as these beasts. Later he would put stars like Vera Miles and Tippi Hedren under contract to him personally, and this would make his enemies fear him, and envy him, even more. Mostly they tried to seduce him and buy him back by offering enormous sums of money at a time when he was struggling to finance his own productions and knew only too well how underfinanced he was. It was a heroic struggle, conducted mostly in secrecy except to his agent, and it went on for years.

The strain on Hitch was enormous. Only Alma, and a few devoted friends, knew how great it was. I think that I love Hitchcock more than all his films, for the struggle that he put up to keep the independence of the filmmaker in Hollywood. And in the end, it was a true Hitchcock picture, *Psycho*—no stars, just know-how—that saved him from going to the wall, and condemned the young actor, Anthony Perkins, to spend the next years playing the same part, again and again, this time without a Hitch.

There were just the three of us at dinner. It was a silent meal. Pat, their daughter, was away in England, and no doubt my presence brought up a few ghosts. It was twenty-four years since I had come to England from the south of France and met, and got a job with, the legendary Alfred Hitchcock. We talked of Anny Ondra, the tall, blond Czechoslovak actress who was Hitchcock's ideal woman. We talked of the huge meals that we used to eat and drink. Hitch was still fat, but nothing like his former twenty-two stone.

"Those were the days, Michael"—Hitch always called me by my given name, as he did when he first knew me—"those were the days. I've forgotten how much a stone is? Fourteen pounds? Really? Are you good at sums, Michael? . . . three hundred and eight pounds . . . thank you."

He looked across at his charming little wife.

"I can't imagine how Alma and I managed on our wedding night."

They were fervent proselytes of California, but it was northern California that they loved the most. Early in their Selznick contract they had gone in their car to see San Simeon, Citizen Kane's castle at the bottom of Big Sur, and had pushed on up that wonderful coast, going crazy about Carmel, and ending up in San Francisco. For citizens of London, the discovery of San Francisco was a lifesaver. Hitch had demonstrated his love for the city in *Vertigo*, and *The Birds* was filmed even farther up that wonderful coast beyond Drake's Bay, where the great admiral careened his ships and the seals play in the fresh water from the mountains. It's a little town called Bodega Bay. I went there for the first time the other day, with Thelma, Pat, and Annie.* We had all been to see George Lucas's Skywalker Ranch, hidden in the hills on the road north, and were still marveling at the wizardry of this modern Jules Verne: George Lucas and Alfred Hitchcock—what a wonderful medium that has room for them both.

I had been of two minds about seeing Hitch on this trip. In wartime, when Emeric and I needed his help, it was a different matter. But now we had gone one way and he had gone another, although he still cherished his strange dream of doing a film of Barrie's *Mary Rose* in Scotland and asked my advice about locations, which was very unlike Hitch. This was delicate ground because of my feelings about *I Know Where I'm Going!* and I held my tongue. Between two craftsmen, criticism is best unspoken. If Hitch and I saw each other's pictures, it was to steal an actor, or an idea, or a technical trick—not that Hitch needed to steal, any more than I did.

I had known and loved Hitch, as a friend and fellow craftsman, for forty years. At first glance, each recognized in the other the same confidence, the same mastery of the medium. For a year or more Hitch held out his hand to me in what had become for me a strange land, England. Abroad, in Europe, Hitch with UFA and I with MGM and Rex Ingram in France had once and for all caught a glimpse of the grail. That glimpse was enough for us for the rest

---

*Pat and Ann Biernacki, longtime friends of mine in San Francisco.

of our lives and careers. Hitch's way was to impose himself upon the world, to exploit that marvelous personality and quick wit; mine—well, we shall see what mine was, when we come to the end of this very long book.

The next day was Thursday, March 21, Academy Awards day. Ferd drove me to the airport to meet Monique, escorted by Hugh French. She hadn't slept for two nights, and said so. I rushed her to the hotel and put her to bed. Chris Mann and Bert Allenberg were waiting for me, and we spent the day in a series of visits to the major studios. Dore Schary at MGM—it was strange to see this tall, thin, bespectacled bourgeois, with pictures of dogs on the walls of the office where Louis B. Mayer had recently reigned supreme. This ex-actor, ex-playwright, ex-screenwriter was now, for no visible reason, president of MGM. Nothing could have shown more clearly how Hollywood had completely failed to understand whence its legendary greatness grew. To be in that office with Louis B. Mayer, with Clark Gable, Greta Garbo, and Spencer Tracy on the walls, was to be in a jungle stockade with a watchful rhino. Louis B. ruled by fear, and conquered by trusting to his instinct. His long reign at Culver City inspired awe. To Howard Strickling, my first friend in movies in Nice in 1925 (when he was publicity rep for Rex Ingram, later becoming personal representative to Louis B.), his boss was always "Mr. Mayer." Small wonder, then, that I, an early alumnus of MGM, with a degree signed by Leo the Lion, should have even less time for Dore Schary than I had twenty-five years later for the son of the Tin Man* on the same throne.

An hour later we were on our way to Paramount to see Don Hartman, head of production, a mild, square man with a track record as a screenwriter and producer. He had all his New York executives on his back and had no time for us. I spent some time in the story department, where the writers welcomed us in and told us that when they had a spiritual flat they ran *I Know Where I'm Going!* So far they had run it nine times. I told this, later on, to Emeric.

"Not enough," he said.

It was time to prepare for the show. The Beverly Hills Hotel was full to bursting, and Hugh French moved in with me. I was retying my bow tie for the third time when I got a panic call from Monique down the corridor— zipper trouble. I galloped along several hundred carpeted yards of corridor, followed, panting, by the little Filipino maid, and managed to zip up the skintight dress by Carven without carving a piece of Monique with it.

"She looks just beautiful," said the little maid.

She did. I dropped a handful of Benzedrine tablets into her bag, and the

*Michael is referring to Jack Haley, Jr., the son of the actor who played the Tin Man in *The Wizard of Oz.*

three of us were driven to the Pantages Theatre, where the show was being held that year. The fans were on the bleachers, and arc lights wheeled overhead. Loudspeakers announced each new arrival. As we drew up the loudspeakers blared, "Deborah Kerr and Leo Genn."

There she was—my dear, my darling, my life, my fate. Her sandy hair was bleached to the color of a scrambled egg. Her dress designer had the waist in the wrong place. She was always too much of an artist to have much clothes sense, but she had a star in her hair, and held it high, and her long body was a perfect match for Leo Genn's dark six feet. The fans roared a welcome as they crossed the carpeted sidewalk. There was a jam at the entrance to the theatre, and we caught up with them. I said, "Hi, you two! This is Ludmilla Tcherina . . . Monique, this is Deborah Kerr."

The two beautiful women, the dark and the fair, looked at each other. Monique said, "Yes, that I know," and they touched hands.

"And this is Leo Genn."

Leo said, "I say, white tie! You'll make us look provincial!"

I riposted, "That was the intention."

Then the jam broke and they moved on, and we didn't see each other again. Well, that's showbiz.

It was nine years since we parted at the Achilles statue in Hyde Park, and the wound, and the desperate feeling of loneliness, were as deep as ever. Monique whispered in my ear, as we looked for our seats, "She is very English, your love, Micky."

I said, grumpily, "She's not English—she's Scottish."

Heads turned as we passed along the aisle. Monique's creamy beauty and impeccable assurance were a standout, even in that assembly. The show was very long and full of private jokes, like our village fête. Various men and women slouched on and off. I remember Jane Wyman making a big hit singing "In the Cool, Cool, Cool of the Evening." Danny Kaye was the efficient and delightful emcee, and without him we would all have died of boredom. Monique was nearly asleep anyway, from lack of sleep, disillusionment, and aesthetic horror. I had spent all the money and brought her here because I thought that now was the moment in her career when she should have a good look at the choices for an artist of world status today. I had a high opinion of her good taste and common sense.

After the show I took her on to Romanoff's, where I had reserved a table. It was the only place to go after an Awards affair. It was a big barn of a room, crowded with tables, each with an unopened bottle of scotch planted in the center—no flowers, just scotch. We were eating a fixed supper, at about twelve dollars a head. I sat Monique down at her table and let the whole, cozy banality of Hollywood break over her. There were the usual men and women, some famous, some infamous, and Humphrey Bogart was eating at a table alone. About 2:00 A.M. I took Monique away, back to the hotel, unzipped her, and said good night.

Next day, she had Robert Taylor on the telephone for an hour, lunch with MCA, and dinner with Robert Taylor—busy girl! I went to see Walt Disney. His studio was in the San Fernando Valley, near Warner Bros., and Walt was always in the studio, and usually in the canteen. He had an office, but he preferred the canteen. He liked to be accessible. Disney employees who had a grievance, or an idea, could get to him easily. When I found him he was surrounded by animators.

"Hi, Micky!"

We might have parted yesterday.

"This is Micky Powell, boys. He made *The Red Shoes.*"

A few nodded.

"We've been running your *Hoffmann*, Micky. Say, that was a great gag, the way you pulled Moira Shearer to pieces. I haven't seen that trick, now, for a long while."

I said I'd seen it for the first time in a silent film during the First World War: it was a Max Linder comedy. Walt scoffed: "Micky likes to pretend that he's as old as George Arliss. Sit down, Micky, have a cup of tea—yes, real English tea! Roy brought back five pounds of it from Fortnum and Mason in London— Earl Grey. Say, what's the difference between an earl and a lord?"

I explained, "An earl is a lord, but a lord is not necessarily an earl. Don't tell me that you're going to animate *Little Lord Fauntleroy?*"

"That would be telling . . . Say, did you ever see Mary Pickford's version of *Fauntleroy* . . . where she played a dual role . . . the young lord and his mother?"

"Of course I did. Sam Taylor directed it, and do you remember the story about Sam Taylor's supposed credit when he directed Pickford and Fairbanks in Shakespeare's *The Taming of the Shrew?*"

"Sure do: 'Additional dialogue by Sam Taylor.' Shaky must have shook in his grave."

Chris Mann and Ferd picked me up and drove us to the airport. By two o'clock we were in Phoenix, Arizona. We drove out to the famous Biltmore Hotel, built and designed by Frank Lloyd Wright. It was owned by Wrigley, of chewing gum fame, who had a white hacienda way back in the hills above the road. The hotel was built of stylish gray bricks inside and out. In the lobby you had a clear view of eight hundred feet or so, with shops and offices in the center. The color scheme was gold and rust red—gold for the ceiling, rust red for the furniture and carpets—which was a brilliant conception. It harmonized with the outside, making the visitor feel that he was in the desert, but in safety and comfort. I looked forward to seeing Frank Lloyd Wright's hotel in Tokyo, the one that withstood the earthquake that flattened the city.

We found Harry Cohn, president of Columbia, in a bungalow in the garden, sitting in the sun on the flat roof. He was in his sixties, short and bulky, with a bronzed, bald head. This was the man who had made Frank Capra into one of the world's greatest directors. I remembered the spectacular films— *Submarine, Dirigible, Platinum Blonde, The Bitter Tea of General Yen*—the explosive arrival, out of what appeared to be nowhere, of *It Happened One Night,* starring Clark Gable and Claudette Colbert in what is still one of the most human, most civilized, and most American of comedies. We talked a while about The Archers' films, and about the wealth of talent in England: Carol Reed, David Lean, Alec Guinness, Robert Hamer, even about Alex Korda and Arthur Rank. He had told me that he had enjoyed *The Tales of Hoffmann,* so I broached Emeric's plan of a film about Strauss, *The Golden Years.*

"Strauss?" he said. "Which Strauss? The waltz one, or the other one?"

"The other one."

And I explained our scheme of the narrator being Strauss himself, and the two big set pieces, which would be *Salome* (with Tcherina as the daughter of Herodias), and *Der Rosenkavalier* for its waltzes and its sensuality and its gorgeous spectacle. Chris had not said a word but had let me ramble on, and suddenly the deal was done, almost too quickly for me to enjoy it. The Archers undertook to deliver a script within four months. Chris had other business to discuss with Columbia, and we agreed that I would leave them alone. I got up to go, when Cohn suddenly asked if we would like to make *Lawrence of Arabia,* which at that time belonged to his company. I rather fancied that the international banks had been wary of it, because of its strong bias in favor of the Arabs, while the establishment of the state of Israel had made the project even less bankable. In any case, we refused it, because we were already committed in our minds to *The Golden Years.*

It makes me smile today (or should I be crying?) to look back at our cocksure behavior. *Lawrence of Arabia* would have been an ideal subject for The Archers at that time in history. We know that now, but we didn't know it then. To an Englishman, it seemed like looking back to World War II. I knew a great deal about Lawrence and the Arabs, had all the books, and had been to Clouds Hill* and had read *The Mint.* It was very much my subject, and Lawrence was very much one of my heroes, but at the time I couldn't see it

---

*The cottage in Dorset where T. E. Lawrence was living at the time of his fatal motorcycle crash in 1935. As Private Shaw he was stationed at a nearby army camp and bought the cottage as a retreat. *Seven Pillars of Wisdom* was written there. The cottage is now a museum.

as a film. I was blinded by this search for music and the composed film, and Emeric wasn't interested in Lawrence of Arabia at all. Hey-ho—*quem deus vult perdere dementat prius*, which can be freely translated as "Sometimes you can have too much freedom of choice." Let me say it, once and for all, that we could never have made a better film than the *Lawrence of Arabia* of Sam Spiegel and David Lean, and not forgetting my beloved Fred Young, whose masterful compositions of the feast at Damascus will never be surpassed for color and vigor.

I drove to the airport and flew back to Hollywood in a haze of self-deception and self-inflicted pats on the back. Up The Archers! Now, with backing from a Hollywood major, we could defy the movie barons of Britain, the John Davises, the Arthur Ranks, the Mickey Balcons, the Robert Clarks—yea, even the might of Alexander Korda. And now I was going to dinner with Mr. and Mrs. Charles Chaplin, with the beauteous Ludmilla Tcherina on my arm.

We were late, but others were later still. Chaplin's house was on Summit Drive. It was a large, white, English-style house. Inside, it was light, spacious, and airy. An aproned maid took our coats. We went into a large room through wide, glass doors. A dozen people were sitting, talking in a normal tone of conversation, which is not the normal tone of Hollywood. In the grate a bright fire was burning. Our hostess, a slim, dark girl, had her arms around two lovely children in pajamas, a boy of seven and a girl of three. They had self-possessed, polite manners. Sidney Bernstein followed us in, and was greeted with rapture by the little girl, whom he picked up. Chaplin danced up to us, a small, thick-set, ruddy, white-haired, elegant figure. His quick eyes darted over Tcherina. There was something French about Chaplin, as well as English. He quickly claimed Irish blood. I had never heard that before.

In a moment we were deep in conversation. Nobody was in a hurry. We were waiting for Hedy Lamarr, and she was always the last to arrive. The other guests were mostly quiet and intelligent. Suddenly, a young girl, white-blond, with makeup like a clown, erupted into the room. Then at last, very late, Hedy.

We went in to dinner. Chaplin sat at the head of the table. A tall, clever man whom I met one day up the Hudson, John MacDonald, sat at the bottom. Mrs. Chaplin was on the side next to him. She was, of course, Oona O'Neill, daughter of Eugene O'Neill. I had Monique on my right, and next to me on the other side the small clown. Hedy was opposite, sitting next to a big man who looked like a publisher.

The dinner was simple and good. It was crowned by a wonderful sweet, a kind of meringue about a foot in diameter. It had caramel on top. It looked and tasted like sunshine on a plate. The talk went to and fro. The publisher hated Doctor Johnson, thought him a bore. I took up the cudgels so conveniently placed at my disposal. I didn't believe that he had ever read Johnson's *Lives of the Poets;* he had probably only read Boswell, whom he extravagantly admired. Chaplin was a delightful host, and was acting all the time. He often got up to make a point, or to mimic somebody, or dance. At one point, he was hanging desperately on to the door handle, trying to keep an imaginary intruder outside, and barking like a West Highland terrier.

"White or black?" I asked sympathetically. He was quite firm in his answer. "White."

Melissa Hayden and André Eglevsky were the main dancers in his film *Limelight,* which was in the editing stage. He told me about Claire Bloom, whom he thought would have a big success. His tales of their battles, of the six weeks' rehearsal in his garden room, plus two more in the studio, were predictable. She sounded a difficult girl, but full of character. Their relationship sounded very like mine with Moira; being on your toes must make you touchy.

And—oh joy! oh joy!—Buster Keaton was in it, doing a double act at the piano with Chaplin. The story was nothing. Chaplin's stories were always the same story, always a tender love story—this time in London in 1912, when he himself was in vaudeville: she a dancer, crippled by arthritis, he a world-famous comedian. She, through love for him, when he falls from favor, recovers the power to walk and then to dance again; in the end he dies.

Monique and Hedy were jabbering away for hours. When the party was over, Hedy drove us back in her car. Peering earnestly into the windscreen, she confessed her secret ambition was to play Esther from the Book of Esther in the Old Testament. I congratulated her. It was an excellent ambition; but who would play King Ahasuerus, and who would play Mordecai the Jew? She looked at me as if I had insulted her, and we nearly ran off the road. I realized that I had said a foolish thing. What did it matter who played King Ahasuerus and who played Mordecai the Jew, so long as Hedy Lamarr played Esther? I admitted the logic of the impeachment.

When Chaplin said goodbye to us at the door he was claiming Gypsy blood for himself as well. He could be anything he liked, for my money. In one and the same week, I had sat at the feet of two of my three idols. D.W. was dead, but Walt and Charlie were still very much alive, revealing to a lifelong worshiper no feet of clay.

> Ah, did you once see Shelley plain,
> And did he stop and speak to you?

The next day I flew to Japan. It was Saturday, March 24, 1952.

It is time to stop and consider what kind of book this is. My publishers call it an autobiography. But it is more than that. I call it a hitherto unrecorded piece of social history—no more than that. The critics call it . . . they don't know what to call it. Proust would call it a novel, Chateaubriand a memoir, Rousseau a confession, Voltaire a joke.

There! I've got that off my chest. Now we can get on. I have no intention of dragging you around the world at my chariot wheels, as David did to Jennifer. (But yes, I did meet Kurosawa.) You can relax. I have described this journey of mine in detail, from London to Greenland, from Greenland to New York, from New York to Hollywood, because I am describing it once and for all. It was typical of my restlessness at the time. I knew what I wanted, but I didn't know how to get it. I had dozens of ideas, but no idea how to present them, or how to get them financed. Now that I am in my eighties—and in your eighties—I haven't changed one iota! But I am resigned to my failure to prove that all art is one. It is enough that I know it myself.

Having circumnavigated the globe, I returned to London and Melbury Road. Emeric had finished shooting *Twice Upon a Time,* and it was in the editing stage. He had written thirty pages of *The Golden Years,* and Ray Massey had delivered the final version of *Hanging Judge* and was anxious to start casting and get into rehearsals. He and Dorothy had already booked their passages on the *Queen Elizabeth. Hanging Judge* was a big production, and once I became immersed in it there would be no time for Emeric. So we agreed together to snatch a couple of days and go to Garmisch-Partenkirchen, where Richard Strauss lived and died.

Columba was now sixteen months old, and an active triped.

"Why doesn't he walk?" said Kevin anxiously, as he watched him scuttle around the garden like a hermit crab with two hands and one leg. "Doesn't he want to? Perhaps he's got polio," he added, moving into panic stations. Frankie intervened.

"His trouble is that he's got a father who would rather go around the world than teach his son to walk," she said, "and now proposes to piss off to Germany and hobnob with a lot of Nazis."

Frankie was nothing if not outspoken. Following up her advantage, she dictated her terms: when I returned from Garmisch I must take the whole family on a caravan holiday to North Cornwall.

"And we'll all go surfing. Columba too," she added, for Kevin's benefit.

My elder son was known in his family as "Mrs. Gummidge." Readers of Charles Dickens will remember that when the soup was burned, everybody was upset, but Mrs. Gummidge was more upset than anybody.

Stapi's office in Munich would make the arrangements for our trip to Austria, and Klaus, his son, would meet us at the airport and drive us up to Garmisch to see the Strauss family. Ever since I had achieved my ambition of making a composed film with *The Tales of Hoffmann,* I was no longer content to tell a story simply, economically, and efficiently, as I had in *Black Narcissus.* I wanted to forget the proscenium arch, cut dialogue to a minimum, plan plenty of action to keep the actors moving, or hold them in close-up to show what they were thinking and feeling, and in general to use the camera the way we were taught to use it in the silent days, and tell the story directly into the lens. It was not a new idea to use the lens as the eye of the storyteller. Several clever movie directors had had a shot at it in the early days, and when movies became talkies, these attempts were not forgotten by directors like Billy Wilder or Robert Montgomery. But they were mostly working in the Hollywood dream factory, where cleverness is highly suspicious, and I felt that I could do better than they had been allowed to be. An autobiography was obviously a good subject for experiment, if Emeric would write the script as if the composer were the camera.

Strauss had died three years before, at the age of eighty-five, but his wife was still alive, and the family still lived at the big villa in Garmisch, with the garden where he and Hugo von Hofmannsthal so often walked up and down discussing their newest collaboration. Inevitably, we too did the same. One of the great attractions for me in the life of Richard Strauss was that it was the story of a successful collaboration between two widely different artists—different in temperament, character, and aggression. I think that this appealed to Emeric too. We never discussed our own collaboration together, and we never drew comparisons between the life of Strauss versus Hofmannsthal and Powell versus Pressburger, but it must have been amusing for Emeric, as the wittier mind of the two of us, to get in a few shrewd digs on behalf of Hofmannsthal, on occasions when his collaborator had completely missed the point of a particularly subtle scene.

The family were helpful, told us many wonderful and valuable things; but the greatest discovery of all was a film, a home movie with sound and picture, that had been made of Richard Strauss on his last birthday. We saw him in his garden, and we saw him at home, receiving presents, and he spoke to the camera and thoroughly kissed his wife for the benefit of the cameraman. Any doubts that Emeric may have had about my idea were dispelled by this wonderful piece of luck. The scheme of Strauss as a camera, telling the story of his life, and seeing everything either through his memory or through his eyes, as if they were the camera lens, all fell into place if we were to finish the film with this touching little home movie of this dear old man at the end of a stormy, creative life, which started with Wagner and finished with Stravinsky as competitors.

What a wonderfully moving finish to the film it would be, after you had loved and hated this extraordinary composer who wasn't just a composer of music, he *was* the music! It had poured out of him like a mountain torrent at Garmisch all his life. He had created masterworks and disasters. He had been called an anarchist, a socialist, a Nazi, a benefactor of the human race. His music was his life and his life his music. He was loved by his enemies, hated by his friends, and adored by his family. What a fitting end to such a film, to show him in the bosom of his family after all the storm and strife of his wonderful career!

Very excited, we went out in the garden to walk up and down, like Strauss and Hofmannsthal, and decided to build the whole film around the creation of *Der Rosenkavalier.* The opera *Der Rosenkavalier,* libretto by Hugo von Hofmannsthal, music by Richard Strauss, is one of the world's great theatrical masterpieces, and Emeric and I had often been tempted by it. At one point in our career we were very near to putting it on film. We had been invited to Vienna by the city fathers to discuss making a film that they would finance, for the greater glory of their city. We met them twice in the historic and beautiful room where the Congress of Vienna was held in 1814.

Their proposal was that we should make a film about how Vienna saved Europe from the Turks in the sixteenth century by holding them at the very walls of the city. We looked at each other and then said, politely, that we didn't think that this was a live issue with the youth of Europe today. They said, equally politely, that this was one of the reasons why they wanted the film to be made. I inquired whether they wished the Battle of Lepanto to be included in the film. They said we could include whatever we liked, so long as the Turks were halted at the walls of Vienna while thousands cheered. We said we would need a week to go through all the museums and visit all the battlefields and historical sites, at the end of which time we would meet again. This was agreed.

A professor of history was appointed our guide, and we spent a wonderful time in the Vienna Woods, drinking the new wines in the cafés and eating great quantities of Wiener schnitzel. At the second meeting we reported that, although it was undoubtedly true that the Turks had run out of steam under Vienna's walls, and that consequently Europe had been saved from the infidel, Europe had forgotten all about it, and that the top executives in the motion-picture business, practically all of whom had been born either in Tiflis or Odessa, wanted to forget it too. We recommended that the city should sponsor a documentary film on the subject, for circulation in the schools. For our part, we said that the greatest compliment we could pay Vienna would be to make a film about Hofmannsthal and Strauss, who through their genius, elegance, and wit and sheer theatrical gusto had made Vienna as famous as she had been in the time of Mozart. We would be prepared to put everything else on one side to make such a film.

They thanked us with Viennese courtesy and showed us the door, and now here we are, only two years later, discussing the plans and planning the steps that should lead to the creation of that theatrical masterpiece of beauty and sensuality *Der Rosenkavalier*, from the original conception of the opera by Hofmannsthal to its one-hundredth performance at La Scala in Milan. We figured it could be done in about seventeen and a half minutes in the film.

Hofmannsthal—I mean Emeric—had already found a device for the passing of time, so essential in a film biography. When it was necessary to tell the audience that time had passed, or that a new work was in progress, we took Richard Strauss to the barber. As the years passed and his dimensions increased, his hair got thinner and thinner. His barber, of course, would get older during the course of the film, and would chatter about the new operas and plays, and criticize them the way that barbers do. It was, of course, easy to avoid seeing Strauss's reflection in the mirror, but I made a mental note to experiment with reflections in curved bottles, or shining silver, which would present a distorted image of the great composer, whose real face and personality we would only see in the little film at the end of the picture.

We said goodbye to the Strauss family and drove back to Munich, rather pleased with ourselves. Stapi wanted a piece of *The Golden Years*. He enquired whether I would like to direct an operetta.

"Only *The Merry Widow*," I answered, "and none of us could improve on von Stroheim's silent version, with John Gilbert and Mae Murray doing the famous Merry Widow Waltz."

Stapi shrugged his broad shoulders and gave me his cunning-fox look. He was prepared to wait.

=

Ray Massey's play from Bruce Hamilton's book *The Hanging Judge* is one of the happiest memories of my life, and I like to think of it as one of Ray's too.

He finished the first draft in record time, and although it went through the inevitable changes, it was never substantially altered. Ray should have written more plays. He was a real professional. He felt the theatre in every line he wrote. The actors loved his writing. He knew how to bring them on, and take them off. He wrote good dialogue, and before the rehearsals were half over the running time of the play was about right.

It was a big production. There was a hung-jury scene, which naturally called for twelve good men and true, and although some of them were understudies and some of them were doubles, that meant a big company to take on tour. The main setting of the London club, based upon the Garrick, called for half a dozen good speaking parts, and then there was the interior of the judge's weekend cottage, and a vignette of the judge himself sentencing a murderer. Guy Shepherd was recommended by Hein as the set designer. Hein knew his work in Germany in theatre and films, and he did a splendid job. We used a big gauze most effectively for changing the scene in about a second and a half.

Who was the judge, then? Godfrey Tearle. And who played Sidney, his nemesis at the club? John Robinson. The rest of the cast were all splendid. There are no actors like English actors. There is a vein of poetry and fantasy in the English that sometimes in a man is never known beyond his family circle. The English character actors have it, and when they have a chance they are unbeatable. Little quirks of character, ad-libs, unexpected movements—"May I suggest that I do this?" or "Can I suggest that . . ."—in this way they build up a riveting performance of what is described as a small part. As I have said before, there are no small parts in acting; there are short parts, there are long parts, there are good parts, and there are bad parts; but small parts?—never!

Even as late as 1952 it was still possible to put a show on in the West End for a few thousand pounds. A new play, with a few known names, could still make money on tour. There was only one woman in the cast, the judge's mistress, and she was in only one scene. I needed a big name for the judge, but I needed a good actor too. We were at the start of the autumn season, and the actors who were all in demand were already demanded. Then I thought of Godfrey. He liked my production of *Héloise*, and although he was seventy he was still a magnificent figure of a man—tall, big, madly handsome. He still had the girls running after him. He accepted.

Ray was half-thrilled, half-doubtful.

"Godfrey? Godfrey Tearle!? Gee, what a great idea! . . . But wait! Isn't he too sympathetic? Ain't he too good-looking? I can see him as the judge, but can you see him in a love nest?"

I began to have misgivings. It was true that, on first sight of Godfrey, certain phrases inevitably popped into one's mind, phrases such as "Keep a straight bat!" and "Women and children first!" But on second thought, Godfrey was very attractive to young girls, and the very fact that he would be so formidable as the hanging judge would make the discovery by the audience that he was human, like the rest of us, a little more telling. Ray saw the force of these arguments, and gave way. But I had a sneaking feeling that he was not entirely convinced, that he would have preferred somebody with more deviousness, or cunning, in his makeup.

Walter P. Chrysler, Jr., came over for the last days of rehearsal and went on tour with the company for two weeks. He was a good companion. He had put up half the money, and I found the other half. He liked to talk about his famous father, and I noticed that he always spoke of him in a slightly lowered voice. It was rather touching. Ray paid his own expenses and took a token fee for the copyright. If the play clicked, he had a big percentage; if not, not.

A new play that is intended for London goes on tour for a few weeks, partly to let the actors play themselves in, partly so that the London theatres can size you up. We needed a big, first-class house if we were to make money, and we had set our sights on the New Theatre. The Alberys, father and son, who ran the New, were looking for a replacement and we thought we had a chance. We rehearsed in town for the last few days before the tour on the stage of the Winter Garden in Drury Lane, now vanished. It was built for musicals, and the stage had such a rake on it that we couldn't set up the scenery. The actors had to hold it up by leaning against it, so we set up out of town.

I think we opened in Newcastle-under-Lyme. We worked all night on the lighting cues, which gave the actors two run-throughs on Monday before the opening night. Guy Shepherd had done such a good job on the lighting and setting that everything went smoothly, and by the end of the week I felt we could ask people to see it. Bronson Albery and his son, Donald, came up to see the show and decided to book it into the New Theatre, now the Albery. I was thrilled, and so was Ray. To have our production thought worthy of the New, the theatre where Larry and Ralph revived the Old Vic, and where Dame Ninette de Valois groomed the Sadler's Wells Ballet for Covent Garden—this was a compliment indeed. To me, it was wonderful to have the run of such a house. I knew all its history. I had seen many shows there. Our setting worked on the big stage, and there was plenty of room behind. I wished that we could have run for months, but we didn't.

I'll never forget the first night in London—the excitement, the applause, and Ray going around like the Phantom of the Opera, pale and muttering questions like "Do they like it? Do they like it?"

Then down below the stalls, "What do they say? What do they say?"

Then round the front, then round the back. Then back to me.

"So-and-so's in the house. He likes it." Or, "That bastard, what's-his-name—he's been in the bar for half the first act!"

Then again, at the end of the play, when the applause for Godfrey was very big: "Do they like it? Do they like it?"

He knew theatre, and he knew that that night would decide whether the play would go or not, hence his feverish questioning. Well, it did go for a month or two, but not long enough for it to be a big success and for Ray to be able to sell the film rights, or transfer the play to New York. Still, nothing to be ashamed of.

=

My father died in September 1952, while we were on tour with *Hanging Judge* before coming into London. He had ignored the minor stroke that he had had some months before, and had driven himself up in his old Citroën *quinze chevaux* from Cap Ferrat to London, as he did every year. He had always enjoyed this trip, always made minor alterations, and it was the big event of the year. In the days before paid holidays, when the seasons were reversed and the Riviera closed for the summer, and the racing started at Chantilly, he used to drive up at Easter after closing the hotel. Sometimes we would take Napoleon's route over the Alps, sometimes we would drive west to Arles and Carcassonne, and then wander north, perhaps through the valley of the River Tarn, in search of that magnificent cheese, a *bleu d'Auvergne*, and across the hills to the valley of the Dordogne. Whichever way we went, we stopped at cheap little hotels and played eccentric card games in the cafés on the street. I loved these journeys, and my father's continual pungent comment on the people and places that we visited gave a flavor to the trip.

Later on, when high summer was the great season and most of it was spent anointing your sleeping partner's back with suntan oil, he would leave the hotel to close itself down, and drive up France in September when the *vendanges* were starting, stopping to visit old friends in the wine culture business, tasting wine and buying it, accepting the hospitality of various châteaux, sipping, with delight, the sugar-sweet golden wines of Château-d'Yquem and Barsac.

"Can't understand people, connoisseurs mind you, who say they don't like the wines of the Sauternes. Say they're too sweet. It's all snobbism. Sit in the sunshine and drink a Château-d'Yquem, you won't find a finer wine, Mick, my boy. Drink it with an omelette, or with fruit, or just by itself! Let's have another bottle! Order an *omelette aux truffes*."

Avoiding Paris and the Île de France at all costs, he would usually swing east to go through the champagne country, by Epernay and Ay and Reims, where he always went to look at the cathedral and talk about the 1914 war, and so by the Somme and the Marne and the war cemeteries to Boulogne-sur-Mer, where he put himself and the car on the ferry to Dover and Folkestone, full of memories for him, and so to London and the Royal Automobile Club.

My father being driven by somebody else across France was unthinkable. He had bought his first automobile, a French-made Darracq, in 1911. I remember him in the lane outside Hoath Farm setting out in this formidable machine, completely transformed by goggles and furs into some sort of monster. My mother sat beside him with a large straw hat on her head, tied on beneath the chin with a green scarf, I remember. She had goggles too. Could such a pioneer submit to being driven, even by his son? The only time he went with me in the Bentley he was pale with fear from beginning to end.

I have allowed a few glimpses of my father during the war, first of all firewatching* at Chester Square and at the bridge room of the Royal Automobile Club, and then at Bratton Fleming in north Devon. From D-Day plus one he was back in London, pulling strings to get back to his beloved south of France: "My word, that fellow Patton is a goer! . . . split-ass across Europe!"

My father was a formidable thruster when he rode to hounds. In an incredibly short space of time he had got back to Saint-Jean-Cap-Ferrat, several weeks ahead of his neighbor Willie Maugham. He soon picked up the threads of his old life on the Riviera. The Normans, mother and daughter, had survived the war—they were great survivors—by running the little bar of the Manor House Hotel in Chantilly, where I cut my teeth as a cellarer and bottle washer. My father had long ago given up the big house with its tall windows looking out on the racecourse. He had only owned it leasehold, while the old bar on the village street was freehold and also had a license.

Chantilly had had a pretty tough war, but Nice and Monte Carlo, where convalescent German servicemen had occupied the villas of English aristocrats and Russian grand dukes, had hardly suffered at all. Some familiar faces had disappeared. There were a few tragedies: "Poor old Bussell. He wouldn't leave when I told him to. Said he had friends who would see him through. You don't have friends in wartime. What's the good of friends, when the Gestapo are on your tail? Poor beggar! I shall miss him." He resumed his life at his beloved Voile d'Or as if a European upheaval had never happened.

The day that my father arrived in England we were scattered all over the map. We had all been to the Edinburgh Festival. The play was on tour before coming into London, and my father had promised himself to be there for the first night "in town." I was with the play, Frankie and Kevin were still in Edinburgh, and Myrtle was at the flat looking after Columba. My father was staying with friends of ours, close by. He walked over to see Columba and pronounced him "top-hole"—his highest form of praise for anyone, man, woman, or child. He accepted lunch, settled down in a chair with a cushion across his stomach as he always did for his daily nap, had a sudden violent spasm, and died. Myrtle was left, literally, holding the baby.

I think that we were playing in Newcastle-upon-Tyne, because he died on Sunday. On Saturday evening, after the show, I had driven along Hadrian's

*When Germany occupied France in World War II, Michael's father had to return to London, where he joined Michael in a small mews cottage in Belgravia. They were designated firewatchers by the local air-raid warden. As Michael puts it in *A Life in Movies*: "Our job was to wander about the roofs of these stately terraces, armed with a shovel and a tin hat, and when the fire bombs showered down we were supposed to shovel them smartly into the street."

Wall to join the road north to Dumfries and on to Tynron, to visit my mother. She had elected to stay in Scotland after the war. Her fans will remember that she had been invited to occupy a shepherd's cottage in the village of Tynron, where she had looked after a series of Land Girls.* After the war Jim Gourlay at the Ford wanted his cottage back, so I bought for my mother the square white house with the walled garden on the lane to the Linn. It had a few acres of level pasture, a rarity in those parts, and two big copper beeches, my favorite tree. We bought two cows, christened Monique and Moira: Monique was a large lady, black and white; Moira a strawberry roan, very quick on her feet.

It was a fine, cool night with stars when I arrived, and I went down to see if there was much water in the burn that ran alongside the kitchen garden. There must have been rain in the hills, for there was plenty of water and I thought I might try for a trout in the morning. When I got back to the house Bill had telephoned. We spoke to Myrtle in London, who told us how Pop died. My mother smiled and said, "That's just like Tommy."

I had to go south and make plans for the funeral, of course, and I decided to drive back to Newcastle, leave the car there, and go down by train. I asked my mother where she thought he ought to be buried. She said, "Ask Jack Powell. He's the only one of the brothers left."

I asked if she wanted to come to the funeral. She said, "No, I don't think so. I'll ask the minister here to pray for him next Sunday."

A little while later she said, "He should never have been a farmer. That was his father's fault. He did it to please him."

I said, "What about you?"

"Oh, I'd have been happy anywhere, with my two little boys."

I went to see him in the mortuary and took off his finger the gold signet ring of which he was so proud. He had ordered me to do this when he died. It had a crest on it which he also used to have embossed upon his notepaper: a lion rampant in a crown proper, and the motto *Vigilanter*. I never knew the origin of it—it may have been one of his fantasies. I was not used to wearing a ring, and lost it almost immediately.

I looked at his strong, clean-shaven face. Now that his glasses were gone and you could no longer see the weak Powell eyes (all the brothers were nearsighted), all the strength of his features could be seen. He made a good corpse. I remembered how I had asked him to run the house at Bratton Fleming during the war, and how, after a contemptuous look into the garden

*Women who went into rural parts of Britain during World War II to pick crops and drive tractors in order to relieve men called up for military service. Sheila Sim played a Land Girl in *A Canterbury Tale*.

shed, he had gone down to Barnstaple and bought a set of the heaviest and most durable garden tools he could find: spade and shovel, rake, fork, etc., and then with a red-hot poker had marked them with my initials before setting to work with them.

"Tools are valuable things, Frankie. Cost a lot of money. Buy the best, but always burn Mick's initials on them—'M.P.'—like that."

The ashwood sizzled under his iron.

"Neighbors are always borrowing things in the country. Trouble is, they never bring them back. But if they see your initials staring them in the face every morning, it shames them into it, eventually."

It took me quite a time to find my Uncle Jack in the village of Martley, in Worcestershire. He had married again and adopted his wife's name, so he was now Dowding-Powell. He proved to be a tower of strength. He arranged for my father to be buried in the old Powell burial ground, in the little churchyard at Crown East, on the Oswestry road. My father had meant to be buried in France, his adopted country that he loved so well, but fate chose an English grave for him. He lies in the shade of the old yew tree, only a few miles from Upper Wick, the ivy-covered manor house where he was born.

In these memoirs, I have tried to give a fair and adequate account of my father. As a father he inspired alarm rather than affection; he was so very energetic. The French didn't pretend to understand him, but they enjoyed him very much. They liked his knickerbocker suits, his stockings and heavy brogues, his yellow woolen waistcoats, his knitted tie with the old Bromsgrove colors, his French beret perched rakishly on his head with the silver dragon of the Buffs, our Kent regiment, pinned on it, and in his buttonhole the ribbon of a Chevalier du Mérite Agricole. They liked the way he played golf, losing no time addressing the ball and smacking it straight down the fairway. He was a great stayer, and the champion of the last nine holes. They didn't so much like his way of playing cards because he so obviously played to win, and then usually won, and then quit while ahead. But they admired his great strides, and the extraordinary brand of Franglais that he spoke. Finally, he was *très sportif,* and that covered everything.

=

Memory is our sixth sense. It is triggered by any one of the other five senses: by the images in a family album, by a little tune, by the smell of wood burning, by a dog's cold nose, by the taste of a madeleine. By some such association of words and images, when I wrote that we first rehearsed the play *Hanging Judge* in the Winter Garden Theatre, there rises up in my mind not just the image of the dirty, neglected old theatre, with the battered green garden trelliswork on its walls—the theatre where, between the wars, Leslie

Henson, Dorothy Dickson, and Heather Thatcher strutted their stuff in imported musical comedies from America, like *Sally*—but the anxious face of Emeric, and the bulky script of *The Golden Years* in his arms, begging me to find time to read it before we vanished to the provinces on the pre-London tour of the play.

I leafed through Emeric's script as the train lumbered northward toward Newcastle-upon-Tyne. I had already read the first thirty pages, and I expected a treat. Emeric loved research, and this was a subject very much in his field. Who but Emeric would have opened *The Golden Years* with two boys playing skittles in a German beer yard? (The Strauss family were famous brewers.) He had made great play of the stuffy ceremonials and stiff protocol at the court of some little German princeling where Strauss had his first professional job as assistant music-meister.

I read on, as the sleeping car rumbled on through the night. He had handled the meeting with Hugo von Hofmannsthal beautifully, and established at once the qualities that each man brought to the other in their future collaboration. I recognized myself as the target, and grinned when the poet had to explain some particularly subtle character analysis to the composer. Then I sat up: his treatment of *Salome* was a triumph, a certain success! The scene is the first rehearsal, with all the stuffy bourgeois in a state of shock and the big *Heldentenor* coming up the stairs, singing his part—this was great stuff! And, of course, *Salome* itself, as a piece of theatre and as a wonderful part for Tcherina, a dancer and actress, was almost enough to carry the film.

But *Rosenkavalier* was going to do that. And as I read Emeric's breakdown and treatment of the magic opera I forgot all about *Hanging Judge*, forgot the engine noises and steam when we stopped at Crewe, and almost cheered aloud when I read the sequence of the hundredth performance of this great artistic masterpiece in Milan, at La Scala. But the last third of the script was a letdown that I couldn't blame on the late hour and the discomfort of my journey. After the triumph of Milan, Emeric should have ended his script with the death of Hofmannsthal, briefly and dramatically. This would have brought the film, and the story of the collaboration, to a fitting close. The script was already at page 100, and our scripts were never much more than 110 pages (and in the case of *A Matter of Life and Death*, 96 American quartos).

But when the poet Hofmannsthal died Strauss had many years ahead of him of musical triumphs and libretto failures, and had even written one autobiographical opera, *Capriccio*, which debated the relative importance of words and music; hours and hours of musical ideas, but never, oh never, did he ever touch the heights of ecstasy inspired by his association with the finer mind of Hofmannsthal. Emeric had wrestled with this nobly, but he failed.

The mainspring of the action was broken; the inspiration was gone. The script plodded to an end, the end we had always envisaged of the little home movie and the composer in the bosom of his family.

"He should have died forty minutes ago," I grunted, as I stuffed the script into my already overloaded briefcase.

We never did make *The Golden Years*. Film audiences never saw this old tyrant, this proto-Nazi, kiss his wife in a home movie. The ball was in our hands, but we let it drop. Our agent, Christopher Mann, distrusted the script. Harry Cohn turned it down, and didn't even thank us for writing it on spec. Ilya Lopert and Bob Dowling, who were scouring Europe for a subject, hated it. Strauss was a great European artist, yes, but hadn't he been a favorite of Hitler's? Once these things are said, there is no going back. It was only 1952. We dropped *The Golden Years*.

Stapi was waiting in the wings. And if Richard Strauss was a nonstarter— how about *Die Fledermaus*? I looked blank.

" 'The Bat'?"

Stapi opened his blue, innocent eyes.

"I thought, my dear Michael, that you did not understand German?"

"That's not German, that's English. We call a bat a flittermouse in Kent. *Fledermaus* . . . flittermouse . . . plain as the nose on your face. What is *Die Fledermaus*? Is it a thriller, like *The Old Dark House*?"

"It is an operetta. Johann Strauss. The story takes place in Vienna, and Emeric has a great idea."

I looked at Emeric, who nodded and produced a familiar little roll of paper. He unfolded it.

"Do you remember, Michael, how Alex sent you and me to Vienna to see *The Tales of Hoffmann* on the stage—"

"—and we took our places in the stage box just as Antonia reached a high C—the last note of the opera? Yes."

"Vell . . ."—this single syllable was an invariable prelude to Emeric expounding one of his ideas to me. "Vell, you remember that since the war Vienna is divided into four military zones, English, French, Russian, American, and that there is a joint council where the Four Powers have their representatives who deal with problems that arise jointly."

"Is there?"

"There is. Now, Michael . . ."—this was another of Emeric's gambits to pin down my wandering attention. "Now, Michael, the plot of *Die Fledermaus* is nothing. It is the usual operetta mixture of husbands deceiving wives and wives cheating on husbands. There is a big party given by a Russian prince, lots of mistaken identity—leave all of that to me to sort out. The score is very good, one of Strauss's best. But if these husbands, wives, and lovers are all members of the occupying forces . . . for instance, Eisenstein could be a French captain, Alfred could be an American colonel, who has been a lover of the French lady who is now Eisenstein's wife . . . you can see the possibilities. This would be a lovely part for Tcherina," he added, with the look of one who throws ant eggs onto the surface of the pond and waits for the goldfish to rise and take the bait.

I felt the pricking of my thumbs.

"And the Bat . . . who is he?"

"The Bat is Doctor Falke, a popular Viennese playboy, and he will be played by a Viennese, because Falke is a Viennese in the play. And Anton wants to play him in the film—if we make it," he added hastily, seeing the look of suspicion spreading over my face.

"Anton!"

This was a different kettle of fish. Anton Walbrook! I had been chatting with him only a few days ago, in the crush bar at the Garden.*

"He never mentioned it to me."

"Of course he didn't, Michael. You know how proud Anton is, how correct! You would have to speak first. But, of course, Falke would be very near his heart. He has played two Germans and a Russian for us, but Anton is a Viennese, a true Viennese. He would like to add him to our collection."

I pondered, while Stapi watched and smiled. We were all drinking coffee in the Bauer-au-Lac, and drinking little glasses of slivovitz no bigger than my thumbnail.

"This Falke . . . the *Fledermaus* . . . Why is he a doctor? Is there a hospital scene?" I added hopefully. I detest hospital scenes. But Emeric was too quick for me.

"Oh, Michael, he's not a real doctor! It merely means he is a distinguished person in Vienna. In Vienna everyone is something, nobody is nothing. If you went to Vienna with Frankie, they would call her Frau Doktor Powell. The Bat is always playing practical jokes on other people. He is the sort of chap who can get champagne from the French, caviar from the Russians, when nobody else can . . . you know."

I grinned in spite of myself.

"And this Russian prince, who gives the big party—would he be a Russian general?" I was thinking of Orson.

"I think so, Michael, but I haven't worked it all out, yet. Do you like the idea?"

I temporized.

"It's like those comedies that Lubitsch made in America, with Maurice

*Covent Garden.

Chevalier and Jeanette MacDonald. I would have to listen to the score, and I don't think that I want to do an operetta."

Nobody said any more. The two conspirators relaxed and changed the subject. I was certainly not going to change it back again. I could think of no contribution that I could make to a Viennese operetta, and anyway, *Ill Met by Moonlight* was nearer and dearer to my heart, not because I wanted to play at cops and robbers but because of Crete and the Cretans. But it didn't seem like the right time for it yet. People were still trying to forget the war and become socially conscious. Big, spectacular war pictures, like *The Guns of Navarone* and *Lawrence of Arabia*, were in the oven but not yet in production, and it was obvious that they would have to be crammed with big names and expensive special effects. Emeric already knew that I wanted to start the film with Crete and the Cretans, and that I proposed to open with the German paradrop on the island: hundreds of armed paratroopers turning the sky black like a crowd of locusts, while the islanders fight and die in defense of their homes and families. He had heard my stories about Xan Fielding and Paddy Leigh-Fermor, and had listened to my pleas for at least three or four subplots, love stories or murders, to crisscross in and out of the main plot of the kidnapping of the German general. An action film like this needed to have big names and daring stuntmen, and the best part would be the German general: the more formidable he was, the greater glory for his kidnappers—and then he would have to make several attempts to escape and nearly succeed.

"Imagine Connie Veidt in the part," I said.

To shoot the whole big splashy production in Crete we would need a big company behind us, and if there was no German actor suitable for the general we should go after Yul Brynner. A film like this had to be fun as well as thrilling; after all, I said, this was where we came in on *The Spy in Black*.

Emeric seemed to agree with me, but he didn't. He was going through a series of domestic upheavals and he needed money, lots of money. He looked upon *Ill Met by Moonlight* as a property we had bought cheap and could sell dear. I was dumb, and he was desperate. But not a word of complaint or plea for help escaped those firm, clean-shaven lips. Magyars don't talk.

Optioning of other men's stories was a new experience for The Archers, not altogether a healthy one. In the crazy world of the movies many stories are optioned, but few are chosen for production. Emeric, who had been selling scripts and story ideas all his working life, even went so far as to say that there are certain stories that are always under option but never made, and that these stories are a writer's homing pigeons that return unerringly to the nest when the option period has expired. Such a story was his own *The Miracle in St. Anthony's Lane*, which had been optioned in Berlin, in Paris, and in London, and had even made one flight to Hollywood for six months before returning to its author, minus a few feathers. Emeric even made one attempt to sell it to me, but I wasn't having any. The story was loaded with Hungarian charm, but it had no substance. It was a tender trap, a good fairy, a marshmallow, the sort of film that attracts and sucks in top talent like Willy Wyler, Margaret Sullavan, and then leaves them foundering in the gooey mess. Emeric knew what I thought about *St. Anthony's Lane*, and so he didn't bring it up now.

Hein rang up in great excitement.

"Micky, is it true about *Die Fledermaus?*"

"Is what true . . . ?" I was grumpy. I felt as if I were the Tin Man and was being hustled. "Is what true?"

"That *Fledermaus* is to be our next picture? It's a marvelous idea to stage it in Four Power Vienna! Rosalinda will be a marvelous part for Monique."

"Who says so?"

By now he had got the message and his voice changed.

"Is it not true? . . . No?"

"Who told you?"

"George Busby. He has been talking to Chris Mann."

"And who has Chris been talking to . . . to Stapi, I suppose?"

"Oh, Micky, is it too good news to be true? It has been such a torture, this dreadful Gilbert and this lousy Sullivan. If you say it is not true, I will jump in the Thames, and Ada will hang herself."

My heart melted.

"I don't know . . . maybe. We'll talk about it. I don't think that I understand musical comedy; there's no plot to speak of, and every now and then the characters all stop and sing, for no reason that I can discover."

"Yes—this is operetta—this is true, but Emeric's idea to bring it up to date is a very good one."

"Good for whom? Do people really want to go and see this crap?"

But I was cheering up. I wanted to believe Hein. I wanted him to be happy. I knew that by now all The Archers had heard the rumor. The thought of all those doggy faces looking up at me hopefully . . . I had better come up with something bigger and better, or I was cornered—in Stapi's corner.

It was a crazy winter, the winter of 1952–53. Everything that we tried to promote got turned down, while *Fledermaus* waltzed steadily on to the sound of applause from potential backers. Stapi was putting up £90,000 as his contribution, and Robert Clark at Elstree was putting up the rest. I grumbled that an operetta like this in Hollywood in the 1930s would be chock full of stars—that's what people would pay for. French Eisenstein would be played by Maurice Chevalier, American Alfred by Bing Crosby, the Russian General by Orson Welles, Dr. Falke by . . . well . . . by Anton Walbrook.

"Great idea!" they all chorused. "They're all available. Go get Maurice Chevalier, Bing Crosby, Anton Walbrook, and Orson Welles . . . we'll pay."

We had a meeting with Bing Crosby in Paris. The Groaner would talk of nothing but golf. I talked to Orson. He was somewhere in Spain, Italy, maybe in Cyprus making *Othello*. In any case, he needed money and said sure, could he have the money now? He'd give us three days' work for £30,000 on three days' notice. I said it was a deal. Emeric and I and Hein met Maurice Chevalier, and he said, "Oh, that's a *sensationelle* idea, to co-star with Bing Crosby. That's *sensationelle* . . . but what about the billing?"

Emeric said, "Well, Mr. Chevalier, you wouldn't expect to come in front of Bing Crosby, would you?"

Maurice stroked his chin, and looked at all of us, "No-ooo, no-ooo, I wouldn't expect to come in front of Bing Crosby . . . of course not . . . but I wouldn't like to come after him either."

We all burst out laughing, and Hein said, "We will bill you as Bing Chevalier and Maurice Crosby."

He laughed and nodded.

"That would be *sensationelle!*"

But he wouldn't do it, any more than Bing would. They didn't need to.

Emeric, knowing that I was less than enthusiastic about the project, loyally came up with some other ideas.

"Michael, have you read about the Domenici case?"

Of course I had. It was a cause célèbre, and had been in the news for several weeks. An English family—Sir Eric Drummond, his wife, and daughter—driving down to the Riviera through the mountains and camping on the way, were found brutally murdered, all three of them, in the hills near Digne. It was a route I often took when I drove down to the south of France, and I could picture the location. The murders seemed completely without motive, and suspicion naturally fell on the male members of the French family living in the valley. Some bright journalist discovered that Eric Drummond had been working for MI-5, or some similar organization, in the war, and put up a theory that he might have been well known in this particular neighborhood during the French Resistance, and that here might lie a motive that could be discovered. It was quite clear that the murder had been a vindictive one. The three victims were lying far apart, as if they had tried to escape the avenger. It was a brutal, disturbing, unnerving case, and it naturally made a big effect on all tourists thinking of driving and camping down through the Alpes Maritimes, mostly uninhabited mountains.

"What makes it different from other similar murders, Emeric?"

"It is not the murder, Michael. It is what the police do about it that is fascinating. This would make a film. I was lunching with a man at Geneva, and there were two men at the next table who, I think, must have been magistrates. They looked like officials, and they thought it was so important to discover the identity of this murderer that the police were prepared to put a man on the case and keep him there in the valley until he knew as much as the people in the valley knew. They said that it was quite clear that everyone in the valley knew the identity of the murderer and nobody would talk, and nobody would ever talk unless they did something about it. So this young policeman would be given a mission, to go and get a job in the valley and stay there until the crime was solved.

" 'What if it takes years?' said one of the men.

" 'Then it takes years,' said his friend. 'Maybe he has to stay there all his life! Maybe he gets murdered too!'

"They both laughed, thinking it a very good joke.

"I thought—wow!" said my partner, who occasionally lapsed into the language of showbiz, "Wow! What a great idea for a new kind of murder mystery, and what a great part for someone like your friend Gregory Peck, who is in Europe and is available."

"I'm afraid John Huston has got him pinned down," I said gloomily. "He's got the money for *Moby Dick,* and Greg was always first choice for Captain Ahab. William Wyler is on his trail, too. Still, I'll try. It's a wonderful idea, old horse. Do you have any more like that?"

The old horse was looking particularly well groomed that morning. He smiled one of his smiles, a deprecating smile.

"Have I spoken to you about *Bouquet,* Michael?"

"No, I don't think so; is that the title?"

"Yes. It is really four bouquets: roses, thistles—"

"—shamrocks, and leeks. I get you, four stories in one."

Emeric looked pained. He always did when I jumped the gun on his surprises.

"Yes, four stories in one. The one bouquet is the United Kingdom, of course, and there is an English story, a Scottish story, an Irish story, and a Welsh story."

"That sounds very nice. But the Irish might not want to be a part of a British bouquet."

"Yes, I have thought of that. But they would not like to be left out, either."

"True. It's a nice idea for an anthology film. Do you suggest we look out for some stories, or write something original?"

"I thought we should find stories that already exist, Michael, stories that will go together into one, big, human bouquet. It could be something we could think about—not to hurry, you understand—but to find the right stories, or the right sort of actors, actors that bring out the national character. We might even get the public in on it. Everybody has their favorite story."

I knew where he had got his idea. Willie Maugham had been recording some of his own short stories, and introducing them himself on film, for the Rank Organisation. I don't know whose idea it was, but it was a good one. They were packaged together and called *Quartet* (1948), *Trio* (1950), and *Encore* (1951). Maugham was very shy and went through agonies while making his recordings that introduced each story. One of the dear old prop-men, one of a sterling bunch that worked at Pinewood Studios, saw and understood his agony, and went over to the tea trolley, filled a filthy cup with the awful brown beverage which is considered essential for British filmmaking, and thrust it into Maugham's hand, saying, "Have a sip, Somerset."

Which Willie did, and felt all the better for it.

Emeric interrupted my musings.

"Michael," he said, "you know everything, but I can tell you something you don't know."

"Tell on."

"Monique is going to get married."

Merde alors! Frankie was right. Frankie is always right. The only mistake she made was marrying me. She had said that Monique would opt for Paris, and give Hollywood the go-by. *Paname! Paname!** How you gonna keep them down on the farm, after they've seen Paree!

Monique returned from Hollywood, was offered a job in Paris, went there, and stayed there. Frankie had said that Monique would marry a Frenchman, a tough Frenchman; and that is exactly what she did.

Meet Raymond Roi! Alas, he died only a year or two ago. He was a good and generous and faithful husband. Otherwise, Monique would have killed him. She adored him. She puzzled him. She delighted him.

We all liked him on sight. He was not French, and claimed to be Italian. But so many people do that. He was rich, very rich. He was tough, strong, and broad—not tall. His eyes were his best feature, clear and honest as a wild animal's. He had made his money after the war by acquiring and selling scrap metal. Rumor said that in one of his deals he had stolen an entire armored train, transported it to North Africa, dismembered it and sold it there, by auction, to countries that were in need of scrap; apparently there were a lot of these, and the demand, and the supply, remained constant for some time after the war.

Next time that Frankie and I went to Paris, or through Paris, we met Raymond. Monique was already planning her new life, and her new career, which was going to embrace theatre, film, and all the other arts, as well as *le tout Paris.* When we returned to the San Regis Frankie said, "He'll do. He's already made an enormous settlement on Monique."

*Nickname for Paris.

I was amused.

"What did you make of that extraordinary house in the Bois de Boulogne, and that huge room full of art magazines and nouveau riche paintings propping up the walls?"

"Oh, that's nothing. Monique will change all that."

"You sound a little disappointed."

Frankie gave me one of her wide-eyed stares.

"Well, she could have had anybody, couldn't she? He's just an ordinary racketeer."

"An extraordinary racketeer, you mean."

And all this is thirty-four years ago, and Frankie is dead, and Monique still has an eighteen-inch waist and is more beautiful than ever, and *où sont les neiges d'antan* . . .

Everybody liked the idea of *Bouquet;* everybody has their favorite short story. David Lean suggested "The Cruise of 'The Breadwinner,' " by H. E. Bates. He had wanted to do a film of it when the war was still on, and the Rank Organisation story department had bought it for him. I approved it. It was one of the best stories since Rudyard Kipling. It is an epic in a small compass, as good as that American short story which was made into a film, "Time Out of War."

Emeric fell in love with a delightful Welsh short story by Rhys Davies. The title: "Gents Only." The hero is an undertaker in a small Welsh village, whose wife runs away with a commercial traveler. He announces that he is through with women, and from now on will bury men only.

I suggested Robert Burns's "Tam O'Shanter," spoken by John Laurie and danced by Moira Shearer. The fourth story we couldn't agree on for a long while. Then I met Frank O'Connor. I was reading a collection of his short stories. Somehow I had missed him before, and now I was reveling in a writer who was as good as Chekhov. Then I read "First Confession," and nearly fell off my chair laughing. It was told in the first person by a little boy—that is to say by Frank O'Connor—and he admitted to me later that it was a personal reminiscence. By that time I had met him, we had become friends, I had learned that his real name was Michael O'Donovan and that he had returned to Ireland to live after many years in America. He was one of many Irish artists whose explorations and experiences, generously shared, have not been appreciated by the Irish Church, although the churchmen and the writers arrived at the same end by different means.

Emeric, for whom de Maupassant was more the master than Chekhov, was delighted by Frank. We all finally settled for his story "In the Train," a novel in miniature, a tragedy in twelve pages. The setting: in the train, traveling at night through the west of Ireland. The characters: members of the *gárdai,* returning to their village after giving evidence at a murder trial in which the murderess has been acquitted. The murderess herself is returning to the same village. The story is a gem—a beautiful, polished gem—an emerald. And what a part for Siobhán! I could hear her voice crying, "He's no more to me than the salt sea . . . than the salt sea! . . ." as hitching her shawl around her thin shoulders she vanishes into the night.

But we never gathered our blooms. We never presented our *Bouquet*. We had overlooked an important point. Our proposal was based upon the fact that everybody had their own favorite short story. But nobody can agree on four of them. So the rose had its supporters, the thistle its doubters, the shamrock had its lovers, the leek its detractors. Nobody had the sense to say, "Great idea! Go ahead and do it."

Emeric's dreams of a quick killing faded; they all just sat on their fat asses. I could feel *Die Fledermaus*'s hot breath on the back of my neck. I could see Emeric's pleading eyes, Stapi's guileless eyes. They whispered to each other, "What the hell is he waiting for?"

"But, doctor," I gasped, "I want Clemens Krauss."

I had seen his *Rosenkavalier* and had been to one of his concerts, and had fallen in love with his *tempi*. We had two meetings and I went to two more concerts. My spirits began to revive. Krauss was such a wonderful chap. He shared my opinion about operetta, and explained that that was half the fun. He loved movies, and had wanted to make one ever since he had seen *The Tales of Hoffmann*. He was quick, elegant, full of energy, incapable of a false quantity or a phony idea. Then he went to Mexico City to give a concert, and, as you all know, Mexico City is eight thousand feet up in the air, rarefied air, and he had a weak heart. Without waiting to get acclimatized, Clemens Krauss took a rehearsal, put down his baton, and died.

I was desolate. I was desperate. I was on the barricades . . . when help came from an unlikely source—the firm of Marks and Spencer.

≡

The new state of Israel came into being on May 14, 1948, and was immediately attacked by Egypt in the celebrated ten-month war, ending in the rout of the invaders. Chaim Weizmann, the first president of the new state, died in 1952; his autobiography had been published in 1949. It had been on my shelves for some time, until one day I took it down and started to read it. He called his book *Trial and Error*. It seemed to me a remarkably civilized title for a book about a revolutionary statesman who had achieved so much. He was a fascinating man and he had a fascinating story to tell, and in a few pages I was hooked. As soon as I finished the book I was off to Charing Cross Road to buy a beginner's handbook to organic chemistry (secondhand, of course), for Chaim Weizmann was a chemist, and thereby hangs the tale.

I dropped the two books into my briefcase, flung the briefcase into the

Bentley, and roared up the heights of Hampstead, where Emeric had established himself in a very large house after the war, at 72 Redington Road. A word here about The Archers' briefcases. They were designed and provided by Emeric Pressburger (for Emeric had an exactly similar one), made of the best calf, saddle-stitched, and stood four-square beside their masters when placed upon the ground, unlike those deceitful Fifth Avenue macho imitation briefcases that, when put down at their masters' feet, roll over like ingratiating puppies. The Archers' briefcases were built by master craftsmen from the Lansdowne leather shop off Jermyn Street, London S.W.1, no longer there. They never wore out, but went into honorable retirement every ten years or so, to give Emeric an excuse to buy new ones.

Into their open mouths would drop scripts, books, newspapers, *Time* and *Life*, radios, cameras, bottles of apricot brandy (and occasionally slivovitz), and at least one Hungarian salami of imposing girth and hard as the heart of a Hapsburg. Independent film producers must be prepared for triumph or disaster, and when we stood up our hands would grope for our briefcases as naturally as a commercial traveler's hands would grope for his samples. I remember vividly the amused but incredulous look that Marlon Brando cast at the sight of my battered old briefcase, squatting beside me on the terrace of his ugly home on Mulholland Drive in Los Angeles.

"What's that?" he said, and although he was a sophisticate, and therefore a friend and ally, we cringed, me and my briefcase, at the implied insult, and have never felt the same again about this wild god of an actor, whose power and imagination can turn the earthy details of human intercourse into a sacred rite.

Brandishing the two books I'd bought, I proclaimed to the rooftops of Hampstead, and to the Heath, that this should be The Archers' next film. Emeric, being a Hungarian Jew, a true Magyar, was disconcerted. He pointed out that the new state was only a few years old, and living from hand to mouth. But I live on opposition, and I insisted that Chris Mann write to the publishers to find out if the rights to the book were free. Meanwhile, I reread the Book of Exodus.

I love my Bible—King James's Bible—commissioned by that shrewd, gangling, driveling Scot, and published contemporaneously with the First Folio of Shakespeare: two mines of vigorous English, of golden words and silver phrases that the writers of English have been quarrying over the last four hundred years. How many of my baby years were spent sitting beside my mother and my brother, John, listening to the roll and cadence of the Old and New Testament, as we sat in our pew in the little church of St. Martin's on the Hill, looking down on Canterbury in the river valley below? Behind my brother's attentive mask, I knew that he was reconstructing the Forth Bridge, girder by girder, or was working out the optimum route (with bridges) for a railway line to connect Hong Kong and Peking. My mother, content to have a son sitting on each side of her, was probably planning a new rose garden. I would be storing away favorite passages of the readings for private recitals:

> Thou shalt not covet thy neighbour's house, thou shalt not covet thy neighbour's wife, nor his manservant, nor his maidservant, nor his ox, nor his ass, nor any thing that is thy neighbour's.

As for coveting this, that, or the other, I think that I had a general idea that a spot of coveting could be a pleasurable thing, and only the week before, my father had thrashed both of us, my brother and myself, for coveting and stealing cherries—from our *own* trees, mark you!—which we considered grossly unfair, not knowing that the crop had been sold on the trees. I wriggled at the thought, and then I wriggled for another reason.

Services were longer in those dear, dusty days before the 1914 war. My mother, listening attentively to the sermon, would feel a tug on her sleeve, and see an agonized face whispering, "Wee-wee, Mummy!" and would bustle me down the aisle and out into the churchyard, where I relieved myself under an old yew tree on a favorite gravestone that had collapsed long ago and now lay at an angle of about twenty degrees, with deeply incised letters that offered a fascinating number of possible channels for my surplus water . . . until I was dragged back to church by my patient mother. Leaving my brother high and dry we scuttled into an empty pew, with the old verger in his tattered black gown a smiling accomplice.

Before I could read, I knew a great deal of the Bible by heart—thrilling scenes that were almost contemporary to me, like the temptation of Jesus:

> And the Devil said unto him: "If thou be the Son of God, command this stone that it be made bread." And Jesus answered him, saying: "It is written, that man shall not live by bread alone, but by every word that proceedeth out of the mouth of God."
> Then the Devil, taking him up into an high mountain. . . .

where else but the Matterhorn—climbed by my grandfather!

> . . . showed unto him all the kingdoms of the world in a moment of time. And the Devil said unto him: "All this power will I give thee, and the glory of them: for that is delivered unto me; and to whomsoever I will I give it. If thou therefore wilt worship me, all shall be thine." And Jesus answered and said unto him: "Get thee behind me, Satan. . . ."

Later on, when I was a King's Scholar at the King's School, Canterbury, playing and whispering on the benches of the great cathedral, sheltered from the eye of my housemaster by the tall, polished, wooden bench-backs, I would suddenly become aware of the descent of a white-surpliced figure from the rood-screen above, fluttering down like an angel from heaven, moving in a stately fashion to the brass lectern, finding the place in the Old Testament, and reading with a sense of drama the scene between Pharaoh and Moses: "Let my people go," while I meditated on my favorite miracle, the parting of the Red Sea, a piece of magic that was to haunt me all my life. The canon had a beautiful voice and read well, except that he was a little too conscious of having a beautiful voice. I preferred the archdeacon, with a voice like a tuba, reading about Joshua and the walls of Jericho:

> So the people shouted when the priests blew with the trumpets: and it came to pass, when the people heard the sound of the trumpet, that the people shouted with a great shout, that the wall fell down flat, and the people went up into the city, every man straight before him, and they took the city.

What small boy would not be stirred by the tale of David and Absalom; how the young man's bright, long hair, of which he was so proud, betrayed him to his enemies, how it caught in the low, sweeping branches of an oak tree, how he was held fast by his hair until Joab came up with him and slew him? And David's lament: "Oh, Absalom, my son, my son! Would that I could have died for thee! Oh, Absalom, my son!"

And there was Solomon with the love songs—for, by now, I could read them myself—likening his beloved's belly to a heap of wheat. I knew exactly what he meant, for I had seen these heaps of wheat on the threshing floor at home, rounded and smooth, with a hole like a navel in their center, and I could appreciate the sensuality of the image. Heady stuff for an eleven-year-old. So, it is no wonder that the names, words, and places of the Bible filled my head as I read Chaim Weizmann's book, *Trial and Error*.

But what fascinated me most of all, as a storyteller and as a filmmaker, was the fact that Weizmann was an organic chemist, and that he used his skill as an inventor to further his political aims. How many countries have been created out of a test tube? He could have said, as he did to his fellow Zionists, "We Jews cannot be guests all our lives; we have to be the hosts sometime," and they would have listened to him as little as they listened to Herzl, that great Zionist and great optimist. Weizmann could have warned his fellow Jews, as he often did, "We are always telling each other that we are the salt of the earth. I don't like that. If there is too much salt in the food, you throw the food out—and the salt with it," and they would still have gone on uneasily seeking assimilation with a culture that was not their own.

But this man, this tall Russian Jew from the Pripet marshes, this child who had seen pogroms, this prophet who had turned the revolutionary Jews away from Leninism to Zionism, this industrial chemist, this far-seeing inventor, whose researches in rayon helped his adopted country, England, to win the First World War, who asked for no reward for himself, only a home for his people—this was a new kind of hero for a film, and one very much to my taste.

Just now, I was writing that the King James Bible is the only translation of the Testaments for me. So I will now contradict myself. There is one other—a Greek Testament—a little black book bound in leather. It was the John Miles Powell Memorial Prize, which I won in my last term at Dulwich College, to the great gratification of Aunt Ethel and all the other aunts, her sisters. My mother and I pretended to be gratified too, but I don't think we were really. We blamed John's death on his housemaster.* I would have rather had my bespectacled, straight-haired, serious elder brother alive, rumpling my curls and calling me "Fuzzy-Wuzzy."

That was the year 1921, when I ceased to be a bookworm and became movie-mad, which I still am in 1986. I am writing this in New York, in Greenwich Village, at 23 West Tenth Street. Thelma and Marty are editing *The Color of Money*. This is the first of July, and next Thursday is the Fourth of July, *the* Fourth of July, the celebration of the arrival of the Statue of Liberty in New York harbor a hundred years ago, enlightening the world. Mitterrand will be there, Reagan will be there, liberty will be there. When darkness falls, at 11:30 P.M., the president of the United States will press a switch and the Statue of Liberty will be illuminated again, and every American man, woman, and child will be murmuring the words that are engraved on its plinth, for they all know them by heart, they are part of the heart of the nation:

> Give me your tired, your poor,
> Your huddled masses yearning to breathe free,
> The wretched refuse of your teeming shore,
> Send these, the homeless, tempest-tossed, to me.
> I lift my lamp beside the golden door.

Just imagine what this must have meant a hundred years ago to the Jews from the European ghettos when they had nowhere else to go but America. For them Ellis Island, with all its terrors, was really a golden door. And now, a hundred years later, ships are coming from all over the world to the port

---

*Michael's older brother, John, was only fifteen when he died tragically of appendicitis while at boarding school. His housemaster failed to recognize the seriousness of John's symptoms until it was too late.

of New York to honor this magnificent gift from the country of *Liberté, Egalité, Fraternité* to the country of "If you want to call me that, smile."

The president of the Republic of France will accept America's thanks for this magnificent present, and trail these clouds of glory with him over the top of the world, to his meeting with the president of the Union of Soviet Socialist Republics.

And then there are the ships: great battleships from the belligerent nations, and beautiful, tall sailing ships, three- and four-masted barks from the seafaring ones, from Denmark, from Norway, from Argentina, from France, from Belgium, from the Dominion of Canada, from Chile, from Colombia, from Ecuador, from Indonesia, from Italy, from Mexico, from the Gulf of Oman (a very sporting effort by the Sultan, for it took this bark one hundred and two days to get from the Indian Ocean to little old New York) to join the other ships in their goodwill fleet. Great tall ships from Venezuela, Portugal, and Spain are still arriving, and from Philadelphia, the cradle of the American republic, there is one very special ship, the *Gazela,* the oldest square-rigger still putting out to sea. This three-masted barkentine was built in Portugal in 1882, her timbers sawn from trees that were planted by Prince Henry the Navigator in the fourteenth century. She is maintained by the Philadelphia Ship Preservation Guild, and you can see her most days at Penn's Landing. She has a crew of thirty, her length is 186 feet, her mast is 100 feet high. This wonderful ship, on her maiden voyage, must have passed close to where the Statue of Liberty was being prepared in her home port in France for her maiden voyage, three years later, to New York. How sweet, and how suitable it is, that these two great man-made images should come together again, in friendship, one hundred years later . . . What's that you say? Why am I taking so much time and trouble to tell you about a lot of ships, when you want to hear about another launch, the launching of the state of Israel? Because it interests me, sir, or madam, and should interest you. This celebration in New York, apparently so casually gotten together in the American way, with a great deal of backstage organization and very little talk, is one of the great events of the century. It is also a great and enjoyable party, and this coming together of all these fine, tall ships from nations large and small, in pride and in friendship, in friendly rivalry, is an inspiration.

I admit that I am prejudiced. I am passionately interested in the great tall ships of the last century, and the great, tall men that sailed them. I have already mentioned our projected film, *The Promotion of the Admiral,* which is one of the two films that I most regret not having made, and which could have been made, with some guts and determination and—yes—tact. So please bear with me a little longer, and let me pick out a few ships for special mention.

The *Bluenose II* from Canada: This two-masted, wood-hulled schooner is a typical member of the Grand Banks fishing fleet, so lovingly and so wonderfully described by Rudyard Kipling in his novel *Captains Courageous,* and so faithfully re-created and directed by Victor Fleming in the Metro-Goldwyn-Mayer film of the book. Do you remember Spencer Tracy as a Portuguese seaman, and Freddie Bartholomew as the spoiled little heir to millions, washed overboard from a passenger liner and picked up by one of these fishing boats? The film of a book, particularly of a great book, very seldom equals it, but in this case I think it did. The Grand Banks fishermen of those days, and in those schooners, came from New England and the Canadian ports, and remained at sea, fishing those huge, submarine reefs full of fish, until their holds were full and they could run for home and try to be first in for the market. They were still fishing on the Grand Banks in the 1930s, right up to the declaration of World War II, and the making of *49th Parallel.* I know that Canada is proud of her *Bluenose*s, and her seamen, but I wish that she would consider renaming this historic ship as *Captains Courageous* instead of *Bluenose II.*

From Latin America allow me to single out the *Esmeralda* from unhappy Chile—I am writing this in 1986. The *Esmeralda* was what seamen would call an unlucky ship. When newly commissioned, there had been a fire on board, and since then she had led a checkered life, until she was bought by the Chilean navy in 1954. It was rumored that she had been used as a prison ship at the time of the coup by General Augusto Pinochet, and that prisoners had been tortured in her holds. Although a training ship, she is armed with four guns. (I'll bet she is, and I'll bet they're pointing inward!) Her steel hull is white, and her figurehead is an Andes condor, that largest of birds of prey. The giant South American condor is known to the Indians by the name of "bone-breaker." Crew, 338, length, 370 feet, height of her topmast 179 feet—she's a big ship.

And now a little surprise for you. You thought I had lost my way among all this shipping . . . You see that brigantine there? She is privately owned, but her blue wooden hull and her white sails are the national colors of Israel. She is *Galaxy,* registered in Israel, sailing out of Eilat—now, at the time of writing, Israel's only port on the Red Sea. *Galaxy* was originally built in Portugal in 1960, where she was a fishing trawler. She was rebuilt and refitted in 1983. Her decks are African hardwood; her panelings are mahogany. She has a crew of eight and an overall length of 120 feet; her mast is 87 feet. She is not a government ship, and yet she is here, representing her country. There is something typical about this, typical of a country that has been created as an experiment in organic chemistry, typical of a country whose first prime minister and president were poles apart: Ben-Gurion, the fighter, the labor leader, and Chaim Weizmann, the statesman, the chemist.

=

We landed at Lydda airport on Saturday, May 16, 1953. Research had begun on the projected film, and the four of us were the advance guard of The Archers: Syd Streeter, Hein Heckroth, Emeric Pressburger, and self. The state of Israel had shaken off the mandate three and a half years before. The new country was on alert, the citizens went armed and full of confidence in their country and in their destiny. The bitter ten-month war with Egypt had ended with the complete rout of the invaders, and the Israelis went about their business with a calmness and efficiency that is always inspired by the knowledge that your fate is in your own hands. Immigrants were pouring into the country—from the United States, from Europe, from Soviet Russia, and from Aden. The city of Tel Aviv was buzzing like a beehive and growing daily, but Jerusalem was still partitioned, the borders of the Arab states that surrounded her were still patrolled on both sides, the Golan Heights were still disputed, and there were still guns and mortars on the cliffs of the Sea of Galilee that face Tiberias. Every kibbutz was an armed camp.

Chris Mann's letter of inquiry to Messrs. Methuen, the publishers of Chaim Weizmann's book, had produced some results. Even better, it had produced Meyer Weisgal. Meyer Weisgal was the administrator of the Weizmann Research Institute at Rehovot in Israel. He was an American citizen, but for years had been one of Weizmann's closest associates and was now his literary executor. He was also one of the most outrageous and dictatorial beggars that the world has ever seen. He had financed the new country with enormous loans that he had no hope, nor intention, of repaying. The world owed the Jews a living, in his opinion, and he went first to the rich Jews, to the great bankers, financiers, capitalists, and industrialists in the United States and Europe—the Rothschilds, the Barings, the Bernie Baruchs—and they gave up their billions meekly, for one does not refuse Meyer Weisgal. Weizmann had dreamed up and created the new state, but it was Weisgal who kept it going from year to year, from day to day, from hour to hour. In appearance he was like the magician in a Russian fairy tale, the kind of legendary figure who lives in the deep forest, to whom you come for advice, and who is both feared and loved.

He was formidably short and alarmingly solid, like a figure in an old woodcut. He wore bright colors. His head was enormous and set on a short neck on broad shoulders. He had extraordinarily bright, observant eyes in this huge, wizard face of his. He wore rings on his thick fingers. He had thick, curly hair, and every hair seemed to have a vitality of its own. He swore continuously and harmlessly, and blasphemously, and on the whole inoffensively. Speech roared out of him like pebbles in a torrent. I am trying to paint his portrait from love and memory. He was a marvelous creation of nature. The only thing that could improve my portrait would be gold teeth, and he may have had those too, I don't remember. But I loved him on sight.

Convinced that we were serious and had the right intentions, he took us to see Simon Marks, chairman of Marks and Spencer, for Simon and his friend and partner, Israel Sieff, had been among the very earliest supporters of Weizmann and of Zionism. They were successful businessmen in Manchester when the young Weizmann came to Manchester University to start the series of experiments that would lead, finally, to the greatest experiment of all, the creation of Israel.

Emeric and I had done a great deal of preparation for this meeting, but now we learned a great deal more, and particularly about the period between the two great wars. Finally it was agreed that we should go with a small team to Israel to "see for ourselves" before writing the script. Arthur Krim, president of United Artists, an old friend of ours who, with his partner Bob Benjamin, had acquired our film *A Matter of Life and Death* from the Rank Organisation and had disguised it under the title *Stairway to Heaven*, now entered the scene and agreed to finance the picture, if Marks and Sieff would finance the script. It all happened very quickly, and now here we were, passing through Rehovot, with its long, tree-lined streets like any pleasant little town in the U.S.A., and leaving it to climb the low hills and drive down an avenue of eucalyptus trees, a tunnel of green shade.

The names of the buildings, as we passed them, were rattled off by our guide, Julian Meltzer, born in London: the Daniel Sieff Institute, the agricultural station, and, after the great white block of the Weizmann Foundation, the living quarters of the doctors and scientists at the institute. There were neat houses, flower beds, apartment blocks, and sprinklers everywhere throwing up pyramids of water that sparkled in the sun. We turned in at one particular house and stopped. This was the home of Meyer Weisgal.

On our way to the Middle East, Emeric and I had stopped over at Cannes, where the film festival was in full swing, and talked to Meyer and his wife, Shirley, a charming woman who seemed to be perfectly satisfied to be married to the archbeggar of all time. They were staying in one of my favorite parts of the coast, near Saint-Tropez, where the Montagnes des Maures drop down to the sea and are covered with beautiful chestnut trees and supply half the world with *marrons glacés*. In the valleys the roads wind through vineyards, the soil is red, and the best wine is the local vin rosé, the wine of Pierrefeu, with that lovely rusty color that the true rosé should have. A dominant feature of the landscape is the umbrella pine. There Emeric and I had met

Meyer for a last chat before we flew on to Israel. He would join us there, perhaps in three weeks' time.

While encouraging us to use his home in Rehovot as a base, he started to throw out dark hints about his daughter Helen and her husband, who were members of a kibbutz. Apparently it was a very strict kibbutz, but Helen and her husband were stricter than strict. They were redder than red, although the fact that Helen was an American who had married an Israeli seemed to indicate a faithful, supportive wife, rather than the tight-lipped commissar portrait he was painting. It sounded as if Helen and her husband had been expelled from the kibbutz and had taken up quarters in Meyer's house, and he half expected us to find the place barricaded and a machine gun in the drive.

However, the coast was clear. A friendly German cook called Erna, a bonny woman, welcomed us with tall glasses of pure orange juice. Still no machine guns, no "Brits go home," no singing of "The Red Flag." Heralded by yells from her eighteen-month-old son, Helen came swiftly and silently. She had two children. She was about twenty-five. She had rather prominent, light-colored eyes, and her skin was the color of amber. She was slender and strong. The most personal thing about her was her walk, with her hands held half clenched, and turned in the direction in which she was going. She moved beautifully.

"I like Helen, the way she walks," confided Hein. "She sends me with her walk."

But although she seemed a slender reed to be the daughter of that oak tree, Meyer Weisgal, she very soon proved to be a thinking reed. Israel is nothing if not political, and we were soon deep in the ramifications of Israel's political parties and divisions. It became clear to us that Helen and her husband were not lonely revolutionaries, but the founders of a new political party drawn from several kibbutzim, including their own, Shuval, where Shmuel, her husband, had been the organizer of the dairy system. He was now organizing secretary of the new party. Helen had been one of his dairy maids—a situation as old as the Bible.

I don't remember that we ever met Shmuel. He was always closeted some-where, writing political manifestos. But we couldn't have had a better intro-duction to the new, young Israel than Helen. She went off to a meeting, leaving us talking with Meltzer. He was an old newspaperman with thirty years' experience of Zionism, and a mine of information about Weizmann's tactics. A heavy dew came down at sunset and there was a thick fog in the valley. I had promised to keep an eye on the children and had left the communicating door open. There was a cool breeze blowing through. The air was full of birds large and small. I could hear the constant cooing of pigeons and rock doves, and the screams of little owls hunting. I had noticed exotic birds, too, with red backs and long tails, and at Lydda airport there were hundreds of migrating storks. The children made no sound, and when Helen and her husband returned I closed the door and went to sleep.

The next day was the Sabbath, when everything stops, so we spent the morning planning our itinerary. It would take three weeks, for we had a great deal of ground to cover if we were to "see for ourselves." I was a bit irked, as usual, by the absence of adequate maps. At 1:00 P.M. we went to have lunch with Mrs. Weizmann at the big house on the hill. It was designed by Eric Mendelsohn. The lunch was a success. Vera Weizmann was a wise, witty, intelligent woman. She was born in the south of Russia, in Rostov-on-Don, but her heart belonged not to Russia, and not to Israel, but to England, her adopted country. There she and her husband had found, from the time of their marriage and settlement in England, the soil most suitable for the great idea of Zionism. New ideas take time to root, and even then they are slow of growth, but if they are coaxed and encouraged, they became accepted in the English way, until that great moment when Mr. Balfour walked down to the House of Commons and, in reply to a prepared question, answered that His Majesty's Government would look with favor on the idea of Palestine as a national home for the Jews.

The years of the Mandate were to follow, years of struggle, civil war, waiting, patience, violence, heroism, until that great day in 1948, when the blue-and-white flag flew over Israel, and Weizmann and Ben-Gurion had a full-scale war on their hands. No wonder, then, that the Weizmanns looked on England as their father and mother; and although there were portraits and sculptures of her late husband throughout the house, Vera's favorite picture was the portrait by Oswald Birley, and the portrait bronze by Jacob Epstein.

On leaving, our hostess said to Emeric, who had been very silent, "Come again, when you have seen enough."

He looked at her with his beautiful eyes, and said, "We can never see enough."

The next ten days were busy ones. We traveled in Meyer's big, comfortable American automobile with the cracked window; by steam train to Jerusalem; by light aircraft to Eilat; sleeping in a new bed every night, and returning two or three times to base. Tel Aviv, a great, sprawling, vital, ugly city between the hills and the sea was only half an hour away. All the energy and inventiveness of the Jewish nature seemed to be continuously exploding out of the city, like the bursting bubbles at the edge of a volcano. We went to the borders with Lebanon, and to the Ladder of Tyre. We saw the mountains on the frontier, still streaked with snow and lined with forts. We wandered, marveling, through Acre, the crusader city, where the Arab way of life had remained unchanged since the time of Richard the Lion Heart. In the valley of the Jordan we stood on the bank and looked at the Arab sentinels across the river, only forty feet away, and Hein crept down with an old Coca-Cola bottle to fill with Jordan water for his mother. The Arab sentry unslung the rifle on his shoulder . . . and then . . . slung it on the other shoulder.

We marveled at Haifa, that beautiful port and city, with a harbor crowded with shipping that is one of the best in the Eastern Mediterranean. We met some relatives of Emeric's who had come down from Nahariya looking for him, and Hein found at Tel Aviv an old friend from Dartington Hall who was running the Habima Theatre there. We stood on the terrace of the hotel at Tiberias, on the Sea of Galilee, and looked across the lake to the thousand-foot cliff on the other side, which was the frontier with Jordan and was a still-disputed and precarious outpost; and at the foot of the cliff, across the lake from Tiberias, we saw and visited Ein Gev.

Music had made Ein Gev more famous than other kibbutzim—music and war. Their concert hall, which was in the open air, used the enemy cliffs for a sounding board. It seated three thousand and Koussevitzky had paid for the chairs and most of the instruments. Menuhin gave a recital to open their first season. We asked what the young artist had chosen to play on such an occasion. Nobody could remember, nor could he, when I telephoned his house in London the other day. "Sir Yehudi can't remember, but it would have been Bach or Brahms," says one of the dear ladies who answers the telephone in the great violinist's house. "And perhaps Tchaikovsky," says the other dear lady, listening on the extension. "He can't remember, he says, but Hepzibah was there. He does remember that."

The next day, May 27, was to be Emeric's last with the expeditionary force. I had known that all along, but I had hoped to persuade him to change his plans, partly out of devilment, and partly by the pricking of my thumbs. But Emeric's plans, when he makes them, are sacrosanct. It would take more than a witch or two to change them. Before we left England, he had been invited to be one of the guests at HM the Queen's garden party at Buckingham Palace around the time of her coronation. To Emeric, this was *the* accolade. I scoffed at this. We had earned official recognition when we created *A Matter of Life and Death* for the first Royal Film Performance in London in 1946. Had anybody spoken up for us? No. We had been introduced as clever little men to the King and Queen of England, and had bowed formally over their hands, and had felt quite happy about the honor. But a royal garden party to which two thousand other guests had been invited was not, in my opinion, the way to reward the services of a naturalized British citizen who had written *49th Parallel, The Life and Death of Colonel Blimp, A Matter of Life and Death,* and *The Red Shoes*—films that had circled the world, films that had admitted no possibility of defeat by Hitler, films that hinted that the British had a sense of humor behind the insolent façade, films that proved that the British could produce artists as well as artisans—films that spoke for England.

The morning of Emeric's last day we all got up early, long before breakfast, and went swimming on the long beaches of Nebi Rubin, which are only two miles away as the hawk flies, but in the dark, groping our way, it took forty minutes. It's a lovely beach, firm sand with bulky outcrops running out into the sea, so flat that the sea just washes over them. The edges of the reefs are sharp and clear as a table. You can walk to the edge and look down into fifteen feet of clear water. Hein and Syd and Helen played swimming-bath jokes on each other. Hein, particularly, made a very good splash when pushed off the edge of a reef. Emeric did not swim, but industriously picked up very ordinary colored stones to add to his excess baggage. I went for a run to the other end of the beach, which is about a mile long. I ran along the firm sand, just clear of the surf, and thousands of little spidery crabs, hearing the thunder of my great feet from afar, like Sabu and the djinn in *The Thief of Bagdad,* rushed back into the sea, screaming and waving their claws. The faster I ran, the faster they ran, but they always won the race. The beach ahead of me was full of flying claws, but never the one I was crossing, and when I looked over my shoulder there was never a laggard on the beach, as you sometimes see a last scared rabbit scuttling out of the grass behind you when out rough shooting. Nebi Rubin beach was suddenly and mysteriously empty. I had cleared it of its millions of crabs, and went back to breakfast.

A tale is told of the beach at Nebi Rubin, a tale of the days of the British Mandate when desperate Jews from all over Europe were trying to find shelter and a home in Palestine. Legally they could, illegally they couldn't. These were the days of the Haganah, the secret Jewish army, of the Irgun and the association of Jewish terrorists who opposed Britain's stern rule of Palestine with reprisals that were even sterner. But the little epic of the beach at Nebi Rubin ended in a comedy worthy of the topsy-turvy world of G. K. Chesterton.

Some hundreds of refugees, men, women, and children, whole families, from great-grandfather Menachem to little three-year-old Chaim, who walked with a limp because of an injured hip, desperate to escape from Cyprus internment camps and encouraged by friends and relatives in the Promised Land, chartered a trawler, whose captain knew every inch of the coast and landed them under cover of darkness on the beach at Nebi Rubin. The weather was fine, and because of the rock formation the captain was able to bring his ship right in to land. I was reminded irresistibly of the evacuation of the island of Foula. When day dawned it revealed a most extraordinary sight. These were mostly city folk, and they carried what little wealth they had left on their persons. The older men wore all their wardrobe and had

238 · MICHAEL POWELL

suitcases in each hand. The younger had enormous bundles and bulging rucksacks. There were even pets in cages, canaries and budgies, as well as dogs and cats. The children were already escaping from their parents and running all over the beach.

As the sun rose, hats and overcoats were discarded, and jackets peeled off like skinning an onion. Meanwhile the coast watchers had given the alarm and the military police were on the way. But the Haganah was on the way too. And now the leaders of the immigrants, who had gathered together for a conference, saw a remarkable sight. The single road to the beach, and the tracks among the dunes, were suddenly alive with townspeople from Tel Aviv. First there were dozens and then there were hundreds. Many of them had friends and relatives among the unlawful immigrants. There was running and calling and shouting and embracing, and in half an hour the group on the beach was like one big family; and miracle of miracles, when the security forces arrived all the newcomers were brandishing residence permits, while the lawful citizens of Tel Aviv had unanimously forgotten to bring theirs. And by another coincidence, all the men and women on the beach at Nebi Rubin that day had the same names.

"What's your name?"

"Ben-Israel."

"And what's yours, sister?"

"Beth-Israel."

"And what's yours, pretty one?"

"Beth-Israel."

"And yours, tough guy?"

"Ben-Israel."

"Must be quite a big family."

A bland look.

"Oh, yes, we are."

As the sun set the police gave up and went home, and the little crabs took possession again on the beach at Nebi Rubin.

The next day, after seeing Emeric off, we returned to Ein Gev. The place is beautiful, stern, and magical. It can never be conquered. On the way we passed several kibbutzim, some of them famous, like Ein Harod, with which a famous painter is associated and where there is a picture gallery that Hein was eager to see. A painter himself, he was anxious to find out whether a painter who was a member of a kibbutz had to toe the line, or whether he went his own way as an artist should. He had never had a convincing answer.

"If I could be sure that I would be free, I would join a kibbutz tomorrow," he announced.

"Helen and her husband were expelled from their kibbutz for being too Communist," I suggested.

"Huh! I am not a Communist, I am an anarchist. All artists are anarchists."

"Tell that to the Royal Academy."

"Royal Academy? I am talking about painters, not illustrators."

We turned up the Jordan River valley. The road climbed a steep hill, giving a splendid view of the Sea of Galilee. In the north Mount Hermon, streaked with snow, loomed through the heat haze. There was a strong westerly breeze blowing, and the surface of the great lake was ruffled; white waves were breaking on the eastern shore. Hein insisted on stopping at a factory where they made veneers for export. The men who tended and guided the machines looked more like intellectuals than carpenters, said Hein, watching in awe as a huge machine stripped an enormous tree trunk down to sheets no thicker than paper.

"See those workmen? Look at the way they cut their hair. See the faces? These are not ordinary workmen!"

Of course they weren't, any more than Hanan, our friend and guide at Ein Gev, was an ordinary fisherman on the Sea of Galilee. When he lived in Vienna he was a wholesale dress designer and manufacturer, and he brought a note of elegance to his pursuit of sardines and the maintenance of a fishing fleet on this strange sea, which is two hundred feet below the surface of the Mediterranean.

The guesthouse at Ein Gev was a gift from American Jews, and there were many distinguished names in the book. The dramatic siting of the kibbutz under the towering cliffs crowned by the enemy, plus the daily fear of seeing it overrun, had made Ein Gev famous and its survival almost miraculous. The guesthouse stands among eucalyptus trees, and beyond the striped trunks we could see the gleam of the water and the waves breaking on the pebbles. The westerly breeze came up every afternoon. In the morning the surface of the lake was calm and still and then, toward midday, when the sun was getting hot, the breeze started to blow, and soon the waves were breaking on the beach. Looking up above us at the towering mass of Susita, we told Hanan that we wanted to visit it and take a jeep up the rough track to the very top. He thought it would be difficult to get permission from the police and from the military; some of the way, yes, to the top, no.

On the top of Susita are the remains of the Graeco-Roman city where, in Roman times, beautiful villas with hanging gardens looked across the water to Tiberias. It was also where the Arab batteries were sited that were stormed and destroyed by the Israelis. In an ancient cistern, deep in the rocks, they had established their new headquarters. There is a photograph of this HQ in *The Book of Ein Gev*, which lay on the table of the guesthouse. There were photographs, sketches, maps, narratives, and the names of "the seven who died." For days before the assault by the Arabs the kibbutz had been plastered with shells and bombs. But they never really found the hidden bunkers where the people were sheltering. I asked Hanan if they were afraid. He answered reflectively, "When you are fighting with the woman you love at your side, I do not know how it is, but you cannot be afraid."

We asked him why the settlers did not all leave Ein Gev when the war started. The road was cut, the Arabs had artillery and tanks, they were besieged on three sides. When they sent out the pregnant women and the children, why did not they all go? The way across the water was open. Did they expect to be able to hold Ein Gev? He groped for an answer.

"No, we could not imagine that we would not be overrun. Our position was impossible. But we had created Ein Gev with our own hands. We had built the houses, planted the trees, and made the fields. It was May, it was nearly harvest time. We knew that if we left Ein Gev, we would never get it back." He hesitated, and thought awhile, and then said, "It was impossible for us to leave."

Hanan himself had been in command of a forward post, about three hundred yards farther along the seashore, a house and garden that belonged to a Persian businessman. There was a banana plantation near it, and trenches and thick cover connected it with the bunker where there was to be a last stand, when it came to it. At night the chicken man used to creep out to feed his fowl. They all survived the war, and he never let anybody forget it. Those who were responsible for the crops and fields also crept out at night and set the sprinklers going during the hours of darkness. In daylight, of course, no one could stir from the bunker. Although it was about eighty yards long and built of reinforced concrete, it was well camouflaged and the attackers could never quite make out where it was, although they plastered the whole area.

"What happened to the cows?" asked Hein. "It's difficult to camouflage a cow."

"They were all near the water tower when the shelling started, and most of them were killed."

We surveyed what was left of Hanan's advanced post.

"Weren't you a bit lonely out here? Rather exposed, wasn't it?"

"You get used to anything, you know."

How often I heard that phrase during the London blitz.

At supper in the big dining hall a table was kept for us. We felt a bit conspicuous. It was rather like dining in college. There were so many people to feed that they fed in shifts. Service in the canteen was obligatory, and popular, and it came round to each person about every two years. When your name came up the duty lasted about two months. The food was good, mostly vegetables and very plain. It answered one of Hein's questions: in a kibbutz any artist, culinary or otherwise, has to fight to exist.

Moving about the big hall were several pretty waitresses, one very pretty, about seventeen, with long legs and a cheeky face. Her short shorts were very short and she went barefoot, like most of the girls, which explained the lack of noise. After supper there were groups all over the garden, and under the trees, and along the shore, chatting and laughing in low tones. Down at the harbor the fishermen were getting ready to go out for the night's fishing. By nine o'clock the kibbutz was asleep.

The next morning, early, a jeep and its driver called for us, and we rocketed across the dusty plain and up the winding road to the pumping station on Susitha. We rode in a sort of sandstorm. Seeing our distress, the driver kept the windscreen wide open to save us from asphyxiation. At the pumping station he turned around and stopped. We tried to persuade him to take us higher, but he had his orders. Ein Gev lay beneath us, spread out like a map on the shore of the sea. We could see how daunting it must have been to the attackers when they realized that the place had not been evacuated, and that somewhere down there there were hidden defenders who would fight. Only one attack was ever made by the Arabs, and it failed because it was made in too great a force. It was a mass attack, or rather an invasion, and their losses were terrible. They got within a quarter of a mile of their objective, and then they had had enough. They turned back and never tried again.

We dashed back down the hill to the kibbutz. It was noon. People were knocking off work in the heat of the day. The roads were crowded with youngsters in working clothes, wearing those absurd round American fatigue hats, which were very popular just then. Hundreds of young people were swimming or sunning themselves. There was a group of twenty naked children under the care of a young teacher. The noon breeze started to blow. Ein Gev is a lovely place.

Before we left in the afternoon we crossed the great field, followed a path through the trees by the surfbound shore, and climbed a low hill above a vineyard heavy with grapes. There is a monument here to the seven from Ein Gev who died during the war. The blue granite slabs stand in a row, looking over the fields for which they fought and died. Happy seven, to be buried here as a witness, and to be remembered.

Meyer Weisgal and Shirley were to arrive that day, on board the steamship *Negba* at the port of Haifa, and we had to be back at Rehovot to meet them.

"Well, you guys, how do you like a real country when you see it? . . . Who the hell has been borrowing my books? . . . Helen! . . . Where the hell is . . . Oh! there it is! Well, tell me something, can't you . . . You haven't been pestered by a lot of goddamn Jews, I hope? Has Helen been looking after you properly? Wonderful . . . I don't believe it! . . . No goddamn red, even if she is my daughter, cares a goddamn about anybody . . . Oh! . . . she's your daughter too, Shirley? . . . and you brought her up well, didya? . . . yeah! . . . Why can't I find anything around here?"

"So Emeric went back? Couldn't wait to see me . . . oh! . . . I know, I know

. . . He had to see the coronation, and when Emeric has anything planned . . . Say, did you convert that guy to this country? The country converted him, did it . . . Hmm! . . . Say, it's not a bad dump, is it? All right, all right, you don't have to use all those superlatives. I believe it . . . half of it. Did you meet any of our 'great men'? Yeah, I know there are plenty of 'em . . . I meant did you meet any of our lousy politicians, the guys who are supposed to be running this goddamn country? . . . Only Gershon Agron? . . . He's no politician! . . . or is he? Have you met Ben-Gurion . . . No? . . . Well, you've got to meet him . . . And Sharett?* . . . You've got to meet him, too . . . Say, what have you done around here, Julian, except use up all the goddamn gas in the country riding around in my car on your asses? . . . Tell me something, can't you? . . ."

The storm of questions, suggestions, planning, advice, objurgations, obfuscations, continued for half the night, and for Shirley probably the rest of the night as well. It continued next morning. Men and women who had been going peaceably about their jobs now ran, or looked uneasily over their shoulders. The whole tempo of life around the Institute changed. Within two days of Meyer's return, we met Ben-Gurion.

Meyer drove with me to the house of the prime minister in Tel Aviv. It was a square, modern, detached, three-story house, distinguished from the others only by a military policeman at the latched gate. Mrs. Ben-Gurion led us into a salon for a moment, in order to chat with Meyer, then directed us to go up to her husband's library on the first floor. It was three rooms, opening into one another, lined from floor to ceiling with books. The door opened into the central room, which was empty. The books were in several languages, and by no means light reading. I had been told that Ben-Gurion was a classical Greek scholar and was entirely self-educated. The man must have had the energy of Napoleon. He spoke Russian, of course, Hebrew, naturally, Yiddish and German with a fluency I couldn't estimate, and he expressed himself well and unhesitatingly in English.

As we looked about, he stirred like a lion in his den and came out of the next alcove in the library. He was short and chunky, yet somehow elegant. His white mane of hair was very fine in texture. He wore one of the white, open-collared, short-sleeved shirts that he had made famous. His head was massive on a short neck. His hands and complexion were well cared for. He looked, and was born, a leader of Labour.

After we had chatted a short while, and I had explained who Powell and Pressburger were (and, in view of certain items in the Israeli press, also who they were not), I became convinced that my job was to explain the scope of the film we were planning, to enlist his sympathy for the project, and, above

*Moshe Sharett, Zionist leader and prime minister of Israel from 1954 to 1955.

all, to explain to him our aim of framing the life of Weizmann within an incident of the war for independence, so that the life would be seen in its true perspective, as the greatest single contributing factor to the creation of a state that was still growing organically, as its first president always maintained that it should. I think I made a fairly good job of it. Ben-Gurion listened to me with attention and intelligence, asked very pointed questions, and seldom interrupted. He took off his slippers and curled himself up in his armchair. When I finished, he spoke for about an hour. This is what he said:

"You seem to be going about it in the right way. If you make a work of art of it, then nothing else matters. You need two things for real creation: a great subject, and the art to handle it. You seem to have a great subject. . . .

"In 1940 I was in London. I shall never forget those days, nor the people. The taxi drivers alone were a miracle. Churchill and the British people—what a combination! They called out the best in each other. If Churchill had led the French—but no!—it wouldn't have worked, and perhaps if you had been led by Chamberlain. . . .

"In 1944 I realized we would probably have to fight for Israel. I was in America at the time, and I called a meeting of twenty men I could really depend upon—twenty friends of Israel, some Jews, some not. This man was there." He pointed to Meyer, who went off like a time bomb.

"There! I got the other twenty there at nine o'clock in the morning. Don't forget that!"

Ben-Gurion waved his hand and nodded.

"Yes. Some came from Florida, from Los Angeles, from Chicago. But they were all there at nine A.M. I told them: 'I want your unconditional help, I don't want your advice. I don't intend to tell you what I am going to do, I want you to trust me, and do what I ask, because it will be life or death for Eretz Israel.' Without exception they bound themselves.

"That was the start of the armament of Israel. They bought machines to make armaments—the U.S.A. was selling off cheap, and they got huge machines for practically nothing—and they shipped them to us, here. One machine looks very like another. We were ready to produce arms, but we couldn't until the Mandate expired.

"Then, I sent two men—they went to Canada, and then to the U.S.A., and to Czechoslovakia. They bought arms, guns, and airplanes, but they couldn't ship them until the Mandate expired.

"The Haganah was armed with rifles, knives, a few Sten guns, and Molotov cocktails. The Arabs had armor: tanks and mobile guns and artillery. We bought a lot of sixty-five-millimeter guns from the French, guns which had never been used in the First World War. But we couldn't get delivery of them until the Mandate expired.

"The war really lasted for fourteen months. First, there was the undeclared war. It started as soon as the United Nations decision in November 1947. It went on all through the winter. Jerusalem was cut off early in the year. Four settlements at Hebron were surrounded and besieged. There were dozens of incidents. We were on the defensive.

"When the Jerusalem road was cut I told the staff of the Haganah that we had to reopen it and keep it open. We were still a secret army, of course. I asked them to make a plan. They came and told me that they were ready to attack with five hundred men. I asked them, were they crazy? They would be annihilated. They said they had no more men. Our troops were dispersed all over the country. I said if we lose Jerusalem, we lose everything. I asked every commander in the country to give us half their men. Only in Galilee I asked for no men, but for half their guns. They all appreciated my reason; however hard-pressed they were, they sent the men and the guns. We mustered fifteen hundred men and we opened the road again. We had gone over to the offensive for the first time.

"That was in April. The Mandate was still in force, but the British did not interfere in our fighting. I don't know why they didn't, but they didn't. The British commander had seventy-five thousand troops in the country. He had promised to keep the Jerusalem road open. He didn't. When the Arabs closed the road, he did nothing. I told him: 'Listen! Open the road, or we will do it ourselves.' I spoke as the commander-in-chief of the Haganah. When we attacked, he let us alone. It was nice of him.

"To hold the road, we had to take the Castell. You know it? It was hard to take. It changed hands several times. Two of our men killed Abd el-Kader, the commander, the son of the Mufti. They did not know who he was when they killed him. We found papers on him after. We lost a lot of men at the Castell. But we held it, and the Arabs of the villages around, who had fled, asked to come back. We said: 'Come back. But no more shooting. No incidents. Or we destroy your villages.'

"So Jerusalem was no longer cut off. During the next month we took control of Tiberias, of Safad, and, at last, of Jaffa, just before the Mandate expired, at midnight on May 14. The day before that, our settlers at Hebron were overrun . . . the day before. Three settlements were massacred. In the fourth was the Arab Legion. They took our people prisoner and saved them from the mass of Arabs. The Arab Legion behaved well. They fought well, and, if they gave their word, they kept it.

"At midnight on the fourteenth, the Mandate ended. The state of Israel was proclaimed by me, first in session of the Knesset, then on the radio at four A.M. The British were still in Haifa, of course, but we were the government. As I broadcast to America I heard bombs not far away. Others followed during my broadcast. The Egyptians were bombing us. As soon as I finished, I asked for news. They had attacked the Rutenberg power station, and the airfield at Lydda. Every reporter in America started to get on to Tel Aviv. I took a car and visited Lydda and Naharayim. At Lydda two people were killed. The power station was undamaged. As I drove back to Tel Aviv it was still early, but there were faces at all the windows. I looked at the faces. They had the same expression which I had seen on the faces of the people in London in 1940. They were serious, but they were not afraid. Then I knew it would be all right.

"Now, the attack started on seven fronts. We had against us Lebanon, Syria, Trans-Jordan, Iraq, and Egypt—and, of course, the fifth columnists among the Arabs in the country. In the cities most of them ran away. All the rich Arabs, the people with property, ran away. Jerusalem was cut off again. Negba was isolated, but held out. Ein Gev the same. The settlers were advised to leave. They dug in and fought.

"Arms were on the way, but they had a long way to come. There were forty thousand of our people who were interned in Cyprus. Seven thousand of the young men came over first. Within two days they were fighting in the battle for Latrun. Latrun commands the entrance to the main road to Jerusalem. 'Who holds Latrun holds Palestine' has always been true. It is the key to the country, the key to the hills, and the key to the plain. The sea is only twenty miles away. The country could be split in half. We decided to take Latrun. We failed. We lost three thousand men. The Arab Legion still held it. They hold it now. But that's all they hold in the Corridor.

"I was in Jerusalem. Then I flew down in a little aircraft. I can't think why nobody shot down that little aircraft! I directed the war from Tel Aviv. On the night when the Latrun attack was planned, an aircraft full of machine guns arrived from Prague. The Arabs held Lydda, and the aircraft couldn't find the emergency landing strip. It took six hours to find it, circling round and round. At last it landed, and we got our two hundred machine guns. Without them we should have been wiped out. Then six of our French field guns arrived. I rushed them up to Kinneret, where they held back the Syrian attack. Then we had an SOS from Jerusalem, and I had to rush two of them up there. A week later, the rest of them arrived.

"Jerusalem was still cut off, so we started to build an alternative road which wound through the hills, out of sight of the enemy's guns. We called it the Burma Road. Then the United Nations forced a truce. The others were as glad to accept it as we were. We needed time; and they needed time to get over their surprise. While the truce was on we were allowed to send supplies of food up to Jerusalem, but no arms. So we sent the arms by the Burma Road. There was an impassable place, a sheer cliff. Our new road ran up to the top, then there was a cliff, and at the bottom was the other road to Jerusalem.

Volunteers carried everything down on ropes. Trucks would come to the top, unload, men took the contents on their backs down the cliffs, then loaded them onto the waiting trucks. I saw those boys swarming down those ropes. You ought to have that in your film . . .

"The war broke out again. We remained on the offensive, even though the Arabs started a day before the truce expired. In those days a deputation came to me from three of our most important settlements. They were more than settlements, they were symbols. It's no use my telling you the names of the three men, but when you know our country better you'll realize what sort of men these were, and what they meant in worth to me and to the country. I'll call one of them Joe. They asked for reinforcements, otherwise they couldn't hold out. I had to tell them I couldn't give them a man or a gun. Joe cried. I saw some terrible things in that year, but I think that was the most terrible. Joe crying! . . . They went back and they held on.

"Things went better. The Egyptians couldn't advance, nor retreat. We held the others on all sides. Jerusalem was still cut off. We chased the Lebanese back into Lebanon. On July 24 there was another truce. By this time, the whole world realized what was involved. The U.N. was getting really busy. We held on. We maintained the offensive in the U.N. as well as at home. The autumn wore on. The other side didn't keep the truce. We had the right to send trucks of food down to our besieged settlements in the Negev. The Egyptians wouldn't let the trucks through. We appealed to the United Nations. We sent a convoy down. They ambushed it, burned the trucks, and killed the drivers. Then we got a strike force together. We went through to Beersheba, and we took it. Then our trucks went through.

"The Egyptians were supplying their force by air. But now we had planes, too. We shot down their planes. We penned them in Faluja. They expected us to attack by the road. But there was another road, a track which one of our men, an archaeologist, knew. We attacked and surprised the fort and took it. We closed in. They lost fifteen hundred men, killed and wounded. The U.N. decided the terms of the armistice. There were three thousand of them left in holes in the ground. There was nothing left of Faluja.

"The armistice was signed in January 1949, nine months after the creation of the state. We had kept alive, and we had taken in one hundred thousand new immigrants. . . ."

We had been there one and a half hours, so we took our leave. Ben-Gurion's last words were "The important thing for your film is that it should be a work of art."

Mrs. Ben-Gurion saw us out. She was a warm and comfortable woman, kind and humble and completely natural, a sweet hostess. Meyer was quite silent, for him, as we drove back to Rehovot. I said I was impressed. He agreed.

"He's a formidable man. He took the decisions. Only a Labour leader would have had the guts to send all those men to their deaths. I couldn't have done it. Weizmann couldn't have done it. People say that Ben-Gurion's decision to take Latrun was a wrong one. But he took the decision, and that's what this goddamn country needed at the time."

"And still needs?"

He was silent again.

We drove straight to the white house where Mrs. Weizmann received us with her extraordinary charm. The others arrived, and we had lunch. As before, it was perfect and homely. She was a hostess in a million. And, what few hostesses could do, she handled Meyer expertly and firmly. That explosive extrovert was clay in her hands, and only said "hell" once and "bastard" twice.

I went down to the grave after lunch and photographed it. The leaves had fallen from the jacaranda tree, and the violet blossoms were clear against the hot sky. The Judaean hills, bleached to a pinkish haze, were invisible. At this time of year the time to shoot them was the early morning, when they were dark against the sky.

Later on we returned with Helen and Shirley and swam in the long, narrow pool under the ceilings of Pompeian red, covered with large, green leaves. The low sun shone in between the pillars. In the library the voices of Meyer and Mrs. Weizmann made a background to our cool splashing. Suddenly it turned quite cold. It was amazing how cool it was in the evenings.

We ran a 16mm film of scenes from newsreels relating to Weizmann. They had been made up by Paramount from the files, and showed us nothing new. Mrs. Weizmann smoked and watched the films with an expressionless face.

=

We never made the film *The Salt of the Earth*, the title Emeric and I had given to the screenplay based upon the autobiography of Chaim Weizmann. We wrote the script, but in 1953 The Archers had lost their glorious arrogance. We no longer snapped, "Put up and shut up!" We found ourselves listening to other people and their opinions. We even started listening to each other: this, after fifteen years of reading each other's thoughts!

There were too many films. The question was, which one to make? My enthusiasm for Chaim Weizmann's book, and my own energy, had been infectious, but the state of Israel, so long a dream of the Zionists, was in being and had found itself in the struggle for independence. For each of us the film was different. For Meyer Weisgal the film was a great political drama, full of intrigue and secret deals of which no one knew more than he. Ben-Gurion saw it as a battle for existence, a battle that had been won, and would have to be won again and again, until Israel, the great scientific and technological state, dictated her terms to the world. Helen's film was a revolutionary clenched-fists-and-all musical, in which the marching thousands of young men and women worked and played, and loved and marched, hand in hand, until the Negev blossomed like the rose. Emeric's film was a full-length biography, told by Weizmann's voice and seen through Weizmann's eyes. There would be no part for a great actor. The camera and microphone would shape the man. Perhaps, when all was done and the pilgrims entered Zion, there might be one tall, stooping figure who saw the new flag flying over Jerusalem and saw that it was good.

And I? For me the film was over with the Balfour Declaration. It was not a drama, and not an epic, it was a comedy. A comedy? Yes. It was the story of a young man, a chemist, one of the teeming millions of Europe, who chose to come to England, to a laboratory in Manchester, without friends, influence, or money, already engaged to his life's partner, already dedicated to the cause of Zion, with nothing to help him but his own genius and a colossal appetite for work, and who created a country out of a test tube.

=

I now had absolutely no excuse for not making *Die Fledermaus*. I would have been lynched by my own unit. We decided on a production date early in 1954, and started to think about casting. The different opinions held by distributors, exhibitors, and even the two producers, as well as their production crew, should have warned me. Here they are:

Cast No. 1 (In a Never-Never-Land)

Colonel Eisenstein	Maurice Chevalier
His wife, Rosalinda	Danielle Darrieux
Alfred, a Yank	Bing Crosby
Adele, a Viennese tartlet	Lilli Palmer
An English colonel	Noël Coward
Frosch, the jailer	Jerry Verno
The Bat	Anton Walbrook
General Orlovsky	Orson Welles

Cast No. 2 (In the Real World of 1954)

Colonel Eisenstein	Michael Redgrave
Rosalinda	Ludmilla Tcherina
Alfred	Kieron Moore
Adele	Anneliese Rothenberger
An English colonel	David Niven

Frosch	We decided on a native Viennese
The Bat	Anton Walbrook
General Orlovsky	Orson Welles ankled our show and later apologized

Cast No. 3 (Final Cast)

Eisenstein	Michael Redgrave (he also sang his own part)
Rosalinda	Ludmilla Tcherina
Alfred	Mel Ferrer
Adele	Anneliese Rothenberger
An English colonel	Dennis Price
Frosch	Oskar Sima
The Bat	Anton Walbrook
General Orlovsky	Anthony Quayle (whom I'd been grooming for it)

Stop! Whoa! . . . Wait a minute . . . Did you say Mel Ferrer as Alfred?
Yes.
Mel Ferrer! . . . That sneak, that black-hearted traitor, that seducer, that phony, that shot in the dark . . . that traitor . . . that dancer who can't dance, that singer who can't sing, that actor who can't act! Are you sure you don't mean José Ferrer?!
No.
But all the books say that you were considering José Ferrer for the part, because he had all the qualities that the other Ferrer singularly failed to possess: charm, humor, honesty; and sex appeal, talent, and a touch of genius.
He wanted too much money.
But you're already in production—you're rehearsing! How did it all happen?
Don't be so noisy—you're interrupting the rehearsals.
Clink! Clink! "Tea or coffee, Mr. Powell? The tea's just been made."
"Tea then, Bessie."
Let's go back to the time I saw Audrey and Mel in *Ondine* in New York. The year before, I had seen Audrey in *Gigi*. So when I saw that she was playing in *Ondine* opposite Mel Ferrer as the knight in a production by Alfred Lunt, I saw there was a matinee and went to it. I had seen the Paris production of the Giraudoux play, with Louis Jouvet as the Knight and Madeleine Ozeray as Ondine, but in spite of that I was quite carried away by Audrey and Mel. Of course, the play is one of Giraudoux's most successful attempts at combining Parisian irreverence with poetic licence; and Jouvet playing a man in his twenties, at the age of sixty, had something of the quality Conrad Veidt

possessed, of portraying burning passion behind a mask of polite indifference. Mel, particularly in the clothes designed for him by Richard Whorf, looked like a monkey on a stick. But his lean height and self-confidence carried him through, just as Audrey's charm and flair made up for her small voice in that vast Forty-sixth Street theatre. At the intermission I left a note at the stage door, saying that I would call around after the final curtain.

As it was a matinee they were staying in their dressing rooms and having some food sent in from Dinty Moore's, so I shared it with them and we had a good half hour's talk. They were madly in love, that is to say that she was wholehearted in her love for him. She is the kind of woman who gives all or nothing. I don't know how he lit this torch, but by heaven it flamed. They were both escaping from other obligations and entanglements. There had been scenes, public and private, and the press had got on to it. It made their performance in the play a delight, and a torture. The public came to love and gloat—envious, salacious, and curious. The play was only on for a limited run, and they yearned to escape out of America and into Europe. Both of them had lived up to the hilt ever since their first appearance in front of the public, and neither of them had any money. Audrey had made a stunning success in William Wyler's *Roman Holiday*, but she was not yet a star, except on Broadway. Mel had been offered a part in a picture to be made in Rome and they planned to escape there, look for work without appearing to do so, and live on his salary. I sized up the situation, and offered them the support of The Archers. The story of *Ondine*, by La Motte–Fouqué, is of course in the public domain, an established classic. But the play by Jean Giraudoux was another matter, and we would have to get the rights before we could say that we would make a film. I thought, privately, that it might be better to write a completely new version of *Ondine*, the published story, which is after all only a grandiose fairy tale. But I could see how wedded they were to each other, and to these parts of the knight and the water nymph, which had brought them both together and cradled them in their arms. They snatched at the offer, and said that their agent was Kurt Frings, adding with a giggle that he had been a lightweight boxer in his time, which made him a very good agent. There was no time for much more. Emeric and I were off the next day. But I put Kurt Frings in touch with Christopher Mann and let the magic work.

The next time that we all foregathered was in Rome—November 1954— after a great deal of water had passed under the bridge. Audrey and Mel had got married in Switzerland in the spring, and had gone to Rome to live while Mel worked on his film. The Archers, after many comings and goings, and inordinate use of other people's trust, had three arrows notched and ready to fly: *Die Fledermaus* (only half-financed, but with vocal and orchestral score ready to record); *The Pursuit of the Graf Spee*, the story behind the Battle of the

River Plate, financed by Twentieth Century–Fox, with cooperation from the Admiralty (it had been Emeric's suggestion, when we were invited by President Perón to a vast international show-business shindig in Argentina); and *Ondine*, which was to follow *Rosalinda* into production on or about June 1, fully financed by Paramount thanks to the maneuvers of Christopher Mann and Kurt Frings, those unlikely bedfellows. It was time for the four of us to meet again, for Emeric had an idea to sell, a magnificent idea, which was fated to bring the whole goldfish bowl of *Ondine* crashing to the floor and leave the two principal goldfish floundering.

But at the moment, all was going as merrily as wedding bells, and Mel came to meet us at the grand new central station in Rome. Our train was early, and at first I thought there was no one there to meet us, but then I saw the tall, elegant figure of Mel thrusting through the crowd and waving, while his nutcracker jaws cracked open in a smile of welcome. He and Audrey were screening a new film for some friends and hoped we might like to come along; we could go out to their villa later on.

What film? *On the Waterfront* . . . Had we seen it? Emeric, yes. Michael, no. It was a private screening, with the usual audience of deadheads. Mr. Levy of Paramount presided. He had neuralgia, poor man, probably from seeing the film several times. It is a film full of phony violence, ugly, sordid, unredeemed by any note of beauty or tenderness. Mel got into a passion over the direction, and I began to take a good view of him, for it was clear that Elia Kazan was out to shock.

After surviving the film we went to a typical Roman nightclub to eat something, and then drove three quarters of an hour into the auburn hills. A Dutch couple, friends of Audrey's who were staying with them, tailed our car. A private road off the main road led to the villa. There was a great barking of dogs. We had a nightcap, and Mel was still taking that Greek to pieces. I was delighted to see him so concerned. May he keep that way. Our rooms had deep wide balconies looking out over the vineyards. Rumbles of thunder could be heard in the west, but the night was full of stars. I left my door open, and a big white-and-gold cat came in and jumped on my bed, trod on my face, and slept on my stomach. In the morning there were four of them.

We had breakfast together at nine. It was a cold, misty morning, and the only sweater I had brought with me was too thin for the job. We talked, wrote, and worked all morning, continually interrupted by telephone calls and hysterical servants. Audrey and Mel were, amiably, the worst listeners in the world. They were always wandering off in the middle of a sentence, and none of us allowed any of the others to finish one. In spite of that, Emeric kept his temper and his head admirably, and we got a lot of work done. We continued after lunch. The sun came out. So did eight cats. A big woolly dog rushed about. The hills, purple and brown, with vines and olives, sloped down to the distant, shining sea.

Jack Cardiff came to dinner and was greeted with shouts by all. He looked very fit, a dear fool of a man, a genius, a dreamer, a baby. He should have been a painter instead of being the best color cameraman in the world. I didn't know that he was such a friend of the house. A danger signal flashed in my mind. Was Mel playing politics—really? Was he planning to depose Chris Challis, our lighting cameraman and an old buddy of Jack's, and hand the lighting scepter with a regal gesture to Jack? Then I dismissed the thought. The company of Archers were incapable of intrigue, and Jack was one of the founding members.

But it was not Jack that I was worried about.

The next morning Emeric was ready to expound the story line. But things didn't go so well as the day before. Mel was beginning to declare himself, and his tactics were only too obvious: the play, the play, and nothing but the play. Somehow every idea, every scene, became inextricably bound up with the play, and Mel was the knight in shining armor defending *Ondine*, defending it from rape and disaster at the hands of the devilish Archers. Audrey looked at him adoringly. There had obviously been extended pillow talk throughout the night. Emeric floundered. Fortunately the knight and his water sprite wandered away on other ploys and gave Emeric time to collect his thoughts. He looked at me. I nodded.

"They don't seem to know the difference between a play and a film."

"Of course they don't. They're actors. They've learned the part and spoken the words to an audience, and it worked. They think that's all there is to it. We have to educate them."

He looked absolutely terrified. Fortunately our hosts returned in a more sociable mood, and Emeric, gathering his forces, launched into a brilliant exposition of the film, which owed little to Giraudoux's play and a great deal to the original fairy tale by La Motte–Fouqué. Emeric's version restored the balance between art and artifice, even Mel could see that, and he listened to his most cherished lines tumbling into the basket, to be replaced by dazzling conjuror's tricks and scenes full of poetry and savagery. Audrey's hand crept into Mel's and stayed there, and at the end they both clapped and Emeric bowed. We all went for a walk up the hill with two of the cats, their tails waving like *oriflammes*, and came back to the villa, battered by the wind and gilded by the sun, to find Jack Cardiff arriving for dinner.

There were four other guests, two Italian producers of awesome magnitude and unimaginable wickedness, with wives of sultry splendor. One of them sat smouldering in a heap of black and silver tissue all the evening. The other was a very large girl with gaps between her front teeth and a red dress gathered into a sash on one splendid hip. Standing with Audrey, who was tall and slender as a boy, they looked two different species, and both of them collector's items. Hearing her loud laugh, I found myself thinking she must be a very expensive woman to feed and dress.

The party was doomed from the start. They had evidently come expecting to rough it, but not to find the fire out. Emeric was the culprit. He had sat making notes until the arrival of the guests warned him of the gathering chill. They sat grimly in their furs while slaves rekindled the fire into a blaze fit to roast Saint Joan. After that we all did our best in three languages, but the evening never really got going. The only bright spot was dinner, which was roast venison—plus a statement by the mountainous red girl that she and her husband lived in a tomb. With thoughts of Romeo and Juliet in our minds, we encouraged her to explain. It really was a historic monument, and millions of lire had passed from hand to hand to make it comfortable to live in. She got quite animated about it. It was obviously chic to live in a tomb.

"What are their names?" I asked Audrey. "It's been a sticky evening."

"The girls were Silvana Mangano and Sophia Loren."

"And the boys?"

"Carlo Ponti and Dino De Laurentiis."

I wrote the names down. One never knows.

The telephone rang. It was Christopher Mann, quietly triumphant. Paramount would put up £250,000 of a £375,000 production, provided that we four idiots, without whom there would be no film, would leave half our fees in the picture, to be recovered from the top of the profits, if any. If we agreed to the terms, we were fully financed for *Ondine.* Paramount would distribute the film in the U.K. for 25 percent, in the rest of the world for 35. It was a good deal. He recommended accepting it. If we all agreed, the sooner that Audrey and Mel came to London to meet the press, the better.

"Good night."

Mel put down his receiver and gave an Indian yell. We were going to make *Ondine*! We joined hands and danced all around the house, accompanied by all the cats and dogs. We were going to make *Ondine*!

In the morning we went on another long stroll around the farms. They were cutting and burning the vines. Mel, his long face puckered in thought, found a new worry. What about Mme. Giraudoux, the widow of the playwright? She was a pain in the neck, and she had outrageous ideas about money. The sooner we did a deal for the film rights of the play, the better. I promised to stop off in Paris and see her. Then it was time to go.

"Goodbye! Goodbye!"

Waving hands and waving tails, and blowed if we didn't meet Jack Cardiff driving in the private gate while we drove out.

In the sleeping car Rome-Paris, we sat in Emeric's apartment, sipping the apricot brandy that he so thoughtfully carried in his briefcase.

"Well, Michael, what do you make of him?"

"Our host? He's a snake."

"I quite agree."

There was a thoughtful silence. The landscape of Piedmont went flashing by.

"There was not one word of truth in what he said. He wants to make a photographed version of the play. This is why you have to see this silly old woman in Paris. If he could afford to buy the film rights of the play, he would. With a film of the play he would be sure of himself and of Audrey. He knows that we could make a beautiful film from La Motte–Fouqué's book without infringing Giraudoux's play. That is why he wants us to buy the rights for him, so that he can cut our bloody throats."

"Quite."

With a scream, our engine plunged into a tunnel. It was the Simplon, twenty-five minutes under the Alps. The lights had been switched on several minutes before. I lay on the bed looking at Emeric's sturdy figure in the half-light. Men were working in the tunnel. They always were. We heard the sound of rock drills. We saw lights flashing and heard voices. I thought of the dreamers who had dreamed up the tunnel, of the engineers who had given their lives to it. In the half-darkness I heard Emeric's voice: "Michael, I have an idea. We cannot let this shit put one over on us. We'll write an *Ondine* that everybody will understand, even he. A twentieth-century *Ondine*, an *Ondine* in modern dress."

"In modern undress, you mean. That won't suit Mel. He's got knobbly knees and a bony chassis. He wouldn't strip for us."

"Michael, be serious. He can wear one of those suits—you know—black rubber and goggles . . . frogmen suits."

"It would suit him, he looks like a frog."

"It looks already like armor."

I nodded. I was already beginning to see the possibilities of the idea.

"You really mean today? And on a lake in Switzerland, or maybe on the Rhine?"

"Michael, how many times have I told you when I was at UFA, when we started to work on a new script, it always started in Monte Carlo? Let us start in Monte Carlo. The Mediterranean is classical, it's sunshine, it's life; the Rhine is dark and cold, and flows north. A love story like *Ondine* must be in the Mediterranean . . . in *mare nostrum*. Instead of dukes and knights and silly little kings, we will have millionaires and racketeers and scuba divers—"

"—and gamblers and fading film stars," I added. "We might even find room for Silvana Mangano and Sophia Loren."

But Emeric refused to be deflected: "We will have lots of wonderful under-water photography, like we have seen in the films of this French naval captain, Cousteau, and tricks of appearing and disappearing: effects of speed, of swimming, and photography of movement will suit a modern aqualung film much better than a medieval romance. We shall bring a whole new world of wonders to people, and empty it into their laps. Do you agree? Do you think that Hein and Arthur and Chris and Ivor can do it?"

I laughed.

"I should jolly well think they could. It's the answer to their prayers. It's the best thing since *The Red Shoes:* Audrey in tights sewn with glittering fish scales, Mel a scuba diver armed with harpoon gun and torchlight, just like a medieval knight, and the Old One a huge fish or octopus! Oh, Imre! . . . you're a genius! Listen, it's my turn now. I'll describe the first sequence to you. It starts with the view from the Voile d'Or, a view that I have loved all my life:

Ondine '55—Sequence 1: The French Riviera. Camera is on a helicopter hovering above the Hôtel de la Voile d'Or at Saint-Jean-Cap-Ferrat. We are out at sea, looking back at the Alpes Maritimes. We are high enough to see the great, colorful cliffs turn into mountains, and the mountains turn into Alps covered with snow. The village of Eze, on its lonely peak of rock, is in the foreground. This is Provence, Savoy, the land of legend, loved by wander-ing knights and troubadours, and celebrated in songs and stories as blood-thirsty as they are beautiful, a land that is just the same today, just as Crete is the same today. We get glimpses of lonely pastures, guarded by sentinel marmots whistling their warnings, of roaring torrents and airy waterfalls, and forests of huge pines. This is the country of the *arrière pays*—the back of beyond, ignored by sun-blistered, bikini-bisected tourists. Camera is drop-ping swiftly down. The old world vanishes, and the new world takes its place. A land of motor roads, and reinforced concrete, of terraced gardens, and modern villas, of casinos and film festivals, of buildings of lath and plaster, fronting on a narrow strip of beach a hundred miles long—the world of *le tourisme.*

Now we are skimming over the surface of the sea, which is covered with every kind of craft—millionaires' yachts, sportsmen's sailboats, every kind of motorboat and motor launch, waterskiers, divers, swimmers—and then sud-denly we are plunged below the surface of the sea, and all that noisy world has vanished, and we are in Captain Cousteau's "silent world." Motorboats roar over our heads, but we leave them behind very quickly. We are back in the mountains now, but they are underwater mountains, underwater cliffs, underwater caves. At first it is really quiet, and then music creeps in—but not like any music you've ever heard. This is a world waiting to be explored, a world of sunken ships, of galleys loaded with amphorae, of giant fish, of treasure troves—a world where goggle-eyed fish stare into the faces of blind, marble gods.

Now, suddenly, this world is invaded too, by scuba divers, by underwater fishermen, by marine archaeologists, alarmed and threatened by dazzling torchlights, which reveal brilliant colors in this silent world of muted tints. In this world, anything can happen. Audrey can flash through the water at the speed of a fish. Mel can be trapped and held prisoner in an underwater cave . . . anything . . . anything! Even the love of a mortal for an immortal, of a fish for a man . . .

I stopped because the train was whistling. We had passed from Italy into Switzerland. We had passed through the Alps. Another miracle! We were in the valley, and the sun was setting.

"Well? What do you think of my first shot?"

Emeric smiled indulgently. "Some shot! But I think we had best go and see Mme. Giraudoux. Tomorrow, in Paris?"

I nodded. "And, for the present, mum's the word."

"Yes, Michael. Mum's the word."

We needn't have worried. She unbolted five locks and two steel bars to let us into her apartment, and then she didn't stop talking for half an hour. It was a lovely, wide apartment.

"What an *emplacement* for a five-pounder," I said, looking over the river to the Palais de la Découverte.

"Yes," she said, it was hers. She had bought it. She owned it. Nobody could take it away from her. "As to my husband's play, let us talk."

She invented an offer of seven and a half million francs that I had not made, and brushed it on one side.

"Not a penny less than ten million for me, net. Deal as you like with the agent for his five or six percent. Mine must be net and ten million from hand to hand, *de la main à la main.* Do you understand?"

I understood. I was not a French *hôtelier* for nothing. She gave cries of indignation on hearing that her representative in New York, Madame Tallon, had mentioned the participation of Mr. Maurice Valency in the film rights. (It was he who had adapted the play into English.) She had all the rights! . . . she thought. Her agent was Mr. Rothschild, 30 avenue des Champs-Elysées. He would know.

Emeric caught my eye. I read the message. All that we could possibly use of the old play in our new scheme would work out at about 50,000 francs a word. We let ourselves out, promised to go and see Mr. Rothschild, and took our leave. Her locks and bolts clicked and banged behind us. Then we exploded.

"Vive la France," sobbed Emeric, wiping his eyes.

"Vive la France," I echoed, "et les pommes de terre frites!"

=

Die Fledermaus was now officially known as *Oh . . . Rosalinda!!* Don't ask me why. Nobody liked it, but nobody cared to think of a better title. We recorded the score in Vienna in November 1954, with Sari Barabas singing Tcherina's part and Anneliese Rothenberger singing Adele. We had the Vienna Philharmonic Orchestra, and the choir, and no Clemens Krauss, alas, and the result was that thing I hate most in an opera—it was a recording, not a performance. Rehearsals were scheduled for January, shooting in February 1955. It was four years since I had directed a film.

In these turbulent pages, I've tried to render a true account of The Archers and of their divergent aims. My father's death, and Emeric's divorce and consequent separation from his beloved daughter, Angela, were two major convulsions in the sea of trouble. I shall write at length and later on about the Hôtel de la Voile d'Or, and how nearly I came to betraying my chosen path, for all art is one, as Kipling has written, and your art chooses you, not you the art. During these fifty months of indecision I traveled around the world, I had become a publican and certainly a sinner, and I had directed two plays. We had written four shooting scripts, none of them produced, Columba had learned to walk (July 30, 1952) and talk (January 1, 1953), Kevin had gone to Gordonstoun,* and Emeric and I went three times to Montevideo. This calls for an explanation.

Dictators say memorable things: "What a city to loot!" or "Give me Hollywood, and you give me the world!" Some such thought must have been in President Perón's mind when he extended invitations to the whole of showbiz to come to a junket at Mar del Plata, Argentina's answer to the Brazilian Copacabana beach, about fifty kilometers down the coast from Buenos Aires. The party was intended to celebrate the power and permanence of the Perónista regime. But in 1955 Hollywood was in a party mood. Films had come to terms with television, and the big bananas were scrambling for the best positions. There was no longer a threat from England, and the idea of combining business with pleasure and a trip with all expenses paid to Argentina caught on like a prairie fire. It was a thorough operation by the publicity department of the Perónistas. Nobody who was nobody was forgotten.

---

*Boys' boarding school in northern Scotland, famous for its dedication to preparing students for the rigors of outdoor life and because Prince Charles was sent there. While Michael might have thought getting up at 5:00 A.M. for a five-mile run was fun, his sons were not so enthusiastic about the school's regimen.

258 · MICHAEL POWELL

In due course, The Archers' invitation arrived. In Latin America *Zapatillas Rojas* still danced: "Señor Powell" . . . "Señor Pressburger . . ."—the invitations were personal ones from President Perón himself. We looked guiltily at each other. We were most definitely without honor in our own country. We were broke. We had just had two huge films—*The Golden Years* and *The Salt of the Earth*—turned down by distributors and by financiers. Our private lives were in a turmoil. We looked at each other. Who knew if we would ever again be considered important enough to be given the chance of licking President Perón's boots?

Emeric loves parties.

"Michael, don't let us go unless we have a reason for going."

"What do you mean, old cock?"

"I mean, my dear cock, that we have spent a lot of time and money researching the Battle of Crete for *Ill Met by Moonlight,* and nobody wants to know . . ."

I nodded. I took up the tale: ". . . And more money on researching the life of Chaim Weizmann, and the founding of the state of Israel, and even more people, particularly the Israelis, don't want to know . . ."

Emeric fielded the pass with ". . . We planned a lovely film about Hofmannsthal and Strauss, and *Der Rosenkavalier,* and even Vienna doesn't want to know. No bidders. Even *Bouquet,* which is one of the simplest and most beautiful ideas that I have ever had, had no takers. The truth is that even Hollywood doesn't know what to make. The old leaders have gone, and the new leaders, like you and me, are confused by television."

I tried to cheer him up by reminding him we had produced one film in Latin America, *The End of the River,* with Sabu and Bibi Ferreira, directed by Derek Twist.

"But that was a small film, Michael, and we make big ones! Perhaps in Latin America we can find a new story and a new theme which can be understood by everybody. I will think about it."

"What about the invitations? We have to answer them."

"They can wait a few days. We must have a reason for going. It's a chance in a million to have everything paid, and then come back with an idea that everyone would like."

Emeric must have talked to Stapi, for in a few days he telephoned me.

"Michael! I've got it!"

"Have what? The flu?"

"No, no, Michael, our South American story—the idea that everybody will like. Do you remember the Battle of the River Plate?"

"Vaguely . . . wasn't it right at the beginning of the war?"

"Yes, it was. And does the name of the pocket battleship *Graf Spee* mean anything to you?"

I was waking up.

"The German pocket battleship? Didn't she blow herself up?"

"Yes, Michael. At Montevideo, the capital of Uruguay—of *neutral* Uruguay."

"Is that why her captain blew her up?"

"Perhaps. That is what we will go to find out. Buenos Aires is on the other side of the Río de la Plata. Argentina was pro-Axis in the war."

"Is that where they fought the battle? In the mouth of the river?"

"No, Michael. That would have been in territorial waters. The battle was fought at sea between the pocket battleship *Graf Spee* and three English light cruisers. There was a running fight between the pocket battleship and the three small British ships. The German captain broke off the engagement and took refuge in Montevideo. He was given twenty-four hours to leave or be interned. When the ultimatum expired, he blew up his ship. It was the first big Allied success. Now, do you see why we can accept President Perón's invitation?"

I reflected. Emeric had certainly been talking to Stapi, who was ex–Imperial German Navy. When I was a boy, the Royal Navy had been my first love, and I'd always wanted to make a film about the navy. Noël had done a good job of making *In Which We Serve*, but he had spoiled the ship with a ha'pence of tar by playing Captain Louis Mountbatten himself: "I'm a snob, I know it. I couldn't bear to have anybody else play Dickie!"

Whether Stapi or Emeric had thought of it, the *Graf Spee* was a good idea, because diplomacy was involved in it as well as heroism. I yelled into the outer office, "Bill! Accept President Perón's invitation."

"For the two of ye?"

"Ay."

"I thought you would. We had a sweep on it. Doris, you owe me ten bob."

The Archers were looked on with favor by the Admiralty because of *The Volunteer*. The Royal Navy didn't have anything so vulgar as a publicity department, but they did have a well-informed civilian, name of R. Holmes, who acted as liaison for film projects, tucked away in an obscure corner of Admiralty Arch, and who promised to bring the project to their Lordships' attention.

"Will Jack Hawkins be in this one?" he asked hopefully.

We frowned at such amateur enthusiasm. After all, we were The Archers.

"It's early days yet. What about the captains of the British ships that fought in the battle? Are they still in the service? Is Commodore Harwood still alive?"

The answer was no. He was older than his three captains, and died at a comparatively early age. His son was in the navy, and his widow lived in Goring-on-Thames. His three captains were alive and kicking: Captain Woodhurst who commanded HMS *Ajax*, Captain Parry, who commanded the Australian cruiser HMAS *Achilles*, and, of course, "Hooky" Bell, who commanded HMS *Exeter*, the biggest of the three cruisers, and which consequently attracted the brunt of the pocket battleships' firepower. Anticipating this, Commodore Harwood had moved his flag to *Ajax*, and fought the battle from the smaller ships. All three of these gallant officers had now retired from the service, but were all living within an hour or so of London, ready to start another war at a moment's notice. They would come into London, if the film company would guarantee their expenses. Aereolíneas Argentinas were flying us down to Buenos Aires, and we were ready on standby, so we told Holmes that we would interview the captains on our return. Meanwhile we made a formal application for Admiralty assistance in making the film.

The flight to Argentina was one of those endurance jobs, from north of the northern hemisphere to south of the southern hemisphere, picking up contingents of guests en route: London to Paris; Paris to Dakar in West Africa; from Dakar skimming along the equator to Belém at the mouth of the Amazon (featured in *End of the River*); Belém to Rio de Janeiro (where I hoped to see Bibi Ferreira); from Rio de Janeiro to Buenos Aires—twenty-nine hours' flying time.

Our eventual departure was ... uneventful. The British, as was their wont, backed steadily out of the limelight so that later they could complain bitterly of being ignored. Paris was a very different matter. A huge French contingent came on board, everybody talking at once and taking about three hours to settle down. I saw several people I knew: I remembered Dany Robin and, to my secret excitement, Jean-Paul Belmondo, whom I had always admired and hoped one day to work with. Walking down the aisle, he saw that I was reading a French book and put his hand on it, to see what it was.

"Memoirs d'outre tombe!"

He murmured something that could have been "Sans blague!," lurched back to his seat, and went to sleep, and I never saw him again. The French are restless travelers but good-humored, and though they would rather talk than eat they slept with a concentration that I envied, for the road from Africa to Latin America is long, very long.

At Belém we stopped long enough for a shave and a meal and to meet the local press, who knew all about Powell and Pressburger, somewhat to the puzzlement of the French, who had never heard of us. I told the local boys I hoped to see Bibi Ferreira, who had starred in *End of the River*, at Rio, but at Rio we never left the plane. In a very short time we were airborne again. The Argentinians had no intention of letting the Brazilians steal their thunder. There was a big reception prepared for us on arrival in Buenos Aires, so "Vamos!" No stopping at Montevideo—there is no love lost between Uruguay and Argentina, any more than there is between Irish and Scot—and here was the Río de la Plata, the River Plate itself, a great wide mouth of a river, and here was my cousin, Dick Walters, and his family dancing with excitement, and here was B.A.—Buenos Aires!

When Emeric proposed that we should use President Perón's gigantic festival to do research for *The Battle of the River Plate*, he reckoned without our host. On arrival at B.A. we were greeted by half a million people who accompanied us to the Alvear Palace Hotel, where we were going to stop the night. These half million cheerful fans never left us. They surrounded the hotel, their faces pressed to the windows and glass doors; they ran alongside the limousines that took us to the railway station; they let us go to Mar del Plata, about twenty miles down the coast, with regret. There were another half million fans waiting for us when we got there.

The hotel where President Perón and his guests were all staying was about the size and shape of Gibraltar, with an underground world of tunnels and secret exits and entrances. It was not safe to walk in the streets, we would have been killed by kindness. The restaurants seated two thousand. The bars were a hundred feet long. It took three hours to get a meal. You could lie down, but you couldn't sleep. Day and night they would play a tune, a kind of patchy jingle resembling Ravel's Boléro. When the music played, everybody danced, wherever they were: on the stairs, in the streets, in the garages, in the limousines, in bed—always this never-ending tune.

When President Perón came into one of the large rooms of the hotel, everyone stood and clapped. In return, he clapped back. He was a big, burly man, not good-looking, but not bad-looking either. He looked a bit like Arthur Rank—in type, not in likeness. He had the slightly bewildered air of a captain of industry. When he spoke to his people it was in a hoarse shout, with no attempt at art or skilled oratory. But he told them what they wanted to hear, and they loved it.

We gave him a copy of *The Red Shoes* book by Monk Gibbon, and he told us that he had seen the film twice. When we spoke of our wish to make a film about the *Graf Spee* he showed interest and said perhaps we should meet his cultural minister, Raúl Apold. This was not as easy as it sounded, because everybody was at Mar del Plata, including our own embassy and its naval attaché. But we managed it on the very last day, and got an encouraging response from the minister, although he could hardly have done anything else.

When the Mar del Plata shindig was over, we had three days in B.A. They were useful and informative ones, but our main discovery was gastronomic: La Cabaña Entre Ríos, a meat restaurant to end meat restaurants. Even to talk of this heavenly restaurant, years later, made Emeric's mouth water. Their rich and dumpling-studded *pucheros* (stews), their endless variations on the theme of *asado* (roast), their steaks, their chops, their sausages, selected and composed, cooked, and presented with an art beyond all artifice, were never forgotten by either of us. And, I dare say, that La Cabaña had a considerable influence over our decision to return later on for a proper recce, if we could find somebody else to pay for it, while a chilling little adventure that happened to me acted as an even stronger spur on our curiosity and on our imagination.

We had all been asked to an *asado* at one of the big *estancias* back in the hills. It made a nice change. There were five hundred people eating under the shade. There were many Perónista police in plainclothes about. I went on a little exploring trip, and met a friend of the family who said, "They've all gone up to the house . . . come."

We left Walter Pidgeon signing autographs.

At the house, the front door was locked. We went in by the back way. He showed me the harness room, and the saddle room, and the coach house, where traps, dogcarts, and buggies, all painted yellow, leaned in the shadows. We saw the men's quarters, with the great central fireplace, and the meat cooking: hundreds of sausages, white, brown, and black, cooking in the ashes, dozens of ribs on spits. We left the men's quarters and strolled up to a modern house, white with white shutters, cool and aristocratic. The door was locked, and so we came in through the kitchen by the backdoor and found all the ladies talking scandal around the long table; shouts of "Michael!" and "Pedro!"; we were given cups of tea, coffee, brandy, and were introduced to all the mothers. Other people, not so welcome, followed our lead, and a Russian lady, without being asked, played the piano and sang.

Pedro took me to see the long, cool bar in the billiards room and the gun room. There were rows of shotguns, mostly British by Messrs. Purdy, and rifles, mostly German Mannlichers. I lingered over the guns until Pedro became bored and left me, cautioning me to lock the door when I went. He left the key in the lock. I was dying to examine a pair of matched Colts, silver-mounted, made in about 1895, in a glass case. On top of the case there was a long, slim hunting knife in a sheath. I collect knives, and drew the blade from the sheath to examine the quality of the steel. On the blade of the knife was engraved, in Gothic letters, *Alles für Deutschland.* It was an SS officer's dagger. I replaced the knife so hastily I pricked my finger a little with the sharp point and left a spot of blood on the sheath. I had suddenly lost all interest in knives and guns, and went to join the others, locking the door behind me as I had been told to do.

The next day we returned to B.A. We met a bewildering number of people and learned a great deal, partly from our embassy and partly from Emeric's numerous cousins. I insisted on making a formal visit to the Teatro Colón, because of its associations with Diaghilev and his company and, later on,

MILLION DOLLAR MOVIE · 263

Pavlova and her dancing partner, Stowitts. It was at the Colón that Nijinsky escaped Diaghilev, who had stayed behind in France, thus ending one of the world's great love stories and starting Balanchine and Massine on the road to fame and fortune. The Colón was, and is, a magnificent theatre, and B.A. was one of the great theatrical touring dates.

We met several local showmen, and particularly one Mentaste, and it was obvious that there was plenty of money available for a film with local roots. Everybody agreed that the battle of the Río de la Plata was a first-class idea. But after that, what next? Why not write a story that was wholly Argentinian, but that would have an appeal for the rest of the world? I had often urged this on Emeric. Hollywood was not the only place to make pictures, particularly for English filmmakers. What was wrong with the Caribbean, Hong Kong, Australia, and India? Before his marital breakup my old stay-at-home of a partner had resisted my persuasions. But now he seemed prepared to listen, especially when Mai Zetterling added her voice to mine.

"What are you doing in Hollywood, Mai, playing straight man to Danny Kaye? What for?"

"For five thousand dollars," she answered with a beautiful Nordic simplicity. "With five thousand dollars and a few promises, I can make a film of my own in Sweden."

"What kind of film, Mai?"

"About sex."

"That old thing?"

"There is no point in making a film unless you have something to say. I have something to say about sex."

"Bravo!"

We were all on the plane to Rio de Janeiro. It was a small local service: DC-4. I was reading *Vol de Nuit*. Like all youngsters of my age and wide interests, I had been swept off my feet by Antoine de Saint-Exupéry, the poet-pilot-author of *Wind, Sand and Stars* and *Flight to Arras*. With incredulous horror I had watched MGM snatch the rights to *Vol de Nuit* and turn it into a talkie-talkie, with a couple of Barrymores. Thanks to NRF,* this great writer was still in print. There is even an opera of *Vol de Nuit* with music by Dallapiccola, whom I met in a mews flat in London's Belgravia. The world never knew how close they were to having a film of it. I suggested that the

*Founded by writers, Editions de la Nouvelle Revue Française (later called La Librarie Gallimard) played a major role in European literary life in the first half of this century by publishing the works of Proust, Malraux, Gide, Sartre, Camus, Breton, and Claudel, as well as Saint-Exupéry. NRF also translated into French the works of Dostoevsky, Dos Passos, Hemingway, and Faulkner.

whole opera should be staged in a set representing the fuselage of the mail plane, and the composer was delighted with the idea.

*Eheu fugaces.** No one who has read Saint-Exupéry's description of a flight through a storm over the Andes will fail to understand my interest and excitement when I realized that a real storm was generating above, below, and behind us. We charged through the wicked thunderstorms like a bull at a gate, banging our way through thunderheads like a lost bumblebee through mushrooms. It began to be a question of which would arrive first at Rio, the storm or us. It was traveling almost as fast. Below us, through gaps torn in the hurtling clouds, we glimpsed black mountains with rounded towers, reaching up to us like a giant's stubby fingers. As we came round over the city to land, the movement took us to the edge of the whirlpool and threw us like a matchstick only a few hundred feet above the skyscrapers, while black witch-clouds twitched their veils around us and screamed curses at us for escaping. Ten minutes after we had landed the storm broke in floods of tropical rain so fierce that, when driving, we had to stop at every crossing to look from the side windows. The windscreen was choked and blinded with water.

Long waves were thundering on famous Copacabana beach where the sand lies golden and clean like maize-flour. I thought the hotel would be long and low, green and colorful, with exotic ornaments and piles of tropical fruit. It looked like Claridge's. Only the center courtyard, with its pool shining with light and lashed by rain, looked exotic.

At 8:00 P.M. Bibi Ferreira came bouncing in to fetch us for dinner. She was having a baby in July, and looked very well on it. Her husband, a beautiful young man of good family, younger than she, was waiting outside in a huge convertible coupé. I took Bibi in my arms, kissed her, and asked the news.

"Four months."

I was very fond of her, and we understood one another. We felt absolutely natural with each other. Of course, in Rio Bibi was the spoiled baby of the town, her father a popular comedian with his own theatre. She had always

*From Horace's *Odes*, II. xiv, I.

> Eheu fugaces, Postume, Postume,
> Labuntur anni.

> Ah me, Postumus, Postumus, the fleeting
>   years are slipping by.

For Michael's own interpretation of the quote, see page 294.

had a success with her vitality, and her talents as an actress, dancer, singer, and producer. She had now turned serious producer in the Brazilian equivalent of the Comédie Française. She drove us to fetch her husband's uncle, Pascoal Carlos Magno.

Now, this was just the man we wanted to meet again. He had been at the embassy in London for three years, a rich man, a poet, a politician—and Bibi had married his nephew! We went to the house of her sister-in-law, Sra. Haydée, wife of a well-known surgeon. We dined there, and more of the family dropped in. They were charming, cultured people. The house was built into the side of a cliff, all height and no breadth, all stairs and balconies and hanging gardens for two hundred meters, delightful on such a hot, still night as this. The daughter of the house, Márcia, was in the corps de ballet of the opera, a tall, slender naiad with arms and waist and legs and a still, pale, passionate face, which one day might make her a great ballerina. She had the ambition and the temperament. She yearned to come with her grandfather to Paris and London. I promised to help her if she did. She stirred the creative impulse in me. I never saw so slender a creature, with such a will and such passion. Márcia Haydée—a good name. She was sixteen.

We had a very good dinner, very light, discussed everything under the sun and moon, which was full, in English, French, Spanish, and Portuguese. Armando and Bibi drove us home in the open coupé. I saw Márcia's wispy figure outlined against the light as we turned the corner of the narrow lane.

=

In twenty-four hours we were in New York and had made a deal with Spyros Skouras, the head of Twentieth Century–Fox, to do research and write a screenplay on the Battle of the River Plate, script to be delivered within three months. We knew and liked Skouras from our days with Rank, and trusted him.

Suddenly, we now had three projects on the fire: *Ondine*, with Audrey Hepburn and Mel Ferrer, *The Battle of the River Plate*, with Jack Hawkins as Commodore Harwood, and *Oh . . . Rosalinda!!*, with an all-star cast—all three to be made and delivered in 1955. This seemed to me a tall order, but anyway, it was a nice change for the better.

I was home in time for Columba's birthday—his third.

There was no time to lose, though we hadn't been exactly idle during the past weeks, months, years. Emeric went to work at once on his research for *The River Plate*, and we had the meetings with the three captains that had been postponed because of the trip to Mar del Plata. First was Parry: He was Admiral Parry now, Royal Navy retired. He lived at Wittersham, one of my favorite villages in the world, which lies on a little hedgehog's back of a hill, down on Romney Marsh in west Kent—but why specify west Kent? Surely everybody knows of the great marsh and of the marshmen, and of Kipling's "Dymchurch Flit." Who can forget Thorndike's Dr. Syn and his smugglers riding through the night? Ellen Terry had a cottage there, and the marsh had its novelist in Sheila Kaye-Smith and her regional romances—one of them, *Joanna Godden*, was made into a film in which my old dear friend Googie Withers starred.

Parry was a gray-haired charmer with a brisk, much younger wife. He struck me as a self-centered, highly political officer, extremely competent, and we could see why he had retired as a full admiral while his fellow officers, their wives and families, had retired on a captain's pension. But although we didn't get the feel of the battle from Parry, he gave us some useful papers and, in particular, a little paperback book called *I Was a Prisoner of the Graf Spee* by Captain Dove, captain of a merchant vessel that had been sunk by Captain Langsdorff of the *Graf Spee*, for whom Captain Dove had a considerable regard, amounting to hero worship. Emeric pounced on this and pocketed it with every appearance of satisfaction, and I knew that he had found the clue that he had been waiting for which would lead him to the personal story within the story of this naval occasion. In the film Parry was played by Jack Gwillim.

Next came Captain Bell, Hooky Bell, an officer of the old school, with a nose on him like William the Conqueror: it *was* a nose, it curved like a scimitar! He came up to London from Tiverton, the capital of Exmoor, Lorna Doone country. His wife was Australian. They lived in half of a farmhouse-cum-rectory on the edge of the moor. He was a clear-thinking, clear-speaking man, and I was able to learn from him how the battle was fought, and what it feels like to be under continuous fire from a pocket battleship with eleven-inch guns. Delighted with our discovery, we took him to lunch at the Étoile, where Emeric filled him up with saddle of lamb and invited him to be the technical adviser on the film. He was played by John Gregson.

The next day Lieutenant Commander Medley came up from the Joint Services Staff College near Chesham Bois. He was tall, very tall, round-headed, and eager to help. He was also a member of the Garrick. He is played in the film by Patrick Macnee. Medley was the perfect staff officer. He told us a lot about Harwood from his point of view, but I got the impression that he didn't understand the older man. The commodore had not been given his command for nothing. He had a strong historical sense, and the eventual confrontation of his three ships with *Graf Spee* was no accident. Fifteen years before, Medley was probably too young and impatient to appreciate these qualities in his chief.

Calling spirits from the vasty deep was an essential part of our research. But Emeric had been right when he pounced upon Captain Dove's *I Was a Prisoner of the Graf Spee,* and so, on a fine, midsummer afternoon, a somewhat flustered film director could have been seen driving an open black Bentley around West Hampstead, looking for St. Anthony's Catholic church. A postman directed me back the way I came, and on the corner of Garret Road I saw him, a tall, massive man, with fine white hair, saying as I drew up, "I thought it was you when you went up just now. I said to my missus, 'A man like him would be driving a sporty job like that.'"

It was a cul-de-sac, so I backed in and turned around, while he went to fetch Mrs. Dove, a sprightly woman with a weather-beaten face and young eyes. I drove us up to Hampstead, and Redington Road. It was a warm afternoon, but Emeric received us in his library so we had to admire the garden through double-locked glass doors.

Dove put us at our ease by announcing that he intended to play himself in the film through the simple expedient of blackening his hair. In the film, Bernard Lee plays Captain Dove. The authentic Dove would work with Emeric on the screenplay.

These interviews had taken place over a period of three or four months, since we had returned from Mar del Plata. Preproduction work on *Oh . . . Rosalinda!!* was going ahead steadily. We had to return to Montevideo for an official visit, to make contact with the government and establish local liaison people, who would swing into action when we arrived to film the scuttling of the *Graf Spee* by her captain, witnessed by the population of Montevideo, sometime in 1955. It sounds an incredibly ambitious program, but it didn't seem so at the time. Things were going our way.

By August 1954 my Lords of the Admiralty had signified their approval of our intentions and their willingness to give us help, both official and unofficial. Early in August I lunched with Captain Clarke, director of naval information at the Admiralty. Clarke was a foxy-faced man, unimpressive to meet, but very soon impressing by his resourcefulness and imagination. He also had a sense of humor. We discussed the policy of attack in the battle, which had been Harwood's—the policy of heading straight for the enemy before he had time to collect his wits. Clarke quoted the great Admiral Cunningham, who was one of his gods, and mine, who was told in the Med in 1942 that he was running his head against a brick wall.

"Can't you see, you miserable defeatist, if I can loosen just one brick, it's worth it?"

It was Cunningham who said on another occasion, "We can build another navy in one hundred years, but it would take three hundred years to build another reputation. We cannot afford to cease from taking the offensive."

Even Nelson couldn't have put it with more elegance, and it was the audacious way that Harwood and the three ships under his command opened

268 · MICHAEL POWELL

fire and headed straight for the enemy that confused Captain Langsdorff for the first few minutes of the battle, so that he lost the initiative and never recovered it.

"What about the movements of ships?" inquired Foxy-Face. "I suppose you'll be using models a lot, and animation?" he added, knowledgeably.

But I had already made up my mind about this. "No," I said firmly, "all movements of ships will be at sea."

He was impressed. "And I suppose you want us to supply them? Don't you realize that most of the ships afloat in 1939 are now at the bottom of the sea, or in mothballs?"

"Then you'll have to help us get them out of mothballs," I retorted. "I'm not going to have a lot of stupid little models in our big, beautiful film."

He grinned, but I could see that he would help.

"What about the *Graf Spee*? The only people today that have a comparable ship afloat are the Yanks. The *Salem* would do you. She'll be the American flagship of the Sixth Fleet next year in the Med."

"Would the Yanks mind if we blew her up?" I inquired.

"I think they might be a little bit peeved."

We had already had a conference with our people about the end of the *Graf Spee*, so I knew what the answer was. The essential thing when using a model for ships at sea is to make one big enough. Our technical people had worked out that the model would be over twenty feet long, and complete in every detail. Of course, they needed only to do one side, the starboard side. She would be wired and prepared for any amount of explosions, and we were sure that we could get away with it.

"Meanwhile, you write to the American secretary of the navy," said Clarke. "And I shall go to the assistant secretary. Never go to the top man for a favor."

"Why so?"

"Because if he turns you down, you've had it. Whereas, if you go to his number two, he—"

"Okay, okay, I get the point. Has *Salem* got eleven-inch guns?"

"Fifteen-inch . . . Have you got Jack Hawkins?"

"That's what Jack Hawkins keeps asking us."

"Well, have you?"

"We're talking about a year from now. That's too far ahead to promise anything, or anybody."

"And you want me to promise you half the British fleet to play with."

"That's different."

"It certainly is. But you two have gone about it the right way, and haven't tried to rush in at a moment's notice. So I'll tell you what we'll do. I have been through your list of requirements: ships firing broadsides, ships refueling at sea from a German oiler, three cruisers operating under a single command, rendezvous with American Sixth Fleet in the Med, scenes at Malta, etc., etc. If you ask for all this and we lay it on for you, it will cost the earth and you won't be able to make your film."

"What do you suggest?"

"Look . . . can you keep your camera crew on standby for three or four months?"

"If it's in the budget, yes."

"Good. Then this is how we plan it: we work out for you times and places, and ships, materials, men, in August and September next year; officially, we're not doing it for you, we're doing it for training, for maneuvers . . . see?"

"I see. Where will all these exercises take place?"

"It may be in the Med, it may be in Scotland . . . it might even be in the Falkland Islands. The hardest thing, of course, is to have three cruisers available to you for twenty-four hours in the Med; that's why we have to plan ahead. When we say 'Come,' you go, shoot your scenes, and it won't cost you a penny. The taxpayers will pay for it."

"Swell."

"Mind you, the essential thing is to have your camera crew all genned up* and ready to go at a moment's notice. And I think you'll have to hold them for at least eight weeks to cover all that you want, including the scenes at Portsmouth. As for the Yanks, of course, I can't speak for them, but I think that they'll play along with us. The Sixth Fleet will be operating out of Malta, or else they'll be along the Mediterranean coast between Naples and Golfe-Juan."

"Suits me . . . I live there."

"They'll probably want you to rendezvous with the flagship at Malta, but don't worry. We'll get you everything you want if you play it our way."

I outlined the plan to Spyros Skouras, who happened to be in London.

"But have you got Jack Hawkins?"

I said, "Oh, shut up, Spyros—we've got the British navy, and the American navy, and you babble actors."

He liked being told to shut up, but he persisted. "Yes, but have you?"

The meeting was taking place at what the Hollywood elite called *The* Claridge's. Darryl Zanuck, who was talking on the telephone, cut in: "What's this about you boys and Audrey Hepburn and *Ondine?* Is it a deal?"

He was a tough little, dangerous little, man—a rough rider over men, a big-game hunter of women. I snarled back, "Why don't you ask Kurt Frings? He's always complaining that nobody will talk to him."

Spyros was bewildered. He knew nothing about the Paramount deal, and

*Fully informed.

at once assumed that we'd been playing a very deep game. As president of Twentieth Century–Fox he could, of course, make deals; but Darryl Zanuck was the titular head of production, and never lost an opportunity to remind his president of it. Spyros had been pleased about the *Graf Spee* deal, but now here was a much bigger deal, with an international star and an international subject, and he knew nothing about it.

We escaped from their suite and laughed. This meeting wasn't about the *Graf Spee;* it was called by Zanuck to find out about *Ondine.* From then on, Spyros treated us with more respect. We were deep, very deep—but had we got Jack Hawkins? He suspected not, and if we hadn't, he would show us who was boss.

=

Audrey and Mel had arrived in London on New Year's Eve. I drove over to South Audley Street where Audrey's mother, the Baroness van Heemstra, was giving a New Year's party. I sounded the horn and Audrey looked out the window and yelled, "It's Micky!," dashed downstairs, opened the door, and leapt into my arms—these arms. Mel had followed her down with his son, a nice, solid boy, who said, "Gee, is that a real Bentley? Four and a quarter?"

"Three and a half."

The Baroness was a bit stiff, and I soon left. The next day Emeric told me that Mel had cast himself to play Alfred in *Rosalinda.* I was not too pleased. It was the first I had heard of it.

"What about Kieron Moore? He's been promised the part."

But even Chris Mann wouldn't go along with it. Of course it made sense, keeping Mel close to us and all that. But since when has sense meant anything in casting? I fancy that it had been Chris Mann's idea. There was no time to argue. I put up a weak defense; they had me against the ropes, and I gave in. I guess I didn't really believe Mel was an actor. He had no warmth, nothing to give: clever, yes—kind, no. We were a happy company. How would he fit in, I wondered?

Actors are kittle* cattle. That was J. M. Barrie's opinion. It is also mine. Also Hitchcock's. Alfred the Great wouldn't even allow them the kittle. He would say, "Bring on the cattle." Of course, he didn't mean it. There were many actors and actresses that he admired, and went out of his way to work with. It was just his way of remaining top dog.

In *Oh . . . Rosalinda!!* I had a special problem that had been created by myself, for myself. It was number three in our series of art films: *The Red Shoes* (art and ballet), *The Tales of Hoffmann* (art and music), *Oh . . . Rosa-*

Kittle is a Scottish word for "intractable" or "hard to handle."

linda!! (the art of operetta, the hunting of the Snark), and it was to be my one failure in this interesting triptych, and the failure was mine: I planned it, I insisted upon it.

It started with the actors, with the casting of the principal parts. With memories of Mamoulian's and Ernst Lubitsch's musical comedies, it was to be an all-star cast. As Emeric would say, "Already a mistake."

An all-star cast usually ends up by being a no-star cast. Let me remind you that we had ended up with Anton Walbrook as The Bat, Monique (Ludmilla Tcherina) in the title role, Anneliese Rothenberger as Adele, Tony Quayle as the Russian general, Dennis Price as the English colonel, Mel Ferrer as Alfred, the Viennese comedian Oskar Sima as Frosch, and Michael Redgrave in the Maurice Chevalier part of Colonel Eisenstein. Have I left anybody important out? I don't think so. It shows you what sort of film it was, that I am not sure.

Besides the principals, we had a permanent company of forty-eight: twenty-four men and twenty-four girls who could play anything, from street cleaners to headwaiters, and who were as much at home in a military barracks as at a fancy-dress ball. Among them cute little Jill Ireland, later to be snapped up by Charles Bronson, and John Schlesinger—"a child amongst us, taking notes"—with *Darling, Far from the Madding Crowd,* and *Midnight Cowboy* only just around the corner. For good measure, he was also going to play a nice little part in *The Battle of the River Plate,* on board the *Graf Spee.* But he didn't know that yet.

My greatest personal disappointment, and I hope his, was that I failed to make contact with Michael Redgrave. We had admired each other's achievements, and we had always, as they say, hoped one day to work together. It started well enough. We shared many memories. I have always been a great theatregoer. I had seen him in 1938, in Gielgud's *Three Sisters* and Michel Saint-Denis's *The White Guard,* in which Peggy Ashcroft had a never-to-be-forgotten outburst. Of course I had seen Michael's films, *Dead of Night* and *The Browning Version.* I had thought his Hotspur at Stratford better than Larry's. *Tiger at the Gates* was another triumph. He even won me away from gazing in rapture at Diane Cilento's lovely naked feet.

But I knew little about Redgrave personally, and discounted tales of his moodiness, wayward genius, drunks, and heterosexual exploits. What actor is not celebrated by such tales? They are usually inspired by jealousy and envy. They are part of an actor's stock in trade—masks and costumes that he can assume at will, especially if you stand on the scales at 176 pounds, are six-foot-two in height, with glorious golden hair, blue eyes, and a way of taking everything and everybody for granted—a Bronzino that has just walked off the canvas, and now stands looking down at you, half puzzled, half contemptuous, well mannered, hot-headed . . . a bloody-minded baby.

In August of the year before, 1955, Frankie and I went down to drink champagne with Michael and his wife, Rachel Kempson, who, as Frankie remarked, would be very nice if she hadn't been so often told that she was like an English rose. As a matter of fact she was nice, very nice, and now that the rose had faded a little but was still as slender as ever on the stem, she was even nicer. Michael had sent me a copy of his book, inscribed with admiration. It was a reprint of lectures that he had given at Bristol University, entitled *The Actor's Ways and Means.*

The house was one of those large Queen Anne houses on Chiswick Mall. There is a Thames eyot* there, and they were at the upper end. The house was spacious, like a country house, and built of dark brick. It had three gardens— three!—and all of them with paved paths and crawling with roses. The third one was across the road, on the very bank of the Thames, and periodically got washed away; this was before the Thames barrage. The Redgrave family had been living there for nine years, ever since the war. The house was called Bedford House, and stood between a bakery and a brewery. Frankie swore that she could smell the hops, and The Dove public house was just around the corner. Just a few hundred yards up the river was the house of William Morris, where he used to keep his boat and take the whole family upriver to Kelmscott, on water all the way. All together, it was the most desirable house in London, and the highly decorative family were well suited to it.

We were late, and it was already getting dusk when we shook hands at the door. I caught a glimpse of two excited children at the end of a passage—tall and slender girls. They were too shy to come out to meet us, but waved and laughed. Why do I remember this evening so well, I wonder. Is it because the potential in art of these four human beings was so strong?

Michael had pretensions to be a singer, and refused to play Eisenstein unless he should also sing in the part. He was right, of course, in one way, wrong in another. It led to Hilde Gueden marching out of the recording in Vienna. But, on the other hand, we replaced her with Sari Barabas, who sang a delightful Rosalinda. Her gaiety and charm fitted Monique as stylishly as the clothes of Jean Desses, whom Frankie had discovered in Paris after an exhausting elimination contest. He was a Greek who understood the body of Frenchwomen and had a great sense of humor. He was one of Frankie's great triumphs, and she got herself a French haircut as well.

We had scheduled *Oh . . . Rosalinda!!* for six weeks' shooting, two weeks' rehearsal. It was an unpopular decision. Actors hate rehearsals, particularly if they are told by the assistant directors that they are expected to know their lines when they report. Actors like costumes, makeup, props—anything they can hide behind until they are ready to declare themselves and stride into the

*A small island in a river.

limelight. Tony Quayle, reporting from Stratford and entering some bitterly cold and bare North London drill hall, exclaimed, "For a moment, I thought I was back in rep," as he watched Syd and the assistant directors chalking lines on the floor to indicate glamorous sets. "I imagined it would be 'Mr. Quayle' and 'Mr. Redgrave' and wonderfully colored sets and lights, and lemonade and, perhaps, champagne before lunch is served . . ."

While he was speaking Mel Ferrer walked in, blandly ignoring dropped jaws and pointed stares. "I know the part already," he announced, and got sour looks from the other men. After a week's rehearsal we moved into the studio and started shooting.

All The Archers regulars were back on the job: Reggie Mills and Noreen Ackland in the cutting room; Syd Streeter and Charles Orme either in the office or on the floor (they alternated the two jobs); Chris Challis and the camera crew clustered around the Technicolor camera—it was their first CinemaScope film.

To Scope, or not to Scope—that was the question in 1955. Chris is swearing that Twentieth Century–Fox has given us a dud set of lenses. He is shooting test after test after test, and then viewing them, walking to and fro from the projector and the screen.

"Law lumme,"* says Bill Wall, trailing him, "you'll have us in the bathtub *with* Monique if you're not careful."

Bill Paton is sitting solidly in my director's chair, because he knows very well that I never sit in it myself. Fred Lewis, bending over a metronome, is tut-tutting over the actors, who will not keep in synch with the singers' voice track. Arthur Lawson is prowling like a hungry wolf, between the shops and the set, between the set and the shops, while Hein is everywhere at once, followed by his gang, sketching and scribbling, tearing the costume off a girl, his mouth full of pins. The setting and costumes are some of the best he has ever done, bright and childish, and designed with the freedom that CinemaScope, if you work with it, can give you. But Chris is trained by Technicolor, and Chris is not happy.

"If the actors move three or four feet upstage they are out of focus. Micky, we've sacrificed everything we ever learnt about Technicolor for this bloody wide screen. I suppose it's all right for Westerns and spectaculars, like *The Robe*, but it's no good for comedy. Comedy has to be dead sharp."

"How about having individual spots for each actor?" I suggest bravely. Chris gives me a look of pure hatred.

"And burn up their silly faces? You know very well, Micky, there comes a time when too much light is no light."

This is my first film in four years. The budget is £278,000, and we have

---

*Dialect for "Lord love me."

£6 in the bank, our bank. We have spent all the rest of our own money getting *Rosalinda* to the start post. We know all about front money, distribution guarantees, and guarantees of completion. We are what is laughingly called "independent." We can't even pay ourselves a salary. Thank goodness, we say to each other, Paramount is going to finance *Ondine* in their wide-screen process, VistaVision, and Twentieth Century–Fox is going to finance *Battle of the River Plate* in their wide-screen process, CinemaScope. Long live Spyros Scopus.

But all was not well along the Potomac. Production was up to schedule, but the chemistry was not working. Mel's Alfred was a clown without charm, and he was proving a partner without charm too. Alfred was a part he could play standing on his head—and frequently did—and then spend half the night intriguing against us over *Ondine*. He and Audrey wanted more consultation, he said. Since I was on the floor all day, Emeric got the brunt of this. Mel told Chris Mann and Kurt Frings that we were difficult.

"They want us to lick their asses," I told Emeric. "You take Mel."

They suspected us, with reason, of still wanting to modernize *Ondine*'s story—to turn it into a twentieth-century fairy tale, to tell Mme. Giraudoux and all residual Giraudoux to go jump in the Rhine, that we didn't want to pay an exorbitant author's fee—and they were quite right. We appreciated the play *Ondine* for what it was—a sophisticated Parisian fairy tale. Mel was certainly no Louis Jouvet. When Jouvet paused, we all paused. When Mel paused, the whole play stopped. It was Audrey, in spite of her small voice in that big theatre, who carried the play. We preferred Emeric's idea of a modern version, and we were only awaiting the moment to spring it.

Hein knew this, of course, and maybe he had battled with them. Maybe he had tried to sell it to them. I never knew for sure. But each meeting was more urgent than the last, and the inevitable confrontation took place on the day that Mel played his last scene in *Rosalinda*. After a long day's shooting we were summoned to a meeting at, of all places, Hein's studio at the Pheasantry, in Chelsea. And who should be there at Mel's invitation but the designer Roger Furse and his sister Margaret. They were always together. They were full of tact, like two cancer specialists called in for a consultation. I had never worked with the Furses.* They were in a different league—more theatre than film—and of course I knew all about the family, and admired their inventiveness and taste. Roger, in particular, with his memories of the original Old Vic, must have seemed impressive to Audrey and Mel.

Audrey never said a word, but Mel spoke for two. They were not satisfied

*Roger Furse was a theatre designer who moved into film and designed costumes and sets for Laurence Olivier's films. He won an Oscar for *Hamlet*. Another sister, Judith Furse, was a director and an actress. She played Sister Briony in *Black Narcissus*.

with the costumes and they didn't believe that we were, or that even Hein was really. He wanted a totally new approach, whatever that meant. It was quite clear that the meeting was about who was going to be boss, and by no means exclusively about costumes. It was a weird experience: the big studio, the half-dim figures sitting or sprawling around, Emeric as solemn and silent as a judge, the fire flickering, the creative partners avoiding one another's eyes, drifting steadily apart, no shouting and screaming. Perhaps it would have been better if there had been.

Emeric and I didn't look at each other. We realized that Mel had been leading up to this for months and was now coming in for the kill. His voice had a little crow of triumph in it. He was acting the part of producer for his new friends. In art there is an unspoken brotherhood, an identifiable aristocracy. We all know it, and recognize it in each other. There are certain names, certain subjects, certain reputations, that serve as passwords when the project is ambitious. We are sure of our own participation in the venture. But what about a certain aspect of it? For a moment there is a check. A name is mentioned . . . the mist clears. A certain quality has been guaranteed, a certain confidence has been inspired. There is no more question of the validity of the enterprise, only how, when, and where. Without this mutual trust, this mutual recognition, an artist cannot live and grow.

I yawned, and apologized.

Of those that belong to this coterie that I have described, one of them, Robert Morley, a young man with talent and ambition, ran a summer theatre in Perranporth in north Cornwall in the 1930s. They did good work. It was such a group as the ones I have been describing. The Furses—Roger, Margaret, Judith, Jill—were active members. Early in my London days I saw Jill Furse at the little Torch Theatre, exquisite in *The Masque of Kings*—which was the first dramatization of the tragedy of Mayerling. Nancy Price was running the little Torch Theatre, giving jobs and good parts to Esmond Knight and Roger Livesey. I smiled as I remembered Charlotte Leigh at the Torch Theatre in a monologue to the stunned audience about how she had been back to visit the house where she had been born, that the people were new and everything was changed, even the front gardens: "Pansies they were, I remember, and now they were all red-hot pokers."

The fire crashed, and burning coals rolled toward Nandi, Hein's daughter, who had gone to sleep in the grate. The meeting broke up. Emeric and I had still not exchanged a word. Mel was whispering to Audrey. Hein and Ada were bursting with suppressed laughter. We all drove off in different directions. The Heckroth family stayed up for another hour, drinking and laughing about the Furses. They thought it was the usual piece of power politics. They didn't realize that it was the end of *Ondine*.

The next morning Emeric came out to the studio around eleven and handed me a draft of a letter from The Archers to Kurt Frings. I handed him an almost identical one. We quoted Chaim Weizmann: that disagreement was the salt of life, but in this case there was too much salt in the soup. The film had to be made our way, and with our people, or not at all. No doubt Paramount would take over the whole production. We wished them luck. A load dropped from our shoulders, and with it £10,000 sterling. The next time that we heard of Audrey and Mel they were in Paris, and a month or two later in Rome preparing for King Vidor's *War and Peace.* Jack Cardiff was the lighting cameraman, of course.

=

We had been neglecting for far too long the half-finished script of *The Battle of the River Plate.* Emeric dusted it off and went to work. I finished up *Rosalinda* in great style. We came in under schedule, and under budget, but not without our dramas. Anneliese proved to have an inferiority complex as big as the Ritz. Her numbers, her dialogue scenes, her dances, all had to end in tears. This had to run its course. Once it was over, she was excellent. Monique astonished everybody by developing a broad vein of slapstick comedy. She was terrific. In the big bedroom drama she stole the scene from Michael Redgrave.

Anton and Mike were in love with each other. It was a love-hate relationship. Michael was better before lunch, Anton after it. When they were playing to each other they were like children. Anton stole the whole picture in the final scene, when he made his speech to the Four Powers and said, "Go home."

It was a beautiful performance of The Bat, but too Viennese for our English audiences. They had seen Anton as romantic hero in *Dangerous Moonlight,* Canadian farmer in *49th Parallel,* German officer Oberleutnant Kretschmar-Schuldorff in *Colonel Blimp,* and, above all, as the cruel, art-loving Lermontov in *The Red Shoes.* All these performances by Anton had been accepted by English audiences because they were part of the struggle we were all determined to win. But after five years of Hitler's war, they were not disposed to see the joke when we offered them a Viennese playboy. Only when Anton made his final appeal to the Four Powers, only then were they disposed to listen and applaud, and by then it was too late. If you please, I'll quote it to you, or even if you don't please. It's quite short:

Ladies . . . sweet, charming ladies . . . and gentlemen. It's four o'clock in the morning, and the air of Vienna is like champagne. When I am soaked in champagne, I love everybody. I love the whole world; in particular, of course, our dear friends the British, the French, the Russians, and the Americans, who have been spoiling us Viennese for so many years, now. And when I say spoiling, I am not thinking only of your champagne . . . *(Cut to Redgrave and Tcherina)* . . . and whisky *(Cut to Dennis Price)* . . . vodka *(Cut to Anthony Quayle)* . . . and Coca-Cola *(Cut to Mel Ferrer).* We are proud that you love us, so much, and we can assure you that we love you, too. But even the dearest friend loses a bit of his attraction, if he . . . overstays his time . . . *(laugh)* . . . don't you agree? So, if you don't mind . . . go home. Come back, as our guests. But, please *(shooing hand gesture)* . . . go home.

Alex Korda hated homosexual actors. It was a surprising admission for a man of taste and experience. He hated Anton Walbrook because he was homosexual, and because he had such good manners. No doubt he was jealous. He had seen this beautiful, glorious youth, Adolf Wohlbrück, take Vienna by storm in the 1920s. He had the world at his feet, while Alex Korda was still being kicked around. Everything came Adolf's way. Paula Wessely, Vienna's favorite actress, was mad about him. He could take his pick of romantic heros: Michael Strogoff, Mazeppa . . . he played them all. Then came the invitation to England, from Herbert Wilcox, to play Prince Albert, the Prince Consort, husband of Queen Victoria, in both of Herbert's Victorian epics, the second in Technicolor. It was *the* accolade. He came, he saw, he played Ivor Novello's *The Rat.* His command of the subtleties of the English language was amazing, unlike Conrad Veidt, who had been a great theatre and cabaret star in Berlin. Anton, for he was now Anglicized into Anton Walbrook, was not afraid to appear on English boards, no more than Elisabeth Bergner had been when she played in Margaret Kennedy's play *Escape Me Never.*

Came the war, and Anton stayed put. Like all actors at this climactic point in their career, he could only offer his services and wait. Then came Emeric Pressburger. It was Emeric's idea to make *49th Parallel* an episodic drama, with new stars arriving in each new episode. He wrote the part of the Hutterite farmer for Anton, and the part of the Hutterite girl for Elisabeth Bergner, who ran away to join her husband in Hollywood and in doing so made a star of Glynis Johns. Each star in *49th Parallel* was paid the same as the others, i.e., £2,000 for two weeks' work, guaranteed. Anton gave half his salary to war charities. Leslie Howard was dissatisfied with his fee and insisted on having a percentage of the profits. We gave it to him out of our share.

Now you see why, when we made *The Life and Death of Colonel Blimp*, the story of a British officer's love and friendship for a German officer through three wars, we didn't have far to go. We loved and trusted each other, we knew each other's mettle. When it came to *The Red Shoes* and that devil, Boris Lermontov, there was no question in our minds as to who should play him, and give a performance filled with passion, integrity, and, yes, with homosexuality, thereby earning the unsolicited but outspoken criticism of Sir Alexander Korda, a supporter of the British establishment. But art has many mouths, and many faces, and all art is one, man, one.

I hadn't seen *Rosalinda* for thirty-two years when Bill Everson ran it for me and Thelma and Martin Scorsese and his class at New York University, in the spring of 1987. It was a 16mm Eastman Color print, a little bit anemic in color, but otherwise in good shape. Bill had obtained the print by devious means, into which I did not inquire. As our film had never been professionally exhibited in the U.S.A., the class evidently thought it was an occasion, and so did a chorus of cleaning women who left whatever they were doing and came to see the pretty costumes and the lights. I enjoyed the film much more than I did in London, sitting among a nest of hostile critics. Monique was every bit as funny and as beautiful as I remember her, and Anneliese sang like a lark. I remembered how my bank manager in London said, after seeing the film, "What's the matter with the critics? What do the public want, anyway? Here are two lovely women, singing and dancing and acting—isn't that enough for them?"

I saw now what I had never seen before, either in rehearsal or in performance: Michael Redgrave was a child. He had the open heart of a child, the innocence and cunning of a child, the obstinacy and the naughtiness of a child. I ran through a list in my head of the films I would have liked to have made with him and now never would. I settled on *Edward Lear.*

I watched Tony Quayle sing and clown his way through General Orlovsky, and although Tony was in magnificent voice and form, I cursed Orson Welles in my heart. After our meeting in Paris, and after repeated promises, Orson had vanished into the Mediterranean sunset somewhere, leaving behind him a sketch of himself singing "Chacun à son goût," a cigar in one hand, champagne glass in the other, with a mocking caption underneath. I had always believed that he would turn up eventually, but dear Orson had too many irons in the fire. He left unfinished films all over Europe that he had to visit from time to time, just as a doctor visits his patients, giving them a shot in the arm, or the ass. Very few actors could follow Orson in, even fewer could follow him out. Luckily, I had Anthony Quayle standing by. He was my second string for Harwood in *The River Plate.* Next in line was Trevor Howard. In spite of Skouras, we knew that Jack Hawkins didn't want to play another uniformed part, and we agreed with him.

What was that? Have I still got Orson Welles's sketch of himself singing "Chacun à son goût"? Yes, I have. Do you think that I would ever part with a self-portrait by the great rebel? Not bloody likely.

My attention came back to NYU and the 16mm print of *Oh . . . Rosalinda!!*

The cleaning women were loving the big musical numbers that bring the film to an end. The students were a bit shy. They liked the film, but nobody had ever told them that they should like it, so they didn't know what to like. And now The Bat was speaking his piece to bring the film to a close: an Edwardian piece in a Tiffany frame—very pretty, but a long time to wait for it. As the champagne flowed on the screen, I thought of Anton and the strange art of acting. Larry said that real acting, the big stuff, is walking a tightrope between the two sexes: sooner or later you fall off one side, or the other. Anton was different. No actor that I have known had such control as Anton had—until he played The Bat. Then, The Bat controlled him. All those great roles that he created with us, including that attractive monster Boris Lermontov, had to be imagined, thought up, created, performed, controlled: three triumphs. The Bat was different. In order to play Dr. Falke, Adolf Wohlbrück had to return to his sources. The clattering of the projection stopped, the class were applauding, the cleaning women were applauding, I was applauding too. But in my heart, I knew that this was Anton's only failure, because he had to play himself.

As for me, I needed a sea change:

> I must go down to the seas again, to the vagrant gypsy life,
> To the gull's way, and the whale's way, where the wind's like
>   a whetted knife;
> And all I ask is a merry yarn from a laughing fellow rover
> And a quiet sleep and a sweet dream when the long trick's over.

=

It would seem to be a long step from Johann Strauss to John Masefield, but The Archers made it without effort. The Royal Navy has its own language of communication and a good ear for a turn of phrase, which suited The Archers fine: "The movements of ships at sea . . ." Could there be a simpler or more beautiful phrase than that? A series of images of ships crowds my inner vision: a great barkentine, all sails set to catch the least breath of wind, lifting slowly to an oily swell; a great battleship at slow speed, crowding alongside an oiler, ropes and commands flying to and fro between the two vessels; a county-class cruiser bearing majestically down upon us with a thousand men swarming over the decks and shrouds, waving and cheering; a lean destroyer, quietly slipping out of a Riviera port at night to a rendezvous off Sardinia; the vast bulk of the American battleship, *Salem*, gathering speed as she leaves Valletta harbor to join the fleet; the dark, streamlined shapes of three British cruisers, proceeding in line beneath the full moon rising over the coast of Anatolia.

Could all these images be more beautifully and simply described than by the phrase "the movements of ships at sea"? It was the use of this phrase by us, when we first visited the Admiralty to request assistance for a film about the Battle of the River Plate, that had attracted the attention of Mountbatten, the First Sea Lord, whose son-in-law, Lord Brabourne, had been his aide-de-camp when he was Viceroy of India. Now Lord Brabourne was to be our liaison with the Admiralty, and later would become our production manager. John Brabourne has often told me The Archers were so used to having every man's hand against them, and to fighting their own battles, that we didn't at first appreciate how lucky we were.

Meanwhile, Spyros Skouras was in New York, cowering in his president's chair, leaving the head of his London office, who was not a production man, to deal with our requests and entreaties, which were fast becoming threats to go somewhere else for what my father would have called "the bees and honey." Spyros was still bleating for Jack Hawkins, who was the only British name he knew. *Rosalinda* was in the editing stage, and would soon be ready for dubbing, and I was being summoned to Cyprus for a conference with the C-in-C* Med, to discuss our plans and timetables. Emeric was completing his final draft of the *Graf Spee* script.

We had frequent conferences between us, at the weekends. At the same time, now that *Ondine* was officially abandoned, Chris Mann was trying to interest other companies, the Rank Organisation among them, in Emeric's *The Miracle in St. Anthony's Lane*, which I suggested should be called *Men at Work*. It was one of those ideas, and one of those scripts, that attracts and repels in about equal quantities. The miracle that took place was a genuine miracle—or was it? The postman, who acts throughout the film as a sort of angelic observer, is not really an angel—or is he? It was the kind of story and script from that period when plays like Molnár's *Liliom* and films like *Here Comes Mr. Jordan* were going the rounds.

Emeric's miracle tale had brought him a handsome little income from frequent options. Now he wanted to get it made and get some cash in the bank. He was moving from Hampstead at this time, leaving his great family house in Redington Road for a flat in Eaton Square, and I had frequent conferences with him at both places. I had no love for *The Miracle in St. Anthony's Lane*, yet I understood Emeric's love for it. But it would need a very firm hand on the tiller to bring it into port: there I go!—using a salty metaphor. But my excuse is that I was mad about the River Plate subject, and Emeric had found a wonderful way to tell the story and keep control of the action. The inspiration for this was, of course, the little book by Captain Dove, *I Was a Prisoner of the Graf Spee*, which revealed how Captain Langsdorff's prisoner became his friend, and a spectator of a great tragedy.

*Naval lingo for commander-in-chief.

On June 7 I went to Emeric's flat for breakfast before going to the studio, and we went through half the script together. I came back for tea and the other half. He had eliminated all scenes with subsidiary characters that detracted from the classical shape of a tragedy. The film fell naturally into four acts:

ACT ONE: Captain Dove, or The Prisoner of the *Graf Spee*
ACT TWO: *Achilles, Ajax, Exeter*
ACT THREE: The Battle of the River Plate
ACT FOUR: Montevideo, and the end of the *Graf Spee*

From the opening scenes, the film moved relentlessly forward, Jules Verne–like, a combination of science, engineering, mystery, and romance. The climax was the deliberate destruction of the great ship and the suicide of her captain, cut off, abandoned, surrounded by enemies. Stapi had been right; it was an epic, and they don't fall into your lap every day. And you can bet that Spyros Skouras was not the man who could stop us from getting it on the screen. We decided to go to someone with more guts, and informed Basil Litchfield at the Fox office that our patience was at an end, that the three navies—British, American, Indian—were converging upon the Mediterranean while his president, that perfidious Greek who had put up the money for the script and never read it, was still screaming for Jack Hawkins.

The two subjects, *The Miracle in St. Anthony's Lane* and *The Battle of the River Plate*, show Emeric at his best and worst. De Maupassant was Emeric's literary godfather, and *St. Anthony's Lane* was an emasculated de Maupassant *conte*—no pun intended. As a film for the 1940s and '50s, it clearly showed its prewar provenance. It was all about the lusty navvy leader of a street-repair gang, the man who handles the drill, up a new girl every night, while the virgin heroine breaks her heart for him and prays for a miracle to happen . . . and it happens . . . or did it? Only St. Anthony in his church at the top of St. Anthony's Lane, and the postman, who knows everything and everybody in the lane and who is in love with the girl himself, knows the true facts of the matter . . . or does he? The script shows its age by the delicate way it steps around sexual relationships; nobody ever fucks anybody. The people in the lane are the usual ethnic types. The only memorable image in the script is the final one, when the boy who is head of the road gang leans upon his automatic drill and says to the girl, "Free tonight?"

She nods, and he grins and plunges his drill into the virgin surface of the road. Get it?

But the Pressburger of *The Battle of the River Plate* was quite another cup of tea (or should I write a cup of *barackpálinka?*),* for his conception of this epic subject showed clearly his Magyar origins; this was a writer with balls. We start in the vast South Atlantic ocean, stay at sea, and remain at sea until we are driven into port at Montevideo and the final confrontation. Before I left for Cyprus for my briefing, Joan Page and I went through Emeric's script for the last time. The budget and schedule depended upon it. Joan and I sat down at two tables, tore two scripts to pieces, and worked with an eye on the clock. There were two big new dialogue scenes that gave me a lot of work, but Emeric's scheme was impregnable and we finished by two o'clock. I left Joan to pick up the pieces and took off for Cyprus.

Cyprus was not like Crete. You could cut the colonial atmosphere with a knife. Perhaps that is why knives were being used to solve the problem of *enosis*—self-government. The Royal Navy, however, still seemed to be popular. I stayed the night at the Ledra Palace and drove across the island next morning to Larnaca, where the cruiser *Sheffield*, Admiral Sir Guy Grantham's flagship, was lying together with *Surprise*, a kind of superyacht instituted by Lord Mountbatten as a supply ship for the C-in-C Med and his guests. Larnaca had a long seafront with piers going out into deep water. We drove out onto one of these and waved to the flagship, and I heard the bos'n's whistle. There was a bustle on the flagship, and the launch came to get me and tore out to the flagship in great style.

I was received by Captain Lewis, the Captain of the Fleet, an important person with a finger in every pie, with whom I would have to deal. I was obviously expected, for there were one or two officers there whom I had met when I was on the *Formidable*,† at the time of the North African invasion. It was evident that I was considered a VIP, thanks to Mountbatten. I did my best to look the part. Admiral Sir Guy Grantham DSO RN was thin, fair, and cordial. He looked more like a bishop than an admiral, but the two jobs have always been interchangeable. He greeted me warmly and gave me a cool drink, then handed me over to Lewis, who at once got down to the script with me and told me he had orders to cooperate with me and try to get me everything I wanted, but of course it all had to be done by Fleet Order. I was to put myself into his hands, and he would see me through. He was a tall, ruddy-faced man with a high color and black eyes. I realized that I was in safe hands, but I got a jolt when I learned that all the dates that we'd been given

---

*Hungarian apricot brandy.

†Michael was shooting a recruiting film The Archers were making for the Fleet Air Arm, on board an aircraft carrier in the Mediterranean in 1942. It was called *The Volunteer* and starred Ralph Richardson, who along with Laurence Olivier had joined the Fleet Air Arm when war was declared.

were wrong. There was only one time that three cruisers could be detached and together, and that was between June 19 and 21. The cruisers were the *Sheffield*, the *Jamaica*, and the *Delhi*, which, as I have already related, had taken part in the Battle of the River Plate as HMAS *Achilles* in the Australian navy, a fact of which we were reminded ten times a day. It was touching to see how these sailors, from midshipman to admiral, were moved by this astounding piece of luck for this battle-scarred veteran.

Lewis explained that the Indian contingent would join the fleet the next day and anchor off Limassol. On Thursday, the combined fleet would sail in company to a favorite little anchorage, Marmoris on the southwest coast of Turkey. The director and camera crew would be taken on board *Delhi*, and would transfer later to the flagship.

"Stop, stop, Lewis," I cried. "I have no camera crew, no cameras, I must talk to Pressburger at once, if not sooner."

We commandeered the Admiralty line to London, and although it was Sunday an excited Pressburger was soon on the phone, reporting that reactions to the script and project were generally favorable, but most particularly from Earl St. John of the Rank Organisation, who was seeing John Davis over the weekend. Earl St. John was John Davis's head of production at Pinewood. He had not blenched at our budget figure of £254,000, nor did he question our production schedule, which was original to say the least of it, and arrived at by Syd Streeter and George Busby after an all-night session. Listen to it: camera crew and director on standby for three months, followed by seven weeks in the studio, five-day week, climaxed by ten days' shooting in Montevideo, the unit to return home to London for Christmas with two days in hand. One week out allowed for Christmas and New Year, followed by the model shots of the *Graf Spee* blowing up—all these shots to be done in the studio tank, which would fill the whole of Stage 4 at Pinewood. Only the Americans, or the Rank Organisation, had the money, the distribution, the studios, and the technical resources to play out this daring plan, which was typical of The Archers at their most self-confident.

"Oh, Michael? . . . British Lion are interested in *St. Anthony's Lane* . . . with Stanley Baker and Diane Cilento."

I said that was nice, but when was he seeing John Davis?

"Four o'clock on Monday, at his office. Oh . . . and Michael? . . . Trevor Howard has read the script, and says he would like to play Harwood. When do you need Chris?"

I looked at Captain Lewis, who was listening sympathetically.

"What's the latest time for Christopher Challis and his camera crew to arrive in Cyprus?"

"Wednesday night. *Delhi* sails on Thursday morning, seven A.M. What's the trouble?"

"No trouble, but we shan't know until Tuesday whether we're shooting the film in CinemaScope or VistaVision."

"Will that affect the movement of ships?"

"No."

"Then, let's get on with the Fleet Orders."

I spent the weekend sightseeing and reading Runciman's *History of the Crusades.* You wouldn't think that any historian could make the crusades sound like a package tour, would you? Tuesday morning, before breakfast, a message from Emeric via the Admiralty. I walked over to read it. Copies of the message had already gone all over the Mediterranean, so the air was full of John Davis, Powell, and Pressburger, and other almost mythical figures. The opening line hit me like a blow: "JD approves project and script."

I stopped reading and took a deep breath. The office cat came over and rubbed against my leg. I resumed my reading. It was a guaranteed takeover by John Davis of all, or any, of the obligations incurred by us with Twentieth Century–Fox, and confirmation that the film would be in VistaVision, not in CinemaScope. Chris Challis, plus camera, plus crew of four, plus Bill Paton, would arrive by Viscount* on Wednesday evening. Here I permitted myself one "Yippee!" Davis approved Trevor Howard, if we wanted him, and didn't care what other names we did or did not have.

"Yippee!" again.

Paramount would distribute in the U.S.A.

"Yippee!!"

Obviously John Davis was thoroughly enjoying scoring off Spyros and Twentieth Century–Fox. But the hero of the occasion was Emeric. When I think of that small, square, neat figure advancing to do battle with these monsters it brings tears to my eyes—a partner in a million! Emeric concluded with a message from John Davis, wishing us luck and asking us to look upon our return to Pinewood as a return home. This was mighty handsome of John and did a little to make up for our eight years in the wilderness, but can the leopard . . . ? We had fought for, and obtained, complete artistic freedom in making our films, by which I mean that no one came between our craftsmen and us. We shared our thoughts and inventions with our fellow craftsmen, with our actors and actresses; and in return they gave us love and loyalty. We smashed conventions and threw out old rotting customs. We paid our audiences the compliment of treating them as equals. There were no secrets, and we were always accessible to each other. When something new—an idea, a

*British passenger aircraft.

gadget—was needed, we invented it. For ten years we always had one film in production, one in preparation, and one in editing: "A Production of The Archers, Written, Produced and Directed by Michael Powell and Emeric Pressburger." In an industry like the movies, this was pure anarchy! The new crop of directors coming up after the war sighed in envy. Who were these Archers, that they should be allowed to get away with this? Martin Scorsese, then in his teens, describes the reign of the toxophilites as the most successful period of subversive filmmaking ever to affront the mainstream of studio film production. And all this we were bringing back to Pinewood, to the studio that had been the home of independents, to the men who had found the money for it, Arthur and John, now known collectively as the Rank Organisation, the Man with the Gong. Well, we said to each other, the fatted calf is being dressed for us now, but there will be trouble later when Earl St. John tries to shove his oar in.

Later in the day, while I was discussing timetables with the Captain of the Fleet and the Captain of the *Delhi*, a further telegram arrived: Chris Challis and VistaVision camera, with camera crew of two and no Bill Paton, would be arriving by Viscount that evening. The Admiralty did remind Michael Powell that our numbers would be limited to four, by agreement. Lord Brabourne would be liaison on the film between the Admiralty, the film unit, and Pinewood. I bristled: already no mention of The Archers. The telegram was signed "Earl St. John."

"Who is this Earl St. John," asked Lewis, "friend of Brabourne's? Are all your gilded staff in *Burke's Peerage?*"

"Earl St. John is John Davis's 'yes-man' at Pinewood," I answered concisely. "He is called Earl St. John because that is the name that the mother who bore him gave him."

"I see."

I was a bit huffed because in my original, pre-Brabourne requests for help in photographing the movements of ships at sea it was quite true that my crew and I had been limited to four in number.

"The ships are full of people . . . Every bunk, every hammock is occupied . . . Can't interfere with training, you know. Even to take four of you is stretching it a bit, but we'll manage, somehow."

I had agreed, knowing perfectly well that if I brought along an extra person, or two even, it wouldn't rock the boat. As for Bill—Bill had been in the navy during the war, Bill the tower of strength, Bill the nonunion man, my personal assistant, who usually acted as if *he* were the boss and I were the assistant—Bill Paton was a must! Who else could carry those blasted twelve-volt batteries that I had been asked to buy in Cyprus? I had been caught out before by those rupturous objects, each one weighing about fifty pounds, or fifty tons (it was much the same, when you were trying to climb a vertical ladder in a warship). I knew that if William Paton were not there to carry the batteries, I would have to carry the batteries, and carrying twelve-volt batteries is not my cup of acid. I am good on ladders, and platforms, and helicopters, and all that sort of thing, but not with a twelve-volt battery in each hand.

When this limitation of four people was broken to me, I naturally assumed that I could smuggle in Bill. He wouldn't count, being ex–Royal Navy, and then the camera would have its own grip. All these extra people could be wangled when they were on the spot, asking for a bunk with pleading, doggy faces. But now that we had "liaisons" and "agreements" and were no longer pirates, I could see it might not be so easy to do a little smuggling, and that one of us was going to be the fall guy—me.

After complete failure on the telephone, I went back to Kyrenia, and located Messrs. Solomonidis, who sold me the batteries that would power the camera. Two big eleven-plate batteries cost £10 pounds each, and weighed—well, you know what they weighed. The clerk in charge of the store took me to a battery-charging place behind the market where they put them on charge and promised to have them ready at 6:00 A.M. on the morrow; what could I do but believe them? By the time I got back to Nicosia, my crew had arrived and it was dark—no Bill. In spite of that, his pal Chris Challis was in great form. With him were Austin Dempster, the camera operator—blond, chunky, sleek, and silent—and, of all people, Jim, Jim Body, who was on *49th Parallel*, and many other Archers' pictures. They had all been working on *Quentin Durward*, and had deserted the Middle Ages in a body to dash two thousand miles to be in at the first shots of *The Battle of the River Plate*.

They had brought a perfect mountain of equipment, two or three tons of it. I never saw so much stuff. We were right back where we had started, now that we had added VistaVision to our quiver. Chris brought me a chit from John Brabourne telling me that John was flying out to Malta with a second camera after the weekend and would meet us there. He would try to arrange shots from the air as our three cruisers approached the island. He would also bring Bill with him. . . . He'd better!

I was so excited, I don't know whether I slept or not. We were called, anyway, at 3:30 A.M. The cars to take us down to the docks were half an hour late. I was in quiet despair. We loaded up and sent the van off first, with half of the material, the rest following in five minutes. I felt ill with worry and lack of sleep. There was no margin for error, and I couldn't know whether the batteries waiting in the marketplace were charged, or whether the ship's boat was still there. I kept saying to myself, "Ten minutes to offload that material into the boat . . . and the fleet sails at seven!"

Fortunately we had a good driver. He was very black, calm, and efficient, making a good contrast with me, the director. We got to the market as the clock struck six. The batteries were ready. We drove across to the customs shed, where Jim Body was standing at bay. I had forgotten to warn customs about our early start, and the office didn't open until 9:00! I brushed the watchman on one side.

"Don't listen to him, and don't argue," I said to my crew. "Just load the stuff on."

Even the naval boat's crew started to look doubtful. But with the driver's help we whipped three tons of material through the shed and into the boat. The watchman was vainly protesting. He ran away and came back with a militiaman who demanded our passports.

"Okay," I said to the others, "give me your passports and get going. Get the stuff on board the ship. Then come back for me," I said to the steersman. He was grinning and nodded. This sort of lawless situation is meat and drink to an Archer. I ran across to the police office where the militiaman was looking with great respect at our much-traveled passports.

"You'd better see Mr. Logan," he said.

"When's he come on?"

"Not till nine."

"Get him on the blower."

A pleasant, Scottish voice on the telephone: I poured out my story. He listened calmly, then said, "Give me my fellow," and with three words set me free.

The police cheered. We shook hands all around. I raced back to the dock. It was 6:50 A.M. I kept repeating, "The Fleet sails at seven!"

I strained my eyes for the boat . . . no boat. Twice I saw a boat pass from one ship to the other . . . no sign of my boat coming for me. I waited. It was 7:30 A.M. at this point, and the Fleet was still there. At last the boat came back, bringing the *Delhi*'s commander.

"Some trouble, Mr. Powell?"

"No, just ulcers."

The *Rajput* had a leaky steampipe, and sailing had been postponed until 9:30 A.M. My heart soared . . . so, after all, I hadn't delayed the Fleet.

We sailed, eventually, in *Rajput* at 9:45 A.M. on a northwesterly course, destination Marmoris. *Delhi*, playing herself as *Achilles*, was our star performer. We figured that the sun would be in about the right position toward 4:30 P.M. At 4:30 we were set up with the camera on the foredeck, looking off to starboard, ready to shoot. *Delhi*—I mean *Achilles*—came up on our quarter looking very fine, in third-degree readiness, forging along through a blue-and-white checkered sea, her ensign flying stiffly in a strong breeze, the low sun lighting her gray sides from almost dead ahead. At 4:45 we shot

Scene 1, Take 1, *The Battle of the River Plate* and radioed the news to Emeric; he deserved it.

But we couldn't afford to waste film and our next shots were at dawn the next morning, so we struck the camera and held a conference. We had thirty-nine shots to get before we arrived with the fleet at Malta, and all these shots, with times and compass-courses, had been worked out by me with the Captain of the Fleet and included in the Fleet Orders during the next few days. There was a fair breeze, and the night was full of stars. We would have to wait for the light in the morning. It meant an early call, so we all turned in, the four of us in the captain's cabin in the stern of the ship, while he slept in his sea cabin under the bridge. I went to sleep immediately.

A crescent moon was hanging low over the coast of Anatolia when we turned out at 3:30 A.M. It was still dark, but the outline of low, jagged mountains could just be seen. We were approaching the rendezvous at the time arranged. *Delhi* had taken up her position and we held her in our sights, waiting for the dawn. As the sky lightened and the coast appeared we started cautiously to shoot—at first ten feet at a time, then longer bursts as the light broadened. *Delhi* looked like a purple ghost against the dark background. At last the rim of the sun appeared over the mountain and we started shooting, and not too soon, for we were driving at twenty-five knots into the Bay of Marmoris, and it would be considered bad form to knock the flagship out of the water. I told *Delhi* to turn sharply off to starboard and make black smoke. She did, the low sun gleaming on her forward bridge and turret. We turned with her, shooting as we went, and were happy.

We went below and shaved, while the squadron re-formed and proceeded at a more sedate speed into the Bay of Marmoris. It was full of great ships, and looked very impressive as we steamed slowly down to our station at the end of the line; all ships were dressed with flags and men. We reached our station, dropped anchor, and had breakfast. We were no longer acting independently, but under the command of Admiral Sir Guy Grantham, who had called a film conference at 9:00 A.M. on the flagship.

Thanks to the presence of Captain West, secretary to the C-in-C, and Captain Lewis, the conference went like a dream. I stopped panicking and began to look forward to the next day. That evening the admiral gave a dinner to all his captains on the quarterdeck, twenty-four of them. He lent me his cabin for the night, and I joined *Diamond* in the morning. She was a clean and happy ship and my crew was happy too, although a little worse for wear because of a party the night before. *Diamond* was one of the new Daring class destroyers. She was to be our camera ship.

Captain Eddison looked familiar, and turned out to be the brother of Robert Eddison, the actor, who later appeared in our children's film *The Boy Who*

Turned Yellow, which means that he was tall, amiable, and good-looking. He had a stagestruck daughter. We sailed at 11:30 A.M. Toward three o'clock we were in the Aegean Islands, and took up our position on *Jamaica's* port quarter. The three great cruisers in line ahead looked splendid in the full sunshine, with the violet-colored misty cliffs beyond them. My moment had come. We started to shoot. I was in telephone communication with *Sheffield* by wireless, and I had a loudspeaker telephone between the bridge and the camera on the fo'c'sle and vice-versa. Captain Eddison handled his ship like a Thoroughbred (she had twin screws), and everything worked to plan. By teatime I was running the Fleet like an old admiral, and with Eddison's enthusiastic cooperation we closed in on the flagship and got a couple of the most spectacular shots, wonderful shots.

There was an unforgettable moment when she steamed slowly by our camera into the low sunlight, the other ships in line abreast, her upper works gleaming; and the final scene was the most extraordinary sight I have ever seen. We had maneuvered the three ships to an easterly course, with the sun setting behind a long, low, violet island. We were steaming in silence, Chris and I watching together the red ball sink lower and lower. Together we said: "Now!" I gave the word, and Eddison put the wheel hard over. We turned the camera amidships and crossed a sea flecked with light. As we swung, the great red sun swung solemnly into our picture and crossed behind the ships to the other side. One by one, they were outlined in front of the fiery globe, and one by one they passed before us, as if in review, and out of our story. The red globe vanished, as majestically as it entered. Everyone on the bridge drew a long breath.

The ships hove to. The flagship lowered a boat by its giant crane, and we lowered our gear into it hand over hand. It took half an hour, and by the time we slid down the jumping-ladder it was dark. There was no sea, only a steady rise and fall. We came up under *Sheffield's* quarter, shackled on, and the crane lifted us all into the air, crew, equipment, and boat. Captain Lewis was waiting as we landed on deck, dirty, sweating, but happy.

"Hurry up! The C-in-C's waiting dinner for you."

"What about the others?"

"They've got dinner in the wardroom."

I raced down, washed and changed, and joined the others, resplendent in their white full dress with medals.

Later on in the night we all went out and chose the position for our next shots, on the gun platform above the quarterdeck. The admiral thoroughly enjoyed himself, climbing ladders like a midshipman with myself following sedately behind.

We were called before 0600, and the launch was loaded with our gear, and with us, and dropped over the side onto a sea like a millpond. The three big cruisers lay with engines stopped. We crossed to the lee side of *Jamaica*, where a tall, bearded commander greeted us at a jumping-ladder. We passed up a lot of our gear (the crew were staying the night on *Delhi*, but the day on *Jamaica*), then set up the camera in the boat. We were soon ready, cast off, drew away from the ship, then gave the prearranged signals. This was the famous "council of captains," which Harwood called at sea on the day before the battle. We passed the bows of *Jamaica* and revealed the flagship, gleaming in the early light, then beyond her *Delhi* with a seaboat pulling for the flagship and a captain (dark—but it didn't show at that distance) in the stern sheets. We went nearer on the boat, and followed her up to the flagship. I could see all the staff on the bridge, looking self-conscious. It was a grand scene, and one of my most difficult ones. To have the time, the place, and the weather all perfect, plus everyone in a good humor, plus three cruisers, was more than you could pay for. You just had to be born lucky.

Last of all, we deployed the cruisers into the setting sun, the whole sea glittering like a carpet of gems. We lowered a pinnace with us and the gear already in it, plus a crew of marines. When halfway to *Sheffield*, they discovered that there was no water in the engine. They thought it a great joke. I went aboard *Sheffield*, where Lewis greeted me with motherly inquiries, while the others were taken to *Delhi*, where they were in no time installed on the B-turret, shooting the flagship making signals. I stood beside the signals officer, feeling rather forlorn and like a staff officer without my camera at my elbow.

So here I was, with the last of my trans-shipments done, and near the end of the ambitious program I had planned. Everything had depended upon timing and upon weather. Well . . . my timing is good, and the weather loves me. "Boldness be my friend."

To arrive in Malta after those wonderful days at sea with the Royal Navy was to leave a world of action and discipline for the world of politics, naval and movie. During the next six months of glorious filmmaking, John Davis and I, although we seldom met, were very much aware of each other. He had welcomed us to Pinewood, true, but for how long, and on what terms? Neither of us wanted the other one's job; it was purely personal. I was a filmmaker, he was an accountant—natural enemies. But I was more than just a filmmaker, and he was more than just an accountant. And I had the Royal Navy in my quarter, thanks to John Brabourne and the First Sea Lord, his father-in-law. Without the help and authority of these two formidable allies, I could never have achieved what I did. As it was, all doors were opened to me. I moved, arrived, and departed with all the authority of the Admiralty. The result is up there on the screen.

When you look back over a long life, a pattern emerges that could not have been foreseen. Chance had brought Frankie and me to the Mullaghmore* in the spring of 1945. Chance and a violent squall of wind and rain which had us hammering at the door of the castle, asking for shelter for ourselves and our horses, with the Atlantic rollers leaping over the harbor wall and swirling to our very feet, for the castle had its feet in the sea. It was then, while we dried off in front of the great log fire, that we first heard tales of the high-born young women who used to come to the Mullaghmore for their holidays and run wild like nobody at all, and one of them, Edwina it was, was to marry the great Earl Mountbatten and be the last Vicereine of India . . . and wasn't that a wonder and an honor to Mullaghmore?

Ten years passed, and I find myself on a high rostrum bawling out my production manager, John Brabourne; bawling out the husband of Edwina's daughter, Patricia. John answers in kind, with an aristocratic bluntness that disconcerts me. He makes his point, and we become friends who are slightly wary of each other. A year passes, and we are all in white tie and tails for the tenth Royal Film Performance, before Her Majesty, Queen Elizabeth II, and her husband, Prince Philip. The Archers have become Blimps and John Brabourne is a producer in his own right.

Twenty years pass. Headlines crash against the stone of the Mullaghmore: "IRA BOMB OUTRAGE . . . A FAMILY IN MOURNING . . . EARL MOUNTBAT-TEN MURDERED."

The Mullaghmore! I could hear the boulders grinding on the rocks. There is blood on the stones. Suddenly, I become intimately connected with those two grieving families. Memory returns to that wild night on the Atlantic seacoast. Months later there is a glimpse of John, wounded, in an invalid chair.

Four years flash by and our paths cross again, and again: in Canterbury Cathedral, in Dallas, Texas. John and Patricia have recovered from their terrible wounds, but there are some wounds that can never heal. The Mullach More has claimed its victims. And now Frankie is dead, and soon there will be no one to remember the Mullach More as we remembered it on that night of storm and rain, so many years ago.

Malta has many beautiful sights, but the most beautiful for me was the

---

*It was during Michael's horseback ride across Ireland in 1948 to research the film he hoped to make about Paddy the Cope that he and Frankie had to take shelter from a storm in Classybaun Castle, the summer home of the Mountbatten family. On August 27, 1979, the IRA detonated a bomb on a boat in the harbor at Mullaghmore, killing Mountbatten and several memebers of John Brabourne's family. Brabourne and his wife were badly injured. Brabourne served as liaison with the Admiralty on *Battle of the River Plate*.

sight of Bill's unmistakable bottom as he stood in the middle of the carpet in the hall of the Hotel Phoenicia, giving out the gospel according to The Archers to John Brabourne, who, to do him justice, was listening with attention. I watched them for a moment, unperceived. John's face is entirely his own. The most remarkable features are his eyes, large and luminous. He is clean-shaven, and his nose and cheekbones are on Plantagenet lines. He would look great in one of those Norman helmets with a thingamabob along the nose: the face of a man used to command, and used to being obeyed; a calm face, quick to react and break into a smile or a frown; a face that, in repose, gives nothing away. He sees me and with a look of relief springs to his feet. Bill turns.

"So there ye are. We were just comin' to look for ye."

He hands me a note written in Emeric's large, round hand:

Dear Michael,

John Davis wants to see us in his new office in South Street, Mayfair, on Monday, July the 4th, four o'clock in the afternoon. He wants to talk about the budget and the cast. Congratulations on starting shooting. Thanks for your cable. Send the rushes back with the second camera crew.

Much love,
Imre

At my request, John Brabourne had brought a second VistaVision camera with him from London, also a full crew of four. So now we had two cameras and seven camera crew. I cannibalized the two crews into one, and sent the second camera odd-bodies home, much to their disgust. One of the new crew was Ginger Gemmell, a camera grip already celebrated for his insubordinate ways and considerable efficiency. He knew all about me and The Archers, of course, and "we iced one another warily." He weighed in at about fifteen stone, and looked and acted exactly like his name.

I looked forward to working in a unit that had Chris Challis and Ginger Gemmell writing their own dialogue. A good week followed, full of picnics. In those days Malta was the property of the British crown, Malta GC,* and the island was the chief station of the British fleet in the Mediterranean. John Brabourne knew the island and all the people well, from spending two deliri-ous long summer holidays there with his wife and family when his father-in-law was C-in-C in the Med. Before leaving for London to confront John Davis

*In recognition of its dogged and successful defense during a German siege, and the heroism of its inhabitants, the island fortress was awarded the George Cross in 1942.

Everybody in show business knew Earl St. John, but nobody but John Davis would have thought of putting him in charge of production at Britain's premiere studio, Pinewood, chosen, as you will remember, by the independent producers as their home in preference to Denham, where so many of them had been nurtured and brought forth. At Pinewood Studios, *Great Expectations* and *Oliver Twist* had been made by Cineguild; Gilliat and Launder had written, directed, and produced *Green for Danger;* David Lean had directed *Brief Encounter;* Anthony Asquith had made *The Way to the Stars;* The Archers had filmed Rumer Godden's *Black Narcissus,* settings by Alfred Junge, costumes by Hein Heckroth, Technicolor photography by Jack Cardiff.

These were all filmmakers. What was Earl St. John? He was a showman, true. Before the war, and before the talkies even, he had produced the live shows that used to precede the main feature on the Plaza Cinema's minute stage. He made many friends in show business, and few enemies. One doesn't kick a dog, and Earl was like a great St. Bernard dog in his desire to please, in his size and shape, in his great, lined face, and in his anxiety to agree with the last speaker. He puzzled artists with whom he had to work. Nobody disliked him, but nobody trusted him either. To put such a man—or such a dog—in charge of creative artists was a joke, or a crime, or both. To call such a man a has-been was a mistake. He had never been; he had just been around. This, then, was the officer of the company called in by John Davis to witness the big reconciliation scene with the stubborn and dangerous Archers. Earl stood up as we came in. John remained seated. He was bright and breezy.

"Well, Micky, long time no see."

I sat down in the chair nearest to John, and said, "Who writes your dialogue?"

He grinned.

"Not Emeric, anyway. But I wish he would . . . eh, Emeric?"

Emeric gave him one of those long, beautiful Emeric looks, perfectly friendly, but delivered from somewhere up in the stratosphere. John said hastily, "I told Emeric that you were to think of yourselves as coming home, and I meant it. It's eight years since you deserted us and went over to the enemy. You'll find a lot of changes at Pinewood. Improvements, I hope, eh, Earl?"

Earl, who had cast himself as an onlooker, hastily got his act together and gave a reassuring mumble directed at me, and fumbled in his briefcase.

John went on, "About casting . . . we should expect you to use some of our contract artists. Yours is an all-male picture, isn't it?"

"Yes," said Emeric, so far his longest speech.

John went on, "A picture like yours needs big names to help sell it. Earl thinks you could use Dirk Bogarde and John Gregson in key roles."

They all looked at me. My touchiness about any interference with the director's functions was common knowledge. I said, "I don't use actors. I work with them. Of course I know Dirk's work, and John Gregson was excellent in the Old Crocks picture *Genevieve*. (The Old Crocks race from London to Brighton every year had been riotously successful as a film, produced by Henry Cornelius, an old friend and admirer of Emeric's, who had burst into tears when Emeric refused to write his script for him.) I went on, "Perhaps Earl will let them read the script and then arrange that they come and see me."

Earl writhed acquiescence. John lit a cigar, and said through the smoke, "Emeric told me that the budget is £254,000, correct?"

I said cautiously, "That's what it was two weeks ago. Do you want us to find a completion guarantor?"

John was on home ground here. He shook his head.

"Nope. We have a good accounts department—the best. Once your budget is approved, we guarantee any overage."

I said, "In that case, add ten percent to our budget."

Earl St. John had passed it over to John Davis, who gave it an accusing stare.

"About £280,000 all in?"

"Yes."

John shook his head. He was enjoying himself.

"I suppose you know that Arthur Alcott, in our accounts department, says that your figure is way below the figure that they have arrived at independently?"

"Of course he does. He's got to cover himself and his department, and then add a percentage all round to cover individual temperaments. We've learned, while we've been in the wilderness, to cut our cloth according to our coats."

"Very well."

He initialed the budget and passed it back to Earl St. John.

"But I shall expect you to stick to this figure."

There was iron in his voice. We were on trial.

That was the Fourth of July. On the sixth, the U.S. secretary of the navy, Mr. Forrestal, surfaced from ten thousand fathoms and, as a favor to Lord Louis Mountbatten, First Sea Lord, gave The Archers permission to cast USS *Salem*, one of the prides of the United States Navy and flagship of the American Sixth Fleet in the Mediterranean, as the German pocket battleship *Graf Spee*, commanded by Captain Langsdorff, of Hitler's navy, in the Battle of the Río de la Plata, December 13, 1939, which climaxed in the suicide of Captain Langsdorff and his ship. We were advised to contact Admiral Ofstie on board *Salem* where she lay at Villefranche-sur-Mer, the deepwater harbor that is the port of call of all large visiting vessels, and that is five minutes' walk across Cap Ferrat from our family hotel, the Voile d'Or.

We were given permission to shoot the *Salem* from all angles where she lay in Villefranche roads. She was set to sail independently to Malta, and we were to sail in a destroyer, the *William R. Rush,* which was lying at Golfe-Juan. We would rendezvous with *Salem* off the coast of Sardinia and complete our shooting at sea. We would then be taken on board *Salem* from the *William R. Rush,* and I and my camera crew would proceed to Malta where we would go ashore to arrange further photography on the British flagship if, when, available. I left immediately for the south of France, followed the next day by Brabourne, Bill, and Chris and a wardrobe master with several hampers of German uniforms.

=

I first came to the little fishing port of Saint-Jean-Cap-Ferrat when I was sixteen years old, in 1921, after my father took over the lease of the Hôtel du Parc, as it was then, and where I later on got my first job in movies from Metro-Goldwyn-Mayer. In 1925 I spent the whole summer there in the closed and shuttered hotel, but after that I only returned at long intervals, and there was the war in between, and when I made *The Red Shoes* Emeric wanted me to share in his delight in making *The Red Shoes* at Monte Carlo and living the life of *les grands palais.*

I arrived in 1955 hardly better known in the little village of Saint-Jean than I had been twenty years before. I was the son of *ce fameux capitaine Powell,* and I was nothing more. So when a Technicolor camera crew and important-looking film executives appeared upon the terrace of the Voile d'Or, while automobiles and motor launches started coming and going, the village was *à go-go.* They rubbed their eyes and inspected a central figure, slim and dictatorial, looking very much at home and in command—*le fils du capitaine Powell. Tiens! C'est un cinéaste, le fils du capitaine. Sans blague!*

Salem sent a launch to pick us up and take us out to the battleship, whose vast bulk seemed to fill the *rade,** which I had known from childhood. We were a small party and I was very conscious of a countess who sat next to me. I very soon found that she was equally conscious of me. She was a tall blonde, with beautiful brown eyes and a lovely body. She was one of those rare women whose beauty is enhanced by nakedness. She wore very short, peach-colored shorts, and I let the back of my hand caress her naked knee as we sat there, jammed against the thwarts of the motor launch. To my delight, my pressure was answered. She neither spoke nor looked at me. We both had the same exquisite pleasure from this first brief encounter.

Everybody in both navies was in awe of Admiral Ofstie, but he was kind to us, although he only gave us five minutes. He agreed to my list of requests and

*Anchorage outside a harbor.

turned it over to Commander Mitchell and Lt. J. G. McNaughton, who took our party on a tour of the ship, finishing in the air-conditioned wardroom—no portholes on the *Salem*. Our new hosts were enthusiastic, and agreed to shoot next morning. *Salem* was to supply two big launches, one for the camera, the other for the extras, with Bill Paton doubling as Captain Dove, master of the *Africa Shell*. I called for volunteers on the ship's radio to play German sailors and the seamen from the captured vessel, and got an enthusiastic response. The ship's armory would supply rifles and small arms.

On our tour of the flagship I had been very impressed by the hangar below deck and the steel doors that closed over it. The aircraft were lifted out onto the deck by a powerful crane. No better illustration of a prison at sea could be imagined if the launch, with its prisoners and the German guard, could all be hoisted out of the sea, swung around, and lowered down into the hangar while the steel doors snapped shut like the jaws of a giant clam. The engineer commander was a bit doubtful whether his crane could take the weight of twenty people, the launch, camera, and crew, but he was willing to try. We arranged to shoot the next morning, and returned ashore singing "Yankee Doodle."

Yes, I dare say. But what about the countess? We want to know more about her.

We do?

Yes, we do.

It's the story of a troubadour who tracks his lady halfway across France, with no idea what he'll do when he gets to where she lives, the name of a little town scribbled on a piece of paper. It's a walled town, somewhere in Touraine, and it's evening when he gets there. Nobody seems to know where his countess lives, and it is almost dark when he comes to a small château with a great door in a wall and a very ordinary-looking bell that says *Sonnez*.

He stands there, hesitating, while the fatal minutes tick by, wondering why he hasn't the courage to ring that bell. *Sonnez, SVP:* surely that is simple enough. But in love you can never hesitate. No use to say to yourself, perhaps she is alone, perhaps her husband is there. What sort of stumbling tale am I going to tell, of losing my way, and remembering her name? How many troubadours in the past six hundred years had set the bell jangling at this postern gate, in the hope of singing for their supper, and perhaps finding the lady in need of diversions?

He is about to ring the bell, but suddenly lights are switched on in the courtyard, the great doors are dragged open, and a Jaguar, which had been purring nastily in the courtyard, now switched on blinding lights, and leapt forward with a roar. Our lover saved his skin by a hair's breadth. The monstrous animal crossed the drawbridge and shot down the hill in an orgy of changing gears. He glimpsed two goggled figures in the front seat. Behind him, the great doors rumbled shut. The single light went out. Our hero stood there with egg on his face, as the words of Danton came back to him: *"De l'audace, et encore de l'audace, et toujours de l'audace"*—in love as in war.

He never again failed in audacity, but the memory of this misadventure lingers still. There is something about a countess. Casanova would have said "a certain flavor." In my time, I have been loved by three of 'em—not all at once—French, Spanish, Roman: three memorable loves. I'm writing this in Thelma's apartment in New York City in Hell's Kitchen. I am in my eighty-third year. I should be ashamed of myself, but, of course, I am not—only for my lack of courage.

Patricia, Mountbatten's daughter and John Brabourne's wife, had joined us in Saint-Jean for a few days. In our riotous company she was a bit stiff and British, and dressed in a distressingly British way. But the crew caught on to her sense of humor, and decided that she wasn't bad at all. Chris and his camera crew had been openly intrigued by John's noble connections and by his title, and when he cut himself shaving, the camera crew expressed themselves as being deeply disappointed:

"What, no blue blood? . . . Only common red, like the rest of us? We thought that you were the aristocracy. Is that what we've fought and died for?"

Kevin came with us, looking very smart and acting as number boy. He held up the slates. Columba, in full naval rig, joined us later, with his mother in very short shorts. The young American sailors thoroughly enjoyed acting German pirates. They were bristling with arms from the armory, and they looked a desperate bunch. We were all through by 4:00 P.M., and left to join the *William R. Rush* at Golfe-Juan.

Golfe-Juan is a little fishing port and yacht harbor halfway between Nice and Cannes. There are a lot of good little restaurants, and it is a great place for bouillabaisse. Napoleon landed here after his escape from Elba, and started his march through the mountains back to Paris and Waterloo. The Fleet was in. There were tall, white-clad figures everywhere, some trying to walk, some prone on the ground, some being sick on their friends' feet. The military police knocked them on the head impartially, and dropped them into barges to be sorted out later. Only Americans can treat Americans that way. Some showed fight, but it was all remarkably good-humored, and the town was fancy-free, except that the poor drunk boys were singing, instead of dancing. It was pitch dark when we arrived and some time before we found our destroyer. It was a bit of a change, after looking up at *Salem,* to look down on the *William R. Rush* lying alongside the mole, there at our feet, a dark and dirty-looking destroyer.

There seemed to be nobody about, but I eventually unearthed a disgruntled but sober young officer who signed us in. Meanwhile the camera crew had got all the gear aboard, and stowed it, and found the wardroom. There was nothing to drink but tomato juice, and there was no sign of the captain, who had gone ashore. So, at our request, the young officer assigned us all bunks—that's to say eighteen inches of breathing space—and we all turned in, while the officers and crew staggered back to their ship. Bill, of course, had found the galley and was making tea.

We sailed during the night, and were at sea when we woke. Griddle cakes and syrup for breakfast—ugh! The young officer who had us in tow had been in the war with the Canadian merchant marine and, liking the life, had transferred to the U.S. Navy, but the U.S. Navy had changed his mind for him. I was curious.

"What's the matter?"

"Oh, they make a drama out of everything."

At about noon we rendezvoused with *Salem* off Sardinia. The weather was calm, and we established communication by a closed WT circuit and started shooting. By sunset we had completed the small ship-to-ship shots. There was one unforgettable moment as we lay with stopped engines. The sun was setting in a great haze as the great battleship loomed up and stole by us, with no noise but the hiss of her bow wave and the sound of her engines like a throbbing heart.

During the day we'd been so busy that I had never found the captain of the destroyer, and began to believe she hadn't got one, so while we packed up and got ready to trans-ship on board the *Salem* I went looking for him, and found him where you would expect to find the captain—on the bridge. He was a redhead, tough and friendly. I mention it to keep the record straight. I don't want to spread the rumor that Yankee destroyers sail themselves.

Although *William R. Rush* had been an interesting experience, it was nice to be back on *Salem*. As we came aboard we were greeted by several old friends last seen at Villefranche playing scowling German sailors, armed to the teeth. The officer of the watch greeted John Brabourne and me and told us that we were messing with the admiral. A film director afloat must be the equal of an admiral in a film studio. Our crew were received noisily in the wardroom, where Chris and Ginger got to work at once, improving their act. John and I dined with the admiral and his staff and Captain Maginnis. The staff were a seasoned and formidable bunch of men who held Admiral Ofstie in great awe. We learned later that he had been a famous carrier captain in the Pacific war.

The *Salem* was steady on her course at about fifteen knots, and I was surprised and impressed, when I came on deck, to see that she was refueling and taking on stores. It's part of the training to do this at sea. It was all done by telpher lines.* There were hardly any orders given. I lingered, fascinated, watching as the fuel from the oiler poured into *Salem*'s hungry tanks. By this means, and in the vast Atlantic, the *Graf Spee* had been able to keep at sea for months. This was obviously of the first importance, and John Brabourne got in touch with the Admiralty, who promised us the same facility in the right latitude, off Invergordon, Scotland.

The next day we completed all the remaining scenes on *Salem.* They were mostly starring Bill Paton, getting more and more like Captain Dove every day. In the evening we had a movie show on the afterdeck. The same crane that had hoisted us and our launch aboard now hoisted a giant screen into the starry sky, and what did they show? They showed *The Red Shoes.* Hundreds of young men lay about on the decks, in all sorts of positions, watching the movie. The sky was full of stars, and the mountains of Sicily were faintly outlined in the afterglow. The sea was calm and as the water rushed by, Moira danced. The strange male audience said never a word, but I felt that they were intrigued and impressed. As Moira died and Massine presented *The Red Shoes* they got up and walked away, always in silence. It was an interesting experience for one of the two makers of the film.

The next day we arrived back at Malta. We had now been the guests of two navies, and as Guy Grantham came in a launch to pay a courtesy call on Admiral Ofstie, John Brabourne and I discussed the difference in tone between them. We concluded that the reasons were historical, financial, and geographical. The Royal Naval man looks on his ship as a home, the American as a ship—that's all. American ships, when afloat, are dry. The Britisher is proud of his ship and likes to entertain you on board. The American, equally hospitable, is more likely to suggest meeting you ashore. John suggested duty-free gin, as against scotch at a hundred dollars a bottle, as another consideration; likewise, the comparative salaries of both navies. But money was not the main consideration, or so we two islanders liked to believe.

The camera unit had gone ashore, and we had stayed behind to take formal leave of the admiral. He unbent to talk about *The Red Shoes,* which had impressed him and which he had never seen before. Later on Bill and I went ashore with several hampers of German uniforms. The customs were now resigned to our appearances and disappearances with different navies, in different ships, and hardly gave us a glance. Arthur Lawson was waiting for me at the hotel. He reported continuous sniping by the Pinewood staff over The Archers' schedule and budget, and particularly over the art department's

---

*A system for transporting fuel and supplies by means of vessels suspended from a cable and moved by means of an electric motor.

estimates. This was no more than we had expected, after our meeting with John Davis.

Arthur Lawson is in heaven and, no doubt, designing a new one. He was a modest, soft-spoken man, but I think he would like me to write about him, and this is the place to do it. He joined us as assistant to the great Alfred Junge and was with us on and off for nearly twenty years. The art department, which should really be called the department of design, is the heart of a film production. In our strange craft there are many dreamers. The art department deals with facts and images. Their draftsmen, their carpenters, their painters, their plasterers and sculptors, make solid facts out of a director's and writer's dreams and fantasies. I don't know where the appellation "art director" came from, but I suspect from the Germans. The Germans were among the first, and certainly among the best, of the early filmmakers who brought fantasy to the screen. I had understood and appreciated this from my first days in the cinema, with great directors like Rex Ingram and Alfred Hitchcock. These great men didn't wait for inspiration. They believed in control, in design, from the start to finish of a film. So Alfred Junge, the greatest of all film art directors and designers, rejoined us from an internment camp to design *The Life and Death of Colonel Blimp* in the middle of World War II. By the end of the war he was our designer, and Arthur Lawson was his art director. Also, from being a rightly feared Prussian tyrant, Alfred Junge, the great and feared, had become Uncle Alfred to The Archers and their collaborators.

Through all these years, until 1947 and *The Red Shoes*, Arthur Lawson was his associate designer. When Uncle Alfred and I no longer saw eye to eye and followed different paths, he went back to MGM-British, who were very glad to get the designer of *Goodbye, Mr. Chips*, *The Citadel*, and *A Yank at Oxford*, while Arthur Lawson stayed with us and was co-designer, with Hein Heckroth, of *The Red Shoes*. This logical development and promotion proved to be a great artistic success, and a happy collaboration between Hein Heckroth, man of the theatre, and Arthur Lawson, man of the cinema. There was no jealousy, either professional or personal. Both of them were already Oscar winners for color and design for *Black Narcissus*, and the harmony with which they worked together, and the generosity by which Hein would say, "I don't know, but Arthur does," and Arthur would say, "I don't know, but I'll talk it over with Hein . . . he will find a way," equaled my own collaboration with Emeric, but perhaps went beyond it. They worked in double harness for eight years until, in 1956, Hein went back to Germany and the theatre, and Arthur stayed with me to triumph with *Peeping Tom*.

The art department's work on *Rosalinda*—artwork, titles, costume, design, props and inserts, all sorts of color work—had overlapped the start of shooting of *The Battle of the River Plate*, with all its dramatic changes of dates and of moods. So it had naturally been assumed by everybody, including Emeric and myself, that Hein and Arthur would continue as co-designers. But it soon became clear that there was very little original design in the film. It was more like a documentary than a feature. Even the important one third of the film that took place ashore, in a Montevideo that was more like a never-neverland, was conventional in design and gave no opportunity to a painter like Hein. It was breaking my heart, and Hein's too, to realize that on *The Battle of the River Plate* Hein was a passenger. But while Hein and I were in despair, as we watched our great collaboration dissolve and vanish and Hein decided to return to Frankfurt as chief designer of opera and ballet, Emeric's heart, I know now, was not even chipped. He had other fish to fry. With the *Graf Spee* picture as bait, he proposed to sell John Davis three sprats to catch a mackerel: *Ill Met by Moonlight, The Miracle in St. Anthony's Lane,* and *Cassia.*

Cassia was a book by Manfred Conte, *Cassia und die Abenteurer,* published in Germany by Fischer-Verlag. We owned the rights, in association with Stapi's company, Carlton Films, and still own them, I believe. The book was translated into English and had some success. It was very easy to read, and no doubt had been written to be optioned and made into a successful and commercial film. The plot and the principals of the story moved from one European country to another smoothly and credibly, and there really did seem no reason why it should not be filmed and forgotten, like many another best-selling book. But this was not Archers film fodder, not by a long shot. It was John Davis fodder, it was Earl St. John fodder, and it was most certainly not Michael Powell fodder, and Emeric was deceiving himself if he tried to maneuver me into his master plan.

From my future knowledge of the lives and deaths of Michael Powell and Emeric Pressburger, and from my love for Emeric and admiration for his mind, I think that I can deduce his master plan. It went like this:

Michael is unpredictable. Or perhaps, it would be more accurate to say that he is predictably unpredictable. He has the world at his feet, and he kicks it in the balls. He has already done this twice: once to Arthur Rank and John Davis over *The Red Shoes;* once to Alex over the third act of *Tales of Hoffmann.* As a result, we have no power, we have no money, we have only our interest in our films, when they go into profit, and this may not be for years.

He was right. Most of our films took twenty years to get into profit, and forty years to be recognized as classics.

Now, after eight years in the jungle, we have been welcomed back, like prodigal sons, by John Davis, and it is clear that Michael is preparing to kick him in the balls again. This is mad! We shall not get a third chance. Michael must be steered away from contact with John Davis until the picture is finished. They are like cat and dog together. But the picture looks like being a winner, now that we have got Peter Finch to play Captain Langsdorff. Trevor Howard would have been better, but Peter Finch is a bigger name. Bernard Lee will be a good Captain Dove, and Anthony Quayle, who Michael is so crazy about, will be all right as Admiral Harwood. The other captains will be Rank contract players. We are up to schedule. We have the establishment, naval and Rank, on our side. Everyone has the feeling that we are on a winner, and a certainty for the Royal Command Performance next year. It is the moment for The Archers, and we must strike while the iron is hot.

Imre loved English similes, and collected them as other people collect postage stamps or old automobiles.

John Davis is bound to ask us to make another film, and we must be ready for him. We have three subjects that we own, and are ready to go into production: the Cretan story that Michael likes, *Ill Met by Moonlight; The Miracle in St. Anthony's Lane,* my dear, old many-times-optioned-but-never-made filmscript; and *Cassia.* Michael will finish shooting with actors on the *Graf Spee* story by Christmas. He will shoot the model shots and the blowing up of the *Graf Spee* in January, in a studio. The script of *Ill Met by Moonlight* will be ready, and can go into production immediately. It's a pity about this *enosis* that the Greeks are all fighting about. It means we can't use Crete or Cyprus, but Michael will find other locations in the Mediterranean. He knows them all.

By the end of the summer that picture will be in the can, and we can go into the studio with *The Miracle in St. Anthony's Lane.* Michael wants to call it *Men at Work,* but I think I shall call it *Miracle in Soho.* The Royal Performance will be in October 1956, and by the spring of 1957 we can be shooting on *Cassia* in Germany—four pictures in a row, all of which we own, all of which are productions of The Archers. Michael *must* be sensible! He must see that we must do this. Of course, I know that all these are not real Archers pictures, but they will be very popular with Earl St. John and Pinewood Studios, because we shall use the studio and the contract actors, and deliver our films on time, and by the end of 1957 we shall be top dogs, with lots of bones in the bank. I shall not try to convince Michael, I shall just let it happen. He will see for himself that it is not necessary that every arrow should be in the gold. It is enough that it should be on target.

Also sprach Emeric Pressburger. Only he didn't *sprach*—not to me, anyway. Perhaps it would have been better if he had. My old acquaintance R. A. Butler used to talk about the art of the possible. Emeric would have savored the phrase. But my art was a proud art, and I still believe in the art of the impossible.

=

Meanwhile, I was in the Highlands of Scotland, preparing to stalk my first red deer. *Whang!* The painted steel image of a stag rocked, and the bullet ricocheted down the glen.

"A bit lower in the shoulder, Mr. Powell," said the head stalker. "Ye missed the heart by just a hand's breadth."

He handed the rifle back to me.

Whang! But this time the animal rocked violently.

"Aye, he's a dead 'un. Give me the gun, Mr. Powell. We've got quite a walk ahead of us."

The unit was in Scotland, at the Fleet anchorage naval base at Invergordon, and Rorie Tarbat* had invited the whole family to stay at Castle Leod. I announced my intention of going after a stag, to the horror of Kevin, who has a tender heart for all living things.

"You'll have a good day," said Rorie. "They'll all be on the hill together. Let the stalker pick one out for you."

"For his head?" I inquired, offhandedly.

"No, for his meat. If you miss today, there will be no dinner tomorrow."

"I will not eat a stag," announced Kevin categorically. Rorie grinned. "Are you a vegetarian, Kevin?"

"A red deer is a beautiful animal," said Kevin.

"I agree. He looks beautiful on a plate," said Rorie, onetime colonel of his regiment, captured at Dunkirk, and a prisoner-of-war for the duration. "I hope you'll never be as hungry as I was then, Kevin, or as I will be tomorrow at dinnertime."

The week before, on August 17, we had had our grand and private showing of the shots so far for the combined staffs of the Admiralty and the American navy. Admiral Cassidy sat next to Earl Mountbatten, and so I boldly pushed in and sat beside them, explaining, mentioning personalities, and making little jokes. The scenes made a great impression. Like us, they had never seen anything like it. There has never been anything like it.

We started with a dozen scenes on the normal screen, which for color and composition were already better than anything they had ever seen, and then,

---

*Viscount Tarbat (Roderick Grant Francis Mackenzie), son and heir of the Earl of Cromartie, chief of the Clan Mackenzie; author of *A Highland History*, the first book to set the Scottish Highlands in a European and world context. He has since succeeded to the title.

suddenly, in the middle of a shot, we opened up the big screen and switched to the other projector—and the whole three rows of naval dignitaries pressed hard back in their chairs for, really, the great ships seemed about to sail out into the theatre. It was colossal. They were like children at a party, and when my shot of Dove on the *Salem*, taken from the bows, came on, showing the whole great ship, shining and bristling with armaments, there was an audible sigh of admiration from everybody.

After that, normal thanks and praise were an anticlimax. The film and publicity section of the Admiralty were quite stunned. A week later I was summoned to Invergordon.

It was a grand day, cloudless and very hot. I let the stalker set the pace, and kept close on his heels all day. At intervals, we would stop and search the corries through the glass. Not a sign of a stag, but plenty of hinds.

"We're early yet. The boys will be all up in the hills, having a fine time. We'll be lucky if we see a stag this day."

So all the morning we raked the hills and the whole glen. At last we stopped by the burn at about two o'clock and had our lunch. The crystal water was leaping down, and I had a wash as well as a drink. It was a heavenly spot, and I cared nothing about stags. The stalker was a grand companion, interested in everything.

After lunch we climbed straight up the watershed. Halfway up he dropped like a hare, and so did I. There they were—a dozen young bachelors, about a mile up the corrie, having a fine time, grazing and gossiping. They hadn't seen us and we were downwind. It was a long, careful stalk up the stream, until we were looking through a tussock of grass within shot of them, about 150 yards. Then they all lay down, and we waited half an hour until the one we had picked stood up. I fired and missed. At once, they were all up and looking around. I fired and again missed. Away they went at a trot, over the burn and up the hill opposite. The stalker said nothing. We were a long way from home—perhaps twelve miles—and they had gone off in the right direction. After a pause to let them out of sight we followed leisurely, continually stopping to watch the distant, steadily moving brown figures. They kept on stopping and grazing, then one would throw up his head and off they would go again and disappear over the next ridge. We followed steadily over the very big country, always getting nearer home, as the stalker approvingly pointed out.

At last, about two miles away, they seemed to have stopped, so we stopped too and held them in the glass for half an hour. They still stopped, so we cast around to windward of them, taking the risk because it was the only side we could approach under cover. We got away with it. As we came sneaking down between huge boulders we saw they were still below us. We stalked the same stag to within 100 yards. He stood up suddenly, and I fired—and missed. He stared, then I fired again, and down he dropped with such suddenness that I stared up at the empty space where he had been.

"Quick! Up the hill after the others! You may still get another shot!" said the stalker, pounding down toward the fallen stag and pulling out his sheath knife. I raced up the hill, nearly bursting my lungs, but there was no more chance. They were gone like shooting stars. I returned, wheezing, to my stag. It was a splendid young animal, in perfect condition, with a good head. The bullet had gone through high on the shoulder. The stalker was complimentary—now.

"Ye hit him just right. The meat'll not be spoilt. Oh! He'll make grand eating."

He did.

We disemboweled him as neatly as a tiger, and dragged him by the horns and hoofs a mile down the hill to the track. It was hard work, and we were both done by the time we got there.

"Lucky ye missed him first time, up the ben,"* he grunted. "It would have taken us two hours to get him down here where the pony can get him."

He put his two fingers in his mouth and whistled, and a fat, old, white pony, pulling a sledge and driven by a shepherd, came bumping up the glen. We told the shepherd where the stag lay. He nodded, and we left them to bring it in.

We set out at a steady swing down the glen. But it was after eight, and dark, before we saw the lights of the castle. We had been out twelve hours, covered about twenty-five miles of the hill, and got our stag. We had a tale to tell.

The next day the unit arrived. The nearest hotel to the naval base at Invergordon was the Tain. I went over for a council of war. Pointed remarks were made by the camera crew about directors of films living in castles while their humble companions were lying three in a bed in a one-star hotel. I concluded that they had been spoiled in Malta and ignored them.

John Brabourne and I drove over to the naval base. On this trip our stand-in for the *Graf Spee* was HMS *Glasgow*. Captain Dawnay proved to be a charmer, and a great sportsman as well as a great handler of ships. He must have been a diplomat as well, for there were rumors that he was first in line for the captaincy of the royal yacht. We mapped out our program, which called for three days: two in brilliant sunshine and everybody in tropical uniforms, and one day overcast for the fueling sequence with the *Altmark*, supposedly somewhere off the main shipping lanes in the southern latitudes.

I wanted fog and rain and a complete contrast with the other scene, and everybody, of course, in blues not whites. This was the program that had

*Scottish word for "mountain peak."

worried the completion guarantee people, but we took it in our stride. My luck with weather is legendary, but there is no luck about it—not in the British Isles, anyway; you simply ignore weather forecasts and local prophets of the weather, and carry out the program as planned. You may have to wait a little, and of course you have to be there at sunrise until sunset, but the weather soon sees that the game is up, and rolls over with its paws in the air. Any determined British picnicker will tell you that there is no other way of dealing with the British weather. When the great novelist Rose Macaulay was commissioned to write a little book about the British character, her four opening words were: "Owing to the weather . . ." She knew . . . She knew where the British character begins and ends . . . with the weather.

Day 1: Gunnery with the fleet. It was a 5:00 A.M. call, and I nearly missed the boat. There was a group of gunnery officers waiting, and John Brabourne was in the middle of the road doing the Sister Anna act.* As we steamed out through the narrow entry to Cromartie Firth we passed between the Two Sutors. We opened up the village of Nigg and spotted Eric Linklater's house, standing on a mound surrounded by trees except on the seaward side. He had a splendid view, the dear chap, of the Moray Firth, but he must sometimes have got bored with so much saltwater. But what am I saying? Eric is an Orcadian, a man of Orkney, an islander, and a Norseman, and a writer of rare and rugged talent, besides being a member of the Savile Club.

"Whom are you waving to?" asked Dawnay, as I saluted Pitcalzean House.

"To the author of *Juan in America*," I answered. "Of *Poet's Pub*, and *Private Angelo*, and *Sealskin Trousers*, and—"

"Oh, Linklater. I had dinner with him last night. He's got a head like teak."

Tugs had gone ahead of us towing an enormous target on a raft, and we very soon opened fire. The whole of the Moray Firth had been cleared of fishing boats for the exercise. We heard for the first time the incredible sound of the projectiles winging away from the ship—"away, away, away"—until the sound vanished and great fountains of water sprung up, straddling the target ten miles away. Another salvo was on the way before we saw the

---

*Music hall ditty about the Salvation Army:

> Who will carry the banner?
> Sister Anna will carry the banner.
> But I carried it last week!
> You'll carry it this week.
> I can't! I'm in the family way.
> You're in everybody's way—clear out!

splashes of the first. Finally *Glasgow* closed all watertight doors and fired two broadsides, a stirring and terrible sight and sound. Chris and his camera crew, in an exposed position on deck, their ears stopped with cotton wool, their eyes protected with tinted spectacles, announced that they had got all they wanted and were coming down, thank you very much.

The next day was a repeat performance, with the camera crew on an escorting destroyer. We trans-shipped the gear at sea, the two ships steaming about seventy feet apart, the sea rushing between. Then they rigged a bos'n's chair and John Brabourne came across to the sound of cheers. The camera crew were delighted to be aboard. They had found that life on big ships was not their cup of tea at all. In a destroyer, dashing along at twenty knots, with a few inches of freeboard, her decks creaming, they felt at home.

The third day was the big day: the refueling of the battleship *Graf Spee* by the oiler *Altmark*, as witnessed by Captain Dove in Atlantic waters. In spite of my legendary luck, John Brabourne came to see me the night before.

"Shall I make the call two hours later, so that we can size up the weather?"

I was shaving.

"No, I don't think so. We need time to get everybody into German uniforms."

"In blues?"

"Yes, in blues."

John glanced at the setting sun.

"The glass is still very high. What about the weather?"

"What about it?"

He gave up, grinned, and went away. The change of weather came in the night. I got the weather I wanted: clouds, mist, a sullen sea, and everybody in blues or oilskins. The oiler came steaming up on our port quarter, up to our camera, and there was no doubt who she was or what she was, although her captain had ordered the name *Altmark* on her bow painted over; but the name *Altmark* was still visible through the second coating of paint—nice touch by the art director. She was a big, black, sinister ship, about eleven thousand tons, the Fleet oiler *Olna* when on her lawful occasions. It reminded me of the scene in *Mare Nostrum*, my very first film, when the German U-boat is refueled by Antonio Moreno's tartan,* a pretty ship like the one in which Edmond Dantes was captain in *The Count of Monte Cristo*.

The doubles for Captain Dove and the others looked good, and all our officer friends enjoyed themselves giving the Nazi salute and standing with very square German shoulders as the *Altmark* came alongside. Rockets boomed,

---

*A single-masted vessel with triangular sails extended by a long tapering yard, like the sails seen on feluccas in the Mediterranean.

ropes flew through the air; we did nineteen shots by teatime and we called it a day at 4:30 P.M. We had arranged to have half a day in hand, but we didn't need it.

The next day the unit returned to London. They were on standby for Portsmouth. John and Chris came to lunch at the castle. They had been living on short commons at the Tain Hotel, and there was roast venison for lunch. I never saw two men eat so much. They had helping after helping; I thought they would never stop eating. The family were returning to London over the weekend, minus Kevin. It was our first official separation. He was going as a boarder to the preparatory school for Gordonstoun.

In the dear, dead, hopeless and heedless 1920s, Kurt Hahn was the founder and headmaster of a boarding school on English public school principles at Salem, in southern Germany. All the best people's sons were sent as boarders to Salem, to take cold showers and early morning runs and cry their little eyes out. The star of the school and head boy, Philip Mountbatten, son of old Lord Louis Mountbatten, né Battenberg, was later on to serve in the Royal Navy under his illustrious father, and marry a queen.

When Hitler and his gang of warlords signaled to the world their intention of taking over Germany by, as a preliminary, burning the Reichstag, Kurt Hahn was permitted to move his school from Germany to Scotland, where he was offered a house and Highland estate as a refuge for his school. He had the right connections, funds were made available, the pupils flocked, or at any rate parents flocked to his banner.

Northeast Scotland is Macbeth country. "How far is't to Forres?" Answer: Just down the road from the school, and the grim Castle Cawdor ("All hail Macbeth, Thane of Cawdor!") guards the southern approaches. The Gordonstoun estate was between Lossiemouth and Nairn, and the northern border was the low, rocky shore of the Moray Firth. There were some two hundred pupils by the time that Kevin and I and Bill arrived in the Bentley to inspect a part of the Highlands that was unfamiliar to us, and put Kevin's name down with the acting headmaster, H. L. Brereton. At this time Kevin was about five, and Brereton looked rather startled that we should want to put his name down so many years before the required age of ten. But he admitted that they were looking for suitable houses for a preparatory school, and they had almost fixed on one on Speyside, at the village of Aberlour, which consisted of one high street pottering along on the banks of the Spey, which makes an erratic curve at this point. Here the village baker, Joseph Walker, no less, was setting up his ovens and his family, and preparing to conquer the world with his full-butter shortbread and other delicacies.

Gordonstoun is 650 miles from London, traveling by Edinburgh and Perth. The nearest city is Aberdeen, whose granite terraces face the North Sea, while

Inverness, the capital of the northern Highlands, stands at the head of the Great Glen about forty miles to the westward, and the rugged Cairngorms have to be crossed, or circumvented, if you are for London. Inverness is a bonny town, and the terminus of the sleeping cars from London, so that you doze off while rumbling over the Home Counties and wake up in the middle of the mountains of Scotland. But it's a big trip to plan and carry out just for the sake of an interview with a schoolmaster, and Kevin took enthusiastically to my plan of going on to Scrabster, parking the car, taking the steamer to the Orkney Islands, and then a motor launch to the northernmost island in the group, in order to see the sun come down on June 20, touch the horizon and then mount up again, by this means proving something about the summer solstice that I, as a fellow of the Royal Geographical Society, should have been able to explain to my son, who explained it to me instead.

So now, four years later, the die was cast and Kevin was going not to the prep school of Aberlour, where Columba a few years later was to make his mark as a draftsman and a storyteller, but to another preparatory school, Wester Elchies. As usual, Kevin had got it all worked out: "Daddy, you are to take me with you in the morning, and leave me before lunch. You are not to stay or hang about. I want to have lunch there, and get used to it, and settle down."

I agreed humbly. Columba had a *crise* in the afternoon and wouldn't go to bed after a terrible career of crime. When he started to defy me from under the tea table, at about 7:00, I hauled him out by the scruff of his neck and carried him like a biting, scratching kitten up two flights of stairs and into the bathroom. By this time he was hanging on to my knees and roaring, "Sorry! Daddy! Sorry! Daddy!" through his tears.

I bathed him and put him to bed with a caution, and a story, of course. He was partly upset by Kevin, and partly by his ear, which had an infection which he had never got over since the day Kevin tried to clean it with a matchstick.

The drive to Wester Elchies took a long while: it was eighty miles, and then difficult to find. It was a lovely, old, hideous, but comfortable house in a fine position about five hundred feet above the Spey. The master, Pares, was a dark, intelligent, wiry man, who was one of the original masters from Salem in Germany and who followed Kurt Hahn to Scotland when he was expelled by the Nazis. I liked him.

Obedient to Kevin's obvious fretting, we soon fled. He was so brave. He stood on the running-board with tears in his eyes, then dropped off at the gate. He kissed Bumba, who said absolutely nothing and refused to kiss him back. Then Kevin said, "Goodbye, Mummy! Goodbye, Daddy! Goodbye, Bentley! Please go!"

We went, and saw him waving, until the road turned and he was hidden. It made us very solemn. But not Bumba. He showed no sorrow at all. I am sure that that Napoleonic mind was already working out what to do with all the books and all the toys when he got back home.

When did Columba officially become Bumba to his intimates? It was at Milnton, my mother's house in the Lowlands of Scotland. It was the day that Kevin made a spirited attempt to cut his own thumb off while playing with a knife. Previous to that the boys had been working under the direction of Dougan, who came over laughing to me and said, "You know what Columba calls himself, now? . . . Bumba!"

And Bumba it has been, ever since, to his intimates and to himself. It is credibly reported in the Book of Bumba that he announced when he was a teenager: "I am not a boy, I am not a girl . . . I am a Bumba," which statement was reported by his mother to one of his numerous girl cousins, who promptly fell in love with him.

While I was enjoying myself by sea and by land, commanding great ships and shooting red deer, Emeric was being given a bumpy ride by John Davis. The first obstacle was, of course, the budget. When Spyros Skouras let us down and Emeric had to go willy-nilly hat in hand to see John Davis, our stalwart George Busby and Syd Streeter had been wrestling with figures, while Emeric and I had been tangling with words. These figures changed daily, around a notional figure of £275,000 all in. The figure on that fateful day in John Davis's office happened to be £280,000. This had been accepted by John, but by the time I came back from Scotland the total cost had risen to £290,000 all in. This gave John something to play with, and he absolutely refused to accept the revised figure. He handled it very cleverly: he just said the sum of £280,000 had been named by Emeric, and accepted by him, and it was up to The Archers, and to Pinewood Studios, to bring the picture in at that figure, and Earl St. John growled his agreement from the steps of the throne.

Meanwhile, I was bagging sequence after sequence, drawing thousands of feet of film on credit, never knowing whether my call would be canceled or not. We gave George and Syd carte blanche in dealing with the Pinewood machine, and with a whoop of joy they threw their hats into the ring. The Pinewood accounts department, of course, didn't have access to all our information and changes of policy, and they also, naturally, kept adding 10 percent on—"just to make sure"—but in about ten days, Syd and George cut them down to size and were back to the new figure of about £290,000.

In the meantime I was still shooting, using our partnership with the Admiralty to obtain lights, cameras, film stock, transport, and general expenses, and turning up each time with huge, spectacular shots of ships, which were already the talk of Pinewood and the envy of other producers. Nobody dared stop us, and finally Earl St. John brought John Davis in again, but this time with a more conciliatory suggestion: that he would agree to the new figure of £290,000 if we, on our side, would agree to leave in a sum of money that was due to us on the foreign sales of *The Red Shoes;* an ironical touch, but we agreed. We were in pretty deep ourselves, but we knew we had a good picture in the making, and perhaps a very good one. It was a most unorthodox beginning to a highly professional job—but that's picture making.

So the fabulous Archers rode again at Pinewood, shooting down the chair polishers with their arrows, while their fellow filmmakers raised their heads and remembered that making films is not only a great adventure but can be the most enormous fun. Unfortunately, in a battle there must be casualties, and as I have indicated, in this case it had been my best friend, Hein Heckroth.

Eight years earlier, in 1947, the best film designer who had ever lived had said to me, "Micky, you want to go too far," when we were discussing the designs for the Ballet of the Red Shoes. I at once set about looking for a new designer who would tell me I didn't want to go far enough, and found him in Hein Heckroth. He took over the art direction of our most ambitious project up to that date, and made it his own. He was not an architect but a painter, a man of the theatre. Egged on by me he designed the costumes, the setting, even the makeup. The Red Shoes Ballet alone involved some six to seven hundred sketches. He surrounded himself with painters, modelers, property makers, sculptors, costume designers—men and women who understood how big the big screen is. Hein understood at once when I announced that there would be no shots of audiences arriving, leaving, gaping, applauding. We were the audience, I said: we were the audience, we who made the film. It was up to our artists to deliver to us. They wouldn't have a tougher audience than that.

Hein and Arthur agreed. The result, the Red Shoes Ballet, was something new that remains unchallenged to this day, and I am writing this in New York, in an apartment on Fifty-second Street and Eighth Avenue, and the date is May 2, 1988. We made *The Red Shoes* in the summer of 1947, forty-one years ago, and as I write (and I am dictating onto tape) every video store in Manhattan has *The Red Shoes* on video. You can see it on film, you can get it on tape, and every week there is an inquiry from some Broadway showman about the legitimate stage rights of our film.* It is no longer a film, it is a legend. And there are millions of fifty-year-old frustrated ballerinas willing to stand in line around the block to see the latest legitimate version of their favorite fairy tale.

Here's to you, Hans Christian Andersen! And perhaps they will find a

*A musical version of *The Red Shoes* did open on Broadway in the fall of 1993, with a score by Jule Styne. Sadly, it closed in a week.

grandmother's part for Moira on Broadway . . . Perhaps they will make a show that will run for years and years, and then, before the turn of the century, it will turn itself into a new film . . . for *The Red Shoes* are immortal. Listen to the tale of those flying feet: Emeric Pressburger and Keith Winter wrote the first script, Emeric Pressburger and Michael Powell wrote the second script, Brian Easdale the score, Sir Thomas Beecham conducted the ballet, Moira Shearer put on the Red Shoes and danced the hearts of the world away, and Hein Heckroth and his team, Jack Cardiff and his crew of Technicolor technicians, were told by us: "The war's over, boys—shoot the works."

It was the word they had been waiting for. From the first shot of the candle flame guttering in the wind to the final shots of Massine's great eyes offering the Red Shoes to all the women in the world, it was magic . . . magic! . . . and Hein Heckroth was the magician who inspired it all. His moment had come, just as it had come to Emeric and me in Korda's office ten years before. Nothing had been impossible for us then, and nothing seemed impossible for us, and for Hein, now. He and I were like brothers; brothers and craftsmen in this renaissance of the art of the movies. Three years later, in 1950, we tackled an opera film, *The Tales of Hoffmann,* the perfect composed film, the film I had always dreamed about. It was the perfect combination of music, dance, song, acting, design, and beautiful women. As Cecil B. DeMille had said, you *can* have everything. The second act of our production is as beautiful as the Venetian lagoon at night, as light as the touch of a moth's wing as it brushes your face on a warm summer evening.

And now all this was coming to an end. Fantasy had fled and the kitchen sink stood squarely in the middle of the academy frame, and The Archers were making a war picture, believe it or not, a naval epic, co-starring the *Graf Spee* and Peter Finch. What was Hein doing *dans cette galère?* He must have asked that question himself. But there was nothing that The Archers could do to rescue Hein—nothing that Hein could do on a British naval epic—to be followed by cops and robbers in Crete, for it was plain that Emeric had already unloaded *Ill Met by Moonlight* on John Davis and Earl St. John, judging by the catlike purrings from that quarter. The more I thought about it, the less I liked it. It was dangerous to make a picture with John Davis and Arthur Rank. But so long as it was one picture only, we were the bosses; they paid the piper and we called the tune.

But even The Archers couldn't find a place for Hein Heckroth on *The Battle of the River Plate,* or in the Cretan mountains. Even Hein admitted this, and I had to agree, though I hankered after my lovely Cretans. I was having a whale of a time as a brassbound admiral in my naval picture, but I could feel the prison irons were beginning to close upon the growing boy.

Emeric (soliloquy): "Michael is himself again. He is happy . . . happy as he was on *49th Parallel* fifteen years ago. We were our own masters then, and we are our own masters now. But not for long, I think. John Davis is not a friend, but he is not an enemy either. He needs us and we need him. He has the money and the studios, the distribution organization and the theatres, and the power that goes with all those things. We have only the power to say no. But John Davis is not a man you can say no to. You say, 'I'll see what Michael says,' or 'I'll talk it over with Emeric.' Michael is not good at this. He is inclined to . . . what was it that George Busby said the other day? 'He flies off the handle.' Yes, that was it, he flies off the handle too easily.

"Of course, he and John Davis hate each other, because John persuaded Arthur to put *The Red Shoes* on the shelf. 'It's an art film,' he said, 'and we are just going to the public for money. You can't go to the public with an art film when we are trying to force the Americans to open their markets to us.' I can understand this, but Michael can't. He looks upon films as a religion and expects everyone else to think so too. We should have stayed with Arthur Rank in 1948. We should have rallied the other Independent Producers. They looked to us for leadership, and when we left Rank and went back to Alex the rest of the film industry fell apart. John and Arthur thought that if the Americans wouldn't let Rank's films into American theatres, they could fight them and keep them out of the English market. But no one can win against the Americans. A good thing, too."

"But the future of The Archers is not in America, it is in England, that is if what Joe Mankiewicz was telling us the other day is right: 'Go for quality, Michael and Emeric. It's the only thing that can compete with television. Go for art. You can't compete with America. They'll murder you. John thinks because the Rank Organisation have all the money and theatres in the U.K. that he can keep the American films out of England, off the British screen. He's nuts. With the whole film business reeling from CinemaScope, VistaVision, and television, he wants to make poverty-row pictures after you fellows, you independent producers, have made *Oliver Twist, The Third Man, Black Narcissus, Brief Encounter, Great Expectations, Henry V, Hamlet, Stairway to Heaven*— that was a beauty, that one, that was art from start to finish . . .'

"Of course, Joe Mankiewicz was right, but he doesn't have to work for John Davis and we do. At present we are on a good course—the course of the pocket battleship *Graf Spee*. Stapi was right when he suggested it. Michael is going to make a very good picture, and it will be followed by *Ill Met by Moonlight*. We have only to wait and let them come to us. Meanwhile, I have Stapi as a backstop, and there is always *Cassia* . . ."

Hein was the odd man out. It was incredible. It was brutal. It was ridiculous. Listen: He had designed and executed the costumes for *A Matter of Life and Death;* he had designed and executed the costumes and props for *Black Narcissus;* together with Arthur Lawson, he had designed and executed the sketches, the sets, the costumes, and the Ballet of the Red Shoes; he had broken his heart over *The Elusive Pimpernel;* he had created grand opera on the screen with *The Tales of Hoffmann;* he did his best to bring operetta to the screen when we made *Die Fledermaus,* and when we failed it was my fault, not his. Like some great spider, he spun a web out of that head like a Roman emperor's, a glittering web of costumes, sets, and properties, and never repeated himself. He saw life and art as a hill that had to be climbed, a wall that had to be crossed, again and again. I call him a magician, but he was more than a magician. He was a man, a child, an artist, a husband, a father, an inspiration, and a friend to all of us, but most of all to me—Judas. I loved him, and I failed him. He was not happy working with someone else, after all we had done together. Korda was a showman, a great impresario, a patron, a prince, but he knew nothing of the way an artist feels and works. When Hein's contract was taken over by London Films, Alex was quite surprised to learn that Hein had turned down an offer from Hollywood to remake the ballet *Le Tricorne.*

"You . . . Heckroth . . . you turned down an offer from United Artists? Why?"

"Because a better artist than I has already designed the ballet."

"And who is this genius?"

"Picasso."

"Hmmm . . . Do you know the *Salome* of Richard Strauss?"

"Yes."

"Would you like to design it for me?"

"Very much. I have often thought of this piece. Do you think, Sir Alex, that Salome should be very young, a young girl—twelve years old, perhaps?"

"What I think, or don't think, is my business, Heckroth. In my company, the designer does not make suggestions to the director until he's asked to do so. Go and see my brother. He is a painter, and mad, like you. He will give you a contract."

Vincent, of course, was a painter, a real painter, a good painter, who knew another good painter when he saw one. He was only too glad to hand over *Gilbert and Sullivan* to Hein. To make a film about the witty poet and librettist W. S. Gilbert and his composer-collaborator Sir Arthur Sullivan was not one of Alex's brightest ideas.

"But the Gilbert and Sullivan operas have their following to this day," you say. "They are full of wit and melody, of big laughs, and even pratfalls."

True.

"And everyone knows some of their famous lyrics. The D'Oyly Carte Opera

Company has toured the world. The lyrics are as well known in New York as in London. Why shouldn't the lives of these creators, and excerpts from their popular works, be a huge popular success?"

No reason why they shouldn't, but they weren't. They belonged where they belonged, and that was not in a London Films presentation, any more than making a film of the original *Beggar's Opera,* with Laurence Olivier not only acting but singing the part of the dashing Captain Mackie, was. I'm sure that Larry would have liked to forget this. None of us who saw it can forget it.

After a production meeting that went on for two days and a night Hein went home and went to bed and refused to answer the telephone. It was then that Korda appeared at Hein's bedside to threaten him.

For the first time, Hein considered returning to Germany. The Frankfurt Opera had been paging him for months, with a contract to design four productions a year, plus teaching at the arts center, plus a free apartment. But neither Hein nor Ada wanted to return to Germany. They were devoted to their Nandi, and she had married Jonathan Routh and had two sons. She was working as a costume designer in television, and this would mean the family splitting up. Hein went to see Emeric, who gave him small comfort. He had enough trouble himself, as we know.

Hein's reputation as a film designer had been growing, and he now had several interesting commissions coming from France and Germany, where they needed his experience in color design. He worked on *Le Rouge et le Noir,* directed by Claude Autant-Lara in Paris. He designed a new *Threepenny Opera,* with Curt Jurgens as Mack the Knife. He did yet another film about the mad King Ludwig, and always he returned to England, hoping against hope that the tide would turn. But fantasy was dead, The Archers were parting company, and he signed a three-year contract with Frankfurt. Later he went to Hollywood to do a film with Alfred Hitchcock, *Torn Curtain,* but he never went back to England, to the country that he now regarded as his home but which had no more use for him. He had been with The Archers for ten years, and in the ensuing years we tried to work together several times. We succeeded at last, with *Bluebeard's Castle,* a one-hour piece by Bartók, a jewel of a piece, but our plans were thwarted, our paths led different ways . . . What else could I have done?

═

Emeric says that there is always a right way and a wrong way to start a story. To quote Wendy Hiller in *I Know Where I'm Going!,* I only know the wrong way. Emeric was tolerant about it: "No, Michael, you see people don't always know what they want, especially female people."

"When you told me the story about the girl and the island, you said that she did know what she wanted."

"She did, but she was mistaken. That is what the story is all about."

"You really want to start the film with a little girl, who can hardly walk, in a comfortable, middle-class nursery, crawling across the floor in a straight line?"

"Yes, Michael."

"Are you sure it won't empty the cinema?"

"Yes, Michael. We will mix shots of the baby and the little girl with the credit titles of the film. *I Know Where I'm Going!* is a good title. The audience will get the idea."

"Okay . . . You know best."

"Yes, Michael, I do. Now, may I ask you a question?"

"Go ahead."

"George Busby tells me that you want to get the film rights of the little song 'I Know Where I'm Going' and have the Glasgow Orpheus Choir, whom you used in *The Edge of the World*, to sing the song. Are we going to have people singing on the screen, in my story?"

"No. I just want to use the soundtrack to create a bit of fantasy around the heroine, on her first trip to Scotland. I remember how excited I was on my first trip to Scotland."

"Very well, you know best."

"Yes, I do."

"But, remember, this is not a musical. It is a love story."

"I agree—a love story to words and music."

The opening shots in any production of The Archers are famous in film lore, and are quoted by every film buff: the majestic mountains and rich prairies of Canada suddenly threatened by a monster from the deep, a German U-boat, bursting out of the depths of the North Atlantic; the terse title "Kiel, 1917" superimposed against a background of rain and mist, startling British audiences in 1939 when we were at war with Germany; the empty Wellington bomber, like a ghostly airborne *Marie Celeste*, flying unmanned back to her base; the military dispatch riders whose thundering machines are carrying the message from Colonel Blimp—"War starts at midnight"; the bells of Canterbury Cathedral, ringing in the pilgrims in *A Canterbury Tale*; David Niven in the doomed aircraft, speaking words of love to a girl that he's never seen; the student riots, led by Marius Goring, at the beginning of *The Red Shoes*, which lead him to a seat in the gods of Covent Garden. These were carefully baited hooks, and *The Battle of the River Plate* was to prove no exception.

It was Admiral Parry who had placed in Emeric's hands the little book by

Captain Dove. The book had produced the man, and now Bernard Lee was playing Captain Dove and Peter Finch was playing Captain Langsdorff, and the strange friendship between the two seamen, which on Captain Dove's part amounted to hero worship, had been developed by Emeric into a saga of two men, linking the thundering broadsides of great ships at sea with the whispers of secret diplomacy on land. Without this imaginative development of the story line by Emeric, the film would have just been a superdocumentary instead of a saga.

We started shooting at Pinewood Studios on October 17, 1955. I decided to kick off with the scenes in the prison ship, and I had been casting for it for a month and rehearsing on the set for three days with the camera crew and full unit, but without shooting a thing. Earl St. John was visibly coming out in pimples but I knew what I was doing, and by Friday morning of the first week we were up to schedule.

The prisoners of the *Graf Spee* were a very select company. They were chosen from films I had made, and plays I had seen, over the last twenty years, and had all worked with me before. They were an extrovert bunch. Here they are: John Schlesinger; Bernard Lee; Nigel Stock from the play *My Three Angels;* Andrew Cruickshank from the play of *Dial M for Murder;* Peter Dyneley from Bobby Helpmann's *The Millionairess;* Gron Davies, an enormous Welshman; Dick George, who played the submarine commander in *49th Parallel;* Jack Faint, a burly, dark man, good type; Alan Beale, from Canonbury Tower Theatre; Eynon Evans, who was actually not an actor but a writer; Brian Worth, the handsome, sulky boy who played the fighter pilot in my flying sequences in *The Lion Has Wings* in 1939; Tony Newley, the Artful Dodger in David Lean's *Oliver Twist* and later the star of *Stop the World—I Want to Get Off;* Edward Powell, a long-nosed, fair-headed Welshman; George Murcell, a pugnacious, bearded character; and Joseph O'Connor, a Dubliner, who brought his guitar. There were a couple of dozen more, but these were the leaders of the pack. Dick George brought a mongoose that bit everybody, including Dick George. It was a good idea to have an animal pet in the film, and the next day Dick turned up with a marmoset, which entailed me in some reshooting, but was worth it.

By now, the scenes in the German prison ship were uproarious. Julian Somers, who had been in my production of *The Hanging Judge,* turned up as the quartermaster of the *Graf Spee.* The big set tilted to order, like the passenger ship I had on *The Spy in Black,* and I had breakaway panels and sliding furniture, and a great time was had by all. We were all thrilled, ahead of schedule, and I put out a rush call to shake everybody up, for the captain's cabin on the *Graf Spee,* and Peter Finch. He arrived in a hurry, just in time for tea. He had grown a little beard, and it suited him. We roughed out the scenes between Captain Langsdorff and Captain Dove. Almost at once, the scenes took off. Peter confided to me a week or two later that it was one of those parts that really send you, as an actor. He felt that he knew more about the way that this man felt than Langsdorff himself. This was a real gift of the gods, for Peter had that magical thing, star quality. The scenes between the two captains are not just good theatre, they probe deeply into what makes a man love and respect another man. I went home on Friday night happy.

Emeric said to me, "What business have you to direct musicals, when you can direct men like this?"

I answered him by quoting Boswell's retort to Johnson: "But what men!"

I had cast John Gregson as Captain Hooky Bell, of the *Exeter*, some weeks before. He was under contract to Rank, and Earl St. John begged me to "use him," as he put it. I repeated to him, "I don't use actors, and they don't use me."

A week or two later, John Gregson came to see me. I was pleasantly surprised. So was the real Hooky Bell, who sat beside me. John was from Liverpool, a blunt, battered young man with charm and a sense of humor.

"He'll do," said Hooky Bell, "if he'll only stand up straight, and forget about that cowboy slouch of his."

John had been giving us his imitation of a naval officer ready for anything.

"What about his nose?" I asked the real Hooky. John was looking in awe at Hooky Bell's commanding beak.

"We'll have to build up your nose. Do you agree?"

John hesitated. "Well . . ."

"You're no John Barrymore," I said cheerfully. "It's either that, or somebody else gets the part."

He groaned. "Okay, it's a deal."

"Okay," I said. "Take John to the makeup department, and get to work."

Tony Quayle was playing Commodore Harwood, flying his flag in *Ajax*, so there were two more captains of ships to be cast. I appointed Ian Hunter to *Ajax*. Tall, lazy, and overweight, he had a lovely light touch for comedy. We were old friends from the quota-quickie days. Occasionally he would catch my eye and wink at me. During the whole sequence on the bridge we hardly exchanged a word. The last of the three captains to be appointed was Captain Parry. He was the only real naval officer in the squadron—Jack Gwillim, six foot two, taciturn, polite, and every inch of him Royal Navy. He could handle blank verse, too, and joined us on the recommendation of Tony Quayle. When he was on deck, the other actors had to mind their p's and q's. A glance from those gray eyes stiffened their backbones.

There were almost two hundred speaking parts in the film of *The Battle of the River Plate*, and many of them were one-liners. Everyone was personally selected by me, and instructed in his duties by Captain Hooky Bell, RN. We were intercutting between the bridges of all three cruisers, and it usually took a whole morning of rehearsal for the different sets of actors to know their duties and their places during the battle.

Today, Saturday, October 8, 1988, Thelma and I were invited to dinner by Antonio, hairdresser to the New York theatre world. There were two other guests: tall, handsome people with an air of suppressed excitement about them. The man burst out, "You gave me my first part in *The Battle of the River Plate* . . . my first part, my first real part! I played the lookout. I spotted for *Graf Spee*."

I stared at him, embarrassed. It could only be Donald Moffat, whose name and features I had carried with me for thirty-three years, for what face could be more important and more memorable than the lookout of the *Ajax*. He was, and yet he wasn't, the Donald Moffat that I remembered. He was now a famous actor, with a name I had often read in notices. I had thought, frequently, can this be my Donald Moffat? When we got home, I went to my diaries, took out 1955, turned to October, and read: "Donald Moffat, one of my intuitive pieces of casting for the lookout Swanston. He was excellent. A lovely, long, Scottish face, and a fine actor. He pronounced his line, 'It was a pocket battleship,' in a voice of doom."

As I closed the diary, thinking of the handsome couple we had just dined with, I thought to myself, well, I sure do know how to pick 'em.

Syd Streeter, that one-man Swiss Family Robinson, and Arthur Lawson, construction genius and architect extraordinary, had built the ships' bridges, after many discussions, to suit all my own requirements, which were to fight the battle as realistically as possible without actually killing anybody. Charles Orme from the production office had been working for weeks on an elaborate cue board, which was to be used to signal gun flashes, water splashes, drifting smoke, loud explosions, turning control towers, and rocking bridges, as well as big bangs and flashes between the cameras and the actors. All this had to be controlled with the electrical panel behind, and above, the camera. I now broke it to him that he would have to work his panel himself because I was sending Syd to Montevideo, to mobilize the government, the police, the army, and ten thousand civilians to come down to the docks on a specified Saturday and Sunday. Charles had led a rather sheltered life up until then, but he rose to the occasion all right. Archers do, and after all he was Emeric's brother-in-law . . . or had been.

Tony Quayle was still shuttling to and fro between Stratford-upon-Avon and Iver, Bucks. He confided to me, "This filming is great."

I grunted. "Yes, that's all very well, when you have the background and experience and discipline that you have. Then, film acting, the instant reaction to emotion, the instant creation of reaction, is exhilarating, like a bout with a master swordsman after you have learned how to handle the foils. We are up to schedule, but I find Pinewood, these days, a bit sticky. Already there is a civil service atmosphere about the studio, and very soon, if we don't laugh them out of it, they will be class-conscious, the permanent staff looking down on intruders as interlopers, treating the creative talent as a nuisance that has to be put up with. After that, there is only one more step to them thinking that they know best, and saying so; and what they know best is the same mixture as before."

Denham was never like that. Denham was never cozy. Those great concrete walls had something piratical about them; those white towers advertised to the world, as it scuttled by in its little automobiles: "Here be dragons." The Archers made several mistakes in their brilliant career, and leaving Denham Studios was one of them. I felt our guilt every time I passed Jack Oakie's great white walls. I remembered *Goodbye, Mr. Chips; South Riding; Knight Without Armour; The Ghost Goes West; The Spy in Black; Colonel Blimp; A Matter of Life and Death;* and bowed my head in shame.

The other day, and I am talking now of 1988, I was around the town and studios of Elstree, with David Puttnam. He confided in me: "Studios don't send me. I prefer to make films on location. On location, it is up to you to create the right kind of atmosphere, and you get everybody working as one. You don't get that when you're making a film from nine to five; you don't get the excitement and loyalty of a film unit on location."

I said: "Yes, that's all very well, but your great cameramen, your wonderful art directors, your marvelous electricians—where have they learned their job? Where is their home base? In the studio. How would you ever have front projection, and back projection, and trick shots, and wonderful model shots, like we had on *Black Narcissus,* without a great studio with a great tradition behind it?"

I thought of Denham, which had become a storehouse, then the home of Xerox, and finally just something to be knocked down by a wrecking crew. Denham—its creation and its destruction—is symbolic of the film business. Oh, ye of little faith!

I had to shoot around Tony quite a bit. He was playing the Moor in Larry Olivier's *Titus Andronicus* with Vivien Leigh, a piece of Grand Guignol and doubtful Shakespeare. Tony's tenderness, as he cradled his little black baby, was the best thing in it, except for Larry's witty idea of casting his wife as the mutilated victim, who has her tongue torn out and is consequently speechless.

On Friday Frankie came home from Paris, bringing Columba and a new Tin Tin book, *The Cigars of Pharaoh.* By breakfast time on Saturday we had been through it three times. It was all about international dope smugglers. After breakfast I wanted Columba to go with me to try on his new saffron kilt. I baited the trap by promising to take him to see the Royal Automobile Club swimming pool, plus a second visit to the late George VI's statue, but when we got to Scott Adie he refused to try the kilt on. The old cutter, who had taken a lot of trouble over it, was mortified. It was a beautiful little job, with buckles and pleats—just like Daddy's. Columba admired it as a piece of art, but would have none of it as a piece of clothing.

Then I wanted him to lunch with us at the Étoile, where Frankie and Rupert Revelstoke joined us. He was outraged. There he was in a silly restaurant, when he could be at home with his new book! Even Nino couldn't make him eat. So back we all trailed to Melbury Road. Bumba dived into his new book and spoke to nobody. Finally I went to bed with two aspirins and hot milk. Frankie joined me.

The next day was Sunday and Emeric telephoned me.

"Michael, can we talk?"

"Where?"

"Here."

I got into the Bentley and drove over to Eaton Square. The plane trees were dropping the rest of their leaves. Very soon they would be bare and beautiful. Emeric poured me out a generous *barackpálinka*. He was quite excited.

"Michael, I have found our commentator for the second half of the film."

"Are you sure we'll need one?"

"Yes, Michael. So long as the story takes place at sea, we are all right. It is a chase story—cops and robbers. But once the battle is over, we go ashore to Montevideo and the secret battle of diplomacy begins, and the only way to keep the audience interested is by narration."

I was horrified. "You don't mean narration!"

"No, Michael. I do not mean voice-over. I mean by commentary—by American commentary. I have discovered from the files of *The Washington Post* that there was an American radio commentator in Montevideo at the time of the battle."

"No!"

"Yes, Michael."

"NBC or CBS?"

"Neither, Michael. He was on his own. He was a freelance journalist, picking up stories. Of course, his equipment wasn't strong enough to broadcast the story of the battle directly to New York, but somehow he managed to relay it back to America, and he will be our commentator for the film."

"Emeric, you're a genius!"

Emeric waved his hand and poured some more *barackpálinka.*

"I was not happy with the second half of the picture. Here are some speeches. Will you work on them?"

"You bet I will. I'll start looking for the Yank tomorrow. Do you think Sinatra would do it?" We now had that very necessary thing for an epic: a commentator, or a chorus.

The next day was Monday. I rang Emeric early.

"He sets up his mike and radio equipment in a café on the waterfront of Montevideo, okay?"

"Okay."

"He just goes blasting on while life goes on around him. I call it Manolo's Bar. I've put a call out for Spanish speakers."

The next day Syd brought a very striking-looking actor onto the set to meet me, for Manolo. He was very tall, and had a remarkably large and long skull. His eyes were beautiful, large and expressive. He vibrated with energy.

"Do you speak Spanish?"

"Sí, señor." He burst into a whole speech in Spanish. "But, I also speak French." He shifted the clutch again. "And German."

He quoted a piece of Heine. The man had the most powerful voice and presence, and all this energy. The way he gave the whole of his attention to me was quite disturbing.

"Do you want me to read the part, Mr. Powell?"

"The part isn't written yet. The scene is a waterfront café in Montevideo. We'll ad-lib most of it."

"Good."

His assurance was impressive.

"Okay, Mr. . . ."

"Lee, Christopher Lee."

We put out a general call for Spanish-speaking girls who could sing or dance or do acrobatics, or something, in the café. My phone rang at home. It was April Olrich, whom I'd last seen dancing Red Riding Hood for the Royal Ballet, Covent Garden.

"How'd you get my number?"

"Bobby Helpmann gave it to me. He said you wouldn't mind."

"Come to Pinewood tomorrow."

"Do I get a car?"

"You do."

Next morning she came to Pinewood, selected a dress from the wardrobe, wriggled into it, and came on the set, accompanied by wolf whistles from the whole company. I said, "I didn't know you could talk Spanish."

"It's not the only thing you don't know about me."

She launched into a torrent of Spanish, coming very close to me, gazing earnestly into my blue eyes. Everyone was enjoying the fun.

"Okay, okay, you're hired."

All we needed now was a Yank to play the reporter. We found him in an American theatre company that was performing *The Teahouse of the August Moon* at Her Majesty's Theatre. Lionel Murton was playing one of the leading parts. He was a Canadian: so what? He came to see me on the set.

"Where's the script?"

"It's not written yet."

"British picture, eh? I want my fee in advance."

We hired him. The three of them, Lionel, April, and Christopher, were given a dressing room, a secretary, and a Spanish-speaking coach, and endless cups of tea. Brian Easdale was asked to compose a couple of Spanish numbers, and we brought in Muriel Smith to record them.

Arthur Lawson came to see me on the set. We were on the bridge of the *Exeter*.

"Here are the set designs for Manolo's Bar, Michael."

"Looks good. How many people?"

"Three hundred."

"Including waiters and barmen?"

"No, Michael."

"Cut it down to two hundred, and include waiters and barmen."

He made a note and went away. I yelled, "Charles—start the effects! Ready everyone, this is the big bang. Action!" Arthur's dignified walk changed to a run. I pressed the button.

Since 1952 I had been keeping a diary, one of those large Dataday diaries, foolscap size. Sometimes I had nothing to say, but on other occasions I had a good deal, and I thought one day they might be useful. But diaries are tricky things, and after twenty years or so I gave it up. I never hid the diaries or kept them under lock or key, and I got rather tired of Frankie tearing out whole sheets of narrative that were too personal to be read by my sons or grandsons. (Incidentally, where are my grandsons, Kevin and Columba?)

From now on, I was too hard-pressed to keep a diary. It lies before me now, page after page, blank. Occasionally there is a scribbled note. It wasn't until December 6 that the diary was resumed: "Airborne to Montevideo."

It had been a hectic five weeks, making this enormous, complicated, technical subject in the studio. I did it, but there was no time for talking about it. From the first week in November the tempo was set. The night gang worked all night erecting our sets, which melted away next day before our onrush. It became clear to all the chair polishers that we were going to do what we said we were going to do.

You must imagine the next few weeks whizzing by, activated by the spirits of challenge, triumph, and esprit de corps. Even our own unit was transformed into a powerhouse, with me as the humming dynamo in the center, coaxing, shouting, suggesting, applauding: audience and dictator in one. And still we were up to schedule on a five-day week, nine-hour working day. We were on a winner, and we knew it. Even a visit to the set by Lady Harwood to see Tony Quayle playing her late husband couldn't shake Tony's confidence and authority. As for Lady H, she was delighted with Tony, and she herself was a delightful, charming, intelligent woman. She said she'd come again. It was quite a little romance. It was not at all like seeing a ghost.

Early in November Emeric came to see me on the set. There was the usual hurly-burly. He looked like a lion tamer entering a cage full of lions at dinnertime.

Chris Challis yelled, "Don't shoot, boys! It's an Archer!"

Charles Orme said, "Would you mind moving, Emeric? You're standing on one of the waterspouts."

Syd said, "Have you seen the rushes, Emeric?"

Emeric signaled that he had, by solemnly turning his thumb upward.

"Michael, can I have a word with you?"

"No."

"How about lunchtime?"

"We're rehearsing Manolo's Bar at lunchtime."

"How about tonight?"

"What day of the week is it?"

"Friday."

"Okay. Where?"

I was already far away. Emeric inflated his lungs and shouted, "At my flat!"

I waved acceptance, and went back on the bridge of the *Achilles*. She was the Australian vessel. Constant readers will remember that she was now in the Indian navy, and had escorted us up the coast of Turkey in July.

There was a third party at the dinner—James Archibald, the personal production assistant of John Davis. He was bright, very bright, and it was a relief to have someone like him in such a key position. I had impressed upon Emeric the importance of letting John Davis come to us, not the other way around, and although I was half-asleep and drank too much, it seemed that this strategy was going to pay off. Archibald and I left together. It was a foggy night. As I stepped over the low door of the Bentley and dropped into the driver's seat, I glanced up and could see that Emeric was still burning the midnight oil.

Emeric (soliloquy): "Michael is impossible. He hates John Davis, and doesn't care who knows it. He cannot forgive John for not being an artist. Think how much worse it would be if he were! As for John, he is not a fool. He understands that he and Michael are like cat and dog, like fire and water, so

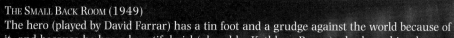

THE SMALL BACK ROOM (1949)
The hero (played by David Farrar) has a tin foot and a grudge against the world because of it, and because he has a beautiful girl (played by Kathleen Byron) who loves him, he suspects, only out of pity. Powell had a special respect for Byron from the time she pulled a gun on him. "A naked woman and a loaded gun are persuasive objects," he said.

THE SMALL BACK ROOM
It's wartime London. Sammy Rice (David Farrar) has a drinking problem, and he keeps a full bottle of scotch around to remind himself that he can't be left alone with it. One night Sue (Kathleen Byron) is late . . . . In a surreal fantasy scene (inset), Sammy fights off a fifteen-foot whiskey bottle.

THE TALES OF HOFFMANN (1951)
Suggested by the conductor Sir Thomas Beecham, it had marvelous parts for three women—Ludmilla Tcherina (left), Moira Shearer, and Pamela Brown (above, with Robert Rounseville as Hoffmann, in a scene later cut). Powell was fascinated by the sight of the gold-painted Brown, "a golden, breathing, sensuous statue," with whom he had a long relationship.

The perfect "composed film," shot freely to a pre-recorded soundtrack, was made possible by a talented team (right) of collaborators. From left to right: chief electrician Bill Wall, director of photography Christopher Challis, Technicolor technician George Minassian (kneeling), camera operator Freddie Francis, assistant director Sydney Streeter, and Technicolor assistant John Kotz.

OH . . . ROSALINDA!! (1955)

In this film version of Johann Strauss's operetta *Die Fledermaus*, Michael Redgrave played Colonel Eisenstein. Powell describes him as "a Bronzino that has just walked off the canvas, and now stands looking down at you, half puzzled, half contemptuous, well mannered, hot-headed . . . a bloody-minded baby." Mel Ferrer (who had just pulled out of a proposed Archers' film of *Ondine* with Audrey Hepburn) was also featured in the cast; a young Jill Ireland and John Schlesinger were among the bit players.

THE BATTLE OF THE RIVER PLATE (1956)
Above, wife Frankie and son Columba pay a visit to the studio set of the film, after the naval action scenes had been shot at sea. Below, Frankie and Michael Powell and a bowing Emeric Pressburger meet Queen Elizabeth, accompanied by Princess Margaret and producer J. Arthur Rank, at the film's Royal Command Performance in 1956.

The Battle of the River Plate centers on the mutual respect between the German commander of the *Graf Spee* (Peter Finch, above right) and his prisoner, the English captain of a merchant ship he has sunk (Bernard Lee, left). The film cleverly combines real naval maneuvers with studio sets and a superb twenty-foot model of the *Graf Spee* (below) that was blown up at Pinewood.

ILL MET BY MOONLIGHT (1956)
In this last production of The Archers,
based on a real wartime exploit, Dirk
Bogarde (above right, with Michael
Powell and David Oxley) plays British
intelligence officer Patrick Leigh-
Fermor, leading a band of partisans
(including Cyril Cusack, far right) on a
mission through occupied Crete to capture one of Hitler's favorite generals.
The film was shot in the south of
France. On location (right), Powell is
seen with camera operator Freddie
Francis (later director of photography
on Martin Scorsese's *Cape Fear*) and,
on his left, Christopher Challis.

PEEPING TOM (1960)
Karl-Heinz Böhm (Carl Boehm for the film), son of the great
Austrian conductor, gave an unforgettable performance as the
young cameraman obsessed with his art. Critics savaged the
film, and the distributor withdrew it from circulation. The scandal ended Powell's career. Today the film is considered a classic.

TRAVELS

From 1956, Powell spent more and more time at his hotel, the Voile d'Or, in the south of France, where David Niven (above), posing here for The Archers' logo, was his neighbor and friend. Another pleasure was trekking across the Scottish hills (left), here with his friend Alastair Dunnett, editor of *The Scotsman,* and Bill Paton, a trusted colleague since *The Edge of the World.*

Powell made two films in Australia: *They're a Weird Mob* (1966), with Walter Chiari (above right) playing an Italian immigrant journalist who ends up as a laborer with a noisy bunch of friends (below right); and *The Age of Consent* (1969), starring (and co-produced by) James Mason (center right, with Powell) and a nubile Helen Mirren as his inspiration, swimming naked off the Great Barrier Reef.

Michael Powell and Emeric Pressburger—The Archers (above) whose seventeen-year collaboration produced films admired for their wit, invention, and passion; Powell (below) with directors Akira Kurosawa (left) and Senkichi Taniguchi in Japan in 1952. Bowled over by Kurosawa's *Rashomon*, Powell made the trip to meet its director.

Above, Powell with film editor Thelma Schoonmaker, his wife, at Lee Cottages in 1987. Below, Martin Scorsese with Powell and Jerry Lewis in New York during the filming of *King of Comedy*, 1981. Powell became a frequent presence on the sets of Scorsese's films, where Scorsese came to value his advice and inspiration.

HOME

When not making entries in his diary, Johnson (above) helps his master read maps. Taking a break during the writing of his autobiography, Powell (below) warns his friends: "You're all in it!"

he sends Archibald to me instead. It is the olive branch extended to The Archers, by the board of the Rank Organisation, and by John Davis, its chairman: 'We need The Archers, and The Archers need a home. We offer you Pinewood for two more pictures, which you will propose. You can bring all your people with you. You will use all the Pinewood services. We want you, and we hope you want us. Then, after these two pictures, let us talk. We will fully finance you up to £350,000 a picture. Well, what do you say?'

"What does Michael say? He says nothing. He goes to sleep. Michael and I have been creative partners for seventeen years—ever since we met in Korda's office in September 1938. Of the twenty films we have made together, only three have failed to recover their costs. But the permanent staff of the big studios at Shepperton, Elstree, and Pinewood are uneasy about us, and no wonder.

"We bring in our own key personnel, we talk about art, we dispute their estimates, their budgets, their schedules, and write our own; worst of all, we prove to be right. But all this does not matter, if we have the backing of the top brass on the board. When John came to our rescue on that terrible weekend three months ago, he stuck his neck out. He had to make a snap decision and justify it later; and now The Archers are proving that he was right; and now the ball is at our feet.

"But the real hero of *The Battle of the River Plate* is Stapi. As an ex–German naval officer, he understood Langsdorff, and he knew that Peter Finch's sympathetic interpretation of the part would make the film a success, even in Germany. Yes, the old fox was right, and now we have *Ill Met by Moonlight* to follow it up, another war story, another big German part, and there is *St. Anthony's Lane,* and *Cassia* . . . although I think Michael has gone off *Cassia.* But there is time for us to consider whatever subjects Rank may own, or propose, and meanwhile we can bait the hook with *Ill Met by Moonlight.*"

Hein and Ada arrived back from Frankfurt, where they had gone to discuss the contract being offered to Hein by the Frankfurt Opera. It meant that he could do a film only during the ten weeks' summer vacation of the opera, and Hein was crazy about film and most particularly with The Archers. Had he not proclaimed, "Films are the folklore of the twentieth century"?

Designing a ballet for Buchwitz, intendant of the Frankfurt Opera, after working with The Archers would be another kettle of fish. Besides, Nandi and her two boys, Jodi and Kiki, were in and out of Hein's Chelsea studio day and night. He hesitated. He was still officially on the picture, and his salary was being paid by The Archers. I asked him to see Reggie Mills in the cutting room and run the cut sequences. When he saw those big VistaVision ships and men he came down to the floor to congratulate me, and took over the dressing of Manolo's Bar from Arthur.

On Sunday we had a rehearsal of the bar scene in Hein's studio at the Pheasantry, with Brian Easdale playing the piano and singing Muriel Smith's part, which she was still learning. April Olrich, being a dancer, picked it up very quickly. Lionel Murton took the whole thing as a great joke, which suited me for the scene. As for Christopher Lee as Manolo, he was everywhere at once, curling and uncurling like a hissing cobra. His entrances were stormy, his exits abrupt. We parted very pleased with ourselves.

A few days later, on November 16, Syd, solemn, pink, and thrilled, left us for New York, the Caribbean, Rio de Janeiro, and Montevideo. The head carpenter of the Joe Rock Studios in 1936, the chief of construction on the island of Foula expedition, had come a long way. He was now an associate producer, and The Archers' ambassador to the Latin American country of Uruguay, where he would lay the groundwork for our ten days of filming in Montevideo. We were hoping thousands of the city's inhabitants would turn up along the waterfront as extras, to be filmed watching the drama of the final hours of the *Graf Spee*. Lionel Murton's scenes, as the American reporter broadcasting news of the event, would be shot at the same time.

Emeric and I were to join Syd on December 6. Passages were already booked. Our return passages were booked, too, for it would be Christmastime. Emeric and I were making a side trip to Buenos Aires, and then I had persuaded him to cross the continent, to Santiago de Chile, where he had a cousin, and return to New York by the western route, with a stopoff at Lima, Peru, to see my old friends Felipe Ayulo and Felipe Beltrán. My family would all be at Saint-Jean-Cap-Ferrat for Christmas, and my big, black, *quinze-chevaux* Citroën was having an overhaul in Paris. I had already planned to part with Emeric in New York, fly to Paris, pick up the car, and drive down to Saint-Jean to arrive on Christmas Eve. I don't seem to have had any doubts about carrying out this hair-raising plan.

Meanwhile, the film went steadily on. It was becoming clear to everybody that we were not only going to finish on time, and on budget, but were also going to have a perfectly splendid show, barring a disaster.

How did we pay for Manolo's Bar? It came out of contingency—that is what a contingency is for. On the Wednesday, in Hein's studio, we had another rehearsal, to record the playback tape, this time with Muriel Smith the singer, Fred Lewis the musical director (with a portable piano), and Brian Easdale. We went all through the sequences and settled the arrangements. Brian and Muriel took turns singing, with interruptions by Christopher Lee in what he claimed to be Spanish. Muriel Smith was first-class. We let her finish and then Brian took her aside and told her the story. She came back and sang quite differently. By now Lionel Murton had got the hang of events.

We were all so happy, and so busy, that the premiere of *Oh . . . Rosalinda!!*

Dancers are wonderful. They are capable of anything. I would rather have a dancer in a film than an actress any day, and if I were an actress I would learn to dance. It's the discipline, the hard work: look at Moira; look at Dany Robin and Odile Versois, both of them Paris Opéra rats for years before they became actresses; look at Cyd Charisse and Rita Hayworth . . . but I won't go on. Some of my best friends are actresses.

The next days were cleanup days, pickup days, back projection setups, all the sets and shots and inserts that remain to be done at the end of a big film's production. By the afternoon of Friday, December 2, we were through. At 5:30 P.M. we staged a unit still photograph, and then The Archers threw a party. We even invited the chair polishers. It was Friday night, there were drinks all round, and by seven o'clock it was all over and everybody was going home. We tried to telephone poor Syd, marooned in Montevideo, but couldn't get through. It was over, all over. What a feat! What a Herculean, Augean, Cyclopean, Gargantuan feat . . . and how timely and tidily it finished. I had beaten so many records that nobody was astonished. But *I* was astonished. My family was astonished. We had a light meal, and then Bill Paton and I got into the car and drove to the Royal Automobile Club and vanished into the marble splendor and comfortable toweling of the Turkish bath. Bill lost seven pounds and I lost two in the steam room. The dirt and sweat of those two years fell off us like the scales of the sea serpents in the "Rime of the Ancient Mariner":

> They moved in tracks of shining white,
> And where they reared, the elfish light
> Fell off in hoary flakes.

"Hoary flakes"—what a lovely phrase, and how exactly it describes finishing a big picture in the studio. Then, wrapped in towels, we slept until 6:00 A.M., when we woke up and forced the night porter to make us tea, and drove back home to bacon and eggs for breakfast.

Emeric had already left for New York. He had arranged with his wife, Wendy, to see his daughter, Angela, in Greenwich, Connecticut. I followed him on Saturday. We had headwinds and it took us nine hours to get to Gander, where they refused to let us land because of the weather—how Gander did repeat itself! We went on to Sydney, Nova Scotia, and refueled there. At New York the ceiling was right down to the ground, but somehow our pilot scraped in over the marshes. They had improved the facilities at the new airport, and we were through in about an hour. I took a Carey transportation vehicle to the terminal. It cost one dollar, I note in my diary. What was that incredulous whistle? It was my dear wife, Thelma.

"It would cost you eleven, now."

I got to the Carlyle at lunchtime, and by two o'clock was eating clams and Emeric joined me. We were to fly in company to Montevideo on Tuesday, December 6. In New York there was the usual round of business, but the only meeting I remember was with Arthur Loew. I was very fond of him. He wanted to see *Rosalinda,* but I told him I couldn't see how it would fit into MGM's program. I asked him what the chances were of making an MGM-British picture, like the splendid ones they made before the war, mostly with Robert Donat. He gave the stock reply, which was that it should all start with Sam Eckman at the office in London and then come to him in New York or on the Coast. I asked him what European films he would be interested in, and after some thought, he said, "Anything with Alec Guinness."

And then, after a little more thought, "Any subject with a British appeal and which didn't call for an American star. Something to do with your empire," he added with a twinkle, "not ours."

I liked Arthur Loew, but he was a prisoner all right. The man in the Loew mask. I said, "Arthur, what are they trying to do to you, making you president of Loews and rushing you to and from from New York to the Coast and back again?"

He sighed and nodded. "I'll have to spend more and more time there."

He meant the Coast. I said, "You know, Arthur, I've always thought of you as the one man who kept on top of the film business, and lived the life he liked. And now, you are letting it get on top of you."

He said, "You're so right. Well, come and lunch with me when you get back from wherever you're going. Have you still got that hotel at Chantilly? Have you seen Laudy lately?"

He meant Laudy Laurence, the fabled Laudy, the friend of every American artist in Paris. I said that the last time I was in Chantilly I tried to see him, but I missed him. He was away, he was living in Paris, somewhere on the Left Bank. Arthur said hopefully, "Yes, but he still has the Lodge at Chantilly?"

I saw Ray Massey at the Century Club and had lunch with him. He was doing a television production of *Hanging Judge* with himself playing Sidney. Cedric Hardwicke was playing the judge. I wished him luck and left him, after a wonderful lunch and two martinis, which were just raw vodka. At the hotel I had a report from London that our camera unit had left for Montevideo by KLM. We were booked to follow them south next day. I had the evening free so I went to see *The Chalk Garden,* Enid Bagnold's excursion into botany and murder. Gladys Cooper was giving a magnificent performance of Enid Bagnold. Siobhán was the companion murderess. She seemed puzzled by the part, and no wonder—it defeated Pamela Brown!

The next day, December 6, Emeric and I took off for Montevideo. There were stopovers at Caracas, Belém, Rio. But in those days the airlines had bunks for their passengers and you could lie there and think of nothing. I found this therapeutic. Syd met us at Montevideo airport with the news that our unit was stranded somewhere in the Azores. They had been coming with KLM by the West African route and a wheel had come off. In those days this was considered a good joke, but this time the joke was on them. They arrived the next day.

I don't propose to give a blow-by-blow account of our ten days' stint in Montevideo. Essentially it was a commando raid in which the raiders were greeted with open houses, cups of tea, and bowls of *maté*. I watched carefully the ritual of *maté*, and here it is: the small gourds are filled almost half-full with powdery tea. The kettle of boiling water is poured, nowadays, into a Thermos that has a spout on it. These are preliminaries. Then the hot, not boiling, water is trickled into the soggy mass, which rises to the brim. Now the *bombilla*, the long, thin, silver pipe with a spatulated end to it, stirs and presses the herbs to one side of the gourd. Soon the level of watery tea sinks a bit and is topped up. Finally, after due deliberation, the owner takes a long pull on the pipe. The gourd is then refilled and passed to a friend. Soon the Thermos needs refilling from the blackened kettle on the fire. The herb is a dusty, green color. The gourds are dark and quite small. They can be held comfortably in the hollow of one hand. Chris Challis proposed to take one, filled with Pinewood tea instead of *maté*, into the canteen at the studio, in the hope that it would make the tea more drinkable.

December 13 was the sixteenth anniversary of the Battle of the River Plate, and although it hadn't been planned that way, we looked on it as a good omen that we were on hand to celebrate it. Montevideo celebrated it too. It was one of their great events, and the children then were our hosts now. Thousands showed up at the waterfront for the crowd scenes. As we shot Lionel Murton setting up his radio equipment outside Manolo's Bar the police held back the crowds.

We fixed camera positions on board the destroyer *Uruguay* in the harbor, and shot the scenes of the prisoners of the *Graf Spee* disembarking with the skyline of Montevideo behind them, and then trans-shipped into a tug to film the crowd as if they were watching the final hours of the *Graf Spee* as she was sailed out of the harbor and scuttled by her captain.

There must have been about ten thousand people, held in order and prevented from drowning themselves by cordons of naval police. The great black hearses, ornamented with crowns and crosses, shining like ebony in the sun, stood out against the white ambulances like islands in the sea of people. We sailed along the mole only fifty feet out, shooting the colorful, excited crowd. There were hundreds of prewar cars brought by special request, and the zealous police had turned back at the gates all later models. They didn't all wave, or do any of the things that I feared: they just stared, which couldn't have been better. People were clustered on cranes, on machinery, on everything high, like bees swarming. We came down on the tug to a position on their own level, and passed by their faces slowly. It was impressive. At last we went out to the other mole at the harbor entrance, where a faithful band had been waiting for hours, and got almost the best shot of all, as if we were the *Graf Spee* leaving harbor, turning the crowded lighthouse with the whole city in the sunlight beyond it.

By now the sun was declining and so was the crowd, and we were all peeling from the fierce sun over the water. We had been at such a stretch of energy and excitement all day that when I said, "Pack up!" they all looked at me with surprise, not quite realizing that the great day was over. We went back to the hotel and drank the largest gin-and-tonics I have ever poured down an aching throat.

On December 18 we all took off—the unit back to England and Pinewood, Emeric and I to Buenos Aires, on the right bank of the Río de la Plata, where we met the press, who had been looking enviously at our high jinks on the other bank of the river. I needn't say that before pressing on next day to Santiago we had an early lunch at La Cabaña with Emeric's cousins.

The weather was clear and the flight, first of all over the pampas and then over the Andes, was a superb geography lesson. Without any preliminary the great mountain barrier, naked of trees, soared up into the cloudless sky, contemptuously permitting a narrow strip of earth called Chile, 2,600 miles long from north to south, to be colonized by men. Not long ago this wonderful coast, from Valparaiso to Santiago, was one of the great trading routes of the world, with the harbors crowded with shipping sailing to and from San Francisco, and the east coast of America by the route around Cape Horn. Nowadays all that had gone, and Chile felt isolated from the rest of America and from Europe. But the pendulum will swing and all that will change again, for Chile is one of the great countries.

An old friend of Emeric's, Nadinska, met us at the airport and swept him away, poor exile, for an hour of European gossip before she returned him to me with apologies. Then we were off again, out over the South Pacific to avoid the dreaded Andes with their sudden storms, and four and a half hours up the coast of Chile and Peru, to land at Lima, where my old friends the two Felipes welcomed us and took us to see Felipe Ayulo's new house and new wife, both of them spectacular. They had no children. Everybody asked after Frankie with sincerity and affection. Frankie keeps her friends. I showed some pictures of Columba, which you can be sure I had ready. At midnight we said goodbye, left for Balboa, Miami, and New York. On the Panagra line you passed through customs in Miami, not one of my favorite places. From the air Miami appeared to be a swamp covered in garages and skyscrapers. A thin line of sandy beach ran along the eastern end of the swamp. It appeared to be overpopulated. For nearly three weeks we had been treating the eastern and western hemispheres so disrespectfully that I no longer knew where I was. As we crossed the James River I said to Emeric, "Look at the surf."

"It's not surf, Michael, it's snow," hardly raising his eyes from his book.

True enough, it was snow, a natural phenomenon that I had forgotten about, and we were heading for New York on the 42nd parallel. The farms and forests and rivers were closing up for the winter. The ice looked very green from the air. Washington shone in the pale gold sunlight. We didn't get out of the aircraft. We pressed on up the sandy seacoast, and reached Idlewild around two o'clock. Emeric went off to see two Hungarian pals. I took myself to see *Oklahoma!*, in Todd-AO. It wasn't a patch on the stage show with Alfred Drake, but I liked it. The images, of course, were wonderful. I thought to myself that anybody who made a film musical in the small academy frame after this would need his head examined. There was a very long ballet in the film by dear Agnes de Mille—dear, dear Agnes de Mille . . . dear, dear! Like all big pictures, it was too long. I set out to walk back to the hotel, but the weather was fantastically cold, down to 15 degrees or something hideous. My ears froze and my nose crackled. I took a cab and went to bed, with Rodgers and Hammerstein in my head.

December 22 was a gray day with a promise of snow. I began to get anxious. I was booked to fly to Paris that evening. If anything happened to delay the plane, I would never be back with the family at the Voile d'Or for Christmas. I had to pick up the Citroën at Paris and drive it down to the south of France, where it would be needed. Syd arrived and reported the unit back in London safe and sound. He was flying on that night. Emeric was leaving at four. I was supposed to leave at six. By now it was snowing hard.

We had quite a good meeting with distributors over *Oh . . . Rosalinda!!* They loved the picture because it was a musical, and musicals were in, but they couldn't decide whether it should be distributed in the theatre or on TV. One of the major television stations had made a bid for Olivier's *Richard III:* a million dollars in cash—sight unseen. A film of this classical eminence, starring Sir Laurence Olivier and a gaggle of theatrical knights in all the major roles, had never been premiered on the box. The question being debated was whether to take the money and run, and risk the effect that a nationwide TV showing would have upon future film audiences, or distribute the film in selected situations as the Shakespeare classic it was, as had been done with Larry's *Henry V* and *Hamlet,* and had proved pretty successful. But times were changing. The old audiences were staying home to watch television. The new audiences could not be spoon-fed.

At first amused, then alarmed, Emeric and I listened to the brutal talk of these two showmen, and we decided that it doesn't do for artists to listen to their dealers pitching sales.

After lunch I was so busy seeing the others off that I quite forgot that I had to go myself. At four o'clock I called for my bill and a taxi and there was not a taxi to be had. I went out to look for one myself. It is hard to believe that I was out in the snow on Madison Avenue for an hour, hoping for a taxi. There were none. At last two cabs arrived simultaneously, and one of them agreed to take me out to Idlewild.

We left at 4:45 P.M., and arrived at 7:45 P.M. You can imagine the state that I was in. The snow was falling thick and fast, and for what seemed like hours at a time we were hardly moving. Cars were massed and stationary along the Triboro Bridge, and all over the parkway. At any time you could see about ten thousand cars massed on the highway, three abreast. The snow fell swiftly. It was dry and powdery and was soon six inches deep.

At the airport, I jumped from the cab and ran to the check-in desk.

"Has one-fourteen gone yet?!!"

A harassed gray-looking man looked at me with distaste, but admitted, "No."

He added with sour pleasure, "It's all loaded; it leaves at eight."

"Can I get on? I'll get my bags!"

There were no porters, and it took me two trips. The man looked at my ticket, and groaned.

"I can tell you, it's all loaded. It's the snow. They've moved out from their berth. You're too late."

I was insistent.

"It's not my fault. You've got to get me on if the ship's still there."

He was a beauty.

"It's all loaded," he repeated, obstinately. "We'll have to reroute you, if we can," he added, walking away.

I almost cried. After that awful taxi ride, it was too much! A girl suddenly appeared at my elbow in a bright Pan-Am uniform. I had seen her face before.

"Don't listen to him. I've got you on," she said with excitement. She came from the backroom, not from the desk, and she had the unusual idea that the passenger who had booked on a flight should be got on board, if possible.

"The ship has gone over to the hangar," she said breathlessly, "she had to be de-iced."

I said, "I don't care if she has to be deloused. You are a jewel!"

Inside three minutes she had me marked in, weighed, and checked. The other fellow had disappeared, probably to put his head down the lavatory.

"Come with me into the backroom," said my sterling good fairy. She seized my bags herself, and tried to lug them in.

"We've got to get you transport over to the aircraft," she panted. "It's two miles."

Inside, a man was talking double-Dutch on the telephone. A tall, thin Scandinavian said, "Sit down, sir. We'll get you on."

I said, "I can't sit down. Could you?"

He smiled benignly. The ground staff were in rubber overalls and galoshes. They knew what they were doing. We stepped over the moving band that carried the luggage—it was like a barrier separating this world of technical efficiency and brotherhood from a world of counters and tickets and Coca-Cola—before we found a small van to transport me to the aircraft. We were joined by three more frantic passengers and all jammed into the truck and drove across, through the driving snow, to a brilliantly lit hangar on the other side of the field. By now it was 8:30 P.M., but what did I care? I was on!

A low door in the belly of the plane was opened, and we entered through the bar and up the stairs. We met the combined staff and all the other passengers, who had been waiting for an hour and a half for us. A man said, "Well, better late than never."

We agreed with him. We now learned that there was a strike in Paris and the aircraft would put us down in Brussels, which is four hours in the train from Paris. I calculated we wouldn't get to Brussels until 2:00 P.M. Any idea of driving to the Riviera overnight would have to be reviewed, always depending on how I felt and whether I could find Jack Sée,* who had the car. Luckily, he knew the U.S., and would have checked with Pan-Am, and would know we were coming on the train. Anyway, I was lucky to be on the plane at all.

I insisted upon knowing and writing down the name of my gruff little good fairy of Pan-Am, Jeanette Hanou, a name that shall be held in honor by my family. I kissed her and said, "Come and stay with us at the Voile d'Or. It won't cost you a penny, even if you bring your husband."

It was an eleven-hour flight to Brussels. By New York time it was about 3:00 A.M., but our bodies, being breakfast bodies, knew better. I watch my body and frequently consult it. I haven't got a watch anyway. Instead I use my body. It's surer and safer.

Brussels, a great, big, noisy town like a Flemish mobile done by Rubens, was *en fête*. Shining faces oozed good humor and prosperity. The street illuminations were stunning. Every bulb shone. In any other country there would have been short circuits or a shortage of juice, but Brussels was full of juice. There was no train to Paris until 7:15 P.M.

We arrived in Paris's Gare du Nord at 11:40 P.M., and after five minutes of

---

*Owner, with his wife, Billie, of a restaurant in Nice. Ludmilla Tcherina introduced the Sées to Michael and Frankie and they became lifelong friends. Michael writes of their tragic end on pages 341–44.

suspense I saw, to my joy, Raymond Roi's chauffeur approaching me through the crowd. Jack Sée had already left for the Voile d'Or, but had given Roi's chauffeur the papers for the car, and French money for me. He drove me across Paris to the Porte Maillot and put me on the right road for the Porte d'Orléans. I left at once, drove 400 kilometers through the night, and decided at Bourg-en-Bresse that I was falling asleep, so I stopped. After knocking up three hotels I found a bed at the Hotel Terminus and fell asleep with five busts of Napoleon watching over me.

I woke at eleven (it was Christmas Eve) and took to the road again. I reached Grenoble at 1:45 P.M., and I was on top of the Col de la Croix Haute at 3:05 P.M. There was no snow, but there was lots of ice on the road in dangerous patches. I crossed over the Pont du Diable, with its awful black gulf. Darkness fell, and I had two very narrow shaves in the darkness on the icy road. Once I went into a skid and crashed, with locked wheels, into the side of the mountain. Lucky it wasn't a ravine! But my father's beloved Citroën was made of sturdy stuff, and we backed out of that one. It left me a little shaky. The second time we were stopped from skidding into the deep waters behind the new dam by a concrete post, placed there by a far-seeing road surveyor.

After that it was plain sailing, and by seven o'clock I was telephoning Frankie from a little bar on the River Var. Three quarters of an hour later, the wheels of the Citroën crunched the gravel of the terrace of the Voile d'Or, and the air was full of flying bodies. Jack and Billie Sée and their daughters Danielle and Joelle were staying with us. It made a real family Christmas. Bumba had already told his mother, "When Daddy arrives, I shan't have much time for you."

=

After the making of *The Red Shoes* had reconciled me with my beloved France, Frankie and I visited my father at Cap Ferrat once or twice, but never in the season, knowing very well that after two days there would be broad hints about occupying profitable beds. The hotel is so well known that it isn't worthwhile describing it, but in those days it had been a small hotel-pension, about twenty rooms, built in the Italian style, with a few balconies and a tiled roof, standing back from an enormous terrace about 150 meters long, one side of which looked down on the little fishing port of Saint-Jean-Cap-Ferrat, while the other side looked across the Bay of Beaulieu to where the stupendous colored cliffs of the Alpes Maritimes plunged down into the sea.

It's a fine view: that great, red, headland is Cap Roux; that high cliff, with military barracks on top (it must be all of two thousand meters high), with a huge, rounded top like the head of an animal, is the Tête du Chien. It's the western boundary between France and the little principality of Monaco. That hill village built on and around a great crag of rock . . . there! . . . where the Moyenne Corniche road crosses the ravine . . . it's the town of Èze, celebrated in the songs of troubadours and tales of Barbarossa the corsair. If you look to the west, and crane out from the wall of the terrace, you can see another cape jutting out into the Mediterranean, maybe twenty miles away. That is Cap Martin, and beyond that those hazy shapes are the Italian Alps and the frontier at Ventimiglia.

I was passing Wildenstein's, the art dealers in Bond Street, and noticed that they had an exhibition of Edward Lear's sketches and watercolors. He's a delicate and friendly painter, so I went in. They were priced rather high for me, but there was one view, a seascape with mountains, that I found particularly attractive, and I returned to it again and again. All of a sudden I realized I was looking at a pen and watercolor sketch of the very view that I have just described to you. In the foreground was a little harbor and a pile of rocks, and I realised it was the view from the pathway between Saint-Jean and Beaulieu, the view from the villa that used to have the verse of Horace painted on the landward side:

Eheu fugaces, Postume, Postume,
Labuntur anni.

The sketch, which was a fair size and nicely framed, was scribbled all over with notes by Lear: color notes and time of day, that sort of thing. But there it was, our coast from Beaulieu to the Cap du Chien, and I decided I could afford this one, whatever the cost. It hung in the hall of the hotel for many years. I wonder where it is now.

My father left no money and no other property, except his Citroën. He at first bought the lease of the hotel in 1921, and carried on like that until he was forced to buy it. He always lived from hand to mouth . . . his mouth. When he found that the freehold was for sale before the war, at a rock-bottom price, he scraped together all he could raise, and was lent the rest of the purchase price by Samuel Courtauld, a longtime friend of his, and one of the most generous men that ever lived. By the personal way my father ran the hotel, he never accumulated any capital, and he never paid back Sam Courtauld, who wouldn't have dreamed of asking for it. He cleared just enough money to keep the hotel running and repaired, and he made enough money out of his bridge winnings and an occasional gamble at the Sporting Club to buy himself a few luxuries. He always played to win.

Of course, this system worked all right as long as he was the resident proprietor, with a little family of servants and one of the restaurant owners in the village running his restaurant for him. But when he died the whole thing threatened to collapse, and we had to go out and take over.

We spent our first winter there in 1952–53, and from then on we became progressively more involved. The children loved it, the staff loved the children, and Frankie, who was a wonderful hostess and manager, saw it as the chance to be fully occupied that I denied her in films. My father—or "the captain," as everybody called him—left a will that was commendably brief, written in his own hand on one side of a sheet of notepaper, but all witnessed and in proper order, with instructions to repay the Courtauld loan when we could afford to, and expressing the hope that we would carry on with the hotel.

Of course, without Frankie that would have been impossible. It would have meant leaving the film business and taking up the job full time, and probably that is what I should have done. I had achieved what I set out to do in my profession, and I had had my share of power and authority. But the pull of the business was too strong. In spite of the disappointments and frustrations of the past five years, I couldn't do it. I was hooked. After what I had achieved, retirement at forty-eight seemed ridiculous, and you must remember that I had not accumulated any capital, nor did I have any regular income from royalties, as I had much later on.

At the risk of repeating myself, we were paid very little for making our biggest films—either by the Rank Organisation or by Alex Korda. All our expectations of big money was in the profits. In the case of Rank, these took nearly twenty years to mature. In the case of Korda, he went bankrupt and we never got anything. I didn't want to end up in a job that had so satisfied my father, as a little hotel keeper, living from hand to mouth. Of course, it was a charming life, but I had moved whole continents and pleased, or displeased, governments. Interesting and talented men and women were my friends. Was I to be reduced to seeing them occasionally on my terrace and standing them a bottle of wine?

Anyway, for the present I brought in money from England and bought francs in Nice at a ruinous rate of exchange, and carried on with the summer season as my father would have done. The first great difficulty was a political one. My father possessed the coveted *carte de commerçant*, meaning a licence permitting him to trade on the same level as a French citizen, which had been easy enough to obtain when he first went into the hotel business in 1919, after the Great War. His record was impeccable. When World War II broke out, he had left France under the threat of internment, at the very last possible moment, and he certainly returned with the first wave of troops. For me it was a different matter. The local restaurant owner, M. Cappa, naturally expected that he would take over the management of the joint. He already ran the restaurant and the bar, so why not the hotel? I had other ideas. He had a short-term contract and I was prepared to sit him out. Meanwhile, I set about pulling strings and talking to my father's friends to get me a *carte de commerçant*. It took me two years, but once I had it my position was impregnable.

My father had a manageress, Alice Wahrmund, a charming Viennese lady. She was shrewd, she was brave, she was loyal. When France collapsed before the German assault in 1940 and was overrun, the big exodus of resident foreigners began, and Britain even sent ships to take off as many as they could. My father was lucky (what he would have called "the luck of the fat high priest"), and he was on the west coast of France when the breakthrough came. He was playing golf at Saint-Jean-de-Luz, left his car and his golf clubs, scrambled on board the *Arandora Star* at Biarritz, and Alice was left in charge of the hotel for the whole of the war.

Her first act was to take all the hotel silver, some of which was family silver, and bury it in the garden. Her second act was to make herself known to the German authorities as a Viennese citizen, and volunteer her services as an interpreter. These were refused, but she was appointed the official manageress of the hotel under the new regime, and since she spoke German both she and her hotel became very popular with German soldiers. I'm sure that, otherwise, the hotel would have been knocked about, looted, and destroyed.

When my father returned she was there to welcome him back, and handed over the silver. She then went to see her relatives in Vienna, and returned to the Voile d'Or. She was a woman of strong character and equable temperament. Naturally, we took her on; we would have been lost without her. The permanent staff consisted of Marcelle, the *femme de chambre*, and Joseph, a local boy and jack-of-all-trades and destined to be assistant manager. As I have said, the restaurant and bar were run by Cappa. For the present, we let this arrangement ride, and for the first season ran the hotel as my father would have done if he had been alive.

Since we were in the hotel business as well as in show business, we had a good many friends and hangers-on. Among the friends were Jack and Billie Sée. They were an attractive couple, still in their twenties when Tcherina introduced them to us outside their teashop, grandly entitled Le Restaurant de la Minaudière.* It was in the Jardin Albert Premier, back of the Hotel Roule, and only a hundred yards from the Promenade des Anglais. I can see them now, Billie all eyes and curls, generous and practical; Jack, quick, powerful, shrewd, and a dreamer.

They had been a famous dance team, Jack and Billie, on both sides of the Atlantic, and had worked with Fred Astaire. But all that lay behind them, and now they thirsted for better things. They had two daughters, Danielle and

Minaudière translates as an affectedly dainty female.

Joelle, who must, of course, marry well. So they had left the nightclubs and gone into commerce. Billie was the moving spirit in all this, and had made a great success of La Minaudière, leaving Jack free to spend all the profits on the inventions of his ingenious and fertile mind. This was to be the pattern of their lives. And of their deaths.

Marriage is a business, no French couple needs to be told that—a business full of checks and balances, moral and physical. Love is love, no one can plan it or organize it. But to fail in marriage is to fail in the business of love. It is not a matter for laughter or tears, it is something to be ashamed of. To overdraw one's marriage is to be bankrupt of emotion.

In a successful, busy marriage, like Jack and Billie's, the partners need a passionate friendship to round out their lives. For Jack Sée, this was his daughter, Danielle. For Billie, it was I. At first sight we became friends. She had a lively mind. We had a mutual interest in books, plays, and people. It was a relationship of mutual trust. Billie adored Frankie, her beauty, and how good she was with people. I admired Jack, how good he was with things. At one time we thought of taking them into partnership to run the hotel. At another time we planned a London-Paris film production company, to make Anglo-French films, the first of which would be *Le Voleur d'Enfants* by Jules Supervielle. But after an initial flurry of excitement we all decided that we would rather be friends than partners.

Billie wrote me long letters, frequently. When they sold La Minaudière she started a dress shop in the rue du Paradis, which was a huge success, until Jack sold it so that they could move to Paris, to Suresnes and a partnership in a machine shop, where he could work out some of his inventions. It stood on the banks of the River Seine, and there was a good little restaurant in a houseboat moored to the bank. Jack had some successful patents, and many failures.

The girls were growing up, and somehow Billie managed to scrape together enough money to buy a doll house in Deauville where *le tout Paris* came for the weekend. For ten desperate years she paid for it, and clung to it, while Danielle was a student in Paris at the Beaux-Arts, and Joelle was astonishing her family with her brilliance and unpredictability. All this was shared with me by Billie, in long letters full of tears and laughter. The two families met from time to time, sometimes in Paris, sometimes in London, but the chain of communication between Billie and me was never broken, although too often neglected on my side.

Years later the decline in my fortunes, the breakup of my marriage, and my adventures in America were shared, and soon followed by the arrival of Jack and Billie in California. Jack's inventions were being taken up, there was important finance available, and there was a house at Malibu instead of

Deauville. After New Hampshire and New York, I was now in California myself, at San Quentin, but not in prison, yet. We still corresponded, or rather Billie wrote long letters, full of comment on life and letters and people, answered briefly by me in postcards. For some years we went on like this, her letters flying up the coast, my short answers sailing down. Several times both Jack and Billie went back to Paris, and came back to California again, for Joelle's boys were in California at university. And now a Pacific Palisades house was their home.

Billie's letters talked always of great fortune and always around the corner, while Jack worked, dreamed, and poured out his ideas over the telephone to Danielle in Paris. When Thelma and I had to go to California to make an important speech, we saw Jack and Billie. Their house was now in Bel Air. They gave us a party. It was obvious that things were not going well, but it was not so obvious that they were going really badly. We no longer had the house in San Quentin, and flew back to New York.

Then came the news that Billie had had a stroke, one of those thunderbolt strokes that smite you to earth and remind you that you are but earth yourself. We telephoned every day, and discussed whether we should go out. But then we heard that she was getting better. At last Jack was coming to take her home from the hospital, and Danielle was coming from Paris to look after her mother. The pattern of hope and disaster, disaster and hope, seemed about to be repeated. But it was the end. Jack had thrown in the cards. He had a loaded revolver and he shot Billie, he shot her little dog, he telephoned Danielle in Paris and told her what he had done, and then he shot himself. He had the last word.

Men and women are as destructive as machines, as terrifying as gods. For thirty years I had walked beside Jack Sée, a charming, intelligent, knowledgeable man—and all the time he was a madman and a murderer. And she knew it, God rest her soul. They had been living on credit and borrowed money for years. Los Angeles was their last chance. In that city of dreams and lost hopes fortune is always around the corner, but it eluded them. Their friends, who loved them, had no more money to lend them. A sea of unredeemed notes threatened to engulf them, and I never guessed . . . or do I convince myself that I never guessed . . . the truth?

Talk about courage! Think of her despair. How could I be so blind? Whenever I looked in Billie's great, luminous eyes, I could always see a question in them. I know now it meant, "Can you help me? . . . Can you save me? . . . Or will you leave me to my fate?" There was no friend to save her, no money to cure her . . . she, who had given everything to her friends in friendship alone, who had pledged herself again and again for the sake of her children, her grandchildren, for Jack, and for her little dog. It was shameful.

But what good is it to talk of shame? It was life. It was death. It was the end of the story for Jack and Billie.

From 1956 onward, we spent more and more time at the Voile d'Or, and it became more and more identified with our plans, or lack of them. High June was now the top of the season, and a star-spangled coterie formed around our unpretentious hotel, where the guests ran the bar and chalked up the drinks when they remembered to: Jack Hawkins and his wife, Trevor Howard, Stanley Baker and his family, David Niven and Hjördis from across the bay, Alec Guinness, always an observer, only reluctantly a player, with Frankie, the most beautiful woman on the Riviera, as their hostess, supported and guarded by her two beautiful children, Kevin chattering in French, his eyelashes on his cheeks, and Columba roaring across the harbor, "Momma— big wee-wee!"

=

1956 started with a bang and ended with a bang. It was the year of *Ill Met by Moonlight*, the year of Mikis Theodorakis, the year of the tenth Royal Command Performance, the year of *Cassia*, the year of *St. Anthony's Lane*, the year of the breaking of the arrows.

It is only now, when I write this memoir, that I realize how completely my steps were guided at this time by Emeric and by Stapi, by my partner and by my friend. Sometimes I shudder, when I think how narrowly I escaped the fate that awaits the artist in the murky shadows of the movie jungle. I am speaking of the English-speaking movie, of London, of New York, of Hollywood; the movie of *Variety*, the movie of the full-page advert, the movie of the Oscars, those statuettes that should be engraved with the words: "So far, and no further."

For when the shouting's over—what next? You have to become bankable, and must repeat yourself. Even Hitchcock, who spoke the language of the cinema better than any of us, could not escape this fate. Nor will you; nor will I. There is too much money involved. The grosses are too gross. The bankers, lawyers, exhibitors, distributors, financiers who carve us up between them hate us for our successes as much as for our failures. In all my experience only Alex Korda knew that you must have failures to have successes. He recognized talent, and spoke to all of us on equal terms. We ne'er shall look upon his like again. I was in a New York office when I heard the news. It was Monday, January 23, 1956. Shirley Harden, David Selznick's secretary, said, "Isn't it sad about Sir Alex?"

My breath was cut off. It could only be a stroke, or he was dead. Yes, he was dead, a sudden heart attack. Well, it was better so. He had lived like a Renaissance prince for too long ever to die in retirement, and he was already

There was a big theme that went with the big naval stuff, but we used Brian's Latin American music and the voice of Muriel Smith singing for the playout of the film. When the lights went up, we all knew we had a big hit. John turned to me, and said, "Micky, why didn't you use that big naval theme of Brian Easdale's for the playout of the picture?"

Emeric said, "Vell, you see, John, the battle is over. The *Graf Spee* is no more, and we felt it would be nice to finish with the song and the music as if it came from the shore of this neutral country who had been so kind to us."

John said tolerantly, "You artists are all the same. You're thinking of this as if it was an ordinary film. I'm thinking of it as a film that I'm going to hold for the next Royal Command Performance, and that film should finish with a naval scene, not with all that South American jazz."

Brian, who was sitting in front of us, screwed round in his seat to see my face. But we were staring at John.

"You don't mean to say you're going to hold the picture up for a year for release—until October!?!"

"Yes. I've seen the list of possible choices to be forwarded to the palace, and we shall win, hands down."

I looked at Emeric, and he looked at me. He nodded. I said, "All right, John. You win."

He said, "Then you'll change the music?"

I said, "We'll change the music."

But I didn't really agree with him, and I don't think Emeric did either. The idea of showing these great ships sailing into the sunset accompanied by this gay Latin American music was a good one. After such a victory, to crow over your defeated enemy would be really a little too much. You see what I mean about the boys in the front office? They're desperate if they don't contribute something. But who asked them? They're not there for that.

Emeric had driven me and Judy and Bill Paton down to Pinewood in his big Bentley limousine, and he drove us back. I sat beside the driver, Judy promptly went to sleep in the back, and Bill sat, solid as a rock, gazing straight ahead of him. We came out of the trees into the Oxford road. Emeric, his eyes on the road, said, "Michael, what are we going to do between now and the Royal Command Performance?"

I knew what he wanted me to say, and I said it: "We'll make *Ill Met by Moonlight*."

What else could I have done?

Judy Coxhead, now Judy Buckland, was my secretary, one of a number of well-educated, well-made young ladies who acted in that capacity over the years. For some time after the war was over I had difficulty in keeping them attached to my person, and the duties that went with it, because as soon as

I had a good one, my friend Jan de Hartog ran away with her. His excuse was always the same. He was a Dutch writer who thought in Dutch and wrote in English, because that was where the money was. Obviously his need for a personable, well-educated English secretary was greater than my own. Although I protested this proposition, I went along with it for years. Eventually, Marjorie Means appeared and soon put a stop to it. She was my secretary at the time that Jan was the rage of *le tout Paris.* Marjorie looked him over, and decided he would suit her as perfectly as she suited him. So I lost Marjorie as a secretary but kept her as a friend. All my other secretaries are friends too. And as I write these words in Avening, in 1988, under the eye of Thelma, Jan and Marjorie are only a few miles away, in the village of East Coker, struggling with Jan's book. But to return to Judy.

Frankie now took a hand in the search for a nonconvertible secretary, and one morning at Pinewood I looked out of the window of my dingy little office where I hardly ever went, for I had my caravan and I had my Bill, and saw a tall young lady standing on the small patch of grass surviving among a film studio's concrete and corrugated iron, her legs well apart, her stance firm, as she addressed a golf ball with a number six iron. She was dressed in tweeds and cardigans and was obviously a product of Roedean.* She swung her club, I opened the window, and she topped the ball.

"Keep your eye on the ball," I said. "Who are you?"

Not a very original opening.

"Your new secretary," she answered. "Haven't you got a better office than this beastly little box?"

I explained about Bill and the caravan.

"This office is for me to hang my hat in and for you to type in. Frankie said you wanted a job. Will this one do?"

"Couldn't be more thrilled. I've read the script. Super!"

"Our next job will be to write a book."

"Brilliant!"

"Are you a virgin?"

"Yes. Why do you ask?"

"Haven't seen one for years. They're not so common in this part of Buckinghamshire."

"Be my guest. What's my first job?"

"Letters and memos. We're still in production. Then when the film's over, we write a book—about the battle."

"Super! I've never written a book."

"I write the book. You type it."

I looked her over.

*Most famous British girls' public school.

"Come on, we'll introduce you to the camera crew. If they approve of you, you'll do."

The book I had decided to write was to be called *Graf Spee*. I had so much material—letters, reports, diaries—I couldn't use half of it, not a tenth of it, in the film; all this lovely material gone to waste, unless I put it into a book. I decided it should be like an early Jules Verne, saying exactly where we were and what we were doing, and going straight into the action. It was just my tidy mind operating, that and my love for an adventure story in which the men are all part of a grand design.

I had already done my reconnaissance to Crete, and written my diary, so while Emeric was roughing out the first script of *Ill Met by Moonlight* I could be writing *Graf Spee*, provided that I could complete the job by Easter, and I decided to do it at the Voile d'Or, where I had a big studio underneath the terrace with no telephone.

Emeric was already scribbling in his thick notebook. I said, "The music is going to be very important, old cock."

"Huh?"

"The music . . . it's important."

"What music, Michael?"

"The *Ill Met* music. The Cretans are always singing and dancing . . . songs, ballads . . . and performing on a lute, or what passes for a lute, a bouzouki. Music should be very important in the film. It shouldn't be all bang, bang, bang."

"Why is it, Michael, when you tell me how the film is going to be, you always say: 'And then it goes bang-bang-bang,' and then when I see it, Michael, the film goes 'ba-bang . . . ba-bang . . . ba-bang.' Why is that?"

"Shakespeare said: 'How doth desire outrun performance.' "

"And you are telling me that you are not Shakespeare."

"I am telling you, that we need a Greek composer. Brian can't do them all."

We stirred up the Greek embassy, at first incredulous, then enthusiastic.

"There's a Greek student of music in Paris. We'll check him out for you."

The Paris embassy were even more enthusiastic.

"The Archers? *Ill Met by Moonlight? Entaxi!* We have a Greek student of music. He won a prize in Moscow, last year. Theodorakis—Mikis Theodorakis."

"Can you send us some tapes?"

They came. We played them together. They were all folk tunes, wild, heady tunes, marching songs, revolutionary themes and ballads.

"What do you think, Imre?"

"I don't know, Michael. It's good as far as it goes, like those early tunes of Kodály . . . all folk tunes."

I spoke to Paris.

"Hasn't he got more serious music? Hasn't he got a symphony?"

"We'll find out."

Next day, a telephone call.

"Yes, he has a symphony that won the prize in Moscow. We'll have a tape made for you. He's only twenty-four, you know."

The symphony arrived and we played it. It was fierce, declamatory, activist, patriotic, and touched with genius, obviously like its author.

"Give him a visa and send him over."

Mikis arrived, glaring about himself as if he expected to be ambushed by capitalists at every corner, but then he was raised a Cretan, and Cretans do expect to be ambushed at every corner. We put him under contract and paid him a retaining fee, and he wished it clearly understood that, beyond the bare necessities of life, the money would go to *enosis*, the Greek revolutionary movement that was sweeping through the islands like Crete and Cyprus. He knew Patrick Leigh-Fermor and regarded him as an interloper. We were interlopers too.

At this time, early in 1956, John Davis increased his attempts to get us to sign a long-term contract with the Rank Organisation. Emeric was for it—I was against it. Give up dreams of autonomy? Join the herd? Our disastrous decision to leave Rank and return to Korda had given us a reputation as untouchables. We bought our way out of the Korda contract, and were in the wilderness for four years. No wonder Emeric was seriously alarmed, and began to lean more and more on Stapi's shoulders. And now fortune had turned. We were bankable, we were in demand, we could speak to the American bosses on equal terms. John Davis expected the *Graf Spee* film to be selected for the Royal Command Performance. The iron was hot. It was time to strike! John Davis offered a five-year contract, for seven films.

"Sign!" groaned poor Emeric.

"That's not the future!" I would shout. "The future is in big films, in special films, in great films. John Davis's dream is an English Hollywood. Who the hell, who cares about his art, wants an English Hollywood, or a Hollywood Pinewood? Those wonderful studios—Shepperton, Denham, Pinewood—with all they've learned, with all they can provide, are a priceless asset. Technical knowledge is power in the film business. We don't want to tell ordinary stories. We want to perform miracles, rewrite history, shoot films all over the world!"

"Oh, Michael, you're impossible! We shall go broke trying to keep our unit together! We have three subjects which we own, and which we can make while we plan the kinds of films you are talking about."

But I was obstinate: "One film at a time was good enough for Arthur Rank and John Davis in wartime, and it's good enough for them now. John Davis is thinking of his shareholders. He has built Rank an empire, and naturally he wants to keep it rolling. But he doesn't see the future in terms of a few wonderful pictures. He wants to copy Hollywood and make too many pictures. I think he even wants to make B-pictures, as well as A-pictures. What is 'A' and what is 'B,' Emeric? You know very well that talent is all that matters . . .''

So the argument swayed to and fro. We signed for one picture: *Ill Met by Moonlight.* John was quite calm at our decision. He had the Royal Command Performance film that year. He could afford to wait.

Frankie had not been too happy about my plan of writing the book at the Voile d'Or. Although she had chosen the attractive Judy as my amanuensis herself, she was not all that keen on sharing her bed and board with her—and Bumba too! But the alternative was to leave me loose in London, which was not to be thought of, and since Bumba had taken to Judy, and vice versa, Frankie decided to give it a go.

The Citroën was already at Saint-Jean, so Judy and I came down by the Blue Train, which arrived at Beaulieu in the morning. There had been some mix-up over the berths, and Judy had to share with a passenger of the same sex instead of having a sleeping berth all to herself. The sleeping-car attendant, sensing a romance, tried to put Judy and me in the double berth, and although I was completely innocent of the mix-up I think that she suspected me of the worst intentions.

The Blue Train in those days was always chatty and conversational, and we made friends with a splendid-looking elderly military man, Major General Sir Guy Salisbury-Jones, who told us that he was cultivating a vineyard to make English wine in the Hampshire Meons. Judy, always well informed, told me that she thought he was the marshal of the diplomatic corps, on his way to Monte Carlo for the marriage of Grace Kelly to the reigning prince.

The studio at the Voile d'Or was ideal for our scheme of work. When the hotel and terrace were originally built, I think it may have been intended for a café or a bar. It was a big, high room, hacked out of the rock, with a huge window looking directly down on the fishing port and the fishermen's boats. The window was about ten feet by twelve and it didn't get the sun until after midday, which made it habitable in the morning. There was a stone sink and running water, a couple of big workmen's benches, and a very long desk, or table, which Frankie and I had bought in Nice when we first inherited the Voile d'Or. It was an ideal worktable. You could spread out maps and lists and things, with plenty of room for Judy's typewriter, for files and photographs, and plenty of room, also, for me to walk up and down as I dictated into a microphone. This was my first attempt at writing by dictation, and I soon got the hang of it. I had always written everything in longhand, and so had

Emeric. At this time neither of us could use a typewriter. He wrote his scenes and dialogue in the thick notebook that I have mentioned, using a pencil and writing very big. I used a Parker fountain pen and wrote very small.

I started work at about eight o'clock, and worked until about twelve, which on the Riviera is time for the *apéritif* and for lunch. At two o'clock Judy took over the studio and typed till four or thereabouts; that was the working day. Bumba, who was always roaming around the port, was of course delighted to have company, and we soon had the studio organized with hideous French colored drinks and Coca-Cola, of course, and all the ingredients that go into making the huge Niçois sandwich, known and beloved by the locals as *pan bagnat.* For this you need a large, flat loaf of bread, which you bisect. You soak the bread with olive oil and garlic, and pile on it the ingredients that you have been able to steal from the kitchen: tomatoes, black olives, radishes, cucumbers, tunny fish, salted anchovies, and lettuce leaves. Clamp the top on all this garbage, press down hard (it's not necessary to sit on it, which Columba sometimes did), cut into four more-or-less-regular pieces, and eat. It's a little snack that comes in handy about eleven o'clock in the morning.

Of course there were other refreshments in between. I had a Primus stove and made tea, and I am sorry to record here that Columba's friends among the fishermen's sons had taught him to dunk, a detestable trick, but truth will out. And since his father greeted his gastronomic lapse with screams of horror, Bumba made a point of doing it with an amused smile on his face at Daddy's overacting.

In London Emeric had finished the first draft of the screenplay of *Ill Met by Moonlight* and sent it to me. I was disappointed. It was exciting only as a documentary is exciting, when one is sure of the facts. There were some good inventions and a few surprises, some of them remarkably similar to other plot devices that Emeric had used on other films, e.g., the final restoration to General Kreipe of his personal property, and the restoration to Conrad Veidt, in *Contraband,* of his musical watch, which plays a tune. And there is the scene in which the general makes a triumphant speech to his captors over his own cleverness in bribing the Cretan boy, Niko, a scene that is remarkably like the scene with the burgomaster and the Quisling in the Dutch town in *One of Our Aircraft Is Missing,* the scene in which Hay Petrie, as the burgomaster, breaks the nerve of Robert Helpmann, the Quisling, by making it seem that he has fooled the German invaders. There were even some scenes reminiscent of *49th Parallel.*

I could see what had happened. *The Battle of the River Plate* was the culprit, not Emeric. We had undertaken to make a superdocumentary, a war story, but essentially a cat-and-mouse story. We had given this an extra dimension by enlisting my Lords of the Admiralty to help us, and by our insistence on making all the movements of ships at sea. But even then it was still a documentary, until we discovered Captain Dove's book. At once, the whole huge, grand, design became alive. Dove's own personality, his sensitive reaction to his captor, and his admiration for Langsdorff in victory and defeat, was the stuff of a real story. Then we had two superlative actors, Bernard Lee and Peter Finch, to bring them alive. The high quality of these and other elements made *The Battle of the River Plate,* known in America as *The Pursuit of the Graf Spee,* one of our biggest commercial successes. And our failure to find or invent similar characters and motives of the same stature as in *The River Plate* makes *Ill Met by Moonlight* one of our greatest failures.

At that time in France things were still pretty chaotic, officialwise, and if you tried to telephone London you were just as likely to get Madagascar, so I wrote to Emeric, suggesting that we meet. The book was half done, and accepted by Hodder and Stoughton, who would publish it in the autumn to synchronize with the Royal Command Performance in October, by which time we would have finished *Ill Met.*

Meanwhile, our company of Archers had their bows strung and their arrows notched, and orders must be given, orders that depended on the script. Emeric replied, saying that he would drive down in his Bentley and would meet me at Les Baux in three days' time, and would I bring my secretary to chronicle our deliberations.

Les Baux is in the wildest, rockiest part of Provence. It is about six hours' drive from Cap Ferrat, and can be approached along the coast or through the mountains. This is some of the most savage and romantic scenery in France; this is the country of the troubadours, of Hannibal and his elephants, of the mighty rivers Rhône and Durance thundering out of the mountains. Naturally, I wanted to see again the gorges that I knew from my boyhood, and we took the mountain road, and it took nine hours instead of six.

It was dusk when we got to the hotel, our necks stiff from craning them back to look upward at those awful cliffs. I fancy that Emeric was pacing up and down the road outside the hotel. It was dinnertime, and Emeric had already chosen his menu. He said, "We'd given you up. They had to give your rooms away. You'll have to share the bridal suite."

We both looked at Judy, who said, "How do you do, Mr. Pressburger. I don't share with anybody."

I said, "Let's have dinner, and then we'll decide what to do."

We checked in. Personally, I thought the bridal suite looked rather nice. The porter brought in both our cases, and dumped them. Judy was about to protest, but I said, "Let them be. There must be a dog kennel somewhere where I can sleep. We'll sort it out after dinner."

Dinner was a rather silent meal. The food was good. The kitchen had four stars, I believe. I ordered quail. Occasionally I caught Judy's eyes, and she went as red as a beetroot. That wicked Emeric ate a hearty dinner. We parted in the baronial hall. He said, "See you at breakfast, nine o'clock."

It was quite a walk to the B.S.* I opened the door. Judy stayed in the corridor. I said, "Now don't tell me that I planned it all along."

She was furious. She said, "I quite believe you did."

I said, "You'll never know."

She swept into the room, and I closed the door. There was a bit of silent unpacking and arranging. She announced, "I shall sleep on the sofa."

I replied, "I shall sleep in the bed."

I undressed, and put on my most virginal set of pajamas—they are white poplin. Judy was rolled up in a blanket. I said, "Good night," and switched off the light.

She didn't answer. An hour or two later I woke up. Somebody was sobbing. I got out of bed and went over to the sofa.

"It's all right, darling," I said. "You can have the bed."

She put her arms around my neck, and I kissed her. She had the bed.

At the breakfast table the next morning Emeric's face was as sober as a judge's. Magyars have no truck with French breakfasts—*croissants et tout ce tra-la-la.* He was eating bacon and eggs.

"Did you sleep well, Michael?"

"Excellently, thanks. Judy's gone for a walk."

He nodded, picked up the final fried egg on the blade of his knife, and slid it down his throat, closing his eyes in order not to miss the final flavor of this rugged *bonne bouche.* How many times, at the Savile Club for breakfast, have I seen the eyes of my fellow breakfast members peering in horror over the top of *The Times,* the *Financial Times,* the *Daily Telegraph,* and even over the *Daily Nudist,* as Emeric sword-swallowed his egg. Breakfast is not one of my meals, and I ordered *oeufs en cocotte.*

"We will work in my sitting room, Michael. Judy has an electric typewriter? I'd better have the hotel electrician check out the fuses. We don't want to blow the main box, like we did at Tours, on *Pimpernel.*"

He stood up.

"Servus."

He bowed solemnly to me, hands at his sides, and I rose and bowed in return. We had been on the same floor of the Carlton Hotel in Cannes as the Japanese delegation who, when parting to their several rooms, bowed to one another, walked down the corridor, came to their own door, turned and bowed again, and disappeared. We felt that it added class to an otherwise

*Bridal suite.

rowdy bazaar. I finished my breakfast, and went in search of Judy. She was in the garden. I said, "Have you had breakfast?"

"I never eat breakfast."

I shook my head. "In the film business, you eat whenever you can, and particularly when someone else pays, in this case J. Arthur Rank. Come on, we're going to work."

We worked for two days, day and night. We ordered and we ate endless meals, and ransacked the cellars for good wine and fiery liqueurs. J. Arthur Rank did us proud, and we repaid him with some rewriting. But the script obstinately refused to come alive for me. My unhappiness over the project was not increased by the news, imparted to Emeric by Earl St. John, that they would expect us to play Dirk Bogarde as Patrick Leigh-Fermor, the hero of the Cretan resistance. In return, they would let us play whom we liked as Captain Stanley Moss. But they were less than enthusiastic about playing the German actor, Curt Jurgens, as General Kreipe, the C-in-C of the fortress of Crete. Why couldn't we play Anton Walbrook, Earl St. John wanted to know?

I threw up my hands. Why?! Because Anton was a Viennese, an artist, an aesthete, who had scored four times for The Archers, who was our friend, and just about the last man in the world to play a professional soldier, a general in the German Wehrmacht. I went on: General Kreipe was not given his command because he was next in line, but because he was a ruthless disciplinarian, and a man without humor who believed that the end always justified the means. He had stamped out all open resistance, he had established a military government that was completely repressive and dictatorial. The actor who played him should be able to create a character larger than life, and as dangerous as a caged tiger. Curt Jurgens, who had made a stir with his performance in *The Devil's General*, would be acceptable to The Archers, and would give Dirk Bogarde a run for his money.

"Jurgens is asking for an enormous fee," grumbled Earl St. John.

"So would you, if you were in his position," I answered. "He'll come down. We're not starting shooting tomorrow. What about this new actor . . . what's his name . . . for the German general . . . Yul . . . Yul . . ."

"Yul Brynner," growled Earl. "Now you really are talking telephone numbers!"

I tried a different tactic.

"Earl, you're a showman. You know what the public wants to see. You think you need big names to compete with Hollywood. Dirk can't carry this picture alone. He'd be at sea . . . a doctor at sea. Give us Dirk, Curt Jurgens or Yul Brynner, and Stewart Granger for Stanley Moss, and we'll give you a picture that will set the world spinning."

Of course, Earl knew very well that I was right, but he also knew that his bread was buttered by John Davis, and that in John's dream of a British film industry there was no room for opposition. The future was beginning to look bleak for the creative artists of the British film industry, who had had a relatively free hand since the war.

So I thought; but not so Emeric. He was first and last a writer, and all that he could see was that we were sitting pretty, with four subjects in a row, all of them our property, and that all of them could be fully financed by the Rank Organisation if we would only agree. We could sign the contract tomorrow. He had done all the thinking that he was prepared to do about these four subjects, and was already planning ahead for the novels that he intended to write. But in this dream of independence, I was the nightmare. I was unpredictable. He knew very well that my art was everything, and that if I were asked to compromise I was perfectly capable of putting my hands in my pockets and walking away. So when I spoke, Imre listened—or pretended to.

We had limited our time at Les Baux to two days. Emeric was going on to see Stapi in his hunting lodge at Thiersee, in the mountains that form the frontier between Bavaria and Austria. Emeric was thinking of building a house there, a chalet, not to hunt but to write. I had to get back to the Voile d'Or and my *Graf Spee* book, and meet Frankie's inquiring gaze. On the morning of the third day we had our last story conference.

I am a feminist. I love women, and I understand women, and I can't believe any story that has no feminine interest in it. Such stories only exist in the minds of writers. Women are in everything—bless 'em! Where were the women in *Ill Met by Moonlight?* You can't tell me that those brave young men, British and Greek, playing tag with death every day and night of their lives, didn't inspire love and hatred, trust and betrayal.

"Michael, that has nothing to do with the main story."

"It has *everything* to do with the main story!" I shouted. "There must be half a dozen love stories that we can find, if we dig deep enough. You're talking from the book. What did Stanley Moss know about the Special Forces in Crete? He was only on the island two weeks. Paddy was there three years!"

"Michael, we are making a film about the kidnapping of General Kreipe— not about the Scarlet Pimpernel."

"Then why don't you write better dialogue for the old bastard? Why don't we have more talks, more conversations, arguments, between him and his captors? Why don't we give him more to do? At present, he's a dead weight. And who the hell are we going to get to play him, anyhow? It will take an actor with real resource to play a part like that. We've got to like him and hate him by turns. He's a man, isn't he, not just a uniform!"

We parted at 11:00 A.M. Emeric had to be at a three-star restaurant at 1:00 P.M. I ordered a "pique-nique" lunch from the hotel and we ate it beside a mountain waterfall. It was quite idyllic.

As we turned off the coast road and on to Cap Ferrat, Judy started to panic. We had been away three days.

"What shall I say?"

"Say? . . . Say it was a wonderful trip."

"But suppose she asks questions?"

"Answer them."

"But how! . . . How?"

"Tell the truth. Always tell the truth. It's so much easier than telling a lie."

At the harbor we picked up Bumba. Frankie was having tea with Willie Maugham beside a blazing fire in the new sitting room. The fireplace had been boarded up for many years. When we liberated it, people came for miles to see it. Frankie said, "Tea, Mikibum? How'd you get on with the old dormouse?"

"The dormouse" was Ralph Richardson's name for Emeric. We'd adopted it, in private.

"The hotel's a bit grim, but they've got a good chef. Emeric made a muck-up about the rooms. I had to sleep on a sofa."

Maugham ("Have a sip, Somerset") was giving Judy the "oh-oh." It was the glance of a surgeon, a novelist, a dramatist, an observer of the human race. But Judy took it calmly as she sipped her tea, standing before the fire. He might be W. Somerset Maugham, the novelist, but he was just a man as far as she was concerned, and men were two a penny. I had only just read *Theatre*, and I congratulated him on it, knowing that he hated to be congratulated, anywhere, and at all times.

Three weeks later we were back in London, and the *Graf Spee* book was handed over to Philip John Attenborough, at Messrs. Hodder and Stoughton, whose little one-shilling, cheap editions of O. Henry—*The Four Million, Cabbages and Kings, The Trimmed Lamp, The Voice of the City*—had been the delight of my life in the 1920s. We summoned all The Archers, and plunged into preproduction meetings. Emeric had had some good new ideas, but not enough of them. Then there was *enosis*. The eastern Mediterranean, and particularly Crete and Cyprus, were full of murders and alarums. The front office advised against going to Greece at all.

"Nonsense, they'll love it," I said. "It's just like Ireland. They're always on active service."

We couldn't have all of our people. Hein had gone to Germany, and Arthur Lawson was working on another film. We settled for Vetchinsky, who had been my art director way back in the 1930s, when I made *The Phantom Light* for Gainsborough Pictures in the Islington Studios. We had Chris and his crew on the camera, of course, and to our horror, J.D. told us that we would have to make the picture in VistaVision. We all roared with laughter: "In black and white?!"

We had already decided, between us, that as the general and his captors were holed up in a cave, or in a village all day, and then marched at night, it would be best to make the film in black and white. But John insisted, because of some agreement with Paramount, and we were stuck with VistaVision, on a picture that called for the utmost mobility. I was getting completely out of tune with the picture; but just then, I met Dirk Bogarde.

He was a charmer, and I fell for it. I have said that I had seen him on stage and screen, and knew what a good actor he was, but I didn't know that he was as subtle as a serpent, and with a will of steel. He had a long-term contract with Rank, and was their number one box-office attraction on the strength of *Doctor in the House* and *Doctor at Sea*. He knew all about me and actors, and he had absolutely no intention of acting in my film. He would smile (he had a charming smile), he would dress up (fancy-dress costume), he had a good figure (light and boyish), and he would speak the lines—or, rather, he would throw them away—with such careful art that camera and microphone would have to track in close to see and hear what he was saying and doing.

I wanted a flamboyant young murderer, lover, bandit—a tough, Greek-speaking leader of men, and instead I got a picture-postcard hero in fancy dress. He would listen with attention to me while I told him what I wanted, and then he would give me about a quarter of it. All the other actors took their tone from him, except for the Cretans, who were great! But alas, they were not my Cretans. The Greek government had decided that to film *Ill Met by Moonlight* in Crete would be a provocative act, and wouldn't give us the permits necessary to bring in a film unit, armed to the teeth.

"But it won't be the same picture at all if I don't make it on Crete!" I said to Emeric. He shook his head.

"I'm sorry, Michael, but I don't think it will make the slightest bit of difference, if you make the picture in the south of France, where you know all the locations, or in Corsica."

"Corsica?!" I snorted. "Corsica is nothing like Crete. Corsica is all maquis. I'd love to shoot a picture in Corsica, but not *Ill Met by Moonlight!*"

The front office issued an ultimatum: make the picture wherever you like, but not in Crete or Cyprus, or cancel the production. They had me with my pants down. I made the film in the Alpes Maritimes, in the mountain country between Savoy and the River Var, where Italy and France share a common frontier that comes up from the sea and then mounts into the sky of Haute Savoie. It's great country and there are no houses, only military barracks and military roads, for the frontier between France and Italy has been altered three times. But the main reason why this huge, beautiful area had not been opened up and exploited with developments and roads, and even towns, is because it was the hunting grounds of the kings of Italy and of Savoy, and it was alive with marmots, chamois, hawks, and wild sheep, and it had been like that for eighty years.

Martin Scorsese has a pretty complete collection of movies, on film, on tape, and now on laserdisc too, and he has most of The Archers' films. I borrowed a copy of *Ill Met by Moonlight* the other day and settled down in his chair to watch it on his private screen. He was away, shooting a video in Milan. I had literally forgotten that the film was in black and white, and when these images came on the screen it was the first shock, but not the last. I was surprised by how bad the film was. It wasn't entertainment, it was like a Ministry of Information documentary film title: "The True Story of the Kidnapping of the German General Kreipe, on the Island of Crete, 1944."

The Cretan atmosphere was perfect, the use of Greek dialogue resourceful, the music of Mikis Theodorakis stirring and patriotic, the acting by all and sundry B-minus, the camerawork a mistake. I should have shot the film in color. By the time the film reached the screens in 1957 it looked like a historical document. Everyone was obviously having a good time. Nobody was cultivating what my friend Robert De Niro describes as "an attitude." The script was underwritten and weak on action, the gags were unoriginal, and the surprises not surprising.

The final two reels of what was, after all, supposed to be a chase film were particularly weak. The direction concentrated so much on creating a Greek atmosphere that the director had no time, or invention, for anything else. The performances of the principals were atrocious. Marius Goring as General Kreipe wouldn't have scared a rabbit; David Oxley as Captain Stanley Moss *was* the rabbit; while as for Dirk Bogarde's performance as Major Patrick Leigh-Fermor, Philidem to the Cretans, it's a wonder that Paddy didn't sue both Dirk and me. Dirk was determined to throw the part away and go under everything, and he succeeded. It wasn't that he couldn't have played it for blood and guts if he'd wanted to. He didn't want to.

It was a sad end to the Company of Archers, and a triumph for the chair polishers, of whom Emeric was now one. Our glorious past, our courage, our independence, our willingness to gamble high stakes, our outspoken determination never to make program films, never to make a film just for the money—these principles had sustained us and our little band throughout the war and the austerity years that followed. We were not alone: great filmmakers like Launder and Gilliat, David Lean, Ronald Neame, and writers like Graham Greene were working beside us, and we all looked to John Davis for a lead, as in the past we had looked to Arthur Rank. It was a fateful moment. John was for war with Hollywood. If they wouldn't show our films, we wouldn't show theirs. He had six hundred Odeon cinemas to fill, more being built abroad, a distribution organization that covered the whole world, and

Pinewood Studios and its contractees to keep busy. It's no wonder that he plumped for quantity, not quality.

But no one can win against Hollywood. Within two years John Davis had his back to the wall. Within five years he was only saved by Xerox. The relentless pressure continued. Television, radio, and all other means of exhibition, known or unknown, did their work, and in ten years the Man with the Gong was only a shadow of his former self. The great British film business was over, and its first victims had been The Archers, who had done so much to create it. Emeric might say, and even think, that the end justified the means, but life is short and art is long. I was bored, and sick at heart.

The main shooting of *Ill Met by Moonlight* was over, and I was picking up a few odd close-ups on the lot at Pinewood. Ahead of me, and in the immediate future, were *Cassia*, and *The Miracle in St. Anthony's Lane*. It was autumn, and the tenth Royal Command Performance was in the offing. The extra shots in Corsica that I had needed to complete *Ill Met* had sent us into the contingency, but my credit was still high. John Davis and James Archibald approached me on the set. They were both smiling, as if they had good news.

"Micky," said John, "James and I have been talking, and we want you to make *Cassia*."

"What stars?" I asked. "It's a picture that needs big names. It moves about all over Europe. It doesn't stay in one spot long enough to develop characters, except the two principals. Whom would you want to play?"

They exchanged glances. John said, "We'd expect you to play people who are on our contract list."

I said, "You can take your contract list and stick it up!"

James Archibald's face changed and he looked at John, who had turned white.

"Come on," he said to Archibald, and they went off to the offices.

And that was the end of The Archers.

And all that, as I write here in New York in 1988, was thirty-two years ago, and my London agent has been telling me by telephone this morning that four of The Archers films have been shown on television during the last ten days and *Peeping Tom* is going to be shown on the coming Saturday. *Peeping Tom*, the film that should never have been made, the film that should have been flushed down the toilet, the film that was never seen for twenty years because its distributor was so scared, scared that he wouldn't get an OBE or a knighthood, scared of distributing what they call now "Michael Powell's best film"—well—all art is one, man, one.

You have only to add the short piece that I have written about the death of Emeric Pressburger, which is partly manipulated, and you would have a complete book.

I hope that I shall be spared to write one or two extra chapters, to go in here before the last episode of Emeric's death. One of the chapters could be called "Pamela," another one "Marty," and the third one would be "Thelma." We shall see.*

The important thing to get down for other filmmakers, and other artists, is the story of The Archers. I may have overemphasised this, and it will have to be watched in the final cutting, but I feel very deeply that we have to give the facts at some length to other writers, producers, and directors, so that they can meditate on them, and say how lucky we were that we never went to work in Hollywood. It would be ungrateful, and untrue, to say that, but I want others to find a moral in my book, if there is one. I would like to write some extra chapters, and I shall start work on them now. But they are not necessary to make a complete book. I hope that you understand that, my darling Thelma, my lovely wife. So far as I remember, the piece I dictated will round off the book very well. If I never complete the other chapters it doesn't matter, as long as we have the death of Emeric at the end of the book, and a footnote of the actual time and place where he did die and where he's buried. If I am dead too by then, then you can add my date to Emeric's.

Oh, thank goodness that's done! I was terrified that I wouldn't finish the story of The Archers before I kicked the bucket. Now, I can go on and live forever, or die tomorrow. And Thelma, darling, you can tell the publishers that the book is complete.

Oh, and there is one thing—when I talk about Peeping Tom, *and quote the awful things the critics said, I would like to do that much more in depth than length. I'd like to quote more of what they said, the more shocking the better, one on top of the other. When I'm left alone I make a film that nobody wants to see and then, thirty years later, everybody has either seen it or wants to see it.*

The Archers have dominated the first half of the second volume, and La Voile d'Or was important when my father died. Now we switch from historical to personal. I mean I am going to use three or perhaps four people to cover the next three decades, and the death of Imre, and the presumed death of myself. This is a film director talking, not an autobiographer. That's why it's different. If carefully edited, by loving hands, I don't see why it shouldn't work. The Voile d'Or bulked big in the lives of me and my family, but I only made one film from there, Ill Met by Moonlight. *So here we go.*

Every artist has a witch, disembodied or very much bodied. Mine was Pamela Brown. For Emeric she was the ugliest woman in the world. For me she was sensual beauty incarnate. That says a lot about me. She was a cripple. The arthritis that had killed her father at an early age struck her down at the

---

*Michael literally kept himself alive until he could reach the end of the first draft of this book. While transcribing the cassette tapes he dictated, I would occasionally find notes from him like this one, advising me on how to complete the book should he not live to finish it.

beginning of her career. The demon sprang upon her and twisted her legs, her toes, and her fingers. For the rest of her short life she had only the two toes on her right foot to walk on, and her fingers were twisted like a mandrake root. She had been tall and strong and tireless until the teeth of the demon met in her leg and twisted her knee, so that she always dragged that leg. She fought back. She suffered agonies, but she fought back. At the height of her career, when *The Lady's Not for Burning* was in its second year on Broadway in New York, every performance was a struggle with death and disaster. John Gielgud was, perhaps, the fastest speaker on the English stage. He never missed a cue, he never lost a line, he never slowed up for a second. Only her dresser could have told how thin the line was between triumph and physical collapse. In order to be able to give eight performances a week, as well as benefits, she took cortisone and gave herself diabetes. Her life as an actress depended upon a strict timetable and regular meals. Just imagine what that meant on Broadway, and in the radio and television studios, and on tour!

She was part of my life, and my love, and we snatched our meetings from time: sometimes at night, sometimes a day, sometimes only a few minutes in the year at the door of an apartment in the Algonquin, sometimes a whole blessed evening in some incredible apartment rented for me by a Hollywood executive, with a sitting room full of flowers and champagne, and a grand piano so that the composers of the music for *Song of Norway* could play me their interpretation of Grieg.

We made four films together, and would have made two more if we hadn't been surrounded by bloody enemies, fangs of serpents spitting withering poison. The ones we got away with were *Never Turn Your Back On a Friend, Tales of Hoffmann, I Know Where I'm Going!, One of Our Aircraft Is Missing.* The parts that she was intended to play were the redheaded mother in *Peeping Tom* (played by Maxine Audley in the film) and the drunken wife in Graham Greene's filmscript of *The Living Room.*

"We never knew about this!" write the fans.

Well, you don't know everything, do you?

The private life of an actress is sometimes easier to conceal than other women's, because it is so public. You don't believe me? I assure you it is so. Limelight has this curious effect of illuminating the actor or actress and leaving the rest in deep shadow. I include actors out of politeness, for, after all, who cares about the private life of an actor? He lives in public, and on the whole that is all he has to give, if he is a real actor like John, or Alec, or Connie, or Leslie, or Marius, or Anton—collect your prizes from the bran tub at the door as you go out. Oh, I forgot Paul*—anyone who saw him in *Venice*

*John Gielgud, Alec Guinness, Conrad Veidt, Leslie Banks, Marius Goring, Anton Walbrook, Paul Scofield.

Preserv'd, or the Charles Morgan plays, all three of them with Pamela, will know whom I mean. I saw him the other day, at the memorial service for Bobby Helpmann at St. Paul's in the Garden, the actors' church in whose porch Eliza Doolittle had been created by GBS. His friends and his fans gave Bobby a good sendoff, and while we waited—for there were still several people who wished to be the last to arrive—I noticed a tall and beautiful fellow mourner seated at some distance away. His hair and his beard were the color of silver. He was slender and tall, and suddenly he rose and strode across the flags of the courtyard where I was sitting, shook hands, and whispered earnestly in my ear. It was Paul, though I only recognized him when he turned to go back to his seat on the bench. He was playing King Lear for the second time, and with his white hair and beard and dark suit he looked like an archangel who had descended into Covent Garden to snatch the soul of Bobby away from the burning coals, which he would have undoubtedly preferred.

Paul and I never met without thinking of, and talking of, Pamela. They were both great gigglers. Proneness to giggle in the theatre is frowned upon by producers and one's fellow actors but it is, to me, an endearing fault, when combined with genius.

I have told in a previous volume how Pamela and I met, and how we became aware of each other, in those long, black nights on the island of Mull, orchestrated with the crash of the hungry waves as they broke over the harbor wall and the suck of the surge as it swept back into the Atlantic, only to return again, and again, and again, until it seemed that the little fisherman's cottage, built on the very edge of the tide line, would dissolve and break up like a house of cards. I can see the feeble light of my torch as I grope my way along the narrow path back to the house and the sleeping unit, and I can conjure up in a moment the image of Pamela in the prow of Iain's big, open cattle boat, as we spin around the boils and eddies of Corryvreckan. *IKWIG* was our matchmaker and the Western Isles our godmother. We parted, but we knew that we would meet again.

Years slipped by. *IKWIG* was in 1945. *Hoffmann* in 1950. Pamela went to New York with *The Lady's Not for Burning.* She had mortgaged her body to pay for her success, to pay for her art. She was in great demand. Critics had remembered her earlier performances in *The Importance of Being Earnest* and *The Gioconda Smile.* She rode the clouds in triumph, and nobody knew how near she was to collapse and death. At last, she returned to England. We each knew that the other was there, but we made no sign. Finally, a message came: "I want to see you." I went.

Rupert Hart-Davis had his publishing house at 36 Soho Square, and he sublet the third floor to Pamela and her constant visitors, who used to steal the new books stacked on the stairway as regularly as Rupert put them there.

He was not only a publisher, he was a writer, an editor, a biographer, a collector, and he is now, at the time of writing, chairman of the London Library. He carried out these various duties and professions with distinction, and a sense of humor.

The house in Soho Square was part of a spec builder's development in the eighteenth century, and was pretty shaky. Pamela had a large sitting room, and a fireplace with a real coal fire, and two big windows looking on the square. You can hardly ask for anything better than that. A door led into the bedroom, which contained an enormous bed. By groping your way aft you came to the bathroom and kitchen and a room at the back, which was usually known as "Judy's room" although Judith Furse no longer occupied it. It was full of junk.

In the sitting room there was a huge divan. It must have been nine feet long and three feet wide, and you never knew, when you called, whom you would find asleep on it. It might be Ken Tynan, it might be Michael Warre, it might be Bobby Helpmann, it might be Peter Shaffer.

I have said somewhere before that Pamela and I loved, but had not made love. She disputed this, and I couldn't remember. It didn't matter, anyway. She and Peter Copley had walked out of their marriage and Peter had married again, successfully. Pamela naturally took up with the first person who offered his service, the agent who jealously guarded her during the making of *The Tales of Hoffmann*. During the roaring years of Christopher Fry this was all very well, and Christopher was already writing his next play for her—I forget what it was called. It was about one of those Plantagenet kings and his queen, and I think Thomas à Becket came into it. It took Christopher ten years, and by that time Anouilh had written *Becket* and had rather cornered the market on medieval subjects, and Queen What's-her-name was no longer considered bankable by the Tennents.

Pamela kept working, pepped up by drugs. She did quite a lot of interesting parts for *Hallmark Hall of Fame*, and for the BBC, and sound recordings for Caedmon, which are still in demand. But 36 Soho Square was not as glamorous as the Great White Way, and Pamela's protector took up with another lady and told Pamela that he was impotent, a favorite device of Restoration comedies, which is probably where he got it and which Pamela should have known. But she believed him and, living as she did, between one hypodermic syringe and another, she was naturally upset to learn that this other lady was about to have a baby. The news sent her into hysterics.

Her mother, who had been an actress in her youth and was alive and well and living in Kensington, was not the most ideal of confidantes. Her sister, Baba, and her brother-in-law were working for the United Nations in New York. Somehow she got a message to me. Number 36 was dark when I arrived, and she threw the keys down from the window. The apartment was dark, too, and Pamela was pacing up and down. She was in what is known as a state. Dobs the Pekingese was in a state too, but accepted my smell. In a shaking voice Pamela told her story. There was obviously only one thing to be done. I said, "Where does that door go to?"

She said, "To the bedroom."

I said, "Come on."

We made love all night. She was a wonderful lover. Her skin was a delicate shell pink, and the hair on her body was as red as the hair on her head. Her great eyes glowed in the darkness like a cat's. They were so large that she claimed that she could always see almost directly behind her, and I think she could, as wild animals do. We could always make love whenever we wanted to, and we always wanted to. We were lovers until the day she died.

She said, "Leave me. I'm a wreck. I can never go to Scotland with you again. I can never swim in the South Pacific, and see the rollers breaking on the coral reef. I shall never see Papua and New Guinea and the Solomon Islands. I shall never see Sydney harbor, shining in the sun. I shall never drive with you in the open Bentley across Spain, across Italy, across Germany. I shall never camp with you in your great caravan Land Rover, parked among the trees. I shall never go to Salzburg with you. I shall never go to Oberammergau, I shall never hear The Ring. I shall never drive with you through New England in the fall, I shall never drive with you to Mystic Seaport, and clamber about those wonderful old ships looming in the sea fog. I'll never go with you to the back of beyond, hunting and fishing, and holding Johnnie in my arms. I shall never cross the Col de la Croix Haute when the snow is still on the ground and you can hear the marmots whistling all around. I shall never cross the Hudson and drive through the Palisades Park. I shall never sail in a stately stateroom to New York on the Queen Elizabeth and the QE2. I shall never fly around the world."

And I said, "All this you shall do, and more."

=

When I told John Davis what to do with Cassia, Emeric, that patient fisherman, was seated on the bank, his lunch box beside him, his hook baited with The Miracle in St. Anthony's Lane, and John, seeing it as an opportunity to divide The Archers and to show me how to make moving pictures, took the bait. The much-optioned Miracle became Miracle in Soho. John Gregson was assigned to play the leader of the work gang, and a television director was assigned to direct the film. Emeric was to write and produce, and of course he had Chris and Arthur and George and Syd. The Royal Performance of The Battle of the River Plate, on October 30, 1956, had been a huge success, and our Archers were tall in the saddle. I said a mental prayer for them and went to Spain, to Madrid. I was the guest of Antonio, who, starting as an errand boy in the streets of Málaga, was now the most famous flamenco dancer in Europe and had his own ballet company in Madrid. He had seen *The Red Shoes*—*Zapatillas Rojas*—and was determined that we should make a film together. I was going to Madrid to discuss it.

On *Mare Nostrum* I had been in Valencia and Barcelona, but these were Mediterranean seaports, not the real Spain, although I did learn the difference between a Spaniard and a Catalan. I knew about Catalans from *The Count of Monte Cristo,* and from Pablo Picasso and his friends Miró and Dalí, but I had only once spent some time in Spain and met the people, and that was thanks to Ernest Hemingway and *The Sun Also Rises,* bowdlerized as *Fiesta.* It was in 1925 on the studio lot at Nice, on the set for *The Magician,* that Frank Scully put a copy of Hemingway's novel in my hands and said, "At last, we have a real writer, and he's American!"

I started reading in the middle of all that lath and plaster, and was at once conquered. Here were people talking as I had heard them talk, and acting as I had seen them act. There wasn't a word to spare, and there wasn't a word wasted. Of course, this man was writing about things and people that I knew, but that wasn't why a shudder of ecstasy passed down my spine and into my balls. I had thought I knew a lot about English; I had thought I knew a lot about style; but this man wrote about what he knew without introduction and explanation, and that was new in the 1920s: "Write it the way it was!"

The whole postwar literary world crumbled into dust on hearing this simple piece of advice: the way it was. Here was the answer, and plainly stated, at last. We had orders, we had a goal. That was in 1925. Then it was the Civil War, and the International Brigade, and Franco, and Hitler's war, and the Marshall Plan, and one day I said to Frankie, "Let's go to Spain. We've never been there. Let's find Hemingway's trout stream. They say that the frontier with France is closed, but I expect that we can bribe our way in. If not, we'll go around. I want to see the village where Hemingway and Mike stayed, and kidded each other about irony and pity. We'll drive down to Saint-Jean-Pieds-de-Port and scout the Pyrenees, and when we're in Spain we'll drive down to Pamplona, where they have the running of the bulls, and we'll see them running through the streets and tossing the boys, just like they did in the book."

We went, and were conquered. Here was an austere, masculine country where even the beggars were hidalgos. Maurice Hewlett had written, in *The Spanish Jade,* "Spain is the land of things as they are."

Chapman Mortimer in his book *Here in Spain* writes that you cannot talk for long with a Spaniard without having him make a pronouncement prefaced by the words "*Aquí en España,*" here in Spain. No wonder that Hemingway, with his love for Spain, and with the harsh Castilian in his ears and on his tongue, wrote, "Write it the way it was," and so was able to create a new literary language in *For Whom the Bell Tolls*, a language like Castilian, harsh and beautiful and close to Shakespeare's English.

"You are making my head ache," said Frankie. "Let's go."

So we went, and were conquered at the first café we visited in Pamplona, when the waiter brought us drinks we had not ordered and, when I protested, explained that they had been bought for us by the gentleman across the room, who bowed with a welcoming gesture and went out the door before he could be thanked, after which it was a bit of a shock for Frankie to be lectured by a priest for wearing very short shorts in the cathedral cloisters. Our time was limited during that memorable holiday, but now I was returning, and by invitation, to Madrid, which for me meant the Prado, Goya, Zurbarán, and Luis Buñuel.

Antonio was at the height of his career. He was the darling of Spain. He eclipsed even the bullfighters. When he entered a restaurant with his entourage the men rose, clapping their hands, and the women stood on chairs. Madrid meant the Ritz, but there was one new hotel, and it was there that Antonio took me. I went down to the bar and was surrounded in an instant. I was astonished at the amount of whiskey that everybody was drinking before dinner. Dinner wasn't until eleven or twelve at night. With the help of the whiskey we all talked English, French, and Spanish. Everybody wanted to see, and meet, the director of *Zapatillas Rojas*.

We all piled into cars and drove to Antonio's rehearsal room, where his entire company was drawn up on a stage, clapping hands, advancing and retreating, their bony figures snapping like castanets. There was one very pretty, plump young girl, but I was more interested to meet Rosario, Antonio's longtime partner. I liked the look of her—tall, bony, magnificent eyes and nose.

Then back to the cars, and to the restaurant for dinner. I was introduced to Luis Escobar, one of the most popular men in Madrid, a dramatist who would collaborate with me on the screenplay. Presiding at the dinner was Cesáreo González, the head of Suevia Films, and Jaime Prades, his chief of production, who was to work with us and later on joined Samuel Bronson to make *El Cid* with Charlton Heston. Cesáreo was a Gallego from Santiago in the north of Spain where they are, reputedly, tough customers. Prades was sympathetic. He aped the English in his clothes and his trim little mustache, good clothes, and good manners. Antonio was everywhere at once, whispering and laughing and by four o'clock in the morning I had agreed to do a Spanish film in Technicolor, with two new ballets: *El Amor Brujo*, with music by De Falla, and *Los Amantes de Teruel*.

The De Falla piece had been Massine's idea when he heard I was going to

368 · MICHAEL POWELL

Spain. It's a good piece of theatre, about forty minutes, a wild, eerie piece about a Gypsy girl who has two lovers. They fight, and one of them is killed by the other, and he returns to haunt them.

"There are caves, Michael, near Granada, where the Gypsies live. It would be wonderful to do the ballet in the caves."

Both Diaghilev and Massine adored Spain, and it was while they were on tour there that Massine created one of his best ballets, *Le Tricorne*, music also composed by De Falla. The play *The Lovers of Teruel* is a Spanish classic, and there's an English translation that I had read in Zwemmer's bookshop. The story is set in the wars that ended with the final expulsion of the Moors from Spain. It was a savage and romantic time. In many families of Spain there is as much Arab blood as Castilian. The town of Teruel is an austere little town. It stands on a rock in the middle of the plain not far from Madrid. The play is a tragedy, and the stage is littered with corpses. Antonio was for rushing off to the public library at once, but was persuaded to wait for the morning.

I liked Antonio. He came from the gutter and had the soul of an artist. He was fiercely honest and wildly generous. He had fine eyes, but no particular good looks. He was just right, and when he danced he had what the Spaniards call *duende*. The great bullfighters have it too.

The next day we went into committee, chaired by Jaime Prades. It was agreed that there would be two versions, English and Spanish. My secretary, Judy, Luis Escobar, and I would write the story and script. For this purpose we would meet at La Toja, near Santiago in the north of Spain, where González was a power in the land. He had luxury hotels with luxury suites, and luxury yachts with luxury crews, which seemed to correspond to what you would find in the Hamptons on Long Island, or Deauville, or Torquay, or Saint-Tropez, or you name it. All expenses in Spain would be carried by Suevia Films. All expenses in England, including Technicolor and the technical crews, and laboratory and editing expenses, would be paid for by an English distributor, which in this case turned out to be British Lion at Shepperton Studios. Shooting would start in the winter of 1958 and last approximately eight weeks. I would bring an English technical crew to work with the Spanish crew, and the principal photography would be in the masterful hands of Georges Perinal, who had photographed *The Thief of Bagdad* and *The Life and Death of Colonel Blimp*. They would agree to Sir Thomas Beecham conducting the ballets.

"But there must be *zapateado*!" interjected Antonio. "Everyone will expect it," he explained to me. "It is my signature."

He stood up and demonstrated all around the room, with amazing footwork and cracking his fingers like steel pistons.

"I must have *zapateado*! And no English conductor, not even Sir Beecham, can conduct *zapateado*. It's a personal thing, you understand, Don Miguel?"

Zapateado is best described as an Andalusian clog dance. It is very noisy, and incredibly fast, and improvised. I reassured him—there would be as much *zapateado* as the Spanish aficionados could possibly want, and he would set the tempo and Sir Thomas would follow him. The De Falla rights to *Amor Brujo* were obtainable, if not exactly free, and Antonio would suggest the composer for *Los Amantes* when he had read the play.

The meeting broke up with everyone well pleased with one another. Finally I stipulated that, as my work with Escobar would take place during the summer holiday months, I would bring my family, Frankie and the two boys, to La Toja, and I was assured that one of the bungalows would be assigned to us. I figured that it would be easier to get things like that agreed to now rather than later, and events proved me right. The secretaries had taken notes of everything, and Prades went off with them to draw up a draft contract. Antonio took me to one side.

"Michael, what about Moira Shearer?"

I had been expecting this, so I said, "What about her?"

"Michael, you know very well what I mean. Can we get her?"

"I don't know. We can try."

"Please, Michael, do try. I would give anything to dance with Moira Shearer. I would even put on the Red Shoes, myself." He laughed.

I said, "I don't know. She's beginning to talk about acting. Maybe she is giving up dancing."

Antonio was shocked.

"Michael, with those looks and those legs, how could she think of such a thing?"

"Well, she signed with Korda, you know, and he was going to produce a film version of *The Sleeping Beauty* with decor and costumes by Oliver Messel. And now Korda's dead and the film will never be made, and Messel is in despair and has retired to the Caribbean, and I guess that this has had an effect on Moira's new dream of becoming an actress. Did you see Korda's *The Man Who Loved Redheads?*"

Antonio snapped those bony fingers. He was disgusted. "Such a talent, such looks, such hair, such legs! Michael, I want to dance with Miss Shearer. You must arrange it, please!"

I thought of this conversation as I returned to London. I had already failed to get Moira for my projected film version of *The Tempest*, not to play Miranda, of course, but Ariel. Moira has a strong vein of fantasy, a love of the grotesque. Her parts should be the Green Woman in *Peer Gynt*, Goneril in *King Lear*, Lady Macbeth, the Water Sprite in *Undine*, but she still yearned after the big, full-length ballet roles, and the *Sleeping Beauty* part offered her by Korda was a compromise between acting and dancing. In a later version of *The Tempest* that I tried to get airborne, it was James Mason who was to play Prospero and Mia Farrow to play Ariel. At this time John Gielgud was to play Prospero. He hadn't done much important film work at this time, and was delighted by my offer.

"Silly girl! Silly girl!" he said, when Moira turned it down.

But the "silly girl" didn't have her red hair for nothing. The death of Korda and the collapse of his projected ballet film had thrown Moira very much on her own resources, and with the support of her husband, Ludovic Kennedy, a fellow Scot, she had now set her heart on an acting career. It wouldn't have fitted in with her plans at all to leave England at this juncture and go to Spain to make another ballet film. Knowing all this, I hadn't discouraged Antonio from his dream of red hair and Red Shoes, but I hadn't encouraged him either. An independent producer, writer, and director has to keep his flanks covered, and a watchful eye at all times.

Back in London from Madrid I went to see my friends at British Lion, who roared encouragement, so I decided to go ahead. I had decided on a story that would be half love story and half travelogue, and that would involve Antonio and his troupe with a honeymoon couple touring Spain, the young wife a ballet dancer who has given up her career in exchange for a jealous husband. It was to be called *Luna de Miel—Honeymoon.* It was to be a comedy.

For the next year or so I was like Gaul divided into three parts: our London home at 8 Melbury Road, the Voile d'Or at Saint-Jean-Cap-Ferrat, and c/o Suevia Films, Madrid. I wrote an analysis of our intentions, which was agreed to by both sides so that the money could flow. Meanwhile I zigzagged about all over Spain in the open Bentley, looking for locations. Sometimes Pamela flew out and joined me, and at Teruel itself we had an adventure.

I never had an ignition key for the Bentley. Instead, there was a chromium-plated handle that started the engine. Have I mentioned that she was a three-and-a-half liter, black with red interior? She had a black hood that was put up, perhaps, six times in her total career. She had side curtains and all sorts of other extravagances, but we never used them. If the weather was bad we just went a little faster, that's all. She had two enormous Lucas headlights and a large manipulable spotlight. She also had two spotlights on her front bumpers. She had more chrome than a dog has fleas. Her chassis was steel, and she weighed a ton.

Judy had an old Bentley, too—not an open Bentley—with a coach body. It was four and a quarter, not three and a half like mine. She was a good driver, but always running out of gas—petrol, not small talk. When the two Bentleys were together we never looked at each other's automobile. There is decorum in such matters.

Pamela and I arrived at Teruel late one evening, and decided to stay the night. We coasted around, and picked a hotel directly on the street. There was no courtyard and no garage, and I parked the Bentley in the street in front of the front door. There was a night porter. About two in the morning I woke up; I knew that something had happened, but couldn't say exactly what. Pamela was in a deep sleep. Suddenly something clicked, and I got out of bed, went to the window and out on the balcony, and looked down into the street. The Bentley was gone.

At first I couldn't believe it. In Franco's Spain, an English sports car should be as safe as houses. It wouldn't get more than twenty miles without being stopped. I thought maybe I'm wrong, maybe the bedroom window looks out into the other street. But I was kidding myself. I knew that the Bentley was gone; stolen—or, sudden wild thought, the porter had telephoned a garage to take the car in. I scrambled into a shirt and trousers, and ran downstairs. The porter was asleep. I woke him.

"Mi automobile! Dónde está?!"

He came with me. The street was empty.

"Teléfono! Teléfono pronto! Teléfono Guardia!"

If you have ever tried to do anything quickly in Spain, particularly in the middle of the night, you'll know how long that took. The police arrived, took notes, took my name, took the number of the car, and said, "By morning, we'll know where they are. They won't go far."

But I knew better. They had stolen the car in the middle of the night, and they had six hours of darkness to get to the coast and run the Bentley into a lock-up garage. In a big city we would never find them. The telephone rang again. The Guardia listened.

"Señor, they have found your car. They have not got far. Two local boys. I know them well, señor. They are bad, reckless boys. I know the mother of one. They are in a village only twenty miles from here. We will call for you in the morning, so that you can identify your car."

"And the boys?"

"Señor, the police has one of them."

"And the other?"

"Señor, es muerto."

The village of Fuentes lined the banks of the shallow river that scrambled through the houses. The car stood in the river, with the dead man at the wheel. There was a babble of voices. The mayor told his story to me and the policeman. The road approaches the village from the east. Then, on the very edge of the bank of the river, the road makes a sharp turn. The thieves were obviously planning to run the gauntlet of the village, and be through it and out of it before anybody could see them or report them. But the Bentley weighed a ton, or a ton and a half, and they were going full speed, probably ninety miles an hour. The car took off. The bank here was about four feet high. The Bentley was, literally, airborne for a second, turned in the air, crashed down into the riverbed upside down, and broke the driver's neck. His companion, stunned, bewildered, half-drowned, badly bruised, was found wandering about concussed, and captured by the first people on the spot.

The villagers were wonderful. They got a gang of volunteers and somehow managed to turn the car right side up as she stood in the shallow stream. They towed her to the ford, and got a truck to tow her up to the road. It wasn't the ruin of her looks that worried me, it was what the damage must have been to the chassis. The wonder was that she could be towed at all. The Guardia shook his head as he took copious notes from everybody, standing by the silent figure at the wheel of the Bentley.

"Manuel was always a wild boy. There was good in him. I knew him well."

We returned to Madrid in less than triumph. I decided to include the incident in the screenplay of *Honeymoon*. The days rushed by, and soon it was July, and time for our rendezvous at La Toja. Judy went ahead to prepare things. Frankie and the two boys came from Cap Ferrat, Escobar and his friends came up from Madrid, and I came down from London to Paris with Bill Paton, in the small, yellow Land-Rover which had once been Emeric's and in which he and a gang of football fans that included the De Grunewald brothers and George Mikes used to go every Saturday to support their favorite football club, Arsenal.

It was my first experience with Land-Rovers, and I became a convert. There is something about Land-Rovers large and small. In all my fifty years of driving, I have really only had three cars: the Auburn Six, the Bentley three-and-a-half liter, and the long-wheelbase Land-Rover. At one time there were five different automobiles parked in Melbury Road outside our house. I remember them with affection: the Citroën Safari, the Mini Moke, the yellow Land-Rover, the green Land-Rover, the red Land-Rover, and then my father's wonderful old black Citroën *quinze chevaux*—oh, and the little green sports car, an MGB, which I bought Frankie and which she almost immediately smashed up. I loved them all, and I remember them all as clearly as I remember my ponies, Old Barney and Fubsy, and my brother's roan pony, Mr. Bun, and the Welsh cob, Umslopogaas, whom my mother and father used to drive in our smart, yellow trap.

I had decided to turn my pilgrimage from Paris to Vigo to La Toja into a pilgrimage devoted not to religion but to art. My two objectives were the cave of Lascaux in France and the caves of Altamira in Spain. Each one was a worthy objective in itself, but they were far apart, and off the beaten track.

My idea was to plan an itinerary that would include both sites, in the hope that one series of cave paintings might be found to illuminate the others.

Of course, all students of paleolithic art and cave paintings and all that jazz had made these comparisons already, but I doubted whether they had made them on the same day, or at least on two consecutive days. I planned to drive down from Paris to the Limousin, accompanied by Bill and Sweep,* both good traveling companions. The next day, we would leave Lascaux, follow the beautiful Vézère down to Hendaye at the frontier, and drive along the north coast of Spain to Santander, where the caves of Altamira are only a few miles inland, then on by Santiago de Compostela, to Vigo and La Toja, while thousands cheered and Sweep snored.

A great deal has been written, and pictured, about the cave of Lascaux, but this is one thing you have to see for yourself. You squeeze your way into the cave, thrilled and excited, and you come out hours later, bewildered and humbled. What is art, if it is not this? And why has it been hidden here for maybe twenty thousand years, until the great war to end wars (and which nearly succeeded in ending art) is over and won, and the world is licking its wounds? Why have these wonderful works of art been revealed, and submitted to the "oooh"s and "aaah"s and "baaah"s of this generation of tourists, to the explosion of flashbulbs, to the heat of incandescent bulbs? Already they were closing the caves and limiting the number of visitors, whose gasps of admiration were bringing down chunks of rock decorated with paintings that were, alas, only too mortal.

I am quoting from my diary in July 1957, and you are reading this almost forty years later. Are the cave paintings of Lascaux still there, as the artist intended? Or are they carefully detached, and exhibited in glass cases by Paul Getty? I don't know. I possess the cave paintings of Lascaux in my eyes, in my head, in my body, in my brain, in my genitals. Go and see them yourself. Write it the way it was. All art is one.

Sweep speaking: "The old man does go on, and on, doesn't he? And all this stuff about art! Sleeping and eating are the only two things that matter—sleeping well, and eating good. So long as I have my lunch break, and my Bonio at five o'clock P.M., and a few bikkies to take to bed with me, I have nothing to complain about. I am a good traveler. All black spaniels are. We just curl up and go to sleep, and thank Sirius (Sirius is the Dog Star, editor) that they don't know that I understand every word that they say. Not that

*Sweep was the Powell family dog, a cocker spaniel whose coat was as black as a chimney sweep.

Bill and Mr. Powell talk much. Their usual conversation is by grunts, although Bill can be quite talkative, when he's on his own.

"Do I realize that, if I want to return to England I will have to go into quarantine for six months? Of course I do! That's the law. We don't want all these French poodles mincing into England, do we? I gather that the plan is this: we are on the way to a place called Spain, where the family (Mrs. Powell, Kevin, and my Bumba) will join us. Judy is also to join us. I shall be with Bumba, so that's all right. At the end of the film, we all go to Saint-Jean, where I shall end my days as concièrge of the Voile d'Or (that's French). Bumba says they put a lot of garlic in the food. He likes it, but I'm not too keen on it, myself. You can't have everything—or can you? I've never lived in a hotel. Bumba says there are seventeen little beds, for little dogs to take a nap on, until Marcelle discovers you. Marcelle is the *femme de chambre*. Bumba says that she likes her lunch at eleven, and she demands *un plat copieux*, followed by *fromage et fruits*. I think I had better cultivate this woman."

There is no mistaking the quality of the north coast of Spain, opening on the Bay of Biscay, that dreaded bay of sudden storms, which has to be crossed by all ships running for English ports. The coast is high, rocky, and dangerous, with few good harbors and many indentations, all of which have to be crossed by the road or circumvented. In this it resembles the northwest coast of Scotland. It is unmistakably the end of Europe and the beginning of the great Atlantic Ocean.

It was getting dark by the time we reached Santander, a sizable town on a peninsula that juts far out into the sea. We went on a few miles, stopped in a village for the night, and in the morning visited the caves. They are high up on a hill like the cave of Lascaux. The caves have been known for a long while, written up and photographed, drawn and pictured, and so didn't have the same shock effect of Lascaux, whose painters seem to have put down their colors yesterday. But in other ways they are more austere, more unexpected, more frightening. The color of the rock, and the quality of the rock, is different, and the centuries have produced great bosses in the rock, some of them in the ceiling in the cave overhead, which suggest the taut muscles and curious shapes of charging animals, which have been realized by the cave painters and worked until they had become a completely original piece of art.

There was one huge boss in the ceiling of the main cave that had all the bunched muscles, huge bulging shoulders, and explosive sexuality of the fabulous Minotaur—so striking that it seemed to explode out of the stone, yet none of the essential symmetry of the animal was lost. It's an image that will haunt you all your days.

In the evening we arrived at La Toja. Judy was there, Escobar was there, and during the next day or two my family would arrive. It is time to take stock.

=

This book is a story of success and failure, more successes than there are failures. It is also the story of a new kind of artist, and a new kind of art. This century, the twentieth century, belongs to the movies, and the movies belong to all of us who were born between 1900 and 2001. Tommy Trinder—I think it was Tommy Trinder—used to come on the stage at the Palladium as if he were alone in the world. When he got to center stage he would turn and suddenly see three thousand people waiting to be entertained. He would grin his nutcracker grin, look at his audience as if he were counting each one of them, and say, "Oh, you lucky people!"

In the whole history of the world, in the history of communications, in the history of entertainment, in the art of storytelling, nobody has had it so good as you born in this century, as I, born September 30, 1905, and still kicking eighty-three years later. And I am here to tell you so.

I have already told, at the beginning of this very long life, how popular magazines and encyclopedias, with lots of illustrations, were delighting us at the beginning of the century, and how, almost overnight, art became part of our daily lives and surrealism was taken for granted. Geniuses from all over the world became our constant two-dimensional companions. Men, women, people, places, legends, fairy tales, were flung at us by that great motion picture screen. Names that had only been names became part of our vocabulary. Clowns and heroes, kings and queens vied for our attention.

At first, it seemed a miracle. Then, we began to take it all for granted, and then we began to ask questions. Who were the high priests of this new religion? How was it we could go from movie to movie . . . English, French, Italian, Spanish, Chinese, Japanese, Russian . . . and understand what people said? They were obviously talking their own language. Oh! . . . I see now . . . It's those printed cards with words on them . . . What do you call them? . . . Titles . . . which we read, though you have to be quick about it . . . And then there are the big films . . . superfilms they call them . . . that need sound effects in the orchestra pit where the little old tinkling piano, which we had had from the beginning, is suddenly souped up with four or five instruments, just like the real theatre. What next, I wonder?

What was next was the greatest clown, Charlie Chaplin; the greatest hero, Douglas Fairbanks; the world's sweetheart, Mary Pickford. And then, from behind the scenes into the light of day, the great film directors: D. W. Griffith,

Abel Gance, Erich von Stroheim, Rex Ingram, Fritz Lang, René Clair, Eisenstein, Pudovkin, Dreyer, Sjöström, Marcel L'Herbier, F. W. Murnau, John Ford, Jean Renoir . . . I shall ask our editor to keep a blank page here, to fill in your candidates.

And then, while we basked in the miracle of this golden silence, and understanding between the nations was being created by the silent film, the even newer miracle of sound radio transformed what was now being called the entertainment world. Oh, you lucky people! All of a sudden, you could stay at home and listen to the radio, or you could go down the village street and see the new movie. And suddenly, all new movies had to have sound, synchronized sound, and all these lovely actors from all over the world suddenly became dumb, because they did not speak American.

And then all movies had to be colored—not colorized—in glorious Technicolor, in Agfacolor, in PrismaColor, in colorcolor; and not content with that, the men who ran the entertainment world decreed that the shape of movies had to change, and so we had VistaVision, CinemaScope, and all the other scopes; and suddenly, like the roar of a breaking tidal wave, television was all over us, in our homes, in our supermarkets, in our bedrooms.

Oh, you lucky people! Lucky you, and lucky me, for I've seen it all. But I no longer take it for granted. I am getting impatient. All around me I see my friends and fellow practitioners in the art taking the art in vain. Is that all there is to this great visual art form? Is money everything? Is greed to be its master—its dictator? Are grosses to be the only measure of a film's excellence, of a director's visionary power? Are writers and composers losing all sense of shame? There are only eleven years to go to 2001 . . . you lucky people!

How many people have we got today who practice the art of the movies? Kurosawa heads the list. Why? Because he is a samurai. He is not competing with other film directors, he's practicing his art. He makes films only to find out more about his art. He is pure; pure cinema, and pure genius. Who else? Visconti, of course, the aristocrat in the movies. Who else? Francis Coppola, the Coppola who made *Godfather I* and *Godfather II*, the George Lucas who made *Star Wars*, the Steven Spielberg who made *E.T.*, the Mike Nichols who made *The Graduate*, the John Huston who made *Wise Blood* and *The Treasure of the Sierra Madre*, Carol Reed, who made *The Third Man* and *The Fallen Idol*, David Lean, who made *The Bridge on the River Kwai* and *Lawrence of Arabia*, Ronnie Neame, who made *Tunes of Glory* and *The Horse's Mouth*, Alec Guinness in every performance he has given, Powell and Pressburger for *The Red Shoes*, Martin Scorsese for *Mean Streets*—make your own list and send it to me, but don't expect me to answer. I am not proposing an anthology, I am making a point.

These are all artists. All art is one, man—one. Artists are human, artists can be seduced by money, luxury, and fame. The greater the bribe, the greater the seduction. In the four hundred years since the Renaissance it has been a matter of pride, of comfort, a matter of avarice. But in this century the world of flesh and the devil are with us every day, and every night. Everything has a cash value. *Variety* reports of a Hollywood executive that his personal worth is $60,000,000. It's sheer gibberish! But artists are simple people. They love money and power, just as businessmen do. But they are not businessmen, they are artists, and the greater the artists, the greater the betrayal.

Do you think that Kurosawa ever compromised in his life? I doubt it. Yet here were Powell and Pressburger, who according to Martin Scorsese were the most subversive filmmakers ever to be financed by a major studio, here were the famous Archers panicking when they found themselves on their own, grabbing at the first subjects that came to hand, as if they were lifebelts in a stormy sea. What was the hurry? It was a recipe for disaster. Nobody liked our screenplays. We didn't like them ourselves. In *Honeymoon* there was too little story, in *Miracle in Soho* there was too much. Evidently there was something to be said for the idea of equal creative partnership.

=

Our casting was odd, to say the least. Luis Escobar had written the parts of our honeymooners for Moira Shearer and Paul Scofield. When they turned it down, we ended up with Ludmilla Tcherina and Anthony Steel. Good God . . . not Anthony Steel, the archetypal British shit! He was already grooming himself for the part of the English baronet, Sir Stephen, in *The Story of O*, and he brought Anita Ekberg with him too!

At Pinewood Emeric had half a dozen vigorous young leading men to choose from, including my recommendation, Stanley Baker. But instead he chose to play John Gregson, dear, soft John Gregson, as the leader of the road gang and the wielder of the automatic drill. But who am I to talk? Didn't I accept and direct Dirk Bogarde as the Scarlet Pimpernel of Crete, and then make the film on the French Riviera? This is the sort of mess you get into when you and your unit are under contract to a major studio.

Why did we play Dirk Bogarde and John Gregson, good actors, but wrong for the parts? Because they were there. They were eating and sleeping on a regular contract salary and they had to be employed, their emoluments had to be written off by the studio accountants, whether they liked it or not. That is why it's such a good thing today that we still have the great studios, with all their machinery and technical assets, on what is called today a "four-wall" basis. We bring in our own people. We don't have to employ staff and actors who are idle between films, as we did in the golden days before television.

John Davis would listen to no advice. He had almost started World War III by thinking he could force the great American distribution companies to yield up a share of the American market. The Yanks murdered him, and when the dust settled British film production was back where it was before Korda, and the writers, producers, and actors of the new generation after the war were looking to the theatre, to Stratford, to the Old Vic, and to the Royal Court

Theatre, which had provided a podium for George Bernard Shaw before the First World War and was doing the same service for Arnold Wesker and John Osborne, while Sergeant Musgrave danced, and Godot waited in the wings. Yes, we betrayed our art, we arrogant Archers, by writing, producing, and directing art that went no deeper than the celluloid.

When I slipped my headstall and joined the herd I had two projects in mind—to commission John Whiting to write a screenplay adapted from Cecil Woodham-Smith's *The Reason Why*, about the Charge of the Light Brigade in the Crimean War, but first of all to film William Sansom's novel *The Loving Eye* from a script already written by the author.

William Sansom was an exquisite artist, a novelist's novelist. Imagine Jane Austen reincarnated as a plump, observant Londoner, endowed with sensual good looks and a square-cut, neat beard and mustache which gave a resemblance to one of those Assyrian kings on a desert tomb. His eyes were large and luminous and his prose good-mannered. He had a good ear and wrote excellent lyrics.

The Loving Eye was a comedy about love and the confusion of identities, and it was acted out in postwar Kensington, in those back gardens of brick walls and high fences where cats prowl at night and where I lived; an intimate, confusing world when you get lost in it. Originally I had wanted Natasha Parry to play the two sisters working in the same nightclub and spied upon over the garden wall by a timid copyright accountant, to be played by Paul Scofield. The two sisters had very different characters and experience, but they looked alike and could very easily be confused by an observer, himself confused. Have I confused you, or do you see what I mean?

Anyway I was having delightful conversations and rehearsals of the two-sister act with Natasha, when Peter Brook suddenly got jealous and whisked her away with him to America, a double kidnapping in the circumstances. So, casting my net around, I entangled Moira Shearer in it. She was enthralled, very naturally, by the prospect of playing opposite Paul Scofield. We three, Paul, Moira and I, shepherded by Bill, of course, with constant cups of tea, mapped out the action in the back garden around my Kensington home in Melbury Road. Once Moira met Paul and they had talked over their parts together, there was no holding her and it was Pike's Peak or bust.

The timid birdwatcher, for which Paul Scofield had the comedy as well as the charm, had a London eccentric living with him in his house, the sort of hanger-on you get around Kensington: actor, journalist, pub crawler—you know the type—who has world-weary comments upon everything and everybody. He also has an eye for the elder sister. I had planned the part for Tony Newley, but everyone had their own suggestions. We all know him, don't we?

I have some stills of this period that make me laugh and weep at one and the same time simultaneously. One is of Natasha dancing on a table, egged on by me. The others are of Paul and Moira in the garden at 8 Melbury Road, and on the corner of Addison Road and Holland Park Road. Just to see these photographs makes my heart bleed, for, believe it or not, I couldn't get finance for this delightful Kensington comedy, and it was only by making *Peeping Tom* in the following year that I was able to immortalize the London world in which I lived, at number 8 Melbury Road, and the red-brick, stone-stepped house opposite it where Mark developed his pictures. At this time I had not yet opened my front door to find Leo Marks with a newly lit cigar between his lips; but he was only just around the corner. Some years later Julie Andrews and her husband at the time, Tony Walton, read the script and loved it and wanted to do a musical of it, and I remember them with affection.

William Sansom and I remained friends, and he bore me no grudge. His last book was, perhaps, the best one he wrote for a film or a play. It was called *The Young Wife's Tale.* The titles of his novels were not his greatest triumph; they tended to be mannered. But as a story this was one of his best. The last time I spoke to him was when I rang him to tell him how much I loved his new novel, and that I thought I could raise the money to commission a film script. A while later, he was dead. But enough of that.

Now for *The Reason Why:*

> Theirs not to make reply
> Theirs not to reason why,
> Theirs but to do and die:
> Into the valley of Death
> Rode the six hundred.

Looking back on it, I really think I was on the right track, and readers of my earlier volume of autobiography will recognize the association of the famous cavalry charge with my own personal cavalry charge, on my pony Fubsy, with the gallant First Sussex Yeomanry on maneuvers in east Kent. Cecil Woodham-Smith, the author of the book, was a friend of our family. Her husband Woodham was Arthur Rank's lawyer. They were loaded with charm and intelligence. Frankie and I shared with them a passion for curry and we met frequently at various Indian restaurants. But I drew the line at drinking red burgundy with the curry, which was one of their *gourmandises.*

I am not going to describe the book in detail. If you don't know it you should get it, at once, from your lending library. It's a classic work. Cecil's researches on Florence Nightingale had introduced her to my Lords Cardigan and Lucan and the reason why Cardigan led the charge. This resulted in quite remarkable full-length portraits of the two noblemen. There would have been a long and distinguished cast of English actors and actresses. And indeed I received a message from Dave Hutcheson and Bob Coote, saying: "Hutcheson and Coote are ready. Have horses, will travel."

I intended the part of Cardigan for Rex Harrison, and James Mason for Lord Lucan. I had such respect for Cecil Woodham, and for the subject, and for her treatment of it, that I wanted John Whiting to write the script. He came from a military family and was the most distinguished playwright of that generation, and had just planned and executed a resounding success with his play *The Devils.* He accepted the assignment.

This will always remain a great disappointment for me. It contained all the elements of a great film, and I could have brought a great deal to it. I had the reading, the imagination and wit, and the military background. Nobody could possibly persuade John Whiting to write anything he did not wish to write and, hoping to convince him, I had sketched out an opening in the Garrick Club, which he accepted with good grace and, no doubt, with a private proviso that he could drop it in the final version.

John Whiting was a dramatist of the first order, but a slow writer. His reputation rested on very few plays, which had, in equal parts, exasperated and rejoiced the critics. He was actually writing *The Devils* when I first met him and discussed *The Reason Why.* Dramatists, critics, and actors were puzzled and fascinated by his plays. They seemed as if written by a god—or a devil. They were austere, and yet they were funny. Repeated attempts were made to find a public for them, but they were all respectable failures.

Meanwhile, he was working on Aldous Huxley's extraordinary book *The Devils of Loudon,* hacking a play out of this arid, thirst-provoking book about the devil among the nuns. I went to the first night, and to the second night as well. I was stunned, repelled, attracted. This was art. This was the kind of writing that I was looking for, to do justice to the work of this other great writer, Cecil Woodham-Smith.

But he died. John Whiting died, and I heard later that one beautiful woman in London committed suicide on hearing the news. He was the most intense spirit with whom I have ever come in contact.

So what are you doing, you ask me, *making a pastiche of* The Red Shoes *in Spain with a flamenco dancer and his troupe, Ludmilla Tcherina, and Anthony Steel? Honeymoon* was not a lucky picture. In everything I did or proposed to do I was frustrated, or nearly so. I wanted Joan Miró to design *El Amor Brujo,* but he refused. Even when I flew to Mallorca and camped outside his villa to persuade him, he refused to come out and I flew back to Barcelona in dudgeon. The Catalan painter Durancamps, a masterful painter who used the colors of Zurbarán, eventually did the job. But it was cruel of Miró not to come out of his guarded fortress.

Antonio and I couldn't agree over the composer for the ballet, *Los Amantes de Teruel,* until I suggested Mikis Theodorakis, whose work delighted him. The costumes and design were supervised by Ivor Beddoes, who had so often in the past substituted for Hein, on *The Red Shoes* and *The Tales of Hoffmann.* Georges Périnal brought with him as his camera operator Gerry Turpin, who was to be my camera operator on *Peeping Tom.*

My dear friend and genius Léonide Massine joined us to dance the Ghost in the ballet *Amor Brujo,* and he choreographed the ballet of *The Lovers of Teruel.* Antonio danced in both ballets, as well as doing flamenco and *zapateado* on the high roads of Spain. The elements were all right, but the organization was raw, and the whole thing never quite came together. I should never have taken it on. Enough said.

My love story, and my lovers in the film, were unconvincing, but there was one love story that was not. She came aboard us in the harbor at La Toja. There was a stiff breeze. Escobar had introduced me to a lean, competent nobleman and amateur yachtsman with his own boat and a working knowledge of all the harbors and the anchorages from Vigo to Cowes. He had many English friends, and dressed and looked like an Englishman. He was brusque but hospitable, and I sailed with him many times. The girl was young and high-colored, with great black eyes and wild hair and the body of an athlete. As she swung herself on board, I said to my host, "Who is this Viking's daughter?"

The appellation stuck. She was the daughter of a very old, distinguished family in the north of Spain, where they had vast estates. Her uncle was a famous regional painter. She taught me how to cook an Irish stew on a gimbal tripod in half a gale. There was no contact then, but a little fire was burning.

When the summer was over and we all came back to Madrid I caught sight of her from time to time. I had made no attempt to get to know her better, or to know her family (she had a charming mother), but it seems to me that our paths were crossing frequently, and she often visited the studio with a crowd of young Madrileños. From time to time our eyes met and locked, and then we knew.

The first contact was in some public garden in Madrid. It was not far from the apartment that Sweep, Bumba, and I had rented. I think I was a bearer of an invitation to her parents and the girl, to our farewell party. I left the message, turned to go, and suddenly there was a scurry of feet and she was in front of me. She looked eagerly at me and said nothing. When I turned to go she fell into step with me. My pulses were racing, my limbs were heavy. There was a big hollow tree in the center of the open space, where the children used to play and where Sweep used to take his daily constitutional. Suddenly we were in each other's arms and sheltered by the tree. We were half-suffocated, rigid as statues. She started to tremble, and then her whole body was singing, asking to be taken. I was shaking all over. I had never known such passion.

"Don Miguel, O Miguel, vamos a su casa."

"The boy is there."

"Where can we go?"

"You know Madrid: nowhere."

A cry of anguish. It was true; someone is always watching in Madrid. It's a village, where everyone among the artists knows everyone.

"Oh, Michael, Michael, Michael! When do you leave?"

"Tomorrow."

A cry of anguish.

"Where will you be?"

"Quién sabe?"

"London . . . the south of France? I'll follow you, where you go. I'll follow you!"

"We'll meet. We'll find somewhere."

We kissed, and I wonder that that old hollow tree didn't burst into flames. I was trembling and sweating as if I had malaria. I was a goner.

She turned up in London, with her mother; they turned up in the south of France.

"That girl has hot pants for you," said Frankie dispassionately.

"Just starstruck," I said. "Movie mad."

She shook her head, and went off humming, "I know where I'm going. . . ."

The Spanish aristocracy have links with Scotland, and particularly with the Highlands of Scotland, through marriage, sport, business, and a general design for living. It was my habit to visit the boys at Gordonstoun at least once during the term. I always drove up in the Bentley, stopping to see friends on the way. Nothing was planned between us, and yet we met about one hundred miles from Aberdeen.

"Come on," I said.

Suddenly, we were shy of each other. She had never known a man. We stopped at a little hotel, a cottage, by the River Dee. It was run by two dear women, who made a great fuss over us. I fancy they thought we were running away. We had supper and went to bed and lay in each other's arms. It was as if we had come home after a long stormy journey. Suddenly I said, I almost shouted, "Now!" and she opened everything. We made love until the sun shone through the curtains.

It took us six hours to drive the next twenty miles. We stopped and pulled off the road at every lay-by. We could never have enough of each other. The mountains, and the lakes, and the stunted oaks, and the rowans, belonged to us. She only had two days before she rejoined her friends, and it seemed an eternity. We stretched to breaking point the hours we had together. Our love seemed inexhaustible. I never knew such loving again.

She was as honest as the day, and as brave as she was honest. When she rejoined her mother, it all came out: they were to go together to see Frankie. She was to divorce me, so that we could be married. I was not consulted. This was women's stuff. To the great relief of her mother, Frankie refused point-blank. They went back to Spain and then on a trip to America.

Ten years later we met in London, in Sloane Square. Neither of us had changed much. We felt a great affection and no passion. We walked hand in hand about the park, and visited the bookshops in Charing Cross Road, and bought each other art books at Zwemmer's. She had become a warm, intelligent woman, a dark beauty. Was there anything of that great consuming love that had once burned so brightly in both of us? Yes, the embers were still bright, but the fire was sulky and would have needed tending, and we were ten years older. We met again, but only in our dreams.

"Con Dios," as the old men say, when you pass them on the road, "vaya con Dios." Go with God, Viking's daughter.

Sweep speaking: "Well, here I am, in quarantine in England. What a mess! It comes of leaving everything to these bipeds. Believe it or not, the day before I arrived in Nice, to take up my duties at the Voile d'Or, the French imposed a quarantine restriction on all dogs entering or leaving France, even black spaniels! And there I was, betwixt and between, in a filthy, French kennel in Nice airport. I need hardly say that the dog lovers in France, and the dog owners, rose in one screaming, barking mass and had the ordinance repealed. But too late for me.

"If we had waited a week, it would have been all right. When the French rise against petty tyrannies they rise as one woman, and every dog in France was yapping its heart out. But we couldn't know this at the time, and Mr. Powell had to put himself into a British plane and fly to London, where my own people slapped me into quarantine for six months. It's an eternity for a little black dog. My Bumba screamed the place down, when he heard about it.

"We were allowed visitors in the quarantine kennel, and Mr. Powell drove Bumba down to see me whenever they had a spare weekend. I pretended to be happy and resigned, but I wasn't! I could have bitten them all. But when I was back in my Bumba's arms, I forgave them."

Animals have always been important members of our families. So they should be, in all families. Horses, ponies, dogs and their puppies, cats and their kittens, canaries, budgerigars, hamsters, rabbits, hares, hedgehogs, tortoises—they all have something to give us, in return for food and shelter and sympathy. Dogs are so direct, cats so devious, that I pity the family that has no animals to look after them. For make no mistake about it, we must seem half-asleep to our animal pets. They live in a wildly exciting world of scents and sounds and sights, through which we stumble, blind, deaf, and destructive. Yet they put up with us, and even love us, while we, who are responsible for their little lives and who live more and more in cities and urban developments, grumble about the time and care that we must spend on our pets, and take for granted the love and devotion that they give us in return and which repays us a thousandfold. It is one of the rules of the universe that there is no love without sacrifice, and the sooner a child learns that the better.

That's enough about the humanities and Our Dumb Friends. This book is about one man's life in art, so let's get on with the job.

The studio work and editing of *Honeymoon* was done at Shepperton Studios, where I met Danny Angel. He had just been producing a film about espionage, about codes and decoding, and about the French underground in the war. Virginia McKenna and Paul Scofield were in it, and it was called *Carve Her Name with Pride*, which sounds like a quotation, and probably is. Anyway, it was a very successful film. Danny said, "Micky, are you still looking for a writer to work with you, like Pressburger did? Because, if you are, you ought to see Leo Marks. He's as crazy as you are."

"How do you know?"

"He's been working with me. Apparently, he was a code breaker during the war, and he tells the tallest stories about it that I've ever heard. But he gave us a lot of good stuff for the film. There's no doubt that he knows all about espionage, and code breaking, and all that stuff."

"I don't know that I want to make a film about espionage. It seems to me you've done that. What else can Leo Marks do?"

"He can write poetry. He's weird, I tell you. You ought to see him. He lives double or triple lives, he's difficult to get ahold of, and he's full of mystery and conundrums. But he's good value. I'll give him your telephone number."

I didn't know it, but this was to change my life and career. This was the birth of *Peeping Tom*.

We met. We shook hands, and I wished we hadn't. He had a grip of iron. It reminded me of the hairless Mexican in Somerset Maugham's memorable short story, but Leo Marks was neither hairless nor a Mexican, like the character Peter Lorre played in Hitchcock's *The Secret Agent*. Mr. Marks was impressive. He had eyes like stones and crisp, curling black hair that looked like a wig but wasn't. He was short, square, and powerful. His clothes gave nothing away.

He wanted to write me a film about a double agent, an agent whom he had known personally in the French underground during the war. I said I wasn't interested in a war story. He changed his tune, and started to talk about psychoanalysis. He knew a lot about it, although he was only about thirty. I said why didn't we make a film about Freud? He said yes, why didn't we? It was one of those subjects I had always had at the back of my mind. He said he'd go away and think about it. A week later John Huston announced he was going to make a film about Freud in Munich for the producer Paul Kohner, an old-timer who later on became one of the top Hollywood agents.

I broke the news to Marks, who had seen it already. It soon became clear that he was remarkably well informed. He was no stranger to the corridors of power, and had had frequent access to Downing Street and MI-5 during the war. He said he was through with all that, but I doubted that he was. In a week or two he rang again: Could we meet? By now there was a certain intimacy between us, although I wouldn't call it friendship. I suggested he come to 8 Melbury Road.

He rang the bell at 9:00 A.M. precisely. He had a flower in his buttonhole and a newly lit cigar between his lips. It was all carefully thought out. I took him into the library, and he cast his eye around at the books and the shelves that went up to the sixteen-foot ceiling. He knew about books. He explained that he was the son of that well-known book dealer, Marks, on Charing Cross Road. He had cut his teeth on an Elsevier Bible. When I knew he was a book lover, I was able to relax. It was clear that the books spoke to him from their high shelves. He sat down, leaned toward me, fixed me with a penetrating gaze, and said, "Mr. Powell, how would you like to make a film about a young man with a camera who kills the women that he photographs?"

I said, "That's me. I'd like it very much."

He said, "How shall we begin?"

"I suggest that you work at home, or wherever you're used to working, and come to see me perhaps twice a week to read me what you've written. Then we can discuss it. An original film script wants to be about eighty quarto pages."

"American quarto, or English quarto?"

"American. I can usually make myself available in the evening. Does nine o'clock suit you?"

He inspected his cigar ash.

"What will you pay, Mr. Powell?"

"A nominal fee for the first script, against an agreed fee for the whole job when the film is made."

"What would you call a nominal fee, Mr. Powell?"

"Five hundred pounds down, five hundred on delivery of the final sequence."

His eyes sparkled. This was in 1959.

"And the agreed fee, Mr. Powell?"

"That would depend on the size of the budget. This will be a low-budget film. It's a tricky subject. We don't want our backers telling us how to make it. When the film goes into production, we'll pay you another fifteen hundred."

He took a long puff.

I wrote him a check for £500. He looked at it with affection, and put it away, carefully, in his notecase.

"Does the word 'scoptophilia' mean anything to you, Mr. Powell?"

This was obviously a test question. I thought fast.

"Is it Greek?"

"Yes, it's Greek."

"Love of looking? Urge to look?"

"Exactly: 'the morbid urge to gaze'—a familiar term to alienists."

"Hmm . . . the morbid urge to gaze . . . . *Peeping Tom*."

He made a wry face.

"I was afraid you'd say that."

"But that's what it means."

He inspected the ash of his cigar, looked at me, nodded his great head. "More or less."

He rose. "Will next Friday suit you?"

"Same hour?"

I wrote the appointment down and saw him into the street. It was a fine night. He looked up and down Melbury Road, with its great houses standing in their own gardens.

"I envy you, living here, Mr. Powell."

I nodded. "When are you going to start, Leo?"

"I have started."

We both laughed, and he strolled away up the street. The tall red-brick house opposite, number 5, Mark's house in the film, was dark. But there was a light in the basement. I went back into the house. As I entered the library there was a scratching noise on the tall window. Bibby, my long-haired tabby cat, had taken a run up the windows on the outside and I always left a gap at the top for him. He pawed himself through it and landed soundlessly beside me. I sat down in my armchair and he jumped on my lap and started to wash himself.

When Holland House condescended to recognize that it was surrounded by Kensington, the park of the great house was bounded by Holland Park Road, Addison Road, and Kensington High Street, on the north, west, and south respectively. On the east, on the rise of Camden Hill, Holland Park was bounded by country lanes that connected Notting Hill Gate to Kensington. It is now called Holland Walk, and is still a charming walk. What's left of Holland House is now a youth hostel, and on the sloping ground to the west there is a restaurant in the original Orangerie, where we celebrated Frankie's wake.

Melbury Road hesitates and curves like a country road, because that is what it is. The house that Lady Holland built for Watts, the painter, is on the site of the old farmhouse, and there was a duck pond. This small area was thick with highly varnished, highly commercial painters. Our house was built for Marcus Stone, who painted *Lover's Walk* and *Parting in Gardens*. Back to back with us was the garden of the palace of Lord Leighton, a passionate Arabist who had built himself a studio in the form of a mosque, domed and tiled and with a fountain playing in a small basement. As you walked down from Kensington you passed the immense house of Holman Hunt, who never despaired of trying to teach Edward Lear to paint in oils. On the corner opposite the handsome house with tall windows is the house of Luke Fildes, painter of *The Doctor*, a print of which used to hang in every kitchen or nursery in Britain.

But the thrill of thrills for me was learning that the tall red-brick house opposite number 8 had been the home of Mr. Bassett-Lowke, maker and designer of scale models of steam engines. It was a name of power and delight to all mechanically minded schoolboys, and his catalogs charmed even unmechanical me. Now his name snatches me away from Melbury Road to the playroom that my father built for us near the backdoor of Hoath Farm in Kent. I think that I have related how my older brother took it over and filled it with his steam engines and working models. Even I could appreciate the models and the beauty of their working parts, but to hear the name again was enough to thrill me. There are certain names from that mechanical period before the 1914 war which, though unpoetical themselves, fill the mind with poetic images—Bassett-Lowke, the Great Western Railway, the Flying Scotsman, Bugatti, Rolls-Royce, Handley Page—they conjure up a vanished world of burnished copper, of shining brass, of clouds of steam, of clumsy, great ideas lumbering about and waiting to be airborne.

When I made *Peeping Tom* I chose this house of Bassett-Lowke's to be the home of Mark Lewis, the shy and compassionate scoptophiliac in the film. When we were shooting some night scenes there I was asked in by the owner of the garden flat, who knew all about Bassett-Lowke and showed me a hatchway specially cut in the wall that allowed the model steam train to leave the house and run out into the garden, over suspension bridges and through tunnels, until brought stately back by remote control into the house of the controller. He made so many people happy, including my brother, that I hope Bassett-Lowke was a happy man himself. I always imagined him as being fat, with a top hat.

The other day the son of my neighbors in that house rang me up. He had just seen *Peeping Tom* on television. He told me that when Mark crossed the hall and looked into his mother's room, it was an almost unbearable moment for him. I was pleased. That single shot had found its mark, its unique audience. Equally, Norman Shaw's architecture, with his finials, pinnacles and chimneys and windows, had created a perfect setting for me. There is something looney about his absorption in ornament and detail, as there is in me. He compels your interest because he is confident of gaining it.

Leo was an ideal creative partner. He knew nothing about films or the theatre, but a very great deal about men and women. He was malicious, inventive, and unshockable. In less than six weeks we had our draft script. Our scoptophiliac, our Peeping Tom, turned out to be called Mark, of course, since Leo himself was the original scoptophiliac. Mark works in the movies, as camera assistant and focus-puller on a big film in production at a major studio. He ekes out his slender salary by shooting front covers for pornographic magazines. His equipment is expensive and extensive. He uses a lot of film. He does his own developing and printing. He has his own projector and his own screen. His camera tripod has a concealed dagger in one of its legs. A distorting mirror locks into a slot above the lens. It is a murderous weapon. He is a camera fiend. He is gentle and sweet and attractive, and quite, quite mad.

"How would you like to open the film, Mr. Powell?" inquired Leo.

"With a kill," I answered.

"Correct. Shall I read it to you?"

"Please."

He read it . . . the street at night . . . the click and whirr of the concealed camera . . . the prostitute's words "It'll be two quid" . . . the high heels clattering on the stones, the clang of metal against metal, the whirr of the camera, the screams of the prostitute, the quick cut to the whirring projector showing the whole sequence on screen, Mark's orgasm and collapse . . . it was all there in the first draft.

Leo was watching me closely. There was a long pause.

"Shall I go on?"

He had placed his cigar carefully on a stand before reading and the ash was now almost an inch in length. He picked it up very carefully, took a long pull, and carefully put it back.

"Shall I go on, Mr. Powell?"

I nodded, without speaking. I was already listening to Brian Easdale's piano track.

Leo said, "Dissolve to the next morning."

I said, "No dissolve—straight cut. We haven't used a dissolve for time-lapse since *A Canterbury Tale*."

He made a note.

390 · MICHAEL POWELL

The final script was about ninety-five pages, a bit long, but we had to start going after the money. I sent a copy to the National Film Finance Corporation: they loved it; another one to Film Finances: they wanted to see a budget; I showed it to the Rank Organisation: they turned it down. Just to pay them out, I decided to make it in their studio. Bill Burnside read the script, and was mad about it. "It's better than *M*!"

I was still doing a little work on *Honeymoon* at Shepperton Studios. On the stage next door Jack Clayton was just winding up his film *Room at the Top*, starring Laurence Harvey. Larry seemed to me to be ideal for the job, and he thought so too. I visited his stage and he visited mine. But the word was already out. The scouts had seen Harvey's performance, and very soon everybody knew what a fascinating film Jack Clayton had made of the novel *Room at the Top*. All the Hollywood leading ladies wanted this new leading man. He suddenly appeared at my elbow in the studio.

"Micky, I'm sorry. I'm off to Hollywood. I'll never get such a chance again to screw all those dames . . . you understand . . . nothing personal. I love your script—but Hollywood, here I come!"

I wished him luck. I saw him later on, in *Butterfield 8*, and felt I had contributed something to it. Nat Cohen came into my bar at the Voile d'Or. He was looking very Riviera and wore a Panama hat with a band.

"Micky, I like your script, and so does Stu.* What's your budget?"

"About £150,000."

"That's a bit high for us. You haven't got any names."

"Don't want them."

"Well, get it down to £125,000, and we'll come in. The National Film Finance Corporation will put up the rest."

So we were financed, and I didn't have to play the Wardour Street names as they suggested. Who was going to play Mark? I had no idea. I wanted Anna Massey for the girl. She was twenty-one, a good actress, and Ray Massey's daughter. Anna had brought theatrical London to its feet, and to her feet, in a play by William Douglas Home, *The Reluctant Debutante*. It was her first professional engagement and it ran for two years. As co-star she had Celia Johnson playing her mother; lucky girl, and lucky producer. Her mother in *Peeping Tom* was to have been Pamela Brown, but Pamela was in a play in the U.S.A. Anna Massey had dark red hair and large, expressive eyes, like Pamela, so I searched around for another redhead to play her mother and finally, after some frenzied last-hope cabling:

DARLING HAVE YOU STARTED OR IS THERE THE SMALLEST HOPE I MIGHT BE BACK IN TIME OR HAVE YOU ENGAGED A LESS LOVING BUT MORE SUITABLE ACTRESS

*Film producers Nat Cohen and Stuart Levy ran Anglo-Amalgamated Films.

COULD YOU PUT MUMS SCENE AT THE END I WONDER FORGIVE NO LETTERS
MORALE VERY LOW WARWICK HOTEL HERE RITZ CARLTON BOSTON NEXT WEEK
I LOVE YOU = PAMELA =

Maxine Audley got the part. She also inherited Pamela's sweaters and filled them nicely. She was a powerful addition to the cast. I had seen and admired Maxine in Larry's production of *Titus Andronicus*. She played the Queen of the Amazons, and was a veritable queen. Next came Brenda Bruce, an old friend of Pamela's of long standing. She gave a deliciously grubby performance as the little Soho tart, Mark's first victim.

Who was to play Mark as an eight-year-old child? Nobody but Bumba Powell, naturally. And his father? His father. I don't approve of directors acting in their own films, but this was a family affair. But who was to play Mark as an adult?

I went to a cocktail party in Shepherd's Market. I think Bill Burnside took me there. He was doing the publicity on the film. He was responsible for those awful eyes that glare at you from the posters of *Peeping Tom*, if you can find one. I was introduced to a charming young man whose name I couldn't catch. He was talking about music. There was something about him; every word he said, every movement he made, betrayed the sensitive artist. He was with a lovely girl, of course. It nagged me that I had seen him before and couldn't think where.

"Are you an actor?"

He blushed. "No . . . yes . . . I mean, you wouldn't have seen it, but I have acted."

"In films?"

He nodded. "A film called *Sissi.* It's short for Elizabeth, but when I say the title of the film in England, everybody laughs."

I said, "Watch me. I'm not laughing. You're Karl-Heinz Böhm!"

"How did you know?"

"But, I've seen the film—both films! You were splendid, you and Romy Schneider . . . *Sissi,* and *Sissi, the Empress.*"

He blushed again. He really was a very sensitive young man. "Thank you."

"And Karl Böhm, the great conductor, is your father?"

"Yes, Karl Böhm is my father."

And rival, I thought. To have the autocratic, passionate Karl Böhm as your father, and competitor, would be a tough nut to crack. Karl-Heinz's real passion was also obviously music, but he had charm and ability—loads of it—and he knew how to handle himself, and, on top of that, was most attractive. He spoke English with hardly any accent, it was more like an intonation. I liked that, for the part. It suited our polyglot movie community. I made a sudden decision.

"Here's my card. Please telephone me tomorrow. I might have a film for you."

He was thunderstruck. "Are you *the* Michael Powell?"

"I believe there is another one, but I haven't met him yet."

He still held my card in his hand, so I took it from him, and stuck it in his waistcoat pocket.

"Don't lose it."

"I won't."

Nat Cohen, hearing the news, threw up. Not only was I not going to star Laurence Harvey, whose films had always made money, but now I was playing an unknown Austrian in the main part!

"He's not unknown. His father is a great conductor, one of the greatest. The *Sissi* films made lots of money. Everyone in the European art world knows Karl-Heinz—ask around!"

He grunted. "You're talking about *my* film, and how to sell it."

I flared up. "We're talking about *my* film, and how to *make* it."

He groaned. "I want you to play that blond girl who was in Stewart Granger's film, and you bring me this Massey girl, who is more like a boy than a girl, and it's her first picture, and nobody knows her, and then you let Larry Harvey walk out on you . . . and now you want to play this Austrian!?"

"It'll work, you'll see. My director of photography, Otto Heller, is a Czech."

"I'll tell you frankly, Michael, if I could get out of it, I would."

"You can't."

Why do films always start this way, with disagreement between the film-makers and their backers? The answer's simple: We know what we're doing, they don't.

Moira Shearer is a case in point. She frightens them, as I do. With us, they know it's a long shot. We aim high, but we land in, or near, the gold. *The Red Shoes* had made Moira a star, which means that she was suddenly known, and adored, from Reykjavík to Valparaiso, from Tokyo to Timbuktu. The admirers of her legs, her hair, and her air of virginal wisdom were fit to be tied. They would have jumped off the Brooklyn Bridge for her, and probably did. Everybody all over the world—American, English, Japanese—wanted to make a film with her. And what film did they want to make? They wanted to make *The Red Shoes* again . . . and again . . . and again. And Moira, what did she want? She wanted to be an actress.

She had worked with discipline, with humility, in her chosen profession of dancer. She had won recognition as an artist. She had tasted stardom and the delirium of the spotlights. She had become, overnight, one of the most admired and envied women in the world. She had married the man she loved and who loved her and who was, thank God, not an actor or a dancer, and she wanted his children, and she wanted to act, and nobody understood this except me. We both thought that we could make something unusual and exciting and entertaining out of William Sansom's *The Loving Eye*. Our names were known all over the world, but do you think we could raise £150,000 in our own country, England, to make this comedy of love and identity? Not on your life! We were artists, we were ART, and we all know, don't we, that art is dead at the box office—until a film like *The Red Shoes* grosses $25,000,000, and this when the dollar was worth, perhaps not a dollar, but worth a lot more than a dollar is worth now.

So we settled for Pop Art: for a spine-chilling film about murder and sexual deviation and scoptophilia and Peeping Tom, and we got our money, and lo! when the film was offered to the public it was discovered by the critics to be art with a capital A, a prostitution of the arts. It was salacious, rapacious, pornographic, and unutterably boring for us critics, who had to sit through this mishmash of sex and murder. It was an insult to the film business, it out-cocked even the worst of Hitchcock, in fact it was all cock. What should be done with a film like this? It should be flushed down the water closet, with every responsible critic in London gleefully hanging on the chain:

> In the last three and a half months . . . I have carted my travel-stained carcase to some of the filthiest and most festering slums in Asia. But nothing, nothing, nothing—neither the hopeless leper colonies of East Pakistan, the back streets of Bombay nor the gutters of Calcutta—has left me with such a feeling of nausea and depression as I got this week while sitting through a new British film called *Peeping Tom* (Plaza). I am a glutton for punishment, and I never walk out of films or plays no matter how malodorous. But I must confess that I almost followed suit when I heard my distinguished colleague Miss Caroline Lejeune say: "I am sickened!" just before she made her indignant exit. . . . Mr Michael Powell (who once made such outstanding films as *Black Narcissus* and *A Matter of Life and Death*) produced and directed *Peeping Tom* and I think he ought to be ashamed of himself. The acting is good. The photography is fine. But what is the result as I saw it on the screen? Sadism, sex, and the exploitation of human degradation. (*Daily Express*, Len Mosley)

=

> It's a long time since a film disgusted me as much as *Peeping Tom*. . . . This so-called entertainment is directed by Michael Powell, who once made such distinguished films as *A Matter of Life and Death* and *49th Parallel*. . . . I don't propose to name the players in this beastly picture. (*The Observer*, Caroline Lejeune)

≡

The only really satisfactory way to dispose of *Peeping Tom* would be to shovel it up and flush it swiftly down the nearest sewer. Even then, the stench would remain. . . . Obviously there's a legitimate place in the cinema for genuine psychological studies. But this crude, sensational exploitation merely aims at giving the bluntest of cheap thrills. It succeeds in being alternately dull and repellent. It is no surprise that this is the work of Michael Powell who displayed his vulgarity in such films as *A Matter of Life and Death*, *The Red Shoes* and *Tales of Hoffmann,* and the bizarre tendencies of his curious mind in *A Canterbury Tale,* where the story consisted of Eric Portman pouring glue into girls' hair. In *Peeping Tom* his self-exposure goes even further. He not only plays the sadistic father, but uses his own child as his victim. (*Tribune,* Derek Hill)

≡

It turns out to be the sickest and filthiest film I remember seeing . . . children's terror used as entertainment, atrocious cruelty put on the screen for fun. And the main character, and madman murderer, is played all through as hero—handsome, tormented, lovable, a glamorous contrast to the heroine's alternative youths . . . and in the end her romantic sprawl beside the beloved killer is implicitly sickening. (*The Spectator,* Isobel Quigley)

≡

Ugh! Obviously, Michael Powell made *Peeping Tom* in order to shock. In one sense he has succeeded. I was shocked to the core to find a director of his standing befouling the screen with such perverted nonsense. It wallows in the diseased urges of a homicidal pervert, and actually romanticises his pornographic brutality. Sparing no tricks, it uses phoney cinema artifice and heavy orchestral music to whip up a debased atmosphere. . . . From its slumbering mildly salacious beginning to its appallingly masochistic and depraved climax, it is wholly evil. (*The Daily Worker,* Nina Hibbin)

≡

Perhaps one would not be so disagreeably affected by this exercise in the lower regions of the psychopathic, were it handled in a more bluntly debased fashion. One does not, after all, waste much indignation on the Draculas and Mummies and Stranglers of the last few years; the tongue-chopping and blood-sucking, disgusting as they may be, can often be dismissed as risible. *Peeping Tom* is another matter. It is made by a director of skill and sensibility: the director whose daring and inquiring eye gave us the superb *camera obscura* sequence and the entry into the operating room in *A Matter of Life and Death.*

The same stylist's view it is which now and then makes the torturer's stuff of the new film look like the true imaginative thing, the Edgar Allan Poe horror, instead of the vulgar squalor it really is.

Then one remembers that even in his best period, Michael Powell would suddenly devote his gifts to a story about a maniac who poured glue over girls' hair. He has got beyond glue here. He has got to the trick knife lovingly embedded in the throat, to the voyeur with sound effects, to a nauseating emphasis on the preliminaries and the practice of sadism—and I mean sadism. He did not write *Peeping Tom*; but he cannot wash his hands of responsibility for this essentially vicious film. (*Sunday Times*, Dilys Powell)

We the critics say so. Thank god we are not artists, we are critics.

And what did Nat Cohen do, the great distributor of this disturbance of the peace? Do? He was scared out of his tiny mind. All of us who had worked on the film had spent a very happy time for thirty days. It was a film full of humor and compassion, and Karl-Heinz had given an unforgettable performance. Laurence Harvey would never have touched the level of his intuition, which is not to say that Larry wouldn't have been good in the part. Anyone who had seen him in Restoration comedy would know that. But Karl-Heinz was more than good, he was great, he reached the heights.

We came, all innocently, to the opening at the Plaza Cinema, just around the corner from Piccadilly. It was owned by Paramount, and is a florid and friendly house. It was not an official premiere, but a lot of people in the business were there. Karl and I wore black tie, and I think I even sported a buttonhole. When the show was over we waited in the lobby for our friends.

But we had no friends. They passed us with averted gaze. It was obvious they just wanted to get off the hook, go home, and forget about it—and us. And Nat? . . . Nat? . . . and Stu? . . . the two executives of Anglo-Amalgamated Films? Wouldn't you have thought that they would have spent a little money, and taken space in the newspapers, and said, "This is what the critics say about our wonderful film. Now you, the public, come and see for yourselves, and see what a wonderful film it is, and what lousy critics we have."

But did they? Not on your nelly! They yanked the film out of the Plaza, they canceled the British distribution, and they sold the negative as soon as they could to an obscure black marketeer of films who tried to forget it, and forgotten it was, along with its director, for twenty years.

Leo Marks was philosophical. After all, he had received, and cashed, his check on the first day of shooting, and was already planning his next film. He made no criticisms, but in a very subtle way he managed to convey that if he, the author of the original screenplay, had been consulted more, and if his two long important dialogue scenes—the one between Mark and his girlfriend, the other between Mark and his starstruck victim—had not been brutally dropped in the editing stage, his film—it was already *his* film—might have had a different reception. However, it was no good crying over spilled milk, and he had enjoyed working with me very much. Might he suggest a film about the "White Rabbit," otherwise known as Wing Commander Yeo-Thomas, the English superspy and underground agent? Leo had known him intimately, in fact he could almost claim to have been his boss. Then there was another very interesting character, whom he would call "Mr. Sebastian." He was a code breaker, and was head of a department consisting of two hundred girls, tirelessly working to break the enemy codes. As an idea, it was fascinating, but it seemed to me to lack action. Or else, he suggested, there was an extraordinary creature who was a double agent and spied for both sides, and got away with it. Leo knew them all.

But although I wanted to work with Leo again, I was already involved with a horse of a different color, a horse called *Imperial.*

But to return to *Peeping Tom.*

Now that *Peeping Tom* is secure in his place in the movie hall of fame (I am writing this in the winter of 1989), I would like to explore for a while my contribution to the battered-child syndrome. It was quite conscious and quite shameless, for an artist should be shameless. When I asked Frankie for her permission to play Columba as the eight-year-old Mark in the film I knew exactly what I was doing, or at least thought I did. And Columba, when he saw the film with me, just giggled.

We had had the usual maddening delays over money and contracts that beset the independent film producer, and I was still casting the picture. By this time, I had rented offices and studio space in a small studio in St. Mary Abbot's Place, which was only a few minutes walk from 8 Melbury Road and made it very handy for interviews with actors. I had been rehearsing in this small studio for a week, and I decided to do all Columba's scenes there, where it would seem more like a game and where he would feel at home. I left the camera crew to line up each shot and ran down to the studio when they were ready. Bumba looked adorable in his gray jacket, his first, with a black string tie and a white shirt. He was thrilled with it. The day had started with a mad dash to Harrods because Frankie had not realized that we would need the jacket for the first shot. The first shot was Bumba saying goodbye to his dead mother. We soon got that in the can. Bumba was appropriately solemn, but refused to be directed: "If you talk to me, Daddy, during the scene, I shall laugh."

Take 1 was okay; a close-up of Bumba followed.

"It's a close-up. Do nothing. That's what a close-up is for, to see what you are feeling, not feel what you are seeing."

Then we re-dressed the set for the nursery bedroom scene. The lizard was a great success as a personality, but Bumba didn't fancy it much, "because it has claws on its feet."

In the final scene he got frightened, to everybody's embarrassment, including his own. I felt like a murderer, deservedly. Needless to say, I used the scene in the film. If my son has lizard complexes late in life, it will be my fault.

Leo Marks had written a scene for Bumba scattering flowers on his mother's grave. But Frankie drew the line on that. She put the flowers in water instead.

As if it hadn't been enough to lose Laurence Harvey, I now lost Natasha Parry, who was my original choice for Mark's second victim in the movie studio. I think that Peter Brook thought that Natasha and I were getting too intimate. I felt Natasha was a neglected actress, and perhaps I made that feeling too plain. Anyway, Peter Brook telephoned from New York. Would I release Natasha from the contract to join him in New York, where he was producing a play with Rex Harrison? They had just fired the leading lady and Natasha knew the part. Rex added his urgent voice to the clamor. It was obvious that Peter was going to get his own way, so I gave way gracefully, and ran down my list of possibilities:

> *Julie Andrews—too famous*
> *Moira Shearer—too glamorous*
> *Joan Plowright—too sympathetic*
> *April Olrich—too exotic*
> *Elizabeth Seal—too sophisticated*
> *Gillian Vaughan—too . . . too . . . too . . .*
> *Noelle Adam—too big a risk*

Oh hell! None of them inspired me the way Natasha did! Moira was the pick of the bunch, but what hope was there of getting her at short notice? Precious little, I thought. I had seats that night for *The Ginger Man,* so I went. Tony Walton had done the set, so Julie Andrews was there with Beriosova.* Richard Harris in the play was terrific, a genuine star, long-bodied, twenty-eight years old, radiating confidence and physical attraction, but it was a girl I wanted, not an Irishman from Limerick.

On Sunday, I had two units working in 16mm black and white: scenes from Mark's private collection. I shot the scene in our back garden, of Bumba peeping on the two lovers kissing in the next garden. The French couple from the flat upstairs, M. et Mme. Le Compte, played the lovers and put plenty of muscle into it. Meanwhile Bill Paton went off with Margaret Neal and Gerry

---

*Svetlana Beriosova, principal dancer with the Sadler's Wells Ballet and the Royal Ballet.

Turpin to shoot the lady in the bikini at Ruislip Lido. It was a cold, windy day in October, but Margaret was a hardy girl. All these scenes shot by Mark's film father were, of course, in black and white, and 16mm, and hand-held.

I had weighed the possibilities and decided to go banco on Moira. She and Ludo were living in Amersham, north of London. It's a lovely old red-brick market town, with one of the widest high streets in England. I telephoned I was coming, and arrived at half past ten. Ludo was banging away at a typewriter in the backroom. Moira opened the door. We looked at each other. It was ten years since *Hoffmann*. She said, "Come in, Michael," and led the way into the front room, which was decorated with ballet posters.

I plunged straight into my subject, and Karl-Heinz Böhm, who he was, and why. She listened, leafing through the script and the list of the cast. I had penciled the name of the actors already cast against the character he or she was playing, and Moira could see already that there were three or four names that she would love to work with. I could see that I was doing all right, so I left her the script, together with the bongo recording that Brian Easdale had slung together. She promised to read the script by lunchtime, and listen to the recording.

I jumped back in the Bentley and raced to Pinewood. Arthur Lawson was all ready to start building as soon as we got our money. Copies of the script had been circulating, and everybody was excited about the new film. I dashed back to London to meet my young lawyer, Laurence Harbottle, who had been recommended to me by Tony Quayle. He was about thirty and full of energy. He had his offices in the same building as the Film Finance Corporation, which was handy—what you might call inspired casting. I arrived back at our office, with everyone standing around me, and telephoned Moira.

I had telephoned Moira once before, but Ludo, typically, gave nothing away, merely said she was "down the village." It was a deal—she loved the part! Two thousand pounds for six days, over two weeks, any extra days £350 a day. The whole office was agog, because until then I had said nothing. Bill Burnside, who was doing the publicity, rushed to telephone the *Daily Express* and all the agencies. We were all there until long past our dinnertime. It was a great coup.

The next day we had a reading of the script. Just for the record, and because of the importance of the picture artistically and historically, I'll print an extract from my daily diary for 1959. Here it is:

October 27. 10:00 at the YWCA in Baker Street. Present, the author, Leo Marks.
Bill Paton.
Ivor, but only for a short while [Beddoes].

Brenda Bruce—Dora [playing the Soho tart].

Karl-Heinz Böhm—Mark, who was introduced to the assembled company [his name would be Anglicized to Carl Boehm in the credits].

Bartlett Mullins—Mr. Peters [The owner of the grimy newspaper shop. I had first seen Bartlett Mullins in Peter Brook's production of *The Dark of the Moon*, at the Lyric Hammersmith. He played one of the Parish Council in *Gone to Earth*.]

Miles Malleson—Old Gent [Miles Malleson was a wonderful writer, actor, and civilized character. He played the old gentleman who comes in to buy dirty photographs in the newsagent. He never turned down a part if he could help it. He was in several of my early films. He played the Caliph in *Thief of Bagdad*, and wrote most of the dialogue. Korda loved him, as I did. Miles and Bartlett Mullins together were a complete vaudeville act.]

Pamela Green—Milly [the cover girl with not much coverage].

Susan Travers—Lorraine [daughter of Lyndon Travers, played the girl with the harelip].

Maxine Audley—Mrs. Stephens [Helen's mother].

Anna Massey—Helen.

Peggy Thorpe-Bates—Mrs. Partridge.

Brian Worth—assistant director in the studio scenes [Brian was in *The Battle of the River Plate*, and also *Ill Met by Moonlight*. He was the fighter pilot in *The Lion Has Wings*, at the beginning of the war.]

Esmond Knight—Baden [film director in the studio scenes].

Guy Kingsley-Poynter—Tate [the cameraman].

Barrie Steel—clapper boy—n.g., too old.

Gillian Vaughan—Pauline—late.

Moira Shearer (*in absentia*)—Vivian, otherwise known as Viv.

Extra Boy—Roland Curram.

Michael Goodliffe—D.J. [the character's name was Don Jarvis, an allusion to John Davis].

Valerie Hovenden—his secretary.

Cornelia Zulver—extra girl [my niece].

Paddy Leonard—extra girl, read Vivian.

Robert Crewdson—trunk assistant.

Durant—publicity man.

Jack Watson—Inspector Gregg.

Nigel Davenport—Sergt.

(Some young actor, I forget his name, he was excellent—a Detective).

Martin Miller—in and out early—Dr. Rosen [psychoanalyst].

Leo sat there with his mouth open, without a cigar for once. I had sprung the whole thing on him, choosing Moira Shearer. Someone gave him the *Express* to read: there was Bill Burnside's story. Interleaved in my diary is a telegram addressed to me:

EVER GRATEFUL I HOPE—NATASHA

I smiled. I could afford to smile. I had Moira.

In the writing and rewriting of a film, in the casting of the actors, in the designing of the sets and costumes, in the composing of the music, in the conferences between director and cameraman, and camera department and sound recordist, in the discussions over makeup, in the excitement over research, in the planning of the shooting schedule, the conferences with the editor, the date of the mix of sound and picture and music, the date of final delivery—from the first day's shooting to the opening night—we bathe in love, we lucky people.

Miracles are performed, new ideas are tested out, new effects are invented. There are no secrets. Everything is shared. After the first two days everyone knows his place, everyone knows his job, our triumphs are their triumphs, our successes, their successes, our hearts beat as one. Sometimes old-timers say to me, "Well, Micky, it's only a job, isn't it?" But they know in their hearts, and in my eyes, that they are liars. At one time or another they have caught what we have been striving for all our lives, and then the crust breaks—and they love this wonderful art too. And what do we get from the folk who put up the money, who own the studios, who own the laboratories, who own the theatres, who own the distribution companies? What do we get from them? Hate. We are paid like princes and treated like slaves. They buy and sell us, body and soul. Fools that we are, we take their cash instead of insisting on a percentage of the gross—not of the profit, of the gross. So the budgets get bigger, and nobody wants to back new ideas, new subjects and new men. A country's films, like a country's poets, are one of its greatest cultural assets. A good film is accepted and digested everywhere. A great film can change the world in a flash of time. I have seen this happen before; I shall live to see it again. Seventy years ago there were not many men like D. W. Griffith, and seventy years later—now—there are not many men like Martin Scorsese. But so long as there is one there will be others, and the art of the cinema will survive.

It is Friday, January 13, 1989, and I am writing about Tuesday, October 27, 1959, thirty years ago, and people are still discovering *Peeping Tom*. In 1936, fifty-three years ago, I made *The Edge of the World*. It suffered the same fate as *Peeping Tom*, but I would not let it die. Only a few independent cinemas booked it in England, the country of its origin. Only two critics saw it for what it was. But the National Board of Review in New York and the National

Geographic Society in Washington praised it, and Joe Rock, its producer, and I, its director, wouldn't let the little film die. After the war was over I tracked down the negative and brought it home to be hospitalized and restored. That was in 1946. Thirty years later I showed the little film in a retrospective in Santa Fe and it got a standing ovation. Films have a short life, do they? We shall see, my friends, we shall see. Only eleven years to 2001.

THREE

WEDDING DAY:
Thelma Schoonmaker
and Michael Powell
in front of Holy Cross
Church, Avening,
May 19, 1984.

W hen I look back at the cast list of three films, *The Battle of the River Plate, Ill Met by Moonlight,* and *Peeping Tom,* I realize that I have failed to get over to you the slowness of the recovery in England of the performing arts and performing artists after the war. I have already indicated how much the English enjoyed the ten-year period of austerity that followed the declaration of the peace. America could slam all the gears of all the arts into high, but not England! Oh no, not England! England had lost her Empire, England had fired Churchill, England had a socialist government, the English people must all pull together! There would be no dancing on the green, and above all very slow demobilization because it might affect the economy . . . but you know all this, don't you? The clever ones, the cunning ones, the lucky ones—dare I say, the sensible ones?—got a good start in the new world that was supposed to have been created.

After the war was over there was a great scarcity of leading men and women in all the lively arts: theatre, film, radio, television. Most of the top talent went off to America, where they claimed to have won the war, not lost the peace. The Albert Finneys, the Peter O'Tooles were waiting in the wings. Their time was coming, but it was not there yet. My cast of actors in *River Plate* was middle-aged and strictly male. It was quite an effort to scrape up the actors for a hundred small parts. Neither of the leading men in *Ill Met by Moonlight* would have got the job in normal times, any more than the gentlemen actors would have been cast in Carl Foreman's *Guns of Navarone.* The sequences of elderly gentlemen climbing cliffs, obviously done in the studio, were hysterical. You should have heard David Niven on the subject: "Who does he think I am, Superman?"

David Farrar was a great discovery, and we should have done more with him; we should never have played David Niven as Sir Percy Blakeney; we never would have met Mel Ferrer if he hadn't been tied to Audrey, and never would have been too soon for me. Peter Finch was a lovely man and a lovely actor, and had that little extra that makes an actor a star, like Conrad Veidt. Dirk Bogarde was . . . Dirk Bogarde; Anthony Steel was Anthony Steel, alas! Which brings us to *Peeping Tom* and Karl-Heinz Böhm, who was both a triumph and a disaster. I have forgotten Christopher Lee, the great Christopher Lee, in his masterful performance of a German soldier in *Ill Met by Moonlight* where he dominates every frame of the scene, and there is Jack Watson, until *Peeping Tom* a radio actor, who played the inspector of police, and Nigel Davenport, who played his sergeant and never seems to have stopped working, and Martin Miller, who played the psychiatrist and with whom I always wanted to work, a great actor; all character actors, you see—no stars, present or potential, except Peter Finch.

The actors, the personalities, were there all right, and very soon were to dominate films like *Lawrence of Arabia,* and *Saturday Night and Sunday Morning,* not to mention *Room at the Top.* But I don't think anybody has ever realized why English films after the war tended to be unexciting. So far as the British film industry was concerned, John Davis had brought the whole thing to a grinding stop, and by the time England resumed production again it was a cottage industry. Alex was dead, Arthur Rank was dead, and but for Xerox John Davis would be dead too.

This long-winded attempt to explain the inexplicable is to explain why The Archers' starry creations were women—Deborah Kerr, Moira Shearer, Kathleen Byron, Kim Hunter, Ludmilla Tcherina—rather than men. Owing to the recent conflict, and our association with the British Ministry of Information, the films that made our names tended to be films of ideas rather than of action. This was really where we came to loggerheads with Arthur Rank and John Davis. We should have slugged it out with them. We should have gone the full twenty rounds with John Davis and come out with some suitable compromise. We should have . . . we should have . . . ah, the hell with it! If we had it all to do over again, we'd probably do exactly the same. But looking back at those days, I must admit that we seem to me to have been a little bit old-fashioned. The Archers' arrows needed new goose feathers.

We are picking up the pieces, and the new generation is at the gates. And my next film was *The Queen's Guards.*

The Brigade of Guards are the personal troops of the reigning sovereign: the King's Guards or the Queen's Guards. In the present case, the Guards are Her

Majesty Queen Elizabeth II's. Her subjects, especially the small boys among them, know the Guards as toy soldiers on ceremonial occasions, in scarlet uniforms, shining breastplates, tall bearskins, and flashing swords. The Changing of the Guard, with ceremonial saluting and stamping, is one of London's most popular sideshows. But it is less well known to the public that the Guards are first-line troops and spend a great deal of their time on active service.

On the first Saturday of June every year the Queen reviews her troops, drawn up on the Horse Guards parade ground. It's a noble setting: on the east is Whitehall, with all the administrative and government offices, and the Admiralty Arch, which leads into Trafalgar Square; to the south is Downing Street and the Foreign Office; to the west, Buckingham Palace and the park. It is a stage fit for this tribute to a queen. There are five regiments of Foot Guards: the Grenadier Guards, the Coldstream Guards, the Scots Guards, the Irish Guards, and the Welsh Guards. In addition there are two regiments of Household Cavalry: the Life Guards, and the Blues and Royals (before 1960 the Horse Guards). Only the Foot Guards and the Household Cavalry take part in the Queen's Birthday Parade, popularly known as Trooping the Colour, before Her Majesty Queen Elizabeth II.

If you are a Londoner and live in London, and if you are lucky enough to live in a mews cottage in Belgravia, as I did once, you would have been agreeably conscious, from time to time, of the clatter of horses' hooves mixing with the roar of the traffic around Victoria Station. The Household Cavalry is passing by, either as the sovereign's escort or merely to exercise the horses in Hyde Park. A friend of mine, Simon Harcourt-Smith, was meditating these matters as he stood outside Buckingham Palace, hat in hand, for Regimental Sergeant-Major Peachy Woodhouse had just knocked a terrified man's hat off with a roar: "Take your hat off, you idle civilian!" RSM Woodhouse's complexion was of a permanent brick red, which explains why he was called peachy. At that moment the idea of a film of the Queen's Guards was formed.

Simon brought the idea to me, and I bought it. I suppose that it was inevitable. Readers of my earlier volume will know that, like Rudyard Kipling, I am a sucker for stories about the services. I will never let it be forgotten that I was an honorary sergeant, attached to the First Sussex Yeomanry, in the 1914 war. Then there was the matter of *Colonel Blimp*, which showed astonishing knowledge of the military animal, to match Emeric Pressburger's intuition and invention.

But alas, I had no longer my Pressburger, although, when *The Queen's Guards* was first being discussed Emeric rang me up, saying he had an idea and would like to discuss it with me. I remember that a small boy was one of the principal characters. But I was just on the point of leaving for North

Africa, and there was no time for more than a hurried conversation. I regretted it at the time, and I regret it now.

A script for *The Queen's Guards* was already in the works at that time, by Roger Milner, a dramatist with a flair for military subjects and a sardonic humor. He had had considerable success in the theatre, but he was more a sketch artist than a full-blown dramatist. I liked him very much, but our collaboration was uneasy. He sent me a Christmas card the other day, in 1989, scribbling that he blamed all his subsequent nonsuccess on his collaboration with me. This could be read two ways, but I think he meant it as a compliment.

Harcourt-Smith's basic idea was to encapsulate the story of a British military family within the ceremony of Trooping the Colour, in which the climax is the arrival of Her Majesty to take the salute. Sounds great. Everybody bought it, including Twentieth Century–Fox, who put up the money. The Queen's consent was sought and granted. It was calculated that nine Technicolor cameras would be needed on that one morning in June. Things were moving at such a pace that I suddenly found myself in production while the script was still being written and *Peeping Tom* was having his trouble with the censors.

It was early spring, March 1960, and the Guards were flying to Libya to join up with other elements of NATO in a vast exercise over World War II terrain, for at this time Colonel Qaddafi was a pain in the neck only to his family. The War Office, perhaps anxious to atone for their stuffy behavior over *Colonel Blimp*, suggested that we might like to come along, too. They would get us there and back, but out there we would be on our own. This happy-go-lucky approach had worked with the Royal Navy, and there seemed no reason that it shouldn't work with the army, so I enlisted Syd Streeter, Bill Paton and me, Gerry Turpin, Bob Kindred, two assistants, and a Technirama camera. The airlift consisted of two Comets and four battalions of troops. Of course there was no room for us, and of course they said we had to leave all of our equipment, and of course we made them all back up and take us. This is normal, when dealing with the services.

We left from Lyneham, a military airfield near Swindon, not far from where I now live. We were put down at daybreak at El Adam military airport near Tobruk. The Brigade of Guards went off in a cloud of dust and left us sitting on our asses on the tarmac. Fortunately the RAF were more hospitable. They packed us into a Beverly transport aircraft and moved us up to Tmimi, where the clans were gathering. We drew our rations, two 160-pound tents, and got them erected before a sudden storm laid the dust. But we still had no transport.

The next morning I commandeered a Land-Rover and sent Syd and Harcourt-Smith off to Derna to get two trucks or else come back on their shields. Helicopters were already moving pallets of stores up to an airstrip. A long line of trucks and troops, "Duke of Edinburgh," were on the march. The Grenadiers to our south were moving off in clouds of red dust. Tomorrow there would be a battle.

Syd and Simon came in late but triumphant: two one-ton trucks. The next step was to be airborne. Moving off, I sent the Land-Rover off again to beg, borrow, or steal a helicopter. This was big country and everything was spread out. I spent the morning stealing petrol for my trucks. A battalion conference was signaled by a little Ferret armored car, which came storming over the ridge followed by a brother Ferret. The conference, held on the edge of the escarpment, was a pictorial success, some officers in bright green canvas chairs, others sitting on the rocks around. All these snapshots are in the film; they are the best part of it.

Next morning, at 5:00 A.M., we drove up to Tmimi to claim our helicopter. The one that had been assigned to us was American. Fortunately, an umpire had grounded another helicopter, which he declared to be shot down, so we bagged it. Syd and Gerry got to work mounting the camera in the open door of the chopper. We used a high hat* for the camera, mounted on the driver's seats of the two trucks to lessen the vibration. The camera could be tilted by the operator. This lash-up job looked terrible, as well as dangerous, but it worked, with acknowledgments to Heath Robinson. It's very tricky shooting out of an open door of a helicopter. Gerry hung on to the camera, and we hung on to Gerry. I directed the pilot over the intercom.

We put down at HQ. It was only then that we found out that there were no overall plans of battle; there was us, and there was the enemy, and they made it up as they went along. The army seemed to have learned something since *Colonel Blimp* and "War starts at midnight." After a look at the war maps we took off again, and flew over the escarpment. The terrain was rock and grass, gray and green, and the advancing infantrymen spread over it like purple lizards. We took a wide sweep around and saw the enemy, and flew over our advancing troops. They came on steadily in extended order; spread out over a large area they looked great.

That night it blew cold, straight off the bitter Balkan snows. Deep in my sleeping bag, I wished that I had Ingrid Bergman to keep me warm. In the morning we caught up with the Guards' headquarters. A tall, fair, mustachioed officer was standing with a falcon on his wrist. It was a peregrine, a tiercel, and he unhooded the savage little bird, which looked around fiercely

*A metal base for a camera that is bolted to a piece of wood so that the camera can sit flat on the ground, allowing for extreme low-angle shots. It resembles a top hat.

for a possible prey. Its master explained that he was attached to the Libyan army and was an instructor at the military academy at Benghazi. While we were talking three helicopters came out of the sky and settled down near us like geese, big ones from NATO. Bugles blew and men ran. I said to Gerry, "Go get 'em."

As we set up the camera a tall figure stepped out of the leading helicopter: Mountbatten, known to us as John Brabourne's father-in-law. He was passably astonished to find me there.

"Mr. Powell, what on earth are you doing here?"

"Doing for the army, what we did for the senior service."

He laughed. "You've got no business here at all."

He led the way into the staff tent. The others followed him, and I followed them. It was a nice little scoop.

We saw the Supreme Commander, NATO, off the premises, and ourselves took the road to Benghazi and the Lasga Pass, where the last battle was supposed to take place. In no time we moved up with the Welsh Fusiliers, old campaigners, who had been training in the hills for the last eighteen months and were watching the enemy through our glasses. The enemy, of course, were our old friends the Guards, who were spread out over the distant hill.

Early in the morning, before daylight, the attack came. Our gunnery officer was splendid, hurling thunder flashes and water bombs all around. The hills were lit up by star-shells. The Grenadiers advanced calmly through the smoke, and we all went to breakfast. Suddenly I realized what a huge concentration of men and materials were around us: twenty-five hundred men and vehicles, all gathered in a shallow saucer in the hills. Columns of men and machines were marching in. It was really big stuff. We shot all that, and then hastily got going, while the going was good. Our objective? Cyrene, that unchanged and enchanting Greek city that hangs upon cliffs that face the sea. We found a good place to pitch our tents, and I took my bedding roll right down to the edge of the waves and slept under a tamarisk tree.

In the morning we let the blessed Mediterranean wash the desert out of our eyes, noses, and hair, hanging on to the limestone edges. Then we took the Derna road, passing the army all the way, bathing, swimming, and playing and arriving at Tobruk in the evening, too late to shoot at the cemetery. It had been a long week of great heat at midday and very cold nights.

The reason we were at Tobruk, at the cemetery, was that in the tentative outline of the story of the film there were two brothers, one of whom had been killed in Tobruk in mysterious circumstances. His younger brother comes to find his grave. Tobruk was like all military cemeteries, orderly and impersonal, curiously undramatic, and very human. Our mission was completed here, and we had to think about getting on. Syd and Simon Harcourt-Smith were trying to get us on the returning transport. Meanwhile Bill had made a landmark stew. My life has been punctuated by Bill's stews, and once tasted, they are never forgotten by the participants.

=

The Queen's Guards is the most inept piece of filmmaking that I have ever produced or directed. I didn't write the story (weak) nor the screenplay (abysmal), but I take all the flak. Just to make sure that I knew what I am writing about, I asked Martin Scorsese (who, as I have said, has the world's more complete collection of Powell-Pressburger movieana) to let me run his videocassette of the film, which is imposed upon the public by Twentieth Century–Fox and me. I don't know what the critics made of it, and I don't intend to look them up. They must have been as puzzled as I was.

Here's the basic plot. A military family—father, mother, two sons—whose eldest son always goes into the Guards lose him in a skirmish at Tobruk, and heap their hopes of fame and military glory onto the shoulders of his younger brother, John, who, when the time comes, joins the Guards not because he wants to but because he thinks he has to, and wants to please his father, who, as often as not, addresses his son as Dawson, the name of his batman when he was the colonel of the regiment. This is no morale builder for John. In addition, his mother refuses to believe that her eldest son is dead. She believes that he was taken prisoner and lost his memory, and may walk in at any time. She is quite sane otherwise, and a charming woman, but on this subject definitely barmy. But, as Torquil MacNeil says in *IKWIG*, "Who isn't?"

Raymond Massey played the father, Daniel Massey, brother of Anna, played the son, thus completing once and for all Powell's obsession with the Massey family. To later-comers to this saga, I should explain that Ray Massey was under contract to Alexander Korda in the great Denham days, and played the chief part in H. G. Wells's *Things to Come,* and also Citizen Chauvelin in Leslie Howard's *Scarlet Pimpernel.* When I made *49th Parallel,* Raymond Massey, who was born a Canadian and had served in the Canadian army in World War I by lying about his age, and who had rejoined the army when Canada joined the British in World War II, was a natural choice for the part of the deserting soldier. He was, again, the natural choice for Abraham Farlan, the American prosecuting counsel in *A Matter of Life and Death,* because he was now an American citizen, while his elder brother, Vincent, who had been Canadian High Commissioner in London all through the war, was heard but not seen in *49th Parallel.* He spoke the prologue.

From that firm friendship it had been a natural step to Raymond Massey's play, *The Hanging Judge,* at a time when Vincent was being summoned back to Canada to be the first Canadian Governor-General. That was in 1952. In

1959 came Anna Massey and *Peeping Tom*, and a year later Daniel Massey playing opposite his father in *The Queen's Guards*. In weaving this web of relationships in art and friendship, I was consciously following the lead of the great theatrical families in the past, and it gave me great comfort to do so. A pity then it was that *The Queen's Guards* should be such a broken-backed feature, when it should have been a family saga and an epic of military glory. ". . . 'Tis true; 'tis true, 'tis pity; And pity 'tis 'tis true."

We shouldn't have tried to compete with A.E.W. Mason, that grand and great storyteller and author of *The Four Feathers*—and when at last it came into the hands of the three Korda brothers, Alex, Zoli, and Vincent, what a magnificent job they made of it! It had been made into a film before, and by another Hungarian, Lothar Mendes, later the director of Conrad Veidt's *Jew Süss*, and a beloved member of the Savile Club. I think that the Hollywood version of *The Four Feathers* was mainly a studio job, and the only actor that I remember was Richard Arlen, one of my favorites. But there was a memorable scene of hippos tumbling like a falling mountain into a river, and it must have been this Hollywood version that inspired Korda to remake it. Will those who saw *The Four Feathers*, and who see it now, ever forget C. Aubrey Smith as the general, and Ralph Richardson and John Clements, and the charge of the Mahdi's troops at the Battle of Omdurman? Never!

> An' 'ere's *to* you, Fuzzy-Wuzzy, with your 'ayrick 'ead of 'air—
> You big black boundin' beggar—for you broke a British square!

But to return to *The Queen's Guards* . . . what a comedown! In my ignorance, and innocence, I had thought that Ray and Dan would be delighted to play father and son. On the contrary, they both screamed in horror at the thought, and only yielded through flattery and to my importuning. Ursula Jeans played the psychotic mother. It called for someone much more scatty and funny—or frightening. You remember her, don't you, in the Berlin nursing home sequence in *Colonel Blimp*, the baroness who had the fat horses? In life she was Roger Livesey's wife, and now they are both dead.

It was a perfect marriage. Neither could have long survived the other. They were in a play together in New York when the blow struck: Roger had cancer of the bowel, and it took all their money and all their savings to pay for the operation and bring him home. The future looked bleak. At one stroke Roger had been deprived of his splendid body. Frankie and I asked them down to stay at the Voile d'Or for a few weeks when we were redecorating the hotel, and Roger painted all the bedroom doors in startling colors.

They struggled on. Friends rallied round, but they were no longer picking and choosing the roles they would play. They were offered less and less work. Roger aged greatly. Then, as so often happens between such a devoted couple, Ursula was struck down by the same killer, and died first. He soon followed her.

You who read this, you who have stood in the golden glow of Roger's performance as Clive Candy, as the Laird of Kiloran in *IKWIG*, as Dr. Reeves in *AMOLAD*, and who will remember with delight Ursula Jeans's verbal duel with Deborah Kerr in *Colonel Blimp*, have a right to know how this love story ended, and what sort of human beings lived and breathed behind the actors' masks.

Robert Stephens, who had made his name at the Royal Court Theatre and the National Theatre, and who was under contract to Twentieth Century–Fox, joined the cast to play Henry Walton, an officer but not a gentleman. Jack Watson, seen as the detective inspector in *Peeping Tom*, crossed over from Scotland Yard to the Guards barracks to play the sergeant-major. Anthony Bushell had one scene especially written for him, and which recalled his sour performance as Colonel Strang in *The Small Back Room*.

The girls in the script were 1960s nonentities, and were cast and played like nonentities; in the 1960s, the only woman was Joan Plowright. Ian Hunter brings up the rear of the column. He gave a sterling performance, as he always did, amiable, unintelligent, and full of charm. Ian personified the "something will turn up" actor, and one of the first films we worked together on was for Irving Asher at Warner Bros., a rehash of a Hollywood script entitled *Something Always Happens*, in which he played a charming wastrel who always landed on his feet. This little film is still around; it was made in 1934. But the very first film that Ian and I worked on together was *The Phantom Light* for Mickey Balcon.* That was the part that I tested Roger Livesey for, but Mickey didn't like Roger's voice and was not impressed by his hawklike profile and wonderful, red-gold Viking upswinging hair. I always thought that it was typical of Mickey Balcon that he lived at Sevenoaks, a town in Kent that is neither town nor country but an uneasy compromise of both.

But I have left *The Queen's Guards* standing on parade too long. Let's dismiss them! "Guards! Shun! Shoulder arms! By the ranks! Quick march!"

Some talk of Alexander, and some of Hercules;
Of Hector and Lysander, and such great names as these;
But of all the world's brave heroes, there's none that can compare,

---

*Leading British film producer from the early twenties to the sixties. Mostly identified with the early Hitchcock thrillers and the Ealing comedies. The actor Daniel Day-Lewis is his grandson.

With a tow, row, row, row, row, row, for the British Grenadier.
With a rah, ta, ta, rah, rah, rah, rah, with a British Grenadier.

=

I think that's wrapped that up rather well. I hope I got away with it. I'd hate to talk any more about The Queen's Guards. *Here we go, then, final stretch of the book. If I don't live to complete it, you'll know how to do it, my beloved amanuensis. The last page or two I have done already, when we talk about being amateurs. They finish with the death of Emeric. We can now add a footnote saying: for the record, Emeric Pressburger died at such and such a time, on February 5, 1988, and by his own request is buried in the churchyard at Aspall, the little Suffolk village where he spent the last twenty years of his life. I would like to bring in Shoemaker's Cottage, too, and quote the Walter Scott poem carved on his tombstone by his grandsons. And if I'm dead, you can do the same for me and Avening and dear Lee Cottages. All clear? So, now I am starting on the final chapter. I had better change the reel. I'd love to have something by Kipling engraved on my stone, but I am afraid it would look like showing off:*

If you can force your heart and nerve and sinew
To serve your turn long after they are gone,
And so hold on when there is nothing in you
Except the Will which says to them: "Hold on"*

=

The Queen's Guards was my last British movie. *Miracle in Soho* was Emeric's. It looks as if we should examine the similarities or dissimilarities between them.

They were both failures: not the sort of failures you can shovel under the carpet, but total failures. When I sneaked a view of my old partner's production of *The Miracle in St. Anthony's Lane*, which he had hopefully dragged from Berlin to Paris, from Paris to London, to Korda, to me, to Rank, and finally to John Davis, at first I writhed and cried out, "No, no, Emeric! No!"

And then I wept for my old partner, for I knew what he was trying to get over in this mixture of fantasy, realism, and superstition. It's a heady mixture that appeals to Central Europeans, and particularly to Hungarians. They like shortcuts to a situation, and they jump from joke to joke. I've already written that one of Emeric's most characteristic remarks in English, when discussing a literary work, was, "Already a joke."

*The poem is on Michael's gravestone in the little cemetery at Holy Cross Church, Avening, Gloucestershire, England.

There is more than a touch of fantasy in *A Canterbury Tale*, even more in the curse that is laid upon the lairds of Kiloran in *IKWIG*, most of all in *A Matter of Life and Death*. When I read Emeric's first outline of the *Matter of Life and Death* screenplay I was seriously disturbed. It was full of mysterious appearances and disappearances, and waving curtains, and spectral voices, and airy-fairy speeches. You could see the wheels going round all the time. I realized that the whole idea of the trial in heaven had to have a solid basis in reality, medical reality, and that the appearance and disappearance of the heavenly messenger would have to be matter-of-fact and realistic if we were to get away with such fantasies at the end of a great war to end wars.

It was the firm acceptance by all the principals of the solid medical reason for the operation on the pilot's brain that made the rest of the plot so satisfying to the audience. I hadn't quite brought this off in *A Canterbury Tale*, and I was determined not to make the same mistake in *A Matter of Life and Death* . . . see what I mean? When the Americans wanted to rename our film *Stairway to Heaven* we knew at once they hadn't understood at all what we had succeeded in doing. They saw it all as a fairy tale. I saw it as a surgical operation. When Dr. Reeves has his motorcycle accident we see him burned alive, one of the most sympathetic characters in the story. It is the same with *The Red Shoes*, when Moira Shearer leaps to her death on the railway line and has her feet cut off by the train, and when Marius kisses her legs and the torn and grimy tights. It shocks the audience into sensibility. Hans Andersen knew what he was doing, and so did I.

When I told John Davis what to do with the script of *Cassia* I knew that I was burning my boats, and so did he. He had sent for Emeric, told him that I was impossible, and offered to finance *The Miracle in St. Anthony's Lane*. Emeric came to me in great distress, and I said, "Grab it."

The moment for *St. Anthony* had come. We looked at each other. We knew it was the end. Emeric said, "I think I shall call it *Miracle in Soho*."

I said, "Great title."

He peered at me doubtfully. "You really think so?"

I said, "Yes. Who will direct it, Imre? You?"

He shook his dear, wise head. "No, Michael. I know the story too well. It belongs to a part of my life that is over. Someone else must bring it to the screen."

I looked doubtfully at him.

"What does the little tin god say?"

"He says I can have whom I like, but why not try one of the new young television directors."

I winced. John was starting already. He was maneuvering Emeric into a position that he could not defend. I said, "Don't do that, Imre. All the members of our group, from producer to clapper boy, know how much you have contributed to us, and to British films. Ask Ronnie or David or Carol Reed to direct it. Any one of them would be flattered to be asked, and then you could go from strength to strength."

"Do you really think so?"

"Would I say so, if I didn't?"

He gave me a long look, with those beautiful, honest eyes. "I don't know, Michael. Perhaps you might."

"How about Jack Cardiff? We gave him three great chances. He owes you a picture. He wants to direct, and a fantasy like *Miracle* would be right up his street . . . up his lane," I finished, laughing.

But I might as well have saved my breath. They assigned one of those new television directors to do it, one that was under contract to the Rank Organisation. He couldn't direct traffic.

What about art direction? The French and the Germans had been building wonderful, fabulous street scenes for years, with alleys and streets and steps and fire escapes and roofs, with dozens of interesting camera angles all arranged for the director. The Pinewood art department built Emeric a street—a solid little street that opened at each end onto traffic and shops, a street where there were about two decent camera angles, and where the camera and director were always backed up against a shop or a wall. The Church of St. Anthony, the church of the title, had to be given a proper place in the decor and in the story, and in addition there had to be room for the road gang to put down a new asphalt surface to the street. It was a shambles. Chris Challis did his best, and the better he lit it the worse it looked. It still gives me nightmares to remember.

The shooting schedule, and the assistant director's job, must have been the most complicated in the history of British films. Alfred Junge, the great Alfred Junge, would have provided for Emeric all that his script needed, and room to work as well. As for plot, the script was all plot and involved an Italian family; and there was a mysterious postman, played mysteriously by Cyril Cusack, who evidently was an angel in disguise, or perhaps a guardian angel for the girl. I know there was a letter he should have brought, or did bring, or something, but by the time they got in all about the Italian family there was no room for anybody else, and the celestial person got short shrift.

Plot? I never saw so much plot in my life; everybody was drowning and swimming in plot, and the Soho atmosphere was laid on so thick that you couldn't care whether St. Anthony was watching over his flock or not. But worst of all was dear, fluffy John Gregson as the chief of the road gang, the man with the mighty forearm muscles, whose drill was plunged vulgarly again and again into the virginal tarmac. This was a young man who was with a different girl every night and who was always starting fights in bars. Stanley Baker was under contract at that time and would have been wonderful in the part. John Gregson was like a pussycat arching his back and tail and waiting to be stroked . . . enough, enough!

John Davis had his way. This was the kind of film he wanted made at Pinewood Studios. He opened it at the Odeon Leicester Square and played it through the entire Odeon circuit, and the public could like or lump it. They lumped it. They stayed away in droves. Of course he turned upon Emeric, the writer and producer, and blamed him for the disaster. There was no more question of *Cassia*, there was no more question of any film with the Rank Organisation. This, to the man who had written two Royal Command performances that had brought fame and glory to the Rank Organisation.

Emeric accepted this outrageous treatment with dignity, and yielded to David Lean's entreaties to go with him to India and tour the subcontinent for several months while they were preparing together a script on—guess what? Right first time—the life and death of Mahatma Gandhi, a film eventually to be made not by David Lean, not by Emeric Pressburger, but by little Dickie Attenborough, coming up from behind in the field to pass all the established favorites to win in a canter, while thousands cheered. But that is another story, and I hope that Dickie will write it some day.

I knew Emeric better than his wife, better than his daughter, better than all his girlfriends, better than his current mistress, but not, I hope, better than his two Scottish grandsons. If you don't know by now that he had a beautiful mind, and knew nothing about women, then you'll never know anything, and I should have failed in my career as a biographer. We remained friends for the rest of our lives, a statement of more importance than any that I have yet made. For twenty years we had been as close as a man and wife. We continued to see each other. Why not? We loved each other; not like brothers, like friends. We even made a film together. And we worked together again on one or two other little jobs that none of you know anything about; but perhaps we'll tell you about them when the time comes. Those painstaking people who collect filmographies—disgusting word—don't know everything!

Alas, the poor Archers!

> I shot an arrow into the air,
> It fell to earth, I knew not where.*

It fell in Spain. The rain in Spain falls mainly on the plain, and on my heart. But nothing of value came of my Spanish venture, *Honeymoon*. Nothing that

*From Longfellow's "The Arrow and the Song."

has happened, before or since, has so convinced me that I am not a writer. I am a film director, and one of my missions in life is to convince my fellow film directors that collaboration is an art, and that the movies are the greatest of collaborative arts.

All art is one, man, one.

Yes, that's true; the end is the same, but putting words together for a reader is not the same art as creating images for an audience. Alfred Hitchcock is the acknowledged master of surprise and suspense, but his best films were written for him by Launder and Gilliat in the years before the war, films like *The Lady Vanishes*, *The Man Who Knew Too Much*. First the word, then the image. Of course Hitchcock knew this; he knew, he knew. But it was never part of his policy to give credit to the creations of his writer-collaborators, and the world took him at his valuation. But give him a poor subject—*Frenzy*, *Torn Curtain*, *Jamaica Inn*—and he could do nothing with it.

On *Honeymoon* I was so convinced of my talents as a showman, I had been made so arrogant by the worldwide successes of *The Red Shoes*, *Black Narcissus*, *The Tales of Hoffmann*, that I thought that I had done it all myself, although I knew jolly well that I hadn't . . . but why go on? I am blaspheming against my own beautiful art. Be honest, Michael Powell, you could have saved your partner of twenty years from disaster, you could have transformed *The Miracle in St. Anthony's Lane* into a touching love story with a tongue-in-cheek premise. You knew what could go, and what could not go, with the tough, disillusioned public of the 1950s and '60s. And even if you felt that Emeric had let you down with *Rosalinda* and *Ill Met by Moonlight*, he had more than made up for it by his contribution to *The Battle of the River Plate*. Instead you ran away to Spain, and got your deserts at Coruña, like General Wolfe before you.

Now, when I look back, I realize that we were both proud, we were both to blame:

> 'Twas love I cannot ride with thee,
> And love I dare not bide alone.
> For both were proud, and both were free
> And both were as hard as the netherstone.*

Before Emeric left for India, he put into my hands his first novel. The title: *Killing a Mouse on Sunday*. It was a small book to come from the house of

---

*Michael carried vast amounts of poetry around in his head. At the age of seventy-six, he once quoted to me from memory all fifteen stanzas of Browning's *The Pied Piper of Hamelin*. But I never asked him the origin of this poem and have been unable to discover who authored it. Some have suggested that Michael may have written it himself.

Collins, one hundred and eighty-nine pages, and the title was certainly no help. In his pursuit of the English language, which made him a lifelong admirer of Lewis Carroll, and particularly of *The Hunting of the Snark*, Emeric had discovered that great tempter, *The Oxford Dictionary of Quotations*, with its memorable introduction by Bernard Darwin. It became Emeric's bed book, and he turned to it again and again. The story that he had to tell was a cat-and-mouse story; French cat, Spanish mouse. So, searching for a title, he looked up "mouse" in the same spirit that he would fling a handful of *jetons* onto the roulette table.

Richard Braithwaite came up, a Restoration poet and journalist and man-about-town. He comes up now and then, and is remembered for a coffee-house joke, as good a way as another's been remembered. It was at the expense of some gloomy Puritan, who one day hanged his cat on Monday for killing a mouse on Sunday. I was worried about the title. I said so. It was the kind of argument we had often had before. I can hear our two voices: "But, Imre, it's about the Pyrenees, and the Basque country. It's a thriller, and a jolly good one, with political undertones."

"It is a cat-and-mouse story, Michael."

"Great! Why not call it *Cat and Mouse?*"

"I have called it *Killing a Mouse on Sunday*, Michael."

And this time, there was nothing I could do about it.

The novel was well reviewed, and the film rights were snapped up immediately and Fred Zinnemann assigned to direct it. It was given a starry cast: Gregory Peck, Anthony Quinn, etc., etc., and was a complete failure at the box office.* With all this Emeric had nothing to do. In his college days Emeric's thing was running; his distance, a quarter of a mile. He took the money and ran.

A copy of the book lies in front of me now as I write. It still has the wrapper on it, with brilliant sketches on it by Papas:† Spanish innkeeper, a priest in his black soutane, a boy kicking his football, a bandit. On the flyleaf is written, in Emeric's firm, large hand: "To Michael, with much love, Imre. London 29 September 1961." My birthday is on the thirtieth of September, but the twenty-ninth is Michaelmas Day, the feast of St. Michael and All Angels. I turned the page and read the official dedication: "To my friend Stapi." I closed the book and sat there thinking. Then I laughed out loud.

---

*The film version of Emeric's novel was called *Behold a Pale Horse*.

†Bill Papas was a political cartoonist for *The Guardian*, *Punch*, and the *Sunday Times*, and had illustrated a book for Emeric's close friend and fellow Hungarian George Mikes. Papas was forced to leave South Africa for England in 1959, when his cartoons for the *Cape Times* caused the government to issue a banning order on his work. He now lives in Oregon and devotes himself to painting.

I had been working for a long time with Günther Stapenhorst, without knowing it. It had started with *Ill Met by Moonlight*, a wartime story in which the German General was the true hero. Next came *The Golden Years*, as spectacular a German musical film as was ever planned. Then *Cassia*, the adventures of a German painter of genius who was flooding the international art market with brilliant forgeries; finally, *The Battle of the River Plate*, whose real hero was the German Captain Langsdorff. How Stapi, who had been a commander in the Imperial German Navy, must have enjoyed starting this particular hare!

What? I missed one out? Which one?

"The Bat!"

The Bat?

"Yes, the Fledermaus *. . . the flitter-mouse . . . the Bat . . . your one and only operetta! . . . that oh, so naughty* Oh . . . Rosalinda!!*"*

I was hoping you had forgotten that. But then I remember Anton's speech at the end of the film, and Michael Redgrave doing an *entrechat* in the hotel corridor, and Tony Quayle singing "Chacun à son goût," and that glorious performance by Ludmilla Tcherina, and dear Dennis Price, sick and broken and always elegant and well mannered . . . these memories give me strength to admit that I was fooled once more by Stapi and Emeric, and it served me right. Because you admire the culture of another country that is no reason for thinking that you can do more than imitate it. If originality and truth are your aim, cultivate your own back garden.

≡

Nineteen sixty-one was a disastrous year; for me, for my friends, for my fellow artists. Scoptophilia was a dirty word, *The Queen's Guards* a big yawn, William Sansom's *The Loving Eye* suspected of being another *Peeping Tom*—it would have had more laughs—and then . . . suddenly . . . blue sky, a great rift in the clouds! Moses, in the shape of John Sutro, wreathed in smiles like an amiable bulldog, descended from the mountain bearing the tablets of the law—in other words, a screenplay by Graham Greene from his play *The Living Room*.

I had seen the play at Wyndham's Theatre, and had been moved to tears by Dorothy Tutin's devoted young heroine. It was a parable of youth and age, and the impossibility of bridging the gap between them by mere words. The girl is seventeen, her lover twenty years older. Her uncle, a Roman Catholic priest beautifully played by Eric Portman, is in his seventies, and her two aunts in their eighties. What chance has she got?

Their much younger brother, the girl's father, a lecturer in psychology in one of the American colleges, has died, and it has been decided by the family that the girl should return to England to live with her elderly relatives until she marries, or takes a job, or takes the veil—for her uncle is a priest, remember. She is escorted back to England by the man who was her father's star pupil and who is now himself a lecturer at Bristol University and is returning there after a long vacation. He is only a few years younger than her father, whom she adored, and all her grief and fear for the future are transmuted into desire and a need for a protector. Their love and need of each other is passionate and inevitable. The lecturer is married to a dipso. The evergreen master knows how to set the stage.

I read the script and was stunned by the possibilities of a real tragedy at last; a tragedy in which the author is in control the whole time; a tragedy like *Troilus*, a tragedy like *Romeo*, sensual, passionate, dramatic. But, of course, being Graham, he had kept his cool and left the passion and violence to be found out, and spelled out, by the director and the two lovers. It was an awe-inspiring script, the kind of script that God dictates in his spare time.

John Sutro telephoned. "Well, Michael?"

"What do you mean, well? It's terrific, isn't it?"

"Yes, Michael."

I could almost hear his bulldog grin. His charming French wife was listening in.

"And the cast? . . . Who's the girl?"

"Samantha Eggar—"

"—and the oldsters?"

"Nobody is settled yet, Michael. I wanted you to be in it at the earliest stage."

"Quite right . . . and the girl's lover?"

John hesitated.

"Can you keep a secret?"

"No, not in show business. Come on, John, what do you have up your sleeve? Who is going to play the sexy schoolmaster?"

"Rex Harrison."

He might as well have set a bomb under my chair.

"Rex!"

"Yes, Michael."

"Sexy Rexy?"

"Yes, Michael."

"You've got it in writing?"

"Better than that, I've got Laurie Evans on our side."

Mr. Evans was Rex's personal representative at MCA, an immensely powerful combination of ten percenters who, like the Cabots of Boston, talked only to God. We have met Mr. Evans before, during the shooting of *The Tales of Hoffmann* as an object of Bill Wall's savoir-faire.

"What does Rex himself say?"

"He loves the part. To him, it's a sort of halfway house between *French Without Tears* and *My Fair Lady*."

John was giggling with excitement, and delighted that he had knocked me off my pedestal. We met.

"John, this is terrific news! Without Rex, I don't think Graham has a chance of his script being made into a film; with Rex . . ."

"Exactly."

"Who will distribute?"

"Ilya Lopert and Bob Dowling."

"Where is Ilya?"

"At Cannes. Ilya and Bob will fully finance, if Rex is in."

I burst into action.

"I must see Rex—you know what a two-timer he is—that's how he got to be a star."

"He's at Santa Margherita."

Santa Margherita is a delicious little port on the Italian Riviera and Rex had a villa there, which he had bought for Lilli Palmer in happier days.

"Get him on the phone, John. I've got to go down to the Voile d'Or. I'll drive over and see him tomorrow."

Rex was looking very relaxed. He tried to set me off balance at once, by criticizing my clothes.

"Micky, what on earth are you doing, wearing that tweed suit? You look like a farmer."

"Sometimes I wish I was."

"Let me buy you a shirt."

He picked out a very colorful one. I said, "I like them without sleeves."

"You're wrong. You've got thin arms."

Rex had thin arms. The villa was spectacular and comfortable, but being an old hand on the Côte d'Azur I was not impressed. We discussed Graham's script. Rex praised it, which was high praise from the man of a hundred affairs.

"Well, are you in, Rex?"

"There's only one thing that worries me."

He mentioned the girl's name. She, too, had committed suicide.

"It's a little near the knuckle, you know."

"That's years ago! These things flare up and are forgotten."

"M-m-m . . ."

"Look here, Rex, you're either in or you're not. Which is it?"

He sipped his Ricard.

"I'm in."

We all swung into top gear; we started casting. John went about beaming.

He had brought off a veritable coup worthy of a pupil of Alex Korda. The news leaked out: Graham Greene, John Sutro, Rex Harrison, Michael Powell, Samantha Eggar; that was something you could call a line-up. We booked the studio, we engaged the art director, every cameraman wanted the job.

Then one morning John met me with an ashen face.

"Rex . . . he's called it off!"

"What do you mean? He's committed!"

"I know but somebody has published the story of that girl . . . you know, the one who committed suicide . . . it's in one of the girlie magazines. It mentions Rex's name and all. You know how actors are. He's scared stiff of his image."

I saw red. "How can he? He's given his word! You can't stop an express train! Where is he now?"

"In Paris . . . Graham is at Antibes."

"Tell Graham to fly to Paris. I'll come up from Cap Ferrat. Where's Rex staying?"

"The Lancaster."

"We'll meet there at ten o'clock tomorrow morning."

The meeting took place. Rex looked ashamed of himself, as well he might be. I said, "All we want to know is—is Rex in, or out?"

John said, "In, aren't you, Rex?"

"What does Rex say?"

Rex hesitated. He pointed to the magazine, of which there were several copies. "Have you seen this piece by——?" He named the journalist.

"Yes, what do you expect? They love to paint you as Don Juan. What's so special about this time?"

Rex muttered, "It's the circumstances. They're so very alike."

I said, "Come on, Rex! Kick it, for God's sake! I can understand you felt bad alone at Portofino, but you're not going to be alone in this picture. We all understand how you feel, and we'll see that you're protected, won't we, Graham?"

Graham looked at Rex and said, "Of course."

He was anxious to get out of this hotel room as soon as he could. I didn't blame him. He wasn't a film director.

Anyway, the upshot was that Rex agreed to stand fast. I met Ilya Lopert after the meeting in the bar.

"Well, Ilya?"

"Well, Micky?"

"Are you happy about *The Living Room?*"

"No, I'm not. If Rex weren't in it, I wouldn't touch it with a ten-foot pole."

"Why?"

"Because it's a tragedy, and the public don't pay to see tragedies. They've got enough tragedy at home."

"Speak for yourself, Ilya. Graham Greene's books sell by millions. What about *The Third Man?* His public don't expect to see Rex come on singing and dancing, and wearing a funny hat."

He gave me a sour grin.

"Very funny. But, I will say this, Micky, if anybody can make a film out of this *Living Room*, it's you."

The crisis seemed to be over. Rex went to London to see about his wardrobe. Then the blow fell. The Royal Court announced that it had signed Rex Harrison to play Platonov, the principal character in the play of that name by Anton Chekhov. He was going into rehearsals immediately. The play would open in four weeks' time, and after the London run it would go to New York. Greatly relieved, Ilya canceled the contract, in spite of all that John Sutro could do.

We shall hear of *The Living Room* again. One memory of this time stays with me. There were several lines in the script that I wanted changed, and Graham had reluctantly agreed to a meeting between the two of us. I took a room in a hotel at Cannes (or it may have been Antibes) where we could meet and work for a day or two. I can see us now: myself keen and respectful but inwardly outrageous; Graham, as grave and detached as the Archbishop of Canterbury, or perhaps I should say the Pope? I would make a suggestion and he would ponder it, sometimes for a good three minutes, before reluctantly stretching out his hand, picking up a pencil, poring over the script, and adding two or at most three words. I would peer at these alterations or additions, nod, and scribble them into my own script. At this rate it took us two days to finish the job. I have the impression that it gave Graham physical pain to alter one word of his dialogue.

By November 1961 I could look back and realize that I had achieved absolutely nothing. *Peeping Tom* had cost £135,000, and in the ordinary course of events would have recovered that cost within three months. Instead, and according to the latest accounts sent to me by the distributor of the film, it has taken twenty-nine years. The American rights were sold, or given, to Astor Pictures, which was trying to distribute European films in art houses and eventually went bankrupt. It is one of the peculiarities of independent film productions that you recover the cost of your venture within the first six months of distribution—or never. If Nat and Stu had jumped into the ring and slammed the critics as fiercely as they slammed me, the film would have become airborne and would have had its champions in England—like Bertrand Tavernier in Paris, where they retitled it, inevitably I'm afraid, as *Le Voyeur*. A better title would have been *Le Cinéaste*. This was before Bertrand became, himself, one of France's most distinguished directors. At the time he was one of its most notable film journalists. He invited me to Paris and interviewed me, and kept the film alive. He saw to it, over the years, that I was not forgotten in France.

The Queen's Guards was out of step, and the cutting copy was being batted to and fro by Darryl F. Zanuck's editor at the Fox Hollywood studios, and by Noreen Ackland, my editor at Shepperton Studios on the Thames. Noreen had been Reggie Mills's assistant for some years, and had become an editor herself with *Peeping Tom.* You don't need me to tell you what a good job that was. I saw her the other day with her husband, Dick Best, a film editor too. Noreen looked just the same—tall, dark, romantic, imaginative, and precise. It's a happy marriage.

=

It will be gathered that, by now, the main base of the Powell family was the Voile d'Or. We were as much there in the winter as in the summer. Besides being an asset to the hotel, with her beautiful face and figure and lovely manners, Frankie thoroughly enjoyed meeting people, and our two boys took it all for granted.

We had a small staff who were devoted to us, and a regular supply of regulars from all over Europe. As a French *hôtelier* I had never tried to exploit my connections with the film business, reasoning with myself that I had no ambition to see Ilya Lopert and Sam Spiegel engaged on my terrace in carving up a deal. As a consequence, the big terrace and the little bar remained a haven for British actors and their families. While my father lived, I had never regarded the hotel as my second home and I had no inclination to do so now. I have a compass in my head and it points north. When I wanted to recover my sanity I turned instinctively not to Saint-Jean-Cap-Ferrat but to the Highlands of Scotland.

I was fortunate in my friends. Alastair MacTavish Dunnett was now one of Roy Thomson's men. He had been offered the editorship of *The Sunday Times,* and had preferred *The Scotsman.* He was one of the great journalists of our day. But I only had to say to him "Can you get away for a few days, Alastair?" and he would manage to do it, don't ask me how. Alastair would say, "Will I alert Seton? He's just sent me a long piece on a piping contest in Inverness. Nobody in Edinburgh will read it, but I'll have to print it and pay him for it. I'll find out whether he's free to meet us."

Alastair, Bill Paton ("Up Helliya, Shetland ahoy!"), Seton Gordon, descending like an eagle from his eyrie in the Isle of Skye, and self, Michael Powell, were continually to be found, singly or together, usually summoned by one of the clan escaping from an office chair—by motorbus, by train, by light aircraft, and on our flat feet—to places like Glen Tilt, or Braemar, Campbeltown, or Lochboisdale, Stornoway, or Auchiltibuie, to Orkney, Shetland, the Fair Isles, Ullapool, Applecross, the Paps of Jura, the banks of Loch Lomond, Cape Wrath, the Treshnish Isles, Wester Ross, the Long Island, the Outer Island, and even to far St. Kilda.

It was November 10, 1961. I said to Bill, "We're off."

"North or south?"

"North. We're following the *IKWIG* trail: Glasgow, Oban, Tobermory."

"I'll pack the rucksacks."

"Do that; plenty of choca and whiskey."

When we pulled up the blinds, we were in the mountains near Tyndrum. A hard frost coated the heather, and the hilltops were covered in snow. The train ran down along the shores of the loch, and we were in Oban by half past nine in the morning. The boat sailed for Tobermory at 1:15 P.M., and there was a motorboat connection to Mingary pier on Ardnamurchan.

"Have you ever been to Ardnamurchan, Bill?"

"No."

Ardnamurchan is a dark, long, sparsely inhabited, and mysterious peninsula, some miles to the north of Tobermory. The nearest of the islands to the peninsula are Eigg and Muck.

"We'll sleep on Ardnamurchan tonight," I said.

Bill looked sceptical. He was still not aware that we were on our way to visit Gavin Maxwell, author of *Ring of Bright Water*. Gavin was nine years younger than I. He came from the Borders. Through his mother he was related to the Duke of Northumberland, and his grandfather was Herbert Maxwell of Monreith, the distinguished amateur naturalist and archaeologist, who was a near neighbor of mine when I held the house of Tynron for my mother. Gavin and I had mutual friends: Peter Scott, Michael Ayrton, and other loners. We had corresponded while he was living abroad, and we met in London when he came back to write what proved to be his finest book. It was published in 1960 and, filled with enthusiasm for its film possibilities, I optioned it for films and distributed copies to all my friends and fellow filmmakers at Shepperton Studios and British Lion. None of them could see what I saw in it, even when I told them that Edal, the otter, with her long lissome body, her huge eyes which could look two ways at once, was the image of Pamela Brown. Meanwhile the book took off and became a best-seller, and Gavin not only had the world at his feet, but at his door.

We sailed on time, on Joan Webster's trail. She knew where she was going. But on arriving at Tobermory we discovered there was no winter boat to Ardnamurchan, but if we spoke to Mr. Cowie at the Macdonald Arms, he and his sons had a boat and maybe they would take us over. The boat was on the mud and hadn't been used for three weeks, but "he would see." Encouraged by opposition, we went into the hotel lounge and had a whiskey. A Scottish whiskey is more generous than an English one, and once you are in the Western Isles there is no limit to the amount that you can pour. By now the boat was floating too, and the three boys went off to find some fuel. We shook hands all around, picked up our rucksacks, and staggered to the end of the pier.

The boat was a thirty-foot lobster boat. The sun had set, but there was so much glow in the sky, and the afterglow, that you could see for miles. Our skipper was twenty-three and had three lobster boats under his command. If we wouldn't mind, they wanted to pick up a few lobsters now, before they landed us on Ardnamurchan. Fortified by Old Mull, we said go ahead, we'll help you haul.

Two hours later we were crossing the sound of Mull. Hauling lobsters, we discovered, is heavy work. Half the Atlantic seems to come in with the lobster pots, and pours down your neck, arms, and shoulders, and into your boots. The pots are on a long chain of ropes, anchored at each end. As the lobsters are snatched out of the pots these are rebaited and hurled back into the sea. The lobsters are snapping and hissing and rattling their big claws against the bars of the pots and fighting each other. But once they are in the boat they go strangely quiet, as if they sense their doom. Lobsters in 1961 fetched nine bob a pound in Oban.

A car from the hotel on Ardnamurchan was waiting for us at the pier. It was pitch dark now. In the bar we found a driver who wouldn't mind driving on the Sabbath and would drive us in the morning across the peninsula, to the end of the road where a track led up the shore of Loch Shiel to a hotel twenty miles away.

The next morning the weather was brilliant, with cold winter sunshine. The path was rough and wet, but had once been good, and the keen frost kept our boots from breaking through the frozen surface. The ice crackled like glass under our feet. We went over burn after roaring burn, which were mostly crossed by stone and turf bridges. We tramped and scrambled, and slid and crept along the side of banks, and eventually at one o'clock came down to Kintra Bay. A car overtook us and gave us a lift to the clean, white Loch Shiel Hotel. The motorboat would take us up the loch in the morning. Bill still snored worse than ever, but you can get used to anything, as Myrtle says.

The run up the loch took about an hour and a half. There was only one stop at a village with a pier. I could just image Prince Charles Edward standing by the mast of the vessel bringing him back to the land of his forefathers. We were in good time for the train. We passed Morar with its white sands—the whitest in the world—and its deep loch. It is quite small and narrow, an awsome cleft in the hills. We tumbled out of the train at Mallaig and onto the steamer, which was just about to leave. I was in a hurry to get to the Kyle of Lochalsh.

We sailed up the sound, with Skye on the port bow. We had never lost sight of the Cuillin for two days. I had the map out and pinpointed Gavin Maxwell's cottage at Sandaig, called Camusfeàrna in the book. It is a glorious position: just a small croft, with a great, wide, sandy, shallow beach in front of the cottage. The steamer hooted, but there was no sign of anybody about. We passed Glenelg, where Dr. Johnson stayed—"the wretched inn at Glen Elg"—and the ferry across the sound at Kylerhea. The sound was quite narrow, and the tide was running black and swift. We arrived at Kyle about two.

"Quick! Where's the motorboat?"

We had been warned to look out for it, and catch it before it went back down the sound to Glenelg. A sailor said, "You'll see 'im, a wee boat on the other side of the pier."

We ran onto the pier, and looked down into an empty swimming pool, perched on a small motorboat. I climbed down a rickety iron ladder into the boat.

"Are ye for Glenelg?" asked a shock-headed youth, in incredibly dirty dungarees. We said we were, and was there any room underneath his swimming pool?

"Ach, plenty! It's for Major Maxwell, and his otters."

"Is Major Maxwell there?"

"He is. We're taking it down to him tonight. I'll bring the boat round to the pier, and we'll pick up the mail, and you can join us there."

"We'll get a cup of tea, first," said practical Bill.

It is always teatime in Scotland. At the tea shop, I telephoned Gavin; he had the telephone now. He gasped on hearing that we were for Glenelg.

"There's no hotel! Where will you stop, tonight?"

"Why don't *you* put us up?"

A long silence. I said, "Don't worry. We'll find a bed," and ran back to my tea.

The fiberglass pool, perched on top of the cabin of the motorboat, looked even larger at close quarters. Most of it was propped up on the wheelhouse, with the skipper and his crew underneath it.

"It only weighs three and a half hundredweight."

We slipped down the sound at a great rate, but at Glenelg we stopped, because they all had to go and get their tea. Meanwhile, the sun, most inconsiderately, went on setting. By the time the skipper and his crew came back, wiping their mouths on the backs of their sleeves, it was nearly dark. By the time we rounded Sandaig Light it *was* dark and you couldn't see a thing.

We nosed in warily to the shallow, sandy beach, and at last two torches on the shore started to blink. We launched the swimming pool with a grand splash, and the skipper jumped inside. Bill grabbed a big oar and jumped in after him. The tide was already carrying them into the open sea. Bill put a stop to that with his oar. They started to pull their way in toward the beach, Bill roaring orders at the captain. Goodness knows, they could have ended with the swimming pool in Corryvreckan.

I carried the mail ashore, and was greeted in the light of our torches by a tall, beautiful youth: Jimmy, Edal's* co-star in the book. The naked child in the photographs by the waterfall had not prepared me for this Greek faun. I seized two cans of kerosene and marched up to the cottage, while the air resounded with Gaelic curses from an old gentleman who had tripped over an outboard motor and several lengths of copper tubing in the dark. Gavin had evidently been on a spending spree.

At the cottage, what did I see? Electric light, a fridge, a washing machine, and, thank heavens, a coal fire burning in the grate. We were starved with cold. Gavin was cleaning mussels in the sink.

"Damn you, Micky," he said. "There is a bed for you with someone else's sheets. There's *moules marinières* for dinner. Did you bring whiskey?"

"Yes."

"Then you're welcome."

Jimmy reported that the swimming pool was enormous. They would scarcely get it above the tidemark, let alone to the cottage.

"Well, that's up to you," said Gavin, feigning a machismo indifference.

As a matter of fact, it was up to Bill, who practically carried the swimming pool up the beach single-handed and dumped it at the door. Bill believes in direct action. Gavin started to give me a dozen reasons why the otter film couldn't be made. Jimmy had vanished into the darkness. As I listened to Gavin, my heart sank. Out came the excuses: the otters were getting unmanageable, Jimmy didn't want to be a film star, the estate didn't want to have a film made, and would injunct us if we made it . . . Finally, he announced that he might be getting married.

"It's a lonely spot for a woman," said Bill judgmentally.

Gavin went on with his tale. He didn't say that two years ago he had needed the option money and the publicity to help sell his books, and now he didn't, with *Ring of Bright Water* a best-seller. I could see that it was serious, and that he had worked himself up into a state about it. Jimmy had gone up to the neighbors for the evening. The mussels were good, but the venison stew, which Gavin warmed up, was uneatable. We drank and played records, while Edal's flat feet tramped up and down on the wooden floor above our

*Edal was one of two tame otters Gavin Maxwell had living in his cottage.

heads, occasionally stopping to chase her toys, mostly marbles, around the room into a corner, while the big dog otter, Teko the Slob, whistled in his hutch outside.

I went up the steep stairs to have a look at Edal over the stable door. Gavin came up and opened the door, and she ran up and kissed him ecstatically, and stared at me, purring, turning at intervals for another bout of kissing. She looked just as wonderful as I remembered her. Occasionally she uttered a high-pitched growl in my direction. But that could mean anything. She seemed quite tame to me, although Gavin swore she was dangerous. Gavin would swear anything to keep his privacy. We went on talking and arguing until one o'clock in the morning.

At 8:00 A.M. Gavin woke us, banging on the wooden ceiling of the room below with a walking stick. We came down and made our own breakfast. It was becoming more and more clear that we were most unwelcome guests. I signaled to Bill and we packed up and got out, leaving Gavin most of the whiskey. Jimmy was nowhere to be seen. We took the rough road up to the burn.

"What way, now?" asked Bill, who had uttered perhaps twenty-two words during the entire visit.

"South," I said.

We were only about three miles from Glenfearch, where there are the three Pictish brochs which had so impressed Eric Linklater.

"Like the ones at Mousa?" asked Bill, anxious to maintain the supremacy of Shetland in every department, historical, cultural, and architectural.

"Aye, but there are three of them."

We walked a while in silence. Then Bill cleared his throat.

"Yon Gavin."

"What about him?"

"He was glad enough to see the back of us."

"He's in love, Bill."

Bill pondered this for a while.

"With his otters?"

"If you like. He's been living alone for too long. He's a very emotional man. He's an artist, so he has to sublimate his love."

"With his writing?"

"Partly. He used to be very much of an extrovert, and got rid of that with his books . . . You remember when we met him in London. Now, he's much more of an introvert. And the success of his book has given him a lot of new things to think about, things that he didn't think about before."

"What things?"

"Oh . . . plans, fame, the future, and who to share it with. Since the war he's gone his own way, and now that his book is a best-seller it will bring the world to his door, and he doesn't know what to do about it."

Bill grunted. "It's a bonny wee place that he's got there. I mind it was a light keeper's cottage, before the war."

I nodded. I was thinking: hardly the place to bring a bride.

Given the circumstances, the life of Gavin Maxwell could hardly have a happy ending; this attractive, passionate and lonely and gifted man—he married, he divorced, he lived, and died. An electrical short circuit caused a fire that burned out Sandaig, and it stood for years as an empty shell, while his books were still delighting readers all over the world, and in every language. He had infinite patience for animals and children; none for men and women. He had married me with a ring, a ring of bright water.

Bill and I took the train to Inverness, hired a car at Macrae and Dick, drove to Gordonstoun and rescued Kevin for dinner at a hotel, and caught the night train to London.

I never made my film of *Ring of Bright Water.* I told Walt Disney that the rights were available, and he took over the option from me. Bill Travers and Virginia McKenna, forsaking Elsa the lioness, assumed this labor of love. Perhaps the key to the film lies in a few lines in the book in which Gavin describes a little expedition in which he, Jimmy, Edal, and a young girl took part. Edal bounded along in front, in high spirits, but she kept on returning to Jimmy to chide him for being so slow.

"She never does that to me," said Gavin.

"It's because he's young," said the girl. "She knows who you are, but she thinks Jimmy is an otter."

We must sorely try the patience of our animal friends. It was about this time that Sweep, our black cocker spaniel, died. But first, I would like to remind you what a character he was. A few years before, Seton Gordon, anxious to show me his part of the islands, arranged to meet me and take me up Glen Tilt and down the other side into the forest of Braemar, where he knew every stick and stone and stalker. The pools were full of dying salmon, still struggling to get up to their birthplace and die. It was a longish walk, twenty-two miles, and I had always wanted to do it again.

Alastair and Bill came, and there were one or two others, but the one I remember most is Sweep. I had forgotten that Seton and I had taken a car up the glen to where the road ends and had then completed the walk on foot. It added about six miles to the tramp. By the time we got to the watershed we had all had enough, and there were still ten miles to go. Suddenly Sweep stood there in the middle of the track and gave out his opinion of what lousy planners we were, how nobody but an idiot would bring a little dog to such a spot in the Cairngorms, with night falling, and he, Sweep, would like to bite all the people concerned.

"Bow! Wow! Wow!"

We all stood there transfixed, while he barked and yelled his opinion; a dog of character, a dog with his own opinions, a dog from whom to learn.

As Sweep conducted his life, so he ended it. It was the Easter holidays; Columba was at home. Sweep had gone on a visit to the vet to have a tumor removed. While Columba was eating his egg the postman rang and delivered a letter from the vet. Myrtle started to read it aloud while Columba ate his egg. The vet wrote what a good little dog Sweep was, how clean and healthy, but unfortunately his heart wasn't strong, and during the operation to remove the tumor his heart had stopped.

Too late, Myrtle realized what she had done. The corners of Columba's mouth had gone down. There was a pause, and then a storm of tears. There was only one thing to be done. I decreed that there would be a state funeral. Invitations would go out, costumes would be worn, the grave would be dug in the garden under the mulberry tree, and Sweep would be interred with full honors. This dried the tears. Columba is a great stage manager, and by the time he had invited all his friends and given them their parts, he was quite reconciled to the death of the star of the show. After all, not many black spaniels are buried under a mulberry tree in the Royal Borough of Kensington.

=

In the year that followed, 1962, my world turned upside down. I went to Australia.

It had been an Irish year. I had met and become a friend of Sean Kenny, one of the very few authentic geniuses that I have met in show business. During his short life he was an inspiration to many people, myself among them. I met him in Pamela's flat, together with other members of the *Martin Luther* company who were playing at the Phoenix nearby. He was stocky, with a round head like a cannonball and the most remarkable eyes that I have seen on a man.

His designs and sets for John Whiting's *The Devils*, and for *Oliver!* at the New Theatre, are famous. He couldn't scribble anything onto a piece of paper without being original. To authors, to ordinary craftsmen, it was a time of ferment in the theatre, and Pamela's apartment on the second floor of 36 Soho Square was often the center of the whirlpool. There were Ken Tynan, Alec McCowen, Alec Guinness, Sean Connery, Diane Cilento, Christopher Plummer, Harold Pinter, milling around Shaftesbury Avenue and the Waterloo Road, hellbent to change everything, dodging the embraces of Binkie

Beaumont and Donald Albery. Sean Kenny was Irish, and I had a number of Irish subjects to suggest, including one musical film, which had been developed on Rupert Revelstoke's Lambay Island; a musical film about the transformation of an island paradise into a nuclear station, at first entitled $E = MC^2$ and changed, as the months went by, to *Sea Birds Don't Sing*. Fortunately these plans, or dreams, were interrupted by Rupert Revelstoke's throwing a paperback book in my direction and saying, "Read it, Micky. That's the sort of film you want to be making."

He had been lying on the sofa reading it all morning and roaring with laughter. I picked the book up. It was entitled *They're a Weird Mob*. It was not a title calculated to ensnare the common reader, and the author was billed as Nino Culotta, which was obviously a *nom de plume*, Nino being short for Giannino, and Culotta meaning "big ass." I looked at the book warily: *They're a Weird Mob*, by John Big-Ass. I was flying down to the Voile d'Or where there was the usual crisis.

Well, I read it, and I was rolling about the plane in my turn. It was a natural! It had to be filmed, and as soon as possible. It was the best thing of its kind since Harry Leon Wilson's *Ruggles of Red Gap*. I have always envied James Cruze, the director of the silent film of *Ruggles*, and Leo McCarey, director of the talkie version, with that golden performance by Charles Laughton as the English supervalet. In the silent version Edward Everett Horton played the valet. It must have been about 1923, sixty-six years ago, that my mother and I saw the film in our local flea palace, and were so delighted by the America, and the Americans, that were revealed to us in that wonderful film that we sat around the program twice.

My mother particularly liked Ma Pettingill, a tough, spherical character in riding breeches, a cowboy hat, and a put-it-there-pardner manner, played by Lillian Leighton. Extra popular with us was Ernest Torrence the Great, whom we had already seen and fallen in love with in *Tol'able David*, in which he played the villain and had a historic scrap with young, boyish Richard Barthelmess. Torrence was a legendary figure to us, for he was one of the two scouts in the spectacular western, *The Covered Wagon*, also directed by James Cruze. The other scout was played by Tully Marshall, who kept on appearing and reappearing in all sorts of parts, which included the husband of the Merry Widow, Mae Murray, in the film directed by Erich von Stroheim.

All these details may seem irrelevant to you, but they were pieces of social history to us, which would always influence our thinking about the Americans. The talkie version of this delightful book was even better. It was directed by Leo McCarey, and when I say directed, I mean *directed*. Every person and every situation was presented with a bubbling enjoyment that it was impossible not to share. The casting of every part was impeccable, from the littlest part to the greatest, in a company triumphantly led by Charles Laughton. Anyone who has not seen the sequence in the saloon with Laughton, Charlie Ruggles, and Zasu Pitts, in which Laughton, the English valet shanghaied to Red Gap, recites from memory Lincoln's address at Gettysburg, can't claim to know anything about acting or direction of comedy.

And what about Roland Young, as the English lord, and his scene with Leila Hyams at the beer bust, when the American girl takes the starch out of the lord . . . and the overall transformation of Charles Laughton from subservient manservant to manager of Red Gap's newest and most exclusive restaurant—what about it, eh? And, I should add, that none of these details, names, and scenes have been looked up by me; I haven't needed to run the film again, or look in the books. The films, silent and sound, have stayed with me during these sixty-six years, because they are full of love and enthusiasm and delight. Every name, detail, and character of these happy memories is engraved on my heart, even the sleepy man on the chair tilted back against the wall who, when the bartender asks what did Lincoln say at Gettysburg, replies, "I don't know, I wasn't there," after which, we follow the barman around the saloon, asking what Lincoln said at Gettysburg, and nobody knows, until finally he comes back to the sleepy man, who has his chair kicked from under him by the frustrated barman with the pregnant line, "You wasn't there!" and the stage is set for Laughton's great speech. All of America seems to me to be condensed into this one, wonderful sequence.

And now, here was just such a chance for me, not in America, but in Australia. *They're a Weird Mob* was told in the first person by Nino Culotta, one of several million Italian immigrants to Australia, and through his ears and eyes we learned about Sydney, Australia, its inhabitants, and their language, which appeared to be a highly spiced mixture of cockney and Liverpool Irish. Whatever it was, it was new and it was exciting and entertaining. The writing was direct, colorful and simple, and so was the plot.

Nino is a young Italian sports journalist who has been sent for by his cousin, who is running a newspaper in Sydney and needs a sports editor. By the time Nino has arrived the paper has folded and the cousin has skipped the country, leaving a lot of debts. The chief creditor of the defunct newspaper is a girl called Kay, whose father is a big builder. Their first meeting is not a pleasant one. Nino has to eat, so he answers an advertisement and goes to work as a bricklayer.

One of the saddest, and funniest, sights in the world is an artist who has to go to work with his hands, and at first Nino is in despair, but he develops a whole new set of muscles, makes friends, and even manages to win Kay around. It's a simple framework, but it works, and the picture which emerges of the Sydneyites, pronounced "Sinnyites," is endearing.

Of course, in the end Nino pays off the debts and gets the girl, in spite of the opposition of the girl's father, a part that obviously could only be played by Chips Rafferty. By the time that my plane touched down in Nice I had finished the book, and was determined. After floundering about for two years my path lay straight ahead and I was glad of it.

The book that I had read was the English edition, and the next morning I telephoned the publisher. He put me on to the author's agent in London. He knew who I was, and was upset to have to tell me that someone else had the option. At first he wouldn't tell me who it was, but then he couldn't resist it: Mr. Gregory Peck, the film actor. This was too easy! Greg was staying in Saint-Jean-Cap-Ferrat with his family, about a hundred and fifty yards up the road from the hotel. I caught him at home.

"So you're a producer now? Don't tell me that Hollywood will ever let you play Nino Culotta!"

He was staggered.

"They're a Weird Mob? . . . How did you know?"

I told him.

"It's a wonderful subject."

"Isn't it?"

He brightened.

"We were in Australia making that Nevil Shute film, *On the Beach.* Fred Astaire read it and passed it on to me. We both thought it was great, and I took an option on it. When I got back to Hollywood nobody wanted to know. They all wanted to do some piece of shit which they owned, first. And they would say, 'We'll let you do it later,' and you know very well they won't. I've had it for a year, and haven't gotten anywhere."

"Give it to me. I'll get it done . . . not with you . . . it has to be an Italian."

He groaned again.

"I suppose you're right. It was so wonderful reading it in Australia, and having all the people around us just like they are in the book, but in Hollywood they've never even heard of Australia."

"Give it to me . . . don't fool around, Greg. It ought to be done. I'll get it done. It should be a coproduction with Australia, a European picture."

"Perhaps you are right. I've still got two or three months left on the option. I'll have another try. If that doesn't work, I'll let you have it."

"You're a prince."

Greg kept his promise, and the film rights of the little book fell into my waiting hands in mid-September. I told the agent and the publisher that I wasn't interested in options; I wanted to buy the film rights. If the author agreed, I would make arrangements to come out to Sydney, Australia, as soon as possible but in any case before Christmas of 1963. I wanted to see what

I'd bought, and find out if I could raise part of the production costs in Australia. I knew that Michael Balcon had made several Australian coproductions like this, and Michael Balcon was no crazy hothead. His budgets were always well padded, and he seldom went into the contingency.

The only Australians that I knew in show business were John McCallum and Googie Withers. I had been to their wedding. I checked them out. They were both in Melbourne, Australia. Then there was, of course, Peter Finch, who had played Captain Langsdorff in the *Graf Spee*. Peter was in a picture in Rome. We had dinner in a little courtyard in the open air. Peter was willing to help, but he didn't want to play Nino Culotta. He had left all that behind him.

"Walter Chiari is your man," he said.

I had never heard of him. Peter explained: "He's a wonderful fellow. Very versatile, lots of talent. He's all the time on tour with theatrical shows; that's why he hasn't made a big name, yet, either in films or television. Everybody in Italy knows Walter Chiari."

"Where is he? Who is his agent?"

"I'll find out for you. He's a great friend of Silvana Mangano. Give me a ring tomorrow at the studio. I'll know by then."

"What's Walter Chiari like?"

"Oh . . . tall, dark, about my age."

"Is he a Milanese?"

"No, I think he's from Verona . . . a touch of the Arab about him . . . very attractive, very funny. Could have been a star long ago, if he had stuck to it. He can't resist going on these long tours around Italy and being popular with the crowd."

"He sounds ideal for Nino."

"Oh, he is! But you'll have to convince him of that."

The next day Peter phoned. Walter Chiari was in Milan, and keen on the idea. I ought to see another comedian, too, called Renato Rascel. He was playing in Turin. I ought to see them both.

I thanked Peter, and took the train to Turin. I managed to get four hours' sleep somewhere. Rascel was idolized in Piedmont, and I could see why. He could handle the audience wonderfully, but it was all local stuff. He spoke very little English, but had great charm. We had supper together at a big, echoing restaurant, and then I took the very early train for Milan and Walter Chiari.

Somehow or other I managed to get another four hours' sleep. The journey across Lombardy took about two hours. Nobody met me and there were no porters. I carried my own bags out, and took a taxi to the Via Donizetti. Number 16 was a tall, old-fashioned house. As soon as I rang the bell, a tall, thin, slim, excited young man rushed into the street, and filled it. In a moment, my taxi was dispatched to the Grand Hotel, with two reckless two-thousand-lira notes stuffed into the driver's pocket, and instructions to check my bags into the room that was waiting for me.

The next second I was in a small dark room, with a balcony opening out onto a small square garden. The room was full of Persian cats. Walter Chiari's charm lit up the room. He spoke excellent English.

"Of course, you must have lunch, now, immediately. We will have caviar. Do you like chopped onion with caviar? And chopped egg?"

I said I did.

". . . and pheasant. We must have pheasant! I shot it myself, on Saturday. I work all night on this film I am making, and then I go hunting; then I sleep for four hours, then I go to work again . . ."

. . . and so on, and on. In everything he said there were flashes of insight and some piece of uncommon knowledge. This man was much more than an actor. I guessed he was in his early thirties, and found him charming. He could play down or up to almost any age. That was his theatrical training. As I watched him, and listened to him talking, I could feel my whole conception of the part changing. Here was the common man that Peter Finch had been talking about. Walter told me that he wrote and produced his own shows, and would write his own reviews. I thought, what an agreeable companion he would be on a film like this one. He was committed to twelve television shows and a play after that: "But that can be arranged," he said in a burst of enthusiasm.

Walter was not a big name in Italian movies, like Vittorio Gassman, or Sordi; that was evident. But once we got him out to Australia he might be better than either. I felt that the Australians would approve of him. And that was important for me. I suddenly realized that, up until now, I had been thinking of this production as a British film with an Italian box-office star, and all that implies in the way of extended schedules, special publicity, and big budgets. Now, thanks to Peter Finch, I was thinking about the film as an Australian film, which, first and foremost, would have to please the American public. I no longer thought about pleasing Hollywood, or Wardour Street. I was already wondering how much of the budget I could raise in Australia, and I was deciding to go there and find out.

We ate the pheasant and drank a good white wine, a Frascati, then Walter had to go to work. He dropped me off at the hotel, a staid, comfortable hotel, like the Ritz. I had a good room on the street, with a balcony. I telephoned home. There was a letter from John McCallum, and Bill read it to me. It was a real tonic. Googie was going to open very soon in Melbourne in a play by Ted Willis, *Woman in a Dressing Gown.* John himself was now the joint managing director of J. C. Williamson Theatres, the biggest theatrical chain in Australia. He was enthusiastic about the idea of filming *They're a Weird Mob,* and was sure that Williamson's would invest in the film, and there were other possibilities. I ought to come out as soon as I could. If the film wouldn't cost more than a million dollars, he was pretty sure that half of that could be found in Australia.

This was great news. I had planned to go down to Rome to see Pamela and Rex, Christopher Fry, and Joe Mankiewicz, Elizabeth Taylor and Richard Burton, who were making *Cleopatra* at the time. It would probably be the last chance to see such a monstrous collection of, well, monsters. I could go on to Australia from Rome. There was also a letter from Sam Ure-Smith, the publisher of *They're a Weird Mob,* informing me that Nino Culotta was only a pen name. The real name of the author was John O'Grady, and he was urging me to come out to Australia and meet everybody. He assured me that the press would give us a great welcome. Everything seemed to be going our way, and I decided to take him at his word. I told Bill to alert John McCallum, and to book me out of Rome to Sydney in a few days' time. The next day, I flew down to Rome, and took a taxi to Cinecittà. Secure beneath my English bowler hat, from Messrs. Locke and Co., St. James's Street, I told the driver not to stop at the gate, but to drive through and up to the restaurant, quite a smart, attractive building. I went into the bar, and there was Rex, magnificently Roman in a very becoming gray wig, receding at the temples, wearing a good costume of soft colors, maroon and green, and a gray overcoat. With his towering height, he looked splendid.

He had left his long, fleshy nose alone, and a bust of him would have done credit to any museum, even though he hadn't got Julius Caesar's nose and skinny frame. Pamela made an entrance, her head high, her hair dressed in curling, golden snakes. Her eyes were outlined with sequins. It was nothing like Egyptian or Cretan, but it was very effective. She looked at me apologetically, so I said I didn't mind. Rex seemed pleased to see me; anyway, he bought lunch, and he seemed relieved that I made no reference to his walking out on *The Living Room.* I had heard that he had admitted it to other people, which was a point in my favor.

He sent me home in his car, but first I had to chat with Dino De Laurentiis about Vittorio Gassman for Nino. The Italian movie industry was riding high, and it was possible to discuss a coproduction deal between a London-based producer and a Rome-based Italian—possible, but not probable. Still, it seemed to me that if I could get a sufficiently big-name actor to play Nino, and a sensible Italian coproduction partner (not so easy, this one) this was a possible way to go about it. De Laurentiis agreed to wait for a script. I said nothing about Walter Chiari.

I was leaving for Sydney at the weekend, so Rex gave a little dinner party. They had rented a villa for him on the Via di Porta San Sebastiano, number 13. The owner was a jeweler, and the house stands above the sunken road along which the traffic roars, day and night. Each side of this narrow road is a steep wall pierced with doors. Number 13 is up some very antique steps, where there was a bell sunk in the wall. After a long interval, a man in a red uniform opened the door.

Apparently the Roman jeweler lived in some style, and when Rex and Rachel Roberts took over, every servant in the place wore white gloves. Rachel said it got on her nerves. We were shown into a long, undistinguished room, with a good fire burning and a lot of bookcases only quarter-filled. Rex's son by Lilli Palmer, a tall seventeen-year-old, was introduced. He was studying archaeology. Rachel came down at last. She had taken to makeup in a big way, after leaving the Royal Court Theatre. She looked a bit weird, but not quite so ugly. She was just as goodhearted and small-time as ever. I never could see what Rex saw in her, but there she is. I wonder what the son told Lilli.

We all got into a huge Cadillac, and drove to the market on the Piazza Vittorio Emmanuele. It was a good enough market, but nothing special. We bought vegetables and fish for the dinner, went back to the house, were given torches, and were taken down to see their own private catacomb in the garden. It was impressive, like a safe-deposit vault, with arched pigeonholes, all for the ashes of Roman fathers and, I suppose, mothers. As a starter for the bizarre vegetarian meal that followed, it couldn't be improved upon. Light was supplied by dozens of candles stuck in empty bottles.

But I digress . . . Come to think of it, my life is one long digression . . . I am in Rome, aren't I? Pamela is waving me off to Sydney, Australia. The time is midnight, the aircraft a Boeing jet. It is crowded, but comfortable. The route tonight is Teheran, New Delhi, Bangkok, Singapore. From Singapore five hours across the China Seas to Perth, capital of Western Australia. It was the middle of the night when we got to Perth, and I was impressed by the relaxed, efficient air of the tall, quiet men who were running the airport. Sydney, the capital of New South Wales, on the east coast of the continent, was quite another cup of tea, according to Nino Culotta—which reminded me that I had better get out his book and read it again, because I was going to meet John O'Grady in another three hours.

When he wrote the book, John was a dispensing chemist in Samoa. He had already broken into print with a hilarious novel about a small native Samoan who was unable to keep out of trouble, called *No Kava for Johnny*. Sam Ure-Smith, the publisher, took it over, and commissioned a similar comic novel about Sydney, Australia—result: *They're a Weird Mob* by Nino Culotta.

Sam Ure-Smith's enormously successful publication (350,000 copies sold) was illustrated by the cartoonist Wep.* His concept of Nino was of a tall, bulky young man, wearing a European-style jacket and trousers, with curly hair over a large moon face. He wore no hat, and was, more or less, a stereotype. He had a big behind, and Wep's drawings emphasized this steatopygous aspect of his manly figure. This was certainly not Walter Chiari; but it was early days yet.

We seemed to be flying over that memory of English schooldays, the Great Australian Bight. How often I have bitten it out of a slice of bread and butter.

We landed at Sydney on Monday morning, November 5, 1962. John O'Grady and Sam Ure-Smith were there to meet me, along with six ladies and gentlemen of the press and a radio recording crew. John was about my age, short and tough, with knobbly knees, dressed in shorts and shirt, no hat, with a bristly beard streaked with gray, and observant blue eyes. We inspected each other, and I liked what I saw. He returned the inspection and made no secret of his relief. I had expected this. He was Irish, of course; probably second or third generation. He talked with an aggressively Australian accent that was a little bit put on. Sam Ure-Smith, young, slick, and quick, was typecast for a successful Sydney publisher. Nino Culotta already had a new book in the shops, *Gone Fishing.* The Nino of this book (there were obviously going to be a string of them) was even less like Walter Chiari, but I said nothing. When in doubt, play dumb animals.

I said I had to lie down, and they left me at my hotel. I didn't know it, but I was suffering from severe jet lag. Around four o'clock John McCallum telephoned from Melbourne. He must have thought I was drunk; I didn't know who he was, or who I was. By this time, the first reactions of the press to the prospective filming of *Weird Mob* were coming in: it was okay—I was accepted. I was a "good bloke."

Next morning more interviews and television. By now, the telephones were ringing every five minutes, and John O'Grady swept me off to his cottage on the George River. The banks were high and rocky, choked with trees and great slabs of rock. John's house was perched on one of them, with a great view up and down the river. More important, the river was full of delicious oysters.

John's wife, Molly, was plump and cheerful, and a great hostess. I had brought her flowers, and we got on well, although I was still so tired from jet lag that I kept falling asleep in the middle of the sentence. Various characters from the book dropped in on us. There was one complete mob of spec builders,

*William Edwin Pigeon was a famous Australian cartoonist and portrait painter who signed his work "Wep."

like the mob in the book, building a house only a few yards away. I met an opossum family, and I was introduced to a kookaburra bird. As I kept on dropping asleep again, they took me home.

The next day I flew to Melbourne (pronounced "Mebbn") to meet with John McCallum and Googie Withers. The weather was much colder than in Sydney; no John and Googie to meet me, but Williamson Theatres had sent a car. The driver took me to a startlingly new, big, and faceless hotel, the Southern Cross, where I learned that I had just missed John McCallum and his board of directors and his joint managing director, Sir Frank Tait, whom John was hoping would invest in *Weird Mob.* They had gone to Adelaide to open a new theatre, but were coming back to Sydney to see a touring show of *Lili* that night. John rang and said that if I wanted to see the show he had a ticket for me. I could meet all the Williamson directors, and Frank Tait, in the interval. I said I didn't mind if I did.

John met me in the lobby that evening, looking incredibly tall and handsome in his part of an actor-manager. He had been an actor at the time he met Googie in England, and had swept her off to Australia with him after they married. Now he was a businessman. He introduced me to five old men and their wives. Melbourne was the home of the big shots of show business and their head offices. Googie was having a run-through of her play and came into the office after the show. She wore slacks and a soft sweater, and looked gorgeous. I love her old face and crinkly eyes. How clever I was to give her that big chance, so many years ago . . . let's see, when did I do *One of Our Aircraft Is Missing?* Googie always remembers that I gave her that break because of her performance as a barmaid in my quota-quickie *Her Last Affaire.* But her career really started when Sergei Nolbandov picked her out of a crowd at Warner Bros. Teddington Studios. Sergei had a remarkable eye for talent.

An old friend, Dave Hutcheson, who you will remember was Roger Livesey's friend and fellow officer at the beginning of *Colonel Blimp,* was in *Lili* that night, playing Schlegel, the showman—superb miscasting. We fell into each other's arms, ordered up a bottle of whiskey and a pile of sandwiches, and finished the lot. I first saw Dave and Googie together in a musical play in London, at the old Strand Theatre. It was called *Nice Goings On* and starred Leslie Henson. Nobody bothered about the plot, and a good time was had by all, and later on they were both in my quota-quickie *The Love Test,* a desperate attempt by me to imitate an American B-feature. We made it at Wembley Studios. Alex Korda was directing *Wedding Rehearsal* on the next stage to us. For the record, it should be noted that *The Love Test* was the first film to feature Bernard Miles. Sir Bernard would have liked to forget it.

I had done some interviews at the airport, and next morning the newspapers gave me very nice write-ups, *The Sun* in particular, and it seemed as if all the Italians in Melbourne had telephoned the hotel. Every other passenger ship that docked at Melbourne had sailed directly from Italy, usually from Naples. In 1962 Melbourne had a population of 1,800,000. In twenty years' time, some estimated, there would be a million Italian-born citizens in Melbourne.

I went for a walk, city tasting, and decided that if Melbourne was strong red wine, Sydney was beer. Several people recognized me and shook hands. It was very friendly. Inevitably I ended up in a bookshop, where the owner picked out for me *Back of Sunset, North by Thursday,* by John Cleary, author of *The Sundowners*—did you see Fred Zinnemann's film with Robert Mitchum and Deborah Kerr? You did? Then I don't have to tell you what a dinkum* job Robert Mitchum made of the Australian accent. The bookshop owner also gave me *Death of a Swagman,* one of a series of detective stories whose main character was called Bony. Chief Inspector Napoleon Bonaparte, aboriginal half-caste, was the property and invention of Arthur Upfield, who in his time had been a swagman, a stockman, and goodness knows what else. I decided I would try to meet him.

John McCallum was a good friend, a showman, and an artist, and he wanted to see *Weird Mob* made in Australia. He could see that it would be followed by other films, if the majority of the costs could be recovered in Australia. Williamson Theatres, with their huge organization and big reputation worldwide, were an obvious target for me. But that meant convincing the board, and a board of old showmen is very hard to convince.

Sir Frank Tait was eighty, and he was the youngest of them all, so far as showmanship was concerned. He asked me, mildly, whether I wanted their investment in the film, and with the relief of a young girl who has finally maneuvered her chosen mate into making a proposal, I said that I would welcome it. Around this time it occurred to somebody to ask me how much money I wanted. I hadn't any idea. Australia's film industry, after a brilliant spurt in the 1920s and 1930s, had fallen into the doldrums except for television and for commercials. I looked to Australian finance to cover the development costs of *Weird Mob* up to the first day of shooting, roughly one third of the total cost.

This was not unreasonable, considering that the Australian investors would own the film rights of the book and of the screenplay as well. The rest of the money would come from England, either from an English or an American distributor, as a direct investment of capital, or in the form of guarantees against completion of the film. I had already bought the screen rights of John O'Grady's book, and after hearing what a hero Nino Culotta had become to

*Australian slang for "true" or "real."

the Australian public, I expected to be mobbed by potential investors. Not so
. . . not so. However, it seemed to me, judging from the costs of *Peeping Tom*,
that £150,000 total would be a reasonable figure.

Of course, I had no idea what sort of a deal I could make with Walter Chiari,
once the film was on the stocks, but I could cover that in my skeleton budget
with a note saying that if anybody wanted stars, the remuneration of said
stars would have to be a matter for discussion, and could not be included in
the budget.

John McCallum and I held a council of war. He thought that he could bring
Williamson Theatres in, but the bulk of the money would come from Sydney.
He wanted me to see Bob Austin in Sydney, an old friend of his, a lawyer, a
good mate.

"If Bob can find the money, we'll marry him to Frank Tait."

Before John saw me off to Sydney I appeared on an evening quiz show, the
Delo and Daly Show. I cut Jonathan Daly down to size. I was very, very relaxed
and wore a light-colored suit and a beige shirt, so came over like a snowstorm
in a cellar. It worked. All next day people were stopping me in the street.

"I saw you last night! Swell! Good luck!"

I was booked on the *Southern Aurora*, the new night train to Sydney. Believe
it or not, until a few months before, passengers had to change at the frontier
of New South Wales because the railways of New South Wales and Victoria
had different gauges. The journey took thirteen hours. The train was all
metal, all chrome, all streamlined, and all cramped. Every sleeping berth had
its own toilet, but for most facilities you had to weigh 140 pounds or less. I
couldn't see how old people or fat people managed it at all. There were no
shelves, no cupboards, no coat hangers, nothing at a convenient height, but
the train went along, and they were very proud of their train. The club car
was fine, very comfortable, and I sat there for some time. I was recognized,
of course, just an old Narcissus. Everybody had steak and eggs for breakfast.

John O'Grady was at the station to meet me. Now things started to happen.
Enter Bob Austin, of Messrs. Harding, Breden, and Austin, bosom friend of
John McCallum and Sydney firebrand. He was big and fair, with shoulders so
broad they almost seemed deformed. We took to each other at once. He gave
me plenty of his time, and I made an impression, especially with my forecast
for Australian sales of the film, which was new to him. Talking to Bob was
such a shot in the arm that it stimulated me into going back to the hotel and
putting my ideas on paper. I worked until dark, and nearly finished it. Only
the timetable of production was a bit airy-fairy. I didn't know enough yet of
local conditions. Film financing, with its stops and starts and checks, is tricky
to explain to novices, but I fancied that Bob Austin, with his formidable
personality and his gray eyes like flints, would not be a novice for long.

I had promised to go out with John O'Grady and see some local color. He took me to the Marble Bar. Everybody at the bar, all men, was drinking beer. We knocked back four schooners apiece. My performance was commented upon. I don't usually drink four schooners of beer, but it was a matter of prestige.

A very drunk man said to me, "Excuse me, sir, but you are impeccably dressed."

I said, "Thank you."

He said, "You are the most impeccably dressed man that I have ever seen."

I began to feel self-conscious, and drank some beer.

He said, "That tweed, I'll bet it's made from the best tweed in Scotland."

I said, "From Donegal."

"That's what I said."

Next morning I had two hours with Austin. He was most shrewd, asked good questions, and I wished I had all the answers. I cabled Chris Mann to send me the figures of all our films that had played in Australia. I knew that *The Battle of the River Plate* had been a big-grossing film, and I also asked for grosses on *A Town like Alice*, and Alec Guinness's films, and Tony Kimmins's comedies. I should have brought all these figures with me, but I was new to the sales side of the business.

Bob was impressed enough to cancel a date to see his son, aged thirteen, play cricket, in order to fly to Melbourne on Saturday and meet John McCallum and Frank Tait. This was noble of him. If Williamson's would put up the development money, which included the script, I could go to a distributor like Rank for the rest of the money. Austin assured me that he could bring in some private investors as well.

Bob Austin and his wife called for me in a sports saloon. Wife was small, brittle, and Australian. Bob looked larger than ever in a pale silk tussah suit and a tiny hat that set off his pale face, red hair, and big shoulders. He drove with decision, but rather jerkily, across Sydney to the airport. Bob got out, and Mrs. Austin insinuated her small form into the huge space recently occupied by her husband and drove off without ceremony. I gathered that she had a party on that night, and Bob would be late for it. I was more than ever obliged to him. He was quick, well read, intelligent, could make up his mind, and act on it. Here was the kind of man that I had been looking for. We sat at the back of the plane and looked at the view. He said, "You're doing me good already. I must have flown from Sydney to Melbourne a dozen times in the last few weeks, and I had my nose buried in papers and never looked out of the window once."

When we landed at the tiny Melbourne airport, the temperature was down from Sydney by about thirty degrees. Bob shivered in his silk suit. John

McCallum met us, gentle, handsome, and courteous as ever. I had always thought of John as unusually tall, until I saw him together with Bob. We drove to John's office. While we talked, Frank Tait came in and out. Bob's announced intention had been to ask Williamson's to put up all the development money, but he must have been tipped off by John McCallum not to fly too high, for suddenly I heard him suggesting that Williamson's put up half. We looked at Frank Tait, who nodded. It was a deal! John beamed. It was a triumph for him too.

I liked Frank Tait. He was shrewd, kind, and had a quiet vein of humor. Things started to move. They decided it would be a private Canberra company for tax reasons in various states. We all went to lunch at the Athenaeum Club. Bob rushed back to Sydney. I stayed to celebrate with John and Googie at their house in Toorak. The new Australian film business was on its way. I then flew back to Sydney. I could hardly believe in my success, and I was still hugging myself. I went to dinner at Vadim's in Kings Cross and ate the inevitable beef Stroganoff. Erik Bruhn came in with Nureyev. It was like watching an eagle mate with a pigeon. Nureyev is really insatiable! By now, people around the Sydney arts knew who I was. Even Vadim knew, and people kept coming to my table.

I had been working on my memorandum and took it to Bob the next morning. Bob at once set to work on it. He called in his secretary and we wrote and typed and tore out pages, and blue-penciled sentences, until at 12:30 we went off in a great hurry to the New South Wales Club, where the first person we saw was Frank Tait, who had come north for a few days. We told him we had just named him on the board of the new company. Bob now considered himself in show business, and gleefully pointed out to me Sir Norman Rydge of Greater Union Theatres, and Ernest Turnbull, who ran the other theatre chain, Hoyts. They little knew that we were their future partners.

I had written to Arthur Upfield, author of the Bony stories. He wrote me back now, saying that his London agents were Hope, Laresche and Steele, and that I could talk to them. I answered at once, saying that I couldn't do business with a man I didn't know, and how much I admired the Bony detective stories and the character of Napoleon Bonaparte, and finished by saying that I was arriving at Bowral, which is about an hour down the line from Sydney, on Monday morning, by the *Riverena Express*. He answered by telegraph, asking me to telephone him. When I did, a deep voice answered, welcoming me but advising me to book my return seat. It made me ashamed of my persistence, but I had been impressed by Upfield the author, and I wanted to meet the man.

Upfield was such a good storyteller. Like Conan Doyle, he only wrote about what he knew, the swagmen, stockmen, policemen, cattlemen, and aboriginals. He knew nothing about women, and treated them with respect, admiration, and fear. My purpose in hunting him out was to see if we could work together, for if I made a success of *They're a Weird Mob* I had seen enough of Australia to know that I would like to see more and know more, and buying the film and television rights from Arthur Upfield for the Bony books would be as good a way as any, and better than most.

I caught the express to Bowral. It was only half full. The train ambled along, gradually gaining height. The country was first pasture, and then rolling hills and thick brush with sandstone outcrops. After Mittagong there was more granite, with wooded valleys and stony creeks. Bowral is a bright little town at two thousand feet, surrounded by high hills. Arthur Upfield met me with a hired car, and we drove to his home, a long yellow bungalow with black stripes, like a wasp. Men were at work, blasting in a quarry in the hills behind. Upfield was over seventy then, and not well, and his wife had arteriosclerosis. They said, cheerfully, that life was difficult for them, but all that mattered was that they were together. They didn't have many visitors, but when they did, they enjoyed them.

I asked Upfield if he was still writing. He said no, but his wife had written his biography. On a sudden impulse she went and got it, and gave me an autographed copy. It was very moving to see how proud he was of her writing. We walked down to the Bowral Hotel for lunch, no three-star job, and walked up Bung-Bung Street, chattering like old friends. Then it was time to go, but I was glad I had come. When I said that the Bony stories ought to be made in color, and we should make a nationwide search for the actor who should play Detective Inspector Bonaparte, they were thrilled.

Upfield walked down with me to the station. I understood why agents, literary and otherwise, are reluctant to permit unchaperoned meetings between their clients and us producer-directors. But they lose more than they gain by it. All art is one, and artistry is a delicate plant that needs manuring by agreement, and by disagreement, and by cross-pollination of ideas. Writing is a lonely profession, and a writer needs encouragement and the competition of like minds. He needs to bask in the warmth of professional appreciation. Above all, he needs to be convinced that what he writes is something of value, not necessarily of permanent value. Only his readers can do that for him.

As the train rattled along back to Sydney, I thought about Arthur Upfield's books, about his hero, Detective Inspector Napoleon Bonaparte, detective extraordinary. When I first picked up *Death of a Swagman*, I couldn't have anticipated the quality of Upfield's mind. By making his hero a half-caste abo he was able to observe and to debunk a whole gallery of Australians, immigrants and native-born. His wit was gentle but it was devastating. He knew the huge island-continent of Australia as very few men did. He had wandered all over it, with his swag on his back and his billy in his hand, and he shared his experiences and his knowledge without condescension. I kept on acquiring a new Upfield, and was hardly ever disappointed. His earliest books had the same quality as the later ones.

Time was getting short, and I was expected in Rome next Monday. John McCallum was coming up from Melbourne to sign the partnership deeds. John O'Grady drove me to the Visatone Studios at Bondi Junction, where Ken Sledge, Hans Wetzel, and Ross Hawthorn were drawn up in a line to be presented. With one voice they assured me that their studio and organization were the only possible ones in Sydney for *Weird Mob.* They went over my budget and laughed with scorn. In their opinion the Australian end of the production should not cost more than £45,000. I listened. I was there to listen. Mentally, I was adding in all the extras like insurance, contingencies, and percentages and bank interests. But I said nothing.

I skipped lunch, and saw a student film with Bruce Beresford, who had made it, and I met all the people who had made it and acted in it. The film was about a student and the devil, of course. It was projected in the hall of a labor organization.

At the final meeting of the directors of our new company, we went through Bob Austin's items and agreed to them all. He suggested that the name of the company should be Williamson-Powell Ltd.: Frank Tait, chairman (alternate, John McCallum), Bob Austin (alternate, John Hunt), Michael Powell (alternate . . . that's the question). Capital: £200,000. I got the impression that John McCallum and Frank Tait were not quite with us, and were prepared to ask questions, but Bob swept the whole thing along.

I needed a production secretary, and Joy Cavill, a lady of immense experience as a continuity girl, production secretary, and producer in Australia, came and did all the paperwork for me. Cost at the end of the day—£12. According to Joy, who had heard me on radio and seen me on television, I had made a very good impression all around, particularly with the younger set.

My last day in Australia had arrived. At three o'clock I signed the articles of the new company, Williamson-Powell Proprietary, Ltd. Only a quarter of an hour previously, the New Zealand partners of Williamson had agreed to come into this daring project. Before we parted, I told John McCallum that I owed it all to him and Googie, which is quite true. He took my love to Googie. "Bread upon the waters."

≡

In the morning, I started home. John O'Grady, faithful to the last, came with his son to see me off. All four of his books were on sale in the airport bookstall:

No Kava for Johnny, They're a Weird Mob, Cop This Lot, Gone Fishing, altogether three quarters of a million sales, hardback and paperback. Not bad, Nino Culotta, not bad! Let's have another schooner!

They waved as I went through immigration, they waved as we went out to the aircraft, they waved as we became airborne. Their wave meant good-bye, come back soon. It took me three years.

You would think, wouldn't you, that an enterprising young film producer, who had bought the film rights of a best-selling novel about the uproarious experiences of an Italian immigrant in Australia, who had had the enterprise to fly out to Sydney himself, meet the press, meet the author, and find Australian partners eager to invest in the Australian costs of the film, and who was himself not unknown, would have no difficulty in raising the rest of the money through English and Italian banks and film distributors. But you would be wrong.

Even though in Walter Chiari I had found, thanks to Peter Finch, the perfect Nino Culotta, even though the Australians went off the pound and on the dollar during the preparation period, even though the Rank Organisation had bought a 50 percent share in Australia's Greater Union Theatres to make sure of getting their money back twice over, even though John O'Grady's book remained at the top of the best-seller list, even though my Australian partners stood firm through crisis after crisis, it took three round trips, and three years, before I stood in Sydney's Marble Bar, blinded and deafened, and yelled "Action, everyone! Scene One! Take One! *They're a Weird Mob* . . . Take it away!"

Excuse me, did I say three years? From November 1962 to November 1965. *Really? How interesting. But how could you afford to spend so much time waiting about and seeing people? You've always been so energetic, Powell. Perhaps you were in Hollywood? . . . Or were you at the Voile d'Or?*

No, although the Voile d'Or figured large in the lives of our friends and of my family. By this time, both Kevin and Columba were at school at Gordon-stoun, in Macbeth country on the shores of the Moray Firth, Kevin in his last term, Columba at the preparatory school at Aberlour. They had to be visited from time to time. Bill Paton held the London fort and ran the office. Frankie ran the Voile d'Or.

In these two summer seasons under Frankie's magical direction, or should I say magical misdirection, none of our guests ever paid for drinks at the bar. Everything was chalked up, as it is in heaven. Jean-Pierre Bertsch joined the Voile d'Or as manager for a season or two about this time, and can a tale unfold of those golden days and nights.

At the same time I was trying to promote another Royal Naval epic, *The Battle of the April Storm*, by Larry Forrester, to star Richard Burton as the captain of the *Glow-worm*. In another part of the forest, Leo Marks was under contract to me to write *Mr. Sebastian,* a semiautobiographical screenplay about a master code breaker. He had written two hundred pages, and showed no sign of stopping.

The script of *Weird Mob* was first of all written by me, then it was written by John O'Grady, and the final version was rewritten, believe it or not, by Emeric Pressburger, and still John Davis couldn't make up his mind. And then . . . and then . . . all of a sudden, the clouds rolled, the sun came out, and I was flying to Australia to clinch the deal. Then back to Europe to return in triumph, on November 17, 1965, arm in arm with Walter Chiari, who would take Australia by storm as Nino Culotta.

Do I make my point? The life of an independent producer, if he hasn't got the backing of a major studio, is rough. Remember what Pierre Levy said to me, in Paris: "I'm going to give it up, Michael. I don't like the life of an independent film producer. First of all, you must be born in Tiflis, or Odessa, and then you must be getting in, or out of, an airplane all the time. That's all right for you, Michael, but it's not for me. My father was a publisher. I shall follow in his footsteps. I shall sit scribbling in a room, surrounded by books, while you are winging through the sky."

And here I was, on my way back from my first trip to Australia, destination Rome. Ostensibly, I had to see De Laurentiis. Both Sordi and Gassman were under contract to him, and both were possible Ninos. I wasn't sure that I could handle De Laurentiis as a partner. Then there was Santi, Walter Chiari's producer. He also produced cheese.

I was expected in Rome. My room had been booked in a hotel that was new to me. It had a wonderful, tall window looking down on a narrow street. I flung my things on the floor, fell on the bed, and went to sleep. Toward evening there was a bang on the door, and a porter marched in carrying a suitcase, followed by Pamela.

Two days later I rang my agent in Rome. She was reproachful.

"Where have you been? We've been looking for you everywhere."

"I needed a rest. Who have I got to see?"

"Suso Cecchi d'Amico. Her husband's a music critic. She's the best screen-writer in Italy. Her name means a lot."

"*The Leopard,* for Visconti . . ."

"Hm-hmm . . . and she did *Rocco and His Brothers.*"

"She's out of my class."

"Don't be stupid. She's dying to meet you."

We went up to the Borghese Gardens and met the lady. She was about forty, tall, broad forehead, generous mouth, obviously out of my class. But she was nice, and we talked about my project. It took her some time to understand what I wanted to do, but she knew and liked Walter Chiari.

"Perhaps your Nino could be a schoolmaster?"

Right then and there, I knew we were in different leagues. But I was sorry. I liked her forehead.

"Where's Dickie Burton?"

"In Paris."

"With Liz?"

"Of course. They had to get away from the paparazzi."

"Out of the frying pan?"

"More or less."

"Where are they staying?"

"The Georges Cinq."

When I arrived, the hotel was in a state of siege, but I got in by a service door. Richard hadn't read the script, but he promised that he would; at least he had it with him. We sat and waited for Liz Taylor. There were faces at all the windows, but they started to drift away at dinnertime. After we had had three brandies and sodas, and Burton and his entourage had made twelve long-distance telephone calls, Liz came down with her hair piled on top of her head. It was midnight, more or less, so I suggested dinner at Fouquet's. The fans outside had gone, except for a few diehards. Liz got into a huge limousine, and Richard into a sports car, and we drove around the corner to Fouquet's. The dinner was good, and afterward I suggested that we take in the town.

"What about the paparazzi?"

"Paris isn't Rome. You'll be all right."

We daringly walked along the Champs-Elysées, and dropped in on several nightclubs. Just for the record, I danced with Elizabeth Taylor. We broke it up about four in the morning, Richard promising again to read *Battle of the April Storm*. Ever since he had discovered that it would be an all-male cast he had been much more enthusiastic.

In spite of the Christmas holidays, I got to work on the script of *Weird Mob*, and finished it by January 28. It was a bit long, 130 pages, but a script from a book always is. I sent it off to John O'Grady, and waited for the fireworks. Then, I got a call from Hein.

"Micky, Micky, are you free?"

"As the air—what for?"

"Good. Oh, thanks be to God! Here is Norman Foster."

"Who?"

"Talk to him, Micky. He wants to do a film of the Bartók couple: *Bluebeard's Castle* and *The Miraculous Mandarin*. You know, they are a couple of one-hour shows, they always go together."

"Do they?"

"Here is Foster, Micky. Talk to him. He would produce and sing, and act Blaubart. It is for German television in the summer. Oh, Micky, it would be wonderful to work together again, on such a thing! Have you got the music?"

"No, I haven't got much Bartók."

"Get it, Micky. Get it, and play it, and then telephone me. I want to know what you think."

A deep baritone: "How do you do, Michael Powell?"

"How do you do? The only Norman Foster that I know was an actor, and is now a director in Hollywood. Are you he?"

"I am an American, Mr. Powell, from Boston, but I am not that Norman Foster. I am a singer and a film producer. Of course, I've seen your wonderful films, and I have talked to Hein Heckroth, here in Frankfurt, about designing the two Bartók pieces. *Bluebeard's Castle* is an opera, and *The Miraculous Mandarin* is a ballet. In both cases, the libretto is the work of Béla Balázs, who was a friend of Bartók's."

"The film critic?"

"Yes, the film critic."

I was very tempted. I didn't know the Bartók pieces, but I loved his music. I had come to it through Kodály. I telephoned my record store and they had a recording of the Berlin Philharmonic, with Dietrich Fischer-Dieskau singing Bluebeard. From the first notes, I was completely sold. I rang Hein back.

"Sold! It's terrific!"

"You really think so, Micky? I would be so happy if we could do it together. We could do it in the *relâche,* when the theatre is closed for the holidays. My students here could do the decor and make the props. Norman wants to make the film in Salzburg."

"Why?"

"There is a new film studio being built there. We would be the first production there. It will be ready in the summer, before the season starts."

"Where would the recording be done?"

"In Vienna, with the Philharmonic."

"And the singers?"

"Norman Foster himself would sing Blaubart, and he knows a woman who he says can sing the other part. There are only two parts, the man and the woman."

"Who is the woman? Is she his girlfriend?"

"He says not. But he has toured with her, and she is good."

"Is the money there?"

"I guess so. He has money from Süddeutscher Rundfunk, and he gets the studio free, and he says perhaps he does the recording in Yugoslavia. It is cheaper there, and maybe better. I'm not all that keen on Vienna, after *Rosalinda.*"

"Do we use Technicolor?"

"We do. I have spoken to George Gunn, and he's very excited to get such an art film."

"The film will be developed at Technicolor, Heathrow?"

"Yes."

"And the cameraman?"

"I do not know him, but I hear he's very good. His name is Hannes Staudinger."

Just so lightly did I enter into a project that was going to keep me zigzagging over Europe for the next six months.

A long letter arrived from John O'Grady. He had learned a lot from my script, but he was now going to write his own.

I got the score of *Bluebeard's Castle* from Boosey and Hawkes and threw it into film shape, without trying to be too clever. Béla Balázs's scheme of the seven doors, opening one after the other, until the final door, which closes, imprisoning Bluebeard's new wife, who wanted to know too much, was a natural for film opera. I sent it to Hein, who got to work on it with enthusiasm and sent me a sketch of the two lovers, to be the cover for the script.

About *The Mandarin* I had reservations. The joke was personal and obscure, and had probably been thought up in a café in Budapest. It appeared to be about an insatiable Chinaman in a whorehouse, but appearances are not always what they seem. It had been done as a ballet on the usual balletic circuit, and there was a picture of Mr. Todd Bolender in the role of the Mandarin on the cover of the sleeve.

I wasn't prepared, at this stage, to do much thinking about it, but it seemed to me that the music conjured up visions of Budapest trams undercranked, ending in a vast pileup of the traffic in the biggest city square. As we all know, a tram is a being that moves in predestinate grooves, not a bus, not a bus, but a tram, and I felt that to see these majestic vehicles leap from their predestinate grooves and all pile up in the middle of the square, as directed by the Mandarin as a traffic cop, could be immensely satisfying. Fortunately I was never called upon to prove it.

As if this were not enough, Christopher Mann was suddenly on the blower.

"Richard Burton has read the Forrester script of *The Battle of the April Storm*, and likes it. Hugh French is his agent, and is asking five hundred thousand dollars and ten percent of the gross. What are your comments?"

I replied that as I was already in discussion with United Artists about *Mr. Sebastian*, it would make sense to let them in on the ground floor, and make it a joint production between Rank and United Artists. I felt pretty sure that John Davis would come in fifty-fifty, on an estimated budget of £400,000. Both Chris and I felt that we could cut Hugh French's quotation for Richard by half.

And as if all that were not enough, John Pellatt came to see me. John had been second assistant on *Oh . . . Rosalinda!!* and now, ten years later, was a producer. Having seen me with a full head of steam, he held me in great awe.

"Micky, I hope you don't think I'm being cheeky, but would you do a television film?"

I said, "What sort of a film?"

And he breathed a sigh of relief.

"It's a series, called *Espionage;* one-hour shows. The producer is Herb Hirschman, who operates in Hollywood, and he is over here setting it up for Herb Brodkin."

"Whoa! Hold your horses, John. Who is Herb Brodkin, and who is Herb Hirschman?"

"They are television tycoons. They are the new rich, and they are over here now in Europe to make the series, and perhaps other series, hoping to get actors and directors on the cheap. Herb Hirschman has produced dozens of shows for television, but Herb Brodkin is a big shot. He has done a lot of shows for *Playhouse 90.*"

"Has he, by God."

Playhouse 90, with its improvisations and its reckless audacity, its use of top talent and its knowledge of the theatre, was already a legend among TV showmen. Apparently the producers commanded top talent, and were top talent themselves, and were not afraid to plan shows starting at one hour that might run to two or three or even four hours. In the early days this was live television, mind you, and required a great deal of skill and daring, and sheer nerve, in both the planning and the performance. These were people that I would like to meet and work with, or even for. So I said, "What do they pay?"

John gulped and said, "Not much, Micky. About a thousand pounds a show. The time schedule is eight days. You get a reading with the cast, but no rehearsal. They're not mean. They want all the top people. They're paying Malcolm Arnold, for instance, to do the music. Wilfred Shingleton is doing the sets, and Rose Tobias Shaw is doing the casting."

"She's the best, and she's not cheap."

"No. What do you say, Micky? Shall I tell them that you're thinking about it?"

"I won't work for less than a thousand a week. If they'll pay that, and pro rata, I'll think about it."

"Great! I'll find out, right away."

"Hang on a moment. Who is writing the scripts?"

"Oh . . . everybody! They're mostly very simple . . . a couple of sets, you know, and exteriors."

"I'd like to read some of them."

"Okay. They'll be at your office this afternoon."

I read them at home that evening. They were trash in a gilded can, but there was one that had the germ of an idea. It was called *Never Turn Your Back On a Friend*, a bit of a smart-aleck title, but it wasn't a bad piece of writing. When John telephoned me, I said, "I'll have to have approval of the script."

He hesitated.

"I don't think Herb Hirschman will give you that."

"What about Herb Brodkin?"

"I don't know. I'll find out."

"And I would want Leo Marks to write one of the . . . shows, do you call them?"

"Yes, Micky."

"Okay . . . to write one of the shows. He's under contract to me at the moment, but I'll loan him to you."

"I think I can do that. They're looking for writers."

"There's one of the shows that I like—*Never Turn Your Back On a Friend*. It's got something, but it needs a rewrite. I'd want Larry Forrester to do the rewrite."

Things were moving a bit fast for John, but he said, "Okay, Micky, I'll try."

I said, "See you," and rang off.

I didn't expect to hear from John again, but he turned up in two days, all smiles.

"Okay, Micky. Buzz Berger has agreed to everything."

"Who is Buzz Berger?"

"He works for Herb Brodkin."

"Then, who's Herb Hirschman?"

"He and Brodkin are old buddies. Hirschman is getting these shows together for Brodkin. He's California-based. Herb Brodkin lives in New York. He's got a long-running series there, *The Defenders*. It's into show one hundred and twenty, already."

"My, my!"

Never Turn Your Back On a Friend had four main characters: a Norwegian schoolmistress, secretly a member of the resistance to the Nazis, and three young men, British, Soviet, and American. Their mission: to destroy a heavy-water plant. The three young men begin as allies, but finish as enemies. I said to Pamela, "You've got an offer."

"When do I start?"

"When we've got the script right. But it's a good part."

Larry Forrester was delighted with the assignment.

"I've got the Yank lying down most of the time, you know the way the Yanks are always lying down and resting?"

Larry is Canadian.

"It's fun to do. When do you want it?"

"In a week."

"Can do."

We shot it in eight days. Malcolm Arnold came to see me.

"I'm supposed to write music for your film. It doesn't need any."

Herb and Herb and Buzz saw the film. Herb Brodkin said, "That looks like Pamela Brown."

John said, "It is Pamela Brown. Michael asked her to play the part."

Herb said, "I always wanted to meet her. She's a great actress."

He thought for a while, and said, "Even in this, she's great."

John said, "I'll tell Michael."

Leo wrote the next script about a Soviet agent who falls in love with the girl on the other side, played by Siân Phillips, and in the end finds that neither side trusts him. I gave it the title *A Free Agent.* Tony Quayle played the agent, and Norman Foster his friend and go-between. Norman brought his beard along with him from *Bluebeard's Castle.* The story called for scenes in the snow in the winter sports in Austria, and there is quite a bit of action around a chair lift, in which all the family took part, Frankie, Kevin, and Columba. We shot the scenes when we went for our skiing holiday.

By this time I had met Herb Brodkin. He couldn't quite size me up. I liked him a lot, and thought I could work with him. I thought he was bound to move on from television to films. If I had a partner like that, I could plan anything, do anything; this was the sort of man I was looking for. Herb had the grandeur of a Caucasian landscape. He was rugged, and he had a splendid head. He was ruthless, one could see that, but there was always humor in his eyes. It was obvious that once he had made up his mind, he was invincible. I could just see him, or his father, or grandfather, charging out of a tremendous mountain pass, brandishing a huge *yataghan,* a fur cap on his head, his mouth yelling curses and threats, his tall body erect in the saddle, and his eyes full of humor and delight at the fight. He was everything that I was not, but I felt we could get on together. I decided to make him a partner in *Mr. Sebastian.*

=

Meanwhile, *Bluebeard* had come and gone, and the road through the Alps and across Lombardy no longer echoed to the thunder of my Land-Rover. This was my red Rover, a short-wheelbase, which I had permitted our chef at the Voile d'Or to use for marketing at the Nice market, until the Syndicat d'Initiative told me to stop. They said it was an English-registered car, and anyway, it was unfair competition. It was also blatant advertising, as everyone in the market wanted to know where this magnificent red Rover came from.

So to save her from the attention of the *douaniers,* I used her for trips across

Europe, which seemed to be essential for the financing of *Bluebeard's Castle*. From the hotel there were several routes to choose from, and I tried them all. You could go through Menton and Ventimiglia and take the road along the Italian Riviera, or you could turn inland and climb over the Col de Tende and down into Lombardy, through Tunio, to Turin and the Italian Alps. This was my favorite way, and I loved to climb up to St. Moritz and the Engadine, and then plunge down the gorges of the River Inn and see this magnificent river grow and spring beneath my wheels.

Another way was by the Tyrol, and yet another through the Alpes Maritimes to Chamonix, the towering Matterhorn continuously in view. I sang and recited poems by the yard, and wished I had a dog with me, and wondered whether I would hear from that lady in North Wales who had advertised black spaniel puppies for sale, and who had promised to let me have the pick of the next litter.

Hein and Ada were in Frankfurt, of course, until the theatre closed for the summer holidays, and I dropped in on them whenever I could, sometimes leaving the Rover in a lock-up garage at the airport. I would get sudden calls to attend a meeting in Vienna, in Munich, in Zurich, or wherever Norman Foster was having the usual difficulty of independent producers in coordinating their finance.

At one of the rallies I met Anna Raquel Sartre, who was to sing and play Bluebeard's seventh wife. She was tall, intelligent, and clumsy-looking in an endearing sort of way. I was agreeably surprised. Most of Norman's suggestions so far had been predictable, but not so this woman. She was an artist, and had a sense of humor. She was a victim, but would never surrender. It was obvious Norman knew that she could do the job for the right price, but had never thought of her as serious competition. I thought otherwise.

I remember one memorable drive through the night in appalling weather, and across the border between Austria and Yugoslavia to Zagreb, to meet a young conductor who was reputed to be the best interpreter of Bartók at the moment. He was also cheap; he was also good. There was no comparison between Zagreb and Vienna, either for quality or for cheapness. I remember that we rehearsed and recorded for ten long hours, and after that the brisk young conductor was to conduct a performance, that night, of *Carmen*. I decided I liked Yugoslavia and its artists. They love and hate, and are not afraid to say so.

So in June, two weeks before the season started, we all met in the enchanting village of Salzburg. I had picked up Pamela along the way, I can't think where, and had parked red Rover outside the café. We came out to find Ada peering in the window. We were all staying on the edge of the village, in private houses covered in flowers and balconies and gables. There were also

At this time my father wasn't seeing much of his family. I was preparing to make and direct a film in the farthest north of Scotland, in the Shetland Islands, and my mother was keeping a home for me. Came the war, my father's exile to England, and then his return to the Voile d'Or to resume the simple and entirely selfish life that he had always pursued. Sydney Courtauld was dead, and Rab Butler had married her cousin. He did his courting in the woods and on the border of Gatcombe Park, in Gloucestershire, which I can see from my window as I write. Rab's father-in-law had bought Gatcombe Park to appease a friend and fellow collector, Viscount Lee of Fareham, who gave Chequers to the nation and was now living in the Old Quarries House in the village of Avening below Gatcombe. This was before World War II, and Lord Lee had built an enormous fireproof strongroom in the wing of the house to hold his valuable collection, now part of the Courtauld Collection, on permanent view to the public.

Lord Lee was in a great state, because he had heard that the county council were thinking of turning the Gatcombe property adjacent to his house into a lunatic asylum. Courtauld intervened by purchasing the property. Everything Sam Courtauld did was on this scale, and yet done with a generous simplicity that was quite unique. He was always very good company, which cannot be said of Lord Lee.

In 1952 my father died suddenly of a stroke, as I have related, and I was sole heir to his properties: two hotels, at Cap Ferrat and Chantilly. It was only then that I discovered how shaky my father's title to the Voile d'Or was.

If I had been able to pay back the original loan at once, that would have been the best thing to do. Emeric and I were living as independent film producers do, from one production to another. If I had had good advice, I could have come out of the situation a winner, but I didn't. I had one good friend, David Niven, who, by coming to the rescue with money in Switzerland, saved me from being sold up and taken over.

Frankie and I had tried to run the hotel ourselves for a couple of seasons, but it was becoming clear that this would be the way to disaster. I still had not the slightest interest in becoming a *hôtelier*. Frankie, on the other hand, was a complete success as a hostess, and even as a *hôtelier*, but she had an alcohol problem and it was unthinkable to leave her there to kill herself, sooner or later. There were plenty of professional *hôteliers* and *restaurateurs* anxious to get hold of the Voile d'Or, and the most professional and reputable was a family that was well known on the coast, who, having failed to get hold of the Voile d'Or by other means, were now prepared to buy me out. It was to conclude these negotiations that I now returned to the Voile d'Or for the last time.

It will be asked why, with powerful friends and the experience of handling budgets worth millions of dollars and hundreds and thousands of pounds, I didn't plan to continue to run hotels and film production in double harness. There were similarities; we both have to please the general public. The answer was, simply, that I was not interested. I would always be that boy who opened his friend's copy of *The Picturegoer* magazine in January 1921 and lost his heart to the movies.

I must now chronicle the arrival of Boswell and Johnson.

A family without domestic animals has no right to be called a family. Very true, but Frankie and Bill, who would have to look after the animals while I was doing my European flying saucer act, were not so sure, pointing out that there was already our magnificent cat, called Bibby because of the white bib under its chin. He was a male black cat. So when I went to Portmeirion with a bunch of scripts under my arm, one of which turned out to be Larry Forrester's *Battle of the April Storm,* I read the local adverts on the notice board and saw that a marriage had been arranged, by a lady who lived in Snowdonia, between her black spaniel bitch and a dog of impeccable ancestry, and that orders were now being received and considered for puppies born of this union. I put my name down for two male puppies, and forgot all about it, thanks to being invaded by Herb and Herb and Buzz: as a consequence of which, I suddenly heard from the lady in North Wales that her spaniel bitch had a litter of six, and two boys had been reserved for me and would be expressed to me by rail in nine weeks' time, subject to receiving a check for eighty guineas.

Frankie was at Cap Ferrat, Bill was with me at Elstree, Myrtle quite definitely turned down the suggestion that she should act as nursemaid to two black babies for the next couple of months, and I was shooting another *Espionage* film, laid in the eighteenth century and starring Roger Livesey as Dr. Johnson. It will be remembered, by admirers of the "great Cham of literature," that he was a fervent Jacobite who openly expressed his opinion that the Hanoverians were usurpers. When he accompanied Boswell, on the latter's insistence, on the Highland journey to the Isle of Skye, a considerable adventure in 1773, he insisted upon meeting Miss Flora Macdonald, who had helped Bonnie Prince Charlie evade his pursuers and escape back to France, and had questioned the lady closely on the capability and ambitions of the Young Pretender and his supporters.

He had made his sympathies known in Edinburgh. There is no doubt that, on his return to London, he would have been regarded with suspicion by the authorities, and with humor by George III, who by this time felt sufficiently secure on his throne to be able to admire the great dictionary maker and wit who had dismissed Lord Chesterfield's letters to his son, on their publication, because, "They teach the morals of a whore, and the manners of a dancing master."

I have always loved Dr. Samuel Johnson, and it may be remembered that

I took him with me on my Burma trip up the Chindwin in 1938; and I have always loved Roger Livesey, as an artist and a man. It was one of the few occasions on which I have directed a film for personal reasons, and the result was as disastrous as one might expect, knowing either Roger or me. There were some good artists involved on the productions, but not even Jill Bennett, playing a boy, could save it. I don't even know now whether I ever saw it put together. But at least the little film serves to date the arrival of the two black spaniel puppies: Boswell and Johnson.

They arrived by the morning train from Portmadoc, and Bill went to meet them at Euston. The guard of the train reported that they had yapped all night, but otherwise had been as good as gold. Bill prudently kept them in their traveling case, returned to the studio, and released them on the set amid the "oh"s and "ah"s of dog lovers present. In about forty-five seconds flat they had licked everybody's faces, raced about the stage, cocked their legs on every conceivable piece of equipment, yelled their heads off when cornered and captured by the propmen, and started a nonstop barking contest in the dressing room assigned to them.

Pamela was a dog lover, and since she was resting between engagements I appealed to her for help. She arrived with a load of books, scripts, sandwiches, and puppy biscuits, and took up residence in the dressing room. I visited her at lunchtime. The two puppies were stretched out, asleep on her tummy, and the room was full of shit. Pamela lifted her glorious eyes from the script she was studying and looked calmly at me. She said nothing. She was, for the moment, a substitute spaniel bitch.

=

Herb Brodkin was a great sportsman, and I decided that I was one too. Fishing was Herb's sport, and he practiced it like a religion. Hannes, my Tyrolean cameraman, had already interested me in game shooting, and I decided that I would become an all-round sportsman, forgetting how clumsy I am. It was not the hunting or the shooting or the eating that attracted me. It was the places that you go to, and the people that you meet, and then the implements that you employ: the guns, the rods, lines and reels, the knives, the cartridge bags, the creels!

A gunsmith's shop is the most seductive place in the world. I bought a huge eight-bore Purdy from Holland & Holland, and took it into Purdy's Gun Shop, in South Audley Street.

"I believe this is one of your guns?"

"Ah, yes, sir."

He reached under the broad mahogany counter, produced a couple of huge ledgers, and flipped the pages over.

"Here it is, sir: 1871. You've kept it very well, sir."

"I'm going to try it after high birds—geese and ducks."

"Should be ideal, sir. Can I sell you a couple of boxes of cartridges?"

Mr. Wetherall, another gunsmith, was even more persuasive, and sold me a beautiful twelve-bore shotgun, and a couple of hundred cartridges. He also sold me a rifle made in 1912, with pointed cartridges that gave less wind resistance. It had many refinements, and was a Stradivarius of a rifle. They ordered for me from America a Colt revolver with a long barrel, for shooting small game when you were on the trail, and a plain simple Winchester '73 that never let me down.

I bought most of my fishing tackle in Scotland, most of it designed and made in Sweden and Norway. I fished the River Spey, and the swift Findhorn, and the lochs of northeast Scotland. I bought my salmon-fishing gear from famous sporting shops in St. James's, and from Hardy in Pall Mall, of course.

Herb scoffed at all my tackle and lent me his, and tried to teach me how to cast. He had started his fishing on Fire Island, that long, low, wonderful sandbar off Long Island, a haven for New Yorkers. He was a magnificent fisherman, and an ambitious one. He was never satisfied, always looking for new places to fish, some of them far afield like New Brunswick in Canada or the River Dee in Aberdeenshire, the River Wye in Wales. He was patient, he was crafty, he was tireless.

He invited me to come to New York and shoot some more television episodes for his company, goodness knows why. It's a highly competitive world, and it was a mystery to me why they were doing it. Pamela was working in New York, and so we took a flat together near the United Nations building, where her sister and brother-in-law were both working.

Herb was fond of Pamela. It was fine to see them together, and we met Herb's wife, Pattie, and his two daughters. Pattie had a lovely face. It was both strong and tender. Her eyes were set beautifully in her head, and the way she stood and the way she walked made you love her. She and Herb had both been at art school together. She was a fine designer and architect, with a gift for interior decoration and faultless taste. Of the two girls, one had inherited her mother's talents, the other was a witch. The happiest times we had together were at Fire Island and on the River Miramichi in Canada. Herb had got it into his head that he would teach me how to fish, not realizing that I was the greatest fool in the world when I was not handling actors or a camera.

Later on, and by force majeure, I discovered that I was a writer. But in those days I just kept a diary about people and things of interest. The camp on the Miramichi was luxurious and practical at one and the same time. There were several cabins, built on a low bluff beside the river, which at this place was about two hundred yards wide, with an average depth of about two feet, a swift current, and a firm, rocky bottom. Above and below the camp there were rapids and deep pools. The river narrowed and animals like deer and moose came to drink there and often cross there.

I was in heaven. Ever since I had read, or rather devoured, all the books of Stewart Edward White about the northern woods, I had longed to explore them, to follow their trails, to fly over the lakes of Canada. Among my fellow guests was Lee Wulff, author of *The Atlantic Salmon* and designer of the White Wulff fly. He was tall and lean, with a beautiful face with high cheekbones, and he could cast seventy feet of line with the greatest of ease, using a seven-foot, six-inch rod. Herb was his admiring disciple. Wulff flew his own float plane single-handed, landing on nameless lakes and distant, lonely rivers.

A huge young man, the local gas agent, brought gasoline for Lee Wulff's plane, which was anchored in a pool downriver. After lunch we all went down to McCluskey's Camp to see him off. There was plenty of wind, but only about six hundred feet to get going. He checked up, said goodbye, taxied down the pool, turned, and then came upstream into the wind. He was overloaded and couldn't get off until he had gone clear around the corner, up some rapids and under some powerlines, half airborne, half-planing. Then he was up and away. He flew back, rolled farewell, and headed north for Seven Islands. We all went back to our cars, shaking our heads and saying he only just made it. And he always has.

I was assigned to James, or rather James was assigned to nurse me how to cast and how to fish. We had a battered old canoe, and I would cast all morning without even frightening a fish, let alone attracting it. James would untangle my lines and give me advice, and talk to me about his life in the woods in the summer and winter, about his fellow workers, and the horse that worked with him.

"Do you work with teams in the woods?"

"Some uses tractors, but horses are better to work with."

"Big draft horses?"

"Clydes. I, and a mate, worked a whole winter through, cutting and sawing with a Clyde. Cleverer than a man, she was."

"We call them Clydesdales."

He accepted the correction: "That's their name, of course."

"Cutting their name short is as bad as hogging their manes."

James chuckled.

"This here Clyde, she would go to and fro between me, where I was cutting the trees, and my mate, where he was sawing them. Soon as I had a log ready, I would clip on the hooks, and away she would go all by herself, through the woods to where the saw was working, to and fro all day. She would come back dragging the chains, all on her own. If the traces caught in a stump, she would just step sideways, and pull it free. No matter where I was, she would find me. Once, I clipped on the hooks, and said "Go!" and she wouldn't move. So I shouted at her. She give me a look, and then she went. Few paces later, the hook pulled out. She stopped, and give me another look . . . Cleverer than a man."

"Did she always work like this?"

"Never had a bridle on her all winter. She was a small eater, too. Always well covered, but she would never eat more than three bushels of oats. Give her five, and she would still eat three, then step back from the manger. She was the best workin' horse I ever seen. She would take bread from my hand with just her lips. She was plumb gentle. She loved bread; bread and molasses. It put a shine on her coat that was pretty to see."

"What was her name, James?"

"Whose?"

"The mare's. She was a mare, wasn't she?"

"Marge."

In another part of the forest, John Pellatt had not been idle. It will be remembered that it was he who introduced me to the *Espionage* group, and during that winter and spring he learned a good deal about my hopes and plans for *They're a Weird Mob*, for *The Battle of the April Storm*, and for *Mr. Sebastian*. It was an exciting trio of projects, and he decided to throw his lot in with me when the thirteen episodes of *Espionage* were in the can.

Until Herb loomed upon the western horizon I had been discussing these projects with Arthur Krim and his associates at United Artists. My association with them dated back to *Stairway to Heaven* in 1946. At this time they were interested in Leo Marks's script of *Mr. Sebastian*, and they were being asked by me to put up 50 percent of the cost of *The Battle of the April Storm* with Richard Burton.

On *Weird Mob* I was asking John Davis to come in with my Australian partners as to 50 percent of the budget of £150,000, but Walter Chiari, whom I now regarded as essential to the film, would not be free until the autumn of 1965, which was one of the reasons why I accepted Herb's invitation to shoot some more television films in New York, where I met David Greene.

David Greene was Brodkin's resident film director in New York, and he looked upon my intrusion with suspicion, tinged with awe. He was certainly the favored son in the Brodkin camp, and he lived with a telephoto finder to his eye and a tape recorder in his hand. He was English in origin, an actor, and I remember seeing him at the Old Vic, in Tyrone Guthrie's production of Christopher Marlowe's *Tamburlaine*, starring Donald Wolfit as the dreaded tyrant. David was one of the petty kings who were dragged at his chariot wheels: "Holla, ye pampered Jades of Asia."

David Greene had been one of the first English directors to think of Canada as a stepping-stone to Hollywood, and he made a big career out of it. He was efficient, had humor and imagination, and had directed a feature film in 1966, called *The Shuttered Room,* and would later direct a few more; I could never understand why he chose to make his career in television, but that's his business. Of course, David, being English in origin, knew who I was at a time when Herb and Buzz had never heard of The Archers or Powell and Pressburger. There was a generation gap somewhere, and it never occurred to them to try and bridge it, and since they got to know me at a time when I had no agent to trumpet my achievements they never did know, until I published the first volume of my autobiography twenty-two years later.

Of our three projects, John Pellatt and I most favored *The Battle of the April Storm.* The script had originally been commissioned by Emile Littler, lessee of the Palace Theatre and great theatrical producer. This was the script I took with me to Paris and gave to Richard Burton to read. He would be free in the spring, and liked the part, and it really seemed that it would go.

United Artists finally agreed to come in for 50 percent of the one-million-pound cost, in harness with the Rank Organisation. There was a very large male cast in the film. A million pounds sounds a lot for those days, but if it wasn't worth that, it wasn't worth anything. The script called for immense technical resources in the studio, which Pinewood certainly possessed. Unlike the *Graf Spee* picture, this naval epic would be made almost entirely in the studio. The style would not be realistic, but epic. Sound effects and a musical score, combined with technical know-how and invention, the use of miniatures and models, plus front and back projection, would have brought this extraordinary epic to stunning life, and death.

Suddenly Arthur Krim and his associates changed their minds. They had a bad habit of holding conferences, and somebody must have remarked that there was no American in the cast, nor place for one. Without warning we in England were told that because of this national or international imbalance, UA would only put up one third of the dough for it. Rank would have to find two thirds. John Davis, very naturally, refused point-blank; and then, very foolishly, refused to negotiate further, which put an end to all hope of production for this magnificent piece of writing.

Larry Forrester was in despair, and finally asked me if I had any objection to us turning the script into a book. Without thinking I said, "None at all," and he took the typescript to a publisher, who gave him a contract. When the book was published he was sued by Emile Littler, who owned the original copyright of the screenplay. No doubt Larry acted innocently and was badly advised, and I could have kicked myself for my carelessness in not looking after him.

Thus passed *The Battle of the April Storm*, and with it my last chance of playing Richard Burton in a film. I had always hoped to work with Richard, ever since he joined the Stratford Shakespeare Memorial Theatre to play Hotspur and then Henry V, giving sensational performances of both for a young unknown Welsh actor. I was staying at that time with Ian Dalrymple, at the Manor House at Little Wolford near Shipton on Stour. Ian was so moved by the magical young actor that he bought Richard Hillary's book, *The Last Enemy*, to be a vehicle for Burton. Negotiations were in progress, but Twentieth Century–Fox and Spyros Skouras had already assigned Richard to play in *The Robe*, which introduced the public to CinemaScope for the first time. Richard had a good business manager in Hugh French, once my friend and now an agent, who immediately added two noughts to every figure in the contract. It was almost like Larry Harvey in *Peeping Tom* all over again.

The Richard Hillary book *The Last Enemy* ("The last enemy to be destroyed is death") would have made a wonderful film. In case you need reminding, Hillary was a young fighter pilot, aged twenty-two, who was shot down and so badly burned that it took the plastic surgeons at East Grinstead eighteen months to give him a new face and hands. During the time he was in hospital he wrote his book. He then rejoined his squadron and died, as he lived, in the air. Ian would have made a wonderful film, and Richard Burton would have made a wonderful Richard Hillary. He had a pagan simplicity about him, and his heart and his head were in the right place. R.I.P. to both Richards.

> Wrap me up in my tarpaulin jacket,
> And say a poor buffer lies low, lies low,
> And six stalwart lancers shall carry me, carry me,
> Their steps solemn, mournful and slow, and slow.*

A script entitled *The Stalwart Lancer* came into my office. It was the script of a television show that had already been produced. I read it and I would have whistled, if I could, but I can't; I never could. Come to think of it, I can't do anything but make movies. It was just about the best bit of screenplay writing since that memorable screenplay of C. S. Forester's, *The African Queen*, that John Huston snatched away from me in the roaring fifties. The writing of this *Lancer* script was spare and patrician; the men were men, and with clearly defined backgrounds and manners; the woman was a woman. I read on entranced.

*From the poem "The Tarpaulin Jacket," by George John Whyte-Melville.

You don't know how dizzy it makes you feel to find a new, good writer in your "in" tray; and this was a master writer, with insight, ambition, feeling. He knew the people that he was writing about, he knew them through and through. Life disgusted him, and thrilled him, but he kept his emotions on a tight rein. He was a born dramatist and they are not made. His name was Richard Vaughan Hughes.

The location of the action was a mews in Belgravia, and I knew all there was to know about a mews in Belgravia, having lived in one throughout the war. A London mews flat over a Victorian coach house with wide double doors and cracking paint, and its narrow stairway to the cosy flat up ahead, with brick-built chimney and coal fire and its general Sherlock Holmes flavor, is a delightful setting for a drama. And when the long, narrow mews, with its brick surface and its patches of cobbles, is a cul-de-sac, then you have a trap from which even James Mason could not escape.

The part of the Lancer spy was played on television by James, and alas, I never saw him play it, although as I read I could see those beautiful suffering eyes and fine body tortured by pain, racked with desire. I could hear his voice pleading for help from his old flame, while she drank martinis from a shaker beside her double bed. I could hear the roar of the four-and-a-quarter-liter Bentley sports car, and see the blood on the cobblestones . . .

This was the writer that I had been looking for to make a workable structure out of Leo Marks's *Mr. Sebastian,* for if ever there was a man who knew too much, it was Leo, and it was time for a writer with some sense of construction to take over and reduce two hundred pages by 50 percent. Like all good writers, this one was hard to nail down. His agent said he had a room in Notting Hill Gate, but preferred to work and live in the country. He was eventually tracked down somewhere in Somerset. He read Leo's script, then asked to meet Leo himself. He proved himself a formidable tactician by convincing Leo to collaborate with him. This left me free for the script of *They're a Weird Mob.*

I can't write and speak too often about the value of collaboration between writer and director when planning a film. *Weird Mob* was no exception. When I read the book I was so sure of its ultimate success that I didn't option the book, I bought it outright. Peter Finch had been my guiding star, and Peter Finch had been right: Walter Chiari was the right man for the part. His English was excellent, and his world was the real world of the struggling artist-journalist-actor, the world of the stand-up comedian. A delightful Italian actor like Alberto Sordi, or a brilliant legitimate actor like Vittorio Gassman, or even an international personality like Vittorio De Sica—none of these would be able to handle the subtleties of John O'Grady's Nino Culotta.

My Australian partners, including John O'Grady, were dismayed and bewildered by my delays and changes of heart and excuses, and by the continual rewrites of the script. But I ignored the appeals from John McCallum, and the threats from Bob Austin, and signed a provisional agreement with Walter Chiari to start shooting in Sydney, Australia, by October 1965.

The first script by me was a straight adaptation of the book, and was like an attempt to put a quart into a pint bottle. The second script, by John O'Grady, on his own suggestion, was funny, authentic, and would have played four hours.

The third, and final, script was by Richard Imrie. At my request, he read the two scripts, and also the book. He rang me up. I said, "Well, Imre? What do you think of Nino?"

"Vell, Michael, I like him."

I breathed a sigh of relief. I waited; dead silence.

"Are you still there, Imre?' "

"Yes, Michael, I am here in Thiersee."

"We can pay three thousand pounds cash, and two and a half percent of the producer's profit."

"Do you think that there will be any profit, Michael?"

"Who knows?"

"That is true."

"Will you take it on, Imre? I bought the rights, and Walter Chiari will be splendid in the part, but I'm not happy about the script."

A chuckle. Then: "There is no story, Michael."

"Isn't there?"

"Oh, Michael, Michael . . . How many times have I told you that a film is not words. It is thoughts, and feelings, surprises, suspense, accident."

I was humbled.

"When could you start, Imre?"

"Do you wish me to start, Michael?"

"Please."

In ten days he brought me a new script, on 114 quarto pages, handwritten in his round handwriting, and all tucked away cosily in a ring book, like the very first script we ever did together, *The Spy in Black*. It was like old times. We made two trips together, the first to Roquebrune, the village above Monte Carlo, where De Laurentiis had a villa. Walter was staying there with Silvana Mangano and a horde of children. Imre was delighted with Walter. We all ate, talked, and drank a great deal. Our second trip was to Rome, to finalize the script.

In London, the National Film Corporation had just been formed, to help British producers, and was headed by John Terry, a clever and sympathetic lawyer. *Weird Mob* was one of their first investments. This brought in Rank, as distributor and part-investor. The budget was now £230,000. I closed my eyes and signed a bond, guaranteeing a first payment of Walter's salary of £8,000, payable in September, and told our Australian partners we were ready to go by the agreed date in October.

But now I struck a real snag. Bob, John, and their partners, disheartened by delays and unfulfilled promises, had run out of steam. Their investors had regrouped; Frank Tait and Williamson Theatres had got cold feet, and Frank had resigned as head of Williamson-Powell.

Action was needed. I told John Pellatt to book us two return tickets to Sydney, and cabled John McCallum and Bob Austin that we were coming, with Walter Chiari in our pocket, to check all facilities, find new finance and, if necessary, new partners. Greatly heartened by this plain speaking, they replied, guaranteeing our expenses—economy class.

We flew the east-west route first-class and put up at the St. Francis Hotel, San Francisco. Crossing the Pacific, John had his first tussle with the international date line. On arrival at Sydney, we went directly into the board meeting that had been planned three years before. It developed into a shouting match, and was most enjoyable. I remember Bob Austin's furious face, saying, "Mates, Michael, mates!" in reply to some furious rebuttal by me. It ended with a pledge from all of us to carry the can, come one, come all.

Williamson's had booked us into a second-rate hotel, and a shared suite, but we soon fixed that. The news of our arrival had gone around, and we would have to meet the press the next day. Then a miracle happened. We all went along to the club for lunch, and there John McCallum met one of the directors of the British Tobacco Company and learned that they had just had a board meeting to decide to go into films and TV, and had already put down purchase money for one of the existing small studios. Of course, John O'Grady's Nino Culotta was just what the doctor ordered, and a deal for 50 percent of the Australian costs was struck, there and then, that same afternoon.

The next morning we met the press, and Bill Bengtsson, one of the directors of the British Tobacco Company, was on the platform with us. The next few days were busy ones for John Pellatt and for me. While I was going over Emeric's final draft of the script with John O'Grady, John Pellatt was racing around Sydney, checking facilities, arranging meetings, cabling DenLabs in England, interviewing technicians, and arranging a casting director to work with me.

Sydney was agog. The men's parts were quickly filled, but casting the women took longer. Obviously, the more Australian actors there were in the picture, the better, not only to save money, but for public relations. Some of the technicians had to be brought from London, and this had to be agreed with the local unions. I was more and more impressed by John Pellatt's efficiency and foresight, and he had his fans among the Aussies as well. At the end of three weeks, John was winging his way back to London—first-class. I followed a week later.

I don't think that I have described John Pellatt and his wife, Marigold. Ladies first: she was slim, black-haired, intelligent, and pretty. She was warmhearted, and had a grin like a boy's. She had a good eye for color, and was social. It couldn't have been easy to be John's wife, and she made a great job of it.

John was medium-sized, quick, and observant. He wore a beard. He was generous-hearted, and had a most attractive smile. He was also observant. He made very few mistakes. He had passed muster, through thirteen stormy episodes for Herb, Herb, and Buzz, and that was no mean feat. He had also not been afraid to invite me to make some television films, and that was no mean feat, either. He was a whiskey drinker, as I am, and drank malt whiskey, as I do. We made four films together, and never had a cross word (I'm counting three *Espionage* episodes as one film).

All was now set to start shooting *They're a Weird Mob* in Sydney in October. I owed this to John. I never could have done it without him. I am not so much a commander-in-chief, as a leader of forlorn hopes. As with Lermontov in *The Red Shoes*, there has to be a rabbit in the hat before I can produce the rabbit out of the hat. I have high ideals, I insist upon top quality, and I make the mistake of believing that everyone concerned in the work in progress shares my taste for quality. Alfred Junge had said it when we parted company over *The Red Shoes*: "Micky, you want to go too far." Yes I do.

Before leaving Sydney I signed Clare Dunne to play opposite Walter Chiari and Chips Rafferty to play her father. Although I was new to Australia I wouldn't have felt happy to play just anyone as Chips Rafferty's daughter. Clare was tall, with a stick of a figure, but with green eyes and red hair. She held her head high and pretended to be afraid of nobody. She didn't claim to be an actress, but she had speed and presence. I reckon that I would have been happy to have somebody half as good; above all, Clare didn't whinge.

There was an Italian family in the film, and Walter was bringing his girlfriend, Alida, to play one of the two sisters in it. She was like a lion's cub. She had tawny skin and gray almond-shaped eyes—the sort of woman that should decorate Flaubert's *Salammbô*. She was a bit too glamorous for the part, and it was hardly fair to Clare.

Judith Arthy came from Melbourne to audition for the leading part, but stayed to play Dixie, Clare's girlfriend, who is also making a little play for Walter. She was cuddly and accessible. As soon as she came onto the screen, Emeric and all his Hungarian friends sat up. She was a sort of Hungarian dream girl: she had brains, but used them sparingly. But the best actress of the lot was the big girl who played Joe's wife, Doreen Warburton, unselfish and unself-conscious, even when cutting her toenails for the camera.

The men came in all shapes and sizes, and were completely satisfactory as men and as types. Except for John Meillon, they made no nonsense about being actors. They had to give what they had to give, and they gave it generously. Ed Devereaux was a bit old for Joe, but he created a real human being. John Meillon was a genius, but far out. He had a striking personality, a big body, but was somehow graceful, and his mind was continually working to find the right reaction, the right mood. I would have loved to see him play Quince, or Bottom, or Falstaff. You might know him as the friend and business partner of Paul Hogan in *Crocodile Dundee*. Oh, and I nearly forgot Jeannie Diamond, the lovely young girl who played Jeannie. She had a very attractive squint, and was as wise and innocent as . . . as a young deer.

One of the great privileges and rewards of filmmaking is that you get, sooner or later, to meet and sometimes work with the men and women whom you admire. I look back over sixty years of filmmaking, and the faces come up, one by one: Martin Scorsese, a pale fanatic, eyes that burn, a close-clipped black beard; Francis Coppola, a riddle to himself, let alone to other people; Robert De Niro, an artist who is really larger than life; James Mason, a face and figure of romance; Karl-Heinz Böhm, a saint if ever there was one; Ray Massey, an enormous child; Peter Finch, a martyr; Charlie Chaplin, the greatest of all clowns; Walt Disney, the twentieth-century Hans Christian Andersen; Bernard Lee, a shaggy dog; Bobby Helpmann, a faun; Léonide Massine, a flame; David Niven, a prince; Anton Walbrook, an archangel; Hein Heckroth, a magician; Roger Livesey, a Christian soldier; Eric Portman, a devil; Conrad Veidt, a legend.

And then the women . . . the women . . . Nancy Price, Joan Maude, Deborah Kerr, Wendy Hiller, Kathleen Byron, Valerie Hobson, Pamela Brown, Sheila Sim, Googie Withers, Kim Hunter, Jennifer Jones, Moira Shearer, Ludmilla Tcherina . . . Ah, the women!

And then, always first, always last: Alice Terry and Rex Ingram.

=

My mother died, on October 20, 1965, in a nursing home in Weybridge, Surrey, where the River Wey joins the River Thames. Mother had always loved the River Wey, which winds through fields and forest, along the Pilgrim's Way, from Guildford to Godalming:

> There runs a road by Merrow Down . . .
> A grassy track to-day it is—

> An hour out of Guildford Town,
> Above the river Wey it is.

It was Kipling's *Just So Stories* that made us love the Wey so much.

Aunt Grace, who lived with the Tomlins family only a few minutes away from where my mother spent her last hours, telephoned me early in the morning. It must have been about 4:00 A.M. in Australia. My bedroom looked out over Rose Bay, and the sun rose out of the sea. Mother left me a letter, in which she apologized for living so long. She was ninety-seven.

"No one should live over eighty, Micky darling. You can no longer fend for yourself, and all your friends drop off, one by one."

And your son drops off too, I thought to myself, bitterly. My Mummy Mouse was dead, and I was on the other side of the world. But she would have been happy that I was doing what I loved to do, and that I had succeeded in launching *Weird Mob*, which had so many things in it that she would have liked to see. She had always loved eccentric people, simple people. She asked that her ashes be scattered on John's grave. It was the first time she had mentioned my brother's name for a long while.

> But far—oh, very far behind,
> So far she cannot call to him,
> Comes Tegumai alone to find
> The daughter that was all to him.

His five daughters adored Frederic Corbett, and when the war came, and he was evacuated from the city where he lived and worked, I was proud to give my grandfather a home. He was ninety-eight. I have a photograph of all five of his daughters: Annie, Grace, Mabel, Muriel, Ethel. They are seated on the stones of a stone circle on Dartmoor; "The grey wethers," my mother had written on it. How could I fail, coming from stock like this?

Before we started shooting, I returned once more to London to sign all the papers, and once again out to Australia to make the film. Altogether, I made five round-trips to Sydney, Australia, for the honor of *Weird Mob*. I took out a cameraman, Arthur Grant, who was Geoff Faithfull's assistant on my first film at the little studio in Walton-on-Thames. Arthur was a square, solemn young man in those days, and thirty-two years later he was a square, solemn young man. He wasn't looking for any Academy Awards. It was a comedy, and he gave me good, clear negative that would print well in Eastman Color.

The editor, G. Turney-Smith, was also from England. Claude Watson was my chief assistant on the floor. He was almost infernally competent. He had been in Malaya shooting a film and came on from there. He had a very critical eye and tone in his voice. I admit that he made me nervous; he was so much more efficient than I; but what a good second-in-command he was! He died of a fever, I heard, but I don't know where, or when. If he had lived, he would have been a good director.

Last to arrive, of course, was Walter Chiari, and his girlfriend, the delicious Alida. She was younger than I expected, and passionate. She was also beautiful and smart. An Australian woman, seeing her walk from the aircraft, said, "You can't tell me that these Italian girls don't have class." I've already described how she looked. Everybody envied Walter, and I wouldn't have minded a cut off the joint myself.

Walter had been post-synching and making additional shots and retakes in Rome up to the eve of his departure, so he was dog-tired before he got into the aircraft, and by the time he arrived in Sydney his eyes were like two burned holes in a blanket, as my old nurse would say. But there was no time to be lost, for, of course, his agent would charge for anything over the scheduled eight weeks, and after a hasty introduction to Clare Dunne, his redheaded leading lady, he went straight into the first scene in the office of *La Seconda Madre.* This was the name that Emeric had given to the sports magazine run by Walter's cousin in the film, being a left-handed compliment to the country of his adoption, Australia. The cousin having skipped, leaving unpaid bills, Nino Culotta finds the office being thrown into the street, and after a blazing row with Kay, played by Clare Dunne, he has to look for another job, and becomes a bricklayer and a member of the "weird mob."

We had bought a plot of land, as an exploitation gag, and announced that the land, and the house that we would build on it, would be raffled on the last day's shooting. This meant several revisits to the site during the shooting of the film. When Nino begins to earn money, he starts to pay back the debt that his cousin owed to Kay and her father. In the end, of course, Nino buys his own plot and builds his house and marries the girl, and becomes a partner in the father's big firm.

Chips Rafferty was as much a recognizable piece of the Sydney scene as Sydney Bridge, and almost as big. When he leapt to fame in *The Overlanders,* in 1946, he was a long, stringy, six foot four of a boy, and proved himself a natural actor. He never gave a bad performance in his life, and the whole world loved him. I remember coming to MGM Studios in Hollywood on a visit and being taken on a tour by Howard Strickling to where Clarence Brown was shooting some extra scenes for *Mutiny on the Bounty,* what else? All the best character actors in the world were lined up against the bulwarks, ready to give me a Bronx cheer and take the Mickey out of me. Chips towered over the rest, not just in size and weight, but in personality.

Of course, as soon as he heard about *Weird Mob* he had earmarked the part of Kay's father for himself, and he took care that I knew it. I wouldn't have dared not play him, but when I returned to Australia on another film I managed to dodge Chips, although I believe it was he who suggested that I make the Norman Lindsay book *Age of Consent* into a film. He was a wonderful actor, a splendid boy, and a great man.

Bill Paton came out to Australia with me, and we took a house on the cliffs above Rose Bay. Bill and I were old hands at this kind of caper. We had no intention of sleeping in a hotel bed and eating somebody else's cooking. On Saturdays we gave lobster parties, and on Sundays we slept. Somewhere around the middle of December, Pamela telegrammed from New Zealand. She had been doing a Hallmark show in New York. We had spoken most mornings.

P BROWN SPEAKING I AM ON MY WAY

she announced blandly in a cable. Nobody in Sydney had any idea who "P. Brown" was, which was the way we liked it.

We had planned a ten-day holiday at Christmas, but it was a near thing. We were still shooting on December 2, at Bondi Beach, the beach with its huge, friendly crowds and enormous surf rolling in. It was almost too much for an ordinary camera. I ran the dailies for the Greater Union Theatres representative, Keith Moremon, and his publicity man, Ray Steele. It was great stuff. In most cases, Take 1 was okay, and I just needed a few extra cover shots, which Claude Watson, the assistant director, was already shooting. Clare Dunne walking out into the surf was a joy to see, and Walter being carried in by the lifeguards upside down and protesting vigorously was a big success. I was showing all this on the screen at the Lyceum Theatre, where they expected to premier the film. It was owned by Methodists, but even they were laughing. The Lyceum had been burned out a year or two before, rebuilt and redecorated, and they were planning to reopen it with *Mob*. It had sixteen hundred seats and was bang opposite the Marble Bar. The new management had been thinking of putting *The Heroes of Telemark* into the theatre, but not anymore. They wanted *Mob*. It would run six months, they said.

I went home to Rose Bay. Bill was having a snooze. I woke him up, and said, "We're on a winner."

He said, "Fine. We're packed and ready to go."

We arrived at Cairns on Christmas Eve: Bill, Walter, Alida, Pamela, and I. We had planned our escape in dense secrecy. Only John Pellatt knew where we were going. Cairns is in North Queensland, about seventeen hundred miles up the coast from Sydney. In those days Cairns was a small, friendly place. It is still friendly, but no longer small. The Great Barrier Reef, which rises out of the sea at Lord Howe Island like the tower of a sea king's palace, ends at Cairns in a gaggle of small islands, most of them inhabited. A better antidote to Bondi Beach can hardly be imagined.

Ray Booker, owner and captain of *Seastar*, crewed by his wife, was anxious to show us the town. We would have none of it. We were all at the end of our tethers. We had no wish to meet anybody or see anybody. We just wanted to get afloat and get away from it all, and bless 'em, they understood.

Within two hours we were chugging over a calm sea, the wine, beer, and whiskey safely stowed, baskets of fresh vegetables, containers of meat and ice, plenty of fishing tackle and bait, Walter and Alida berthed for'ard, Pamela and I aft, Bill below. For eight weeks our lives had belonged to the population of Sydney. Now they were returned to us, and we sprawled on the deck and slept in the pale sunshine, until we nearly knocked Fairbanks Island out of the water.

A huge dugong, a manatee, greeted us at the quay. He expected to be fed, and waved his flippers at us affably. He must have weighed a thousand pounds. Walter and Alida had a bungalow reserved for them, but Bill and Pamela and I stayed aboard. For the next eight days we were either in the sea or under it. Walter became a mighty hunter under the reef and spent all day fishing, his slender bottom in the air. He brought in giant lobsters, crabs, and shellfish, until Alida decided that she was being neglected and made a scene.

I met a manatee* on the Barrier Reef, a white manatee that waved its flippers politely. We swam together, so that I could see its red hair and white skin and great, staring eyes. No wonder that the ancient fishermen took them for mermaids and jumped overboard into their waiting arms, to be kissed and fondled and drowned in the great underwater caverns.

Seastar was a sturdy and comfortable boat, and Captain Ray knew the reef like his backyard. We went out to Michaelmas Quay, where there were hundreds of seabirds, we cruised around between Fitzroy Island and Green Island and Dunk Island, where there were fruit-eating bats. We saw the New Year in and then flew back to Sydney, where nobody had missed us, and Cairns and the Barrier Reef were like faces in a dream. But, unknown to me, I had cast my bread upon the waters, and it would return to me after many days.

When I make a movie I expect the editor to keep up with the shooting, and to have a rough assembly of the picture within a week of the end of shooting. This one was no exception, and Turney-Smith showed me a first cut on January 10. It was long, of course—the first cut in comedies is always long—but within a week we had taken twelve hundred feet out of it, and we

*Michael is describing Pamela Brown here.

could see we had a picture. More important, we had a comedy, and a real star in Walter. My plan was to finish the editing in England and return with Walter on the opening night in April. In fact it took place in August. "The best laid schemes o' mice and men gang aft a-gley."

The first news that greeted me, on our return from Cairns, was that the Methodists, who were the principal shareholders of the Lyceum Theatre, had turned our picture down. They did it with regret, as men and as Australians, but as Methodists they couldn't sponsor a film that was so full of "bloody bastards" and "moody buggers." We saw their point, and showed our rough-cut to Keith Moremon, and the chief booker of Greater Union Theatres. The film was received in dead silence, although there were one or two smothered laughs.

When the lights went up, Keith said, "Well, boys?"

The chief salesman said, almost as if he were apologizing for it, "It'll go ten weeks at the State."

Now, the State was the flagship of Greater Union Theatres, and seated about twenty-two hundred. On a good Saturday, it could take five thousand dollars. Even Keith Moremon's jaw had dropped. But the other men agreed with their spokesmen.

"It'll go ten weeks," they said. "It might go to twelve."

In actual fact, it went to fourteen. That settled it. It was like a tonic to me after all I had been through. If our film could go ten weeks at the State, I didn't give a bugger what anybody else thought. I told Turney-Smith to pack up the film and get back to England and complete the fine cut as soon as he could. We had some sound recording to do, particularly the big song, "It's a Big Country," and I would arrange to direct Walter's post-synching in Milan, or wherever he might be found. The English technicians could return home, John Pellatt would clear up everything and follow us, and I would get the hell out to New York, to consult with Herb about *Mr. Sebastian*.

I gave a final press conference, and away!

In New York, Herb was being encouraging. He had been offered the job of head of film production at Paramount, in Hollywood, but was not sure whether he would take it or not. Meanwhile he had sold them his entire television output, which would make him financially independent, even with two daughters. I doubted that this would be good for him. What showman wants to be financially independent? Half the fun is coaxing money out of other people's pockets into your own. I told him that the new script of *Mr. Sebastian*, by Vaughan Hughes, would be ready in a month or two, or three, or four, and maybe we would meet again on the Miramichi, but I had to get *Mob* out first. Meanwhile he was planning to work in the field he knew so well and make big shows for television, of two, three, or four hours—they were called "specials"—with the financing and backing of the big television networks.

Once I had seen Herb, I didn't stay in New York, but took off for home, for I had received notice from Messrs. Martin Walter Ltd. that my long-wheelbase Rover had been converted and was now awaiting my approval. It was to become the dominant passion of my life for the next twenty-two years.

> Land-Rover, long wheelbase, hard top, one owner, only 1,850 miles on the clock, side and rear windows, rear door with fixture for spare wheel, also fixture on bonnet. Price £850. A bargain.

It was; add special high-powered headlights, adjustable spotlight, curb-level sidelights and interior lights. I had discussed the conversion of the interior with Messrs. Martin Walter Ltd. before I left for Australia to make the film, on the understanding that it would be ready within ten weeks. They accepted the challenge, and this magnificent new traveling home was waiting for its master on my return.

Important modifications were as follows: the hard top was gone, and in its place was a roof that could be raised and locked off, and which contained a bunk. There were two five-gallon cans in special mounts on the front bumpers, to carry spare petrol or water. All doors had pull-down steps; the galley was by the back entrance, and contained a stove and a basin. There was a cupboard amidships, big enough to hold half a dozen coats, blankets, pillows, etc., and there was an equally big square metal one on top of the van, jutting out truculently in front over the driver's seat, and which contained all the bedding. It also contained the tripod, the salmon rods, two shotguns and a rifle, and, of course, ammo; and designed and planned to be unostentatious.

There was a bookcase that could hold about a dozen books, including, of course, Boswell's *Life of Johnson*, *The Concise Oxford English Dictionary*, *The Oxford Book of English Poetry*, *The Oxford Dictionary of Quotations*, and *The Holy Bible*. The long interior seat could be slid over to make a double bunk. The driver and his passengers were in the front compartment, but there was, of course, a sliding glass panel to connect the two apartments, fore and aft, and if you were agile, you could scramble through the front compartment to the back and have a little snooze. This was Johnnie's favorite position, for he was able to keep an eye out over my shoulder as I drove, and at the same time bark hideous threats at some other dog in an overtaking car.

> "Johnnie, is me."

Is I.

> "That's what I said . . . It's me, Johnnie. My real name is Johnson. I am a little black spaniel, a cocker spaniel, from Wales. I used to have a Welsh

accent, look you, but I don't anymore. My brother from the same litter, Boswell, barks with a Highland Scottish accent, but then he's a sporting dog. He likes to go out with the guns. I don't. Mr. Powell, my master, says I'm the only dog he's ever heard of who is a gun-shy gun dog.

"When I am in London, I live at number 8 Melbury Road, Kensington, W.8, and there are good smells in the neighborhood. I have a kennel in the garden, but I prefer to sleep in Rover: there's nowhere like Rover. It is a dog's paradise. There is no garage, so we park our cars on the curb. When other dogs come down the pavement, I stick my head out suddenly, and say the most awful things to them, and they can't do a thing about it; there's nowhere like Rover.

"When my brother and I came down from Wales, at first we weren't very popular. We weren't housebroken, you see, and boys will be boys. We had a kennel in the garden, but we didn't like it, and we said so, night and day. When we were six months old it was decided that we should be trained as gun dogs. This was while Mr. Powell was away in Australia, where he says all the gun dogs are upside down. Does that mean that the smells are upside down, too?

"Bossie and I were being trained by Mr. Clark, in Derbyshire, at a place called Woodley, near Outerbridge. Mr. Clark had told us that Mr. Powell was coming, so we knew who it was when he came driving Rover down the bumpy road over the moor. Mr. Clark was standing in front of the old manor house, and we yelled our greetings from our kennels. Our old master was a bit startled by the look of us. He hadn't seen us for two months, and we were fully grown, and pretty rough. I think that I can say that I am a good, quiet little dog; but Bossie is bossy.

"It was getting late and would soon be dark, but Mr. Clark wanted us to show off our paces as gun dogs. Of course, Bossie showed off like anything, while I just looked miserable. Well, what's so special about being a gun dog, anyway? It was agreed that a sporting home would be found for my brother, and that Mr. Powell would come for me in a few months' time. I sneaked up to him and licked his hand. Afterward, Bossie called me an ass-licker. What's wrong with that? I am not like those stinking Dobermans, nor murderous Rottweilers. I am a spaniel, and we are in Shakespeare, so there! Mark Antony, my master says:

> The hearts
> That spaniel'd me at heels, to whom I gave
> Their wishes, do discandy, melt their sweets
> On blossoming Caesar.

"And Mark Antony was a king, or general, or something—so there!"

This is an extract from Johnnie's diary, who is entirely responsible for its content. We shall be quoting from it, from time to time.

$=$

I was in a hurry, so by the first week in April we had a final cut on *Weird Mob* and a rough mix on the dialogue, to show the British censor, John Trevelyan. He wouldn't let me sit in with his board of viewers, so I waited outside.

Trevelyan said, "Oh, there you are, Micky! Come into my office and shut the door."

I said, "Well, John?"

"Well, Micky, it's full of rather unusual language, but I have persuaded my advisers to look on it as they would a foreign-language film, since the expressions you have recorded throughout seem to be sui generis."

I said, "Oh, they are!"

He said, "We shall give a Universal certificate, and if we are attacked by parents, I shall defend myself."

I could have kissed him for his generous and broad-minded approach. He said, "We all thank you, for showing us a glimpse of Australia which is quite new to us."

I took him for lunch at the Étoile. Nowhere else would have been good enough. I had left John Pellatt and Turney-Smith, the film editor, biting their nails in the cutting room. When John heard the news he couldn't stop laughing. He had expected a tough fight with the censor board. I explained the success of my tactics.

"If you leave in a couple of 'bloody's, and a 'bugger' or two, they're going to ask you to cut them out. But, if every other line of dialogue has a 'bloody' or a 'bastard' in it, they'll accept it, like John Trevelyan says, as a foreign language. I'll bet you here and now, that the Australian censor will give us a Universal certificate too, and for the same reason."

De l'audace, encore de l'audace, and *toujours de l'audace.* Boldness is all.

Not to be outdone, the Australian censor passed the picture without a single cut. Everyone was jubilant, except John Davis and Rank Film Distributors in England. They thought that it was a vulgar film about common workingmen, and they asked for extensive cuts in nearly all the reels. I refused. I was prepared to make an issue of it, and John Terry of the National Film Finance Corporation, who were the other investors, supported me.

I showed our film to the British critics, who received it in dead silence. I was there. As the lights went up, the critics in front of me turned around in their seats, and said, in the tone of one asking for information, "Micky, why did you make this film?"

"Because I had never been to Australia before, and I liked the book."

"Ah . . ."

When Fred Thomas, head of distribution for the Rank Organisation, saw the film, he tried to stop it going to Australia. Too late. I had one print already airborne to Keith Moremon and another with me in Milan where Walter had done his post-synching. I took Emeric along for the ride, and Walter took us to see a lady who said she was Puccini's daughter. She was a vigorous old lady of seventy-five, she claimed, but she could have been any age.

By May 3, I was in Sydney with Kevin, who had elected to come with me, and intended to stay if Australia liked him. It was the first showing of *Mob* to the Australian backers. I sat next to Norman Rydge, with Bob Austin on my right. Keith Moremon sat in front of Rydge within easy reach. John McCallum sat next to him. An awful hush reigned. I started to sweat. The projection was perfect and the sound magnificent. The level was a bit low, but Keith had that corrected. The film never seemed so slow to me, nor so underplayed.

But the reaction of the small audience was very different from mine. I never saw film distributors so impressed. They rocked with laughter every ten seconds. The scenes between Walter and Slim DeGrey had them in the aisles. They said, "If *The Sundowners* ran for twenty-eight weeks in Sydney, this film will run a year."

Deborah, are you listening? The atmosphere was electric. The feeling of success, of big success, was in the air. Bob Austin was grinning like an alligator. John McCallum had forgotten that he was a top executive and was laughing like an ordinary man. At the end of their dialogue scene, when Slim said to Walter, "I don't give a bugger how you look, come on!" the theatre rocked. When Slim said, "Why didn't you bring me Prince Philip?" I knew we would never hear Joe's reply. The meringues got applause.

As the lights went up, Norman said, "Well, Michael, you've done it. Congratulations! It's a winner!"

The others echoed him, but with such sincerity you couldn't suspect them. Their notebooks were blank, like Keith's. They wanted no cuts, they had no criticisms.

Keith Moremon took Bob Austin and me to a French restaurant in a cellar and seated me on his right hand, Bob on his left. In spite of a deafening concertina player, we managed to bubble our excitement. Keith said, "When I met you with Norman Rydge, he said that you were a dedicated man, it'll be all right. Then I watched you work, and I knew that you were a perfectionist. When I met your star at the airport, I knew that he would panic the women of this country. I suddenly realized that you were going to make a great picture, and I admired the way that you handled the press. Nobody has ever had such a press here. And now, it's all come together, and it *is* a great picture. It will be the start of a new Australian film industry, in wide screen and color. You can have what you want from us. Every Australian will want to see this film. They will drive a hundred miles to see this film . . . five hundred miles! It's a picture for the whole family . . . it's a picture for the drive-ins! It will run a year in Sydney . . . it will run as long as we want!"

Kevin was thrilled. He liked what he saw. He made a very good impression on everyone he met. I said it was up to him whether he stayed; Keith Moremon would put him to work right away, preparing for the premiere in August. He was a beautiful, serious-minded boy, and he was now a handsome young man with an inquiring mind. He is also the only practical man in our family. He has made Australia his second home.

We spent the rest of the day with John O'Grady's family. They were riding high, and you couldn't blame them. We were late getting home. You can't expect to spend a day with the O'Gradys and have anything left over.

I saw Kevin comfortably settled and took off for London, promising to be back for the premiere in August. On the way I had lunch with Herb in New York. The Paramount situation was ripening. His plan was to get capital into the company by a massive sale of films for television. After that, make films all over the world, no barriers, but only make subjects worth making; turn the West Coast studio over to making television films; buy up British, Continental, and films worldwide, to keep the distributor from going broke. I believed he would do it, too, although he hadn't quite made up his mind to take the job. His mind was too much on fishing. He had the Miramichi again that year, and he dreamed of going north to the coast of Labrador, to Ungava, where the salmon were enormous.

"So are the mosquitoes!" I said, remembering our trip down the coast of Labrador on *49th Parallel* in 1940. He was not impressed. Herb thought that all feature film makers were sissies.

On to London, where I called a meeting with my British partners on *Weird Mob*. They were expecting a fight, so I was very jolly, making jokes, and making Fred Thomas laugh. Since they had received reports from Australia they were no longer so sure of their ground. They even began to realize—and even to say—that a British-Australian picture could get back its costs in Australia! In fact *Weird Mob* turned out to be the highest-grossing film that had ever played Australia at that time, with the exception of one or two of the big Disney animated features. They actually began to believe that their investment in the film was safe, and they agreed to let Sydney have the world premiere of the film, which was very nice for Australians, and for me. As hope dawned on their silly faces they got up saying, "See you in September," and left the room, laughing immoderately. I had no more time to spend on *Weird Mob*. I had other fish to fry.

=

Vaughan Hughes had delivered his shooting script of *Mr. Sebastian*, adapted from Leo Marks's original story and script. It was a good job. It had a beginning, a middle, and an end. It had an attitude. It moved in a world of authority, discipline, and brilliant guesswork. This Mr. Sebastian had become a brilliant part for an actor as resourceful as Rex Harrison. Laurie Evans, Rex's agent, read it, and agreed with me. I said, "Even the love story is more believable now. The girl makes all the running, in fact she practically rapes the professor."

This cheered Laurie up. "You know how sensitive Rex is about making love to young girls on the screen."

"Do I not!"

I rang Vaughan Hughes, congratulated him, and suggested that we meet Leo together. Without hesitation he agreed. Leo arrived at eight in the evening. He implied that he had had to rearrange the nation's affairs, and all his own appointments, in order to be there on the dot. Besides the inevitable cigar, recently lit, he carried a briefcase. Out of it poured a couple of publications, and one in particular, entitled *The SOE* in France.* He claimed to have access to these and other secret documents, because he was referred to by name as head of agents' codes in SOE during the war.

He sat brooding behind his smokescreen until Vaughan Hughes arrived at 8:30, when he attacked him savagely for his handling of the scenes between Sebastian and the two hundred girls in his coding department. In fact, the only good word he had for Vaughan Hughes's script was for his creation of Becky, the heroine, a troublemaker and troubleshooter in the department.

Vaughan Hughes was furious. No author likes to defend his inventions in the open market, but I didn't see why I should go to the bat for him, and I was getting valuable information from both authors for nothing, so I moved about, making coffee and adding fuel to the flames. This went on until midnight. Leo, that secretive man, had no secrets from me, and I could see that his main purpose was to find out whether I approved the new shape of the script or not.

Sure enough, next morning Leo phoned. Was this to be the new pattern of the script? Because if it were, then he had important advice and notes to impart to Mr. Vaughan Hughes. I said that it was, and gave Vaughan Hughes Leo's various numbers, which were all heavily shrouded in secrecy.

That evening we had a double-headed preview of *Weird Mob*, at the Slough Granada. That sounds like a missing chapter from John Bunyan's *Pilgrim's Progress.* I wonder how many people in the audience recognize John Bunyan

---

*Special Operations Executive. A clandestine British force operating in France during the German occupation.

in *A Matter of Life and Death*, when he enters heaven with Dr. Reeves, played by Roger Livesey. And I wonder how many people know

> A tinker out of Bedford,
> A vagrant oft in quod,
> A private under Fairfax,
> A minister of God.

Bunyan and Kipling have conducted me all my life, and they will conduct me into the other world, or that part of it reserved for me. I only hope that there will be no previews.

At Slough there was quite a good turnout. John Terry was there, representing the NFFC investment; there was a deputation from Australia House; there was a group from Pinewood; and various kibitzers and supporters. None of them expected to be entertained. The preview was typical of the parochial British film industry then and now. The regular program that night was a film by Morecambe and Wise, so the house was half full. To their surprise, they found themselves laughing again and again at *Weird Mob*. John Terry was surprised and relieved, and ready to accept the film, and indignant about the attitude of Fred Thomas and Rank toward it. I told him that at the sight of anything unfamiliar, the sales forces on both sides of the Atlantic call a meeting to panic stations and ask each other, "How are we going to sell this one?"

It is hard to believe that Rank was still nagging me to cut down what they called the "work scenes" and "the beer scenes," and the scenes of the drunk man on the ferryboat. All these scenes soured their delicate stomachs. It's very interesting to look back on those days and realize that we all, myself included, thought we were making a British film in Australia, not an Australian film in Australia, which was the real novelty of my approach. It is this that had fascinated me when I read John O'Grady's little book—the Australian self-love, the Australian self-mockery, the self-awareness that American films used to have and that brought millions of immigrants to her shores.

June 12, 1966, is a date that will be remembered by anyone who loves the theatre. It celebrated the reopening of the Royal Court Theatre, Sloane Square, London S.W.1, ten years before. Ann Jellicoe* said to meet her at the theatre, but at 7:30 the Royal Court was dark; the front doors on the square were locked, and even the stage door was locked. After some thought, and after investigating around the back among the dustbins, I crossed the river to

*Playwright and director who is best known for writing *The Knack* (1962). *The Sport of My Mad Mother* was an experimental drama about a London street gang, written in 1958.

the Old Vic and found the forecourt full of TV vans, and an entire audience waiting in the lobby for the show to start. Ann and I came face to face in the crowd.

"I'm going to have a baby," she announced. I congratulated her, but claimed no responsibility for the event.

"In December," she added, "so I won't be able to work on the play, unless you postpone it. I'm thirty-nine, and I won't have another chance."

"I expect it will all work out," I said. Ann Jellicoe was one of the stage managers of the Royal Court, and the author of *The Knack*. The play by her that I was interested in was *The Sport of My Mad Mother*. "What are you giving us tonight?" I asked.

"Oh, it's a shambles. Albert Finney is doing his bit from *Luther*, because he has to get back to the show in the West End, and he can't be in the performance tomorrow. But he'll be in the TV, and that makes five thousand pounds' difference. Now *that's* what being a star is."

I agreed. Dress rehearsals had started at 9:30 P.M. It was an anthology of the ten Royal Court years. All the actors who could appeared in their original parts. John Osborne himself appeared in the bedroom scene from *A Patriot for Me*, with Jill Bennett. J.O. was tall and fine-looking. He looked well in uniform, and spoke the difficult lines with fine shades of meaning.

Lindsay Anderson, rolling about like a good-humored ape, compèred the show, with the help of a wild-looking schoolmaster who turned out to be John Arden. One of the best things in the first half of the show was a solemn reading out by Lindsay Anderson of what was on in the London theatre the week that the Royal Court opened its doors. It was hilarious!

Larry appeared twice as Archie Rice, *The Entertainer*. Alec Guinness did the cat monologue in *Exit the King*. Nicol Williamson and James Dale did *Waiting for Godot*, and Nicol appeared again in *Inadmissible Evidence*, in which a young girl with honey-colored hair and gray wool stockings that left her knees bare lent an ear to his amazing tirade.

Finally the whole company did Arnold Wesker's *The Kitchen*. Everyone took a part. At the climax, when the restaurant is going full tilt, there were forty stars on the stage. Robert Stephens was better than ever as the cook. Rita Tushingham was in her old part as the waitress. The other waitresses were Vanessa Redgrave, Maggie Smith, Jill Bennett, and Sybil Thorndike. Larry made another brief, and wonderful, appearance as the headwaiter, with a frock coat down to his ankles and really wonderful boots. It was all very exhausting for the audience, but the actors had a wonderful time.

I had sent the new script of *Mr. Sebastian* to Herb. He reported that Paramount were interested in the Bony books, as a series of films. Before leaving Australia I had driven up to Bowral with Bob Austin and John McCallum and offered to meet the executors of Arthur Upfield's estate. The tall, kind, simple author was dead. He had followed his wife to the grave. It had been their wish that they should go together.

Arthur was a great man. I don't think the public in Australia realized how great he was. In Germany his books sold as well as Simenon, which means that they were steady sellers. Heaven knows how many millions of people have been influenced by the originality, the color, and the honesty of his books.

We signed the contracts and handed over the check in the room where he and his wife had entertained me, and where he had proudly shown me his biography which she had written, praising her writing and never talking about his own. Heaven bless you, Arthur Upfield. Your books and your characters will be dramatized again and again, and Detective Inspector Bony will be as famous in his own country as Sherlock is in London.

I remember one thing of that day that makes me smile wryly today. Bob Austin and John McCallum both signed the check, and were about to hand it over when I said, "If you don't mind, I would like to sign it too."

They hastily put it across and I added my signature. It was a symbolic act. Much good did it do me.

While I was still fighting my English partners, Brodkin telephoned me from New York. Oddly enough, it was not about *Mr. Sebastian*, it was about *Bony*. Paramount was interested in going ahead with a deal for the whole series. Herb had Alan Morris, his business manager, on the phone with him. I said that Larry Forrester was writing a treatment. Herb asked if I could come to the Miramichi, like last year. Could I not! Canada was, and will be, my first and last love.

John Pellatt, who had been my rod, my staff, my comforter throughout *Weird Mob*, now landed a very good job on a film about a cowboy in Africa, which would bring him in £4,000 net. We swore eternal friendship, and off he went. He had been a wonderful partner, tough and tireless, resourceful, inventive, and the more responsibility I heaped upon his shoulders the more he seemed to like it, and the best of it is that we are still friends.

Herb rang again, this time about *Mr. Sebastian*. He had read the script, and he more or less agreed with me and my views, but what won my heart for him as a partner was what he said: "Paramount will finance the film, you and I will approve the script. Let's get on and do it."

You can't ask more of a partner than that; and we would make the film in England.

Meanwhile, we were in July, and I bought my ticket for Fredericton, New Brunswick, where I would be picked up and driven down to the Miramichi.

Gerry Munn met me, polite about my endless baggage. Besides fishing and photographic tackle, I had four bottles of whiskey, two boxes of cigars, two Irish whiskey cakes, two hundred cigarettes, two rods, twenty pounds of books and scripts, and various presents such as Irish tablemats, horn mugs, and bottle openers shaped like Spey salmon.

Somewhere there had to be a cold beer. It was about 9:00 P.M. Gerry startled, and said there was a tavern in a backstreet of Fredericton. We drove cautiously to a plain door in a plain house, went in, and found a big match-boarded room and bar, with dozens of fellows drinking a good, cold beer. It was much quieter than a Sydney pub. The beer was a godsend. With its help I sat quiet for an hour, while Gerry drove soberly to the Miramichi.

"The Mounties are very hot on the speeders Saturday night," he explained.

We rolled over the familiar roads, up the lovely, winding Nashwaak, over the divide, down and round by Boiestown, over the wooden, Swiss-type covered bridge ("They're doing away with it, soon," said Gerry), along the narrow highway to the Miramichi bridge.

I could see the lights of the camp on the bluff on the other side of the river. We crossed the iron bridge, swung over the wooden one across the creek, turned down the dusty, stony road to the camp, past the two graying log huts of the old camp where the trail goes down to the river, and up the rise to where the new camp stood on a level space, two hundred feet above the bend of the river.

It was quite dark. Herb came out of the big lighted room, and we met in the shadow of the camp, where hundreds of moths and flies beat their brains out on the edge of the screen door. When he greeted a friend, Herb had a sort of light, airy geniality, partly shyness, which was quite charming from such a big man of overpowering strength and personality. It had the effect of making you reassess and like him all over again, and put you on your best behavior.

He read the script of *Bony*, by Larry Forrester, after we came up from a fruitless, or rather fishless, morning. By page thirty-seven he had decided it was old-fashioned, corny, and "lacked a point of view." Bony was looked at, rather than through; the audience failed to find points of identity; in fact, the author tried too hard, because Bony always said just a line too much, and his pomposity was overdone rather than endearing.

More or less my own feeling at the first reading, although the second half of the script was much better. Herb doubted whether Larry could do any better. Whoever did it should go there, and get the feeling on the spot. He had a young writer with a sardonic but lyric quality, who could probably have a shot at it. I said we had such writers. If Forrester was wrong, it was my mistake; obviously the writer had to be English. Possibly I could bring Larry to see our point, but it meant collaborating on every line as I did with Emeric. I doubted whether Forrester could change Herb's first impression.

In the morning there were no fish rising, perhaps no fish at all. Herb and

Million Dollar Movie. Marty had seen plenty of foreign-language films with subtitles in movie theatres, particularly Italian ones, but some of the English these actors spoke on *Million Dollar Movie* was nothing like the English that you heard in Little Italy. Still, it was English, and understandable, although the films were quite different from the big, splashy Hollywood films shown on the same program. Marty had known before that there were people making films in English, not necessarily in Hollywood or New York. These films must be from England, and a careful study of the small print on the main titles confirmed this. More and more films, old and new, were crowding onto the television screens. Marty became a film buff.

Ten years later the passionate little boy had become a passionate young man and had made his first film, *It's Not Just You, Murray,* and had won the National Student Film Award. He was already a legend in his class, and outside it. There had been and would be others like him at New York University. But already his baby films had something for the discerning critic; they had a life of their own.

And there were quotes; quotes that he explained to his astonished professors were from some British films on television, on a program called *Million Dollar Movie.* He remembered the themes, the images, the jokes, and the leisurely pace. The men who made these pictures were supremely confident. Who were they? The ones he particularly remembered, because their credits were unusual, were The Archers.

Their films were written, produced, and directed by Michael Powell and Emeric Pressburger, and their logo was a target, and an arrow thudding into it. Marty had no idea who Powell and Pressburger were, but the name stuck, just as the arrow stuck in the target. P & P must be some unimaginable age today: in their fifties—or even (in horror) in their sixties! Or, perhaps they were dead, a burned-out case. Meanwhile his own movies were getting nominations for Academy Awards, and one day he made a trip to London, where a miracle happened: Michael Powell was alive and well, and living in Kensington.

I was indeed living in London, and had just decided that my career in film was over.

From the time that I had made my first film, in 1931, I had been my own master. I had never had to compromise. Any mistake that I made was my own, and I could take credit for some of the triumphs, too. For sixteen or seventeen of those years, Emeric and I worked together in close harmony; but the casting vote was always mine.

Now that I look back on it, I think that I was a bit too sure in my belief that someone must lead. Even in our last film together, a children's film made from Emeric's story "The Wife of Father Christmas," someone had to make the decision to call it *The Boy Who Turned Yellow,* and that someone was me. The final decisions in any film, big or little, are just as important as the first ones, for a film is a gamble, a dare: you work blindly and lovingly for months and months, and sometimes for years and years. It took me six years to get *The Edge of the World* onto the screen. Emeric had to wait ten years to see Moira Shearer put on the Red Shoes and dance her dance of death. I could never get the money to make Shakespeare's *The Tempest,* and so the world never saw Mia Farrow as Ariel and James Mason as Prospero. We never heard that deep voice, like a golden bell, intone:

> "We are such stuff
> As dreams are made on;
> and our little life
> Is rounded with a sleep."

But it were better never to hear it, than to be untrue to a great poet.

Once you surrender control of your films to another, or to a committee, you are being false to the public, who know as well as you do what they have come to see. Emeric and I had left the Rank Organisation, which we had partly created, because John Davis wanted control of production by committee. We had left Spyros Skouras, at Twentieth Century–Fox, because they thought putting up the money gave them the right to the last word. We had gone back to Rank and John Davis because they gave us this, subject to completion guarantee. But that didn't last long.

Emeric and I parted company because he was willing to compromise over *Miracle in St. Anthony's Lane* and *Cassia,* and I wasn't. Since then I had made mistakes, but they had been my own. I bore no grudge to anyone. My biggest gamble had been to make *They're a Weird Mob,* to make an Australian film in Australia, where showbiz was traditional and rooted deep in the past, and where there was a limited film industry and where television was just getting under way, where theatre owners had to look to England and the U.S.A. for product. I had triumphed, and the investment of my partners was safe. I turned to *Mr. Sebastian* and was betrayed.

It had never occurred to me that collaboration with Herb would be any different from collaboration with any of my other partners—artistic collaboration, I mean. Even Alex Korda never questioned my technical supremacy: "Micky is the greatest technician in the movies. When he and Poppa Day* get together, they can do anything . . . anything!"

Even Harry Lachman, my first employer, and my first master, Rex Ingram,

*Percy Day was the French-born special effects wizard long associated with Alexander Korda. Michael had immense admiration for his great gifts as a matte painter and film illusionist.

never failed to turn to me for solutions to difficult problems. And Harry Lachman was to direct, years later, *Dante's Inferno*, which, next to the Ballet of the Red Shoes, was one of the greatest technical triumphs of the cinema. Even Hitchcock, when we were both young and new, trusted me as an equal.

The two greatest technical wizards that I or the cinema have ever known, Alfred Junge and Poppa Day, treated me as an equal when they came to discuss the trick scenes and effects for *A Matter of Life and Death*, and the creation of this world and the next. Who but I had created the whirlpool of Corryvreckan, and the Stairway to Heaven, and the Ballet of the Red Shoes? Who but I would have decided to make all the movements of ships at sea in *The Battle of the River Plate*? Who but I would get inside the lens of a camera and become a Peeping Tom?

I don't mean that I could paint, draw, sketch, and project like that great genius, Alfred Junge. Nor that I could create costumes and makeup and the inside of people's heads like that great painter, Hein Heckroth. Nor that I could create the whirlpool of Corryvreckan, or the Himalayan snows single-handed. Nor that I could create a golden, moving stairway between heaven and earth. Nor could I, myself, create a camera obscura for Dr. Reeves to watch the daily life of his village, where he could spy on them and their symptoms like a god in the heavens.

But I was the inspiration of these lovely fantasies, of these celestial jokes, and through me these wonderful craftsmen, with whom I surrounded myself, surpassed themselves and achieved miracles that delighted the world and warmed the heart of little Martin Scorsese, dreaming of future films and future power over magic, like Powell and Pressburger.

But all this was a closed book to my partner, Herb Brodkin. It was not his scene. It never would be his scene. Television was his scene, and he had a literal mind. He was a teacher, a prophet, a preacher. He was what the doctor ordered for a captive audience: "Take it, and don't make a face, because it's good for you. And what's good for you is good for me, and good for the networks. They are going to pay for it, and I know how to handle them. My films will not be films, they will be shows. They will be sermons. I have made millions out of television series: *The Doctors*, *The Nurses*, *The Defenders*, even *Espionage*. My new shows will be whatever length it takes to say what I have to say, and the networks will pay for it. Leave that to me.

"Do you see that stack of scripts, over there? That's *The Holocaust* . . . yes, the Holocaust. We'll go into the field, and we'll go into the death camps, and the world will never quite be the same, Michael. Isn't that better than witch-hunting? See this bundle of scripts? That's *The Missiles of October*, the Cuban missile crisis, the Bay of Pigs. Ernie Kinoy wrote that for me. He's still writing for me. He's working on a big subject now."

"What does Charlie Bluhdorn think of your production plans for Paramount, Herb?" I inquired. "He won't like your turning the West Coast studios over to television. He won't like your financing films in Europe and India and China and Japan. He won't like your saying, 'No film should be made unless there is a reason for making it.' Or will he?"

Herb frowned. Dear Herb.

"Get on with it, Michael," he said. "If you can't get Rex for *Mr. Sebastian*, get O'Toole, or that boy with the glasses. And get Julie Christie, and let's make it!"

Dear Herb. How right he was. Half the pictures are never made, because the partners don't have the guts to say to each other, "Let's do it." If you approach the art of the movies on your knees, you go out on your ass.

Pamela had left a note for me, after reading the script of *Mr. Sebastian*.

"Sam Eggar could do it, or Sarah Miles? Rex is too old. There is always Trevor, looking lazy and lovely."

I thought to myself, for Brodkin's prestige with Bluhdorn at Paramount I should go for the big fish first, especially in this case where the big fish were first-rate actors. Pamela added, "You have a fine script. All you have to do is get some spanking good actors, plus Hein Heckroth in his simplest mood, and make it!" She would get along fine with Herb.

In that busy year, actors and actresses were scattered all over the map. I located Christopher Plummer in the south of France, Peter O'Toole in Dublin, Patrick McGoohan at MGM, and I gave Rex an ultimatum. I was able to deliver it in person, because he was at Castle Coombe, in Wiltshire. I found him in the park, sitting on a grassy mound, surrounded by two hundred sheep. He was carrying a blue and yellow macaw that, for some reason, was called Polynesia.

It was raining gently and a bored and wet unit sat about. Rex looked fine in frock coat and a stovepipe hat. I don't think I ever felt so strongly before the essential insanity of our profession. A few years before I had been trying to persuade Rex to play in a magnificent script by Graham Greene, a part that might have been made for him, and that undoubtedly would have helped his career. Now here I was on location in the west of England trying to persuade this charming shit to play a cryptographer whose brain worked about two hundred times as fast as an ordinary man's; and he was trying to persuade me to postpone my film another six months, for his benefit.

And for what? So that he can play Doctor Dolittle. I felt as if I were sleepwalking. Solemnly we discussed possible leading ladies: Julie Christie was in *Far from the Madding Crowd*, Sarah Miles was on an extended holiday with Robert Bolt (some holiday), Vanessa was in a play and then the film of *Camelot*. Maggie Smith? Where, oh where, was Maggie Smith? It was becoming painfully clear that I was being treated as only one of Rex's options. We were in different leagues, and I said so.

Johnson was getting restive. "They stink," he said. "The sheep, I mean."

So we went down to Dartmoor and camped near the Steps. Some ponies came in the night and blew through the window.

Next day, I was back in London, phoning Herb. I broached David Warner, and suggested postponement until May. Herb was enthusiastic.

"What sort of contract should I give him?"

"Two pictures, with an option for a third one."

I was delighted. What did he think of *The Russian Interpreter?* He loved it.

"With David Warner?"

"Perfect."

Things were going too fast. Then, in an offhand tone, which didn't deceive me for a moment, Herb said, "I've quarreled with Bluhdorn."

Now Charles J. Bluhdorn was the chairman, or president, of Gulf and Western, and consequently chairman and president of Paramount Pictures, and not a character to tangle with lightly.

"I lost my temper," Herb confided. "But don't worry, Michael, it won't affect our picture. I'll see to that."

No, but it might affect future pictures, I thought, and who was this character called Evans whom Herb was talking about, who was going to be in charge of British production for Paramount—who was *he?* I resumed: "If I talk to Michael Caine, what shall I offer his agent?"

"Two thousand dollars, against forty rising to seventy thousand."

"And David Warner? What is he worth, by U.S. standards?"

"It changes week by week; seventy-five to one hundred fifty thousand."

"What contract?"

"Oh, the usual."

This was a bit glib. I had better watch my step. This was not the Herb that I thought I knew.

We planned to start shooting *Mr. Sebastian* in February and go to the spring. Rex just dropped out of sight, and nobody seemed to mind. This is the essential difference between making an English film and an American movie. In Pinewood, in Shepperton, in Elstree, we know that the money boys are going to say, "Who's in it?" And we will name with faltering voice some waning star, like Rex, whom we have been courting for eighteen months, upon whose promises our life, our dreams, our careers, seem to depend; and we have no alternative, if they say that his last picture is still in the red. In Hollywood, in New York, the field is open. It is not a matter of art, it is a matter of box office, and there are probably half a dozen names to choose from. Decisions are made for purely financial reasons, and you have to make the best of it. Your timid suggestions are ignored until a Moira Shearer, a Deborah Kerr, a Wendy Hiller, a David Farrar, appears from what our American partners call "nowhere."

All the same, when we gathered in London for preproduction conferences, I was not overjoyed to be told by Herb that Paramount was keen to have Dirk Bogarde play Mr. Sebastian and that he thought it was a splendid idea. Dirk Bogarde! I was in a quandary (for "quandary" see Robert Benchley, *My Ten Years in a Quandary, and How They Grew*). What was I to say? This was to be a British film, made in England, directed by an Englishman, written by an Englishman, fully influenced by Paramount as a Paramount-British production, and the distributor asks for Dirk Bogarde as the romantic lead! The sophisticated and sardonic lover, Mr. Sebastian! I liked Dirk, and he liked me, but we never wanted to work with each other again after the fiasco of *Ill Met by Moonlight*. But could I admit this to a party of enthusiastic Americans?

True, the part of Mr. Sebastian was much more in Dirk's line than the charming, swashbuckling thug Major Patrick Leigh-Fermor. I hesitated, and I was lost, the picture was lost, and I lost control of the picture.

Blow followed blow. David Greene was to join us in England, and it was clear that he was expected to direct the film. I had forgotten that, to men like Herb, a director was just a director—a servant, a butler. And Leo Marks had been talking, first on the phone and then at meetings, with David Greene and with Herb. The Vaughan Hughes script, which had taken me nearly three years to wrench out of Leo, and had cost me about £10,000, was no longer our Bible.

I came to meetings where it had already been decided we should borrow such and such a sequence from the Leo Marks script, and marry it with the Vaughan Hughes script. I came to other meetings, and found myself involved in casting sessions with a casting director who looked to Herb and Buzz and David Greene for information and decision. I couldn't blame David Greene. For him it was a chance in a million to be the director, at last, of a feature of this quality and size. I could, and did, blame Leo for sneaking his way in, and for his determination to bring back into the script certain characters and action that he had been nursing in his wounded breast for months.

When casting sessions started I was no longer the sole arbiter. There were no disputes but, somehow, I found myself overruled. Maggie Johnston, my old friend who had married Al Parker and was now running his talent agency, brought some candidates to see us and found herself cast as one of the superintendents of the decoding department. Other actors that I had fancied for minor roles vanished. There were no arguments. There were no fights. Everybody was delightful to the old man, Michael Powell, this suddenly aged Brit director.

John Pellatt joined us and very soon saw what was going on. John was a sensitive and imaginative man, not tough and brutal as I so often have to be, and he never managed to get his own way or pull his weight on the film. In their terms the invaders spoke to me often about John Pellatt, how useful, how imaginative, how informative he had been when they came to make the *Espionage* series, and how much he had changed, now; he didn't seem to have his heart in it, they said.

He went ill, and after several weeks, in and out, he had to leave the picture. Herb and Buzz couldn't understand what had happened to him. It wasn't as if he was an artist. He was an executive, and executives had no right to be ill! Buzz said to me, "What happened to John? He's not the same man that he used to be." He wasn't.

This mixture of good intentions and of cross-purposes went on until the end of February, when we started to shoot the film. By then it had become just an ordinary film. Nobody but me could say exactly how, or why, this conjuring trick had been achieved; but instead of starting the film with one object in view, we were all pulling in different ways and different directions.

Dirk is a good actor, but he didn't like the part; he wasn't right for the part, and he didn't hesitate to say so and think so. The one bright thing was the presence of Susannah York. This enchanting girl had rolled the whole world on its back in Victor Saville's production of the delightful film *The Greengage Summer*, and she had gone her own way ever since. Maggie Parker was her agent, as she proved to be the agent for all the promising girls in the next ten years. Susannah was beautiful, strong, tough, and delightful; she took things in her stride. Physically she was adorable, moving as light as a feather and warm as the morning sunshine. She had one of those faces and spirits that belong to all time. She could be any color she pleased. Her expression seemed to change and shift like the water in a mountain stream. She was a stunner.

Mr. Sebastian proved to me, once and for all, that I was not a producer. I was a director. As a director, after the statutory first three days of sailing into the wind, it was all sails set with no hesitation until I crossed the finishing line. I was supremely confident. I knew too well how much a foot of finished film cost to produce, and it was a joy to me to finish the day and know that I was ahead. I didn't have to explain my reasons, because they were all resolved into action.

As a producer I made, or participated in making, the major decisions; but after that I was bored. I could leave all that behind me while I was making the picture, and turn up in the cutting room when the job was done to find out what kind of film I had directed. What mattered was that our fate was in our own hands.

Thelma is a film editor, but she only works with one director, Martin Scorsese. While they work, they talk, and the whole mysterious craft of writing, producing, directing, and distributing movies passes under review. Their room is large, but it is filled with editing machines, television screens, and tape decks. Marty must not be allowed to be bored for a second. That screen there is running an old silent film, and this screen is occupied by one of his current favorite hates.

Thelma has two picture heads on her flatbed editing machine, and together they cut and slash through performances to the bare flesh, to the exposed nerve.

"How's the book going?" asks Marty, and in this way he learns the facts behind the inexplicable inclusion of *Mr. Sebastian* in the work attributed to Michael Powell and Leo Marks.

"What!" he screams. "It was Herb Brodkin who deprived us of another Michael Powell film!? Never mention that man's name to me again. He must be mad . . . insane!"

Anyone who disagrees with Martin Scorsese about movies is automatically insane.

"Whatever happened? Didn't he know who Michael was?"

"No."

"What do you mean, no??"

"Just no . . . He knew that Michael had directed for him *Never Turn Your Back on a Friend*, he knew that Michael had made a film in Australia, wherever that might be, he liked Michael Powell personally, and was still hoping to teach him to fish. Buzz and David Greene would make the film, and Herb and Michael would go fishing."

"You're joking!"

"It's no joke."

"You mean to say he'd never seen *The Life and Death of Colonel Blimp*, or *A Matter of Life and Death*, or *I Know Where I'm Going!*, or *Small Back Room*, or *The Red Shoes*, or *Peeping Tom*??"

"He's a television man, Marty. He's not like you and Michael. He sees things on a small screen."

"I don't want to hear any more about it! . . . Wait! Stop! Stop—didn't he ever explain to Michael that he was taking over the picture?"

"No."

"And didn't Michael ask for a showdown?"

"No."

"You mean . . . it just happened?!?"

"Sort of . . . yes. Michael says it was like that scene in *Lawrence of Arabia*. He just disappeared in the sand . . . no motion . . . it was like moving, or swimming, in molasses. He wasn't exactly ignored . . . he was just unnecessary. You see, these were television people, captive-audience people. They weren't making a film, they were going from one show to the next. David Greene knew better, but he had learned to keep his mouth shut. He wanted to direct a big film. So it was nothing to do with the kind of films that you and Michael make. Michael says they were all so happy. It was like a bad dream."

"I don't want to hear any more about it . . . What do you think happened, really happened, I mean?"

"Michael thinks there's a clue in what Herb says about having a row with Bluhdorn. Everyone had rows with Bluhdorn. He was president, that's why he was there. But this must have been a big row. You remember that Herb said to Michael, 'I lost my temper.' That, from Herb, is a pretty strong statement. It would seem that Bluhdorn had changed his mind about Herb becoming head of production after listening to his ideas, but Herb had already told everyone he had the job. They must have had a blazing row. It must have been quite an occasion, and it left Herb more or less decided to be his own boss, to woo the networks, and get them to finance his shows. And then fools like Michael and you go on talking about art, and practicing it. No other explanation fits, and Brodkin didn't have to explain himself to anybody, except Pattie. Meanwhile he was committed by Michael into making *Mr. Sebastian* in England, and he had to see it out the only way he knew; and Michael was the victim of Herb's great plans and ambitions, which he couldn't talk about to anybody."

"Except Pattie."

"Except Pattie. For Herb, there was no longer any reason to make *Mr. Sebastian,* but now everybody was committed, the money was there, the film had to be made. No other explanation explains the appearance of *Mr. Sebastian,* the film."*

Which reminds me, they even took away from *Mr. Sebastian* his appellation, or prefix, the "Mr." *Mr. Sebastian,* at least, had some style about it, some mystery. Plain *Sebastian* only had Dirk Bogarde.

The film was made at Twickenham Studios, one of the early British studios, dating back to silent films and even earlier. It was famous for its "quota-quickies." There were two shifts: day and night. I had made *Lazybones* there, with Ian Hunter and Claire Luce. It was built bang on the railway line, and you had to get used to the sound of trains arriving and departing on the soundtrack. By the time we made *Sebastian* this little matter had been attended to, partially.

It was a very popular, chummy studio. Production and administration worked cheek by jowl, because they had to. The Thamesside town of Twickenham had a good shopping street, and the beer is good at both of the pubs. But it's a busy street, and the studio yard was small, and there was nowhere

---

*It was uniquely Michael that he remained a close friend of Brodkin's until the end of their lives.

to park my beautiful brand-new camping Rover. I had also just bought a secondhand Rolls-Royce Silver Ghost limousine, in mint condition, for £800, and had nowhere to put it. But I had recently bought a cottage in the Cotswolds, and I decided to park it there. Herb would drive it, now that he was a British producer, and I would drive Rover, with Johnnie. Herb and I would then proceed in the Rover over the Welsh Marches to Hay-on-Wye. The notable River Wye, which rises high in the Welsh mountains and joins the River Severn at Chepstow, is one of the best sporting salmon rivers in the British Isles, and the stretch belonging to the hotel at Hay-on-Wye was considered the best of the best. The town of Hay is also famous for its bookshops, which are reputed to have a million books always on sale . . . but I'm not writing a guidebook, and Hay is too well known already.

The M4 to the West of England and Wales was not completed in 1967, so we took the old road up the Vale of the White Horse, following the invisible Thames all the way to the watershed, where the Thames is linked to the Severn by fabulous Sapperton Tunnel, nearly two miles long, and by a series of locks that can compete with the Panama Canal. It was hacked out of the limestone by human hands, and was opened in 1787 by George III. The boatmen on the canal used to lie on their backs and push their boats along the tunnel with their feet against the vaulted roof.

Once we were over the watershed we were in the Golden Valley, which runs down to the River Severn. The little valley of Avening creeps out of the hills beside it. Our cottage was under the hill, looking south and west. It was sheltered from the northwest by huge chestnut trees, but it was open to the west wind that comes roaring up the valley from the Atlantic. Avening had a post office, two shops, two pubs, a bakery, and a leading citizen, Arthur Udall of Pike House Garage. But we must press on to Hay-on-Wye: Herb, Pamela, self, and Johnnie.

Johnnie had a good nose; you might say that, being a cocker spaniel, he was all nose, like the Duke of Wellington, or Julius Caesar, or William the Conk. On arrival at Hay-on-Wye he quartered the town at high speed and decided there was nothing to it. He then went to sleep in the Rover. Second-hand books were not his scene. As to salmon, Mr. Powell would catch one, and then we would see.

But Mr. Powell didn't catch one. Nor did Herb. The Wye at Hay is swift and deep; no wading knee-deep in sparkling water! You fish from a low bank into a turgid stream lined with huge willows to catch your fly. The banks are sculpted by the swift stream, and the pools are deep and dark. Herb could make nothing of all this. Nor could I, but then I never expected to. I came for the books and the romantic river and the mountain air, and Johnson came because of Rover. He loved Rover.

And Pamela? Pamela said, "While you two boys enjoy yourselves, I think I'll have a nap." Pamela believed in first things first.

Another time was in northeast Scotland on the River Dee. It was early in the year, and cold; too cold and too early. It was a favorite beat, and we stayed in luxury in the great house that owned it. The house was large, square, ugly, and comfortable, with wide, carpeted stairs and huge tasseled curtains to pull across the great high windows to keep out the cold. My, but it was cold!

The fish were cold, and lay on the bottom of the river and wouldn't come up. You could see them lying there, squinting up at you through the water, but rise they wouldn't. I have never admired Herb more. Every day of the week he was out there in that icy water, casting every fly in the book, and to no purpose. I have a snapshot of him that I took at the time. He is like a man of stone; but he never got a bite, not even with a White Wulff. Pattie would drive down from the house to the river sometimes, but she had been through this before. There was a stalker's hut on the riverbank, a comfortable little place with a big fire and paneled walls, like the ones in our cottage. It was Pamela who decided to have paneled walls, bless her!

Occasionally I would go out and make a great show of casting, too, but I jolly soon came back again. We really felt sorry for Herb, but "the fish did not know him."

And Johnson? Johnson was in love! And, like his master, he kept a diary, which got him into trouble. I quote:

"She was the most excellent, exquisite thing that I have ever smelled. She had something in her of the bitches of all time. She was all curves, small, intimate curves. She was black all over, not a speck of white anywhere. She was never still for a moment. Her eyes were large and lustrous, and peeked coyly at me, as she tossed her beautiful, silken ears. Her legs were slender, and adorned coquettishly with curls. Bow-woooow! I've said nothing, yet, about her nose. Oh, that adorable nose, slightly moist, as she sniffed enquiringly in my direction through her delicate nostrils! Where she was narrow, she was narrow as an arrow, and she was broad, where a broad should be broad. Bow-wow!

"Mr. Powell, Mr. and Mrs. Brodkin and me were all staying at the big house. So was P. Brown, and so was I. We had a gorgeous big kennel, with Brussels carpets on the floor and Staffordshire china washbasins, and, I must say, the pickings around the kitchen were pretty good. But on the second day *she* arrived in company with her two humans, and from the moment that I smelled her across the room, I was a goner.

"What a flirt she was! It was: 'I want you . . . I dare you . . . I hate you . . .' Then, it was streaking up the broad steps of the hall, and round and round the landing, scattering the mats, down again at full speed, suddenly stopping to piddle on the tapestry curtains . . . Off again! Round and round the great hall, playing peekaboo around the tall doorways, running to the huge fireplace, where the great logs were burning, and flinging ourselves down in exquisite abandon, daring me to approach her with eyes that spoke of nothing but love . . . It was hell, it was heaven . . . It was love!

"During the daytime, we saw little of one another, but in the night . . . ah, the night! . . . Oh, those nights! In the daytime I was with Mr. Powell and P. Brown in the stalker's hut, brewing continual cups of tea and munching bikkies, while Mr. Brodkin drowned flies. But by five o'clock in the evening, we were back in the big house, and she! . . . she was waiting for me, though she pretended she wasn't. She would be lying, provocatively stretched out on a tiger's skin, at the fireplace, pretending to ignore me—bow-wow! I soon showed her who was master. Off we would run, paw in paw, up the stairs, along long corridors, pausing to water the curtains, as she would allow me a glimpse of her exquisite *derrière* (that's French for it), before rushing downstairs and playing 'come and catch me' from under her mistress's skirts.

"And then the nights! Oh, will I ever forget those nights, when we would steal tiptoe along the corridors to our rendezvous in the marbled hall. Sated with love, but only temporarily, we wandered through the sleeping house, and, if we had the luck to find the kitchen door left ajar, we would steal into the kitchen and were sure to find some dainty bone or other for my mistress to have first crack. And then, slowly and lingeringly, back to our baskets, before the house was stirring.

"Great news! I have learned that her humans are not Scottish humans. They are London humans. In fact, they live in a flat, not far from Knightsbridge. We must make sure that our humans continue to keep in contact. London is not too large for lovers to find each other. Standing in Holland Park, where I live, I could smell her in Hyde Park, if the wind were in the right quarter.

"We parted in tears, but I promised her that Mr. Powell would see to it that we met again. Ah, that lovely little creature . . . those black, erotic curves . . . those delicate curls, that feathered behind . . ."

And here I have a confession to make. Two lovers so happily and so suitably suited should be mated, should bring forth proof of their passionate love. In imagination and ambition I could already see five shining little black heads, with long, pendulous ears, sitting in a row in their basket, whining to be taken out by their proud parents, and licked all over. I agreed with Johnnie that this was a consummation most devoutly to be wished. I had the address of the owner of the little spaniel bitch, and I wrote to her a passionate love letter, in Johnson's name and in Johnson's style, urging her to meet me in London and achieve this consummation. It was couched urgently, and in earthy language, and it is possible that I offended her, for she never answered. Or perhaps the letter fell into the hands of her lover (charming women are so careless at leaving letters about), and he may even have been her husband. In any case, it was plain that the letter was misunderstood. He must have been her husband.

Anyway, neither he, nor she, ever answered the passionate canine's letter, and that row of little black heads and large, pleading eyes and huge crumpled ears was only a dream to Johnson, as he whimpered by the dying fire.

≡

The scene now shifts to Australia.

Both John Pellatt and I wanted to make another Australian film. He had intended to make Arthur Upfield's *The Bone Is Pointed*, and then follow it up with other Bony films. But in January Bob Austin and Lee Robinson, two of our partners in *Mob*, came to London to see the National Film Finance Corporation and the Rank Organisation and ask them why, when an Australian film like *Mob* was obviously going to make $2,000,000 and more in the Australian market, its producers and director should only get $600,000 of it and would have to wait a couple of years for that? It was particularly obnoxious to them, because the Rank Organisation were part owners of the Australian Greater Union Theatres and were getting their cut from that, as well as the 30 percent from us. Of course, we had made a bad contract; but when it was proved that *They're a Weird Mob* was going to gross two million or more in the Australian market, John Davis should have rewritten the contract, so that we would get our money back earlier to finance other films. When I told him so, he was highly indignant. "A deal is a deal, Micky," he said.

So to make another film it was obvious we had to find other finance. I had read a book written by one of the artistic and prolific Lindsay family entitled *Picnic at Hanging Rock*, and in spite of similarities to other unsolved-mystery novels, I thought it would make a marvelous film and made a note to seek out the authoress and find out what her own solution of the mystery might be, for the plot was based upon an actual event, involving the disappearance of three schoolchildren on a picnic. They had been chaperoned by nuns to a famous spot near Melbourne—a mystery still unsolved.

But I left it too long, and Peter Weir, an Australian director, made it instead of me. I have always regretted it. Such an adult and beautiful story, following up *Weird Mob*, would have been good for me, and good for Australian film production. So I never made *Picnic at Hanging Rock*, and I have no idea how

I would have ended it, for I don't like unsolved mysteries, any more than Sir Arthur Conan Doyle did. Sir Arthur was inspired to write *The Adventures of Sherlock Holmes* by reading Poe's *Tales of Mystery and Imagination*, and Poe in his time was inspired by Sir Thomas Browne, who wrote:

> What song the Sirens sang, or what name Achilles assumed when he hid among women, though puzzling questions, are not beyond all conjecture.

I then became interested in Norman Lindsay's *The Magic Pudding* as the basis of a musical film on the lines of *The Wizard of Oz*, starring Liza Minnelli as the heroic koala bear. All of Australia's fantastic and lovable animals would be pressed into service, to become parts for comedians and acrobats. Kangaroos would cross the Pacific, jumping from island to island. The kids would go mad about it.

But I was met with sturdy faces in Australia. They'd all been brought up on slices of *The Magic Pudding*, the same argument that the distributors put up to MGM when the studio proposed to make a new film of *The Wizard of Oz*, the best film for children ever made, except, of course, *The Thief of Bagdad*. A couple of years later I broached the idea to Liza Minnelli, who was doing one of those lightning club tours around Australia.

"Screw that," she said. It was her most frequent line of dialogue; some people say her only line of dialogue. "Who would want to see me and a lousy bunch of Australian animals?"

I said that I would, but that cut no ice with Garland's daughter.

Then fate, or Michael Pate, or Chips Rafferty, or Jack Lee took a hand.

"What about *Age of Consent?*"

What, indeed? I had never done one of those Girl Friday stories, but that was no reason why I shouldn't make one, now that I was in my dotage. Norman Lindsay had obviously written the book for money, but that was no reason why it shouldn't make a film. It would depend upon who played the painter. It would have to be a name, a big name, and the girl would have to be quite a girl . . . luscious, intelligent . . . a hot number . . . eighteen, played down to sixteen, an impatient virgin on the brink of being a woman.

Hey, wait a minute! Where have I seen such a woman recently? Tall, strongly built, gray eyes, blond, and a remarkable actress for a girl of eighteen. She had humor, a glint in her eye, a jaw that showed character, a girl who could take her place worthily in that long line of actresses from Peg Woffington to Helen Mirren.

Helen it was. She had come with dozens of other girls to audition for *Mr. Sebastian*, and David Greene, who directed the tests, thought she should have played the lead part. He asked her to read a difficult scene two different ways, an old trick but a good one, and she passed it with ease and humor. She moved smoothly and easily from one character to the other. She was no prodigy. She admitted later on that she had been scared to death, but that didn't stop her doing a good job on both girls. And now it got her the lead in *Age of Consent*, opposite James Mason.

It was Margaret Johnston, Mrs. Al Parker, who brought James and me together again. It was a far cry from our first meeting in 1934. That was in Shepherd's Bush Studios, in Lime Grove. I was directing *The Phantom Light*, and Roy Kellino was my cameraman, a wild, dark, handsome boy. He introduced me to another wild, dark, handsome boy, James Mason. Later they would both be in love with a wild, dark, striking-looking girl who would have been very good-looking if it hadn't been for her nose. She was the daughter of Isidore Ostrer, the head of the Ostrer family that controlled Gaumont-British Studios. Pamela Ostrer married Roy Kellino. In 1938 James and Roy formed a partnership to make a film starring Pamela Kellino and James, to be photographed and directed by Roy. During the filming Pamela and James had an affair and her marriage with Roy broke up. James and she subsequently married.

She kept her professional name, Pamela Kellino, until James Mason became famous, when she became Pamela Mason. They had two children, and went to Hollywood. James became a great star, Pamela became a name in radio and television. They divorced and James returned to England, where he made a second career, and an even greater name, as an actor. This was when we met again, under the auspices of Maggie Parker.

James was proud, sensitive, and suspicious, but in spite of that, he was lovable. He was a big fellow; you remember that he was an oarsman at Cambridge and was physically attractive, almost with a woman's power. He was also beautiful. I think that I may have said that I saw him first on the stage at the Little Arts Theatre, in a play whose title and plot I have clean forgotten, and I felt that I had never seen such a beautiful man in all my life. The only actor to match him for masculine beauty was Gérard Philipe, the French actor, and, perhaps, Robert Donat. I caught sight again of this wonderful creature in a production at the Haymarket where he had quite a small part, I think it was *Love for Love*; he was a valet, I believe. On a crowded stage you just looked at nobody else.

Now, thirty years later, he had kept his looks, but it was his voice that people loved and remembered. I may be wrong, but it seemed to me that when he spoke verse he was not more intelligent than other verse speakers, but in movies that voice was supreme. It was cultivated, tender, masculine, and irresistible to women. In England he reminded us of his roots by a subtle but uproarious performance as a Yorkshire businessman who finally eloped with a teenager after a rugged courtship. The title, and theme song, was *Georgy Girl*, and its leading lady was the younger of the two Redgrave sisters, Lynn. It was brilliantly and tenderly directed by Silvio Narizzano. It woke everybody up with a bang. "Hey there! Georgy Girl," sung by an Australian group, was an instant hit, and took years off James's published age. James was a Yorkshireman, of course—Bradford—which helped. Come to think of it, Arthur Rank was a Yorkshireman too.

James read *Age of Consent* and liked the part of the painter, Brad, and liked the idea of a picture in Australia. All of a sudden, the picture was on, and things started to move in the magical way that they do in show business when the wind changes direction. Several people had spoken to me about *Age of Consent*, but it was Michael Pate who brought with him the film rights to the book. He was an Australian actor who had worked in Western films in Hollywood. He had a striking face and made out quite well as an Indian. He had always loved the Lindsay book, and we put Peter Yeldham onto writing the script. At the sound and scent of another Australian production, John Pellatt had returned to me, pronto. One day Michael Pate said to me, "You know, Michael, I am the son-in-law of Joe Rock."

I stared at him. Joe Rock? Joe Rock?! The man who had put me on the rails, at last, to my cherished project, *The Edge of the World*—the little, bouncing, kindhearted, imaginative man who really loved movies, and who had made a film out of the volcanic explosion of Krakatoa; the patient, humorous ex–Hollywood comedian, who had been the only man who looked at me when I told my story?! He had come from Hollywood to England before World War I, and had bought the little Ideal Studios at Elstree, and was on the way to fame and fortune when World War II sent all Americans home.

I had no idea whether he was alive or dead after the war, and now here he was, very much alive, according to his son-in-law. Joe Rock! Foula! *The Edge of the World*—the little eighty-minute film that I made in the Shetland Islands, ignored by most of the British critics but given a new life in America—and here was my Maecenas, my Rock, whose son-in-law had brought me Norman Lindsay's *The Age of Consent*. I told Michael that he would have to work on the picture right through.

Helen Mirren had just signed a three-year contract with the Stratford-on-Avon Shakespeare company. It was the start of a splendid classical stage career. But at the time all we could think of was how to get her out of it. Her prospective legitimate employers were naturally not pleased, but finally it occurred to somebody that if a girl they already had under contract was going to play opposite James Mason in a film, there might be something in it for Stratford.

James had already agreed and, moreover, had proposed himself as coproducer of the venture. I was already at work rewriting the script. There were a lot of good cameo parts in the film, but the most important was a little pest who latched on to "his old pal, Brad," now that Brad was a famous painter, and who followed him to his hideout on Dunk Island, on the Great Barrier Reef, where Brad was proposing to cleanse his palette and refresh his painter's eye.

From the beginning James wanted to play Jack MacGowran in this part, first of all because he longed to be in a film with Jack MacGowran—and who wouldn't?—and secondly because he thought he was ideal for the part, whether he was Australian or not. I rather favored somebody else, but James was right, as usual; and James was prepared to fight for his right of choice, with the result that Jack stole every scene they were in together. Nobody who ever saw the film will forget Jackie MacGowran staggering home to the cabin at sunset, wailing to his host, "Brad! Brad! I've been raped!"

But the real star of the film was Godfrey.

There is a dog Friday in Norman Lindsay's book, and he is Brad's only companion on the island until Jackie MacGowran turns up. There is also an art dealer, Brad's art dealer, played by Frank Thring. The art dealer's name was Godfrey, and the dog in the film had to have a name, so we called him Godfrey too. We sent out a call for a dog and his trainer, and in due course they turned up. They were both rough-haired. The trainer's name was Scotty, and his dog had an intelligence that was uncanny; you could see him think. He had a whole repertoire of tricks, and could learn a new one at the drop of a hat.

His owner was a character. He was about the size and shape of a bear, or sea lion. He was polite, disciplined, sardonic, monosyllabic, and spent a good deal of time alone with his dog, who would listen to him with attention. The trainer was ex-army, or ex-navy. When he brought Godfrey to show his paces it was fascinating to see the close relationship between man and dog. They exchanged thoughts and words and ideas, and they both had the same sense of humor. The dog's kennel name was Lonsdale.

"Will he do all that, with Mr. Mason?" I asked.

"He will, sir."

"Will he learn new tricks, if I want him to?"

"He will, sir."

"Will he follow Mr. Mason, and obey him, just the same as he does with you?"

"He will, sir."

There was a scene where Brad goes ashore in a motorboat and leaves Godfrey tethered to a stake in the ground by a long rope. I explained, "The dog can still run around, but he gets bored, and slips his collar while Mr. Mason is ashore; that leaves the collar attached to the rope. When Mr. Mason comes back, the dog has to run back to the collar, slip the collar on, and sit

506 · MICHAEL POWELL

down as if he has been tied up all morning. Do you think he can do that? Can your dog put his own collar on?"

A long pause. Then: "I'll have a word with him, sir."

A few weeks later, on the island, in the full heat of production, I suddenly found Scotty standing close to me. He saluted. "The dog would like to show you something, sir."

"All right, Scotty—at lunchtime."

When we broke for lunch Scotty was waiting, and we hurried over to the other side of the sandspit, passing my son Kevin's unit manager's office en route. Godfrey was sitting, waiting for me, tethered by a long cord to a stake in the sand. He acknowledged my presence, but his attention was all for his master. His collar was loose on his neck, and Scotty slipped it off, and hurled it away on the sand, still attached to the rope. Godfrey's eyes followed the collar, then returned to his master, who whistled to him, and they both walked about twenty yards away, Scotty said, "Now, Godfrey!"

Godfrey ran back to the collar, wriggled his nose under it, slipped his head through it, and sat down in triumph, with his collar on. I applauded, and he jumped.

"Don't applaud him, sir. It puts him out. Just give him a pat, and say, 'Well done, Godfrey.' "

I obeyed, and was rewarded by a glance from those bright eyes. Then, they turned again to his master.

I said to Kevin, "We're made! The dog can put his own collar on. People will say, 'Have you seen the film where the dog puts his own collar on?' Fame at last!"

But, would you believe it, nobody said a word about it? They all liked Godfrey; a few people even said, "I liked the dog." But nobody ever said: "Oh, it's a wonderful picture, where the dog puts his own collar on!" Nobody. Not even Max Setton.

DEAR MICKEY THOROUGHLY ENJOYED ROUGH CUT WHICH SAW WITH JAMES WHOM WE CONGRATULATED ON THE SPOT INCIDENTALLY CORA WILL WOW THEM ON 42ND STREET BUT WOULD APPRECIATE YOUR ADVISING ME IF YOU HAVE COVER SHOTS INVOLVING NUDITY WHICH WILL BE UNACCEPTABLE FOR US TV AND IN THEATRICAL EXPLOITATIONS IN SOME AREAS MACGOWRAN EXCEL-LENT GODFREY NE PLUS ULTRA ALL KEEPING OUR FINGERS CROSSED FOR BIG SUCCESS ASSUME YOU WILL LIAISE WITH JACK MACGRAW OF COLUMBIA SCREEN GEMS MUSIC FOR MUSIC AND ESPECIALLY NUMBERS PLEASE PHONE ME TOMOR-ROW AS WOULD LIKE TO TALK TO YOU URGENTLY RE FINISHING PROCESS LOVE AND CONGRATULATIONS AGAIN

MAX JOHN AND ALL AT LONDON

Max Setton was head of British productions for Columbia Pictures. He was a lawyer. As an independent producer he had several films to his credit, *Footsteps in the Fog* (1955) and *I Was Monty's Double* (1958) among them. He was kind, he was enthusiastic, and he wasn't afraid to speak his mind, until one day he and I had to run the picture for the board of Columbia Pictures and without James Mason at our side. They sat there, these diminutive executives, chewing their cigars and hating every minute. At the end they went into a huddle and announced they wanted a new music track, and they wanted some Hollywood hack to do it.

It was *Sebastian* all over again. When you don't know what to say, say you want a new music track. I reminded them that Columbia was only putting up 25 percent of the cost, and other people hadn't been consulted, particularly the Australian composer, Peter Sculthorpe. They snarled their way out of the projection theatre; 1968 was not a vintage year for Columbia executives.

I won't insult your intelligence by telling you the plot of Norman Lindsay's book, but there was a painter, Brad (James Mason), a girl, Cora (Helen Mirren), her ma (Neva Carr-Glyn), a pest (Jackie MacGowran), the store-keeper, Cooley (Slim DeGrey), Clarissa Kaye, as Meg, and what the trade papers described as a "strong supporting cast." Led by James, who was loved and venerated, it was a very happy company.

The film was 90 percent made on the coast opposite Dunk Island and on the island itself. The sequences remaining were on a racecourse in Brisbane (Albion Park), a hotel room in a city, a street in New York, and Brad's studio in Greenwich Village. The last person to be cast was Clarissa Kaye. Gloria Paton, the casting director, had introduced her to me with trepidation, and stammered that it was a long shot for the part of Brad's girlfriend.

"Will she take her clothes off?" I asked.

"Oh, yes. She's played in revue, and in *Kismet.* She's slim, and she's ugly, but she comes over strongly."

"Wheel her in."

Clarissa entered. I took one look at that long, slim body, that beautiful mouth, those lovely eyes full of experience, and said, "Okay, give her the part."

Gloria is a hardened casting director, but the two women confessed later that they had both nearly collapsed shrieking on each other's shoulders. And that was how James met his second wife. I put them into bed together, in the Brisbane bedroom scene, and gave them both years of happiness and fun.

The film was full of nudity, but it is a painter's nudity. Goya has shown us in *La Maja Desnuda* that most people are more interesting without their clothes. Even the most unsophisticated person must laugh at seeing that "forked radish" in the mirror. Norman Lindsay's book had been a bit of a romp. My film belonged to the age of innocence, and the most innocent of all was James Mason's Brad, the Australian primitive painter who had strayed too far from his origins. The reaction of the Columbia board of directors to our Garden of Eden scenes was typical: "Have you covered the nude scenes in long shot?" they inquired.

The underwater scenes on the Barrier Reef were staged and photographed by possibly the best team in the world: Ron Taylor and Val Taylor. They took Helen down with them and she blindly obeyed, although she confessed to me much later that she was crying with fright the entire time. If you have ever swum out from the Barrier Reef and hung motionless over the abyss, filled with busy, silent life, an upside-down world full of terror and beauty, you will admire Helen's nerve.

I had discovered Dunk Island on the previous holiday, with Walter Chiari and Pamela and Bill, and the name given to the island by Captain Cook had always intrigued me. Now I had made *Age of Consent* there. I no longer believed in coincidence. I believed that some things are intended, and others are not, and that man is not the master of his fate, he goes to meet it.

Accordingly, when James said to me, "Let's make another film, together," I said. "Let's! But let's do something really worthwhile. Let's do *The Tempest.*"

I had always longed to do a film of Shakespeare's *The Tempest.* His play contained all the things I most loved and most believed in. Prospero, the magician of the isle, is the crowning part of an actor's career. I have seen John Gielgud fail in it, I have seen Michael Hordern triumph in the part. What actor would not trade a year of his life to speak those lines, in answer to his daughter, Miranda's, speech:

. . . How many goodly creatures are there here!
How beauteous mankind is! O brave new world
That has such people in't.
    PROSPERO
'Tis new to thee.

Four words were all that Shakespeare needed.

And what a part Caliban is, for an actor who loves his fellow men, who loves animals, who loves women, like dear, beloved Roger Livesey, who gave such a memorable performance as Caliban before the war at the Old Vic . . . And Ariel, Prospero's slave, neither male or female, but wholly magical . . . What priceless prizes these parts are for actors! . . . What imagination is needed, what physical strength, what beauty, what lightness, what terror, what horror!

I said to James, "Let's do *The Tempest,* James. I'll bring you a script in a month."

With these words, I said goodbye to the movies.

=

I had the separate plays in pocket editions, so I carried *The Tempest* with me wherever I went, in buses, in tubes, in the train to Gloucestershire. I cut the play, I transposed scenes, and I roared Caliban's speeches as I drove my Land Rover through the lanes of Gloucestershire to Avening, scattering pheasants as they walked sedately toward Cherington.

CALIBAN

Be not afeard. The isle is full of noises,
Sounds, and sweet airs, that give delight, and hurt not.
Sometimes a thousand twangling instruments
Will hum about mine ears; and sometimes voices,
That, if I then had wak'd after long deep,
Will make me sleep again; and then, in dreaming
The clouds methought would open and show riches
Ready to drop upon me, that, when I wak'd,
I cried to dream again.

I have always felt that I understood Caliban better than anyone, except Roger Livesey. He had something in his blood and makeup that could turn him into an endearing animal, as well as a murderous monster, a slave. Surely Caliban is one of Shakespeare's great creations, after hearing some New World explorer in a pub describe the cannibals of the southern seas.

In less than a month I told Maggie Parker I was ready to talk to James again, and I flew down to Geneva and drove a hired car along the lake to Vevey, to the villa where James lived, with Charlie Chaplin his neighbor up the hill. We had lunch, and James settled himself to listen as I dashed into the opening scenes.

OVERTURE

The orchestra is placed upon a curving platform which, like a great wave, breaks against the front-curtain of a theatre; the design of the curtain is in the style of the Renaissance, inspired by the patterns of controlled violence of the frescoes of Piero della Francesca in the Church of San Francisco at Arezzo: arrogant banners, formidable men, fantastic head-dresses and armour. We examine it in detail during the Overture.

The conductor takes his place to the usual brief applause. He bows, raises his baton, starts the overture. (Estimate two minutes for the overture.)

Towards the end of the overture the house-lights dim, the curtains start to open.

Cut to:

SCENE 1. *Milan (the Duomo—model or painting)*
   The curtains open to show the façade of the marble cathedral of the Visconti. It is night and the fantastic pinnacles rise against a starry sky.
SCENE 2. *The Starry Sky (model and painting)*
   As seen through Galileo's telescope. We see the planets, nebula the moon. The music continues under the words:

GALILEO (*off*)
My Lord Duke, see how the pallid moon
Has mountains, valleys, seas, and water-ways.
This is a world, like ours.

SCENE 3. *An observatory in the Palace. Night.*
Prospero and Galileo discovered at the telescope. The philosopher is about 40. The Duke, magnificently elegant, a few years older.

GALILEO (*continues*)
This is no lamp
Hung in the sky to inspire the sighs of lovers,
This is a World that turns around the Sun,
The sole and fixed centre of our universe,
As our World turns. So writes the wise Copernicus
Here in this book *De Revolutionibus Orbium
Coelestium*. This dusty handful,
This little earth of ours, is but a speck
I' th' universe. Why then should we yield
To Rome infallibility? The right
To burn, to sanctify, to sty men's minds
In ignorance and darkness? To deny
The natural laws with Papal Bulls? These lenses
Set men free!

ALARUMS. *Enter Gonzalo and Neapolitan Soldiers, armed and with drawn swords. Torches.*

(*Music ends.*)

GONZALO
Seize them!

Prospero and Galileo are arrested.

GONZALO
My Lord Prospero, you are deposed.

PROSPERO
By whose warrant?

GONZALO
By your brother, the Lord Antonio, who by alliance
With my master, Alonso, King of Naples,
Holds your fair city of Milan.

PROSPERO
Upon what charge?

GONZALO
That, rapt in secret studies, you do neglect the State.

PROSPERO
Now I see the pursuit of my knowledge leaves
Me with no dukedom but my books.
Farewell, Galileo!

GALILEO
My Lord Duke, farewell!
And fare you well that we may meet again.

GONZALO
Galileo, you and your arts are banished
To Florence where the Grand Duke of Tuscany
Has you in his protection.

GALILEO (*to Prospero*)
Fear not, my Lord!
Princes fall, tyrants rise, and there in Rome
They say the earth is fixed. And yet it moves!

Galileo is hustled out by guards.

GONZALO
My Lord Prospero, you must go with me.

PROSPERO
To execution?

GONZALO
No. Into banishment.

PROSPERO
And the Lady Miranda?

GONZALO
Goes with you.

At this point, James interrupted, and said, "That scene with Galileo . . . is it Shakespeare?"

I said, "No, it's Powell," and read on.

I could see his approval of the voyage in the Mediterranean tartan, the ship that Monte Cristo uses, with his baby daughter cradled in a nest of ropes while he struggled, with his books and spells, against the elements and the wide Sargasso Sea; and I could feel his doubts and questioning when the island rises out of the sea, and crabs and sea serpents scutter around his feet as he brings the boat in, but he interrupted me no more. He had abandoned himself to the delights of this glorious adventure that I was planning. And when the film ends, and the sails of the great ship are hauled up in the chilly morning air, and Prospero throws his great book into the depths of the sea, James sighed, and congratulated me, and echoed me when he said, "Let's do it!"

But we never did.

For several years we struggled on. James married Clarissa and he had, at last, the happiness that he had earned and deserved. The need to prove himself as the leader of a great company, in a great subject like *The Tempest*, was less urgent, because he was happier. But he remained as enthusiastic as ever, and our friendship remained unbroken. One season he grew a real Prospero beard, an impressive great spadelike affair, which covered his chest. I have a snapshot of him standing with Clarissa in some Mediterranean landscape. He looked magnificent, but above all he looked happy.

I sought finance for our project in Greece, in Egypt, even in Wardour Street, but the combination of Micky Powell, that harebrained genius, and James Mason ("he didn't exactly pull them in in *Age of Consent*") was too much, even when we added Topol as Caliban, and Michael York as Ferdinand. Then, Mia Farrow and André Previn came to town, Mia to have the twins and André to consolidate his Californian reputation as a composer and a popularizer of music and a television showman. I rushed to their flat in Eaton Square, and later on brought James, whom they treated like a god, these two charming Hollywood children, thirsting to have a share in an artistic venture eight thousand miles away from Hollywood. André was to write and conduct the music, and Mia would have been an airborne Ariel to remember. It was not their fault that we never made *The Tempest*.

Meanwhile two Greeks had flung their hats into the arena, Costas Carayanis and Frixos Constantine. Being Greeks, they didn't run away from a classical subject; being Greeks, they ran toward it. They had a small but active company in Athens, which produced comedies, documentaries, wild Westerns, and even porno films. I envied them. I should have such a company! If I would direct the film in Greece—they pointed out that they had plenty of islands—they would put up half the money.

Frixos was a Cypriot-born Greek. Costas, his partner, a Greek on the spot. These two young showmen understood our project as well as James and I did, but Mia's agent in Hollywood had something else for her to do, and we couldn't commit our small Nautilus, British-born company, without British support; after all, Shakespeare was English, wasn't he? The moment passed, we lost André and Mia, and the whole glorious project slid into oblivion.

Costas and Frixos took the whole thing to heart, as if it had been their own cherished project. Their courage and enthusiasm reminded me of my early days in the Mediterranean. There was warmth and laughter, a great eating of salads and drinking of wine, in any project with which they had to do. They knew and had seen some of my films, and treated me as a little god of the cinema. Perhaps the cinema is, after all, a more intimate art than I had been led to believe. Perhaps I should not have sold the Voile d'Or, but made it a center for cinéastes. We could have discussed projects in the heat of the day, and carried them out in the cool months of winter and spring. But a voice inside me says, "No, Micky. The trouble is that you are a bad salesman. You're as big a liar as most men, but you don't know how to lie to an exhibitor, or a distributor. Secretly, you feel that you have a right to be financed by the film business, and, no doubt, on the record, you are right. But this enormous, multimillion-dollar/pound industry, which is sprouting out of our modest multilingual European film, needs special handling, and you are not that kind of showman, and the quality of your projects makes them uneasy."

Alex Korda and Mickey Balcon laid the foundation for an English film business. The war consolidated it. The Rank Organisation was created by Powell and Pressburger, and David Lean and Ronnie Neame, Anthony Havelock-Allen, Launder and Gilliat, Carol Reed, Ian Dalrymple, the Boulting brothers, Bryan Forbes, Alec Guinness, Peter Sellers, Arthur Rank, John Davis—yes, by John Davis, too—and then we destroyed it, we let it tumble into ruins, we let personality get in the way of art. And I, who should have known better, who did know better, had helped to destroy all this credit and goodwill. I was famous, and infamous. I was an embarrassment to people. I was broke.

=

During these years, my old partner's life was undergoing a metamorphosis. You might call it the Kretschmar-Schuldorff–Emeric Pressburger syndrome. Aficionados of *Colonel Blimp* will recognize the symptoms. For some years Emeric had needed a change, and Alex's gradual decline and death had made it a matter of urgency. Emeric's two marriages had failed, his two grandchildren were growing up in Scotland. He had decided to write the novel that he had always wanted to write, and which he had been encouraged to write by the success of *Killing a Mouse on Sunday,* and by the successful and immediate sale of the film rights to Fred Zinnemann. He could be pardoned for thinking that he had it made.

The Glass Pearls, his next novel, was less well received and got no film offers, so he decided to carry out the plan he had been cherishing for some time: if he were to remain his own master he would have to cut down expenses, give up his flat in Eaton Square, and retire to the country, where he could write his novels in peace and quiet and do an occasional film script. This had been in the back of his mind ever since Stapi reappeared on the film scene, as producer, distributor, studio owner, and potential employer in Munich, Bavaria. This, naturally, called for several meals at the Kronenhalle.

Emeric had already been a guest at Stapi's hunting lodge in Thiersee, Austria, just over the border from Munich, and he was very fond of Stapi. He liked Thiersee, both as the setting for a projected supernovel and for its seclusion and quiet; and for its proximity to the great city of Munich. The main railway line north and south was only thirty miles away, and the railway station was a frontier post. Emeric's sports car made mincemeat of the twisting, turning road to Thiersee. Munich had its aerodrome, and he could be in London in an hour and a half. For a man who before the war had always been an exile, it seemed a perfect European design for living. But there was one catch. Imre was no longer a European. He had become an Englishman.

It took some while for this to dawn on him. England is like that. She bides her time. He bought a piece of Stapi's land, adjacent to Stapi's hunting lodge, and built a delightful Austrian-style cottage with room for guests. Being Imre, the cottage was a supercottage and the kitchen a superkitchen. He'd laid out the elaborate plan for his masterwork, and started his researches and interviews. He saw Stapi nearly every weekend and acted for him as adviser and script editor, and soon I arrived, demanding his services on *The Russian Interpreter.* It was all working out exactly as he had planned, but there was something missing, and that something was England.

Magyars are very special people. There are not many of them, they talk a language unlike any other European language but Finnish, and when Magyar meets Magyar, they enter together into a secret world. In any country in the world where Hungarians become naturalized as citizens, when Magyar meets Magyar they talk Magyar. It is one of those languages, like Gaelic, where every second word is a pun or a joke, and when you see two Magyars talking together they will be laughing, conscious of the delicious fact that only Magyars know what they are saying.

For a hundred years Magyars put the paprika into the Central European stew concocted by the Hapsburgs, but their writers sought a wider audience in the English-speaking world, and when the new diaspora began in Austria and Nazi Germany and scattered all the Hungarian Jews overseas, Alex Korda was their prophet and Denham Studios their Mecca; so much so, that the British screenwriting guild protested that the little, weedy River Colne that ran through Denham Studios and Denham Park should be renamed the Danube.

But when these invaders were proved to be a creative force like the three Korda brothers; when the head of the story department was Lajos Biró, a playwright and screenwriter of European reputation; when Bill Hornbeck became head of the editing department; when actors like Charles Laughton, Ralph Richardson, Larry Olivier, Robert Donat, were given their heads; when a program of features to rival Hollywood was announced; when Miklós Rózsa was writing the music for *The Thief of Bagdad;* when the greatest artists of Europe were summoned and told to give free rein to their imaginations; when, finally, a writer like Imre Pressburger found a refuge at Denham on the Danube, where he could write the screenplay for Günther Stapenhorst's *The Challenge,* Alex Korda's project for *The Red Shoes,* and Powell and Pressburger's *The Spy in Black*—there was no more talk of foreign invaders, and even the film journalists began to realize that Alex Korda was creating a European cinema that could compete with Hollywood's best and worst.

The seeds that Alex had sown became other men's flowers. If you go to Denham today, go into the great white industrial chemical building that stands where Denham's white towers once stood. There, proudly displayed, you will see all the titles of the great films made at Denham by Alex and his successors. It is a splendid memorial. But all that is left today is Denham Laboratories on the hill on the edge of the trees, and the ruins of Alex's mansion on the banks of the River Colne still stand, although the roof has fallen in.

As I stand on the bank today, images of *Knight Without Armour, The Ghost Goes West, Goodbye, Mr. Chips, Fire over England, Elephant Boy* come to mind: the parade is endless. I have seen Russia, France, India, Egypt, and the Persian Gulf reproduced on the banks of the Colne . . . and then I remember Anton Walbrook and the other German officers in the prison camp at a concert by the river. Here it was all through World War II, from 1939 to 1945, that I had my caravan on the banks of the River Colne, and here it was, in this very English setting, that Emeric Pressburger wrote and thought, and thought and wrote, in the way he always worked, and invented Lieutenant Hirt, Colonel Blimp, and a dozen other characters. All that time he was, technically, an enemy alien who had to report to the police once a week. But the characters and themes and situations that he was creating were so true, so inventive, and so English, that it was a surprise to his fellow producers after the war when he applied for British citizenship and became an Englishman.

"But Emeric is more English than any of us!" said David Lean.

But Imre knew better, himself; he was a Magyar, and like the cat that walks by himself, all places were alike to him—or so he would have liked to think.

But England is not part of the continent of Europe. England is an island, and islands have a way with them. How many times I have written, or said, that islands great or small, each has its own personality. Oh, Imre! . . . Imre! . . . I saw you so happily installed in the Austrian mountains on the border of Bavaria, with your friend, Stapi, as you would have been if the European war had never taken place. But your own country, Hungary, was forbidden to you, and in Thiersee you were a rootless Magyar with a British passport. The years passed, and gradually the world around you changed . . . or was it that you had changed, and Austria not at all?

The great novel was nearly finished, but Thiersee was no longer the quiet place it had been, with the famous Passion Play as its only excitement. Stapi's and Emeric's cottages were no longer a setting for quiet talks with intimate friends. There were new cottages where there had only been one before, and there was even a shop, and a beer hall, and television, and rock and roll, and the nights were no longer peaceful. Stapi was old. The tremendous energy with which he had helped to re-create a German movie industry after the war was no longer needed. He was ready to hand over to younger men, and it must have been then, I think, that Emeric began to remember the words that he had written for Anton Walbrook in *Colonel Blimp*, spoken by Anton as a German refugee seeking asylum in England, to A. E. Matthews, as the British examining officer, who had the power to send him into internment as an enemy alien for the duration of World War II:

> The truth about me, is that I am a tired old man, who came to this country because he's homesick. Oh, please don't stare at me—I'm all

right in the head. You know that after the war, we had very bad years in Germany . . . we got poorer, and poorer . . . money lost its value, the price of everything rose—except of human beings. We read in the papers, of course, that after the war years things were bad everywhere, that crime was increasing, and that honest citizens were having a hard job to put the gangsters in jail. But I needn't tell you, sir, that in Germany, the gangsters finally succeeded in putting the honest citizens in jail.

My wife was English. She would have loved to come back to England, but it seemed, to me, that I would be letting down my country in its greatest need, and so she stayed at my side. When, in the summer of '33, we found that we had lost our children to the Nazi party, and I was willing to come, she died . . . none of my sons came to her funeral. Heil Hitler!

Then, in January '35, I had to go to Berlin on a mission for my firm. Driving up in my car, I lost my way on the outskirts of the city, and suddenly . . . the landscape seemed so familiar to me . . . and slowly, I recognised the road, the lake, and a nursing home, where I spent some weeks recovering . . . almost forty years ago. I stopped the car, and sat still, remembering . . . and . . . you see, in this very nursing home, sir, I met my wife for the first time, and I met an Englishman who became my greatest friend, and I remembered the people at the station in '19, when we prisoners were sent home, cheering us, treating us like friends . . . the faces of a party of distinguished men around a table, who tried their utmost to comfort me, when the defeat of my country seemed to be unbearable . . . and . . . very foolishly . . . I remembered the English countryside . . . the gardens, the green lawns, the weedy rivers, and the trees . . . she loved so much . . . and a great desire came over me to come back to my wife's country . . . and this, sir, is the truth.

But that time, for Imre, had not yet come.

I had come to Thiersee in 1967 to persuade Imre to involve himself, be it ever so little, in the film adaptation of Michael Frayn's book *The Russian Interpreter*. I read the review, rushed into Hatchard's, read it in a sitting, and was on the telephone to his agent, all in the same day. His publishers said that he was represented by a Lady Elaine Greene, who had an office in Bloomsbury, not far from the British Museum. I made no attempt to conceal my enthusiasm, and she knew very well what she had got. We worked out the deal.

I met Michael, by appointment, at his house on Blackheath. The address, and the day, were pleasant, and so was Michael. He was about twenty-five.

He was tall and slim and charming. He had designs on the theatre; he thought it might be his medium. Meanwhile he was overwhelmed by my praise, although he absolutely agreed with me.

"But, who . . . who can play Proctor Gould?"

"Only Peter Sellers," I said.

"Peter Sellers!" he gasped. "Of course! He would be perfect!"

"I've already spoken to him," I said. "He's reading it now."

We walked all over Blackheath that morning; we spurned the earth beneath us; we were in Moscow, on the Sparrow Hills, in the International University, and then we were loving and laughing over Raisa, the loveliest, rudest, splendidest heroine of Michael's book, and my film.

"But, can you really make the film in Moscow?" marveled Michael.

"Of course not," said I. "But we've asked them, all the same."

"You mean, you would do it all in the studio?" asked Michael professionally.

I explained that we would go to some other Communist city, where they were not so particular.

"Somewhere in the Balkans," I said largely, explaining at the same time about glass shots, and the way large chunks of Moscow could be superimposed on Bucharest.

"But you must have the old women sweeping," cried Michael, "or it wouldn't be Moscow!"

I assured him that we would have the university, and the Moscow woods, and the old women sweeping under our very feet, and that he would be allowed to choose every book in Raisa's bookcase in the film; for Proctor Gould, you must know, was a great smuggler of books, books that did not always contain printed matter.

We parted, still full of excitement, and I went off to talk to Peter Sellers.

In those days, you could still talk to actors. But Peter Sellers and Stanley Kubrick were going to change all that. Ten years before, when I was preparing to make *Ill Met by Moonlight*, Peter came for an interview as one of the partisans. He is described in my notes as "a sort of India rubber owl." And now he was, demonstrably, the greatest actor that the electronic age had produced. He was a master of all the emotions, he was comedian, clown, tragedian, mimic, his wit was spontaneous and inimitable. He rode the sound waves with the same confidence that he had brought to tragedy and comedy. His only peer was Jean-Louis Barrault, who had the misfortune, or good fortune, according to the way you look at it, to be French.

Charles Chaplin was the greater clown, but he never learned to speak the words. Frozen-faced Buster Keaton was the greater director, but the character he created was all on one note—he was not an actor, he was a reactor. Even

Walt Disney's *Flying Mouse* could not compete with Sellers at his best. Who can ever forget Peter's tragic yet human mask as the shop steward in *I'm All Right, Jack;* who can forget *Dr. Strangelove;* who can forget *The Mouse That Roared;* who could ever forget *Lolita;* who will ever forget the wrench to his heartstrings when he learned that *Being There* was to be Peter's last movie?

Peter Sellers was a client of MCA, and the doges of Venice themselves have nothing on the Music Corporation of America. MCA are agents, but this simple statement includes invisible strings of power that encircled the whole world and, no doubt, the moon as well. Peter and I had agreed to meet at his house in the country over the weekend. He had a house at Elstead in Surrey, near Tilford and near the River Wey. This made me feel friendly and off my guard at once, for this is Conan Doyle country, the Conan Doyle of *The White Company* and *Sir Nigel,* and you already know how I feel about the River Wey. We settled on Saturday, around 4:00 P.M. Within minutes, Harvey Orkin* came on the blower.

"What's this about you and Peter meeting!"

"Oh, hello, Harvey. I didn't know you were here. Why don't you come, too?"

"You bet I'll come! Look, why don't you come to the Connaught at six, and meet David Begelman and me?"

At six I was ushered into a first-floor suite at the Connaught. I was already adding a few noughts to my budget. D.B. was a tall, dark, New York smoothie; in the hierarchy of MCA, he ranked high—I mean high. I gave him a run-down on proceedings so far, and made it clear that I was in the market, had my option signed and sealed, and Peter liked the book. We arranged to meet, all of us, at Peter's house next day.

Eventually I escaped. I rang Elaine Greene, Michael Frayn's agent, and told her that I would like to take Michael with me to meet Peter. She agreed. Still later Sandy Lieberson telephoned me. Peter would like Danischewsky† for the script. So would I. Danny was one of the three writers already submitted, by me, to Peter.

It seemed to be an occasion for the Rolls Bentley, and Bill polished her up. At 2:30 Michael Frayn arrived in his car. It was a cold day, and he looked askance at the quivering, black, open Bentley. However, he allowed me to wrap him up in scarves and rugs and hats, and I drove him down to Surrey. He proved to be good with the map, and spotted Peter's house by instinct.

*Peter Sellers's American agent at MCA.

†Monja Danischewsky (known as Danny) was a White Russian who for many years was in charge of publicity at the Ealing Studios. He became a producer on *Whisky Galore!* (called *Tight Little Island* in the United States), and while at Bryanston Films produced the Peter Sellers film *The Battle of the Sexes*.

"It looks so expensive," he said, "it must be Peter's."

Two girls in jeans and carrying saddles confirmed his diagnosis. We drove through high wrought-iron gates and I tooted my horn. Nobody came. I drove over expensive flagstones into an open barn. We got out, and a blond boy, about ten years old, appeared.

"Is this Sellers's?" I inquired.

He nodded, and led the way through a rose garden, into a Stockbroker Tudor great hall. There are more of these in Surrey than you would believe. Peter, clamlike, greeted us. He was playing it gray and slim, dark and quiet this Saturday afternoon. Harvey and the Beagle-man then made an entrance. We had a spot of tea. It was served by a fully dressed chef, who had left his hat in the kitchen. We all looked respectfully at Michael Frayn, and talked about his wonderful book.

All of a sudden, I said, "That's all very well, but is Peter in?"

Peter, who was standing and wandering about, visibly paled. The other two, whose 10 percent of $750,000 hung on Peter's reply, blenched. Peter stammered: "How do you mean . . . I like it very much . . . I want to do it . . . it should be done . . ."

I said, "That's all right, Peter, I agree with you. But are you in, subject to approval of the script?"

His face cleared, and he said, "Oh, I see . . . yes . . . you want a piece of paper."

I said, "Yes, I want a piece of paper."

And everyone was very happy, not least I. A young blonde in jeans, looking about sixteen, was introduced as Mrs. Sellers.* Even for a Scandinavian, she was just a child. Her English was good. Some genius proposed drinks, and they brought on the whiskey in a decanter. I tasted it, and murmured, "Glenfiddich."

The Beagle-man said heartily, "Michael is a connoisseur of the best."

I said, "Of course, that's why I'm here."

And Peter bowed.

Driving back, Michael complained of the cold, but I told him he had his book to keep him warm.

Our next meeting was at the Dorchester in Peter's suite a couple of weeks later, March 4 to be exact. Peter seemed jumpy. There was music playing, pouring out of invisible loudspeakers. Danischewsky, who was the focal point of this meeting, hadn't arrived yet. My heart sank when Peter announced that we were dining in the Terrace Room. Sandy Lieberson arrived, and he seemed to be as nervous as a cat. Britt arrived, and my heart sank even further. How could we talk sense with such a crowd?

*Britt Ekland.

Emeric shook his head. "No, not in Belgrade . . . in London."

Emeric had those supercomfortable chairs that are more like beds than chairs. Michael would have sat up straight at Emeric's bombshell, but he couldn't, so he squeaked from a half-reclining position, "In London!"

Even I was taken aback, although I am used to Emeric's flights of fancy. Emeric condescended to explain.

"You see, there are three ways of making the film from the book. Naturally, the best way would be to make it in Moscow, with Soviet cooperation, but I think that we can rule that out. Next would be to make it in Belgrade, and lay ourselves open to attack from the press on both sides. The third way would be to make it in London, and make a big publicity about it. I think that that would be the best way."

By this time Michael had picked himself up. I could see that he had had a severe shock. "I don't think I could agree to that. I don't like that idea at all."

I said, "Can't you make your suggestion a little clearer, Imre?"

"Vell," said Imre, "you both thought that my first alternative, to make the film in Moscow in the English language, would be the most acceptable to our audiences, but there is nothing realistic about that. We simply ask our audience to accept a convention, in which everybody speaks English. There is nothing realistic about that. The second convention, that our story takes place in an Eastern European country, where half the people are talking Serbo-Croatian, and the other half English, is even less satisfactory. Then I said to myself, like Gertrude Stein: a park is a park is a park, a city is a city. Why not say to the audience from the beginning, our story takes place in Moscow, but we can't make it there, so we are making it in London. You will see. Everyone will accept it."

"I shall not accept it," said Michael firmly. He had now got to his feet and was pacing up and down.

"Vell," said Emeric, "what does the other Michael think?"

By this time, I had made the mental back-somersault necessary to understand Emeric's reasons. "Logically, Emeric is right," I said. "I think we could get our English-speaking audience to accept it, particularly in America."

Michael snorted. He was really upset. "Do you seriously mean," he said, "that when one of our characters boards a bus in Piccadilly, it has Moscow destinations on it?"

"Yes," said Imre simply. "But, of course, the destination signs would be in Cyrillic characters."

"I think that I am going mad," announced Michael. "Excuse me, Mr. Pressburger, but your idea is too much for me."

Emeric nodded. "Of course, what I am suggesting is only a convention," he said. "All drama is a convention."

Michael telephoned his agent, Lady Greene, in London, and then announced that he was returning by air. We saw him off.

"Don't worry, Michael," I said. "Emeric and I will discuss this together, and then I'll report back to you. Meanwhile, think about Dickie Attenborough for the part of Proctor Gould."

But the project was dead, and we knew it. Imre and I discussed it, on and off, for the next few weeks and months. We even produced a lengthy adaptation of the scheme. But it was all dead wood. A scheme like that, even a subject like Michael Frayn's *Russian Interpreter*, should never be allowed to slow up for a moment. When Peter Sellers as Proctor Gould, currency smuggler, that smuggler of fair ladies, leapt into my mind; when Peter himself stammered: "I want to do it . . . it ought to be done . . ."; when Danischewsky, the discoverer of Kay Kendall, the inspiration for *Genevieve*, was bubbling with suggestions for the script, I should have fed the flames.

> "The play's the thing
> Wherein I'll catch the conscience of the King."

Instead I put the fire out.

=

Now that I am writing this autobiography, events that seemed to me at the time to be successive, and excessive, blows of fate, are revealed as part of a plan. The career of an independent producer in the jungle called movies is nothing if not political, and I am not a political animal. The big agents are our natural enemies. It is not their fault any more than it is the fault of the Bengal tiger when his slavering jaws close on the jugular vein of his victims.

Alfred Hitchcock had his own solution for this, sitting up there in his *machan* in that stout tree called Bel Air, watching the carnage below. He picked out the likeliest winners in this game of life and death in the Hollywood jungle and made personal contracts with them, for he believed in being friends with everybody, so long as it got him his own way. His foes respected this, and as a result, when he was no longer bankable, MCA treated him with all the honors of war. But this was a Hollywood game. It wasn't a game you could play at Elstree or Pinewood or Shepperton.

Occasionally there would be a flare-up in the business, heads would roll, and big names would come from Hollywood to Europe to play the power game for a year or two, and then move back again to Hollywood, California, leaving Rome and Paris and London a shambles. I could only offer quality, which nobody cared about, or new ideas, which frightened everyone, and myself, as director. I was the hunted rather than the hunter, the prey rather than the predator.

In our long-drawn-out duel, John Davis had twice given me the option to come into the sheepfold or stay outside with the wolves. Twice I bit the hand that fed me. Little wonder that he didn't seek to have it cauterized the third time. Because I wanted to keep my independence, I was a rebel. I wanted my own way, I didn't fit into the pattern. And I was old. I was sixty-three, and looked twenty years younger.

Retire? On what? The Archers, in their financial deals with Rank and Korda, had always gone for more percentage and less cash. It was good thinking in wartime. But when John Davis went to war with the American distributors, and when television became a license to print money, it took twenty years, and sometimes forty years, for our films to go into profit. *Peeping Tom*, whose certified cost was £135,000, is not in profit yet!

I had had the choice of two careers, hotel owner and film director, and I had plumped for one without keeping the other to retire to. Both Emeric and I had never owned a house in London; they'd all been bought on mortgage, and now, when mortgages were being called in and lease owner was being converted to property owner, we hadn't got the money to invest. I had always been prepared to make sacrifices to get a film made, and now I was the sacrificial object. I had made many reputations, and blasted my own.

I was only too conscious that my own career had been a matter of choice, and I had steadily abstained from encouraging my sons to follow me in my chosen profession, or rather the profession that chose me. I had imposed the discipline and ideals of Gordonstoun on Kevin and Columba when they were too young to resist it. If Kevin had gone into the army he would have been a general by now and running some giant relief organization, and Columba would have been a happy bum, with a touch of genius, as he is today. Frankie, alas, is dead. I became her executioner when I married her. We had been lovers for ten years. It was too long a courtship. We knew each other too well. There was nothing left to discover. We both asked too much of each other.

She was an ideal wife. She had a wonderful sense of humor, and the most beautiful bones that I've seen in any woman. She was brave, honest, unselfish, and drank like a fish. She smoked heavily, but gave it up when she was told that it was bad for the children. She never smoked again. Her sons were jealous of her, because I came first in our lives and they were second. She was always trying to make me jealous about her love affairs, real and imaginary, but when I only laughed she would throw something at me. Her last words to me were "I suppose I really do love you, Micky." We were walking up Kensington High Street to see a doctor she insisted on seeing, who said there was nothing wrong with her. Two days later, on July 5, 1983, she was dead.

Near the turn of this century, when I was gobbling up the contents of the bound *Strand* and *Pearson's* magazines in our local public library, there was a great to-do among novelists about what they called "sacred and profane love." Profanity I knew, for I passed my days among laborers. But profane love was new to me as a concept. I looked it up in the dictionary, a custom of mine that I cannot recommend often enough to you. My dictionary said: "Profane: unholy, heathen, pagan."

Of course! What did that scholar say? *"Odi profanum vulgus"*—"I hate the common herd."

The common man, who is he? As for women, there are no common women. Pamela was "the ugliest woman in the world" (Emeric Pressburger), or "the most beautiful" (John Gielgud and Laurence Olivier). It was the difference between a candle, and a candelabrum, between a steady flame, like Deborah, and a blaze of light like Pamela. The great Continental actresses were her models: Rachel, Bernhardt, Duse. She was blessed with a big voice, and a magnificent chest and lungs upon which she could strike organ notes. Her eyes were like two flames, lighting up every corner of the theatre, and above all she had intelligence, which burned upon her brow and illuminated every move she made and every word she said. No wonder Imre hated her! She was everything that he suspected about women.

But the cold, burning fingers of rheumatoid arthritis were probing that creamy flesh. They said she would never act again, but she did; they said she would never love again, never swim in the Pacific breakers, never walk, or run, or ride a bike, or climb a mountain again, and hear the marmots whistling their signals to one another as they bounced and leapt from rock to rock. But you did!

Only drugs could keep her going. She was slowly killing that magnificent body, cell by cell. We met, with or without planning. We passed in the night, we burned the roads of Europe together. We snatched every hour, every day, every month that we could. We could go anywhere at the drop of a hat. We had big Rover always full of food and drink and bedding. We fished on the Barrier Reef, we cruised to Norfolk Island, explored the Solomon Islands, and decided that there was nowhere like the Western Isles of Scotland, no movie like *I Know Where I'm Going!*, no cottages like Lee Cottages.

They stand together under the wood, on the lane which winds up the hill to Gatcombe Park. It is narrow and deep. It is the old packhorse road out of Avening, down there in the trees below us. The windows face southwest, looking down into the leafy valley of Avening brook, which is hurrying down to join all the other little brooks that have come running through Nailsworth and Stroud, to join forces in the Golden Valley and run, skipping, into the Bristol Channel and the great Atlantic Ocean.

For we are on the very edge of the Cotswolds, where they break and tumble into the sea. Over there, on the other side of the Channel, lies Wales. On a clear day, if you climb up the hill to Rodborough Common, you can see the whole valley of the River Severn, and the Malvern Hills on the far bank, and beyond that the mighty shapes of the Welsh mountains. It's great country to take off from and come home to. Avening was our secret harbor for ten years.

For Johnson it was his private, personal kingdom; his courtiers, we. He waited patiently while we were working our way through the works of Anthony Trollope for breakfast. He's good, solid stuff, is Anthony Trollope, and we liked the country novels best. Then I would go to my study upstairs to work, and Pamela and Johnson would take their morning constitutional. Pamela only had two and a half toes on her left foot that were usable, but every morning, rain or shine, Pamela and Johnnie would walk to the gate at the top of our lane, before it comes out onto the main road, and there she would wait patiently until Johnson turned once, twice, perhaps even thrice, and then did his business. Then once done, oh! what rejoicing, what bouncing, what congratulations, and then speed back home to have a few bikkies, and then—what's for lunch?!

It was a simple, satisfying program, broken occasionally into weeks or months. When Pamela was doing a television show in the U.K. or the U.S.A. I would be doing research at the London Library and staying at the Savile Club, of which, by special arrangement with the House Committee, Johnson was a Country Member. He knew very well that little dogs are not allowed in the bar, or in the Sandpit, or in the dining room, and he would sit in our entrance hall, which has a rather fine circular staircase and a black and white marble floor. He always sat on a black square, so that members tripped over him and had to apologize. He had a great admirer in Colonel Stephenson, chairman of IPC, and high muck-a-muck of Lord's cricket grounds,* who confided in me: "I do admire that spaniel of yours. He sits there in the hall, as the chaps go up to dinner, and several of them speak to him, and even try to pat him, but unless they are out of the top drawer do you think that he pays them any attention? Not a bit of it. He just turns up his nose at them, and looks away."

When big Rover was parked outside in Brook Street, Mayfair, everyone knew, of course, that this was Johnson's kennel and that he slept the night there. Did he sleep there? Not a bit of it! He slept with me. This is how we organized it. When it was time to lock the front door, he and I would go for a little walk around Grosvenor Square. I would make the derogatory remarks of a seasoned birdwatcher about the ugly eagle that presided over the American Embassy on the west side of the square, and Johnson would scuff the leaves and pee on the plinth of the Roosevelt statue.

By the time we returned to the club, the front door would be shut and the

*The premier London cricket ground and headquarters of the game.

night porter gone, but I had a key. We shot through the hall and around the corner to the cloakroom and lift. Johnnie knew the drill, and as soon as the lift door slid open he was inside, followed by me. I pressed the knob for the third floor. Johnson knew all the moves. My room was at the end of a long corridor, by the valet's room. Johnson would pelt ahead of me, down the corridor, come to my bedroom door, and wait for me. The moment I opened it he was inside, and under the bed.

Of course, the valet knew what we were up to, but he was sworn to secrecy, although that didn't stop him from tripping over Johnnie in the morning with the morning tea. After tea we were out and into big Rover before the earliest members were stirring. And at breakfast Colonel Stephenson would look over my shoulder, as I read *The Times*, and whisper, "How is he?"

For some years at this time my credit was completely exhausted, and I had no income but a trickle of royalties from films and books and an occasional article or interview for the BBC. When I tried to get a film off the ground, like Graham Greene's *The Living Room*, it was blocked. Bryan Forbes was running Elstree at that time, and he was a great fan of Graham Greene, and of me. But when he tried to get it through his board, it was blocked by Bernard Delfont.

Robert Clark had finally decided not to make the *Bony* series in Australia, and Bob Austin and John McCallum were reduced to making a television series of Arthur Upfield's splendid stories.

The Tempest had blown itself out. James had grown his magnificent beard in vain. My project for Henry James's *Daisy Miller* was done by somebody else. Nobody wanted Bill Sansom's *Loving Eye*. I was an outlaw. My only contact with the British film business in these days was the monthly board meeting of the Children's Film Foundation, of which John Davis was chairman. All sides of the industry were represented on the board, which was an extremely able one, and I was the representative of the British Film Producers' Association. I made a point of attending these monthly board meetings. I didn't want John to think that I was dead—yet. But what had been merely a move for self-preservation turned into the final collaboration of Powell and Pressburger: *The Boy Who Turned Yellow*.

The CFF met monthly in the magnificent boardroom of the Rank Organisation, number 49 South Street, Mayfair, just around the corner from the Dorchester Hotel and Hyde Park. John was an excellent chairman, and it was pleasant to see the whole British film industry, exhibitors, producers, distributors, working together and speaking as one voice, even if it was only for a few hours and once a month, and as an advisory board. The executive producer of the CFF was Henry Geddes, who handled his advisory board adroitly. The Producers Association kept me on as their representative long after I had ceased to be active, and without them I would have vanished from sight altogether, even though our films were beginning to be rediscovered by a new generation of filmmakers.

The average budget for a children's film of approximately one hour was between £40,000 and £60,000, and it was perfectly possible to make an acceptable children's film for that kind of budget. Geddes had too many amateur producers anxious to do their stuff. He should have gone for the best talent available. There were plenty of excellent directors and writers starving, like Pat Jackson and Tony Pelissier. We all read stories and scripts, and reported our findings to the chairman, but the films never rose above a certain level.

I knew how much Emeric would have loved to write for children, and one day I suggested it to an appalled board: Powell and Pressburger together again? Henry Geddes looked down his nose. John grinned. But I pushed it through, sold Emeric on the idea, and presently he came up with a story. It was called *The Wife of Father Christmas*.

"Is that the title, Imre?"

"Yes, Michael."

"What's it mean?"

"You see, Michael, there is a little schoolboy who goes with his friends on a guided tour of the Tower of London. He has two white mice as pets, Father Christmas and his wife, and he loses the wife of Father Christmas in the Bloody Tower."

"Go on, it sounds terrific!"

"Do you think so? Then, on the way home in the underground, the school-boy turns yellow, between Chalk Farm Station and Hampstead, where he lives."

"Yellow?"

"Yes, Michael, yellow all over, the boy, and his clothes, everything—yellow."

"What next?"

"He runs home to show his mother, and a doctor is sent for but can offer no solution. Then, in the night, he has a dream that he has a strange visitor who comes out of the television box and claims to be responsible for turning the boy yellow. He guides the boy into the television box, and the boy finds that he can travel along the wireless waves because he is yellow. He finds his mouse in the Tower and reunites her with Father Christmas, but he is arrested by the Beefeaters and is about to have his head cut off when he is saved, at the last minute, by another little boy who has a good idea, and at the last moment he escapes back into the television set, and arrives back home cured and the right color."

"I love it! Let's do it! But what about the title?"

"What about the title, Michael?"

"It ought to be called *The Boy Who Turned Yellow.*"

"Michael, I have called it *The Wife of Father Christmas.*"

"Yes, I know, but *The Boy Who Turned Yellow* is a better title."

"You may call it what you like, Michael, but I shall call it *The Wife of Father Christmas.*"

Of course I found a part for Johnson in the film, as our hero's dog. The doctor in the film turned out to be Esmond Knight, and the strange visitor was played by Robert Eddison. The other little boy in the film was a very good part for the kind of boy who is an electronic wizard and understands all about . . . all about . . . well, all about things that electronic wizards are supposed to know about. He is rung up from time to time by our hero, or by his guide, and gives them good advice. This part was played by R. B. Kitaj's son, Lem, who now writes screenplays under the weird alias of Lem Dobbs.

The film suffered the usual fate of our films, particularly when John Davis was anywhere in the offing. The story was approved and everybody said they liked it, but when I made it they got scared and said the children wouldn't understand it. I had to fight to save it from going on the shelf. Then at the end of the year the children of England voted for the best children's film and we won first prize. Not only that, next year they voted for us again, so we won the prize two years running. But that didn't convince the chair polishers. They didn't understand the film, and they didn't like it. It was the story of The Archers all over again, but this time not in VistaVision, not in CinemaScope, just plain old 35mm.

≡

Made bold by the success of this white mouse of a film, I suggested that we ask Emeric for another story and he came up with one that I called *The Magic Umbrella;* I forget what Imre called it. But it was about a bunch of boys who find an old umbrella in a rubbish heap, and when they put it up, rain starts to fall within the circumference of the umbrella. Maybe it was called *The Rainmakers.* The story involved two gangs of boys, and one of the gangs of course steals the umbrella from the other, etc., etc. For some reason, the board turned it down, I don't remember exactly why. I fancy Henry Geddes felt that I was getting a bit too big for my boots.

> I've got a little list,
> I've got a little list.*

*From Gilbert and Sullivan's *The Mikado.*

You won't be surprised if I tell you that Imre was, by this time, back in England. He had finished his great novel about Thiersee and its Passion Play, and its effect upon the cast of local amateurs who act in it. It was a very big and ambitious work.

"You see, Michael, they have this Passion Play there, and at Oberammergau, and they only have it every three years, and this story is about the young man who is chosen to play the Christ in the Passion Play, and how it affects his life."

"Sounds a great idea. You must call it *Passion Play*—it's a great title."

"Michael, it is called *The Passion of Jules Stein*."

"*Passion Play* would be a better title."

The novel was never published. I don't know any of the details, but when he had finished his great novel he may have shown it to local people, whose reactions may have been contrary to his expectations. Certainly he was always very bitter about the Austrians, or, at any rate, at least their racial prejudices. I have never read the novel, and he never asked me to.

Thiersee had changed. It was no longer the Shangri-la that he had hoped for. The weekends were long and noisy with people from the city. Stapi was no longer active and his wife, Charlotte, had died, changing his life. Imre was working on a script for Joshua Logan, adapted from a best-selling novel by an Australian author, *Careful, He Might Hear You*. The story concerned a small boy whose young mother had died, leaving four or five maiden aunts to fight over his custody. The setting was Sydney, Australia, and the climax included the big ferryboat disaster in Sydney Bay.

Emeric's thoughts were returning to England. I encouraged him to come to the west of England and said that I would look out for a cottage for him, but Imre had friends everywhere, Magyars, and he was beckoned to the other side of England, to the east coast, to Debenham, to the River Deben, a small river made great by the early history of East Anglia. There a thatched cottage rose magically from the ground with a nice bit of land, and the Deben trickling a field or two away. It was a small, beautiful cottage, just the right size for a small, beautiful writer, and he kept it spick-and-span and was so particular about locks, keys, bolts, and bars that he frequently locked himself out of his own house.

He had a garage, which is more than I had, so there was room for his German sports car, too. And there he stayed until the day he died. He is buried in the churchyard at Aspall, with the lines from Sir Walter Scott engraved upon the stone by his two Scottish grandsons:

Love rules the court, the camp, the grove,
And men below, and saints above,
For love is heaven, and heaven is love.

I shall be buried in Avening churchyard, in the southwest corner, where there is a place kept for me. The gravestone will read:

Here lies Michael Powell
1905–
Film director and optimist

With Emeric's return to England our friendship, which had survived so many crises, took a happier turn. The old rivalry and jealousy were gone. It was not Powell and Pressburger anymore; it was The Archers. I said to Emeric, "A change is coming, old horse. I see it hovering in the air. We may not have received from Her Majesty the recognition due to us for our two Royal Command Performances; The Archers, and their associates, may not have been smothered by Orders of the British Empire; the British Association of Film and Television Arts may not have recognized our contribution to world cinema, our contribution to British films, but there is talk at the British Film Institute of a retrospective of some of our films, not a total retrospective, but a respectable retrospective—say five or seven Archers films.

"Nobody knows these films, today. They languish in the dungeons of the Rank Organisation. If you agree, old cock, I shall bang the drum and get our films shown in private if they can't be shown in public. Our own critics and film historians have hated us and ignored us, but there is a young American director in town who knows all about our films, though God knows where he got the prints, and what sort of a state the prints were in—whether they were complete, or not, I don't know. He says he saw some of them first on the telly, in a series called *Million Dollar Movie* edited down to a uniform length for the TV slot. There were foreign films, Yank films, and British films in the series, but the ones he remembered, and saw again and again, were The Archers' films, with the target, and the arrow banging into the bull's-eye. His name is Martin Scorsese."

Marty was triumphantly touring the world, after completing the shooting of *Taxi Driver*, which would win the coveted Palme d'Or at Cannes a year later. He was preparing to make *New York, New York*, to star Robert De Niro, who had played the haunted taxi driver in *Taxi Driver*. Rusticated in the

Cotswolds, I had seen none of Marty's films. Mike Kaplan* brought us together. Marty seized my hand and shook it.

"Mr. Powell, it is an honor, it's a pleasure to meet you. I thought you were dead. I love your films, yours and Mr. Pressburger's. 'Written, Produced and Directed by Michael Powell and Emeric Pressburger'—that's the finest credit title in the world. How did you manage to get away with it? You must see my film *Alice Doesn't Live Here Anymore*. The opening sequence is a tribute to *The Red Shoes*. I'll arrange for you to run it tonight. I want to have your opinion."

I saw the film and I was stunned by its quality, by Marty's handling of the actors, by the cutting and the speed, and the acting of the two marvelous women in the fast-food emporium.

"Oh, that? Yes, Ellen Burstyn got the Academy Award for that. Who? Oh yes, Harvey, he's an old friend. Haven't you seen him before? He's the star of one of my first films, *Mean Streets*. But what did you think of the opening of *Alice*? Did you recognize the tribute to *Red Shoes*?"

I confessed that I saw not the least resemblance. He laughed, heartily.

"Mike Kaplan here has a print of *Mean Streets*. Warner Bros. couldn't sell it. It's too brutal, and nobody was in it. But Bob De Niro was in it, Harvey Keitel was in it . . . What? . . . You haven't seen *Mean Streets*? I'll arrange for you to run it tonight. Mike, Mr. Powell is going to see the film, tonight."

Meeting Martin Scorsese in Ladbroke Grove was like meeting a twister in Kansas. He talked a mile a minute, his mouth full of exclamations, explanations, opinions, questions, and contradictions. He was short and dynamic. He gave out energy. He had eyes like a snake, seeing everything, adopting and discarding in the same moment. He had a pale, handsome face, which was mostly buried in a spectacular, closely clipped beard that accentuated the beauty of his eyes.

He was formidable. One minute he was booking projection theatres for me, the next minute he was treating me with veneration. And he knew our films!

*When Scorsese was unsuccessfully trying to track down Michael, he telephoned Kaplan, an American then living in London, for any leads he might have. Kaplan replied: "He's coming to my flat at three-thirty today." Kaplan had met Michael a few years earlier while representing the actor Malcolm McDowell, whom Michael hoped would play Caliban in his never-made film of Shakespeare's *The Tempest*. At the time of the historic meeting between Scorsese and Michael, Kaplan was distributing *A Bigger Splash*, a film about painter David Hockney. He had earlier been one of those involved in the creation of the "Ultimate Trip" ad campaign for *2001*, which saved the film from box-office disaster. This began a long association with director Stanley Kubrick and involved Kaplan in the ad campaign for Kubrick's *A Clockwork Orange*. Now an independent producer living in Los Angeles, Kaplan produced Lindsay Anderson's last feature film, *The Whales of August*, and most recently a documentary about the making of Robert Altman's film *The Player*.

He knew our films through and through! He knew why we made them, he knew what they were about, he was an artist. What on earth was such a man doing making his films in Hollywood? He agreed. No more, no more. *Taxi Driver* settled that.

"After *Taxi Driver*, I can do what I want; Bob can do what he wants. We're going to do another film together after *New York, New York*, but this time it will be a New York film. Do you know the name of Jake La Motta? Well, he's a fighter. A boxer? No, he's not a boxer, he's a fighter, a slugger. He can take punishment, like me," and he laughed uproariously. "He's written a book, himself, about his life. I'll give it to you. It's called *Raging Bull*."

I felt life returning to me. I felt the blood coursing through my veins. I felt every cliché in the world happening simultaneously, to my body and brain. Here was the movies, and here was a real king of the movies; he knew what he was doing, and why he was doing it. Here was the art, and here was the artist that had been lost for so long after the war. We haven't got over it yet. We need a dozen Scorseses. They're waiting in the wings.

I ran *Mean Streets* that night in a little projection room in Wardour Street. There was just me and a couple of young technicians and the projectionist. I was stunned. Here was great filmmaking, the kind of filmmaking that only happened in Europe before the war, except for an occasional Howard Hawks production. Here was no Hollywood complacency, although the film had been shot in Hollywood. Here was life, naked and raw, here was art in the hands of a master artist.

When you saw it you never knew what, or who, was coming next: De Niro, from being an obscure young actor, suddenly dominated the screen, Harvey Keitel was like an avenging angel, but they were all puppies in the hands of this extraordinary genius. When the film was over, the projectionist came out of the booth, and we all looked at each other, silent. Nobody said anything until I said, "Let's go over to the pub and have a drink."

When I saw Emeric next I said, "It's all right, old boy. We haven't wasted our time. The new generation are as good as we were, and better."

Emeric looked doubtful. We were at breakfast at the Savile Club, and he had just arrived from the country. He was about to perform his famous egg-swallowing act. A taxi from Liverpool Street Station deposited him at 69 Brook Street at 8:31 A.M., when I and my fellow members were deep in our newspapers. Emeric always ordered bacon and two eggs sunnyside up, nodded to me, selected a newspaper and sat down opposite me; all this in silence, of course. When his breakfast order arrived he would leave the eggs until last and then, with exquisite skill, balancing each egg on the blade of the knife, he would swallow them one after the other, his eyes half-closed in appreciation, as if he were swallowing a Whitstable oyster. Only then would he whisper, "When is your first appointment?" For at that time, twenty or thirty years after the first showings of our films, we were beginning to receive a trickle of royalties, which were paid to our agent, Christopher Mann, who very prudently held on to the principal as long as was possible, before splitting it three ways.

You will have gathered that I had four homes in this stage of my career: room number 10 at the Savile Club; a flat in Eaton Place, to which Pamela moved after the collapse of Soho Square; Lee Cottages, in the west of England; and the two apartments in Melbury Road. There was also an office, at number 4 Albemarle Street, over Messrs. Agnew, the famous art gallery and print shop, where Bill Paton was king.

At that period of my life I was not in any one of them for any time, but could be contacted through Bill at the office. Columba had left Gordonstoun by mutual agreement to come south, to the relief of his housemaster and head-master. He said that the only thing he enjoyed at Gordonstoun was Prince Charles's performance as Macbeth in the Gordonstoun production of the play. Columba was now at art school, encouraged by John Piper, discouraged by Ron Kitaj. The school was in Lime Grove, on the opposite side of the road from Shepherd's Bush Studios, where I had directed my first four films for Mickey Balcon, and which were now occupied by the BBC, producing television films.

Frankie zigzagged between Vera Burton's flat in Knightsbridge, which was their old stamping ground when they were model girls and, of course, 8 Melbury Road. It was a French farce situation, with people exiting and doors slamming, but it held in it the seeds of tragedy.

I see that I have omitted one other address, which was to become more important as the years rolled on: 52 Shaftesbury Avenue.

Three of London's most important theatres, the Lyric, the Apollo, and the Globe and, peeping around the corner in Great Windmill Street, the Windmill Theatre, stand cheek-by-jowl on the north side of the avenue, with their neon lights and their posters and their stars, screaming for attention. So you might be excused for overlooking a tall, ugly building on the corner of Glasshouse Street and bang opposite the theatres in question.

It is a very narrow, very tall, very ugly house; so narrow, that they had only just room for a staircase and a lift, which was frequently under repair. The offices, two to a floor, were small, the windows were rarely cleaned, the plumbing was basic, but the address—52 Shaftesbury Avenue, London W.1—is super, and the view of the other side of the street, where the theatres stand with those big names in neon lights, is encouraging. Here little Christopher Mann, a talent scout from Manchester, come to London from his native city to try his luck with one client, Madeleine Carroll—who believed in him and he in her—set up shop in 1928. It was here a month or two later that little Micky Powell, a freelance stills cameraman by profession, and self-styled assistant to the American movie director Harry Lachman, came with the 8-by-10 prints of stills from Miles Mander's production of *The First Born*, featuring Madeleine Carroll and Miles Mander himself, and which Chris Mann needed to get Madeleine more work.

Nobody stayed long at number 52, and by the time that talkies were talking and studios were converting, Madeleine was already a big star in British movies. She had the clear, calm, blond beauty that always sent Mr. Alfred Hitchcock up the wall. In no time, she was being directed by Mr. Victor Saville, on a horse (Victor on a horse, not Miss Carroll), in a spectacular film about a Belgian nurse, Martha Cnockheart, who was almost shot by the Germans for spying in World War I.

Alice Terry, another cool, calm blonde, had, I remember, suffered the same fate in Rex Ingram's *Mare Nostrum*, only to be eclipsed by Garbo as Mata Hari, the German spy. There is something sadistic about the delight that their directors had in shooting these tall, beautiful, blond women, and it showed that Alfred Hitchcock was not the only director to get his kicks out of it. And sure enough, a year later, Madeleine was working for Alfred Hitchcock, who had her embarrassingly handcuffed to Robert Donat for most of *The 39 Steps*, a more subtle way of reducing your heroine to tears than by shooting her.

That was in 1934. Let us skip forty years, to number 52 Shaftesbury Avenue, and a tenant of half the top floor is Poseidon Films, and the office of Poseidon Films is my only refuge in an indifferent, if not actively hostile, British film industry, and the managing director, chief producer, associate director, and office boy of Poseidon Films is Frixos Constantine, my only friend.

Frixos, as I have said, is a Greek Cypriot, which means that he was born a British subject on the island of Cyprus, for Cyprus was British in those days, casually added to the British Empire about a hundred years before. He was born into a small, tight group of family, and his father was an icon painter, a painter of the interior of churches. That's one of his father's daubs, on the wall there . . . good honest workmanship, not a brick amiss in it.

But although the small family was happy, the times were stormy. Cyprus was seeking her own identity, with or without Greece, certainly without Turkey. Frixos and his school friends were partisans, chased and imprisoned by the local British occupying forces. Given the choice of going to jail or joining the British army, Frixos opted for military service and became a cook in Alexandria. He still cooks well, but in army style—there is always a lot left over.

When Cyprus gained her freedom, so did Frixos. He had a British passport, so he came to England to complete his education. He married in haste, and never repented it; they are still friends. In no time he was on the fringe of the film business, with a partner in Athens. That's his photograph up there on the wall, Costas Carayanis. Then when I was planning *The Tempest* with James, and Maggie Parker was looking for money, Frixos met me. It was a fortunate meeting for both of us. He saved me. He gave me a refuge. Without him I would have had no home in the industry which I had helped to create, no *point d'appui.* I, and my papers and my films and books and photographs, would have vanished, leaving nothing but a name. It has happened to others, it could have happened to me; and he never said a word about it, or even mentioned it. Do you wonder that I love him?

It was to the office of Poseidon Films that Bertrand Tavernier, marveling at *Peeping Tom,* came looking for Michael Powell, to show the director the articles that he had written in *Midi-Minuit Fantastique* about poor, disgraced *Tom,* praising the film to the skies and inviting Michael Powell, this genius, to come to France and join their study group at Saint-Etienne for a few days to discuss the art of the film.

It was to the Poseidon offices that Roland Lacourbe and Daniele Grivel groped their way down Wardour Street to interview Michael Powell and propose that they add *Une Question de Vie et Mort* (*A Matter of Life and Death*) to the series that they were publishing on classic films. It was to Poseidon Films that Pierrette Matalon and Claude Guiguet, two much younger and even keener French students, both of them schoolteachers, came at their own expense to propose that they write a thesis on this great filmmaker, whom nobody in France had ever heard of; and these two students followed up their visits by articles in *Positif.* It was a much needed shot in the arm. It meant so much to me because it was French, this love and interest. By now I had hit rock bottom.

The big apartment at 8 Melbury Road, with its pictures and its books and its period furniture and its sixteen-foot-high ceilings, had gone. Frankie had moved into the small apartment, and Bill and Myrtle had retired to the country, to their own cottage in Shottenden, in Kent, where I had made *A Canterbury Tale,* and where Bill and Myrtle had met when Bill was on leave from the Royal Navy during the war. With Bill went all the books and files and photographs from the office, forty or fifty boxes of them, all deposited in number 2, Lee Cottages, Avening, Glos.

Gone was 4 Albemarle Street, and the window of Agnew's, and the big window of the Marlborough Gallery where Messrs. Marlborough would wave to me as I passed on my way to the Savile for lunch. Gone was Pamela's new apartment in Eaton Place. She could no longer afford to run two apartments, and she opted for the cottage in the country. All her books, costumes, memorabilia, as well as furniture and pictures, joined my collection at number 2, Lee Cottages. I would have given up everything to keep my subscription to the London Library, with its quarter of a million books and wonderful librarians, and the Royal Automobile Club with its Turkish baths. But how long would I be able to do this? Gone was the three-and-a-half-liter Vanden Plas–body Bentley, the Rolls-Royce Silver Ghost, the red Land-Rover, and the Mini Moke. Only dear, faithful big Rover remained.

Pamela's illnesses were closing in on her: diabetes, arthritis. Only constant injections of lifesaving drugs, which were also death-dealing drugs, kept her alive and still working.

"I never thought I'd make fifty," she told me, "and here I am, waiting for offers."

But her strength was going, and her power to resist the onslaught of other mysterious enemies was fading.

"I want to be a bouncing marmot again!" she cried.

Alas! Alas!

By now Frixos knew my real situation, and Pamela's, and he was as tender as a woman. A man of many love affairs, he had one going now, with a Japanese student. Besides being attractive, intelligent, and delightful to be with, she was also a formidable woman.

"You think you're having just another affair. She's going to marry you, boy."

He laughed boastfully, but there was pride in his eye. What happened? She married him, of course. Who could ever resist a charming, intelligent Japanese student when she had made her mind up. Dear Ikuko! I knew you were the one for him, long before he did. But that's as it should be.

In those Shaftesbury Avenue days Frixos had a tiny flat on the other side of the river, Surreyside. When I had to be in town he and Ikuko would take me back and feed me, and then sleep on the floor while I slept in their bed. When the first baby came she joined them on the floor. It was a tiny flat, and they had the next baby there too. Heaven knows how many times they looked after me, lodged me, and fed me, while I was still doing the rounds, still hoping that someone would understand, like me, that film was an art, and artists were needed and should be given their heads.

I still had the capacity, heaven knows how, of getting enthusiastic about new subjects, new ideas, a new play, a new book, and rushed around to bored executives to try and sell them on the idea. I still read the *Times Literary Supplement* at the Club, and *Variety* in Frixos's office. I helped Frixos to make a horror film in Greece, and a porno, God knows where, and a documentary about the destruction of the island of Santorini, with a commentary by Michael Hordern, which was so brilliant that Frixos couldn't understand a word of it.

And then one day I saw somebody reading a bulky book called *A Biographi-*

cal *Dictionary of the Cinema* and out of tired curiosity I looked to see if I was in it, and what they said about me. And this is what I read, in David Thomson's book:

Michael Powell, b. Canterbury, Kent, 1905 [a filmography followed]. There is not a British director, working in Britain, with as many worthwhile films to his credit as Michael Powell. Yet in an age of Richardson and Schlesinger, Powell has had hardly any adequate critical appreciation. The sadness is that he can easily be written off as an eccentric decorator of fantasies. Against persistent British attempts to dignify realism Powell must have seemed gaudy, distasteful, and effete. All three ingredients contribute to his vision, but so do an imaginative evocation of the erotic and the supernatural, a pioneering enthusiasm for visual autonomy always likely to break out in passages of stunning delight, the adherence to what Raymond Durgnat once called "High Tory" values, a wicked sense of humour and private jokes, and, most distinctive—like Colonel Blimp's dreams—an unsettling mixture of emotional reticence and splurging fantasy. Thus, as late as 1969, *Age of Consent*, a mild beachcombing anecdote, is lit up by baroque passages of Helen Mirren, naked, and underwater.

It is revealing that *Peeping Tom* was dismissed in Britain as wayward nastiness. Worst of all, Powell may have been inhibited by the feeling that his imagination was un-British. Powell has stayed English—despite the merry excursion to Australia—when he cried out for the geography of light and shade that von Sternberg illuminated on the Paramount sound stages. Even when Britain rediscovered horror in the late 1950's, as O. O. Green has remarked, Powell was ignored. Green compared Powell and King Vidor, whose *Duel in the Sun* Jennifer Jones was reduced to *Country Life* fretfulness by Powell in *Gone to Earth*: "Vidor, intellectually, perhaps, less sophisticated, or at least less cautious, than Powell, has retained just that Wagnerian authenticity of emotional excess which gives his films that genuine mysticism, a Nietzschean pantheism. But Powell lived in a class and a country which suspects, undermines, is embarrassed by, emotion; his diversity of qualities rarely find their holding context."

As if in early accord with that verdict, Powell left Dulwich College for the studio Rex Ingram had set up in Nice. He assisted the ex-Dubliner, ex-Hollywood director, on *Mare Nostrum* ('26), *The Magician* ('26), and *The Garden of Allah* ('27). Undoubtedly that experience encouraged his interest in the expressionist treatment of the supernatural; Ingram's splendid isolation may also have confirmed a young man's belief in "artistic" cinema. It was several years before Powell's own films showed such strange fruit. He slogged away for some time in England as a cameraman, writer, and director; only in the late 1930s do his films seem his own.

Thereafter, they struggle with great clashing virtues—with marvellous visual imagination and uneasy, intellectual substance: *I Know Where I'm Going* [sic] is excused by its resort to faery; *49th Parallel* is a strange war odyssey, with escaping Germans wandering across Canada—naive, very violent, at times unwittingly comic, but possessed by a primitive feeling for endangered civilisation; an interesting sequel is *One of Our Aircraft Is Missing*—English fliers getting out of Holland; yet *A Matter of Life and Death* is pretentious and tedious. But the two Conrad Veidt movies—*The Spy in Black* and *Contraband*—are exciting and atmospheric studies in Langian intrigue; *The Thief of Bagdad* is delightful; *The Life and Death of Colonel Blimp* a beautiful salute to Englishness. After the war, Powell expanded, attempting to fuse the talents of painters, designers and dancers. In fact, *The Red Shoes, Tales of Hoffman* [sic] and *Oh Rosalinda* [sic] underline the search for respectability in his work. Visually, they are too often silly, overdressed, inspired by what Green calls "Ye Olde Junke Shoppe" aspect of British visual culture. *Black Narcissus* is that rare thing, an erotic English film about the fantasies of nuns, startling whenever Kathleen Byron is involved. *The Small Back Room* profits from the use of unexpected expressionism on an ostensibly realistic subject and quivers with nervous tension. Equally, *The Elusive Pimpernel* has gorgeous moments despite a routine swashbuckling story.

After about 1950, dejection seemed to set in, only to be dispelled by *Peeping Tom*, Powell's most completely realised and intellectually sombre film. Full of dark jokes—including his own presence as the cruel father—it also shows Powell's sense of the cinema's own contribution to frenzy. The central character is a moving portrait of the imaginative young man who is unsociable with real people but familiar with the stars of movies. He is a shy focus puller who takes film of girls using a tripod that contains a swordstick. The stuck victims goggle horribly at the picture they make in the reflector above the camera; and so reaction stimulates the spectacle even further. The film was reasonably criticised as an exercise in De Sade's principles, and it is the one work in which Powell has discarded all inhibitions.

I was staggered, overwhelmed. I had taken myself at the world's valuation for so long now that any praise tended to bring tears to my eyes, and here were not just the standard phrases, the ordinary short, quotable piece. Here was the opinion and the report of a real scholar, a scholar of English, and a scholar of film. What he said about me, I knew was true. Who should know, but I? But that somebody else had understood, and was so percipient, and so generous; it bowled me over, staggered me.

I read it again, and again, and as soon as I had a little money, instead of buying a bottle of whiskey, I bought Thomson's book. I thought of nothing but gratitude, and the wish to talk to this scholar, whose opinions were so pithy, trenchant, and bubbling with concealed laughter, and sometimes suppressed fury.

I wrote to him. If he believed what he had written, I thought he might be pleased. He was. He answered by return, a long letter. And finally he explained that he was Director of Film Studies at Dartmouth College, New Hampshire, and, as head of the department, he had some say in the invitations the college were able to issue, occasionally, to distinguished artists in other mediums, and he would like to know if he could propose me for this honor, and this post of "artist in residence."

It was one of those boiling hot summers that England sometimes allows to happen. It was a scorcher. Day after day, the thermometer was in the nineties. Johnnie, in his coat of curly black hair, lay about gasping. But when I went for the daily visit to Pamela in hospital, he always insisted on coming too, although big Rover was like an oven. After the second operation they had given her a private room where we could talk. I was writing a story to keep her alive and keep her amused, about one thousand words a day, and every day I read her what I had written.

The nurses were kind, and sometimes let Johnnie in to say hello. Sometimes I would look up from the words, and see those great eyes fixed on me. I think that they never expected her to survive the second operation. But she held out, week after week, and then I did a very foolish thing. An invitation came from Sydney, Australia, to fly out and appear in Bobby Helpmann's "This Is Your Life." This is your life, what irony!

Kevin telephoned, urging me to go and saying it would make all the difference to Australian film production if I came in for a few days; there were people who wanted to discuss coproductions.

Pamela said, "Go! You must go, Michael! Australia has always brought us luck."

I flew out by Qantas. When I was in the studio rehearsing for the show that night, our doctor came on the telephone: "Return at once." I spoke to her at the cottage, where she had been moved, with two young nurses beside her bed. She was very weak, but she said, "Do a good show, and give Bobby my love."

Some hours later, the older of the two little nurses said to the other, "She's going, Maisie."

Her head fell back and her arms dropped, and the ring that I had given her slipped off her finger and rolled away across the boards; and I was thirteen thousand miles away in a huge hotel room and the lights of Sydney through the window in the background.

=

When we bought the cottages, we bought them on mortgage. I happened to have some money at that time, and Pamela was broke. I put up £1,500 for a mortgage in her name, and a lawyer's letter between our two lawyers was exchanged saying that we both owned the cottage and whoever died first, the other would inherit it. During the years when the payment became due whichever of us had enough money in our account paid the bill. When she knew she was dying, Pamela told me that she had borrowed about £1,500 from her sister and brother-in-law, and she was worried that she wouldn't be able to pay it back. So we made a new agreement, exchanging letters, saying that if she died, I would have the use of the cottage until my own death, when the title would revert to her sister or her family. When death is in the room, you don't argue with it, you sign on the dotted line.

As for life, it didn't seem worth living.

Her mother and sister and brother-in-law came. But they had no pity for me, only pity for themselves. Pamela lies in the corner of the churchyard of Avening Parish Church. She never liked cultivated flowers, so I planted primroses and snowdrops and rooted heather, all sweet, natural things. I wanted to bring a granite gravestone from the Western Isles, but the vicar wouldn't agree. He said all stone in the graveyard must be white, so there is a plain, white, stone, with plain PAMELA BROWN, and plain the date of her death. I would have liked to have inscribed on her tombstone:

A quiet woman is like still water under a great bridge

So for a year I was alone, except for Johnnie. But he was old, and an old dog is older than an old man. Death is very patient with an old dog. He comes up on him slowly. At first it's a stiffness in those black, feathery legs. Then it's shortness of breath, and the old dog finds that the path over the meadow from the village below is a bit steep for him, and he has to stop a couple of times and pretend to be looking at the view.

Then there comes the day when he can't manage the hill at all, the hill where he used to bounce up and down so cheerily. Now he has to stop and sit, and let his master pick him up and carry him to the gate of the cottage, where he struggles to be put down on the level pathway. At night, when he wants to go out to do his business and his master lets him out, he stays there and has to be called and found and carried in. He could no longer do it by himself.

That last night, instead of sleeping in his basket, he came over to where I was lying on the big sofa in the downstairs room, where I was spending the night. He lay down beside the sofa and slept next to me. He had never done this before. In the morning he suddenly woke up, stood up panting, then he made a rush across the room to where his water was in his trough by the kitchen door, and he collapsed with his mouth in the water. He was dead.

I buried him by the little oak tree on the edge of the road. The ground was very hard and stony, and with many tree roots, and it took me a couple of hours to make it deep enough, to keep his body safe from the badgers and the foxes, who would know all about it and would want to dig him up. But I could see where he lies from the window of the cottage.

Pamela's two Abyssinian cats, Ab and Syn, were still alive on the day she died. They must have been seventeen or eighteen years old, and were as wild and independent as ever. They lived in the boiler house. When Pamela died, Syn, the male cat, died too. Ab survived for another year. She had always treated me like an interloper, a stranger. But on the day she died, I brought her some liver. She couldn't eat it, but she licked my hand. Abyssinians are never wholly tamed. When Pamela was away in New York or Hollywood or wherever, she would leave them always with the same vet and his wife, in Wimpole Street, who adored them and for whom the cats showed some signs of affection. When Ab died, she was just skin and bones . . . just skin and bones.

Bad times followed. Pamela's relatives wanted their money back, and when I told them they would have to wait for it, they sued me. I had other debts, too. When I couldn't pay I was summoned to meet the local magistrate at Stroud to explain and I asked time, which he granted me. This seemed to me a very human way of dealing with misery and sorrow.

My *Graf Spee* book suddenly produced some German royalties, which enabled me to keep my head above water, but it looked as if I would lose the cottage. I went to see Chris Mann, who was practically the only one left of his wonderful office team. In his great days I had brought him all the independent producers, so that he handled most of them as well as many new ones. I offered to turn over certain rights to him in certain properties, but he refused. He said that once an agent starts that kind of thing for his client there is no end to it. He was right, of course.

Frixos came with me when I went to see Chris Mann, but he stayed downstairs. He didn't come in. But when I told him that Chris wouldn't help, he was incredulous. He couldn't believe it.

"But you made him hundreds of thousands of pounds, Michael! Can't he do this for you? It's your home, it's your life! You're a great man, you've had dozens of Academy Awards, you're famous! It's a disgrace!"

I said, yes, we had had four Academy Awards for The Archers' films, though personally I'd never had one myself, and we may have had a dozen nominations for the technical departments. We were walking along Davies Street and came into Berkeley Square. Suddenly, Frixos exploded: "Leave it to me. I'll get the money for you. Don't ask me where . . . just . . . I'll get it! I'll get it, if I have to steal it!"

I hadn't any plan. I had been like a zombie since Pamela died. We met Erwin Hillier coming out of a side street. He was glad to see me: "Meekee, Meekee!"

Nobody else ever called me "Meekee"—only Erwin.

"I've just come back from Africa, for Darryl Zanuck. I want to make a film in Russia. Are you free?"

"As the air."

"I will telephone you at your club in the morning. I must run. I have an appointment. Please, excuse me."

Erwin was always very polite, a true Continental, a true artist. I think that his photography on *I Know Where I'm Going!* is a high-water mark of black-and-white photography in the 1930s and '40s. It's so delicate and emotional, and he has complete control of every inch of the screen.

"Who was that?" said Frixos.

"Erwin Hillier. He's a great cameraman. He says he wants to make a film in Soviet Russia."

Frixos grunted: "Good for him."

This was not a night when Frixos felt tolerant of the establishment.

In the morning he had gone out before breakfast. Ikuko told me to wait for him, he was coming back. He reappeared in triumph.

"I have it! You can sleep well, Michael. I have it, the two thousand pounds! But don't give it to them all at once. Only give them half."

We all rejoiced, and then I pestered him with questions, where he had been. I suspected him of visiting his auntie or his uncle somewhere in Camden Town. He refused to tell me.

"I have my methods," he said grandly.

What a breakfast that was! I could breathe again.

"And what about your friend, Michael, this Hillier? Don't you want to make a film in Russia? Make a film about Stalin. He was a great man. When I was a boy in Cyprus, I used to pray for him."

"I dare say you did, but I don't want to go to Russia, and I don't want to make a film about Comrade Stalin. I wouldn't mind making a film about Diaghilev."

"Go to your club, Michael, and find out. Leave the money to me."

"I have another idea, Frixos. It's nearly forty years since I made *The Edge of the World*, on the island of Foula. You remember, it was the first film that I really wanted to make. It was my first good film. How would it be to revisit the island, and see what has happened in those forty years?"

Frixos was enthusiastic.

"You must do it, Michael. You must talk to the BBC. *I* will talk to the BBC. They would like such a picture. But who owns the rights? Who owns the film?"

"I do. That's one thing I'm very sure about. I would never give anybody else the negative of *The Edge of the World.*"

"Great! Great, Michael! You have your cottage, and we will all make a film in Russia."

And we did, but not with Erwin, and not for some years yet.

Frixos was right again. The BBC were interested in my *Return to the Edge of the World* film, and I went to see Mr. Alan Howden, head of Programme Acquisitions at Shepherd's Bush. They put up £15,000 to make it. I rushed out a script, and put out inquiries to find out how many of my actors were still alive. John Laurie was first choice, of course.

"Well, Michael, I'll do it, if I can. The doctor gives me two years."

"What?"

He tapped himself on the chest.

"Emphysema, Michael, it's slow but it's sure. But it doesn't show, so we might as well relive our green days together, Michael. You can count on me."

Niall MacGinnis was next. The beautiful, young fisherman from Foula, the loyal, puzzled Nazi sailor and baker of *49th Parallel,* the actor who had brought Martin Luther alive to the screen, had taken his medical degree and had almost given up acting altogether. He had married happily, had a son, and was second string in a medical practice in the Wicklow Hills, south of Dublin. I have written before how I found him there, one foggy evening with Frankie, and how, stumbling in the dark, we saw him through the window of the farmhouse, kicking the fire with his boot. I was dashed when I learned that he couldn't, or wouldn't, come back to Foula with me. The Niall MacGinnis that I remember would never say no to a friend.

"But you see, Michael, I'm not the Niall MacGinnis that you remember. I'm not the roaring boy in the fight on the trawler, who instructed you how to clean out the deep wound in my head with a toothbrush. I'm not the beautiful lover of Belle Chrystall, and of Geraldine Fitzgerald in *The Turn of the Tide.* You'll have to go without me, Michael"—with a slow smile—"and see if any of the boys on the island look like me."

Eric Berry was now a naturalized American. The clumsy young engineer from *The Edge of the World,* the discreet Dimitri, confidant of Lermontov in *The Red Shoes,* the cardinal from Albee's *Tiny Alice,* was still treading the boards, and was on tour with a musical play when I needed him. Oh, well!

Finlay, dear Finlay Currie, was dead, together with his wife, Maud, who used to sing at our concerts: "You are my honey, honeysuckle, I am your bee." They were on the road, in heaven. Those two old troupers could never settle down. What troupers they were! What an actor Finlay was, what a part he made out of the old fisherman in *I Know Where I'm Going!* and what power he brought to the part of the Hudson's Bay factor in *49th Parallel.* Hollywood had taken him up, this grand, six-foot-four, one-eyed saint, with his mane of hair and his thunderous voice, and he had played nearly every apostle in the calendar, before he stumped off and up those stairs with Maud panting behind him.

Grant Sutherland was next. The young catechist in *The Edge of the World,* the night watchman, Bob Bratt, of *The Spy in Black,* had given up acting and opted for business. He had made a success of it, and at the call to go to Foula his blood warmed and he escaped out of his accounting house to go with us. He was still the same young catechist who could preach for two hours without the book.

And Belle? Belle Chrystall? Well, she wouldn't do it. It's hard for a woman to admit that she is sixty. But I think that she made a mistake. I saw her jumping off a bus in Oxford Street the other day, a sprightly seventy. So that left Frankie, and me.

You may remember that in the film *The Edge of the World,* three people came to the island in a small yacht and put into Ham Voe. They were Niall MacGinnis, Frankie Reidy, and Micky Powell. Forty years later we were all kicking, but medicine had claimed MacGinnis, while Frankie was more beautiful than ever. It's the bones, you see, and the soul inside them. I was much the same, except that I had learned to act. In movies you do absolutely nothing, and the camera does it all for you. Frankie refused to go back to the island.

"Never go back," she said mutinously, shaking her mane, but she agreed to be in the film. It was up to me how I did it. We shot her close-ups at Melbury Road, two of them in the garden, two of them on the flat roof next door, to avoid the trees of Holland Park. There are no trees on Foula.

Now for the technicians. Bill Paton, born and bred in the Shetland Islands, refused to go back there. Probably he was afraid of being sued for breach of promise. Chief cameraman Ernie Palmer had passed on. A bright young 16mm Fujicolor crew took over picture and sound. I have left to the last the most important member of the crew: Syd Streeter.

In the book I wrote about the making of my film *The Edge of the World,** Syd was prominently featured; he was the Admirable Crichton. He was the master carpenter at the Joe Rock Studios, and we met for the first time in those studios while making *The Man Behind the Mask,* a thriller starring Tam Williams and dear Jane Baxter and Maurice Schwartz, of the Yiddish Art Theatre of New York. I noticed how remarkably disciplined he was. But that was all I could notice at the pace we were going in those days, to get our pictures made within the budget.

---

*The book was reprinted in paperback in 1990 by its original publisher, Faber and Faber. The original title, *200,000 Feet on Foula* (the amount of film exposed on the island), has been changed to *The Edge of the World.*

But in the next film with Joe Rock, my expedition north to make *The Edge of the World*, Syd came into his own. We were the amateurs, he was the professional. Besides being the master carpenter, who with his own hands took the roof off the church so that we could film in it, and then put the roof back on again, he also planned and built the base camp: five huts, with beds for twenty, and the main dining hut so well and solidly built and anchored to the stony ground that even 90- and 100-mile-an-hour winds couldn't budge them. He was also head of construction for the many harebrained enterprises on the edge of the precipitous cliffs and waterfalls that I initiated and he carried out without one fatality. And when we had a concert, which we did every Saturday night, Syd Streeter was always called upon to sing "Trees."

I've talked a lot about Syd in my book *200,000 Feet on Foula*, which I understand is being reissued by its original publishers, Faber and Faber, under the new title *The Edge of the World*, so I won't go on and on about him. I shall just say that at the sound of *Return to the Edge of the World* Syd sprang to attention. I offered him the job of associate producer. He took it at once.

"You know, I've got a ticker in my heart, Michael. So I'm not quite the man I was, but the doctor says I can go, so long as you don't ask me to build any submarines."

Submarines? Well, yes. Syd Streeter and David Rawnsley, the art director of *49th Parallel*, built a mockup of the submarine we used in the film in the dockyards of Halifax, Nova Scotia, and you can read about it in Volume I, and except for a brief period in the RAF, Syd had been with The Archers until we broke up. Who else but Syd Streeter should head the *Return to the Edge of the World?*

Well, we did it, but we went over budget, and Frixos had to come to the rescue again. I paid him back in rubles.

So there it is—two films in one—*The Edge of the World* and *Return to the Edge of the World. The Edge of the World* is in splendid black and white, and *The Return* is in equally splendid Fujicolor. But the two islands that are featured are not the same. Color does not add to the beauty or the truth of exterior scenes. It is color of one kind or another: Fujicolor, Technicolor, Eastman Color; beauty, but it is not truth. Truth lies in black and white, and it always did and always has.

On our second trip to Foula we had a small airplane, we had facilities that we wouldn't have dreamed of in 1936. We flew over seacliffs that were inaccessible to us in those days, and we marveled at the color of the island. But the film's colors were not the colors of the island; they were the colors of Fujicolor. The island, stern and wild and in black and white, had a character of its own. It was beautiful in an entirely different way.

Sometimes I think that all color is an illusion. Maybe that is why some of my films are different from other people's films, because I see them in the bones of black and white. How lucky I was to start with a master craftsman, a master artist like Rex Ingram, and work for three years in black and white on epic themes. Film technicians are always debating about black and white, but when the crunch comes they are afraid to fight it out with their backers, who only know, or think that they know, that the public desires color. The public knows very well the difference, but is not prepared to go to the bat about it.

So I learned one thing of importance from returning to the edge of the world: flesh and blood, "the pride of the eye, the blood that colors the inside arm" . . . all that's nothing; it's the bones beneath that matter.

But I have left Erwin Hillier in Berkeley Square. He came to see me at the Savile Club, and I took him up into the library, which is usually empty before lunch.

"Meekee, what do you know about Anna Pavlova?"

"Not much. I can tell you more about Karsavina. She wrote the book *Theatre Street,* you know, about St. Petersburg in the days of the Imperial Ballet; or Nadia Benois, she's Peter Ustinov's mother, you know; or Alexander Benois, "great uncle Shoura" Peter calls him. I knew Nikitina in Monte Carlo. I know Massine, and Lifar, and Bobby Helpmann. Bobby was in Pavlova's company in her last year. I know Margot Fonteyn, and Moira Shearer, and Mme. Rambert, and Dame Ninette de Valois . . . Anna Pavlova? Why?"

Erwin literally wrung his hands. I had never seen anybody do that before.

"Because I have been working for years to make a coproduction on the life of Pavlova, and now I've got Armand Hammer, the big American industrialist—you know, he is crazy about doing business with Soviet Russia—and I have been twice to Moscow, and now the Americans won't let me direct it! They say they want a big name for director. All this, while they've accepted the subject, and accepted me as the director, and now, suddenly, they want a name! You know what happened to *Bluebird,* * Meekee, with all those stars and with George Cukor as director. They gave him those awful studios in Leningrad where the roof leaks. George Cukor has always had the whole of MGM at his back. It was a disaster!"

"So I hear."

"Mosfilm know all about me and my work. They know how closely I work with Zanuck. They know that I shoot and direct all those big African locations, all those big exteriors, and I've spent all this time and money to set it up, and now they want a *name!*"

"Tough luck."

*The pioneering U.S.-Soviet coproduction based on Maeterlinck's play.

"Isn't it?"

"But what can I do?"

"Come with me! We will make the picture, together. They will accept your name. They've seen *The Red Shoes*. You gave me my first chance as a lighting cameraman, you know what I can do."

I looked at him doubtfully. Yes, I knew he could do it. Erwin is a splendid technician; but he was a difficult man on the set, just like I was. What would happen when we were together? What would happen when there was a clash! I said, "What's the billing?"

"Oh! Codirection, Meekee, codirection, of course . . . 'Directed by Michael Powell and Erwin Hillier.' "

I was very fond of Erwin. I admired him very much for his high standards, high ideals. We'd known each other ten years, twenty years. We both respected each other . . . but, codirectors? I wasn't sure whether that would work. I said, "Let me think it over; and meanwhile, stay to lunch."

Anna Pavlova was a name to conjure with, especially when she was associated with *The Dying Swan*, which Michel Fokine had set for her to the music of Saint-Saëns and which she had danced all over the world. For the first twenty years of the century she had the biggest name in show business; first of all as one of the chief ballerinas of the Russian Imperial Ballet, then with her own company.

When Diaghilev took Paris by storm in 1909 he invited her to go with that fabulous company, which included Stravinsky, Fokine, Karsavina, and a dozen others. Jean Cocteau, then a boy of eighteen, trumpeted their triumphs. Léon Bakst, with his wonderful costumes and fantastic colors, altered the ladies' fashions. And Nijinsky! What about Nijinsky! . . . that famous jump of his into the wings on the first night of *The Firebird*, which left the audiences applauding for ten minutes. This visit of Diaghilev's, with the pick of the Russian Imperial Ballet, was sensational. Ballet became Russian ballet forever after. The art of Europe has never been quite the same since! Rimsky-Korsakov, Tchaikovsky, Scriabin were now the great names.

I said to Erwin, "But it's a wonderful chance, Erwin! It's one of the great art events of the century. You should build the whole film around that Paris season in 1909—it changed the fashions, it changed the shape of the women . . ."

Erwin looked doubtful. I could see, already, that I frightened him.

"But there is so much more, Meekee . . . much more! You know, she toured all over the world . . . you know she went everywhere! She spoke to the Sphinx, she went to India, she went to Japan . . . it could be a wonderful film, Meekee."

"When did she die?"

"In 1931. You know that she had a house in Hampstead, with a tame swan in the pond in the garden."

"Of course, but she didn't die there, did she?"

"No, Meekee, she died when she was just starting a new tour at The Hague, in Holland, and when she died, the whole town was in mourning . . . the whole world!"

"Death of a swan, eh?"

"Yes, Meekee, *The Dying Swan* . . . that is what I want to call it."

I made a mental reservation. All very well for Mr. Saint-Saëns to call his lovely short piece *La Mort du Cygne*, but for a film title *Anna Pavlova* would be the best.

It was in this casual way that I became involved, willy-nilly, in the various battles that six years later regurgitated in the film *Anna Pavlova*, a Soviet Russian–Poseidon Films coproduction, which lost me the friendship of Erwin Hillier and opened a great career for Frixos Constantine. For when it was clear that the film would die of inanition unless it got a shot in the arm from one of us, Frixos declared that the only thing to do was to learn to speak and write Russian, and in two years he succeeded in doing that.

When I was in and out of London, and in his office at the end of the day, he would settle down for an hour's conversation with a Russian teacher, and I never knew him to break that rule. Gradually he reconciled the warring protagonists. Armand Hammer and his representatives were dropped. Erwin, game to the last but incapable of compromise, found himself dropped.

A Soviet director, one Emil Lotianou from Moldavia, was promoted to provide the necessary Sturm und Drang, which are inevitable when making a coproduction with either the Germans or the Russians. I found myself being drawn inexorably into Frixos's net, to be the English codirector of the film, bringing with me James Fox, one of the big little Foxes, of London's West End, son of Robert Fox, showman and agent. James would narrate as well as act, and he would play Victor d'André, the husband of Anna Pavlova and a necessary link and leitmotiv between the Russian and English audiences. The film also gave me the opportunity to get to know my future wife.

===

Meanwhile my prophecies to Imre were coming true. Kevin Gough-Yates, one of the top officers of the British Film Institute, adopted our cause and sponsored a limited retrospective, which stirred the pot of our reputation. Thanks to this we were "discovered," and seven years later, in 1978, Ian Christie, also of the BFI, organized a complete retrospective of all our films that could be found. We were fortunate in our negatives, because so many of our films had been in Technicolor, and had therefore survived.

In our good days, we had always presented a copy of our current film to the BFI. They, too, had taken care of them. Other members of our group of independent producers were equally worthy of revival, but their films were mostly in black and white, and at that time it was not clearly understood, even by film historians, that black and white was one thing and color was another, and that comparisons between the two were odious.

Meanwhile, David Thomson, of *A Biographical Dictionary of the Cinema*, had successfully proposed me to Dartmouth College as a candidate for the post of Senior Artist in Residence, an honorary and delightful compliment, which paid the artist a fee and lodgings for a whole term, in return for which the said artist was expected to give one or two lectures, make an appearance at any important functions, contribute to the fame and beauty of Dartmouth College, and in my particular case, to teach a class of aspiring film students—and if all this activity were to result in a film for the Dartmouth Archive, so much the better. I confided to David Thomson that I was in correspondence with Ursula Le Guin and that I would seek her permission to make a five-minute film of her novel *A Wizard of Earthsea*.

Ursula K. Le Guin is usually described as a science-fiction writer, but she is more than that. The three novels of which Ged is the principal character, *A Wizard of Earthsea*, *The Tombs of Atuan*, and *The Farthest Shore*, are usually lumped together with the Hobbit novels, with the egregious rabbits of *Watership Down*—but they are more than that. In style, in simplicity, in invention, her books rank with George Macdonald's *The Princess and the Goblin* and John Masefield's *The Midnight Folk*.

I met her, head on, in the *Times Literary Supplement*, where the editor had given her *Wizard of Earthsea* a half page:

> If a book as remarkable as this turns up in the next twelve months, we shall be fortunate indeed.
>
> The story tells of Ged, a bronzesmith's son on a mountainous island, who, when still very young, shows a natural gift towards wizardry. His aunt, a witch in a small way, begins to teach him this and that, starting with the core of all magic, that, to have power over any creature or thing you must first know its secret name.
>
> This was [his] first step on the way he was to follow all his life, the way of magery, the way that led him at last to hunt a shadow over land and far to the lightless coasts of death's kingdom.
>
> But, ignorant how to use what he has learnt, he almost destroys himself. . . . The great Mage of the region, Ogion of Re Albi, hears of the boy, restores him, names him with his secret name, and invites him to be his disciple. Yet even with this wise Master, whom he loves, Ged is impatient and rebellious

and almost wrecks himself once again by peering into the Mage's book, and studying the most proscribed of all runes, that of raising the dead. . . . He uses it to summon up from the unknown dark the Queen Elfarron, dead a thousand years. But something else besides the sad, faint glimmering lady slides out of the crack—a shapeless thing, which fights to enter Ged's body.

Ged lives, for the Archmage himself comes to save him, but he is scarred and changed. He takes small posts on humble islands, looking always for what he has loosed into the world, afraid to encounter it, afraid to lose its tracks. It is his old master who counsels him at last to turn pursuer.

It is doubtful if a more convincing and comprehensive account of a sorcerer's training exists anywhere in fiction outside the *Earthsea* chapters . . . and what comes out of them all is a new quest-story, an original allegory. Curiously, while there is almost nothing local or datable in its machinery, yet every piece of mage-advice seems immediate and topical. (Most learning skills and crafts that come our way are, after all, a form of wizardry.) One finds in *Earthsea* none of the private and scratchy hates, and theological quiddities that even a marvellous yarn cannot cover over in the stories of C. S. Lewis. The matter of the true and secret Name which every creature and thing possesses goes back into the furthest reaches of myth. (Was it not by this secret Name that Egypt's Ra first held then lost his power?) But it is as valid today as ever it was; need one point to its uses in the field of advertising and politics? The advice to change the role of pursuer and pursued: to look for the fear instead of running away from it, is again wholly sound. Nor is the warning against using magic needlessly and without considering its results (which may disturb the world's Equilibrium) a dictum merely for fairy tales.

There are many memorable passages . . . Ged's defeat of the great dragon of Pendor, not by butchery but by counter-moves of power, should be added to every dragon-anthology. . . . But the book is more than a sum of its parts. An image used by Ged himself about the boat he takes on one of his expeditions, comes to mind. Was it "illusion" that made it watertight, he was asked? Partly (he replies):

> because I am uneasy seeing the sea through great holes in my boat, so
> I patched them for the looks of the thing. But the strength of the boat
> was not illusion . . . but made with another kind of art, a binding spell.
> The wood was bound as one whole, one entire thing, a boat.

The book has this kind of wholeness.

Very few new authors had received such praise from the *TLS*, and this was a book published by Penguin, in paperback, ostensibly for children. This was obviously a big occasion, and I rushed out and bought the little book, and read it at a sitting.

It was wizard! The critic in the *TLS* had not oversold Ursula K. Le Guin. This was one of the great imaginative novels, and there were two more to come. All my good resolutions were forgotten. If I never made another film, and I clean forgot that I probably never would, I must make this one. It is me, me, me, in its style, and careful attention to detail, and its good manners.

I wrote to Mrs. Le Guin, telling her how good she was, and asking why her book was published as a children's book, by Penguin. She answered in a short, pert note: "Because Kaye Webb is a smart cookie." Note, for those who are not in the book trade, Kaye Webb is the brilliant and resourceful publisher who was, at that time, the Queen Penguin. I made a note to buy the two sequels that were promised, and put *A Wizard of Earthsea* on that shelf where all my projects jostle with one another, and prayed for the day when Ursula Le Guin and I would meet.

That had been some years ago, and although we had become pen pals we had never met. During these years the fame of The Archers spread. The retrospective of our films being planned in England by Ian Christie was to be followed by one at the Museum of Modern Art in New York. Frixos and Poseidon Films had taken over the *Pavlova* venture from Erwin, and I had accompanied Frixos twice to California to meet Jack Nicholson, Marlon Brando, Robert De Niro, and other fabled monsters, one or all of whom Frixos seemed to be planning for a leading part in his production.

On one of these trips we stayed at a hotel in the real old Hollywood, and I was able to walk down the road and see George Lucas's *Star Wars* and Steven Spielberg's *Close Encounters of the Third Kind* both on the same day.

On another occasion Frixos and I got involved in a party on fabulous Mulholland Drive, which winds its sinuous way along the Hollywood Hills, and where all the houses are fortified. I remember meeting our host carrying a tray with various sauces and bottles on it and saying, "What is your particular high?" And at one point I found myself picking my way through the shrubberies into one of the neighboring villas, where Jack Nicholson wanted to show us scenes that he had directed personally—I think the film was called *Going South.* Anyway, it consisted of shots of a gentleman riding south—not into the sunset—just south, getting smaller and smaller, and, so far as I was concerned, he could have kept on going. Frixos and I could never afford to stay more than a couple of days, so I never knew whether Jack ever finished his picture, or decided that he had gone far enough south and could turn west. In those days the name of Laker was great in the land, and it was possible to fly nonstop from Gatwick to L.A. for a derisory sum.

Now there was a new development in the career of The Archers. A theatrical producer in New York, one Wendell Minnick, wanted to make a Broadway musical out of our film *The Red Shoes,* and cables and letters started to fly to and fro between our agents and this prospective showman. Similar conversations with yet another optimistic showman are taking place now, in 1989.

I was beginning to be known in New York, if not in Hollywood, thanks mainly to Martin Scorsese, who spent his own money to bring a print of *Peeping Tom* over to the New York Film Festival, to the delight of the critics, who quoted all the awful English reviews. Because of that I got an invitation from Francis Coppola, maker of *The Godfather,* to join a select group of filmmakers in taking over and running one of the big, old studios, to be named the Zoetrope Studios, in Hollywood.

I also had an invitation from Toronto, to visit and work with a study group in Niagara Falls, and as I always had a soft spot for Canada I had accepted it. It also meant that I could stop off on my way from Niagara Falls, fly to Rochester, and from Rochester take a small plane to the airstrip at Dartmouth where David Thomson said he would meet me and put me up, and would arrange for me to meet the bursar next day and discuss the details of fees, income tax, and work permits, after which I could return to England and put the cottage in mothballs.

Later on, when I was more sure of my ground, I hoped to get Columba to join me, and go with me to Zoetrope Studios to join Francis Coppola and his group. After the showing of *Peeping Tom* in New York earlier in the year, Francis had asked me to dinner, and had come to meet me across the floor of the restaurant singing Sabu's song from *The Thief of Bagdad:*

> I want to be a bandit, can't you understand it?
> Happy as can be, that's the life for me.

He couldn't sing, any more than Sabu could, but it was obvious that his heart was in the right place, somewhere under his ample beard.

In Toronto I had two emotional experiences. The first was an old love— Paddy Browne. She had been the sweetest and funniest and almost the earliest of my loves, and you may catch a glimpse of her in the film *Contraband,* sometimes known as *Blackout,* starring Conrad Veidt and Valerie Hobson and made in the first year of the war. There is a sequence with Conrad Veidt searching for Valerie Hobson in a nightclub and Paddy is singing her signature tune, "Paddy, You're a Caution," and here she was, in Toronto, the life and soul of an artistic group. In the 1930s we spent all night making love, and now we spent it talking.

The second surprise was *Dante's Inferno.* One of the movie buffs said, "Didn't you work with Harry Lachman?," and when I admitted it, said, "Did you ever see *Dante's Inferno?"* I said that I had always wanted to. I had been in on the creation of the Witch's Sabbath in Rex Ingram's *The Magician,* based on Somerset Maugham's short novel, in which the portrait of the magician was based on Aleister Crowley. In the film Alice Terry has a vision in which she is raped by a faun, danced by Stowitts, who was one of Anna Pavlova's partners. It had been an elaborate sequence, but Rex had not made the most of it because he was so disappointed in Paul Wegener, the German actor who played the magician. They didn't get on at all. Rex had admired him in *The Golem.* He should have given him his head.

Anyway, in the end Harry Lachman designed and prepared most of the sequence, and ten years later, when he was becoming known in Hollywood, he persuaded his producer (I think it may have been Sol Wurtzel) to let him go to town on an imaginary sequence of a descent into hell, a visualization of the story of Dante's *Inferno,* which is being told to the leading character, played by Spencer Tracy. I'm not sure that I quite understand this rather involved explanation myself, but I hope that you do. Anyway, my acquaintance in Toronto turned out to be—guess what—a projectionist, a film projectionist, and he had a print of this sequence in mint condition, which he ran for me.

I had always known that projectionists nip off little bits of scenes that they rather fancy, and project them, but I had never realized that the larceny of sequences was on such a grand scale. Anyway, I can tell you that I recognized the origin of practically every shot in the sequence, only this time carried out with all the resources of a great studio, and directed by Harry Lachman.

=

I don't remember a thing about the seminar in Niagara Falls, and I don't expect that they remember anything about me—what is a seminar, anyway? But the rest of my program worked out, and late one autumn evening I landed on the pocket-sized airstrip that serves Dartmouth College. David Thomson was there to meet me, with his future wife, Lucy Gray. I was at home at once. I had fallen on my feet again. We started talking shop, and went on talking it until about two in the morning. Lucy cooked a magnificent dinner.

The next day we visited the bursar, who offered me the choice of either the winter term or the summer term. Of course, I said the winter. What's the good of being in New Hampshire in the summer? It was agreed that I should arrive on December 30, 1978, which suited me, because Wendell Minnick, who had his heart set on making *The Red Shoes* into a musical, had asked Emeric and me to be his guests at a New Year's party that he and his wife and two sons were giving at their home in Westchester County.

"You take the local plane from Dartmouth," he said, "which flies direct to

La Guardia Airport, and my driver will meet you there, and bring you out to the house."

I accepted for both of us, but I didn't think that Emeric would come. He was keen enough on the idea, and promised that if things developed he would come to New York later.

Dartmouth has great charm. The campus is intimate and leafy, with great trees. It is set upon rising ground. The Inn is set back to back to a magnificent theatre and cinema. The high street leads naturally into and out of the town, down a slope to the splendid, rushing Connecticut River, the boundary between New Hampshire and Vermont.

David Thomson had his own apartment. It was a good-sized block, built of red brick, and he had excellent storage facilities. Too good for me, by the way, because I had brought my cherished print of *49th Parallel* with me to show the class, and I never saw it again.

The apartment destined for me was on a road lined with trees, and was in a block that contained perhaps eight apartments in all. Mine was on the ground floor. It looked battered and was comfortable. I was very happy there. I wrote or read every morning, and watched the students wend their weary way up the hill to work. I was reading every morning, the second volume of *Les Misérables*, and it was there that I started to write my autobiography. I would never find a better place to start it.

There were only ten to twenty men and women in my class, so I had an easy time of it. I soon persuaded David to let us write a script of Ursula Le Guin's *Earthsea* novel, and design and shoot it during the term. After all, to try and tell a two-hour book in five minutes must teach a young student a lot about construction. I told Ursula Le Guin what we were doing, of course, and she was delighted, but not so her agent in Hollywood. However, she calmed down and was more reasonable when I explained it was only an academic exercise.

But the highlight of my time at Dartmouth was meeting Lillian Gish! I told her how I felt about D. W. Griffith, and then we both cried. She said it was only about twenty miles downstream that, in the depths of the winter, with ice six feet thick in the river, they had shot those wonderful scenes in *Way Down East*, where the heroine drifts down on an ice floe and Richard Barthelmess, that hero of heroes, rescues her and carries her ashore.

Have you seen the famous scene in *Way Down East*? Don't worry if you haven't. It is just as exciting to hear about it as to see it, and Miss Gish gave me a cardboard booklet containing a key ring. Attached to the ring was a piece of plastic that enclosed the stamp that the United States Post Office issued in commemoration of the great D.W., a recognition, and a stamp, which she had to fight for for many years before she triumphed. But then

Lillian Gish is like that. She never gives up. On the booklet she wrote in her own hand this little note:

Dear Michael Powell,

Our meeting seemed only a second, but the joy endures. May the keys on this ring always open doors of happiness for you.

With fondest wishes, always,

Lillian Gish
March 1980

I was seventeen in 1922 when I saw Lillian and Dorothy Gish in *Orphans of the Storm*. Under D.W.'s direction the extras did a magnificent job, led by Monte Blue as Danton. Rex Ingram, when he made *Scaramouche* from Rafael Sabatini's novel a couple of years later, made an elegant job of the assembly sequence, and of the Battle of the Louvre. He had a strong sense of period. Already I was beginning to compare one style against another, and to take notice of how the director made his point—in Ingram's case a personal creation, in Griffith's a sort of stagy realism that gave great opportunities to the actors.

Dartmouth lies off the beaten track, as so many good universities do in the U.S.A., whether by accident or design I am not sure. Thelma claims that at Cornell University, where she spent four years, while the soft stuff in her brain was hardening, the students there joked that Ezra Cornell, the founder of the university, stated grimly that his college would be near enough to New York to claim some shreds of civilization, and far enough away to keep the students with their noses in their books.

Dartmouth was a like case, so although the little light airway service now meant that New York was within an hour's journey, there was lots of social activity, and as a mysterious senior artist in residence I was included in all the goings-on. But on my second night at the college, on New Year's Eve, I was already playing truant. I had taken the airbus to La Guardia Airport, where Wendell Minnick's driver, as predicted, met me and drove me by the Merritt Parkway to his house in the Westchester woods. It was a two-hour drive, and one that I was to know very well later on. But at the moment all I got was an impression of the endless, beautiful parkway and our headlights illuminating the naked trees.

The Minnick household was humming when I arrived, and I was introduced to my sleeping bag, where I would sleep on the floor. Wendell Minnick was tall, dark, and shy but obviously a businessman, or at any rate a promoter. His wife, Vicky, was also tall, dark, and better-looking than Wendell.

She was an actress in television. My driver had told me, rather mysteriously, that she was his favorite "soap" actress. The two boys, round about ten or twelve years old, were tall and good-looking too; altogether, a very present- able family. It was evident to me that whatever soap Vicky Minnick was selling, it wasn't soft soap.

It was a handsome, two-story house in a clearing in the chestnut woods, with trails all over the hills around. There was a brook, and a pond on the little estate, and some good outbuildings, which I envied. Nobody got much sleep. It was a good party, with the usual family row backstage that besets all New Year's parties. Wendell drove me back into town in the morning and talked all the way about his plans for *The Red Shoes*. He had two very talented young men he wanted to work on the musical. One was a choreographer and dancer with the New York City Ballet, the other was a teacher at Juilliard. He said I would meet them later. This all sounded very good to me, and it was agreed that I come up to town again, after settling into my post at Dartmouth.

So now I had two reasons for coming to New York: to arrive at an agree- ment over the Broadway production of *The Red Shoes*, and to keep in touch with Martin Scorsese. This pocket dynamo was to become my mentor. With his own money, he had helped arrange the final finance for a distribution contract in the U.S.A. for *Peeping Tom*, after its enthusiastic reception at the New York Film Festival.

Throughout Marty had behaved like a friend and more than a friend, a brother. He could never quite believe that the living, breathing Michael Powell was sitting or more likely walking about the room, talking, moving; and I could hardly believe that this gifted porcupine, bristling with likes and dislikes, could really be the Martin Scorsese of *Mean Streets*, *Taxi Driver*, and *Raging Bull*.

Marty and his editor were cutting *Raging Bull* now, in Marty's apartment on the thirty-sixth floor of the Galleria, an extravagant and unlikely apart- ment house on Fifty-seventh Street, where there was a continual turmoil of friends and fans arriving, jabbering, and departing. Isabella, Ingrid Bergman's daughter by Roberto Rossellini, was Marty's wife at the time. Film flowed out of the bedroom, across the sitting room, and into the bathroom, and back again. There was no difference between day and night.

Frixos, marveling at all these developments, dropped in whenever he could wangle his way to New York. Emeric came later and said that it reminded him of the very worst days at UFA in Berlin, when Erich Pommer's film business was taken over by the intellectuals. Irwin Winkler, the producer of *Raging Bull*, kept wandering in and out, wondering. He had also produced *New York, New York*.

Marty's editor was a woman. In America the women had been very quick to specialize in the editorial side of film production, much more than in England. It's nothing to do with special sensibility, or anything like that. It's just that in America women are more ruthless about getting power. Marty's editor was an old friend, and a young woman, called Thelma Schoonmaker. Like every film buff of a certain age she had been at Woodstock and had ended up being the chief editor for the film of that event, a position that had taught her to deal with almost any emergency that can happen to a can of film. The guest bedroom in Marty's apartment had become her editing room, and she and Marty were chopping this masterpiece to bits without turning a hair. The room was full of bins and film trims, and film was draped around the room and into the bathroom. Elsewhere in this editorial nightmare you never knew whom you would find and where, but Thelma was always in the same place, and always had time for a chat. I had found a friend.

And then there was Robert De Niro. James Hanley wrote a book, and a play, entitled *Say Nothing*. Marty should have bought it and made it with Bob. The combination of the title with Robert De Niro would have been irresistible. Can't you see it up there on the screen?

Robert De Niro

in

SAY NOTHING

He had fine features, but he wasn't beautiful. He had fine eyes, but they didn't seem to be looking at anything in particular. He could change color, and shape, just like a chameleon, and it interested him to do it. He looked at other people, he spoke to them, he even answered sometimes, but he was really looking all the time at himself. He had two sides to his head, and he gave nothing away. He confided in nobody except Marty, and Marty trusted nobody but Bob.

Together they took me down to Little Italy, to the mean streets where Marty was born and brought up. They hailed a taxi and said, "We'll tell you where to go."

The driver said, "You're Robert De Niro, aren't you?"

Bob said, "Yeah, could you take us to the East Side?"

The man said, "You were in *Taxi Driver*. Can you drive a taxi, honest?"

Bob said, "Yeah, could you take us to Fourteenth Street?"

The driver drove with his head over his shoulder. Several people leapt for safety, with a scream of protest.

"Take a right," said Bob.

"Right?" said the taxi driver.

"Right," said Bob. "Now take a left. When we get to the corner, stop."

Marty said, "This is where we shot the graveyard sequence."

"Drive on," said Bob.

"Okay," said the driver.

"Make a right," said Bob. "Take another right," said Bob. "There it is. That's where the guy got shot, do you remember?"

"Where do we go now?" said the driver.

"Straight on," said Bob.

"How did you know about that house, where the women are?" asked the driver.

"Take a left," said Bob, laughing, "and shut up."

"That's my old school," said Marty.

It was like reliving some ancient tale of blood, some battle that took place in the misty past and was brooded upon by the heroes who had survived the holocaust.

Bob is a serious actor. Like Laurence Olivier, his thoughts, his personality, his physical peculiarities, are secret; he is only interested in being someone else, in successfully appropriating another man's emotions and physical peculiarities—this is their gift, and their pleasure.

But, you say, *I thought actors were show-offs.*

You're talking about show-offs, I reply. (Don't worry, I won't name you!) When Bob sets about losing weight, or putting it on, for a part, he does it with the consciousness, and the single-mindedness, of a Savonarola. When Larry Olivier played Mr. Puff in *The Critic* and *Oedipus Rex* on the same night he achieved the impossible, but it was only possible because he had a sense of mischief. When Bob De Niro had to put on forty pounds—do you hear that?—for the final sequences of *Raging Bull,* when Jake La Motta, the great champion, the man who could take it, becomes the laughingstock of his own nightclub, when all Jake La Motta's fearful fights had been recorded, on that very day Bob started to eat pasta, and he went on eating four meals of pasta a day until he put on forty pounds and they shot the final sequence.

I was shocked. It wasn't necessary, it wasn't right, it was a very risky thing to do. But Bob is the kind of actor who when he plays Othello blacks himself all over. When I think of all that pasta! Yuk! I was back in England when they planned this sequence, and Marty asked me how I managed Roger Livesey's weight gain in *Colonel Blimp.* How did we turn a young, fit, springy, guardsman into an old, pink, sweating walrus? I told him it was partly makeup, and partly by using doubles. But Bob insisted on doing it for real. That's the kind of actor he is—the kind of man he is, too.

This was the time that Marty slammed the door of the hired limousine on Frixos's hand, and Frixos never made a sound. He was lucky not even to lose the nail. I don't think that Marty knows about it to this day. Frixos wouldn't want him to. And this was the time that I went with Frixos in a huge yellow

New Hampshire. Dartmouth is an exceptionally friendly and generous university, and I enjoyed every minute of my time there. The atmosphere was relaxed and aristocratic, and there seemed to be friendly groups meeting, forming, and dissolving, always new arrivals and new acquaintances. I seem to remember that there were love affairs. There was one, in particular, that might have caused a peck of trouble, if all the parties involved had not had a sense of humor. Such experiences, such memories, are the salt of life, or should I say its perfume? When love is turned to friendship, when you dip into that packet of letters, you search in memory for a name, and then a face dimly lit in the room comes to your mind, and you lock the letters away, smiling.

My class agreed to go along with my fantasy of making a potted version of Ursula Le Guin's *Earthsea* trilogy, but wanted to know what their credits would be at the end of the term. I said that they would all, including me, be producers, and would get ninety out of a hundred, which is what most producers get away with. A romantic, rough-looking young Jewish boy played the hero Ged, and we borrowed a little dancer from a ballet class in the town, to play the High Priestess. When we actually started shooting, our activities, because of the costumes, provoked some interest, and several of the technical departments got involved in sound effects. Besides that, there was an exhibition, and we showed some films, and the poster department of the art department photographed me and turned me into a poster, which is one of the best portraits I have ever had. I am scowling.

So long as Marty was editing, I knew that I could get him for a chat anytime after midnight. He usually started work about two in the morning; Dan, the cook, answered the phone, and sometimes Marty's editor, who never seemed to sleep. I knew her as "Oh, hello!"

"Oh, hello, it's me, Michael Powell."

She always said, "Yes, I know."

I could picture her pale face, shining in the darkness in the apartment with the sound of the flatbed editing machine chattering in the background. I asked her about Marty's use of color in *Raging Bull.* The home movies were to be in color, home-movie color, and the opening of the film, where Robert De Niro does a slow, thoughtful, creative dance to his doom, would have red titles over it. But the film was basically in black and white, and she told me that they all blamed it on me. When I had seen the early tests of Bob training as a fighter, and the red boxing gloves, I said, "There's something wrong about the color of the gloves." And Marty had said, "You're right! The film should be in black and white."

Thelma was nice to chat with. Her voice was low and sweet, "an excellent thing in woman," and our chats became longer and longer, when Marty was not there. I had arranged with Francis Coppola that when term ended I would fly over to Zoetrope and look the joint over. It was a whole city block on Santa Monica. We discussed production plans.

The newly named Zoetrope Studios were the old Edward Small Studios in the real original Hollywood, not far from where there used to be the Metro lot. These were the studios where Alex Korda took refuge with *The Thief of Bagdad* to finish, when there was fire over England. Here he had stayed for a couple of years, making *The Jungle Book* and *Lady Hamilton* (which got him a knighthood from Churchill) with Vivien Leigh and Laurence Olivier. Francis told me that when he used to go to school, he and his brother, they crossed the studio where *The Jungle Book* was being made, and once all the monkeys had escaped and there was havoc all around the district. No wonder he loved *The Thief of Bagdad*, which was finished there by the three Kordas.

Columba, coming from England, joined me at Dartmouth for a week and then flew with me to Hollywood. He had been a conundrum all his life to those who were set in authority over him, which includes his father, mother, and brother. His patron saint, St. Columba, is also said to have had a hot temper. He built the church and monastery on Iona and converted the Scots, and made a thorough job of it. Colonsay, Columba's isle, is the Kiloran of *I Know Where I'm Going!*, and my Columba is the young Mark in *Peeping Tom*. I love him dearly.

At L.A. we were met by a limousine so big that Columba said with a giggle, "You can roller-skate in it." I was expected, but not Columba, and this caused a panic. We ended up sharing a bedroom in Dean Tavoularis's* house. I should explain that Francis's headquarters in California were in San Francisco, and his home was in the Napa Valley, where he was coproprietor of a vineyard. Francis and George Lucas shared this kingdom between them. Francis had his head office in an incredible skyscraper in downtown San Francisco, called the Sentinel Building. It soared up to a point like a needle, and always looked like it was about to fall down. It reminded me of Maurice Leblanc and one of his Arsène Lupin stories.

Zoetrope was already in production on a new Dashiell Hammett film, starring Freddie Forrest as Hammett himself—the title: *Hammett*. It was being directed by Wim Wenders. They had already shot about a third of it, in San Francisco, and Dean Tavoularis was in downtown L.A. when I arrived, turning L.A. into San Francisco's Chinatown. It was a glorious muddle. Half

---

*Production designer, mainly associated with Francis Ford Coppola, whose early work included *Bonnie and Clyde*, *Zabriskie Point*, and *Little Big Man*. For Coppola he designed (among others) the three *Godfather* films (winning an Oscar for *Godfather II*), *The Conversation*, *Apocalypse Now*, *One from the Heart*, and *Rumble Fish*.

the unit were in San Francisco cleaning up, and people were continually taking fast airplanes to meet someone else where they weren't wanted.

However, I rather approved of this. It put people in a good humor, and Columba, of course, was delighted. I proposed to leave him in L.A. with the few hundred dollars I could scrape together. He wanted to go to Colorado. From there he hoped to get a lift to Santa Fe and visit Mexico. I had to get home to see if the cottage was still there, and meet Frixos and discuss his production plans for *Anna Pavlova*.

He was getting alarmed. The script had been written, and rewritten, a couple of times. Moscow and Paramount were financing the picture, and Emil Lotianou was ready to direct. But I was to codirect it, and make sure the picture would go in the English market. And now here I was gone Zoetrope.

I reassured Frixos that all would be well, and after all, it couldn't do him any harm that I was associated with such an exciting, new, young venture, with a producer-director like Francis. I was coming home now, and would return to Zoetrope in September. I was to be "senior director in residence" at Zoetrope Studios. After nearly fifty years, I was going to be living and working in Hollywood—the real, old, early Hollywood of my dreams, the Hollywood of Rex Ingram, the Hollywood of Erich von Stroheim, of John Ford and William Wyler, the Hollywood of D. W. Griffith, Douglas Fairbanks and Mary Pickford and Charles Chaplin, of Mack Sennett and his bathing beauties, and of the Keystone Cops, of Laurel and Hardy, of Buster Keaton, of the wild Westerns, and of the even wilder Sunset Boulevard. This was the Hollywood where my old friend Grant Whytock remembered seeing Rex Ingram strolling down through the olive groves to work at the old Metro Studios in the valley. This was the Hollywood of the Brown Derby, of Ramon Navarro, of Rudolph Valentino, and Alice Terry . . . This was where I came in.

≡

I should really end this autobiography here, but I have a reason not to. In fact two reasons: I haven't summed up the facts and fancies of my partnership with Emeric Pressburger; and I'm in love, I'm in love, I'm in love, I'm in love, I'm in love with a wonderful girl—a statement that Mark Twain would have described as "interesting but tough."

Ladies first.

When Marty went on his world tour, selling *Raging Bull* and color negative preservation, he took his editor with him, for they had finished the stupendous job of editing the film. If Bob De Niro had been allowed to have his own way he would have fought all the fights, including all the scraps with Sugar Ray Robinson, for real. But when Marty pointed out to him that by the time they finished he would be punch-drunk, or dead, he consented to listen. *Raging Bull* is one of the most romantic films ever made. There are hundreds of cuts in the fight scenes, hundreds.

"What are we shooting today?" Bob would ask Marty, on reporting to work.

"Hitting you on the left side of your head, all morning," was the answer. "We'll go on hitting you on the right side of your head, in the afternoon, too."

"Good."

The painstaking care, and the vivid imagination of the director, paid off. The editing of *Raging Bull* was nominated for an Oscar, and got it. Bob De Niro was nominated for an Oscar, and got it. Martin Scorsese was nominated for an Oscar, and didn't get it. No sense in that, you say, and you are right.

Raging Bull had been editing in New York, where Marty was already preparing his next film, *King of Comedy*, to star Robert De Niro and Jerry Lewis. I was at Zoetrope, writing this autobiography, and saw Marty and his gang again on the day of the Oscars. I went to meet them at their hotel. They were milling around like a flock of sheep, several of them in hysterics. I saw a familiar face among the crowd, a face that was glad to see me, an eager face. She seemed to know me. Where had I seen her before? I associated her with light and shadow, and whirring machines, and a small hour in the morning on Fifty-seventh Street.

That day someone tried to assassinate Ronald Reagan and the Oscars were canceled. I had no tickets for the Oscars, but had been invited by Marty and Bob to their party after the event. I went to the restaurant about one o'clock in the morning, expecting to find them all there. The place was bolted and barred. It didn't just look shut, it looked as if it was shut forever.

But I am used to making a hash of my appointments, and I assumed that I was the one who was wrong. At Zoetrope in the morning I was told what had happened, and that the Oscars were on again that night, and Marty's and Bob's party too. But by this time I was moody, and I didn't go to the party. I enjoyed my misery. It was intensified by the fact that I had no telephone in my apartment.

At Zoetrope in the morning I learned that Bob De Niro had won his Oscar, and that Marty had been passed over. The editor of the film also got an Oscar. Her name was Thelma Schoonmaker. The telephone rang. A familiar voice.

"I thought you'd like to know that Marty was really upset that you weren't at his party last night. It was a good party. We were all looking for you."

The way that she said "we" started a computer clicking in my body.

I said, "Would you like to come to dinner, and tell me about it?"

She said, quite simply, "Yes."

I made an Irish stew. I congratulated her on her Oscar. She was outraged.

"I didn't deserve it, and you know I didn't deserve it. Marty should have gotten the Oscar, not me."

I walked down with her after dinner to Highland, and we picked up a passing taxi. I said, "What about tomorrow night?"

She hesitated. "I've got to go to San Francisco. I'm expected there." Then she said, "I'll go in the morning, the next morning."

She had hired a car. She picked me up and drove us to Venice, to a Thai restaurant that she said was very good. By this time signals were flying to and fro, and it didn't matter whether the food was good or not. It was good.

I seem to remember that we had left the car parked under a tree close to the restaurant. We got into it. She was in the driver's seat and sat there, looking straight ahead. All of a sudden, she was in my arms. All my loneliness and resentment, and frustration with Francis, with Zoetrope, exploded into love. It was a complete surrender, from both of us, one to the other.

After a long, long, time underneath the tree, I said, "Let's go home."

I felt as if it were a newly minted phrase, one that had never been said before. Luckily the boulevard was nearly empty. We left the car in the road and went to the apartment.

"Off with your clothes!"

We made love all night.

When Marty heard about it, in the cutting room, he cleared his throat and said, "I'm only going to say this once. . . . I think it's great about you and Michael."

Who would have thought that when I joined Rex Ingram's Hollywood company in the south of France, fifty-five years ago, that I would find, fifty years later, in that same Hollywood, the love of my life.

Some years later, after Frankie's death, we were married, on May 19, 1984. Columba was best man at Holy Cross Church, in Avening. When we knelt at the altar, the congregation observed with interest that Thelma had a lucky penny taped to the sole of her shoe (it had been put there by the salesman who sold her the shoes to wear to the Oscars) while the groom and the best man both had holes in theirs.

=

I have said that I am going to say a lot more about my partnership and friendship with Imre, but I'll leave it to him to say the last word.*

The other day, Thursday, February 5, 1988, I paid a visit to Emeric Press-

---

*Michael was not with Emeric when he died, but he wanted the book to end with the two of them together. He created this imaginary episode from details of an earlier visit.

burger. It was fifty years since we first sighted each other, in the canteen in Denham Studios, and I felt something ought to be done about it. As usual, I had to go to him and not he to me; always a host, never a guest, that was Emeric's statement to the world. He was a Jew, born in Miskolc, Hungary, on December 11, 1902. That was sufficient reason. You could have friendship, but only if he chose to give it. You could not claim it. He sought love, and often inspired it, but he was incapable of humility, and without humility, love withers on the stem. As a friend and partner, throughout our long lives, he was the better man of the two.

You have to lay aside a whole day if you want to have a short chat with Imre, so I spent the night at the Savile Club, and thought of him at breakfast the next morning. Conversation at breakfast at my club is unthinkable. Every head at the long, polished table is buried in a newspaper, to the frustration of American members from the Coffee House or the Player's Club in New York, who try to start a conversation and get snubbed.

I caught the 9:30 train from Liverpool Street Station to Ipswich, which I believe to be the capital of the county of Suffolk, and which I have known from babyhood as a tongue twister:

> Which switch is the next switch for Ipswich?
> It's the Ipswich switch that I require. . . .

It goes on for a lot more tongue-twisting lines, but I am sure that this sample will satisfy you. It is, on the whole, a tedious journey. British Rail does not actually claim that it is the worst journey in the world, but they do not claim it to be the best, either. If you are visiting Emeric, you get out at Ipswich, and in the days of old you were met by him, in his ancient Porsche, which dated back at least twenty years, to his sojourn at Thiersee, in Austria.

But today I take a taxi, and am driven through the quiet lanes of Suffolk and Norfolk, to the village of Debenham, which has its name from the River Deben, which has its source near Emeric's cottage, in the village of Aspall, famous for its apple juice, a fact that must be very painful for a beer drinker. He is feeding the goldfish in the pond in the garden as I arrive at his white-painted gate, ornamented with the sign "Shoemaker's Cottage."

I told the taxi driver to get lost, and come back for me at three.

I think that I have described Emeric's cottage before, and I have probably made it clear that it is a little number that looks as if it had been run up by the Brothers Grimm, of the celebrated fairy tales. It is small and sturdy, like Emeric. It has a thatched roof, unlike me and Emeric. It has latticed windows and crooked chimneys, and all the fixings of a fairy tale. It also had locks, bolts, and bars on everything, and it is a risky business to sally out for a morning stroll if you are staying with Emeric, because everything shuts behind you with a click and a bang that is final, and you can only get in again by rapping on the kitchen window, where Emeric is busy preparing a boiled beef for lunch. I always laughed at the way Emeric had everything bolted and barred, but he was very serious about it; a relic of the pogroms.

We eat a stupendous lunch, and he has to caution me, several times again, about my handling of the bottle of beer from Prague.

"You don't understand, Michael. You must uncork the bottle, which is very cold. The beer is very cold, too, of course. And, then you leave the bottle on the table for three or four minutes before you pour it out. That gives time for the foam to rise. Yes . . . s . . . s . . ."—deliciously draining the last few suds in his glass, and delicately wiping the top of his lip. "You will never be a beer drinker, Michael; not a serious beer drinker."

Although it's so early in the year, it's quite warm on a sunny afternoon, and we drag out two canvas chairs and sit down on the crazy paving, outside the cottage. We don't talk, much. There is no need of it. Our lives and fortunes are so intertwined that we have hardly any news to give each other. As we sit musing about this, there is a crash and a cry in the tall, thick hedge between the cottage and the farmhouse next door.

"What the hell is that?" I inquire, mildly.

"It's only my old pheasant," says Emeric. "He lives there, in the hedge, and he's probably after one of his wives. Don't you remember? You've often seen him under the apple tree in the little orchard, there . . . and look, there he is now."

Sure enough, a fine, big cock pheasant, in full color, with his tail erect, was marching across the grass, keeping a beady eye on us, but otherwise not alarmed at all.

"I'll get him some corn in a minute. That's what he's waiting for. What news, Michael, of those crazy people who want to make a Broadway musical out of our *Red Shoes?*"

"They seem serious about it."

We both smiled.

"Imagine, Michael, if Hans Christian Andersen had not written *The Red Shoes* somewhere around 1850, this cottage would not be called Shoemaker's Cottage, and we would not be sitting here together."

"What about the pheasant? He would be here, and the cottage would be here. Things go on, you know, Imre, even though we are not there to see it."

The old boy looked at me.

"If you have found that out, Michael, you've found out a very great deal. And now, I will tell you what I have found out. We are amateurs."

"I beg your pardon?"

"You know that all these writers on film that you have set to writing about us—you've written about it yourself, in your own autobiography— you know, Michael, how they are always trying to explain: 'Written, Produced and Directed by Michael Powell and Emeric Pressburger'? You and I know what it means, but they don't. They think there is some secret about it. I'll tell you what it is, Michael. The only secret about it is that we are amateurs. When films were silent, films were an art. We all know that. We all knew that. But when they learned to talk, people tried to turn them into a business. Telling a story, Michael, is not a business. It is an art, and we are different from other artists, because we were left alone by Arthur Rank for nearly ten years to go our own sweet way, thinking we were professionals. But we were amateurs, Michael. That's why our films were different from other people's, and now that I know that, I can die happy. And now I must go and get some corn for that damn bird, who is kicking up such a row."

"Let me go. I know where you keep the corn: in the garage, in a tin. As for being amateurs, I'm not sure you're not right. In fact, now that I think about it, I'm sure you're right. We're amateurs, not Archers."

"That's right, Michael. We shouldn't try to reform the world. It is enough that we remain amateurs."

I walked out to the garage. Of course, it was locked. Everything was locked and bolted. I started laughing, and walked back. Emeric was still slumped in his chair, watching the pheasant. At sight of me, the big bird scuttled off into the hedge.

"When I get back to London, I'll go to the office of Who's Who, and ask them to alter our two entries to 'Recreation: films. Profession: amateur.' What do you say?"

But Emeric Pressburger was dead.

=

For the record, Imre Pressburger died on February 5, 1988, and is buried in Aspall, almost in sight of the little thatched cottage that he loved so well.

> For he might have been a Roosian,
> A French, or Turk, or Proosian,
> Or perhaps Italianne,
> Or perhaps Italianne,
> But, in spite of all temptations
> To belong to other nations

He remained an Englishman
An En-gli-sh-man.

   The time is noon. The place, Fifty-second Street, corner of Eighth Avenue, New York City. The date is August 25, 1989. It's the first day of fall weather. It is very clear and quite cool, and a pretty day.

MICHAEL POWELL

A FILMOGRAPHY

PARTNERS: Michael Powell (left)
and Emeric Pressburger
(right) on the set of
Oh . . . Rosalinda!!
Between them is Alastair
Dunnett, then editor of *The
Scotsman.*

Compiled by Ian Christie and Markku Salmi

NOTE: This filmography lists all the known released films on which Michael Powell was credited as director, producer, and/or supervisor. It does not include all his television work or any of his private, uncredited, or pseudonymous work.

Main credit abbreviations are as follows:

d.—director. *p.c.*—production company. *p.*—producer. *exec. p.*—executive producer. *assoc. p.*—associate producer. *p. sup.*—production supervisor. *p. manager*—production manager. *asst. d.*—assistant director. *sc.*—screenplay. *scen.*—scenario. *adapt.*—adaptation. *dial.*—dialogue. *addit. dial.*—additional dialogue. *cin.*—cinematography. *addit. cin.*—additional cinematography. *cam. op.*—camera operator. *sp. ph. effects*—special photographic effects. *sup. ed.*—supervising editor. *ed.*—editor. *asst. ed.*—assistant editor. *p. designer*—production designer. *sup. a.d.*—supervising art director. *a.d.*—art director. *asst. a.d.*—assistant art director. *set dec.*—set decoration. *m.*—music. *m.d.*—music director. *sd.*—sound. *sd. rec.*—sound recordist. *cost.*—costumes. *choreo.*—choreography. *t.s.*—date of trade show. *rel.*—date of release. *U.K./U.S./other dist.*—original distributor in the country named.

Wherever possible, credits are given in the order and style that appears on the film. Additional information is in square brackets. The country of production is Great Britain unless otherwise stated. Films marked with an asterisk are not at present known to exist in any accessible form.

Powell and Pressburger Collaborations

The Spy in Black · 1939

d.—Michael Powell. [p.c.—Harefield.] presented by—Alexander Korda. p.—Irving Asher. [asst. d.—Patrick Jenkins.] sc.—Emeric Pressburger, from Roland Pertwee's adaptation of a novel by J. Storer Clouston. cin.—Bernard Browne. sup. ed.—William Hornbeck. ed.—Hugh Stewart. asst. ed.—John Guthrie. p. designer—Vincent Korda. a.d.—Frederick Pusey. m.—Miklós Rózsa. m.d.—Muir Mathieson. sd.—A. W. Watkins.

Conrad Veidt (Captain Ernst Hardt), Sebastian Shaw (Cdr. Davis Blacklock), Valerie Hobson (Joan, the schoolmistress), Marius Goring (Lt. Schuster), June Duprez (Anne Burnett), Athole Stewart (Rev. Hector Matthews), Agnes Lauchlan (Mrs. Matthews), Helen Haye (Mrs. Sedley), Cyril Raymond (Rev. John Harris), George Summers (Captain Ratter), Hay Petrie (engineer), Grant Sutherland (Bob Bratt), Robert Rendel (Admiral), Mary Morris (Edwards, the chauffeuse), Margaret Moffatt (Kate), Kenneth Warrington (Cdr. Denis), Torin Thatcher (submarine officer), [Bernard Miles (Hans, hotel receptionist), Charles Oliver (German officer), Skelton Knaggs (German orderly), Esma Cannon, Diana Sinclair-Hall].

82 mins. t.s.—March 15. U.K. rel.—August 12. U.K./U.S. dist.—Columbia. U.S. rel.—October 7 [77 mins.]. U.S. title—U Boat 29.

Contraband · 1940

d.—Michael Powell. p.c.—British National. p.—John Corfield. assoc. p.—Roland Gillett. p. manager—Anthony Nelson-Keys. [asst. d.—William Reidy.] sc.—Emeric Pressburger, from his own story. scen.—Michael Powell and Brock Williams [based on a story by Pressburger]. cin.—F. A. Young. [cam. op.—Skeets Kelly.] ed.—John Seabourne [and Joseph Sterling]. a.d.—Alfred Junge. m.—Richard Addinsell, John Greenwood. "The White Negro" cabaret des./executed—Hedley Briggs. m.d.—Muir Mathieson. sd.—A. W. Watkins, C. C. Stevens. [stills—Frank Buckingham.]

Conrad Veidt (Captain Andersen), Valerie Hobson (Mrs. Sorensen), Hay Petrie (Axel Skold, mate of SS Helvig/Erik Skold, chef of "Three Vikings"), Joss Ambler (Lt. Cmdr. Ashton, RNR), Raymond Lovell (Van Dyne), Esmond Knight (Mr. Pidgeon), Charles Victor (Hendrick), Phoebe Kershaw (Miss Lang), Harold Warrender (Lt. Cmdr. Ellis, RN), John Longden, Eric Maturin (passport officers), Paddy Browne (singer in "Regency"), [Henry Wolston, Julian Vedey, Sydney Monckton, Hamilton Keen (Danish waiters), Leo Genn, Stuart Latham, Peter Bull (brothers Grimm), Dennis Arundell (Lieman), Molly Hamley Clifford (Baroness Hekla), Eric Berry (Mr. Abo), Olga Edwards (Mrs. Abo), Tony Gable (Miss Karoly), Desmond Jeans, Eric Hales (the Karolys), John Roberts (Hanson), Manning Whiley (manager of "Mousetrap"), Bernard Miles (man lighting pipe), Torin Thatcher (sailor), Mark Daly (taxi driver), Frank Allenby, John England, Haddon Mason, Johnnie Schofield, Townsend Whitling, Ross Duncan, Albert Chevalier].

92 mins. *t.s.*—March 20. *U.K. rel.*—May. *U.K. dist.*—Anglo. *U.S. rel.*—November 29 [80 mins.]. *U.S. dist.*—United Artists. *U.S. title*—*Blackout.*

49th Parallel · 1941

d./p.—Michael Powell. *p.c.*—Ortus Films [and Ministry of Information]. *assoc. p.*—Roland Gillett, George Brown. *in charge of prod.*—Harold Boxall. *assoc. d.*—A. Seabourne. [*continuity*—Betty Curtiss.] *sc.*—Emeric Pressburger, based on a story by E.P. *scen.*—Rodney Ackland and E.P. *cin.*—Frederick Young. *cam. op.*—Skeets Kelly, Henty Henty-Creer. *sp. backgrounds*—Osmond Borrowdaile. [*cam. assts.*—D. Mason, C. Holden, J. Body. *2nd unit cam. asst.*—D. Fox.] *ed.*—David Lean. *assoc. ed.*—Hugh Stewart. [*original ed.*—John Seabourne. *asst. ed.*—Hazel Wilkinson.] *a.d.*—David Rawnsley. *assoc. a.d.*—Sydney S. Streeter, Frederick Pusey. *m.*—Ralph Vaughan Williams. *m.d.*—Muir Mathieson. *sd. sup.*—A. W. Watkins. *sd. rec.*—C. C. Stevens, Walter Darling. [*sd. mixer*—Gordon K. McCallum. *sd. cam. op.*—J. B. Aldred.] *Canadian adviser*—Nugent M. Clougher.

The U-boat crew

Richard George *(Captain Bernsdorff)*, Eric Portman *(Lt. Ernst Hirth)*, Raymond Lovell *(Lt. Kuhnecke)*, Niall MacGinnis *(Vogel)*, Peter Moore *(Kranz)*, John Chandos *(Lohrmann)*, Basil Appleby *(Jahner)*.

The Canadians

Laurence Olivier *(Johnnie Barras, the trapper)*, Finlay Currie *(Albert, the factor)*, Ley On *(Nick, the Eskimo)*, Anton Walbrook *(Peter)*, Glynis Johns *(Anna)*, Charles Victor *(Andreas)*, Frederick Piper *(David)*, Leslie Howard *(Philip Armstrong Scott)*, Tawera Moana *(George, the Indian)*, Eric Clavering *(Art)*, Charles Rolfe *(Bob)*, Raymond Massey *(Andy Brock)*.

Theodore Salt, O. W. Fonger *(U.S. Customs officers)*. [Lionel Grose.]

123 mins. *t.s.*—October 8. *U.K. rel.*—November 24. *U.K. dist.*—GFD. *U.S. rel.*—April 15, 1942 [104 mins.]. *U.S. dist.*—Columbia. *U.S. title*—*The Invaders.* *Prizes*—Academy Award to E.P. for the script.

One of Our Aircraft Is Missing · 1942

d./p./sc.—Michael Powell, Emeric Pressburger. *p.c.*—The Archers. A British National Films Presentation (with the cooperation of the Royal Air Force, the Air Ministry, and Royal Netherland Government, London). [*p.*—John Corfield.] *assoc. p.*—Stanley Haynes. *unit p. manager*—Sydney S. Streeter. *p. secretary*—Joan Page. *assoc. d.*—John Seabourne. [*asst. d.*—W. Mills. *2nd asst. d.*—P. Seabourne. *3rd asst. d.*—E. Coventry.] *cin.*—Ronald Neame. *assoc. cin.*—Robert Krasker. [*cam. op.*—Guy Green. *cam. asst.*—David Mason.] *ed.*—David Lean. *assoc. ed.*—Thelma Myers. *a.d.*—David Rawnsley. [*asst. a.d.*—John Elphick. *draftsman*—H. White.] *sp. effects*—F. Ford, Douglas Woolsey. *sd. sup.*—A. W. Watkins. *sd. rec.*—C. C. Stevens. [*sd. cam.*—J. B. Aldred. *boom op.*—Gordon K. McCallum. *sd. asst.*—R. Morgan. *stills*—Fred Daniels.] *tech. advisers*—M. Sluyser, James P. Power, RBA.

Crew of "B for Bertie"

Hugh Burden *(John Glyn Haggard)*, Eric Portman *(Tom Earnshaw)*, Hugh Williams *(Frank Shelley)*, Bernard Miles *(Geoff Hickman)*, Emrys Jones *(Bob Ashley)*, Godfrey Tearle *(Sir George Corbett)*.

People of Holland

Googie Withers *(Jo de Vries)*, Joyce Redman *(Jet Van Dieren)*, Pamela Brown *(Els Meertens)*, Peter Ustinov *(priest)*, Alec Clunes *(organist)*, Hay Petrie *(burgomaster, Piet van Dieren)*.

and on the North Sea

Roland Culver *(naval officer)*, David Ward, Robert Duncan *(German airmen)*.

[David Evans *(Len Martin)*, Selma Vaz Dias *(burgomaster's wife)*, Arnold Marle *(Pieter Sluys)*, Robert Helpmann *(Julius de Jong)*, Hector Abbas *(driver)*, James Carson *(Louis)*, Bill Akkerman *(Willem)*, Joan Akkerman *(Maartje)*, Peter Schenke *(Hendrik)*, Valerie Moon *(Jannie)*, John Salew *(German sentry)*, William D'Arcy *(German officer)*, Robert Beatty *(Sgt. Hopkins)*, Stewart Rome *(Cmdr. Reynolds)*, John Longden *(man)*, Gerry Wilmott *(announcer)*, Michael Powell *(dispatching officer)*, John Arnold, John England, James Donald, Gordon Jackson.]

103 mins. *t.s.*—March 18. *U.K. rel.*—June 27. *U.K. dist.*—Anglo. *U.S. rel.*—October 16 [86 mins.]. *U.S. dist.*—United Artists.

The Silver Fleet · 1943

d./sc.—Vernon C. Sewell, Gordon Wellesley. *p.c.*—The Archers. A Michael Powell and Emeric Pressburger Presentation (with the cooperation and advice of the Royal Netherland Government and of the Royal Navy). [*p.*—Michael Powell, Emeric Pressburger.] *assoc. p.*—Ralph Richardson. *p. manager*—George Maynard. [*asst. d.*—Dennis Kavanagh. *2nd asst. d.*—John Arnold. *3rd asst. d.*—W. Herlihy. *continuity*—Phyllis Ross.] *cin.*—Erwin Hillier. *cam. op.*—Cecil Cooney. [*cam. asst.*—E. D. Besche.] *sp. effects*—Eric Humphriss. *ed.*—Michael C. Chorlton. [*asst. eds.*—Betty Orgar, Sidney Samuel.] *p. designer*—Alfred Junge. *m.*—Allan Gray. *sd.*—John Dennis, Desmond Dew. [*sd. cam. op.*—H. Raynham. *boom op.*—Stan Lambourne, D. N. Barclay.] *adviser*—M. Sluyser.

Ralph Richardson *(Jaap van Leyden)*, Googie Withers *(Helene van Leyden)*, Esmond Knight *(von Schiffer)*, Beresford Egan *(Krampf)*, Frederick Burtwell *(Captain Muller)*, Kathleen Byron *(schoolmistress)*, Willem Akkerman *(Willem van Leyden)*, Dorothy Gordon *(Janni Peters)*, Charles Victor *(Bastiaan Peters)*, John Longden *(Jost Meertens)*, Joss Ambler *(Cornelis Smit)*, Margaret Emden *(Bertha)*, George Schelderup *(Dirk)*, Neville Mapp *(Joop)*, Ivor Barnard *(Admiral von Rapp)*, John Carol *(Johann)*, Lt. Schouwenaar RNN *(U-boat captain)*, Lt. van Dapperen RNN *(U-boat lieutenant)*, John Arnold *(U-boat navigator)*, Philip Leaver *(chief of police)*, Laurence O'Madden *(Captain Schneider)*, Anthony Eustrel *(Lt. Wernicke)*, Charles Minor *(Bohme)*, Valentine Dyall *(Markgraf)*, and personnel of the Royal Netherland Navy.

88 mins. *t.s.*—February 24. *U.K. rel.*—March 15. *U.K. dist.*—GFD. *U.S. rel.*—July 1, 1945 [77 mins.]. *U.S. dist.*—Producers Releasing Corporation.

The Life and Death of Colonel Blimp · 1943

d./p./sc.—Michael Powell, Emeric Pressburger ("with acknowledgement to David Low, creator of the immortal Colonel"). *p.c.*—The Archers/Independent Producers. *management*—Sydney S. Streeter, Alec Saville [*p. manager*—Tom White.] *asst. p.*—Richard Vernon. *floor manager*—Arthur Lawson. *asst. d.*—Ken Horne, Tom Payne. [*p. runner*—Roger Cherrill]. *cin.*—Georges Périnal. *col.*—Technicolor. *col. control*—Natalie Kalmus. *chief electrician*—Bill Wall. *cam. op.*—Jack Cardiff, Geoffrey Unsworth, Harold Haysom. *sp. ph. effects*—W. Percy Day. *ed.*—John Seabourne. *asst. ed.*—Thelma Myers, Peter Seabourne. *p. designer*—Alfred Junge. *m.*—Allan Gray. *m. cond.*—Charles Williams. *sd.*—C. C. Stevens, Desmond Dew. *cost.*—Joseph Bato, Matilda Etches. *makeup*—George Blackler, Dorrie Hamilton. *military adviser*—Lt. General Sir Douglas Brownrigg. *period advisers*—E.F.E. Schoen, Dr. C. Beard.

James McKechnie *(Spud Wilson)*, Neville Mapp *(Stuffy Graves)*, Vincent Holman *(club porter, 1942)*, Roger Livesey *(Clive Candy)*, David Hutcheson *(Hoppy)*, Spencer Trevor *(Period Blimp)*, Roland Culver *(Colonel Betteridge)*, James Knight *(club porter, 1902)*, Deborah Kerr *(Edith Hunter)*, Dennis Arundell *(café orchestra leader)*, David Ward *(Kaunitz)*, Jan van Loewen *(indignant citizen)*, Valentine Dyall *(von Schonborn)*, Carl Jaffe *(von Reumann)*, Albert Lieven *(von Ritter)*, Eric Maturin *(Colonel Goodhead)*, Frith Banbury *("Babyface" Fitzroy)*, Robert Harris *(embassy secretary)*, Arthur Wontner *(embassy counselor)*, Count Zichy *(Colonel Borg)*, Anton Walbrook *(Theo Kretschmar-Schuldorff)*, Jane Millican *(Nurse Erna)*, Ursula Jeans *(Frau von Kalteneck)*, Phyllis Morris *(Pebble)*, Muriel Aked *(Aunt Margaret Hamilton)*, John Laurie *(John Montgomery Murdoch)*, Reginald Tate *(Van Zijl)*, Capt. W. H. Barrett, U.S. Army *(the Texan)*, Cpl. Thomas Palmer, U.S. Army *(sergeant)*, Yvonne Andree *(nun)*, Marjorie Gresley *(matron)*, Deborah Kerr *(Barbara Wynne)*, Felix Aylmer *(bishop)*, Helen Debroy *(Mrs. Wynne)*, Norman Pierce *(Mr. Wynne)*, Harry Welchman *(Major John E. Davis)*, A. E. Matthews *(president of tribunal)*, Deborah Kerr *(Angela "Johnny" Cannon)*, Edward Cooper *(BBC official)*, Joan Swinstead *(secretary)*, [Diana Marshall *(Sybil)*, Wally Patch *(sergeant clearing debris)*, Ferdy Mayne *(Prussian student)*, John Boxer *(soldier)*, John Varley, Patrick Macnee].

163 mins. (later cut to ca. 131 mins.). *t.s.*—June 8. *U.K. rel.*—July 26 (charity premiere June 10). *U.K. dist.*—GFD. *U.S. rel*—May 4, 1945 [148 mins.]. *U.S. dist.*—United Artists. *NFA restoration*—1985.

The Volunteer · 1943

d./p./sc.—Michael Powell, Emeric Pressburger. *p.c.*—The Archers. A Ministry of Information Film. *p. sup.*—Sydney S. Streeter. *cin.*—Freddie Ford. *ed.*—Michael C.

Chorlton [and John Seabourne]. *p. designer*—Alfred Junge. *m.*—Allan Gray. *m. cond.*—Walter Goehr. *sd.*—Desmond Dew.

Ralph Richardson *(himself, the star)*, Pat McGrath *(Alfred Davey, the dresser)*, [Laurence Olivier *(man outside window at Denham Studios canteen)*, Michael Powell *(man taking snapshots outside Buckingham Palace)*, Anna Neagle, Herbert Wilcox *(people leaving Denham Studios canteen)*, Anthony Asquith *(film director)*, Tommy Woodroofe].

24 mins. *t.s.*—November 5. *rel.*—January 10, 1944. *U.K. dist.*—Anglo.

A Canterbury Tale · 1944

d./p./sc.—Michael Powell, Emeric Pressburger. *p.c.*—The Archers. A Michael Powell and Emeric Pressburger Presentation. *p. manager*—George Maynard. *asst. d.*—George R. Busby. [*2nd asst. d.*—John Arnold, George Aldersley. *3rd asst. d.*—Parry Jones. *continuity*—Patricia Arnold]. *cin.*—Erwin Hillier. [*cam. op.*—Cecil Cooney. *focus puller*—Eric Besche. *clapper loaders*—Derek Browne, S. Shrimpton, J. Body, J. Demaine. *2nd cam. ops.*—George Stretton, Desmond Dickinson. *models*—W. Percy Day. *back projection*—Charles Staffel.] *ed.*—John Seabourne. [*asst. eds.*—David Powell, Roger Cherrill.] *p. designer*—Alfred Junge. [*draftsmen*—Elliot E. Scott, William Kellner, Harold Hurdell, H. Westbrook.] *m.*—Allan Gray. *m. cond.*—Walter Goehr. *sd. rec.*—C. C. Stevens, Desmond Dew. *sd. rec. exteriors*—Alan Whatley. [*sd. maintenance*—S. Hayers, J. Stirton *(interiors)*; R. Day, W. Day *(exteriors)*. *sd. cam. op.*—Winston Ryder *(ints.)*, S. Hayers *(exts.)*. *boom op.*—George Paternoster *(exts.)*, Gordon K. McCallum *(ints.)*. *boom asst.*—P. Lloyd. *sd. asst.*—Alan Thorne.] *period adviser*—Herbert Norris.

Eric Portman *(Thomas Colpeper, J.P.)*, Sheila Sim *(Alison Smith)*, Dennis Price *(Sgt. Peter Gibbs)*, Sgt. John Sweet, U.S.A. *(Sgt. Bob Johnson)*, Esmond Knight *(narrator/Seven Sisters soldier/village idiot)*, Charles Hawtrey *(Thomas Duckett)*, Hay Petrie *(Woodcock)*, George Merritt *(Ned Horton)*, Edward Rigby *(Jim Horton)*, Freda Jackson *(Prudence Honeywood)*, Betty Jardine *(Fee Baker)*, Eliot Makeham *(organist)*, Harvey Golden *(Sgt. Roczinsky)*, Leonard Smith *(Leslie)*, James Tamsitt *(Terry Holmes)*, David Todd *(David)*, Beresford Egan *(P.C. Ovenden)*, Antony Holles *(Sgt. Bassett)*, Maude Lambert *(Miss Grainger)*, Wally Bosco *(A.R.P. Warden)*, Charles Paton *(Ernie Brooks)*, Jane Millican *(Susanna Foster)*, John Slater *(Sgt. Len)*, Michael Golden *(Sgt. Smale)*, Charles Moffatt *(Sgt. Stuffy)*, Esma Cannon *(Agnes)*, Mary Line *(Leslie's mother)*, Winifred Swaffer *(Mrs. Horton)*, Michael Howard *(Archie)*, Judith Furse *(Dorothy Bird)*, Barbara Waring *(Polly Finn)*, Jean Shepheard *(Gladys)*, Margaret Scudamore *(Mrs. Colpeper)*, Joss Ambler *(police inspector)*, Jessie James *(waitress)*, Kathleen Lucas *(passerby)*, H. F. Maltby *(Mr. Portal)*, Eric Maturin *(Geoffrey's father)*, Parry Jones, Jr. *(Arthur)*, [U.S. version only: Kim Hunter *(Bob's fiancée)*].

124 mins. [later cut to 95 mins.]. *t.s.*—May 9. *U.K. rel.*—August 21. *U.K. dist.*—Eagle-Lion. *U.S. rel.*—January 21, 1949 [93 mins.]. *NFA restoration*—1977.

I Know Where I'm Going! · 1945

d./p./sc.—Michael Powell, Emeric Pressburger. *p.c.*—The Archers. A Michael Powell and Emeric Pressburger Presentation. *asst. p.*—George R. Busby. *asst. d.*—John Tunstall. [*2nd asst. d.*—Bill Herlihy. *3rd asst. d.*—Parry Jones. *continuity*—Patricia Arnold. *asst. continuity*—Ainslie L'Evine.] *cin.*—Erwin Hillier. *cam. op.*—Cecil Cooney. [*focus puller*—Eric Besche. *clapper loader*—Harold Case.] *sp. ph. effects*—Henry Harris. [*add. sp. effects*—George Blackwell. *models*—Gilleran. *back projection*—Charles Staffel.] *ed.*—John Seabourne. [*2nd asst. ed.*—Sidney Hayers, James Pople.] *p. designer*—Alfred Junge. [*asst. a.d.*—Warde Richards. *draftsmen*—Eliot E. Scott, Harry Hurdell, William Kellner, Mr. Buxton.] *m.*—Allan Gray. *m. cond.*—Walter Goehr. *songs*—sung by members of the Glasgow Orpheus Choir. *(choir) principal*—Sir Hugh Roberton. *sd. rec.*—C. C. Stevens. [*sd. cam. op.*—T. Bagley. *boom op.*—Gordon K. McCallum. *boom asst.*—Fred Ryan. *sd. maintenance*—Roy Day. *dubbing crew*—Desmond Dew, Alan Whatley. *tech. adviser*—John Laurie. *Gaelic adviser*—Malcolm MacKelloig. *stills*—Max Rosher.]

George Carney *(Mr. Webster)*, Wendy Hiller *(Joan Webster)*, Walter Hudd *(Hunter)*, Capt. Duncan MacKechnie *(captain of "Lochinvar")*, Ian Sadler *(Iain)*, Roger Livesey *(Torquil MacNeil)*, Finlay Currie *(Ruairidh Mohr)*, Murdo Morrison *(Kenny)*, Margot Fitzsimmons *(Bridie)*, Capt. C.W.R. Knight, FZS *(Colonel Barnstaple)*, Pamela Brown *(Catriona Potts)*, Donald Strachan *(shepherd)*, John Rae *(old shepherd)*, Duncan McIntyre *(old shepherd's son)*, Jean Cadell *(postmistress)*, Norman Shelley *(Sir Robert Bellinger)*, Ivy Milton *(Peigi)*, Anthony Eustrel *(Hooper)*, Petula Clark *(Cheril)*, Alec Faversham *(Martin)*, Catherine Lacey *(Mrs. Robinson)*, Valentine Dyall *(Mr. Robinson)*, Nancy Price *(Mrs. Crozier)*, Herbert Lomas *(Mr. Campbell)*, Kitty Kirwan *(Mrs. Campbell)*, John Laurie *(John Campbell)*, Graham Moffatt *(RAF sergeant)*, Boyd Stevens, Maxwell Kennedy, Jean Houston *(singers in the ceilidh)*, Arthur Chesney *(harmonica player)*, "Mr. Ramshaw" *(Torquil, the eagle)*.

91 mins. *t.s.*—October 30. *U.K. rel.*—December 17. *U.K. dist.*—GFD. *U.S. rel.*—August 9, 1947. *U.S. dist.*—Universal.

A Matter of Life and Death · 1946

d./p./sc.—Michael Powell, Emeric Pressburger. *p.c.*—A Production of The Archers. *unit manager*—Robert C. Foord. *asst. p.*—George R. Busby. *asst. d.*—Parry Jones, Jr. [*2nd asst. d.*—Paul Kelly. *3rd asst. d.*—Patrick Marsden. *continuity*—Bunny Parsons. *asst. continuity*—Ainslie L'Evine]. *cin.*—Jack Cardiff. *col.*—Technicolor. *cam. op.*—Geoffrey Unsworth. [*2nd cam. op.*—Chris Challis. *focus pullers*—Chris Challis, Eric Besche. *clapper loader*—D.R.E. Allport.] *chief electrician*—Bill Wall. *motorbike shots*—Michael Chorlton. *col. control*—Natalie Kalmus. *assoc. col. control*—Joan Bridge. *sp. ph. effects*—Douglas Woolsey, Henry Harris and Technicolor Ltd. *add. sp. effects*—W. Percy Day [and George Blackwell, Stanley Grant. *back projection*—Jack Whitehead.]. *p. designer*—Alfred Junge. *asst. a.d.*—Arthur Lawson. [*draftsmen*—W. Hutchinson, Don Picton, William Kellner.]

ed.—Reginald Mills. *liaison ed.*—John Seabourne, Jr. [*asst. ed.*—Dave Powell.]
m.—Allan Gray. *m. cond.*—Walter Goehr. *asst. m. cond.*—W. L. Williamson. *sd.
rec.*—C. C. Stevens. [*sd. cam. op.*—Harold Rowland. *boom op.*—Dave Hildyard.
boom assts.—G. Sanders, M. G. Colomb. *sd. maintenance*—Roy Day. *dubbing crew*—
Desmond Dew, Alan Whatley. *pre-dubbing*—John Dennis.] *cost*—Hein Heckroth.
makeup—George Blackler. *hair*—Ida Mills. [*table tennis trainer/adv.*—Alan Brook.
operating theatre tech. adv.—Capt. Bernard Kaplan, RAMC. *stills*—Eric Gray.]

David Niven (*Peter David Carter*), Kim Hunter (*June*), Robert Coote (*Bob Trub-
shaw*), Kathleen Byron (*an officer angel*), Richard Attenborough (*an English pilot*),
Bonar Colleano (*Flying Fortress captain*), Joan Maude (*Chief Recorder*), Marius
Goring (*Conductor 71*), Roger Livesey (*Dr. Frank Reeves*), Robert Atkins (*vicar*),
Bob Roberts (*Dr. Gaertler*), Edwin Max (*Dr. McEwen*), Betty Potter (*Mrs. Tucker*),
Abraham Sofaer (*the judge/the surgeon*), Raymond Massey (*Abraham Farlan*).
[Tommy Duggan (*American policeman*), Roger Snowden (*Irishman*), Robert Arden
(*G.I.*), Joan Verney (*girl*), Wendy Thompson (*nurse*), Wally Patch (*ARP Warden*).]

104 mins. *t.s.*—November 12. *U.K. rel.*—December 30. *U.K. dist.*—GFD. *U.S.
rel.*—March 1947. *U.S. dist.*—Universal. *U.S. title*—Stairway to Heaven.

Black Narcissus · 1947

d./p./sc.—Michael Powell, Emeric Pressburger. *p.c.*—A Production of The
Archers, for Independent Producers Ltd. *asst. p.*—George R. Busby. *asst. d.*—Syd-
ney S. Streeter. [*2nd asst. d.*—Kenneth Rick. *3rd asst. d.*—L. Knight, Robert Lynn.
continuity—Winifred Dyer. *asst. continuity*—Joanne Busby.] *sc.*—Based on the
novel by Rumer Godden. *cin.*—Jack Cardiff. *col.*—Technicolor. *col. cons.*—Natalie
Kalmus. *assoc. col. cons.*—Joan Bridge. [*cam. op.*—Chris Challis, Ted Scaife, Stan
Sayer. *focus pullers*—Ian Craig, Ronald Cross. *clapper loaders*—H. Salisbury, M.
Livesey. *Technicolor cam. asst.*—Dick Allport. *lighting electrician*—Bill Wall.] *ed.*—
Reginald Mills. [*1st asst. ed.*—Seymour Logie. *2nd asst. ed.*—Lee Doig, Noreen
Ackland.] *sp. ph. effects*—W. Percy Day. [*sp. effects cam.*—Douglas Hague. *synthetic
pictorial effects*—Syd Pearson. *foreground miniatures*—Jack Higgins.] *p. designer*—
Alfred Junge. *a.d.*—Arthur Lawson. [*draftsmen*—Eliot E. C. Scott, Don Picton,
William Kellner, J. Harman, G. Beattie, A. Harris. *scenic artist*—Ivor Beddoes. *set
dresser*—M.A.S. Pemberton. *Indian set dresser*—E. Harvinson. *chief construction
manager*—Harold Batchelor.] *m./sd. score/m. cond.*—Brian Easdale. *m. perf. by*—
London Symphony Orchestra. *sd. rec.*—Stanley Lambourne. *dubbing mixer*—Gordon K. McCallum. [*chief production mixer*—John H. Dennis. *sd. cam. op.*—H.
Roland. *boom op.*—George Paternoster. *boom asst.*—Mick Stolovich. *sd. maintenance engineer*—Fred Hugheson. *dubbing crew*—J. B. Smith, Bill Daniels. *dubbing
ed.*—John Seabourne, Jr. *music rec.*—Edward A. Drake. *asst. sd. rec.*—J. G. De
Coninck.] *cost.*—Hein Heckroth. [*dress sup.*—Elizabeth Hennings. *wardrobe mistress*—Dorothy Edwards. *wardrobe master*—Bob Raynor. *makeup*—George Blackler. *asst. makeup*—Ernest Gasser. *hair*—Biddy Chrystal. *asst. hair*—June Robinson.
stills—George Cannon (color), Max Rosher (b/w), Fred Daniels (portrait).]

Deborah Kerr *(Sister Clodagh)*, Flora Robson *(Sister Philippa)*, Jenny Laird *(Sister "Honey" Blanche)*, Judith Furse *(Sister Briony)*, Kathleen Byron *(Sister Ruth)*, Esmond Knight *(the old general)*, Sabu *(Dilip Rai, the young general)*, David Farrar *(Mr. Dean)*, Jean Simmons *(Kanchi)*, May Hallatt *(Angu Ayah)*, Eddie Whaley, Jr. *(Joseph Anthony)*, Shaun Noble *(Con)*, Nancy Roberts *(Mother Dorothea)*, Ley On *(Phuba)*.

100 mins. *t.s.*—April 22. *U.K. rel.*—May 26. *U.K. dist.*—GFD. *U.S. rel.*—December. *U.S. dist.*—Universal. *Prizes*—Academy Award to Jack Cardiff for color cinematography.

The End of the River · 1947

d.—Derek Twist. *p.c.*—The Archers. *p.*—Michael Powell, Emeric Pressburger. *asst. p.*—George R. Busby. *asst. d.*—Geoffrey Lambert. *sc.*—Wolfgang Wilhelm. *cin.*—Christopher Challis. *ed.*—Brereton Porter. *a.d.*—Fred Pusey. *asst. a.d.*—E.E.C. Scott. *m.*—Lambert Williamson. *m.d.*—Muir Mathieson. *sd.*—Charles Knott.

Sabu *(Manoel)*, Bibi Ferreira *(Teresa)*, Esmond Knight *(Dantos)*, Antoinette Cellier *(Conceicao)*, Robert Douglas *(Jones)*, Torin Thatcher *(Lisboa)*, Orlando Martins *(Harrigan)*, Raymond Lovell *(Porpino)*, James Hayter *(Chico)*, Nicolette Bernard *(Doña Serafina)*, Minto Cato *(Doña Paul)*, Maurice Denham *(defending counsel)*, Eva Hudson *(Maria Gonsalves)*, Alan Wheatley *(Irygoyen)*, Charles Hawtrey *(Raphael)*, Zena Marshall *(Sante)*, Dennis Arundell *(Continho)*, Milton Rosmer *(judge)*, Peter Illing *(ship's agent)*, Nino Rossini *(Feliciano)*, Basil Appleby *(ship's officer)*, Milo Sperber *(Ze)*, Andreas Malandrinos *(officer of the Indian Protection Society)*, Arthur Goullet *(peddler)*, Russell Napier *(Padre)*.

83 mins. *t.s.*—October 23. *U.K. rel.*—December 1. *U.K. dist.*—Rank. *U.S. rel.*—July 7, 1948 [80 mins.].

The Red Shoes · 1948

d./p./sc.—Michael Powell, Emeric Pressburger. *p.c.*—A Production of the Archers. *asst. p.*—George R. Busby. *asst. d.*—Sydney S. Streeter. [*2nd asst. d.*—Kenneth Rick. *3rd asst. d.*—J. M. Gibson.] *continuity*—Doreen North. [*asst. continuity*—Joanne Busby. *p. asst.*—Gwladys Jenks.] *sc.*—From an original screenplay by Emeric Pressburger. Based on a story by Hans Christian Andersen. *addit. dial.*—Keith Winter. *cin.*—Jack Cardiff. *col.*—Technicolor. *col. cons.*—Natalie Kalmus. *assoc. col. cons.*—Joan Bridge. *cam. op.*—Christopher Challis. *Technicolor composite cin.*—F. George Dunn, E. Hague. [*focus puller*—George Minassian. *cam. assts.*—Robert Kindred, John Morgan.] *ed.*—Reginald Mills. *liaison ed.*—John Seabourne, Jr. [*asst. ed.*—Noreen Ackland. *2nd asst. ed.*—Tony Haynes, Laurie Knight.] *p. designer*—Hein Heckroth. *a.d.*—Arthur Lawson. *painting*—Ivor Beddoes. *sp. painting*—Joseph Natanson. *scenic artist*—Alfred Roberts. [*asst. a.d.*—Elven Webb. *draftsmen*—Don Picton, V. B. Wilkins, V. Shaw, Albert Withy, G. Heavens, B. Goodwin. *masks*—Terence Morgan II.] *m./m. arr./m. cond.*—Brian Easdale. *m. played by*—Royal Philharmonic Orchestra. *"Red Shoes" ballet seq. cond.*—Sir

Thomas Beecham. *singer*—Margherita Grandi. *m. of "Café de Paris" seq.*—Ted Heath's Kenny Baker Swing Group. *sd.*—Charles Poulton. *m. rec.*—Ted Drake. *dubbing*—Gordon K. McCallum. [*dubbing ed.*—Len Trumm. *sd. cam. op.*—H. V. Clarke. *boom op.*—Al Burton. *boom asst.*—G. Daniels. *sd. maintenance*—Richard De Glanville. *dubbing crew*—Gordon K. McCallum, J. B. Smith.] *cost*—Miss Shearer's dresses: Jacques Fath of Paris, Mattli of London; Mlle. Tcherina's dresses: Carven of Paris. *wardrobe*—Dorothy Edwards. [*makeup*—Eric Carter. *sup. makeup*—Ernie Gasser.] *choreo. of the ballet "The Red Shoes"*—Robert Helpmann. Part of the Shoemaker created and danced by Léonide Massine. [*stills*—George Cannons. *asst. stills*—Alistair Phillips.]

Ballet of "The Red Shoes"

solo dancer and asst. maître de ballet—Alan Carter. *solo dancer and asst. maîtresse de ballet*—Joan Harris. *with*—Joan Sheldon, Paula Dunning, Brian Ashbridge, Denis Carey, Lynne Dorval, Helen ffrance, Robert Dorning, Eddie Gaillard, Paul Hammond, Tommy Linden, Trisha Linova, Anna Marinova, Guy Massey, John Regan, Peggy Sager, Ruth Sendler. *accompanist*—Hilda Gaunt.

Marius Goring *(Julian Craster)*, Jean Short *(Terry)*, Gordon Littman *(Ike)*, Julia Lang *(balletomane)*, Bill Shine *(balletomane's mate)*, Léonide Massine *(Grischa Ljubov)*, Anton Walbrook *(Boris Lermontov)*, Austin Trevor *(Professor Palmer)*, Esmond Knight *(Livingstone "Livy" Montague)*, Eric Berry *(Dimitri)*, Irene Browne *(Lady Neston)*, Moira Shearer *(Victoria Page)*, Ludmilla Tcherina *(Boronskaja)*, Jerry Verno *(George, stage-door keeper)*, Robert Helpmann *(Ivan Boleslawsky)*, Albert Basserman *(Ratov)*, Derek Elphinstone *(Lord Oldham)*, Madame Rambert *(herself)*, Joy Rawlins *(Gladys, Vicky's friend)*, Marcel Poncin *(M. Boudin)*, Michel Bazalgette *(M. Rideaut)*, Yvonne Andre *(Vicky's dresser)*, Hay Petrie *(Boisson)*. [Richard George *(doorman)*.]

134 mins. *t.s.*—July 20. *U.K. rel.*—September 6. *U.K. dist.*—GFD. *U.S. rel.*—October 1, 1951. *U.S. dist.*—Universal.

The Small Back Room · 1949

d./p./sc.—Michael Powell, Emeric Pressburger. *p.c.*—A Production of the Archers. A London Film Presentation. *asst. p.*—George R. Busby. [*assoc. p.*—Anthony Bushell. *p. asst.*—Charles Orme.] *asst. d.*—Sydney S. Streeter. [*2nd asst. d.*—Archie Knowles. *3rd asst. d.*—Jackie Green.] *continuity*—Doreen North. *sc.*—Based on the novel by Nigel Balchin. *cin.*—Christopher Challis. *cam. op.*—Freddie Francis. [*focus puller*—Will Lee. *clapper loader*—John Kotze.] *ed.*—Clifford Turner. *sup. ed.*—Reginald Mills. [*asst. cutter*—Tom Simpson. *junior cutter*—Frankie Taylor.] *p. designer*—Hein Heckroth. *a.d.*—John Hoesli. [*asst. a.d.*—Ivor Beddoes. *set dresser*—Dario Simoni. *chief draftsman*—Wallace Smith. *draftsmen*—Edward Clements, Henry Pottle. *junior draftsmen*—Pat Sladden, Peter Childs. *production buyer*—Charles Townsend.] *m.*—Brian Easdale. *nightclub m.*—Ted Heath's Kenny Baker Swing Group and Fred Lewis. *sd.*—Alan Allen. *dubbing*—Bill Sweeny. [*sd. ed.*—

Cyril Swern. *sd. mixer*—K. Allen. *sd. maintenance*—George Stevenson. *sd. cam. op.*—Alec Rapstone. *boom op.*—Peter Butcher. *asst. boom op.*—P. Myers.] *cost.*—Josephine Boss. [*wardrobe master*—Jack Dalmayne. *wardrobe assts.*—Arthur Skinner, May Walding. *makeup sup.*—Dorrie Hamilton. *makeup asst.*—Peter Evans. *hair*—Constance Pyne. *asst. hair*—Iris Tilley. *casting*—Madeleine Godar. *publicity*—Vivienne Knight. *stills*—Anthony Hopking. *tech. observer*—Cmdr. George E. Mills.]

Michael Gough *(Capt. Stuart)*, Henry Caine *(Sgt. Major Rose)*, Milton Rosmer *(Professor Mair)*, Cyril Cusack *(Cpl. Taylor)*, Kathleen Byron *(Susan)*, Sidney James *(Knucksie)*, David Farrar *(Sammy Rice)*, Leslie Banks *(Col. Holland)*, Sam Kydd *(Crowhurst)*, Emrys Jones *(Joe)*, Michael Goodliffe *(Till)*, Jack Hawkins *(R. B. Waring)*, Geoffrey Keen *(Pinker)*, June Elvin *(Gillian)*, David Hutcheson *(Norval)*, Robert Morley *(the minister)*, Roddy Hughes *(Welsh doctor)*, Bryan Forbes *(Petersen, dying gunner)*, Walter Fitzgerald *(Brine)*, James Dale *(brigadier)*, Elwyn Brook-Jones *(Gladwin)*, Roderick Lovell *(Don Pearson)*, Anthony Bushell *(Colonel Strang)*, James Carney *(Sgt. Groves)*, Renee Asherson *(ATS cpl.)*, [Michael Powell *(gunnery officer)*].

106 mins. *t.s.*—January 27. *U.K. rel.*—February 21. *U.K. dist.*—British Lion. *U.S. rel.*—February 23, 1952. *U.S. dist.*—Snader Productions.

Gone to Earth · 1950

d./p./sc.—Michael Powell, Emeric Pressburger. *p.c.*—London Films. The Archers (London). Vanguard Productions (Hollywood). A Michael Powell and Emeric Pressburger Production. An Alexander Korda and David O. Selznick Presentation. *asst. p.*—George R. Busby. *p. asst.*—Charles Orme. *asst. d.*—Sydney S. Streeter. *2nd asst. d.*—Archie Knowles. *continuity*—Doreen Francis. *asst. continuity*—Joanna G. Busby. *sc.*—Based on the novel by Mary Webb. *cin.*—Christopher Challis. *col.*—Technicolor. *cam. op.*—Freddie Francis. *focus puller*—Bill Lee. *Technicolor tech.*—George Minassian. *Technicolor asst.*—Dick Allport. *Technicolor cons.*—Joan Bridge. *process shots*—W. Percy Day. *chief electrician*—Bill Wall. *p. designer*—Hein Heckroth. *a.d.*—Arthur Lawson. *asst. a.d.*—Ivor Beddoes. *set dresser*—Bernard Sarron. *draftsman*—Maurice Fowler. *ed.*—Reginald Mills. *m.*—Brian Easdale. Played by the Boyd Neel Orchestra. *sd. rec.*—Charles Poulton, John Cox. *boom op.*—Peter Butcher. *sd. cam. op.*—Charles Earl. *sd. maintenance*—P. R. Stephenson. *cost.*—Julia Squires. *dress supervision*—Ivy Baker. *wardrobe mistress* [*sic*]—Bill Smith. *wardrobe master*—Michael Hart. *wardrobe assts.*—Dick Richards, May Walding. *makeup*—Jimmy Vining. *makeup asst.*—Connie Reeves. *hair*—Betty Cross. *asst. hair*—Eileen Bates. *animals*—Capt. C.W.R. Knight, FZS. *animal trainer*—Jean Knight. *puppeteer*—Alec Mozeley. *publicity*—Vivienne Knight. *stills*—Bert Cann.

Jennifer Jones *(Hazel Woodus)*, David Farrar *(Jack Reddin)*, Cyril Cusack *(Edward Marston)*, Sybil Thorndyke *(Mrs. Marston)*, Edward Chapman *(Mr. James)*, Esmond Knight *(Abel Woodus)*, Hugh Griffith *(Andrew Vessons)*, George Cole *(Al-*

bert), Beatrice Varley (Aunt Prowde), Frances Clare (Amelia Comber), Raymond Rollett (landlord/elder), Gerald Lawson (road mender/elder), Bartlett Mullins, Arthur Reynolds (chapel elders), Ann Tetheradge (Miss James), Peter Dunlop (cornet player), Louis Phillip (policeman), Valentine Dunn (Martha), Richmond Nairne (Mathias Brooker, Martha's brother), Owen Holder (brother minister). [U.S. version only: Joseph Cotten (narrator).]

110 mins. t.s.—September 19. U.K. rel.—November 6. U.K. dist.—British Lion. U.S. rel.—July 1952. [82 mins. addit. d.—Rouben Mamoulian.] U.S. title—The Wild Heart. U.S. dist.—RKO Radio.

The Elusive Pimpernel · 1950

d./p./sc.—Michael Powell, Emeric Pressburger. p.c.—London Film Productions [and The Archers]. A Michael Powell and Emeric Pressburger Production. A London Films Presentation. asst. p.—George R. Busby. [p. asst.—Charles Orme. p. secretaries—Gwladys Jenks, Marjorie Mein. accountant—P. Corbishley.] asst. d.—Sydney S. Streeter. [2nd asst. d.—Archie Knowles. 3rd asst. d.—David Tomblin. French asst. d.—Paul Pantaleon. asst. to Mr. Powell—Bill Paton. French unit man—M. Charlot.] continuity—Doreen North. [asst. continuity—Joanna G. Busby]. sc.—Based on the romance by Baroness Orczy. cin.—Christopher Challis. col.—Technicolor. cam. op.—Freddie Francis. [focus puller—Bill Lee. cam. asst.— Gerry Anstiss. Technicolor tech.—George Minassian. Technicolor asst.—Dennis Bartlett.] process shots—W. Percy Day. chief electrician—Bill Wall. Technicolor color d.—Natalie Kalmus. p. designer—Hein Heckroth. asst. des.—Ivor Beddoes. a.d.— Arthur Lawson. location a.d.—Joseph Bato. set dresser—Scott Slimon. sup. scenic artist—W. S. Robinson. [asst. a.d.—Elven Webb. chief draftsman—Maurice Fowler. draftsman—John Peters. jnr. draftsman—Patricia Sladen.] ed.—Reginald Mills. [assembly ed.—Noreen Ackland. asst. ed.—Derek Armstrong. 2nd asst. ed.—Francis Taylor, S. Rowson.] m./m. cond.—Brian Easdale. Played by the Philharmonia Orchestra. [m. asst.—Fred Lewis.] sd.—Charles Poulton, Red Law. [sd. mixer— George Adams. sd. cam. op.—Bernard Hesketh. boom op.—Peter Butcher. boom asst.—Brian Coates. sd. maintenance—Norman Bolland, George Barrett. dubbing crew—Bob Jones. cost.—Ivy Baker. asst. cost.—Bernard Sarron. jnr. cost.—Nandi Heckroth. wardrobe master—Jack Dalmayne. wardrobe mistress—Ethel Smith. French cost.—M. Decrais]. makeup—Jimmy Vining. [studio makeup—Harold Fletcher.] hair—Betty Cross. [master of horse—A. G. Parry Jones. nautical tech. adviser—Lt. Cmdr. G. E. Mills. publicity—Vivienne Knight. stills—Richard Cantouris.]

David Niven (Sir Percy Blakeney), Margaret Leighton (Lady Marguerite Blakeney), Cyril Cusack (Chauvelin), Jack Hawkins (Prince of Wales), Arlette Marchal (Comtesse de Tournai), Gerard Nery (Philippe de Tournai), Danielle Godet (Suzanne de Tournai), Edmond Audran (Armand St. Juste), Charles Victor (Colonel Winterbottom), Eugene Deckers (Captain Merières), David Oxley (Captain Duroc), Raymond

Rollett *(Bibot)*, Philip Stainton *(Jellyband)*, John Longden *(Abbot)*, Robert Griffiths *(Trubshaw)*, George de Warfaz *(Baron)*, Arthur Wontner *(Lord Grenville)*, Jane Gil Davies *(Lady Grenville)*, Richard George *(Sir John Coke)*, Cherry Cottrell *(Lady Coke)*.

The Gentlemen of the League

David Hutcheson *(Lord Anthony Dewhurst)*, Robert Coote *(Sir Andrew ffoulkes)*, John Fitzgerald *(Sir Michael Travers)*, Patrick Macnee *(Hon. John Bristow)*, Terence Alexander *(Duke of Dorset)*, Tommy Duggan *(Earl of Sligo)*, John Fitchen *(Nigel Seymour)*, John Hewitt *(Major Pretty)*, Hugh Kelly *(Mr. Fitzdrummond)*, Richmond Nairne *(Beau Pepys)*. [Peter Copley *(tailor)*, Howard Vernon *(Comte de Tournai)*, Peter Gawthorne *(Chauvelin's servant)*, Archie Duncan, James Lomas *(men in bath)*, Sally Newland.]

109 mins. *t.s.*—November 9. *U.K. rel.*—January 1, 1951. *U.K. dist.*—British Lion. *U.S. rel.*—1955. *U.S. dist.*—Caroll Pictures. *U.S. title*—*The Fighting Pimpernel.*

The Tales of Hoffmann · 1951

d./p./sc.—Michael Powell, Emeric Pressburger. *p.c.*—British Lion Film Corporation [with Vega Productions and The Archers]. A Michael Powell and Emeric Pressburger Production. A London Films Presentation. *asst. p.*—George R. Busby. [*p. asst.*—Charles Orme. *p. asst. and secretary*—Gwladys Jenks.] *asst. d.*—Sydney S. Streeter. [*2nd asst. d.*—Leslie Hughes. *3rd asst. d.*—Fred Slark.] *dial. coach*—Molly Terraine. *continuity*—Pamela Davies. *sc.*—From Dennis Arundell's adaptation of the French text by Jules Barbier. *cin.*—Christopher Challis. *col.*—Technicolor. *cam. op.*—Fred Francis. *composite cin.*—E. Hague. *chief electrician*—W. Wall. [*Technicolor asst.*—John Kotze.] *p. designer*—Hein Heckroth. *a.d.*—Arthur Lawson. *asst. des.*—Ivor Beddoes, Terence Morgan II. *scenic artist*—E. Lindegaard. [*draftsmen*—Maurice Fowler, Don Picton, Kenneth McCallum Tait, Peter Moll. *set dresser*—Bernard Sarron. *property buyer*—George Durrant.] *ed.*—Reginald Mills. [*assembly ed.*—Noreen Ackland. *2nd asst. d.*—Andreas Michailidis.] *m.*—Jacques Offenbach. *m. cond.*—Sir Thomas Beecham, conducting The Royal Philharmonic Orchestra. *asst. m.d.*—Frederick Lewis. *sd. rec.*—Ted Drake. *rec. sup.*—John Cox. *cost.*—Josephine Boss (Miss Shearer and Miss Ayars). *wardrobe*—Ivy Baker. [*dress liaison*—Terence Morgan II. *wardrobe master*—Michael Hart. *wardrobe mistress*—Bill Smith. *wardrobe assts.*—Fred Cook, Mrs. Attride.] *makeup*—Constance Reeve. [*asst. makeup*—Tom Smith.] *hair*—Joseph Shear. [*asst. hair*—Eileen Bates.] *marionettes*—John Wright. *choreo.*—Frederick Ashton. *asst. choreo.*—Alan Carter, Joan Harris. [*publicity*—Vivienne Knight. *stills*—Bert Cann.]

Prologue and Epilogue:

Robert Rounseville *(E.T.A. Hoffmann, a poet)*, Pamela Brown *(Nicklaus, his faithful friend and companion [sung by Monica Sinclair])*, Robert Helpmann *(Councillor Lindorf, sinister opponent of Hoffmann throughout his life)*, Moira Shearer *(Stella, prima ballerina, loved by Hoffmann, desired by Lindorf)*, Philip Leaver *(Andreas, Stella's servant, a rogue)*, Frederick Ashton *(Kleinzach)*, Moira Shearer *(his lady-love)*, Meinhart Maur *(Luther, of Luther's Tavern [sung by Fisher Morgan])*, [Edmond Audran *(dancer)*, John Ford *(Nathaniel [sung by Rene Soames])*, Richard Golding *(Hermann [sung by Owen Brannigan])*].

The Tale of Olympia

Moira Shearer *(Olympia, the doll [sung by Dorothy Bond])*, Robert Rounseville *(Hoffmann as a young student)*, Robert Helpmann *(Coppelius, maker of magic spectacles [sung by Bruce Dargavel])*, Léonide Massine *(Spalanzani, a fashionable creator of puppets and automatons [sung by Grahame Clifford])*, Frederick Ashton *(Cochenille, half human, half puppet [sung by Murray Dickie])*.

The Tale of Giulietta

Ludmilla Tcherina *(Giulietta, a courtesan [sung by Margherita Grandi])*, Robert Helpmann *(Dapertutto, her satanic master, collector of souls [sung by Bruce Dargavel])*, Robert Rounseville *(Hoffmann, now a man of the world, traveling through Venice)*, Léonide Massine *(Schlemil, who has lost his shadow and his soul for Giulietta [sung by Owen Brannigan])*, Lionel Harris *(Pitichinaccio, a hunchback [sung by Murray Dickie])*.

The Tale of Antonia

Ann Ayars *(Antonia, a young opera singer fatally ill with consumption)*, Mogens Wieth *(Crespel, her father, a great conductor now living on his memories [sung by Owen Brannigan])*, Robert Rounseville *(Hoffmann, now a famous poet)*, Léonide Massine *(Frantz, a deaf servant [sung by Grahame Clifford])*, Robert Helpmann *(Dr. Miracle, demonic physician who fans the flames of ambition which destroy Antonia [sung by Bruce Dargavel])*. *[mother's voice sung by Joan Alexander.]* [Sir Thomas Beecham *(himself)*.]

Singers: Robert Rounseville, Owen Brannigan, Monica Sinclair, Rene Soames, Bruce Dargavel, Dorothy Bond, Margherita Grandi, Grahame Clifford, Joan Alexander, Murray Dickie, Fisher Morgan, Sadler's Wells Chorus.

138 mins. [reduced to 112 mins. before release]. *t.s.*—May 17. *U.K. rel.*—November 26. *U.K. dist.*—British Lion. *U.S. rel.*—June 13, 1952. *U.S. dist.*—United Artists. *Prizes*—Special Jury Prize, Prize of the Commission Supérieure Technique, Cannes Festival, 1951.

Oh . . . Rosalinda!! · 1955

d./p./sc.—Michael Powell, Emeric Pressburger. *p.c.*—An Associated British Picture Corporation Presentation. A Michael Powell and Emeric Pressburger Presentation. *assoc. p.*—Sydney S. Streeter. *p. manager*—Charles Orme. *asst. d.*—John Pellatt. [*2nd asst. d.*—Alec Gibb. *3rd asst. d.*—David Mycroft. *continuity*—June Faithfull.] *sc.*—Based on Johann Strauss's operetta *Die Fledermaus*. *cin.*—Christopher Challis (CinemaScope). *col.*—Technicolor. *cam. op.*—Norman Warwick. [*focus puller*—Kelvin Pike. *clapper loader*—Peter Hendry. *2nd cam. op.*—J. Stilwell.]

ed.—Reginald Mills. [*assembly cutter*—Alan Tyrer. *asst. ed.*—Nick Gurney. *2nd asst. ed.*—Henrietta Gordon.] *p. designer*—Hein Heckroth. *asst. designer*—Terence Morgan II. *assoc. a.d.*—Arthur Lawson. [*2nd asst. a.d.*—Bernard Sarron. *draftsman*—Peter Pendrey.] *m.*—Johann Strauss. *lyrics*—Dennis Arundell. *m.d.*—Frederick Lewis. *m. perf. by*—Wiener Symphoniker Orchestra. *m. cond.*—Alois Melichar. *sd. rec.*—Leslie Hammond, Herbert Janeczka. *dubbing ed.*—Noreen Ackland. [*sd. cam. op.*—Bud Abbott. *boom op.*—Dennis Whitlock. *boom asst.*—Hugh Strain. *dubbing crew*—Len Shilton, Len Abbott, H. Blackmore, M. Bradbury.] *Ludmilla Tcherina's clothes created by*—Jean Desses of Paris. *makeup*—Constance Reeve. *hair*—A. G. Scott. *choreo.*—Alfred Rodrigues. [*stills*—Ronnie Pilgrim, Bert Cann.]

Anthony Quayle *(General Orlovsky)*, Anton Walbrook *(Dr. Falke, the Fledermaus [singing dubbed by Walter Berry])*, Richard Marner *(Colonel Lebotov)*, Ludmilla Tcherina *(Rosalinda [singing dubbed by Sari Barabas])*, Michael Redgrave *(Colonel Eisenstein)*, Mel Ferrer *(Captain Alfred Westerman [singing dubbed by Alexander Young])*, Nicholas Bruce *(hotel receptionist)*, Anneliese Rothenberger *(Adele)*, Dennis Price *(Major Frank [singing dubbed by Dennis Dowling])*, Oskar Sima *(Frosh)*.

The ladies: Barbara Ash, Hildy Christian, Caryl Gunn, Griselda Hervey, Jill Ireland, Olga Lowe, Ingrid Marshail, Alicia Massey-Beresford, Eileen Sands, Herta Seydel, Anna Steele, Dorothy Whitney.

The dancers: Betty Ash, Yvonne Barnes, Pamela Foster, Patricia Garnett, Annette Gibson, Eileen Gourla, Prudence Hyman, Maya Koumani, Sara Luzita, Jennifer Warmsley, Igor Barczinsky, Cecil Bates, Denis Carey, Peter Darrell, David Gilbert, Robert Harrold, Jan Lawski, William Martin, Kenneth Melville, Morris Metliss, Kenneth Smith.

The gentlemen: Michael Anthony, Richard Bennett, Nicholas Bruce, Ray Buckingham, Rolf Carston, Terence Cooper, Robert Crewdson, Edmund Forsyth, Roger Gage, Raymond Lloyd, Orest Orloff, Robert Ross, Frederick Schiller, John Schlesinger, Frederick Schrecker. [Arthur Mullard *(Russian guard)*, Roy Kinnear.]

101 mins. *t.s.*—November 15. *U.K. rel.*—January 2, 1956. *U.K. dist.*—Associated British-Pathé.

The Battle of the River Plate · 1956

d./p./sc.—Michael Powell, Emeric Pressburger. *p.c.*—Arcturus Productions. A Michael Powell and Emeric Pressburger Production. *assoc. p.*—Sydney S. Streeter. *exec. p.*—Earl St. John. *p. controller*—Arthur Alcott. *p. manager*—John Brabourne. *asst. d.*—Charles Orme. *continuity*—Betty Harley. *cin.*—Christopher Challis (Vista-Vision). *col.*—Technicolor. *cam. op.*—Austin Dempster. *sp. effects*—Bill Warrington, James Snow. *ed.*—Reginald Mills. *p. designer*—Arthur Lawson. *asst. a.d.*—Donald Picton. *artistic adviser*—Hein Heckroth. *m.*—Brian Easdale. *m.d.*—Frederick Lewis. *sd. ed.*—Arthur Stevens. *sd. rec.*—C. C. Stevens, Gordon K. McCallum. *makeup*—Geoffrey Rodway. *naval adviser*—Capt. F. S. Bell, CB, RN Ret. *tech. adviser on prison sequences* (Graf Spee)—Capt. Patrick Dove of the *Africa Shell.*

John Gregson (*Captain F. S. Bell, HMS* Exeter), Anthony Quayle (*Commodore Henry Harwood, HMS* Ajax), Ian Hunter (*Captain Woodhouse, HMS* Ajax), Jack Gwillim (*Captain Parry, HMNZS* Achilles), Bernard Lee (*Captain Patrick Dove, HMS Africa Shell*). HMS *Sheffield* (HMS Ajax), HMS *Delhi* (formerly *Achilles*) (HMNZS Achilles), HMS *Jamaica* (HMS Exeter), HMS *Cumberland* (HMS Cumberland), U.S. heavy cruiser *Salem* (the German pocket battleship Admiral Graf Spee), Lionel Murton (*Mike Fowler*), Anthony Bushell (*Mr. Millington-Drake, British minister in Montevideo*), Peter Illing (*Dr. Guani, foreign minister, Uruguay*), Michael Goodliffe (*Captain McCall, British naval attaché, Buenos Aires*), Patrick Macnee (*Lt. Cmdr. Medley, RN*), John Chandos (*Dr. Langmann, German minister, Montevideo*), Douglas Wilmer (*M. Desmoulins, French minister, Montevideo*), William Squire (*Ray Martin*), Roger Delgado (*Captain Varela, Uruguayan navy*), Andrew Cruickshank (*Captain Stubs*, Doric Star), Christopher Lee (*Manolo*), Edward Atienza (*Pop*), April Olrich (*Dolores*), Peter Finch (*Captain Hans Langsdorff*, Admiral Graf Spee), [Maria Mercedes (*Madame X*), John Schlesinger (*German officer*), John Le Mesurier (*Padre*), Anthony Newley, Nigel Stock (*British officers aboard* Graf Spee), Richard Beale (*Captain Pottinger*, Ashlea), Brian Worth, Ronald Clarke].

119 mins. *t.s.*—October 29. *U.K. rel.*—December 24. *U.K. dist.*—JARFID (Rank). *U.S. rel.*—November 1957 [106 mins.]. *U.S. title*—Pursuit of the Graf Spee. Selected for the Royal Film Performance, 1956.

Ill Met By Moonlight · 1957

d./p./sc.—Michael Powell, Emeric Pressburger. *p.c.*—A Michael Powell and Emeric Pressburger Production for The Rank Organisation Film Productions [and Vega Productions]. *exec. p.*—Earl St. John. *assoc. p.*—Sydney S. Streeter. *p. controller*—Arthur Alcott. *p. manager*—Jack Swinburne. *asst. d.*—Charles Orme. [*2nd asst. d.*—Harold Orton. *3rd asst. d.*—David Tringham.] *sc.*—Based on the book of the same title by W. Stanley Moss. *cin.*—Christopher Challis (VistaVision). *cam. op.*—Austin Dempster. [*focus puller*—Steve Claydon. *cam. asst.*—Ronald Anscombe.] *sp. ph. effects*—Bill Warrington [and F. George, H. Marshall, Cliff Culley, D. Hume]. *ed.*—Arthur Stevens. [*assembly cutter*—Noreen Ackland. *1st asst. ed.*—Jack Gardner, A. Godfrey. *2nd asst. ed.*—Norman Wanstall.] *a.d.*—Alex Vetchinsky. [*asst. a.d.*—Maurice Pelling. *draftsmen*—Lionel Couch, Harry Pottle, Bruce Grimes.] *m.*—Mikis Theodorakis. *m.d.*—Frederick Lewis. [*m. rec.*—Ted Drake.] *sd. ed.*—Archie Ludski. *sd. rec.*—Charles Knott, Gordon K. McCallum. [*sd. ed. asst.*—D. Lancaster. *sd. cam. op.*—Martin McClean. *boom op.*—Basil Rootes. *boom asst.*—Ken Reynolds. *dubbing crew*—Gordon K. McCallum, W. Daniels, C. Le Messurier.] *cost.*—Nandi Routh. *makeup*—Paul Rabiger. [*stills*—Harry Grimes.] *tech. advisers*—Micky Akoumianakis of Knossos, Crete; Major Xan Fielding, DSO.

Dirk Bogarde (*Major Patrick Leigh-Fermor, DSO, OBE*), Marius Goring (*Major General Karl Kreipe*), David Oxley (*Captain William "Billy" Stanley Moss*), Demetri Andreas (*Niko*), Cyril Cusack (*Sandy*), Laurence Payne (*Manoli*), Wolfe Morris

(George), Michael Gough *(Andoni Zoidakis)*, John Cairney *(Elias)*, Brian Worth *(Stratis Saviolkis)*, Rowland Bartrop *(Micky Akoumianakis)*, George Eugeniou *(Charis Zoghraphakis)*, Paul Stassino *(Yanni Katsias)*, Adeeb Assaly *(Zahari)*, Theo Moreas *(village priest)*, Takis Frangofinos *(Michali)*, Christopher Lee *(German officer at dentist)*, Peter Augustine *(dentist)*, John Houseman, Phyllia Houseman, [Andrea Malandrinos, Christopher Rhodes, David McCallum].

104 mins. *t.s.*—January 29, 1957. *U.K. rel.*—March 4, 1957. *U.K. dist.*—Rank. *U.S. rel.*—July 1958 [93 mins.]. *U.S. title*—*Night Ambush*.

They're a Weird Mob · 1966

d./p.—Michael Powell. *p.c.*—Williamson (Australia)/Powell (G. B.). A Michael Powell Production. *assoc. p.*—John Pellatt. *unit manager*—Bruce Bennett. *p. sup.*—Lee Robinson. *location manager*—Jefferson Jackson. *asst. d.*—Claude Watson. *2nd asst. d.*—David Crocker. *continuity*—Doreen Soan. *sc.*—Richard Imrie [pseud. EP]. Based on the novel by Nino Culotta [pseud. John O'Grady]. *cin.*—Arthur Grant. *col.*—Eastman Color. *cam. op.*—Keith Loone, Graham Lind, Dennis Hill. *ed.*—G. Turney-Smith. *a.d.*—Dennis Gentle. *set dec.*—David Copping. *m.*—Laurence Leonard, Alan Boustead. *m.d.*—Laurence Leonard. *songs*—"Big Country," "In This Man's Country" by Reen Devereaux; "I Kiss You, You Kiss Me" by Walter Chiari. Cretan dance from *Ill Met by Moonlight* by Mikis Theodorakis. *sd. rec.*—Alan Allen. *sd. re-rec.*—Ted Karnon. *sd. ed.*—Don Saunders, Bill Creed. *cost.*—Chris Jacovides. *wardrobe mistress*—Barbara Turnbull. *makeup*—Joan Adelsteine, Barbara Still. *hair*—Leon Daunais. *casting*—Gloria Payten.

Walter Chiari *(Nino Culotta)*, Clare Dunne *(Kay Kelly)*, Chips Rafferty *(Harry Kelly)*, Alida Chelli *(Giuliana)*, Ed Devereaux *(Joe)*, Slim DeGrey *(Pat)*, John Meillon *(Dennis)*, Charles Little *(Jimmy)*, Anne Haddy *(barmaid)*, Jack Allen *(fat man in bar)*, Red Moore *(texture man)*, Ray Hartley *(newsboy)*, Tony Bonner *(lifesaver)*, Alan Lander *(Charlie)*, Keith Petersen *(drunk man on ferry)*, Muriel Steinbeck *(Mrs. Kelly)*, Gloria Dawn *(Mrs. Chapman)*, Jeanne Dryman *(Betty)*, Gita Rivera *(Maria, sister of Giuliana)*, Judith Arthy *(Dixie)*, Doreen Warburton *(Edie)*, Barry Creyton, Noel Brophy, Graham Kennedy.

112 mins. *t.s.*—October 7. *U.K. rel.*—October 13. *U.K. dist.*—Rank.

The Boy Who Turned Yellow · 1972

d.—Michael Powell. *p.c.*—Roger Cherrill Ltd. for the Children's Film Foundation. A CFF Production. *asst. p.*—Drummond Challis. *p. manager*—Gus Angus. *asst. d.*—Neil Vine-Miller. *sc.*—Emeric Pressburger from his own story. *cin.*—Christopher Challis. *col.*—Eastman Color. *ed.*—Peter Boita. *a.d.*—Bernard Sarron. *electronic m.*—Patrick Gowers, David Vorhaus, *sd. ed.*—Roger Harrison. *sd. rec.*—Bob Jones, Ken Barker.

Mark Dightam *(John Saunders)*, Robert Eddison *(Nick)*, Helen Weir *(Mrs. Saunders)*, Brian Worth *(Mr. Saunders)*, Esmond Knight *(doctor)*, Laurence Carter *(schoolteacher)*, Patrick McAlinney *(Supreme Beefeater)*, Lem Kitaj *(Munro)*.

55 mins. *U.K. rel.*—September 16. *dist.*—Children's Film Foundation. *Prize*—Children's Film Foundation award, "Chiffy," 1978.

Powell Without Pressburger

*Two Crowded Hours · 1931

d.—Michael Powell. *p.c.*—Film Engineering. *p.*—Jerome Jackson, Henry Cohen. *sc.*—J. Jefferson Farjeon. *cin.*—Geoffrey Faithfull. *ed.*—A. Seabourne. *a.d.*—C. Saunders.

John Longden *(Harry Fielding)*, Jane Walsh *(Joyce Danton)*, Jerry Verno *(Jim)*, Michael Hogan *(Scammell)*, Edward Barber *(Tom Murray)*.

43 mins. *t.s.*—July 8. *U.K. rel.*—December 28. *U.K. dist.*—Fox.

*My Friend the King · 1931

d.—Michael Powell. *p.c.*—Film Engineering. *p.*—Jerome Jackson. *sc.*—J. Jefferson Farjeon, from his own story. *cin.*—Geoffrey Faithfull. *ed.*—A. Seabourne. *a.d.*—C. Saunders.

Jerry Verno *(Jim)*, Robert Holmes *(Captain Felz)*, Tracy Holmes *(Count Huelin)*, Eric Pavitt *(King Ludwig)*, Phyllis Loring *(Princess Helma)*, Luli Hohenberg *(Countess Zena)*, H. Saxon Snell *(Karl)*, Victor Fairley *(Josef)*.

47 mins. *t.s.*—September 23. *U.K. rel.*—April 4, 1932. *U.K. dist.*—Paramount.

Rynox · 1931

d.—Michael Powell. *p.c.*—Film Engineering. *p.*—Jerome Jackson. [*sc.*—Jerome Jackson, Michael Powell, J. Jefferson Farjeon, Philip MacDonald.] From the novel by Philip MacDonald. *cin.*—Geoffrey Faithfull, Arthur Grant. *ed.*—A. Seabourne. *a.d.*—G. C. Waygrove. *construction*—W. Saunders. *sd.*—Rex Howarth.

Stewart Rome *(F. X. Benedik)*, John Longden *(Anthony X. "Tony" Benedik)*, Dorothy Boyd *(Peter)*, Charles Paton *(Samuel Richforth)*, Leslie Mitchell *(Woolrich)*, Sybil Grove *(secretary)*, Cecil Clayton, Fletcher Lightfoot *(Prout)*, Edmund Willard *(Captain James)*.

48 mins. *t.s.*—November. *U.K. rel.*—May 7, 1932. *U.K. dist.*—Ideal.

*The Rasp · 1931

d.—Michael Powell. *p.c.*—Film Engineering. *p.*—Jerome Jackson. *sc.*—Philip MacDonald, from his own story. *cin.*—Geoffrey Faithfull. *a.d.*—Frank Wells.

Claude Horton *(Anthony Gethryn)*, Phyllis Loring *(Lucia Masterson)*, C. M. Hallard *(Sir Arthur Coates)*, James Raglan *(Alan Deacon)*, Thomas Weguelin *(Inspector Boyd)*, Carol Coombe *(Dora Masterson)*, Leonard Brett *(Jimmy Masterson)*.

44 mins. *t.s.*—December 3. *U.K. rel.*—April 11, 1932. *U.K. dist.*—Fox.

*The Star Reporter · 1931

d.—Michael Powell. *p.c.*—Film Engineering. *p.*—Jerome Jackson. *sc.*—Ralph Smart, Philip MacDonald. Based on a story by MacDonald. *cin.*—Geoffrey Faithfull. *add. cin.*—Michael Powell. *a.d.*—Frank Wells.

Harold French *(Major Starr)*, Isla Bevan *(Lady Susan Loman)*, Garry Marsh

(Mandel), Spencer Trevor *(Lord Longbourne)*, Anthony Holles *(Bonzo)*, Noel Dainton *(Colonel)*, Elsa Graves *(Oliver)*, Philip Morant *(Jeff)*.

44 mins. *t.s.*—December 10. *U.K. rel.*—May 9, 1932. *U.K. dist.*—Fox.

Hotel Splendide · 1932

d.—Michael Powell. *p.c.*—Film Engineering. A Gaumont-British Picture Corporation Ltd. Presentation. *p.*—Jerome Jackson. *story*—Philip MacDonald, Ralph Smart. [*sc.*—Ralph Smart, from a story by Philip MacDonald.] *cin.*—Geoffrey Faithfull, Arthur Grant. *ed.*—A. Seabourne. *a.d.*—Charles Saunders. *sd.*—M. Rose.

Jerry Verno *(Jerry Mason)*, Anthony Holles *("Mrs. LeGrange")*, Edgar Norfolk *("Gentleman Charlie")*, Philip Morant *(Mr. Meek)*, Sybil Grove *(Mrs. Harkness)*, Vera Sherborne *(Joyce Dacre)*, Paddy Browne *(Miss Meek)*, [Michael Powell *(eavesdropping device operator)*].

53 mins. *t.s.*—March 23. *U.K. rel.*—July 18. *U.K. dist.*—Ideal.

*C.O.D. · 1932

d.—Michael Powell. *p.c.*—Westminster Films. *p.*—Jerome Jackson. *sc.*—Ralph Smart, from a story by Philip MacDonald. *cin.*—Geoffrey Faithfull. *a.d.*—Frank Wells.

Garry Marsh *(Peter Craven)*, Hope Davey *(Frances)*, Arthur Stratton *(Briggs)*, Sybil Grove *(Mrs. Briggs)*, Roland Culver *(Edward)*, Peter Gawthorne *(detective)*, Cecil Ramage *(Vyner)*, Bruce Belfrage *(Philip)*.

66 mins. *t.s.*—March 17. *U.K. rel.*—August 22. *U.K. dist.*—United Artists.

*His Lordship · 1932

d.—Michael Powell. *p.c.*—Westminster Films. *p.*—Jerome Jackson. *sc.*—Ralph Smart. Based on the novel *The Right Honorable* by Oliver Madox Heuffer. *cin.*—Geoffrey Faithfull. *a.d.*—Frank Wells. *m./lyrics*—V. C. Clinton-Baddeley, Eric Maschwitz.

Jerry Verno *(Bert Gibbs)*, Janet McGrew *(Ilya Myona)*, Ben Welden *(Washington Lincoln)*, Polly Ward *(Leninia)*, Peter Gawthorne *(Ferguson)*, Muriel George *(Mrs. Gibbs)*, Michael Hogan *(Comrade Curzon)*, V. C. Clinton-Baddeley *(Comrade Howard)*, Patrick Ludlow *(Hon. Grimsthwaite)*.

77 mins. *t.s.*—June 2. *U.K. rel.*—December 5. *U.K. dist.*—United Artists.

*Born Lucky · 1932

d.—Michael Powell. *p.c.*—Westminster Films. *p.*—Jerome Jackson. *sc.*—Ralph Smart. Based on the novel *Mops* by Oliver Sandys. *cin.*—Geoffrey Faithfull. *a.d.*—Alan Campbell-Gray.

Talbot O'Farrell *(Turnips)*, Renee Ray *(Mops)*, John Longden *(Frank Dale)*, Ben Welden *(Harriman)*, Helen Ferrers *(Lady Chard)*, Barbara Gott *(cook)*, Paddy Browne *(Patty)*, Roland Gillett *(John Chard)*.

78 mins. *t.s.*—December 5. *U.K. rel.*—April 6, 1933. *U.K. dist.*—MGM.

Perfect Understanding · 1933

d.—Cyril Gardner. *p.c.*—Swanson Productions Ltd. A United Artists Picture. [*p.*—Richard Norton.] *p. manager*—Sergei Nolbandov. [*sc.*—Michael Powell.] *dial.*—Miles Malleson, Garrett Graham from a story by Miles Malleson. *cin.*—Curt Courant [and Léonce-Henri Burel, Georges Périnal]. *ed.*—Thorold Dickinson. *a.d.*—Oscar Werndorff. *m.*—Henry Sullivan. *m.d.*—Philip Braham. *orchestration*—Leonard Hornsey. *sd. rec.*—A. D. Valentine. *gowns*—Ann Morgan. *film titles*—E. McKnight Kauffer.

Gloria Swanson *(Judy Rogers)*, Laurence Olivier *(Nick Randall)*, John Halliday *(Ivan Ronnson)*, Sir Nigel Playfair *(Lord Portleigh)*, Michael Farmer *(George Drayton)*, Genevieve Tobin *(Kitty Drayton)*, Charles Cullum *(Sir John Fitzmaurice)*, Nora Swinburne *(Lady Stephanie Fitzmaurice)*, O. B. Clarence *(Dr. Graham)*, Mary Jerrold *(Mrs. Graham)*, Peter Gawthorne *(butler)*, Rosalinde Fuller *(cook)*, Miles Malleson *(announcer)*, Ben Webster *(judge)*, Herbert Lomas *(Nick's counsel)*, Charles Childerstone *(Judy's counsel)*.

87 mins. *U.K. rel.*—January 11. *U.K. dist.*—United Artists.

The Fire Raisers · 1933

d.—Michael Powell. *p.c.*—Gaumont-British. *p.*—Jerome Jackson. *asst. d.*—Bryan Wallace. *sc.*—Michael Powell, Jerome Jackson [from an original story]. *cin.*—Leslie Rowson. *ed.*—D. N. Twist. *a.d.*—Alfred Junge. *cost.*—Gordon Conway. *sd.*—A. F. Birch.

Leslie Banks *(Jim Bronson)*, Anne Grey *(Arden Brent)*, Carol Goodner *(Helen Vaughan)*, Frank Cellier *(Brent)*, Francis L. Sullivan *(Stedding)*, Laurence Anderson *(Twist)*, Harry Caine *(Bates)*, George Merritt *(Sonners)*. [Joyce Kirby *(Polly)*, Wally Patch *(Pride, the trainer)*, Ben Welden *(Bellini, Stedding's henchman)*, Danny Green *(Stedding's henchman)*.]

77 mins. *t.s.*—September 18. *U.K. rel.*—January 22, 1934. *U.K. dist.*—Woolf & Freedman.

The Night of the Party · 1934

d.—Michael Powell. *p.c.*—Gaumont-British Picture Corporation. [*p.*—Jerome Jackson.] *asst. d.*—Bryan Wallace. *sc.*—Ralph Smart. From the play by Roland Pertwee and John Hastings Turner. *dial.*—Roland Pertwee, John Hastings Turner. *cin.*—Glen MacWilliams. *a.d.*—Alfred Junge. *cost.*—Gordon Conway. *sd. rec.*—S. Jolly.

Malcolm Keen *(Lord Studholme)*, Jane Baxter *(Peggy Studholme)*, Ian Hunter *(Guy Kennion)*, Leslie Banks *(Sir John Holland)*, Viola Keats *(Joan Holland)*, Ernest Thesiger *(Adrian Chiddiatt)*, Jane Millican *(Anna Chiddiatt)*, W. Graham Browne *(General Piddinghoe)*, Muriel Aked *(Princess Maria Amelia of Corsova)*, Gerald Barry *(Baron Cziatch)*, Cecil Ramage *(Howard Vernon)*, John Turnbull *(Inspector Ramage)*, Laurence Anderson *(defending counsel)*, Louis Goodrich *(the judge)*, Disney Roebuck *(butler)*. [Gordon Begg *(Miles)*.]

61 mins. *t.s.*—February. *U.K. rel.*—July 16. *U.K. dist.*—Gaumont-British. *U.S. rel.*—1935. *U.S. title*—*The Murder Party.*

Red Ensign · 1934

d.—Michael Powell. *p.c.*—Gaumont-British. *p.*—Jerome Jackson. *dial.*—L. du Garde Peach. Adapted from a story by Michael Powell, Jerome Jackson. *cin.*—Leslie Rowson. *ed.*—Geoffrey Barkas. *a.d.*—Alfred Junge. *cost.*—Gordon Conway. *sd. rec.*—G. Birch.

Leslie Banks *(David Barr)*, Carol Goodner *(June MacKinnon)*, Frank Vosper *(Lord Dean)*, Alfred Drayton *(Manning)*, Campbell Gullan *(Hannay)*, Percy Parsons *(Arthur Casey)*, Fewlass Llewellyn *(Sir Gregory)*, Henry Oscar *(Raglan)*, Allan Jeayes *(Emerson, aka Grierson)*, Donald Calthrop *(MacLeod)*, Henry Caine *(Bassett)*. [John Laurie *(wages accountant)*, Frederick Piper *(bowler-hatted man in bar)*.]

69 mins. *t.s.*—February 2. *U.K. rel.*—June 4. *U.K. dist.*—Gaumont-British. *U.S. rel.*—1935/36. *U.S. title*—*Strike!*

Something Always Happens · 1934

d.—Michael Powell. *p.c.*—Warner Bros.–First National Productions Ltd., Teddington Studios. *exec. p.*—Irving Asher. *sc.*—Brock Williams. *cin.*—Basil Emmott. *ed.*—Ralph Dawson. *a.d.*—Peter Proud. *cost.*—Louis Brooks. *sd.*—Leslie Murray, H. C. Pearson.

Ian Hunter *(Peter Middleton)*, Nancy O'Neil *(Cynthia Hatch)*, Peter Gawthorne *(Benjamin Hatch)*, John Singer *(Billy)*, Muriel George *(Mrs. Badger, the landlady)*, Barry Livesey *(George Hamlin)*. [Millicent Wolf *(Glenda)*, Louie Emery *(Mrs. Tremlett)*, Reg Marcus *("Coster")*, George Zucco *(proprietor of the Café de Paris)*.]

69 mins. *t.s.*—June 21. *U.K. rel.*—December 10. *U.K. dist.*—Warner Bros.–First National.

*The Girl in the Crowd · 1934

d.—Michael Powell. *p.c.*—First National. *exec. p.*—Irving Asher. *sc.*—Brock Williams. *cin.*—Basil Emmott. *ed.*—Bert Bates.

Barry Clifton *(David Gordon)*, Patricia Hilliard *(Marian)*, Googie Withers *(Sally)*, Harold French *(Bob)*, Clarence Blakiston *(Mr. Peabody)*, Margaret Gunn *(Joyce)*, Richard Littledale *(Bill Manners)*, Phyllis Morris *(Mrs. Lewis)*, Patric Knowles *(Tom Burrows)*, Marjorie Corbett *(secretary)*, Brenda Lawless *(policewoman)*, Barbara Waring *(mannequin)*, Eve Lister *(Ruby)*, Betty Lyne *(Phyllis)*, Melita Bell *(assistant manageress)*, John Wood *(Harry)*.

52 mins. *t.s.*—December 4. *U.K. rel.*—May 20, 1935. *U.K. dist.*—First National.

The Love Test · 1934

d.—Michael Powell. *p.c.*—Fox British. *unit p.*—Leslie L. Landau. *sc.*—Selwyn Jepson, from a story by Jack Celestin. *dial.*—Selwyn Jepson. *cin.*—Arthur Crabtree.

Judy Gunn *(Mary)*, Louis Hayward *(John)*, Dave Hutcheson *(Thompson)*, Googie Withers *(Minnie)*, Morris Harvey *(company president)*, Aubrey Dexter *(company vice-president)*, Jack Knight *(managing director)*, Gilbert Davis *(chief chemist)*, Eve Turner *(Kathleen)*, Bernard Miles *(Allan)*, Shayle Gardner *(night watchman)*, James Craig *(boiler man)*. [Thorley Walters, Ian Wilson *(chemists)*.]

63 mins. *t.s.*—December 2, 1934. *U.K. rel.*—July 1, 1935. *U.K. dist.*—Fox British.

Lazybones · 1935

d.—Michael Powell. *p.c.*—A Real Art Production. A Julius Hagen Presentation. *asst. d.*—Fred V. Merrick. *adaptation*—Gerald Fairlie, from a play by Ernest Denny. *cin.*—Ernest Palmer [and Arthur Crabtree]. *ed.*—Ralph Kemplen. *a.d.*—James A. Carter. *m.d.*—W. L. Trytel. *sd. rec.*—Leo Wilkins. *hair*—Charles.

Ian Hunter *(Sir Reginald Ford)*, Claire Luce *(Kitty McCarthy)*, Bernard Nedell *(Michael McCarthy)*, Denys Blakelock *(Hugh Ford)*, Mary Gaskell *(Marjory Ford)*, Michael Shepley *(Hildebrand Pope)*, Pamela Carne *(Lottie Pope)*, Bobbie Comber *(Kemp)*, Fred Withers *(Richards)*, Sara Allgood *(Bridget)*, Frank Morgan *(Tom)*, Fewlass Llewellyn *(Lord Brockley)*, Harold Warrender *(Lord Melton)*, Paul Blake *(Viscount Woodland)*, Miles Malleson *(the pessimist)*.

65 mins. *t.s.*—January 17. *U.K. rel.*—June 24. *U.K. dist.*—RKO.

The Phantom Light · 1935

d.—Michael Powell. *p.c.*—A Gainsborough Picture. A Gaumont-British Picture Corporation Ltd. Presentation. *assoc. p.*—Jerome Jackson. *sc.*—Ralph Smart. Based on the play *The Haunted Light* by Evadne Price and Joan Roy Byford. *dial.*—J. Jefferson Farjeon, Austin Melford. *cin.*—Roy Kellino. *ed.*—D. N. Twist. *a.d.*—Alex Vetchinsky. [*m.*—Louis Levy.] *sd. rec.*—A. Birch.

Binnie Hale *(Alice Bright)*, Gordon Harker *(Sam Higgins)*, Donald Calthrop *(David Owen)*, Milton Rosmer *(Dr. Carey)*, Ian Hunter *(Jim Pierce)*, Herbert Lomas *(Claff Owen)*, Reginald Tate *(Tom Evans)*, Barry O'Neill *(Captain Pearce)*, Mickey Brantford *(Bob Peters)*, Alice O'Day *(Mrs. Owen)*, Fewlass Llewellyn *(Griffith Owen)*, Edgar K. Bruce *(Sgt. Owen)*, Louie Emery *(station mistress)*.

75 mins. *t.s.*—January 9. *U.K. rel.*—August 5. *U.K. dist.*—Gaumont-British. [Re-issued 1950.]

*The Price of a Song · 1935

d.—Michael Powell. *p. c.*—Fox British. *sc.*—Anthony Gittens. *cin.*—Jimmy Wilson.

Campbell Gullan *(Arnold Grierson)*, Marjorie Corbett *(Margaret Nevern)*, Gerald

Fielding *(Michael Hardwicke)*, Dora Barton *(Letty Grierson)*, Charles Mortimer *(Oliver Broom)*, Oriel Ross *(Elsie)*, Henry Caine *(Stringer)*, Sybil Grove *(Mrs. Bancroft)*, Eric Maturin *(Nevern)*, Felix Aylmer *(Graham)*, Cynthia Stock *(Mrs. Bush)*, Mavis Clair *(Maudie Bancroft)*.

67 mins. *t.s.*—May 24. *U.K. rel.*—October 7. *U.K. dist.*—Fox British.

*Someday · 1935

d.—Michael Powell. *p.c.*—Warner British. *p.*—Irving Asher. *sc.*—Brock Williams. Based on the novel *Young Nowheres* by I.A.R. Wylie. *cin.*—Basil Emmott, Monty Berman. *ed.*—Bert Bates. *a.d.*—Ian Campbell-Gray.

Esmond Knight *(Curley Blake)*, Margaret Lockwood *(Emily)*, Henry Mollison *(Canley)*, Sunday Wilshin *(Betty)*, Raymond Lovell *(Carr)*, Ivor Bernard *(Hope)*, George Pughe *(milkman)*, Jane Cornell *(nurse)*.

68 mins. *t.s.*—July 17. *U.K. rel.*—November 18. *U.K. dist.*—Warner Bros.–First National.

Her Last Affaire · 1935

d.—Michael Powell. *p.c.*—New Ideal Productions Ltd. *p.*—Simon Rowson, Geoffrey Rowson. *asst. d.*—Sidney Stone. *sc.*—Ian Dalrymple. Based on the play *S.O.S.* by Walter Ellis. *cin.*—Leslie Rowson. *cam. op.*—Harry Gillam. *ed.*—Ian Dalrymple. *a.d.*—J. Elder Wills. *sd. rec.*—George E. Burgess.

Hugh Williams *(Alan Heriot)*, Francis L. Sullivan *(Sir Julian Weyre)*, Viola Keats *(Lady Avril Weyre)*, Sophie Stewart *(Jody Weyre)*, John Laurie *(Robb)*, Googie Withers *(Effie)*, Felix Aylmer *(Lord Carnforth)*, Cecil Parker *(Sir Arthur Harding)*, Henry Caine *(Inspector Marsh)*, Eliot Makeham *(Dr. Rudd)*, Shayle Gardner *(Boxall)*, Gerrard Tyrell *(Martin Smith)*.

78 mins. *t.s.*—October 21. *U.K. rel.*—May 25. *U.K. dist.*—Producers Distributing Corporation.

*The Brown Wallet · 1936

d.—Michael Powell. *p.c.*—Warner Bros.–First National. *exec. p.*—Irving Asher. *sc.*—Ian Dalrymple, from a story by Stacy Aumonier. *cin.*—Basil Emmott.

Patric Knowles *(John Gillespie)*, Nancy O'Neill *(Eleanor)*, Henry Caine *(Simmonds)*, Henrietta Watson *(Aunt Mary)*, Charlotte Leigh *(Miss Barton)*, Shayle Gardner *(Wotherspoone)*, Edward Dalby *(Minting)*, Eliot Makeham *(Hobday)*, Bruce Winston *(Julian Thorpe)*, Jane Millican *(Miss Bloxham)*, Louis Goodrich *(coroner)*, Dick Francis, George Mills *(detectives)*.

68 mins. *t.s.*—February 25. *U.K. rel.*—July 20. *U.K. dist.*—Warner Bros.–First National.

Crown v. Stevens · 1936

d.—Michael Powell. *p.c.*—Warner Bros.–First National Productions Ltd., Teddington Studios. *exec. p.*—Irving Asher. *sc.*—Brock Williams. Based on the novel

Third Time Unlucky by Laurence Meynell. *cin.*—Basil Emmott. *a.d.*—Peter Proud. *ed.*—Bert Bates. *sd. rec.*—Leslie Murray, H. C. Pearson.

Beatrix Thomson *(Doris Stevens)*, Patric Knowles *(Chris Jansen)*, Glennis Lorimer *(Molly Hobbs)*, Reginald Purdell *(Alf)*, Allan Jeayes *(Inspector Carter)*, Frederick Piper *(Arthur Stevens)*, Googie Withers *(Ella Levine)*, Mabel Poulton *(Mamie)*, [Morris Harvey *(Julius Bayleck)*, Billy Watts *(Joe Andrews)*, Davina Craig *(Maggie the maid)*, Bernard Miles *(detective)*].

66 mins. *t.s.*—March 26. *U.K. rel.*—August 3. *U.K. dist.*—Warner Bros.–First National.

The Man Behind the Mask · 1936

d.—Michael Powell. *p.c.*—Joe Rock Studio. [*p.*—Joe Rock]. *p. manager*—Stanley Haynes. *sc. adaptation*—Syd Courtenay, Jack Byrd [and Stanley Haynes] from the novel *The Chase of the Golden Plate* by Jacques Futrelle. [*dial.*—Ian Hay] *cin.*— Ernest Palmer. *camera*—Erwin Hillier. *ed.*—Sam Simmonds. *a.d.*—George Provis [and Andrew L. Mazzei]. *m.d.*—Cyril Ray. *sd. rec.*—William H. O. Sweeny.

Hugh Williams *(Nicholas "Nick" Barclay)*, Jane Baxter *(June Slade)*, Ronald Ward *(Jimmy Slade)*, Barbara Everest *(Lady Slade)*, George Merritt *(Inspector Mallory)*, Henry Oscar *(chief of International Police Bureau)*, Reginald Tate *(Hayden)*, Kitty Kelly *(Miss Weeks)*, Donald Calthrop *(Dr. H. E. Walpole)*, Ivor Barnard *(Hewitt)*, Hal Gordon *(sergeant)*, Gerald Fielding *(Harah)*, Syd Crossley *(postman)*, Maurice Schwartz *(the Master)*, [Peter Gawthorne *(Lord of Slade)*, Esma Cannon *(Emily, waitress)*, Wilfred Caithness *(butler)*, Moyra Fagan *(Nora)*, Esmond Knight].

79 mins. *t.s.*—March 24. *U.K. rel.*—August 24. *U.K. dist.*—MGM.

The Edge of the World · 1937

d./sc.—Michael Powell. *p.c.*—A Joe Rock Production. [*p.*—Joe Rock.] *p. staff*— Gerard Blattner, A. Seabourne, Vernon C. Sewell, W. H. Farr, George Black. [and Sydney S. Streeter.] *cin.*—Ernest Palmer, Skeets Kelly, Monty Berman. *ed.*—Derek Twist. *asst. ed.*—Bob Walters. *props.*—W. Osborne. *m.d.*—Cyril Ray. *choral effects*—women of the Glasgow Orpheus Choir. *cond.*—Sir Hugh Roberton. *orchestrations*—W. L. Williamson. *sd.*—L. K. Tregellas. *sd. rec.*—W.H.O. Sweeny.

The Manson family

John Laurie *(Peter)*, Belle Chrystall *(Ruth, his daughter)*, Eric Berry *(Robbie, her brother)*, Kitty Kirwan *(Jean, their grandmother)*.

The Gray family

Finlay Currie *(James)*, Niall MacGinnis *(Andrew)*.

and

Grant Sutherland *(John, the catechist)*, Campbell Robson *(Dunbar, the laird)*, George Summers *(trawler skipper)*, "and all the people of the lonely island of Foula where this story was made." [Margaret Grieg *(baby)*, Michael Powell *(Mr. Gra-*

ham, the yachtsman), Frankie Powell *(Mrs. Graham)*, Sydney S. Streeter *(man at dance)*.]

81 mins. *t.s.*—July 6. *U.K. rel.*—January 10, 1938 [pre-release in London: September 1937]. *U.K. dist.*—British Independent Exhibitors (Distribution). *U.S. rel.*—September 9, 1938 [74 mins]. *U.K. dist.*—Pax Films. *U.K. re-issue*—December 1940 [62 mins.]. *NFA restoration*—1990 [74 mins.].

The Lion Has Wings · 1939

d.—Michael Powell, Brian Desmond Hurst, Adrian Brunel [and Alexander Korda]. *p.c.*—London Film Productions. *p.*—Alexander Korda. *assoc. p.*—Ian Dalrymple. *p. manager*—David Cunynghame. *sc.*—[Adrian Brunel, E.V.H. Emmett.] From a story by Ian Dalrymple. *cin.*—Osmond Borradaile, Harry Stradling, Bernard Browne. *a.d.*—Vincent Korda. *sup. ed.*—William Hornbeck. *ed.*—Henry Cornelius, Charles Frend. *m.*—Richard Addinsell. [*orchestration*—Roy Douglas.] *m.d.*—Muir Mathieson. *sd. rec.*—A. W. Watkins. [*tech. adv.*—Squadron Leader H.M.S. Wright.] *narrator*—E.V.M. Emmett (Eng. version); Lowell Thomas (U.S. version). *extracts from*—*Fire Over England, The Gap.*

Ralph Richardson *(Wing Cdr. Richardson)*, Merle Oberon *(Mrs. Richardson)*, June Duprez *(June)*, Robert Douglas *(briefing officer)*, Anthony Bushell *(pilot)*, Derrick de Marney *(Bill)*, Brian Worth *(Bobby)*, Austin Trevor *(Schulemburg)*, Ivan Brandt *(officer)*, G. H. Mulcaster *(controller)*, Herbert Lomas *(Holveg)*, Milton Rosmer *(head of Observer Corps)*, Robert Rendel *(chief of Air Staff)*, Archibald Batty *(air officer)*, Ronald Adam *(bomber chief)*, Bernard Miles *(observer)*, John Longden *(controller)*, Ian Fleming, Miles Malleson, Charles Carson, Carl Jaffe, John Penrose, Frank Tickle, Torin Thatcher.

76 mins. *t.s.*—October 17. *U.K. rel.*—November 3. *U.K./U.S. dist.*—United Artists. *U.S. rel.*—January 19, 1940.

The Thief of Bagdad · 1940

d.—Ludwig Berger, Michael Powell, Tim Whelan [also: Zoltán Korda, William Cameron Menzies, Alexander Korda]. *p.c.*—Alexander Korda Films Inc. [London Films.] An Alexander Korda Presentation. *p.*—Alexander Korda. *assoc. p.*—Zoltán Korda, William Cameron Menzies. *p. manager*—David Cunynghame. [*p. asst.*—André de Toth]. *assoc. d.*—Geoffrey Boothby, Charles David. [*2nd asst. d.*—Jack Clayton.] *sc. and dial.*—Miles Malleson. *sc.*—Lajos Biro. *cin.*—Georges Périnal. *col.*—Technicolor. *assoc. cin.*—Osmond Borradaile. [*cam. op.*—Robert Krasker. *cam. asst.*—Denys Coop.] *sp. effects design*—Lawrence Butler. [*sp. effects*—Tom Howard, Johnny Mills.] *col. consultant*—Natalie Kalmus. *sup. ed.*—William Hornbeck. *ed.*—Charles Crichton. *p. designer*—Vincent Korda. *scenic backgrounds*—W. Percy Day. [*assoc. a.d.*—William Cameron Menzies, Frederick Pusey, Ferdinand Bellan.] *m.*—Miklós Rózsa. [*orchestration*—Albert Sendrey.] *m.d.*—Muir Mathieson. [*songs*—"Since Time Began" by Nick Roger, William Kernell; "I Want to Be a Sailor" by Miklós Rózsa, R. Denham. *cost. des.*—Oliver Messel, John Armstrong, Marcel Vertes. *sd.*—A. W. Watkins.

Conrad Veidt *(Jaffar)*, Sabu *(Abu)*, June Duprez *(Princess)*, John Justin *(Ahmad)*, Rex Ingram *(Djinn)*, Miles Malleson *(Sultan)*, Morton Selten *(the old king)*, Mary Morris *(Halima)*, Bruce Winston *(merchant)*, Hay Petrie *(astrologer)*, Adelaide Hall *(singer)*, Roy Emmerton *(jailer)*, Allan Jeayes *(the storyteller)*, [Viscount *(the dog)*, Glynis Johns, John Salew, Norman Pierce, Frederick Burtwell, Otto Wallen, Henry Hallett, Cleo Laine].

106 mins. *t.s.*—December 24. *U.K./U.S. rel.*—December 25. *U.K./U.S. dist.*— United Artists. *prizes*—Academy Awards for Color Cinematography, Color Art Direction, Special Effects.

An Airman's Letter to His Mother · 1941

d./sc./cin.—Michael Powell. *addit. cin.*—Bernard Browne. *narr.*—John Gielgud. 5 mins. *U.K. rel.*—June. *U.K. dist.*—MGM.

The Sorcerer's Apprentice   U.S./W. Germany · 1955

d.—Michael Powell. *p.c.*—Twentieth Century–Fox Film Corporation/Norddeutscher Rundfunk. *p. manager*—Harald Voller. *sc.*—Based on a story by Goethe. *Eng. text*—Dennis Arundell. *cin.*—Christopher Challis (CinemaScope, Technicolor). *cam. op.*—Freddie Francis. *ed.*—Reginald Mills. *p. devised/designed*—Hein Heckroth. *set constr.*—K. H. Joksch. *m. perf.*—Hamburg State Opera Orchestra. *choreo.*—Helga Swedlund.

Sonia Arova *(solo dancer)*.

13 mins. [cut from ca. 30 mins]. *U.K. rel.*—July 14. *U.K. dist.*—Twentieth Century–Fox.

Luna de Miel [Honeymoon]   Spain/GB · 1959

d./p.—Michael Powell. *p.c.*—A Michael Powell Production for Suevia Films–Cesáreo González (Spain)/Everdene (G.B.). *director general of p.*—Jaime Prades. *assoc. p.*—Sydney S. Streeter, Judith Coxhead, William J. Paton. *p. sec.*—Samuel Menkes. *asst. d.*—Ricardo Blasco. *sc.*—Michael Powell, Luis Escobar. *cin.*— Georges Périnal (Technirama). *col.*—Technicolor. *addit. cin.*—Gerry Turpin. *Technicolor tech.*—George Minassian, Ronald Cross. *chief electrician*—William Wall. *ed.*—Peter Taylor. *assembly ed.*—John V. Smith. *a.d./cost.*—Ivor Beddoes. *asst. a.d.*—Eduardo Torre de la Fuente, Roberto Carpio, Judy Jordan. *m.*—Mikis Theodorakis. *m. cond.*—Sir Thomas Beecham. Antonio's "Zapateado" by Sarasate, arr. Leonard Salzedo; "Honeymoon Song," arr. Wally Stott, sung by Marino Marini and his Quartet. *sd.*—Fernando Bernaldez. *sd. ed.*—Janet Davidson. *sd. sup.*—John Cox.

Ballets

El Amor Brujo: sc.—Gregorio Martínez Sierra. *m.*—Manuel de Falla. *sets*— Rafael Durancamps. *choreo.*—Antonio. *soloist*—Maria Clara Alcala, Pastora Ruiz *(sorcerer)*.

Los Amantes de Teruel: m.—Mikis Theodorakis. *cond.*—Sir Thomas Beecham. *choreo.*—Léonide Massine.

Anthony Steel *(Kit Kelly)*, Ludmilla Tcherina *(Anna)*, Antonio *(himself)*, Léonide Massine *("Der Geist")*, Rosita Segovia *(Rosita Candelas)*, Carmen Rojas *(Lucia)*, Antonio's Spanish Ballet Troupe *(themselves)*. [Juan Carmona *(Pepe Nieto)*, Maria Gamez, Diego Hurtado.]

109 mins. *France*—March 18, 1961. *U.K. t.s.*—January 31, 1962 [90 mins.]. *U.K. rel.*—February 8, 1962. *U.K. dist.*—BLC. *Prize*—Special Prize of Commission Supérieure Technique, Cannes Festival, 1959.

Peeping Tom · 1960

d./p.—Michael Powell. *p.c.*—Michael Powell (Theatre) Ltd. A Michael Powell Production. [*assoc. p.*—Albert Fennell.] *p. manager*—Al Marcus. *p. assts.*—Judith Coxhead, William J. Paton. *asst. d.*—Ted Sturgis. [*2nd asst. d.*—Dennis Johnson. *3rd asst. d.*—Carl Mannon.] *continuity*—Rita Davison. [*asst. continuity*—Diane Vaughan.] *sc.*—Leo Marks, from his own story. *cin.*—Otto Heller. *col.*—Eastman Color. *cam. op.*—Gerry Turpin. *chief electrician*—Victor E. Smith. [*focus puller*—Derek Browne. *clapper loader*—Jimmy Hopewell.] *ed.*—Noreen Ackland. [*asst. ed.*—Alma Godfrey. *2nd asst. ed.*—John Rushton.] *a.d.*—Arthur Lawson. *asst. a.d.*—Ivor Beddoes. *set dresser*—Don Picton. *constr. manager*—Ronald Udell. [*draftsman*—Maurice Pelling. *prop. buyer*—Harry Hanney.] *m./m.d.*—Brian Easdale. *percussion number*—Wally Stott. *solo piano*—Gordon Watson. *sd. rec.*—C. C. Stevens, Gordon K. McCallum. *sd. ed.*—Malcolm Cooke. [*sd. cam. op.*—Simon Kay. *boom op.*—Gus Lloyd. *sd. maintenance*—J. Johnson.] *cost.*—Miss Massey's dresses: Polly Peck; Miss Shearer's dress: John Tullis of Horrockses. *wardrobe*—Dickie Richardson. [*wardrobe asst.*—Vi Garnham.] *makeup*—W. J. Partleton. *hair*—Pearl Orton. *hats*—The Millinery Guild. [*publicity director*—William Burnside. *unit publicist*—Lillana Wilkie. *stills*—Norman Gryspeerdt.]

Carl Boehm *(Mark Lewis)*, Moira Shearer *(Vivian)*, Anna Massey *(Helen Stephens)*, Maxine Audley *(Mrs. Stephens)*, Brenda Bruce *(Dora)*, Miles Malleson *(elderly gentleman)*, Esmond Knight *(Arthur Baden)*, Martin Miller *(Dr. Rosan)*, Michael Goodliffe *(Don Jarvis)*, Jack Watson *(Inspector Gregg)*, Shirley Anne Field *(Diane Ashley)*, Pamela Green *(Milly)*. [Bartlett Mullins *(Mr. Peters)*, Nigel Davenport *(Sgt. Miller)*, Brian Wallace *(Tony)*, Susan Travers *(Lorraine)*, Maurice Durant *(publicity chief)*, Brian Worth *(assistant director)*, Veronica Hurst *(Miss Simpson)*, Alan Rolfe *(store detective)*, John Dunbar *(police doctor)*, Guy Kingsley-Poynter *(P. Tate, the cameraman)*, Keith Baxter *(Baxter, the detective)*, Peggy Thorpe-Bates *(Mrs. Partridge)*, John Barrard *(small man)*, Roland Curram *(young man extra)*, Robert Crewdson *(tall shop assistant)*, John Chappell *(clapper boy)*, Paddy Edwardes *(girl extra)*, Frank Singuineau *(first electrician)*, Margaret Neal *(stepmother)*, Michael Powell *(A. N. Lewis, Mark's father)*, Columba Powell *(Mark as a child)*.]

109 mins. *t.s.*—March 31. *U.K. rel.*—May 16. *U.K. dist.*—Anglo Amal-

gamated. *U.S. rel.*—May 15, 1962 [86 mins.]. *U.S. dist.*—Astor. *U.S. reissue*—1980 [Corinth Films, "presented by Martin Scorsese," 109 mins.].

The Queen's Guards · 1961

d./p.—Michael Powell. *p.c.*—Imperial. A Michael Powell Production. *assoc. p.*—Simon Harcourt-Smith. *p. sup./assoc. d.*—Sydney S. Streeter. *p. manager*—John Wilcox. *continuity*—Eileen Hildyard. *sc.*—Roger Milner, from an idea by Simon Harcourt-Smith. *cin.*—Gerald Turpin (CinemaScope). *col.*—Technicolor. *cam. op.*—Derek Browne, Austin Dempster, Skeets Kelly, Robert Walker, James Bawden, Robert Huke, Dudley Lovell, Norman Warwick. *ed.*—Noreen Ackland. *a.d.*—Wilfred Shingleton. *m./m.d.*—Brian Easdale. *sd. rec.*—Red Law. *sd. ed.*—James Shields. *cost.*—Bridget Sellers. *wardrobe master*—McPhee. *ladies cost.*—Mattli. *makeup*—James Hines. *hair*—Anne Box.

Daniel Massey *(John Fellowes)*, Raymond Massey *(Capt. Fellowes)*, Robert Stephens *(Henry Wynne Walton)*, Jack Watson *(Sgt. Johnson)*, Peter Myers *(Gordon Davidson)*, Ursula Jeans *(Mrs. Fellowes)*, Frank Lawton *(Cmdr. Hewson)*, Anthony Bushell *(Major Cole)*, Jess Conrad *(Dankworth)*, Cornel Lucas *(photographer)*, Ian Hunter *(Mr. Dobbie)*, Elizabeth Shepherd *(Susan)*, Judith Stott *(Ruth)*, Duncan Lamont *(Wilkes)*, Jack Allen *(Brig. Cummings)*, Laurence Payne *(Farinda)*, Eileen Peel *(Mrs. Wynne-Walton)*, William Fox *(Mr. Walters)*, Patrick Connor *(Brewer)*, William Young *(Williams)*, Roland Curram, Nigel Green *(Abu Sibdar)*, Anthony Selby *(Kishu)*, John Chappell *(Private Walsh)*. [Jack Watling *(Captain Shergold)*, Andrew Crawford *(Biggs)*, René Cutforth *(commentator)*.]

110 mins. *t.s.*—October 9. *U.K. rel.*—October 23. *U.K. dist.*—Twentieth Century–Fox.

Never Turn Your Back On a Friend · 1963

[TV film for the *Espionage* series.]

d.—Michael Powell. *p.c.*—Herbert Brodkin Ltd. *exec. p.*—Herbert Hirschman. *p.*—George Justin. *assoc. p.*—John Pellatt. *p. manager*—Tom Sachs. *asst. d.*—Bruce Sharman. *continuity*—Doreen Soan. *sc.*—Mel Davenport. Series based on an idea by Charles N. Hill. *cin.*—Ken Hodges. *cam. op.*—Herbert Smith. *ed.*—John Victor Smith. *p. designer*—Wilfred Shingleton. *a.d.*—Tony Woollard. *m./m. cond.*—Malcolm Arnold. *sd. rec.*—David Bowen. *sd. ed.*—Dennis Rogers. *cost.*—Kim Zeigler. *makeup*—Alex Garfath. *hair*—Daphne Martin. *titles*—Maurice Binder. *casting*—Rose Tobias Shaw.

George Voskovec *(Professor Kuhn)*, Donald Madden *(Anaconda)*, Mark Eden *(Wicket)*, Julian Glover *(Tovarich)*, Pamela Brown *(Miss Jensen)*.

54 mins.

A Free Agent · 1964

[TV film for the *Espionage* series.]

d.—Michael Powell. *p.c.*—Herbert Brodkin Ltd. *exec. p.*—Herbert Hirschman. *p.*—George Justin. *assoc. p.*—John Pellatt. *p. manager*—Tom Sachs. *asst. d.*—Jake

Wright. *continuity*—Joy Mercer. *sc.*—Leo Marks. *cin.*—Geoffrey Faithfull. *cam. op.*—Alan McCabe. *ed.*—John Victor Smith. *p. designer*—Wilfred Shingleton. *a.d.*—Anthony Woollard. *set dec.*—Peter Russell. *m./m. cond.*—Benjamin Frankel. *title m.*—Malcolm Arnold. *sd. rec.*—Cyril Smith. *sd. ed.*—Dennis Rogers. *wardrobe*—Jackie Cummins. *makeup*—Alex Garfath. *hair*—Alice Holmes. *titles*—Maurice Binder. *casting*—Rose Tobias Shaw.

Anthony Quayle *(Phillip)*, Sian Phillips *(Anna)*, Norman Foster *(Max)*, George Mikell *(Peter)*, John Wood *(Douglas)*, John Abineri *(town clerk)*, Ernst Walder *(watch factory mechanic)*, Gertan Klauber *(innkeeper)*, Vivienne Drummond *(Miss Weiss)*, Jan Conrad *(chief mechanic)*.

52 mins.

Herzog Blaubarts Burg [Bluebeard's Castle]   W. Germany · 1964

d.—Michael Powell. *p.c.*—Süddeutscher Rundfunk. Eine Norman Foster Produktion. *p.*—Norman Foster. *p. manager*—Walter Tjaden. *libretto*—Béla Balazs. German trans. of libretto—Wilhelm Ziegler. *cin.*—Hannes Staudinger. *col.*—Technicolor. *ed.*—Paula Dvorak. *p. designer*—Hein Heckroth. *a.d.*—Gerd Krauss. *m.*—Béla Bartók's opera *Herzog Blaubarts Burg* (1911). *m. perf.*—Zagreb Philharmonic Orchestra. *cond.*—Milan Horvath. *cost.*—Helga Pinnow. *makeup*—Franz Göbel. *sd.*—Karl Wohlleitner.

Norman Foster *(Bluebeard)*, Ana Raquel Satre *(Judit)*.

60 mins. *U.K. premiere*—November 9, 1978.

The Sworn Twelve · 1965

[TV film for *The Defenders* series.]

d.—Michael Powell. *sc.*—Edward DeBlasio. *cast.*—E. G. Marshall, Murry Hamilton, King Donovan, Ruby Dee, Jerry Orbach.

50 mins.

A 39846 · 1965

[TV film for *The Nurses* series.]

d.—Michael Powell. *sc.*—George Bellak. *cast.*—Michael Tolan, Shirl Conway, Joseph Campanella, Jean-Pierre Aumont, Kermit Murdock.

50 mins.

Sebastian · 1967

p.c.—Maccius Productions Ltd. A Herbert Brodkin–Michael Powell Production. *p.*—Herbert Brodkin, Michael Powell. *assoc. p.*—John Pellatt. *p. manager*—Clifton Brandon. *p. exec.*—Buzz Berger. [*p. accountant*—Peter Lancaster.] *d.*—David Greene. *asst. d.*—Gordon Gilbert. *sc.*—Gerald Vaughan-Hughes from a screen story by Leo Marks. *continuity*—Ann Skinner. *cin.*—Gerald Fisher. *col.*—Eastman Color. *cam. op.*—James Turrell. [*focus puller*—Wally Byatt.] *m./m. cond.*—Jerry Goldsmith. *songs*—"Comes the Night" by Jerry Goldsmith (m.), Hal Shaper (l.),

604 · A FILMOGRAPHY

sung by Anita Harris. "I Need You Baby" by Derek Philips (m.), Ainsley McKenkie (l.), "Out of My Mind" by Alex Nesbitt (m.), John Cassidy (l.), both recorded by Max Baer & The Chicago Setback. "You Gotta Let Me Go" by Bobby Bowers (m.), J. Butler (l.), recorded by The Happeners. *ed.*—Brian Smedley-Aston. *asst. ed.*—Keith Palmer. *p. des.*—Wilfred Shingleton. *a.d.*—Fred Carter. *set dresser*—Terence Morgan II. *cost. cons.*—Sue Yelland. *wardrobe*—Bridget Sellers. *makeup*—Bob Lawrance. *hairdresser*—Gladys Leakey. *titles*—Richard Williams Films. *casting*—James Liggat. *prop. master*—Alf Pegley. *dubbing ed.*—Don Challis. *sd. rec.*—H. L. Bird, Gerry Humphreys. *electronic sd. effects*—Tristram Cary. [*sd. cam. op.*—Michael Silverlock. *boom op.*—Bill Burgess.]

Dirk Bogarde *(Sebastian)*, Susannah York *(Becky Howard)*, Lilli Palmer *(Elsa Shahn)*, John Gielgud *(head of intelligence)*, Janet Munro *(Carol Fancy)*, Nigel Davenport *(General John Phillips)*, Margaret Johnston *(Miss Elliott)*, Ronald Fraser *(Toby)*, John Ronane *(security head Jameson)*, Hayward Morse *(Gavin)*, Donald Sutherland *(Rosenau, the American)*, Portland Mason *(the "Ug" girl)*, James Belchamber *(man with dog)*, Charles Farrell *(taxi driver)*, Charles Lloyd Pack *(the chess player)*, Alan Freeman *(the TV chairman)*, Ann Beach *(Pamela)*, Susan Whitman *(Tilly)*, Ann Sidney *(Naomi)*, Veronica Clifford *(Ginny)*, Louise Purnell *(Thelma)*, Lyn Pinkney *(Joan)*, Jeanne Roland *(Randy)*, Jennifer Lautrec, Sally Douglas *(girls)*, David Toguri, Stuart Hoyle, Ann Norman, Edwina Carroll, Robyn Tolhurst *(party people)*.

100 mins. *t.s.*—March 6, 1968. *U.K. rel.*—April 7, 1968. *U.S. rel.*—December 15, 1967. *U.K./U.S. dist.*—Paramount Pictures.

Age of Consent Australia · 1969

d.—Michael Powell. *p.c.*—Nautilus Productions (Australia). *p.*—James Mason, Michael Powell. *assoc. p.*—Michael Pate. *p. sup.*—Brian Chirlian. *p. manager*—Kevin Powell. *asst. d.*—David Crocker. *continuity*—Rita Cavil. *sc.*—Peter Yeldham, based on a novel by Norman Lindsay. *cin.*—Hannes Staudinger. *col.*—Eastman Color. *cam. op.*—John McLean, Graham Lind. *underwater cin.*—Ron Taylor. *chief electrician*—Tony Tegg. *ed.*—Anthony Buckley. *a.d.*—Dennis Gentle. *m./m. cond.*—Peter Sculthorpe [released outside Australia with a score by Stanley Myers]. *sd. ed.*—Tim Wellburn. *sd. rec.*—Paul Ennis, Lloyd Colman. *boom op.*—Alfred Wiggins. *cost.*—Anne Senior. *makeup*—Peggy Carter. *hair*—Robert Hynard. *casting*—Gloria Payten. *New York paintings*—Paul Delprat. *"Lonsdale" trained by*—Scotty Denholm.

James Mason *(Bradley Morahan)*, Helen Mirren *(Cora)*, Jack MacGowran *(Nat Kelly)*, Neva Carr-Glyn *(Ma Ryan)*, Antonia Katsaros *(Isabel Marley)*, Michael Boddy *(Hendricks)*, Harold Hopkins *(Ted Farrell)*, Slim DeGrey *(Cooley)*, Max Meldrum *(TV interviewer)*, Frank Thring *(Godfrey)*, Clarissa Kaye *(Meg)*, Judy McGrath *(Grace)*, Lenore Caton *(Edna)*, Diane Strachan *(Susie)*, Roberta Grant *(Ivy)*, Lonsdale *(Godfrey, the dog)*, Prince Nial *(Jasper)*, [Dora Hing *(receptionist)*,

Hudson Frausset *(New Yorker)*, Peggy Cass *(New Yorker's wife)*, Eric Reiman *(art lover)*, Tommy Hanlon, Jr. *(Levi-Strauss)*, Geoff Cartwright *(newsboy)*.]

103 mins. [U.K./U.S. 98 mins.]. *U.K. rel.*—November 15. *U.S. rel.*—May 14. *dist.*—Columbia.

Return to the Edge of the World · 1978

d./sc.—Michael Powell. *p.c.*—Banco Credit and Commerce International. Presented by Frixos Constantine. Poseidon Films Ltd. A Michael Powell Presentation. *p.*—Michael Powell, Sydney S. Streeter. *post-production facilities*—Roger Cherrill Ltd. *cin.*—Brian Mitchison. *ed.*—Peter Mayhew. *m./m. cond.*—Brian Easdale. *sd.*—David Hahn.

A return visit to the island of Foula with members of the cast and crew of *The Edge of the World*, including Powell, Sydney Streeter, John Laurie, Grant Sutherland, and Frankie Reidy. In the form of a prelude and epilogue to the 1940 version of *The Edge of the World* (62 mins.).

85 mins. *U.K. premiere*—October 3.

Pavlova—A Woman for All Time   U.S.S.R./G.B. · 1983

Powell was credited as "Western Version Supervisor" on this G.B./U.S.S.R. co-production, written and directed by Emil Lotianou and coordinated by executive producer Frixos Constantine. Its origins lay in a project on the life of Pavlova that Powell had taken up at the instigation of Erwin Hillier.

Note: Page numbers followed by *n.* indicate material in footnotes. *Italicized* page numbers indicate information in the Filmography at the end of the book.

ABOUT THE TYPE

This book was set in Photina, a typeface
designed by José Mendoza in 1971.